GILES COUNTY TENNESSEE

County Court Minutes

- 1823-1825

By:
Work Projects Administration

Southern Historical Press, Inc.
Greenville, South Carolina

Copyright 1942
By: Works Projects Administration

New Material Copyright: 2018
By: Southern Historical Press, Inc.

All rights reserved. No part of this publication may be reproduced, stored in a retrieval system, transmitted in any form, posted on to the web in any form or by any means without the prior written permission of the publisher.

Please direct all correspondence and orders to:
www.southernhistoricalpress.com
or
SOUTHERN HISTORICAL PRESS, Inc.
PO BOX 1267
375 West Broad Street
Greenville, SC 29601
southernhistoricalpress@gmail.com

ISBN #0-89308-590-1

Printed in the United States of America

GILES COUNTY

COUNTY COURT MINUTES VOL. H.
1823-1825

P-1   At a Court of Pleas and Quarter Session held for the County of Giles at the court house in the Town of Pulaski on Monday the 17th day of November A. D. 1823 Present Alexander Black, James Dugger, John H. Camp. Hezekiah Jones, Robert Read, John Laird, John B. Armstrong, Thomas Marks, John Dickey, Arthur Hicks, Edward D. Jones, William B. Pepper, Thos. K. Gordon, William Mayfield, James Paine, Thomas Batte, Thomas Harwood.

Ordered that Thomas Grubbs be appointed overseer of the road in the room of Henry T. Croft resigned and that he have the same district of hands.

Ordered that Elizabeth Scott be released from the payment of a double tax on one lot in the town of Pulaski.

Ordered that Ira Atkins be released from the payment of a Poll tax on account of his being over fifty years of age.

Ordered that William Brown, Thomas Harwood & John H. Camp be appointed commissioners to settle with Samuel Bradley Executor of Joseph Bradley decd. and that they make return of said settlement to the next term of this court.

Ordered that the part of the Buck Creek road which was lately altered and cut out by Josiah Lester and the hand under his direction be established and the part from which the same is turned be discontinued as a Pulaski highway.

Ordered that James Willeford be appointed overseer of the road in the room of George Hillhouse resigned and that he have the same district of hands.

On motion of German Lester Clerk of this court Charles G. Willcox was duly qualified as his deputy.

Ordered that Sarah Poinor widow of David Poinor late of this County of Guilford & State of North Carolina be appointed guardian to Nathaniel Poinor and John D. Poinor minor children & heirs of said David Poinor decd. she having entered into bond and security according to Law.

Ordered that Isaac Allen, John C. Camp & Larken Carden be appointed commissioners to settle with William Lansford administrator of the Estate of Luke Addus deceased and that they make report of said settlement to the next term of this court.

Ordered that Matthew J. Black be appointed overseer of the road in the room of Eliab Vinson resigned and that he have the same district of hands.

P-2   Monday 17th November 1823

Ordered that William Rivers be appointed overseer of the road in the room of Beverly Brown resigned and that he have the same district of hands.

A Deed of conveyance from Josiah Phelps to Kinchin T. Bass for one Hundred and twenty acres of land was produced in court and fully proven by the oath of Daniel Leatheman a subscribing witness thereto and ordered to be certified for registration.

A Bill of sale from Joseph Saunders to Robert Tennen & Lucy Tennen his wife was produced in court and the Execution thereof was acknowledged by the said Joseph Saunders and ordered to be certified for registration.

A Deed of conveyance from John Dabney to Robert Cox for Seventy & a half acres of land was produced in court and the Execution thereof acknowledged by the said John Dabney and ordered to be certified for registration.

Ordered that the County Trustee of this County pay to Davis Browning the sum of ninety eight dollars for building a bridge across Yancys Creek let by an order of this court.

John Young, Paul Childs, Henry Hagen, Anderson Hagen, James McCafferty, and Cary T. Kelly Gentlemen who were commissioned by his Exellency the Govenor of this State to act as Justices of the peace in and for this County appeared in court and were qualified as the law directs.

Ordered that the County Trustee of this County pay to German Lester Clerk of this court the sum of twenty two for a minute book which he furnished for the use of this court.

A Deed of conveyance from Bennet Creesy to Josiah Phelps for one hundred and twenty acres of land was produced in court and the Execution there of fully proven by the oath of John Akins a witness thereto and ordered to be certified for registration.

Ordered that Hugh Bratton overseer of the Lambs Ferry road have in addition to the hands formerly allotted him the hands of Charles Marlow on Buck Creek and the hands of Owen Hardy on Sugar Creek and all the hands from James Bunchs to the head of Agnew Creek including said Bunchs hands to work on said road under his direction.

P-3   Monday 17th November 1823

A deed of conveyance from Martin Lane to Thomas K. Gordon for six hundred and thirty three acres of land was produced in court and the Execution thereof proven by the oaths of Stirling Graves & Andrew Gordon the subscribing witnesses thereto and ordered to be certified for registration.

Ordered that the County Trustee of this County pay to Robert Read Esquire the sum of sixty dollars for the support & Maintainance of William Harris & Elenor his wife paupers of this county for twelve months from this time.

John Washington Weis an orphan boy is bound an apprentice to John A. Nichols an indenture to that effect having been entered into and filed and that the order heretofore made binding said apprentice to be reieved.

Ordered that the order heretofore made appointing Joseph C. Hartin guardin of _____ Carpenter minor orphan of Richard Carpenter decd. be received.

Ordered that William Sheppard Egbert Sheppard, John Tinnen, James Tennen, William Lee, Matthew Johnston and Richard Johnston or any five of them be appointed commissioners to view a mill road from Tyree Rodes the nearest and best way to Tinnen's Mill, and make report to the present term of this court if practicable if not to the next term of this court.

At least five Justices being present Elijah Meadows produced in court a wolf scalp over four months old which was ordered to be burnt.

Ordered that the County Trustee of this County pay to Robert Hunnicut the sum of Fifty dollars at any time after one year from this time for keeping Emmon Cheatam a pauper of this county for twelve months from the date hereof.

A Deed of conveyance from Daniel Frazer, James Raine & Edward D. Jones to John McMillin for one hundred and fifteen acres of land was produced in court and the Execution thereof proven by the oaths of Richard Briggs & Samuel Day two of the subscribing witnesses thereto and ordered to be certified for registration.

Alexander Black Esquire was appointed chairman of this court Pro Term.

P-4   Monday 17th November 1823

Ordered that Tyree Rodes be appointed overseer of that part of the road leading from said Rodes lane to Mayfields Mill which lies between said lane & pigeon roost Creek and that he have under his direction for the purpose of opening the Same all the hands that now work under said Rodes on the Bigby road and the hands of Giddeon Pillow, and that the hands of said Rodes & said Pillow work on said road for the purpose of keeping the same in repair.

Ordered that Robert Anderson be appointed overseer of that part of the road which lies between Pigeon roost creek and Mayfield Mill and that he have for the purpose of opening the same all the hands from the mouth of Pigeon roost creek to the ford of said creek near John Porters thence to run with the road as to include Robert Rankin thence so as to include William Mayfield and that said overseer be allowed a proportionable part of said hands to keep said road in repair.

A Deed of conveyance from William Hunnicut to Guston Kearney for one Hundred and nine acres of land was produced in court and the Execution thereof acknowledged by said William Hunnicut and ordered to be certified for registration.

Ordered that David Bridgeforth be appointed overseer of the road in the room of Guston Kearney resigned and that he have the same district of hands.

A power of attorney from James Farquhar to John Jackson was produced in court and the execution thereof acknowledged by the said James Farquhar and ordered to be certified.

Ordered that Thomas B. Haynie be appointed constable in Captain Watsons Company whereupon he took the oath required by and executed bond & security according to law.

Ordered that Joseph Anthony be appointed coroner of this County who was qualified and gave bond and security according to law.

Ordered that William Buchanan James L. Hendry, William Hendry and Charles Dever or any two of them be appointed commissioners to settle with Sally Taylor & Arthur Hicks administrators of the Estate of Tekle T. Taylor deceased and that they make report of said settlement to the next term of this court.

The administrators of the Estate of William Kyle deceased returned into court an Inventory of said Estate which was ordered to be recorded.

P-5 Monday 17th November 1823

Ordered that the hands of William B. Brooks, David McCallum & Duncan Brown be added to the hands of Edmund Shelton to work on the road of which he is overseer.

A Deed of conveyance from Thomas Rivers to John Brooks for Seventeen acres and thirty seven poles of land was produced in court and partly proven by the oath of Samuel Munerief one of the subscribing witnesses thereto.

For good reasons shown to the court it is ordered that Elijah Meadows be released from further attendance as a Juror at this term.

Stephen Loyd administrator of the Estate of Jeremiah Woodward deceased returned into court an Inventory of said Estate which is ordered to be recorded.

Ordered that the hands of Archibald McFatten David Stovall and John McCormack be added to the hands of William B. Brooks overseer of the road.

A Power of attorney from John Walthall to Henry Hagen was produced in court and the Execution thereof acknowledged by the said John Walthall and ordered to be certified for registration.

The administrators of the Estate of John K. Gibson deceased returned into court an account of the sale of said Estate which was ordered to be recorded.

Letters of administrations on the Estate of Austin Smith Junr. deceased is granted to Thomas Marks and Allen Abernathy whereupon they took the oaths required by and executed Bond and security according to Law.

A Licence to keep an ordinary for the term of twelve months and no longer is granted to Henry Hanison who was qualified and gave bond and security according to law.

Ordered that the County Trustee of this County pay to William R. Davis the sum of thirty one dollars & twenty five cents for sweeping the court house for the term of fifteen months last past.

Ordered that Christain Zimmerman be appointed overseer of the road from Samuel McKnights leading from Leatherman's Mill to the County line in a direction to Hightowers Mill in the room of Robert Webb resigned & that he have the same district of hands.

Ordered that Robert McLaurine be appointed overseer of the Lawrence court house road from William Parkers to Shoals Creek & that he have under his direction for the purpose of working said road the following hands towit, William Mick, Adam Pellick, George Bratten, James Bratton, Wm. Chambery, Robert McLaurine,   (p-6)   (Monday 17th November 1823) W. Porter, Charles Dever, William Fisher, Richard Brandon, John S. Brandon, Robert Black, Millen Tidwell, and Rode Tidwell.

Ordered that the County Trustee of this County pay to Robert Reed the sum of Fifteen dollars for the support and maintainance of James Wilsons daughter Nancy for the term of twelve months from this date.

Ordered that Monday next be set apart for County Business.

Ordered that William B. Pepper, Marcus Mitchel and German Lester be appointed commissioners to let to the lowest bidder the building of a bridge across crooked creek on the Huntsville road and that they take an obligation from the undertaken to keep the same in repair for the ___ of seven years.

Ordered that John S. Brandon, Richard Brandon, David W. Porter, Charles Dever, John Black, Elias Tidwell and Jefferson Chambers, or any five of them be appointed a Jury to view a private way from the land of Robert McLaurine on Egnews Creek to the nearest public road in this County and that they make report to the next term of this court.

Ordered that John Newton, Littleberry Webb, Peter Satterfield, Robert Smith, William Hayes, James Kelso and William Smith or any five of them be appointed a Jury to view that part of the Lincoln County road which lies between William Ezells and Rolley Harwells and see if it be proper to turn said road and if in their opinion it be that they make out the same and that they make report to the next term of this court.

Ordered Samuel Harwell, George Brown, Thomas Harwell, Richard Brandon, Robert Read, Arthur Hicks & James Wilson, or any five of them be appointed a Jury to view that part of the Lawrence court house road which lies between Isaac Purvis and the County line and see if be proper to turn said road and if in their opinion it be proper that they make out the same and that they make report to this court if practicable if not to next court.

A Power of attorney from Samuel Wesson to Robert B. Edmonson was produced in court and the Execution thereof proven by the oaths of James McCafferty & William Edmonson the witnesses thereto and ordered to be certified.

Ordered that court be adjourned till tomorrow morning nine oclock.

               A. Black
               James Dugger
               John Laird

P-7 Thursday Morning November 18th 1823

Court met according to adjournment Present Alexander Black,)
              James Dugger &) Esquires
              John Laird) Justice

The Sheriff of this County returned into court the names of the following persons summoned to attend as Grand and Petit Jurors at this term towit, Archibald Young, Junr. Thomas East, James Hannah, Thomas Cole, James Shelton Junr., William W. Wood, Edward M. Brown, William H. Moore, Marshall Moody, Thomas Wilkinson, Henry J. Cooper, John O. Graves, Robert B. Harney, Ralph

Graves, William W. Thornton, Henry M. Newlan, Homer Rainey, Archibald, Smith, Marcus Mitchell, Isaac Mayfield, Allen Pitts, Thomas Wells, Spencer Clack, and Thomas Williams of whom the following were elected empanneled and sworn a grand Jury of inquest for the body of this county of good and lawful men to wit, Robert B. Harney foreman, Henry M. Newlan, Isaac Mayfield, James Hannah, John O. Graves, Marcus Mitchell, Thomas Wilkinson, Edward M. Brown, Archibald Smith, William W. Woods, James Shelton Jr., Thomas Williams and Spencer Clack who having received their charge withdrew to consider presentments.

Nathaniel Young a constable of this County was sworn to attend on the Grand Jury at the present term of this court.

A Deed of Trust from Richard Bennett to Thomas Batte & John H. Camp was produced in court and the execution thereof proven by the oath of John Bass.

A Bill of sale from Thomas Woodward to Hannah Woodward for certain negros therein named was produced in court and the execution thereof was acknowledged by the said Thomas Woodward and ordered to be certified for registration.

A Deed of gift from Thomas Smith to Fanny Jopling for certain property therein named was produced in court and the Execution thereof proven by the oath of George Brown one of the witnesses thereto and ordered to be certified for registration.

Thomas Lane administrator of the Estate of Martin Land decd. returned into court an account of the sale of the Estate of said Martin Lane which was ordered to be recorded.

The last will and Testement of John Maclin decd. was produced in court and the Execution thereof was duly proven by the oaths of Thomas East and Nathan Farmer the subscribing witnesses thereto & ordered to be recorded and thereupon Sally Maclin and Sackfield Maclin the Executors therein named appeared in court and were qualified and gave bond and Security as the Law directs.

The Execution of the last will and Testement of John Maclin decd. returned into court an Inventory of his Estate which is ordered to be recorded.

P-8 Tuesday November 18th 1823

John Dickey Esquire a Justice of the peace for this County tenders in writing his resignation to the court which was received and ordered to be entered on the minutes.

A Deed of conveyance from William Maclin to B. P. Maclin for one thousand acres of land was produced in court and the Execution thereof proven by the oaths of James Z. Maclin & Willis Pillow the witnesses thereto and ordered to be certified.

At least a majority of the Acting Justices of the peace in and for this County being present & settling as a court the court proceeded by Ballot to the Election of a Sheriff and collector of this County and upon counting the votes Lewis H. Brown was found to be duly Elected who thereupon Executed Bonds & security and was qualified as the law directs.

Rebeccah Hunter Plt.)   In Case
    Against   )
John Maynes ... Deft.)   By consent of the parties in this case
)   by attornies general leave is given to
take the deposition of witnesses to be read as evidence in this cause. On the plaintiffs giving to Defendants and the Defendants giving the plaintiffs Attorney twenty days notice of taking depositions out of this State & of the time & place and ten days notice of the time and place of taking those in the State.

Edmund Shelton Plt.   )   On an original Attachment.
    Against   )
Dudley Smith ... Deft.)
)   Thomas Wilson a Garnishee Summoned to
)   appear at this Term came into court and
being duly sworn according to law deposed on his oath in the following manner to wit, Question 1st by plaintiffs attorney, What are you indebted to Dudley Smith? Answer I am indebted to him Fourteen dollars & forty cents and knowing of no goods or chattles of the Defendants was discharged Except as to the above sum of fourteen dollars and forty cents and that the plaintiff recover of the said Thomas Wilson the aforesaid sum of fourteen dollars and forty cents & that Execution therefor be awarded.

On the petition of Joseph Calvert who undertook as security for Samuel Bradley Executor of Joseph Bradley decd. it is ordered that a summons issue to the said Samuel Bradly requiring him to appear at the next Term of this court and give oaths and counter security to be approved of by the court in said case and further to be dealt with as the law directs.

P-9   Tuesday 18th November 1823

On the petition of William Richardson who undertook as security for Samuel Bradley Executor of Joseph Bradley decd. it is ordered that a summons issue to the said Samuel Bradley requiring him to appear at the next Term of this court and give oaths and counter security to be approved of by the court in this case and further to be dealt with as the law directs.

Ordered that court be adjourned till tomorrow morning 9 oclock.

John Laird
E. D. Jones
Robert Reed

Wednesday Morning 19th November 1823

Court met according to adjournment Present John Laird,)
                                  Edward D. Jones   ) Esquires Justices
                                  Robert Reed   )

Edmund Shelton, Plt.   )   Original Attachment
       against   )
Dudley Smith ... Deft.   )   John N. Smith a Garnishee summoned to
)   appear and answer on oath in this case
after being first duly sworn makes the following statement that previous
to the service of the Garnishment in this case, on him he had sold articles
for Defendant to the amount of something more than four hundred dollars,
that defendant was indebted to him Eighty dollars which he retained out of
the above sum, that he paid by order of the defendant to Lewis H. Brown the
sum of forty three dollars ninety two and a half cents, and that previous
to the service of this Garnishment an attachment was levied on him by the
Sheriff of Limestone County for the sum of three hundred dollars as he was
informed, or there about. The court being of opinion from the above Examination that said Garnishee hath nothing in his hands belonging to the defendant is thereupon discharged Stephen Loyd a Garnishee summoned to appear
and answer on oath in this case after being first duly sworn makes the following statement. That at August Term 1823 of this court administered on
the Estate of Jeremiah Woodward decd. who died intestate in the Summer of
1822 leaving his widow and five children that since the death of said Woodward said defendant hath intermarried with his widow that at the present
term he returned an Inventory of his estate marked A. He does not know the
value of the Estate of said Woodward.

P-10   Wednesday 19th November 1823

In as much as he has not made sale of the property, Question 1st What
goods or Effects of the defendants do you know of in the possession of any
other person? Answer there is on the premises at the late dwelling of the
defendant and in possession of his wife one bed and scant furniture, one
broad ax one pair leather saddle bags, one small trunk, one easy plow, one
pair of drawing chains, one pair of small pistols, one note of hand on
Grabiel Bumpass for eleven dollars, one debt on Robert Webb the precise
amount not known, one pair of large Steelyards in the possession of Zelwlon
Rainey one horse in the possession of Edmund Shelton.

Owen Smith ... Plt.   )   Petition for certiorari
       against   )
Joseph B. Pillow   )   The petition of the defendant for Writs of
& John Pillow   Deft.   )   Supercedeas and certiorari to stay proceedings and remove to this court the record of
a Judgment rendered on the _____ day of _____ by Thomas K. Gordon a Justice
of the peace for this county in favor of the plaintiff against the defendants
Being read and burnt. The granting of the same being opposed by Harris &
Fields attornies for the plaintiff and matured deliberation thereupon being
had it is the opinion of the court that said petition shall not be granted
and that the plaintiff recover of the defendant the costs in this behalf
Expended.

On the petition of David Browning it is ordered that Writs of Supercedery and certiorari issue to stay proceedings and remove to this court the record of a Judgment which Thomas Martin Surviving partner of the late firm of Meredith & Martin recovered against Martin Davenport before John H. Camp a Justice of the Peace for this County on the day of March 1823 for the sum of Forty six dollars or there abouts & costs to the stay of which Judgment the petitioner States that his name was Fraudalently put.

On the petition of David Browning it is ordered that Writs of Supercedeas & Certiorari issue to Stay proceedings and removed to this court the record of a Judgment which James Perry recovered against Martin Davenport before John H. Camp A Justice of the peace for this County on the 22nd day of March 1823 or as near that time for the sum of forty four dollars and forty cents or thereabout & costs to the stay of which Judgment the petitioner states that his name was fraudalently put.

P-11 Wednesday 19th November 1822

Sufficient reasons having been shown to the court Thomas East was discharged from further attendance as a Grand Juror at this term.

Rebeccah Kyle administratrix) Plts.
Clayborn Kyle administrator of)
the estate William Kyle Decd.) Original Attachment
    against)
Thomas Jameson . . . Deft) This day came the parties by
) their attornies and by consent
this cause is ordered to be continued till the next court, and leave is given each party to take depositions upon the plaintiffs giving to the defendant & the defendant giving to the plaintiffs twenty days notice of the time and place of taking said deposition out of this State and ten days notice of the time and place of taking those in this State.

The Governor to the use of &c Plt.) In Debt
    Against)
Thomas Goff . . . . Deft.) This day came the parties by
) their attornies and thereupon
came a Jury of good and lawful men towit, Henry J. Cooker, Homer Rainey, Bazel Compton, Thomas Cole, John Black, Isaac S. Crisman, James W. Wheeler, John E. Holden, Ambrose Cobb, Merry Carter, Caleb White & Thomas Wells who being elected tried and sworn well and truly to try the issue Joined in this case upon their oaths do say that they find said issue in favor of said plaintiff and assess his damages by reason of the detention of the debt in the declaration mentioned to one Hundred & nineteen dollars and Eighty nine cents besides costs. It is therefore considered by the oath that the plaintiff recover of the defendant his debt aforesaid to be discharged by the payment of the sum of one hundred & nineteen dollars & eighty nine cents the amount of his damages aforesaid by the Jurors aforesaid in form aforesaid assessed and his costs by him about his suit in this behalf expended.

Robert Farmer & John Howson Exon. A. Plt.)
        Against)   Covenant
John Browning . . . .)
) James Hannah who was
bound for the appearance of John Browning aforesaid came into court and surrendered said defendant and is thereupon Exhonerated and discharged from his obligation and thereupon David Browning came into court and being considered by the court good and sufficient Bail agrees that if the said John be convicted at the suit of the said plaintiffs that he shall pay and satisfy the condemnation of the court or surrender his body in discharge of the same or he will do it for him.

The Grand Jury returned into court the following Indictments towit the State against John B. Armstrong for an assault and Battery and which is indorsed a true Bill.

P-12   Wednesday 19th November 1823

A Deed of conveyance from Alexander McDonald to Charles Dever for two hundred and twenty four & a half acres of land was produced in court and the execution thereof acknowledged by the said Alexander McDonald and is ordered to be certified for registration.

Charles Boyles to the use of &c. Plt.)   In Debt
        Against)
Sterling C. Robertson and) . . . Defts.) This day came the parties
Eldridge Robertson) by their attornies and
) thereupon came a Jury of
good and lawful men towit, Henry J. Cooper, Homer Rainey, Bazel Compton, Thomas Cole, John Black, Isaac S. Crisman, James W. Wheeler, John E. Folden, Ambrose Cobb, Merry Carter, Caleb White and Thomas Wells, who being Elected tried and sworn well and truly to try the issues joined Between the parties in this case having heard part of the evidence and because a further consideration of this cause continued and postponed untill tomorrow morning nine oclock the Jurors aforesaid are permitted to disperse to meet at that time.

Thomas Goff . . Plaintiff)   On motion
        Against)
James Ashmore Defendant) On motion of said Thomas Goff by Alfred M.
) Harris his Attorney suggesting to the court
now here that the Govenor of the State of Tennessee for the time being, who send for the use of James W. Comby Gdn. of heirs of Chap Choat decd. did at the present Term of this court recover against the said Thomas Goff the sum of one hundred and nineteen dollars and eighty nine cents debt together with the further sum of $7.55 the costs by said Govenor who sued for the use aforesaid about his suit in that behalf expended and further suggesting that said Judgment so recovered as aforesaid was recovered against said Thomas Goff in conveyance of his securityship for James Ashmore & paying a Judgment against said Ashmore for the amount thereof according to the Act of Assembly in such case made and provided whereupon the court now have proceeded to inspect the record of the Judgment aforesaid together with the bond upon wich said Judgment was recovered which

constitutes a part of said record and it therefore appearing to the satisfaction of the court now here that the Govenor of the State of Tennessee for the time being did at the present Term of this court towit on the 19th day of November 1823 recover in this court against the said Thomas Goff for the use of said Comby Gdn. as aforesaid the sum of one hundred and nineteen dollars and eighty nine cents debt together with the further sum of $7.55 costs by the said Govenor who sued for the use aforesaid about his suit in this behalf expended and it further appearing from said record to the satisfaction of the court that said judgment was obtained against said Thomas Goff in consequence of his securityship for James Ashmore it is therefore considered by the court now here that said Thomas Goff recover against said James Ashmore said sum of one hundred and nineteen dollars 89 cts. the debt in the Judgment aforesaid specified with intent thereon to be computed at the rate of 6 per cent from the 19th day November 1823 till paid together with the further sum of $7.55 the costs aforesaid specified and his costs by him about his motive in this behalf expended.

Ordered that court be adjourned till tomorrow morning 9 oclock.

R. Hagen
James Dugger
Thos. Clark

P-13 Thursday Morning November 20th 1823

Court met according to adjournment Present Edward J. Jones,)
John Laird &) Esquires
Thomas K. Gordon) Justices

Norvill & Hill ... Plts.)   In Debt
    Against)
Elisha B. Mayfield Deft.) It appearing to the satisfaction of the court that at the last term an order was made for this suit to be dismissed at the plaintiffs costs, which was not entered. It is thereupon ordered by the court that this suit be dismissed Nunc Protunc and that the defendant go hence without day and recover of the plaintiff his costs by him about his defence in this behalf expended.

William Ball . . Plt.)   In Case
    Against)
John Heman .. Deft.) This day came the plaintiff in his proper person and directs that this suit be dismissed, which is by this court ordered accordingly and that the defendant go hence without day and recover of the plaintiff his costs about his defence in this behalf expended.

A Deed of Trust from Elisah B. Mayfield to Spencer Clack for certain property therein contained was produced in court and the execution thereof proven by the oaths of A. McKissack & L. M. Yancy the witnesses thereto and ordered to be certified for registration.

13

William Hoges . . Plt.)   In Covernant
      Against   )
Isaac Mason . . Deft.)   This day came the plaintiff by his attorney
)   and directs that this suit be dismissed at
defendants cost which is by the court ordered accordingly and that the
plaintiff recover of the defendant his costs about his suit in this behalf
expended.

The State . . . Plt.)   Upon an Indictment for an affray & an As-
      Against   )   sault & battery Abraham Irvine came into
James Lane Deft.)   court and acknowledged himself indebted
)   to the State of Tennessee in the sum of
one hundred dollars to be levied of his goods and chattles lands and
tenments to the use of the State. To be void on condition that he appear
here on the first tuesday after the third Monday in February next and
prosecute and give evidence in behalf of the State against the defendant
for an assault & battery upon the body of said Abraham Irvine and not
depart without leave of this court.

P-14   Thursday 20th November 1823

     A Deed of conveyance from George F. Hamilton agent for Hannah P. Hamilton to William Brown for two hundred and forty nine acres of land was produced in court and the execution thereof proven by the oaths of Baker P. Potts and John H. Rivers the subscribing witnesses thereto and ordered to be certified for registration.

     A Deed of conveyance from George F. Hamilton to William Brown for two hundred and forty nine acres of land was produced in court and the execution thereof proven by the oaths of Baker P. Potts & John H. Rivers the subscribing witnesses thereto and ordered to be certified for registration.

     A Deed of conveyance from William Brown to Baker P. Potts for one hundred and twenty acres of land was produced in court and the execution thereof acknowledged by the said William Brown and ordered to be certified for registration.

     The Grand Jury returned into court the following Indictments towit the State against James Lane for an assault & battery on the body of Abraham Irvine on which was considered a true bill and withdrew to consider of further presentments.

     On motion of Lewis H. Brown Sheriff of this County William C. Mayfield was duly sworn as his Deputy.

The State . . . Plt.)   Upon a presentment for an affray
      Against   )
Aaron Miller Deft.)   This day came as well Solicitor General for the
)   State as also the defendant in his proper person
who being charged on the presentment in this case pleads guilty and because

he will not contend with the State agrees to submit himself to the Justice and mercy of the court It is therefore considered by the court that he make his fine with the State to the amount of fifty cents and that he pay the costs of this prosecution.

The State . . Plt.   )   Upon a presentment for an affray
    Against   )
Thomas Scruggs Deft.   )   This day came as well the Solicitor General for
)   the State as also who being charged on the presentment in this case pleads guilty and because he will not contend with the State (p-15) (Thursday 20th November 1823) agrees to submit himself to the Justice and mercy of the court. It is thereupon considered by the court that he make his fine with the State to the amount of fifty cents and that he pay the costs of this presentment.

The State . . . Plt.   )   Upon an Indictment for an assault &
    Against   )   battery on the body of Willis Willi-
John B. Armstrong Deft.   )   ford.
)   This day came as well the Solicitor
General for the State as also for the Defendant in his proper person who being charged on the Indictment in this case pleads guilty and because he will not contend with the State agrees to submit himself to the Justice and mercy of the court. It is therefore considered by the court that he make his fine with the State to the amount of one dollar and that he pay the costs of this Indictment.

    A Deed of conveyance from Aaron Brown to John H. Rivers and William W. Rivers for two hundred acres of land was produced in court and the Execution thereof & partly proven by the oaths of William Brown one of the witnesses thereto.

The State Plt.   )   Upon an Indictment for an affray and an
    Against   )   assault and battery.
Isaiah Maxey Deft.   )   This day came as well the Solicitor Gen-
)   eral for the State as also the defendant
in his proper person and for reasons made known to the court by the Solicitor General. It is ordered that a Nole prosqui be entered in this case on the defendant assuming upon himself the payment of all costs as on condition and thereupon the Defendant assumes upon himself the payment of the costs as on conviction. It is therefore considered by the court that the State recover of the Defendant the costs of this prosecution in manner & form as above assumed.

The State . . Plt.   )   Upon an Indictment for an affray and an
    Against   )   assault and battery.
Abraham Irvine Deft.   )   This day came as well the Solicitor Gen-
)   eral for the State as also the Defendant
in his proper person and for reasons made known to the court by the Solicitor General It is ordered that a Nole prosqui be entered in this case on the Defendant assuming upon himself the payment of all costs as on conviction and thereupon the Defendant assumes upon himself the payment

of the costs as on conviction. It is therefore considered by the court that the State recover of the Defendant the costs of this prosecution in manner and form as above assumed.

P-16   Thursday 20th November 1823

The State . . . Plt.) Upon an Indictment for an affray & an
    Against   ) assault & Battery.
Washington Bolling. Deft.) This day came as well the Solicitor
) General for the State as also the De-
fendant in his proper person and for reasons made known to the court by the Solicitor General. It is ordered that a nole prosqui be entered in this case on the defendant assuming upon himself the payment of all costs as on conviction and thereupon the Defendant assumed upon himself the payment of the costs as on conviction. It is therefore considered by the court that the State recover of the Defendant the costs of this prosecution in manner & form as above assumed.

The State . . Plt.) Upon a Recognizance to keep the Peace
    Against   )
Lewis Martin Deft.) This day came as well the Solicitor General
) for the State as also the Defendant in his
proper person and for reasons made known to the court by the Solicitor General. It is ordered that Nole prosqui be entered in this case on the Defendant assuming upon himself the payment of all costs as on conviction and thereupon the Defendant assumes upon himself the payment of the costs as on conviction. It is therefore considered by the court that the State recover of the Defendant the costs of this prosecution in manner and form as above assumed.

Charles Boyler to the use of &c. Plt.) Debt
              Against   )
Stirling C. Robertson & Defts.   ) This day came the parties by
Eldridge B. Robertson   ) their attornies and thereupon
) came the Jury empannelled and
sworn well and truly to try the issues Joined between the parties in this case, who not having heard the whole of the evidence are permitted to disperse to meet again tomorrow morning 9 oclock.

Ordered that Court be adjourned till tomorrow morning 9 oclock.

                                           H. Hogen
                                           James Duggar
                                           Thomas Marks

P-17   Friday Morning 21th November 1823

Court met according to adjournment Present Henry Hagen,)
                                       James Dugger   ) Esquires
                                       Thomas Marks   ) Justices

A Deed of conveyance from James Graham to James McDonald for one hundred acres of land was produced in court and the execution thereof proven by the oaths of Alexander McDonald & Lewis Grant two of the subscribing witnesses thereto and ordered to be certified for registration.

A Deed of conveyance from James McDonald to William Owen for one hundred acres of land was produced in court and the Execution thereof acknowledged by the said James McDonald and ordered to be certified for registration.

Charles Boyler to the use of &c. Plt.) In Debt
    Against   )
Stirling C. Robertson &) Defts.) This day came the parties by
Eldridge B. Robertson)   ) their attornies and thereupon
) came the Jury empannelled and
sworn well and truly to try the issue joined between the parties in this case who not having heard the whole of the evidence in this case are again permitted to disperse to meet again tomorrow morning 9 oclock.

The State . Plt.   ) Upon a presentment for neglect of duty as
  against   ) overseer of the road.
Henry T. Croft. Deft.) This day came as well the Solicitor General for the State as the defendant in
his proper person who being charged on the presentment in this case pleads not guilty and for his trial puts himself upon the Country and the Solicitor General for the State likewise therefore let a Jury come who as well &c. to recognize &c. and thereupon came a Jury of good and lawful men towit, William W. Thornton, William Pullen, Andrew Burns, Samuel Maltsby, Benton R. White, Ralph Graves, Jesse Hicks, Francis Smith, Joseph B. Pillow, John D. Riddle Ransom Wells & Claud Neal who being elected tried and sworn well and truly to try this issue of traverce between the State and the Defendant on their oaths do say that the Defendant is not guilty in manner an form as he is charged in the bill of presentment. It is therefore considered by the court that the Defendant be acquitted and discharged from the neglect aforesaid and that he go hence without day.

P-18 Friday 21st November 1823

The State..Plt.   ) Upon a presentment for neglect of duty as
 Against   ) overseer of the road.
Henry T. Croft Deft.) The Defendant having been acquitted on a
) trial on the merits by a Jury. It is ordered
that Judgment be entered up against the County of Giles in favor of the Several Claimants on the part of the State for all costs to which they are entitled and that the Clerk certify the same to the Trustee of Giles County for payment.

The State..Plt.   ) Upon a presentment for neglect of duty as
 Against   ) overseer of the road.
Joseph Goode Deft.) This day came the Solicitor General for the
) State who saith he is unwilling further to
prosecute the Defendant for reasons made known to the court now here. It is therefore ordered by the court that a Nole prosqui be entered in this case and that the defendant go hence without day.

The State Plt. Against Joseph Goode & Deft.	Upon a presentment for neglect of duty as overseer of the road. A nole prosqui having been entered in this case under the direction of the court.

It is ordered that Judgment be entered up against the County of Giles in favor of the several claimants on the part of the State for all costs to which they are entitled and that the Clerk certify the same to the Trustee of Giles County for payment.

The State .. Plt Against Jacob Couch Deft.	Upon a presentment for neglect of duty as overseer of the road. This day came as well Solicitor General for the State as the defendant in his proper person who

being charged on the presentment in this case pleads guilty and because he will not contend with the State agrees to submitt himself to the Justice and mercy of the court It is therefore considered by the court that the defendant make his fine with the State to the amount of six and one fourth cents and that he pay the costs of this prosecution.

The State...Plt. Against Jacob Couch Deft.	Upon a presentment for neglect of duty as overseer of the road. Jonathan Moody who was summoned to attend at this term and give evidence in behalf of the

State against the Defendant in this case, being Solemnly called came not but made default. It is therefore considered by the court that a Judgment Ni Si for the sum of one hundred and (p-19) (Friday 21st November 1823) Twenty five dollars according to the tenor of this Supena and the act of Assembly in such case made and provided and that a Scire issue against him returnable to the next Term of this court.

The Grand Jury returned into court the following indictments towit, The State against Benjamin S. England for an affray with and an assault and battery on the body of James L. Hendry upon which is Indorsed a true bill and withdraw to consider of further presentments.

Rebeccah Kyle administratrix & Claiborne Kyle administrator of Plt. the Estate of William Kyle decd. Against Mary D. Price ... Deft.	Appeal On the affidavit of James Coldwell agent for the Defendant It is ordered that a commission issue to any

of the two acting Justices of the Peace in and for the County of Lauderdale and State of Alabama to take the deposition of William Price to be read in evidence on the trial of this case and that the Defendant give to the plaintiff ten days notice of the time and place of taking said Deposition.

The State .Plt. Against Jesse Edgar Deft.	Upon a Indictment for an affray and an assault & Battery. This day came the Solicitor General for the State who saith he is unwilling further to

prosecute the Defendant for reasons made known to the court now here. It is therefore ordered by the court that a Nole prosqui be entered in this case.

The State Plt.   ) Upon an Indictment for an affray and Assault
    Against   ) & Battery.
Jesse Edgar Deft.   ) A Nole prosqui having been entered in this
) case under the direction of the court. It is
ordered that Judgment be entered up against the County of Giles in favor
of the Several claimants on the part of the State for all costs to which
they are entitled, and that the Clerk certify the same to the Trustee of
Giles County for payment.

The State .....Plt.   ) Upon an Indictment for an affray and an assault
    Against   ) & battery.
Philips Wartman Deft.   ) This day came the Solicitor General for the
) State who saith he is unwilling further to
prosecute the defendant for reasons made known to the court now here. It
is thereupon ordered by the court that a Nole prosqui be entered in this
case.

P-20   Friday 21st November 1823

The State ....Plt.   ) Upon an Indictment for an affray and an
    Against   ) Assault & Battery.
Philip Whortman Deft.   ) A Nole prosequi having been entered in
) this case under the direction of the
court. It is ordered that a Judgment be entered up against the County of
Giles in favor of the several claimants on the part of the State for all
costs to which they are entitled and that the Clerk certify the same to the
Trustee of Giles County for payment.

The State Plt.   ) Upon a presentment for a Riot Rout &c &c .
    against   ) This day came the Solicitor General for the
James Moore Deft.   ) State who saith he is unwilling further to
) prosecute the defendant for reasons made known
to the court now here. It is therefore ordered by the court that a nole
prosqui be entered in this case.

The State Plt.   ) Upon a presentment for a Riot Rout &c &c.
    Against   ) A Nole Prosqui having been entered in this case
James Moore Deft.   ) under the direction of the court. It is ordered
) that a Judgment be entered up against the County
of Giles in favor of the Several Claimants on the part of the State for all
costs to which they are entitled, and that the clerk certify the same to
the Trustee of Giles County for payment.

The State . Plt.   ) Upon a presentment for a Riot Rout &c &c .
    Against   ) This day came the Solicitor General for the
David Houston Deft.   ) State who saith he is unwilling further to
) prosecute the Defendant for reasons made known
to the court now here. It is thereupon ordered by the court that a Nole
prosqui be entered in this case.

The State Plt.) Upon a presentment for a Riot Rout &c &c.
   against) A Nole prosqui having been entered in this
David Houston Deft.) case under the direction of the court. It is
) ordered that a Judgment be entered up against
the County of Giles in favor of the Several claimants on the part of the
State for all costs to which they are entitled and that the Clerk certify
the same to the Trustee of Giles County for payment.

P-21 Friday 21st November 1823

The State Plt.) Upon a presentment for a Riot Rout &c &c.
   Against)
Bird Nolin Deft.) This day came the Solicitor General for the State
) who saith he is unwilling further to prosecute
the Defendant for reasons made known to the court now here. It is thereupon
ordered by the court that a Nole prosqui be entered in this court.

The State...Plt.) Upon a presentment for a Riot Rout &c. &c.
   Against)
Bird Nolin Deft.) A Nole Prosqui having been entered in this case
) under the direction of the court. It is ordered
that a Judgment be entered up against the County of Giles in favor of the
Several claimants on the part of the State for all costs to which they are
entitled and that the Clerk certify the same to the County Trustee for
payment.

The State . . . . .Plt.) Upon an Indictment for an affray & An
   Against) assault & battery on the body of James
Benjamin S. England Deft.) Hendry.
) This day came as well the Solicitor General for the State as the defendant in his proper person who being charged
on the Indictment in this case pleads guilty and because he will not contend with the State agrees to submits himself to the Justice and mercy of
the court. It is therefore considered by the court that the defendant make
his fine with the State to the amount of Six & one fourth cents, and that
he pay the costs of this prosecution.

The State . . . Plt.)   Scire Facias
   Against)
Andrew Burns Deft.) This day came as well the Solicitor General
) for the State as the Defendant in his proper
person and for reasons shown to the court on the affedavit of the defendant
it is ordered that he be released from the forfeiture heretofore taken
against him on the payment of all costs.

   On the petition of Robert Shadden setting fourth that James Donaldson
died intestate in this County leaving his widow Mary Donaldson and eight
children towit, Polly Donaldson, Alfred Donaldson, Nancy Shadden, wife of
said Robert Shadden, Betsy Donaldson, Sally Donaldson, Harriet Leigh wife
of Thomas Leigh, Robert Donaldson, Margaret Dunnegan, heirs and distributors
of the said James Donaldson and that he is entitled to the whole of the

interest of all said heirs and distributers in the Estate of said James
Donaldson decd. he having acquirred the same by purchase from said distributers and that John Dickey of this County administered more than five
(p-22) (Friday November 21st 1823) years ago upon the Estate of said
James Donaldson decd. It is ordered that a summons issue directed to the
said John Dickey administrator as aforesaid notifying him to appear at
the next Term of this court and pleads answer or demur to said petition.

Mary Merit ....Plt.) In case
    Against)
James Turnbean Deft.) This day came the parties by their attornies
) and it appearing to the satisfaction of the
court that the security heretofore given for the prosecution of this suit
is sufficient. It is thereupon ordered that the order of last term requiring the plaintiff to give additional security be set aside and for
neglect hold.

Ordered that court be adjourned till tomorrow morning 9 oclock.

                                                    James Duggar
                                                    H. Hagen
                                                    Paul Chiles

Saturday Morning November 22nd 1823

Court met according to adjournment Present Henry Hagen,) Esquires
                                              James Dugger) Justices
                                              Paul Chiles)

The administrators of the Estate of Anthony Samuel deceased returned
into court an account of the sale of said Estate which is ordered to be
recorded.

The commissioners who were appointed at the last Term of this court to
lay off and allot to Annas Samuel widow of Anthony Samuel deceased one years
provisions for the support and maintainance of herself and family out of
the Estate of her late husband decd. this day made report thereof which is
ordered to be recorded.

The State ....Plt.) Upon an Indictment for an affray & As-
    Against) sault and battery.
Alexander Lockheart Deft.) Thomas D. Dillon, and Aaron B. Miller
) came into court and acknowledged them-
selves indebted to the State of Tennessee in the sum of one hundred dollars
(P-23) (Saturday November 22nd 1823) each to be levied of their goods and
chattles lands and tenments to the use of the State To be void on condition
that the said Thomas D. Dillon make his personal appearance here on the
first Thursday after the third Monday in February next and prosecute and
give evidence in behalf of the State against the Defence for an assault &
battery on the body of said Thomas D. Dillon and not depart without leave
of the court.

The State Plt.   ) Upon an Indictment for an affray &
    Against   ) an assault & battery Thomas D. Dillon
Alexander Lockheart Deft.) and Aaron B. Miller came into court
) and acknowledged themselves indebted
to the State of Tennessee in the sum of one hundred dollars each to be
levied of their goods and chattles lands and tenments to the use of the
State to be void on condition that the said Thomas D. Dillon appear here
on the first Thursday after the third Monday in February next and prosecute and give evidence in behalf of the State against the Defendant for
an assault & battery on the body of said Thomas D. Dillon and not depart
without leave of the court.

The State . . . Plt.   ) Upon an Indictment an affray & an assault
    Against   ) & battery Thomas D. Dillon and Aaron B.
Robert Lockheart Deft.   ) Miller came into court and acknowledged
) themselves indebted to the State of Tenn-
essee in the sum of one hundred dollars each to be levied of their goods
and chattles lands and tenments to the use of the State to be void on condition that the said Thomas D. Dillon appear here on the first Thursday
after the third Monday in February next and prosecute and give evidence
in behalf of the State against the defendant for an assault & battery on
the body of said Thomas D. Dillion and not depart without leave of the
court.

Charles Boyles to the use of &c Plts.)   In Debt
        against   )
Stirling C. Robertson &) Defts   )
Eldridge B. Robertson   )   ) This day came the parties by
) their attornies and thereupon
) came the Jury empanneled and
sworn well and truly to try the issue between the parties in this case who
not having heard the whole evidence in his case were permitted to disperse
to meet again on Tuesday morning ten oclock.

P-24 Saturday November 22nd 1823

Thomas C. Porter . . Plt.   )   In Debt
        Against   )
William Mayfield & Defts   ) On motion of Benjamin W. Edwards and it
Thomas McKissack   ) appearing to the satisfaction of the court
) now here upon due proofs that William
Mayfield & Thomas McKissack did on the 28th day of October 1823 execute
their joints bonds under seal to Benjamin W. Edwards theirby appointing
authorising and empowering the said Benjamin W. Edwards for them and in
their names to confess a Judgment in the court of pleas and quarter session
for the County of Giles and State of Tennessee in favor of Thomas C. Porter
against them for the sum of five Hundred dollars debt together with the
further sum of Seven dollars & fifty cents damages occasioned by the detention of said debt the same being the principal and Interest due said Thomas
C. Porter upon a Written obligatory executed by Wm. & Elisha B. Mayfield &
Thos. McKissack to said Thomas C. Porter for the sum of five hundred dollars
dated the 23rd day of July 1823 and payable on or before the 15th day of
August thence next ensuing, and It also appearing to the Satisfaction of
the the court that the said Thomas McKissack & William Mayfield have had ten

days notice of the intention of said Benjamin W. Edwards to confess a Judgment in favor of said Thomas C. Porter against the said Wm. Mayfield & Thomas McKissack and thereupon said Benjamin W. Edwards says that the said William Mayfield & Thomas McKissack are justly indebted to the said Thomas C. Porter in the sum of Five hundred dollars & fifty cents damages and occassioned by detention of said debt and prayes the court now here to render Judgment in favor of said Thomas C. Porter against said Wm. Mayfield & Thomas McKissack to the amount of their debt & Damages aforesaid. It is therefore considered by the court that said Thomas C. Porter recover of said Wm. Mayfield & Thomas McKissack his debt and damages aforesaid in form aforesaid confessed & his costs by him about his suit in this behalf expended.

Ordered that court be adjourned till Monday morning ten oclock.

B. Black
Jas. Duggar
Anderson Hagan

P-25   Monday Morning 24th November 1823

Court met according to adjournment Present Alexander Black, Archibald McKissack, James Dugger, Robert Read, Edwin D. Jones, William Usery, William B. Pepper.

Ordered that John Abernathy be appointed overseer of the road in the room of Lewis Smith resigned and that he have the same district of hands.

A Deed of conveyance from Archibald Smith to Edmund Lumpkins for Sixty two and ahalf acres of land was produced in court and the Execution thereof acknowledged by the said Archibald Smith and ordered to be certified for registration.

A Deed of conveyance from Hardy Hightower to Edmund Lumpkin for two hundred and fifty acres of land was produced in court and the execution thereof proven by the oaths of Archibald Smith, and Archibald Smith the subscribed witness thereto & ordered to be certified for registration.

Ordered that the County Trustee of this County pay to Hezeciah Jones the sum of thirty dollars for support of Geddeon Pannell a pauper of this County for one from this time.

A Deed of conveyance from Jacob Cochran to Archibald Crocket for eight acres of land was produced in court and the execution thereof acknowledged by the said Jacob Cochran and ordered to be certified for registration.

A Deed of conveyance from James David to Jacob Cochran for five acres of land was produced in court and the execution thereof acknowledged by the said James Davis & ordered to be certified for registration.

Ordered that William M. Shields be appointed overseer of the road in room of Archibald Crocket resigned and that he have the same district of hands.

A Deed of conveyance from Elisha Dodson to Samuel H. Dodson for one hundred sixty acres of land was produced in court and the Execution thereof acknowledged by the said Elisha Dodson and ordered to be certified for registration.

A Deed of conveyance from Samuel H. Dodson to Elisha Dodson for one hundred and sixty acres of land was produced in court and the execution thereof acknowledged by the said Samuel H. Dodson and ordered to be certified for registration.

P-26   Monday 24th November 1823

A Deed of conveyance from John P. Taylor to Andrew Yokley for one hundred acres of land was produced in court and the execution thereof acknowledged by the said John P. Taylor and ordered to be certified for registration.

Matthew J. Black came into court and resigned as constable in Captains Potts Company and thereupon the court appointed John Whitfield constable in said Company who was qualified and gave bond and security according to Law.

Ordered that William Brown son of Isham Brown be appointed overseer of the road in the room of Larkin Webb resigned and that he have the same district of hands.

Ordered that Edward D. Jones & Thomas K. Gordon Esquires be appointed commissioners to settle with John Goff who is Guardian to the minor heirs of George Goff deceased & that they make report to the next term of this court.

Ordered that Nathan Young be allowed the sum of fourteen dollars as per acct. filed and that the same be certified to the County Trustee for payment.

A Deed of conveyance from Thomas Stewart to Jacob Bodenhammer for one hundred & fifty acres of land was produced in court and the Execution thereof proven by the oaths of C. Long & W. Bodenhammer two of the subscribing witnesses thereto and ordered to be certified for registration.

Ordered that Robert McKnight be appointed overseer of the road in the room of James McKnight resigned and that he have the same district of hands.

Ordered that Thomas Harwood be appointed overseer of the road in the room of John Ross resigned and that he have the same district of hands.

Ordered that Robert Fenner be appointed overseer of the road in the room of Henry F. Steel resigned and that he have the same districts of hands.

Ordered that Keenan McMullen be appointed overseer of the road in the room of John Porter resigned and that he have the same district of hands.

William R. Davis is appointed constable in Captain John Browns company who was qualified and executed Bond and security according to law.

P-27 Monday November 24th 1823

Ordered that Charles C. Abernathy be appointed commissioners to settle with the County Trustee and sheriff of this County in the room of Henry Hagen resigned.

The State ...Plt.	)	For failing to attend as a witness
Against	)	
Jonathan Moody Deft.	)	This day came as well the Solicitor General
	)	for the State as the defendant in his proper

person and for reasons shown to the court now here It is ordered that the Forfeiture taken against the defendant at this Term be set aside and that he be released from the payment of the costs that has occured in this case.

Ordered that a Venire facias issue to the Sheriff of this County commanding him to summon the following persons to attend at the next Term of this court to be held at the court house in the Town of Pulaski on the first Tuesday after the third Monday in February next then and there to serve as Grand and Petit Jurors, towit, Charles Edwards, Edward Marks, Joseph Reed, John Young Jr., Gerald Irby, Jacob Cochran, Samuel Perkins, John D. Reddell, Thomas Clark, William Maxwell, John Seal, Marshall Moody, John Balch, Simpson H. White, Stephen Reading, Stirling Graves, Ephraim A. Young, Nathan Bass, George Bowers, Parker P. Potts, John Butter, Henry J. Cooper, John E. Holden, Charles Myers Senr., Matthew Cunningham, and Jarrett Young.

Ordered that Thomas McNight a constable of this county be Summoned to attend at next court.

The Jury who were appointed to view a road from Tyre Rodes to Tinnons Mill made report which was received by the court and thereupon the court ordered that Tyre Rodes be appointed overseer to open and keep inrepair the same and that he have under his direction for that purpose four of his on hands.

A Deed of conveyance from George Holas to Charles Myers Senr., for fifty acres of land was produced in court and the execution thereof proven by the oaths of C. Myers & Robert Reed two of the subscribing witnesses thereto and ordered to be certified for registration.

Ordered that the County Trustee of this County pay to Thomas E. Abernathy the sum of seventeen Dollars for the support of James Preston Paine a pauper of this County for the term of twelve months from this time.

The commissioners who were appointed to settle with the administrators of the Estate of Abner Davenport decd. made return of said settlement which was ordered to be recorded.

P-28   Monday 24th November 1823

Ordered that Thomas Batte Esquire be appointed to take a list of taxable property and polls in Captain Bass company for the year 1824 and that he make return thereof to the next term of this court.

Ordered that Thomas Harwood Esquire be appointed to take a list of taxable property and polls in Captain Kernass Company for the year 1824 and that he make return thereof to the next Term of this court.

Ordered that Miller S. McLaurine Esquire be appointed to take a list of taxable property and polls in Captain McCormack Company for the year 1824 and that he make return thereof to the next term of this court.

Ordered that Robert Oliver be appointed to take a list of taxable property and polls in Captain Crofts Company for the year 1824 and that he make return thereof to the next term of this court.

Ordered that Anderson Hagan Esquire be appointed to take a list of taxable property and polls in Captain Barnes Company for the year 1824 and that he make return thereof to the next term of this court.

Ordered that William Brown Esquire be appointed to take a list of taxable property and polls in Captain Potts Company for the year 1824 and that he make return thereof to the next term of this court.

Ordered that Archibald McKissack Esquire be appointed to take a list of taxable property and polls in Captain Watson's Company for the year 1824 and that he make return thereof to the next term of this court.

Ordered that Henry Hagen Esquire be appointed to take a list of taxable property and polls in Captain John Brown's Company for the year 1824 and that he make return thereof to the next term of this court.

Ordered that Robert Reed Esquire be appointed to take a list of taxable property and polls in Captain Henrys Company for the year 1824 and that he make return thereof to the next term of this court.

Ordered that James McCafferty Esquire be appointed to take a list of taxable property and polls in Captain Brooks Company for the year 1824 and that he make return thereof to the next term of this court.

P-29 Monday 24th November 1823

Ordered that Peter Swanson Esquire be appointed to take a list of taxable property and polls in Captain Ruffs Company for the year 1824 and that he make return thereof to the next term of this court.

Ordered that John Bramlett Esquire be appointed to take a list of taxable property and polls in Captain Whites Company for the year 1824 and that he make return thereof to the next term of this court.

Ordered that Edward D. Jones Esquire be appointed to take a list of taxable property and polls in Captain Livingston's Company for the year 1824 and that he make return thereof to the next term of this court.

Ordered that John Laird Esquire be appointed to take a list of taxable property and polls in Captain Try's Company for the year 1824 and that he make return thereof to the next term of this court.

Ordered that Carey T. Kelley Esquire be appointed to take a list of taxable property and polls in Captain Youngs Company for the year 1824 and that he make return thereof to the next Term of this court.

Ordered that John C. Walker Esquire be appointed to take a list of taxable property and polls in Captain Montgomery Company for the year 1824 and that he make return thereof to the next term of this court.

Ordered that Drury Smith Esquire be appointed to take a list of taxable property and polls in Captain Anderson's Company for the year 1824 and that he make return thereof to the next term of this court.

Ordered that John Young Esquire be appointed to take a list of taxable property and polls in Captain Chiles Company for the year 1824 and that he make return thereof to the next term of this court.

Ordered that Thomas Marks Esquires be appointed to take a list of taxable property and polls in Captain Edward M. Browns Company for the year 1824 and that he make return thereof to the next term of this court.

A Plat & Certificate of servey in the name of William Menefee for nine acres of land was produced in court and the assignment thereon from the said William Menefee to Alexander Hood was acknowledged by the said Wm. Menefee & ordered to be certified.

P-30   Monday 24th November 1823

Ordered that Timothy Ezell be appointed Guardian to Isaac G. Johnson minor orphan of Isaac Johnson deceased who gave bond and security according to Law.

Ordered that Francis Guthrie be allowed the sum of Eight dollars and twenty five cents as per account filed which is ordered to be certified to the County Trustee for payment.

A power of Attorney from James Lester to John H. McKeathen was produced in court and the Execution thereof acknowledged by the said James Lester and ordered to be certified.

Charlotte Hicks was bound an apprenticed to John Tacker an Indenture to that effect having been entered into between the chairman of the court and said John Tacker.

Ordered that the County Trustee of this County pay to James Perry late Sheriff of this County the sum of fifty dollars for his Exofficio services for one year last past.

Ordered that the order of last term binding Jones Potston an apprentice to William Maxwell be received and set aside.

Ordered that Henry Hagen, James Buford & Charles C. Abernathy be appointed commissioners to settle with Gilham Harwell Executor of Buckner Harwell decd. and that they make report of said settlement to the next term of this court.

Ordered that Polly Carvell widow of the late William Carvell a pauper of this county deceased receive for her support and maintainance the ballance of the money which was allowed for the support and maintainance of her deceased husband the present year.

Ordered that the following tax lists be received by the court and the double tax thereon remitted towit, Levi Sherrill 210 acres of land.
              1 white poll
              3 slaves.

P-31   Monday 24th November 1823

Ordered that Joshua Horn, Jessee Allen, John Beaver, William Beaver, Jonathan Moody, James Russell & Thomas Horn or any five of them be appointed a Jury to view a road near the plantation of Jacob Couch and see if it be proper to turn the same and make report thereof to the next term of this court.

Nathaniel Williams Guardian to the minor children of Henry Scales returned into court an account against his wards which was ordered to be recorded.

Gray H. Edwards in right of his wife Susan formerly Susan Jones and Daughter of the late Wilson Jones decd. filed his petition in Writing against Thomas McKissack administrator of the Estate of the said Wilson Jones deceased for a distributive share of said Estate and disclosure of the amount thereof which petition was granted by the court and an order made that a Subpoena should issue to the said Thomas McKissack requiring him to appear at the next term of this court and answer said petition and that copy thereof accompany said Subpoena.

Samuel Smith in right of his wife Jane formerly Jane Porter came into court on the first Saturday after the third Monday in November & filed his petition against John Poter former Guardian of his wife Janes and Eleanor W. Porter and Reece Porter Junr., for a distributive share in three hundred and sixty & a half acres of land in Giles County conveyed by Reece Porter Senior deceased to said Minors which was granted be the court and thereupon Robert McLaurine, Robert Reed, Alexander Black, Archibald McKissack, and Robert Davidson were appointed commissioners to lay off and set apart to the said petitioner in right of his wife his proportion of said land agreable to his petition and under their hands and seals returned two fois platts representing the division of said land.

Ordered that Court be adjourned till tomorrow morning 9 oclock.

           E. D. Jones
           William Ussery
           Robert Reed

P-32 Tuesday Morning 25th November 1823

Court met according to adjournment Present Edward D. Jones,) Esquires
               William Ussery) Justices
               Robert Reed)

A Deed of conveyance from Fountain Lester to Isaac Morris for one hundred and fifty nine acres of land was produced in court and the Execution thereof acknowledged by the said Fountain Lester and ordered to be certified for registration.

Letters of administration on the Estate of David Steel was Granted to Thomas Steel who was qualified and entered into bond and security according to law.

On the petition of Robert Shadden setting fourth that Mary Donaldson died intestate in this County on the 13th day of October 1823 leaving eight children to wit, Polly Donaldson, Alfred Donaldson, Nancy Shadden wife of Robert Shadden, Betsy Donaldson, Harriet Leigh, wife of Thomas J. Leigh Robert Donaldson, and Margret Dunnegan wife of Martin Dunnegan heirs and distributers of the said Mary Donaldson decd. that he is entitled to the whole of the Interest of all said heirs and distributees In the Estate of the said Mary Donaldson decd. he having acquired the same by purchase from said distributees and that Charles Perkins of this County administered on the Estate of the said Mary Donaldson decd. on Monday the 26th day of November 1821 It is ordered that a summons issue to the said Charles Perkins administrator as aforesaid notifying him to appear at the next term of this court and plead answer or demur to said petition.

A Deed of conveyance from Lewis H. Brown Sheriff of this County to Henry Brown for three hundred and fifty acres of land was produced in court and the execution thereof acknowledged by the said Lewis H. Brown and ordered to be certified for registration.

Ordered that Alexander Black and Tyree Rodes be appointed commissioners to settle with Charles Perkins administrator of the Estate of Mary Donaldson decd. and that they make return of said settlement to the next term of this court.

The Grand Jury returned into court an Indictment against Alexander Lockheart for an affray with and an assault and battery on the body of Laurence W. Pendergrast endorsed thereon a true bill also an Indictment against Robert Lockheart for an affray with and an assault and battery on the body of Francis B. Kerr endorsed thereon a true Bill Also a Bill of Indictment against Alexander (p-33) (Tuesday 25th November 1823) Lockheart for an affray with and an assault on the body of Thomas D. Dillion endorsed thereon "   " Also a Bill of Presentment against Meredith Bunch for an affray with and an assault & battery on the body of John Croft. Also a bill of presentment against Edmund Gatlin for an affray with and an assault and battery on the body of Cammell Mayfield and withdrew to consider of further presentments.

The State . . . Plt. against Robert Lockheart Deft.	Upon an Indictment for an affray with & an assault & battery on the body of Frances Kerr.

This day came as well the Solicitor for the State as the defendant in his proper person who being charged on the bill of Indictment in this case pleads guilty and because he will not contend with the State agrees to submit himself to the justice and mercy of the court. It is therefore considered by the court that the defendant make his fine with the State to the amount of fifty cents and that he pay the costs of this prosecution.

A Deed of conveyance from Stephen Anderson & Andrew M. Balentine Executors of the last will & testament of John Samuel decd. to William C. Graves for three hundred acres of land was produced in court and the Execution acknowledged by the said Stephen Anderson and Andrew Ballentine & ordered to be certified for registration.

Charles Boyles to the use of & Plt.)   In Debt
         Against)
Sterling C. Roberts &   )   Defts.) This day came the parties by
Eldridge B. Roberts   )   their attornies and by con-
)   sent of parties and with the
assent of the court Merry Carter one of the Jurors empanneled and sworn
to try the issue joined between the parties in this case is withdrawn and
Stephen Samuel a good and lawful Juror of the County aforesaid was duly
qualified well and truly to try the issue joined between the parties in
this case in the room and stead of said Merry Carter In the case of the
examination of the evidence in this cause the plaintiffs attorney tendered
the following bill of exception to wit,

State of Tennessee)   Court of Pleas & Quarter Session Nov. Term
Giles County Jail   )   1823

Charles Boyles for the use of   )   In Debt
Brice M. Garner & Robert Dixon)
         Vs   )   Be it remembered that upon the
S. & E. B. Robertson   )   trial of this cause the   (p-34)
)   (Tuesday 25th November 1823)
Depts aforesaid in evidence the following notes & protests towit,

Protest and note marked C. Do. Marked E. Do. Marked F. Do Marked G. Do
marked H. Do. Marked J. Do. Marked K. Do. Marked L. Do. Marked M. Do.
Do Marked N. Do. Marked O. Do. Marked P. Do Marked Q. to the reading all
of which the plaintiffs by his counsel objected, but the court overruled
the objection & suspended all said notes and protests to be read in evidence to the Jury to which opinion of the Court the plaintiff by his counsel excepted and preys this his bill of exception to be signed sealed &
enrolled and made a part of the record in this case and the same is accordingly ordered.

E. D. Jones (Seal)   Robert Reed (Seal)   William Ussery (Seal).

     And the Jurors aforesaid upon their oaths do say that they find the
issue joined between the parties in this case in favor of the defendant
It is therefore considered by the court that the defendant go hence without
day and recover of the plaintiff their costs by them about their defence
in this behalf expended. Whereupon said plaintiff by his attorney moved the
court now here for a rule to show cause why a new trial should be granted,
and the same is granted.

     Ordered that Court be adjourned till tomorrow morning 9 oclock.

                                                            James Duggar
                                                           H. Hagen
                                                           A. McKissack

P-35   Wednesday Morning 26th November 1823

     Court met according to adjournment Present Henry Hagen,)   Esquires
                                                    Robert Reed   )   Justices
                                                    William Ussery   )

John M. Preston Plt.) In Case
    Against)
Ira C. Goff Deft.) The Referees to whom were refered the matter
) in controversy between the parties in this case returned their award in the following words and figures towit,

State of Tennessee)
)
Giles County) "Pursuant to an order of the Worshipful court of the County aforesaid appointing us to arbitrate and settle a certain matter in controversy now pending in the County Court of the County aforesaid where in John M. Preston is plaintiff and Ira C. Goff is Defendant we have on day of the date hereof proceeded to the discharge of said duty when the parties were heard and all testimony before us fully examined and we do award adjudge & say that the said Defendant Ira C. Goff is indebted to the said plaintiff John M. Preston thirty dollars and 84 cents which we say he owes him.

Given under our hands and seals this 20th day of September 1823.

                               E. D. Jones   (Seal)
                               Alfred Flournay (Seal)
                               Wm. Mayfield   (Seal)
                               A. M. Ballentine (Seal)

It is therefore considered by the court that the plaintiff recover of the defendant the aforesaid sum of thirty dollars and Eighty four cents his debt aforesaid by the jurors aforesaid in form aforesaid awarded and his costs by him about his suit in this behalf expended.

Ordered that Alexander Black & Henry Hagen Esquires be appointed commissioners to settle with John Paule Executors of John Paul decd. and that they make return of said settlement to the next term of this court.

James W. Wheeler Plt.) In Covenant
    against)
Elisha White Deft.) This day came the parties by their attornies
) and thereupon came a Jury of good and lawful men towit, Henry J. Cooper, William W. Thornton, George Everly, Thomas Wells, John McCracken, Ambrose Cobbs, Merry Carter, John Keenan, George Malone, Robert Lockheart, Ralph Graves, & Larkin Mayfield who being elected tried and sworn well and truly to try the issue joined between the partie s in this case upon their oaths do say that the (p-36) Wednesday 26th November 1823, Defendant hath not kept and performed his covenant as the plaintiff in his declaration hath alledged and they do assess the plaintiffs damages by occasion hereof to seventy six dollars and Eighty cents besides costs. It is therefore considered by the court that the plaintiff recover of the defendant the damages aforesaid by the Jurors aforesaid in form aforesaid assessed and his costs by him about his suit in this behalf expended.

A Deed of conveyance from Joseph Scott to James Derr for two hundred & twenty five and one fourth acres of land was produced in court and the execution acknowledged by the said Joseph Scott and ordered to be certified for registration.

George W. Campbell Plt.) In Debt
    Against)
Eldridge B. Robertson Deft.) On the affidavit of the Defendant It
) is ordered that the trial of this
cause be continued and postponed till the next term of this court, and that
the Defendant pay the costs of this term, and that a commissioner or commissioner's issue to take the deposition of Francis Porterfield, Benjamin
Patterson & Evander McInver to be read in evidence on the trial of this
cause and that the defendant give to the plaintiff fifteen days notice of
the time and place for taking said deposition.

    The Grand Jury returned into court a bill of Indictment against Bartlett
Yancy for an affray with and an assault and battery on the body of James
Johnson on which is endorsed a true bill also a bill of Indictment against
Henry Yancy for an affray with and an assault and battery on the body of
James Johnston on which is endorsed a true bill also a bill of presentment
against John Marler for an affray with and an assault and battery on the
body of William Phifer also a bill of presentment against William Phifer for
an affray with and an assault and battery on the body of John Marler also
a bill of presentment against John Defoe for an affray with and an assault
and battery on the body of James Pillow also a bill of presentment against
Elisah Riddle for an affray with and an assault and battery on the body of
John Edwards, also a bill of presentment against John Edwards for an affray
with and an assault and battery on the body of Elisah Riddle also a bill
of presentment against James Pillow for an affray with and an assault and
battery on the body of John Defoe, also a bill of presentment against
Willis Pillow for an affray with and an assault and battery on the body of
James Bunch also a bill of presentment   (p-37)   Wednesday 26th November
1823 against James Bunch for an affray with and an assault and battery
on the body of Willis Pillow also a bill of presentment against George
Kirk for an affray with and an assault and battery on the body of John
McKissack, also a presentment against John McKissack for an affray with
and an assault and battery on the body of George Kirk, and withdrew to
consider of further presentments.

    The following tax list was received by the court and the double tax
thereon remitted to wit,

Sterling C. Robertson &) 68 00 acres of land
Eldridge B. Robertson) 2 white polls
) 20 slaves.

    A Plat and certificate of survey in the name of Jesse West, Daniel Puryear
and James N. Phillips was produced in court and an assignment thereon from
said Jesse West, Daniel Puryear & James N. Phillips to William Woods was
acknowledged by the said Jesse West, Daniel Puryear, & William Woods attorney in fact for the said Phillips and ordered to be certified.

Thomas Martin Surviving Plt.) In Case
Partner &c.)
    against)
Washington Croft ... Deft.) This day came the parties by their
) attornies and thereupon came a Jury
) of good and lawful men towit, Thomas

Cole, Bazel Compton, William S. Neal, William Pellen, John A. McKinney, George Rice, John Black, Samuel Craig, James Turnbean, Joseph Bridges, John W. Perry & Jordan Whitley who being Elected tried and sworn well and truly to try the issue joined between the parties in this case upon their oaths do say that the defendant did assume upon himself in manner and form as the plaintiff in declaring against him hath alledged and they do assess his damages by occasion of the non performance of said assum set to seventy two dollars and seventy five cents, besides costs.

It is therefore considered by the court that the plaintiff recover of the defendant the damages aforesaid by the Jurors aforesaid in form aforesaid by the Jurors assessed and his costs by him about his suit in this behalf expended.

Ordered that court be adjourned till tomorrow morning nine oclock.

H. Hagen
William Usery
Robert Reed

P-38 Thursday Morning 27th November 1823

Court met according to adjournment Present Henry Hagen,) Esquires
                                    William Usery &   ) Justices
                                    Robert Reed   )

Thomas Martin Surviving Partner & Plt.) Debt
           Against   )
John Keenan . . . . Deft.   ) This day came the parties by
) their attornies and thereupon
came a Jury of good and lawful men towit, William W. Thornton, Thomas Wells, Henry J. Cooper, Thomas Cole, Bazil Compton, Madison Riddle, William Maultsby, Joseph S. Ellison, James Conner, Henry Butler, Robert Lockhart, and Thomas Hallum who being elected tried and sworn well and truly to try the issue and joined between the parties in this case upon their oaths do say that the defendant hath not paid the debt in the writing obligatory in the declaration mentioned as the plaintiff in his replecation hath alleged and they do assess the plaintiffs damages by reasons of the detention of said debt to three dollars and eight cents, Besides costs It is therefore considered by the court that the plaintiff recover of the defendant the sum of Fifty six dollars and forty three cents the amount of the Debt aforesaid by the Jurors aforesaid in form aforesaid assessed and his costs by him about his suit in this behalf expended.

Frances Chambers Plts.) Dept.
    Against   )
Edward O. Chambers Deft.) This day came the parties by their attor-
) nies & thereupon came a Jury of good and
lawful men to wit, William W. Thornton, Thomas Wells, Henry J. Cooper, Thomas Cole, Bazil Compton, Madison Riddle, William Maultsby, Joseph S. Ellison, James Conner, Henry Butler, Robert Lockhart & Thomas Hollum who being elected tried and sworn well & truly to try the issue joined between the parties in this case upon their oaths do say that he the Defendant hath not paid the debt in the writing obligatory in the declaration mentioned

but that there remains a balance of said debt unpaid to the amount of fifty three dollars and seven cents and they do assess the plaintiff damages by occasion of the detention of said ballance of said debt to one Dollar & fifty nine cents and that he hath no other set offs. It is therefore considered by the court that the plaintiff recover against the said defendant the ballance of her debt aforesaid together with her damages aforesaid by the jurors aforesaid in form aforesaid assessed and her costs about her suit in this behalf expended.

P-39   Thursday 27th November 1823

William C. Graves Plt.   )   In Debt
    Against   )
John Phillips . . Deft.   ) This day came the parties by their attorneys and thereupon came a Jury of good and lawful men towit, William W. Thornton, Thomas Wells, Henry J. Cooker, Thomas Cole, Basil Compton, Maddison Riddle, William Maltsby, Joseph S. Ellison, James Conner, Henry Butler, Robert Lockhart, & Thomas Hallum who being elected tried and sworn well and truly to try the issue joined between the parties in this case upon their oaths do say that the defendant hath not paid the debt in the writing obligatory in the declaration mentioned as the plaintiff in his application hath alledged and they do assess the plaintiffs damages by reason of the detention of said Debt to three dollars & ninety three cents besides costs. It is therefore considered by the court that the plaintiff recover of the defendant the sum of eighty three dollars and thirty nine cents the amount of his debt aforesaid together with his damages aforesaid by the Jurors aforesaid in form aforesaid assessed and his costs by him about his suit in this behalf expended.

William C. Graves Plt.   )   In Debt
    Against   )
John Phillips Deft.   ) This day came the parties by their attornies and thereupon came a Jury of good and lawful men to wit, William W. Thorneton, Thomas Wells, Henry J. Cooper, Thomas Cole, Basil Compton, Maddison Riddle, William Maultsby, Joseph S. Ellison, James Conner, Henry Butler, Robert Lockhart and Thomas Hollum, Who being Elected tried and sworn well and truly to try the issue joined between the parties in this case upon their oaths do say that the defendant hath not paid the debt in the writing obligatory in the declaration mentioned as the plaintiff in his replication hath alledged and they do assess the plaintiffs damages by reasons of the detention of said debt to three dollars and ninety three cents, besides costs. It therefore considered by the court that the plaintiff recover of the defendant the sum of eighty three dollars and thirty nine cents the amount of his debt aforesaid together with the damages aforesaid by the Jurors aforesaid in form aforesaid assessed and his costs by him about his suit in this behalf expended.

William C. Graves Plt.   )   In Debt
    against   )
John Phillips . . Deft.   ) This day came the parties by their attornies and thereupon came a jury of good and lawful men towit, William W. Thorneton, Thomas Wells, Henry J. Cooper,

Thomas Cole, (p-40) Thursday 27th November 1823, Bazil Compton, Maddison, Riddle, William Maultsby, Joseph S. Ellison, James Conner, Henry Butler, Robert Lockhart, and Thomas Hallum, who being elected tried and sworn well and Truly to try the issue joined between the parties in this case upon their oaths do say that the defendant hath not paid the debt in the Writing obligatory in the declaration mentioned as the plaintiff in his replication hath alledged and they do assess the plaintiff damages by reasons of the detention of said debt to three dollars and ninety three cents besides costs. It is therefore considered by the court that the plaintiff recover against the said defendant the sum of Eighty three dollars and thirty nine cents, the amount of his debt aforesaid together with his damages aforesaid by the Jurors aforesaid in form aforesaid assessed and his costs by him about his suit in this behalf expended.

Jacob Felmith Plt.   )   In Debt
   Against   )
William Rose Deft.)   This day came the parties by their attornies,
)   and thereupon came a Jury of good and lawful
men to wit, William W. Thornton, Thomas Wells, Henry J. Cooper, Thomas Cole, Bazil Compton, Maddison Riddle, William Maultsby, Joseph S. Ellison, James Conner, Henry Butler, Robert Lockhart and Thomas Hollum who being elected tried and sworn well and truly to try the issues joined between the parties in this case upon their oaths do say that the defendant hath not paid the debt in the writing obligatory in the declaration mentioned and that he hath no set off as the plaintiff in his replication hath mentioned and they do assess the plaintiffs damages by occasion of the detention of said debt to ten dollars sixty two and one half cents besides costs. It is therefore considered by the court that the plaintiff recover of the defendant the sum of two hundred and fifty dollars the amount of his debt aforesaid together with his damages aforesaid in form aforesaid by the Jurors aforesaid assessed and his costs by him about his suit in the behalf expended.

Lunsford M. Bramlett Plt.)   In Debt
   Against   )
William Barnes Deft.   )   This day came the parties by their attor-
)   neys and thereupon came a Jury of good
and lawful men to wit, William W. Thornton, Thomas Wells, Henry J. Cooper, Thomas Cole, Bazil Compton, Maddison Riddle, William Maultsby, Joseph S. Ellison, James Conner (p-41) Thursday 27th November 1823, Henry Butler, Robert Lockhart, and Thomas Hallums, who being elected tried and sworn well and truly the issue joined between the parties in this case upon their oaths do say that the defendants have not paid the debt in the Writing obligatory in the declaration mentioned and they do assess the plaintiffs damages by occasion of the detention of said debt to four dollars & ten cents besides costs. It is therefore considered by the court that the plaintiff recover of the defendant the sum of one hundred and fifty dollars the amount of his debt aforesaid together with his damages aforesaid by the Jurors aforesaid in form aforesaid assessed and his costs about him in his suit expended.

Mary Merit Plt.   )   In Case
   Against   )
James Turnbean Deft.)   On the application of the defendant it is

ordered that a commission issue to any two Justices of the peace for the County of Davidson to take the deposition of Benjamin Capps to be read in evidence on the trial of this cause and that the defendant give the plaintiff twenty days notice of the time and place for taking said deposition.

James Woodfin &) Plts.)
George Malone Exors. &c.)) In Debt
    Against)
Isaac Mayfield)) This day came the parties by
Nathaniel Young &) Defts.) their attornies and thereupon
Elisah B. Mayfield)) came a Jury of good and lawful
) men to wit, William W. Thornton, Thomas Wells, Henry J. Cooper, Thomas Cole, Basil Compton, Maddison Riddle, William Maultsby, Joseph S. Ellison, James Conner, Henry Butler, Robert Lockhart and James Hallums who being elected tried and sworn well and truly to try the issue joined between the parties in this case upon their oaths do say that the defendants have not paid the debt in the Writing obligatory in the declaration mentioned as the plaintiffs in their replication have alledged and they do assess their damages by occasion of the detention of said debt to twenty six dollars and forty cents besides costs. It is therefore considered by the court that the plaintiffs recover of the defendants the sum of six hundred & sixty dollars the amount of the debt aforesaid together with their damages aforesaid by the Jurors aforesaid in form aforesaid assessed and their costs by them about their suit in this behalf expended.

P-42 Thursday 27th November 1823

William B. Martin Plt.) In Debt
    Against)
John Bridewell Deft.) This day came the parties by their attornies
) and thereupon came a Jury of good and lawful men to wit, William W. Thornton, Thomas Wells, Henry J. Cooper, Thomas Cole, Bazil Compton, Maddison Riddle, William Maultsby, Joseph S. Ellison, James Conner, Henry Butler, Robert Lockhart, and Thomas Harlum, who being elected tried and sworn well and truly to try the issue joined between the parties in this case upon their oaths do say that the defendant hath not paid the Debt in the writing obligatory in the declaration mentioned and that he hath not set off as the plaintiff in his replication hath alledged and they do assess the plaintiffs damages by occasion of the detention of said debt to eight dollars besides costs. It is therefore considered by the court that the plaintiff recover of the said defendant the sum of two hundred dollars the amount of his debt aforesaid together with his damages aforesaid by the Jury aforesaid in form aforesaid assessed and his costs by him about his suit in this behalf expended.

Robert B. Harney assignee & Plt.) In Debt
    Against)
Elizabeth Williams . . . . Deft.) This day came the parties by
) their attornies and thereupon came a Jury of good and lawful men to wit, William W. Thornton, Thomas Wells, Henry J. Cooker, Thomas Cole, Bazil Compton, Maddison Riddle, William Maultsby, Joseph S. Ellison, James Conner, Henry Butler, Robert Lockhart and Thomas Hallum, who being elected tried and sworn well and

truly to try the issues joined between the parties in this case upon their oaths do say that the defendant hath not paid the whole of the debt in the Writing obligatory in the declaration mentioned but that these remain yet unpaid of said debt the sum of one hundred and seventy six dollars and seventy cents besides costs, and that the defendant hath no other set off and they do assess the plaintiffs damages by reason of the detention aforesaid debt to $43.56 cents. It is therefore considered by the court that the plaintiff recover of the defendant the balance of this debt aforesaid by the Jurors aforesaid in form aforesaid assessed and his costs by him about his suit in this behalf expended.

The Grand Jury returned into court a bill of presentment against George Kirk for an assault on the body of John L. Brandon and withdrew to consider of further presentments.

P-43   Thursday 27th November 1823

Richard Bently Assignee & Plt.) In Debt
　　Against   )
James H. Pickens &   Defts.   ) This day came the parties by their
Elisha B. Mayfield   ) attorneys and thereupon came a Jury
) of good and lawful men towit, William W. Thornton, Thomas Wells, Henry J. Cooper, Thomas Cole, Bazil Compton, Maddison Riddle, William Maultsby, Joseph S. Ellison, James Conner, Henry Butler, Robert Lockhart, and Thomas Hallum who being elected tried and sworn well and truly to try the issue joined between the parties in this case upon their oaths do say that the defendants have not paid the debt in the Writing obligatory in the declaration mentioned and that they have no set off as the plaintiff in his replications hath alledged and they do assess the plaintiffs damages by occasion of the detention of said debt to seven dollars and twenty cents besides costs.
　　It is therefore considered by the court that the plaintiff recover of the defendant the sum of Eighty dollars the amount of his debt aforesaid together with damages aforesaid in form aforesaid by the Jurors aforesaid assessed and his costs by him about his suit in this behalf expended.

Harrison Hicks Surviving partner & Plt.) In Debt
　　Against   )
Ralph Graves &   )   ) This day came the parties
Charles Perkins   )   Defts.   ) by their attorneys and
) thereupon came a Jury of
good and lawful men towit, Homer Rainey, Thomas Wells, Henry J. Cooper, Thomas Cole, Bazil Compton, Maddison Riddle, William Maultsby, Joseph S. Ellison, James Conner, Henry Butler, Robert Lockhart and Thomas Hallum, who being elected tried and sworn well and truly to try the issue joined between the parties in this case having heard the evidence and agreement of counsel and retired out of court to consider of further verdict and after some time return into court and say they cannot agree by consent of parties, said Jurors are permitted to disperse to meet again at tomorrow morning nine oclock.

A Deed of conveyance from James McCord to Wade Barrett Executor of Thomas Barrett decd. for twenty acres of land was produced in court and the execution thereof proven by the oaths of William Jones and James Walker the subscribing witnesses thereto and ordered to be certified for registration.

P-44 Thursday 27th November 1823

James Rainey Assee &c. for the use of &c Plt.
Against
John Edwards & Alfred Flournoy Defts.

In Debt

This day came the parties by their attornies and thereupon came a Jury of good and lawful men towit, William W. Thornton, Ralph Graves, John Goff, John Black, James Yancy William Henry, Larkin Mayfield, John Phillips, John Hamilton, Henry White, John O. Graves, and Thomas Wilkinson, who being Elected tried and sworn well and truly to try the issue joined between the parties in this case upon their oaths do say that the defendants have not paid the debt in the Writing obligatory in the declaration mentioned, and that they have no sett off as the plaintiff in his replication hath alledged and they do assess the plaintiffs damages by occasion of the detention of said debt to four dollars ninety six and three fourth cents, besides costs. It is therefore considered by the court that the plaintiff recover of the defendants the sum of two hundred and sixty five dollars the amount of his debt aforesaid together with his damages by the Jurors aforesaid in form aforesaid assessed and his costs by him about his suit in this behalf expended.

John Graves Assignee &c Plt.
Against
Lunsford M. Bramlett &
Elisah Eldridge Exors. of
Thomas N. Meredith decd.

In Debt

This day came the parties by their attornies and thereupon came a Jury of good and lawful men towit, William W. Thornton, Ralph Graves, John Goff, John Black, James Yancy, William Hendry, Larkin Mayfield, John Phillips John Hamlett, Henry White, John O. Graves and Thomas Wilkinson, who being elected tried and sworn well and truly to try the issue joined between the parties in this case upon their oaths do say that the defendant have not paid the debt in the Writing obligatory in the declaration mentioned and the plaintiff in his replication hath alledged and they do assess his damages by occasion of the detention of said debt to one hundred and fifteen dollars and twenty nine cents besides costs. It is therefore considered by the court that the plaintiff recover of the said defendants the sum of twenty five hundred and sixty two dollars and nine cents the amount of said debt together with the damages aforesaid by the Jurors aforesaid in form aforesaid assessed and his costs by him about his suit in this behalf expended to be levied of his goods and chattles rights and credit the said testators Estate off so much they have, if not of the proper goods & chattles lands & tenments of said defendants (p-45) From which Judgment the defendants prayed an appeal to the Honorable the Circuit Court to be held for the County of Giles which was granted them.

John Green Assignee & Plt.
Against
William H. Field . . . Deft.

In Debt

This day came the parties by their attornies & thereupon came a Jury of good and lawful men to wit, William W. Thornton, Ralph Graves, John Goff,

John Black, James Yancy, William Hendry, Larkin Mayfield, John Phillips, John Hamlett, Henry White, John O. Graves and Thomas Wilkinson, who being elected tried and sworn well and truly to try the issue joined between the parties in this case upon their oaths do say that the defendant hath not paid the debt in the Writing Obligatory in the declaration mentioned as the plaintiff in his replication hath alledged and they do assess the plaintiffs damages and by occasion of the detention of said debt to twenty five dollars besides costs. It is therefore considered by the court that the plaintiff recover of the defendant the sum of five hundred dollars the amount of his debt aforesaid together with his damages aforesaid by the Jury aforesaid assessed and his costs by him about his suit in this behalf expended.

For reasons shown to the court now here it is ordered that Spencer Clack be released from further attendance as a Juror at this Term.

A Deed of conveyance from John Gilleylan to William M. Shields for fifty acres of land was produced in court and the Execution thereof proven by the oaths of William Jones & Henry Stegall the subscribing witnesses thereto and ordered to be certified for registration.

A Deed of conveyance from George Shields to Wade Barrett Executor of Thomas Barrett deed. for seventy eight acres of land was produced in court and the execution thereof proven by the oaths of William Usery and William M. Shields the subscribing witnesses thereto and ordered to be certified for registration.

Hugh Torrance Assee &c Plt.) In Case
    Against)
John Keenan . . . . . Deft.) On the affidavit of the defendant It is ordered that the trial of this cause be continued and postponed untill the next term of this court and that a commission issue to any two of the Acting Justices of the peace in & for the County of Franklin and State of Alabama to take the deposition of Michael Dickson & James Frazer (p-46) to be read in evidence on the trial of this cause and that the defendant give to the plaintiff twenty days notice of the time and place for taking said depositions.

The Administrators of the Estate of Austin Smith deceased returned into court an inventory of said Estate which was ordered to be recorded.

Isaac Tidwell . . . . Plt.) Certiorari
    Against)
William P. A. McCabe Deft.) On the afidavit of Alexander S. Jones the defendants attorney It is ordered that the trial of this cause be continued and postponed untill the next term of this court and that the defendant pay the costs of this term.

Henry Palmer Plt.) Certiorari
    Against)
John Maclin Deft.) It appearing to the satisfaction of the court

that since this cause was brought to this court the defendant hath departed this life and that Sally Maclin & Shackfield hath qualified as Executors of his last will and testament. It is thereupon ordered by the court that this suit be revived against said Executioners.

William C. Graves Plt.) In Debt
    Against)
John Phillips Deft.) From the judgment of the court in this case
) rendered the defendant prayed an appeal to the Honorable the Circuit Court to be held for the County of Giles and having given bond and security according to law the same was granted him.

William C. Graves Plt.) In Debt
    Against)
John Phillips . . . Deft.) From the judgment of the court in this case
) rendered, the defendant prayed an appeal to the Honorable the Circuit Court to be held (p-47) for the County of Giles and having given bond and security according to law the same was granted him.

Daniel Nance . . . Plt.) Scierifacias
    Against)
Matthew Cunningham Deft.) This day came as well the plaintiff by his
) attorney as the defendant in his proper person and the defendant assuming upon himself the payment of the costs of this case as also the costs of the original suit of the plaintiff against John Simpson the plaintiffs attorney directs that this suit be dismissed.

Thomas Henderson .....Plt.   Original Attachment
    Against
William Cannon Admr. of) Deft   By consent of parties It is ordered
William Cannon decd.)   that the trial of this cause be continued and postponed untill the next term of this court and that the defendant be permitted to file a plea of no assets and that the plaintiff be permitted to reply between now and next term and go to trial then or not at his election and that a commanding issue to any two of the Acting Justice of the Peace in and for the County Coldwell & State of Kentucky to take the depositions of Jordon Harris and William Harris and that a commission issue to any two of the Acting Justice of the Peace in and for the County of Trig & State aforesaid to take the deposition of John J. Cannon all of which depositions are to read in evidence on the trial of this cause and that the defendant give to the plaintiffs attorney twenty five days notice of the time and place for taking said depositions.

Thomas Hudson ....Plt   Original Attachment
    Against   By consent of parties, It is ordered
William Cannon Admr. of)   that the trial of this cause be con-
William Cannon decd.) Deft.   tinued and postponed untill the next term of this court and that the defendant be permitted to file a plea of no assets and that the plaintiff be permitted to reply between now and the next term and go to trial then or not

at his election and that a commission issue to any two of the Acting Justices of the Peace in and for the County of Coldwell and State of Kentucky to take the depositions of Jordan Harris and William Harris and that a commission issue to any two of the Acting Justice of the Peace in and for the County of Trig and State aforesaid to take the deposition of John J. Cannon all of which deposition all to be read in (p-48) evidence on the trial of this cause and that the defendant give to the plaintiffs attorney twenty five days notice of the time and place for taking said deposition.

Ordered that Court be adjourned untill tomorrow morning nine oclock.

M. McKissack
H. Hagen
Jas. Dugger

Friday 28th November 1823

Charles Boyles for the use of &c Plt.	)	In Debt
Against	)	
Stirling C. Robertson &) Deft.	)	This day came the parties
Eldridge B. Robertson)	)	aforesaid by their attornies and thereupon the

rule of the plaintiff to showcause why a new trial should be had in this cause being agreed & by the court now here fully understood. It is the opinion of the court that no new trial ought to be granted in this cause. It is thereupon considered by the court that said rule be discharged and that said defendant depart hence without day & recover of the said plaintiff their costs by them about their defence in this behalf expended. To which opinion of the court overruling said motion for a new trial the plaintiff excepted & filed his bill of exception which is ordered to be made part of the record in this cause.

Edward Shelton Plt.	)	Original Attachment
Against	)	
Dudley Smith Deft.	)	This day came the plaintiff by his attorney and the defendant being solemnly called to

come and replevy the property attached & pleade, came not but made default. It is therefore considered by the court that the plaintiff can recover against the defendant the damages occasioned by reason of the now performance of the assumpsion in the declaration mentioned, but because the court now here are not advised as to the amount of said damages therefore let a jury come who as well and to recognize &c & this cause is continued till next term.

P-49   Friday 28th November 1823

The Grand Jury returned into court and say they have no other presentments to make were discharged.

Harrison Hicks Surviving partner & Plt.	)	In Case
Against	)	
Ralph Graves & Clark Perkins Deft.	)	This day came the parties by

their attorneys and thereupon came the Jury who were elected empanneled and sworn well and truly to try the issue joined between the parties in this case, who again retired out of court to consider of their verdict and after some time returned & say they cannot agree and thereupon they were discharged and this cause is continued till the next term of this court.

Ordered that the order of last term appointing commissioners to settle with Ralph Graves & John Kennan administrator of the Estate of Masterson C. McCormack decd. be in all things revived and that second commissioners make return of second settlement to the next term of this court.

A deed of mortgage from John Edwards to John H. Rivers for certain property therein contained was produced in court and the execution thereof acknowledged by the said John Edwards and ordered to be certified for registration.

John Graves Assee & Plt.)   In Debt
    Against)
William H. Field Deft.)   From the judgment of the court in this case
)   rendered the Defendant prayed an appeal to the Honorable the Circuit Court to be held for the County of Giles in the nature of a Writ of errors and he having executed bond & security according to law the same was granted him.

James Rainey Assee &c to the use of &c Plt)   In Debt
    Against)
John Edwards & Alfred Flournoy Deft.)   From the judgment of
)   the court in this case rendered the Defendant prayed an appeal in the nature of a Writ of error to the Honorable the Circuit Court to be held for the County of Giles and having executed bond and security according to law the Same was granted them.

The State . . . Plt)   Upon an Indictment for an affray & an
    Against)   assault & battery.
Alexander Lockhart Deft.)
)   This day came as well the Solicitor General for the State as the defendant in his proper person who being charged on the Indictment in this case pleads guilty and because he will not contend with the State agrees to submit himself (p-50) to the parties and mercy of the court. It is therefore considered by the court that he make his fine with the State to the amount of one dollar and that he pay the costs of this prosecution.

The State . . . Plt)   Upon an Indictment for an affray & an
    Against)   assault & battery.
Alexander Lockhart deft.)   This day came as well the Solicitor General for the State as the defendant in his proper person who being charged on the Indictment in this case pleads guilty and because he will not contend with the State agrees to submit himself to the Justice & mercy of the court. It is therefore considered by the court that he make his fine with the State to the amount of one dollar and that he pay the costs of this prosecution.

William & John Montgomery Plts.) In Debt
    Against)
Nathaniel Young & James Perry Defts.) This day came the parties by
) their attorneys and the Defendants filed their demurrer sure in which having been agreed by counsel on both sides was sustained and on motion of plaintiffs leave is given them to amend by paying the costs up to the time the declaration was filed and also the costs of the amendment.

Thomas Wilkinson Plt.) On motion
    Against)
John McDonald Gdr. to minor heirs) This day came the plaintiff and
of Arch Alexander decd.) moved the court for one exception
) to issue against the real Estate of said Arch Alexander decd. upon a judgment rendered in this court on the 23rd of August 1822, and for good reasons shown to the court. It is ordered that said execution issue accordingly.

A deed of conveyance from Nathaniel Young to Patrick H. Braden for a lot in the Town of Pulaski was produced in court and the execution thereof acknowledged by the said Nathaniel Young and ordered to be certified for registration.

An account of the sale of the Estate of Thomas H. Meredith decd. was returned into court and ordered to be recorded.

P-51 Friday 28th November 1823

Margaret Bratton widow of the late) Petition for a distributive
William Bratton decd. Elizabeth) share of the Estate of Will-
Bratton in her own right and) iam Bratton decd.
as Guardian of James Bratton   Plts.)
George Bratton, John Bratton,)
Peggy Bratton, Lucinda Bratton,) This day being the 28th of
& Malinda Hugh Bratton Junr.) November 1823 this cause
all heirs of Wm. Bratton decd.) coming on to be heard before
    Against) the worshipful the County
Hugh Bratton & Thomas Bratton   Deft.) Court upon petition answer
Administrators of Wm. Bratton decd.) replications and testimony
) and upon Solemn agreement
first being heard thereon and fully understood by the court It is thereupon ordered by the court now here ordered adjudged and decreed that the complainants recover against the defendants the sum of of six hundred and ninety five dollars sixty one and a half cents the amount of sale as appears of record, with legal interest thereon at the rate of six per centure per annum from the 17th day of November 1821 together with all costs expended in serving out and prosecuting this petition and that execution issue accordingly.

Ordered that Court be adjourned till tomorrow morning 9 oclock.

                                            Wm. Mayfield
                                            Thos. Marks
                                            H. Hagen

P-52   Saturday Morning 29th November 1823

Court met according to adjournment Present Henry Hagen, ⎫ Esquires
                                    Thos. Marks   ⎬ Justices
                                    William Mayfield   ⎭

A Deed of conveyance from Lewis H. Brown Sheriff of Giles County to John W. Perry for a lot in the Town of Pulaski was produced in court and the execution thereof acknowledged by the said Brown Sheriff as aforesaid and ordered to be certified for registration.

A deed of conveyance from John W. Perry to John E. Holden for a lot in the Town of Pulaski was produced in court and the execution thereof acknowledged by the said John W. Perry & ordered to be certified for registration

Nicholas R. Smith Plt.)   On an attachment
        Against   )
Dudley Smith Deft.   ) This day came the plaintiff by his attorney
) & the defendant being solemnly called to
come and replevy the property attached & plead, came not but made default.
   It is thereupon considered by the court that the plaintiff recover against the defendant the damages occasioned by reason of the non performance of the assumpsion in the declaration mentioned but because the court now here are not advised as to the amount of said damages, therefore let a Jury come who as well &c to recognize &c & this cause is continued till next term.

Abel Oxford Plt.   )   In Debt
      Against   )
Gabriel Hensley Deft.   ) This day came the defendant by his attorney
) and the plaintiff being Solemnly called
came not but made default therefore it is considered by the court that the defendant go hence without day and recover of said plaintiff his costs by him about his defence in this behalf expended.

Margret Bratton widow of the late)Plts.)
Wm. Bratton decd. & Elizabeth Bratton   )   Upon a Petition &c.
in her own right & as Guardian to the   )
minor heirs of William Bratton decd.   )   From the judgment of the
        Against   )   court in this case rendered
Hugh Bratton & Thomas Bratton Admrs.   )   (p-53) the defendant pray
of the Estate of Wm. Bratton decd.) Defts.) an appeal to the Honorable
)   the Circuit Court to be hel
for the County of Giles and having executed bond and security according to Law the same was granted them.

Thomas C. Porter Plt.   )   In Debt
      Against   )
William Mayfield &   )
Thomas McKissack   Deft.) This day came the plaintiff by his attorney
) & moved the court to sit aside the judgment
) heretofore entered in this cause It is

therefore ordered by the court that said judgment be set aside & that said plaintiff pay the costs in and about his said motion in this behalf expended

Ordered that Elisha Eldridge be appointed Guardian to the minor heirs of Thomas H. Meredith decd. who having bond and security according to law.

James Woodfin &
George Malone Exors & Plts.
      Against   )   In Deft.
Isaac Mayfield)
Nathaniel Young &) Defts.   From the Judgment of the court in
Elisha Mayfield)   this case rendered the defendants
                                      prayed an appeal to the Honorable
the Circuit Court to be held for the County of Giles and having Executed bond and security according to law the same as was granted them.

Ordered that court be adjourned till court meets in course.

                                                          Robert Oliver

                                                          A. Black

                                                          Thos. Marks

At a Court of Pleas and Quarter Session begun & holden in and for the County of Giles at the Court house of said County in the Town of Pulaski on the third Monday in February being the 16th day thereof in the year of our Lord 1824 Present Alexander Black, Dewey Smith, Thomas Brown, Robert Reed, William Brown, Arthur Hicks, James Dugger, Willis S. McClaurine, James Paine, Joseph Rea, Robert Oliver, Hezekiah Jones, Paul Chiles, Jonathan Moody, Anderson Hogan, Peter Swanson, John H. Camp. Thomas E. Abernathy, William B. Pepper, John Laird, Richard McGee, John Bramlett, John Young, Henry Hagen, and Edward D. Jones, Esquires Justices of the Peace of said County Presiding German Lester Clerk of said Court & Lewis H. Brown Sheriff of said County.

A Mortgage from Hugh Bratton to George Brown for certain property therein named was produced in court and the Execution thereof acknowledged by the said Hugh Bratton and ordered to be certified for registration.

Ordered that Nathaniel Graves be appointed overseer of the road in the room of Joseph Alsup resigned and that he have the same district of hands.

Ordered that Joseph F. Barnett be appointed overseer of the road in the room of John B. Anthony resigned and that he have the same district of hands.

Ordered that Hartwell Harwell be appointed overseer of the road in the room of Robert Adams resigned and that he have the same district of hands.

A bill of sale from James Smith to Leonard Smith for certain property therein named was produced in court and the execution thereof proven by the oaths of John B. Wilson & John Y. Smith the subscribing witnesses thereto and ordered to be certified for registration.

A Deed of conveyance from James Conner by his agent and attorney in fact to Thomas Reed Jr. & John Butler for Four thousand five hundred acres of land was produced in court and the Execution thereof proven by the oaths of Robert L. Cobbs & James Hannah the subscribing witnesses thereto and ordered to be certified for registration.

A Deed of conveyance from Edward Smith to Isaac Smith for fifty six acres of land was produced in court and the execution thereof proven by the oaths of Jacob Smith and Joseph Rogers two of the subscribing witnesses thereto and ordered to be certified for registration.

P-55   Monday 16th February 1824

A Deed of conveyance from James Bright to Mark Eves for ten acres of land was produced in court and the Execution thereof proven by the oaths of James Rogers and Joseph Rogers the subscribing witnesses thereto and ordered to be certified for registration.

The Commissioners who were appointed to settle with John Goff Guardian of John W. Goff this day made return of said settlement which is ordered to be recorded.

Alexander Black Esquire was appointed chairman to this court Pro - tun.

Henry Hagen Esquire who was appointed at the last term of this court to take a list of taxable property and polls in Captain John Brown(s Company for the year 1824 made return thereof which was ordered to be recorded.

Peter Swanson Esquire who was appointed at the last term of this court to take a list of taxable property and polls in Captain Ruffs Company for the year 1824 made return thereof which was ordered to be recorded.

Ordered that William F. Brown be appointed overseer of the road in the room of Isaac Mason resigned and that he have the same district of hands.

Ordered that Thomas Gordon & Edward D. Jones Esquire be appointed commissioners to settle with John Goff as administrator of the Estate of George Goff decd. and that they make report to the next term of this court.

John Laird Esquire who was appointed at the last term of this court to take a list of taxable property and polls in Captain Frys company for the year 1824 made return thereof which was ordered to be recorded.

John Mimms Gentlemen produced in court a License to practice Law in the several courts of law and Equity with in this State and was qualified and admitted in this court.

Ordered that John King be appointed overseer of the road in the room of Benjamin Williams resigned and that he have the same district of hands.

On the petition of Bazil Compton it is ordered that William Steel, Robert Guthrie, Merry Carter, Hensley Carpenter, Samuel Weis, Shands Golightly and John Moore or any five of them be appointed a Jury to view and mark out a private way from the land of Bazil Compton to the Columbia road in this County and that they make report thereof to the present term of this court.

P-56 Monday 16th February 1824

Ordered that Alexander Black and Henry Hagen Esquire be appointed commissioners to settle with John Dickey & William H. Cook administrator of the Estate of James Donaldson.

A Deed of conveyance from John Pate to George Dodson for seventy five acres of land was produced in court and the execution thereof proven by the oaths of Jordon Dodson and Moses Patterson two of the subscribing witnesses thereto and ordered to be certified for registration.

A Deed of conveyance from Samuel Montgomery to Elisha Dodson for one hundred acres of land was produced in court and the execution thereof proven by the oaths of Jordon Dodson & Moses Patterson the subscribing witnesses thereto and ordered to be certified for registration.

A Deed of conveyance from James Campbell to Goodhope Thorp, Fifty six acres and one hundred and forty poles of land was produced in court and the execution thereof proven by the oaths of Moses Patterson & Jordon Dodson the witnesses thereof and ordered to be certified for registration.

A Deed of conveyance from Robert Robson to Archibald Smith for two acres of land was produced in court and the execution thereof proven by the oaths of John Young and Edward Lumpkin the subscribing witnesses thereto and is ordered to be certified for registration.

Dewey Smith Esquire who were appointed at the last term of this court to take a list of taxable property and polls Captain William Fraziers Company for the year 1824 made return thereof which was ordered to be recorded.

A Deed of conveyance from Robert Robson to Archibald Smith for sixty two acres of land was produced in court and the execution thereof proven by the oaths of John Young and Edward Lumpkin the subscribing witnesses thereto and ordered to be certified for registration.

A Deed of conveyance from Alexander McDonald & John McDonald to Joseph Jones for Fifty acres of land was produced in Court and the execution thereof acknowledged by the said Alexander McDonald & John McDonald and ordered to be certified for registration.

P-57 Monday 16th February 1824

A Deed from John Elliss & Nancy his wife to Francis Beard for fifty two acres of land was produced in court and the Execution thereof proven by the oaths of Paul Child & John Young two of the subscribing witnesses thereto and thereupon John Young & Paul Child Esquires, two of the Acting Justices of the peace in & for this County were appointed to take the privy examination of the said Nancy Elliss touching the execution of said Deed.

John Young Esquire who was appointed at the last term of this court to take a list of taxable property and polls in Captain Paul Chiles Company for the year 1824 made return thereof which was ordered to be recorded.

A Deed of conveyance from Robert W. Green to Robert Anderson for one hundred acres of land was produced in court and the execution thereof proven by the oaths of David Bridgeforth & Samuel R. Anderson the subscribing witnesses thereto and ordered to be certified for registration.

A Deed of conveyance from John L. Smith to Hugh Reynolds for sixty acres of land was produced in court and the execution thereof fully proven by the oaths of Willie Boyakin a subscribing witness thereto and ordered to be certified for registration.

Ordered that John Williams be appointed overseer of the road in the room of David Read resigned and that he have the same district of hands.

Ordered that H. M. Livingston be appointed overseer of the road in the room of Richard Bentley resigned and that he have the same district of hands.

The last Will and testament of William Martin decd. was produced in court and proven by the oaths of William Dearing & Moses Patterson the subscribing witnesses thereto and ordered to be recorded, and thereupon John G. Braden & Samuel Davis the executors therein named appeared in court & were qualified and gave bond and security as the law directs.

A Deed of conveyance from Hugh Reynolds to Robert Yarbrough for sixty acres of land was produced in court and the execution thereof proven by the oaths of Ambrose Yarbrough & Hensford Tutt two of the subscribing witnesses thereto and ordered to be certified for registration.

P-58   Monday 16th February 1824

A Deed of conveyance from Jacob Cochran to Samuel Cochran for 40 acres of land was produced in court and the execution thereof acknowledged by the said Jacob Cochran & ordered to be certified for registration.

Ordered that Moses Garrison be allowed the sum of forty dollars towards supporting & maintaining himself and family for the present year.

Ordered that Robert Reed & Peter Swanson be appointed commissioners to settle with John W. Bodenhammer as administrator of Peter Bodenhammer decd. and that they make report of said settlement to the next of this court.

An Additional sale of the Estate of Anthony Samuel decd. was returned into court and ordered to be recorded.

A Deed of conveyance from Thomas Reed & John Butler to Richard Morris for four hundred acres of land was produced in court and the execution thereof acknowledged by the said Thomas Reed & John Butler and ordered to be certified for registration.

Ordered that John W. Bodenhammer be appointed overseer of the road in the room of William Riddle resigned and that he have the same district of hands.

Anderson Hogan Esquire who was appointed at the last term of this court to take a list of taxable property and polls in Captain Jeremiah Barnes Company for the year 1824 made return thereof which was ordered to be recorded.

William D. Jennings Guardian of Samuel W. Weaver returned an account against his said ward which is ordered to be recorded.

James K. Murrah Guardian of John W. Weaver returned an account against his said ward which is ordered to be recorded.

Ordered that James Willsford be appointed overseer of the road in the room of George Keltner resigned and that he have the same district of hands with the addition of Jesse Edgar and Philip Wortman.

P-59 Monday 16th February 1824.

A Deed of conveyance from Thomas Bowman to Roland Hunnicutt for eighty acres of land was produced in court and the execution thereof proven by the oaths of James Hammons & Ira Magee the subscribing witnesses thereto and ordered to be certified for registration.

A Bill of sale from Asher Myers to Elnathan G. Brown for certain property therein named was produced in court and the execution thereof proven by the oaths of John Abernathy the subscribing witness thereto and ordered to be certified for registration.

A Mortgage from Micajah Ezell to Elnathan G. Brown for certain property therein named was produced in court and the execution thereof proven by C. E. Parrish the subscribing witness thereto and ordered to be certified for registration.

A Deed of conveyance from Alexander McDonald & John McDonald to Felker Cox for forty acres of land was produced in court and the execution thereof acknowledged by the said Alexander McDonald & John McDonald and ordered to be certified for registration.

Ordered that Ephriam A. Young be appointed constable in Captain James Kearneys Company whereupon he was qualified and gave bond and security according to law.

Ordered that Henry Laird be appointed constable in Captain Lairds Company whereupon he was qualified and gave bond and security according to law.

Ordered that Thomas W. McKnight be appointed constable in Captain Paul Childs Company whereupon he was qualified and gave bond and security according to law.

Ordered that Buckner Madra be appointed overseer of the road in the room of William B. Brooks resigned and that he have the same district of hands.

A Deed of conveyance from Alexander McDonald & John McDonald to John D. Riddle for one hundred & eighty two acres of land was produced in court and the execution thereof acknowledged by the said Alexander McDonald & John McDonald and ordered to be certified for registration.

Ordered that Robert Reed, Alexander Black and John Dickey be appointed commissioners to settle with Fountain Lester as Guardian of Alfred White & Newton White and that they make report of said settlement to the present term of this court if praticable if not to the next Term of this court.

P-60 Monday 16th February 1824

A Licence to keep an ordinary for the term of twelve months & no longer is granted to Wilton F. L. Jenkins whereupon he was qualified and executed Bond and Security according to law.

A Deed of conveyance from Nathaniel Young to Edward Garrett for twenty five acres of land was produced in court and the execution thereof acknowledged by the said Nathaniel Young and ordered to be certified for registration.

John C. Walker Esquire who was appointed at the last term of this court to take a list of taxable property and polls of Captain Montgomery's Company for the year 1824 and made report thereof which was ordered to be recorded.

A licence to keep an ordinary for the term of twelve months and no longer is granted to David Simms, whereupon he was qualified and executed Bond and Security according to law.

Francis Lynch Plaintiff)
Against) Nathaniel Douglass who was bound for
Thomas Compton .. Defendant) the appearance of Thomas Compton the
) defendant aforesaid at this term
comes into court and surrenders the body of said deft and is thereupon exhonerated and discharged from his obligation and thereupon Bazil Compton and Isaac Compton comes into court and being considered by the court good and sufficient bail agree that if the said Thomas be convicted at the suit of the said Francis in his plea aforesaid that he shall pay and satisfy the condemnation of the court or surrender his body in discharge of the same or they will do it for him.

William Walker Plt.   )   Nathaniel Douglas and John S. Todd who were
        Against   )   bound for the appearance of Thomas Compton
Thomas Compton Deft.   )   the defendant aforesaid at this term came
)   into court and surrendered the body of said
defendant and are thereupon exonerated and discharged from their obligations
and thereupon Bazel Compton and Isaac Compton came into court & being considered by the court good and sufficient bail agree that if the said Thomas
convicted at the suit of the said William in her plea aforesaid that he
shall pay and satisfy the condemnation of the court or surrender his body
in discharge of the same or they will do it for him.

P-61   The court proceeded to class the magistrates of this County agreeable
to an Act of the Legislature of this State in the following manner towit,

Class number one composed of Esquires James McCafferty, Thomas Batte, Alexander Black, Dewy Smith, Thomas Brown, Robert Read, William Brown, Arthur
Hicks, and James Dugger to hold the present term of this court.

Class Number two composed of Esquires Willis S. McLaurine, William Mayfield, John B. Armstrong, James Paine, Joseph Rea, John Henderson, Robert
Oliver, John C. Walker, and Hezekiah Jones, to hold the May term of this
court.

Class number three composed of Esquires Thomas Marks, Paul Childs, Jonathan
Moody, Anderson Hogan, Peter Swanson, John H. Camp, Thomas Harwood, Thomas
K. Gordon, Thomas E. Abernathy to hold the next August Term of court.

Class Number four composed of Esquires William B. Pepper, John Laird,
William Usery, Richard McGee, Archibald McKissack, John Bramlett, John
Young, Henry Hagen, Edward D. Jones, and Nelson Petteson to hold the next
November term of this court.

    Ordered that Amos Vernon be appointed overseer of the road from John
Dailey's to John Manefee's in the room of Josiah Davidson removed and that
he have the same district of hands.

    A Deed of conveyance from Henry Brown to Stephen Anderson for three
hundred and fifty acres of land was produced in court and the execution
thereof proven by the oaths of Samuel Day and Richard McGee the subscribing witnesses thereto and ordered to be certified for registration.

    A Bill of Sale from Harrisson Hicks for himself and as administrator
of the Estate of Francis Hicks decd. was produced in court and the execution thereof acknowledged by the said Harrisson Hicks and ordered to be
certified for registration.

    Ordered that the County Trustee of this county pay to German Lester
Clerk of this County the sum of forty dollars for his exofficio services
for one year prior to this time also twenty five dollars for recording the
tax list for the year 1823.

    For good reasons shown to the court It is ordered John Butler be release
from attending as a Juror at this term.

Ordered that Robert Reed, William W. Thornton, John W. R. Graves, Robert McLaurine, Charles Dever, David Porter, & John S. Brandon or any five of them be appointed a Jury to view that part of the road leading from Pulaski to Moria Meeting house which run's on the land of the heirs of Reece Porter decd. and see if it be proper to turn said road and if in their opinion it be, that they mark out the same, and that they make report to the present term of this court.

P-62   Monday 16th February 1824

On the petition of Gilbert D. Taylor there being nine Justices present Setting forth that he owns a black slave named John Rollins aged about forty eight years whom he wishes in consequence of his long faithful & meritorious services to set free.

It is thereupon ordered and required by the court that said Gilbert D. Taylor give bond with security in the penalty of Five hundred dollars on conditioned as the Act directs whereupon the said Gilbert D. Taylor, Henry Hagen and Alfred M. Harris acknowledged themselves in debt to the State of Tennessee in the sum of Five hundred dollars to be levied of their goods and chattles lands and tenements to be void on conditions that the said John Rollins become not chargable to this County and that they save the County from all damages which may be sustained on account of his becoming to this County which said security is approved and accepted by this court and thereupon Alexander Black Esquire Chairman proterm of said Court reported on said petition that the same is granted and Signed his name to the same It is ordered by the court that said John Rollins be emancipated.

It appearing to the satisfaction of the court that at the last term letters of administration on the Estate of David Steel deceased was granted to Thomas Steele and that the security given by said Thomas Steel is insufficient to secure the faithful administration of said Estate. It is thereupon ordered by the court that the said Thomas Steel appear here on or before Monday next and give good and sufficient security on said administration will be made null and void.

On the petition of George Brown & William B. Pepper It is ordered that a summons Issue to Elisha Eldridge Guardian of the orphan Children of John W. Edwards requiring him to give other good & sufficient security on said guardianship and release the said George Brown & William B. Pepper from their securityship or the court will proceed to the appointment of another guardian to said minor.

Ordered that an order of sale issue to James Caldwell and William A. Brown administrators of the Estate of Henry Neal decd. commanding them to advertise and sell the following negroes belonging to said Estate for the purpose of paying the debts against said Estate towit, Rain Viney, and Harriet Backen, and Nat. It appearing to the satisfaction of the court that the perishable property is insufficient for that purpose and that said administrators require the payment at the time of sale and the balance on the usual ordit.

P-63   Monday 16th February 1824

John Young & Paul Chiles Esquire who were appointed to take the privy examination of Nancy Elliss touching the execution of a Deed of conveyance from John Elliss and the said Nancy his wife to Francis Beard returned said examination into court and said deed together with the examination is ordered to be certified for registration.

It appearing to the satisfaction of this court that Alexander Barron to whom . . . . Strickland an orphan girl under the age of twenty one years was bound by this court has removed out of the Jurisdiction of this court into another County.
It is therefore ordered that said Alexander Barron produced said . . . . Strickland before this court at next term on the third Monday in May next and show cause why she shall not be surrendered up to the court and be rebound and if he fail herein that suit be instituted against him upon his obligations and such other measure be taken by this court as may be expedient.

Ordered that Tyre Rodes, John P. Taylor, Isaac S. Crisman, George M. Gibson, William Rea, Hamilton C. Campbell, & Richard H. Allen, or any five of them be appointed a Jury to view and mark out a road the nearest and best way from the little Tom Bigby road at or near Stephen Reddings to the South end of Isaac Morriss lane thence with the old road so as to intersect the dry creek road at or near Hamilton C. Campbell's and that they make report thereof to the next term of this court.

The commissioners appointed to settle with the administrator of the Estate of Luck Adam's decd. made return of said settlement which is ordered to be recorded.

Ordered that Court be adjourned untill tomorrow morning 9 oclock.

                                                 A. Black
                                                 William Brown
                                               H. Hagen

P-64   Tuesday Morning 17th February 1824

Court met according to adjournment Present John H. Camp, Alex Black, and Edward D. Jones Esquires Justices of the peace in and for the County of Giles German Lester Clerk and Lewis H. Brown Sheriff of said County of Giles.

Abraham L. Caruthers gentlemen produced in court a License to practice law in the several courts of law and equity within this State and was qualified and admitted to practice in this court.

Thomas Batte Esquire who was appointed at the last term of this court to take a list of taxable property and polls in Captain Bass company for the year 1824 and made return thereof which was ordered to be recorded.

A License to keep an ordinary for the term of twelve months and no longer is granted to John H. Camp whereupon he was qualified and executed bond and security according to law.

A Mortgage from Hugh H. Whithers to Alfred M. Harris for certain property therein named was produced in court and the execution thereof proven by William H. Field the subscribing witness thereto and ordered to be certified for registration.

Vaulton Childress ... Plt.   )   In Debt
       Against   )
James K. Murrah & William   ) This day came the plaintiff by his at-
D. Jennings Guardian to &c.   ) torney who saith he will not further
) prosecute this suit. It is therefore
considered by the court that the Defendants go hence without day and recover of the said plaintiff their costs by them about their defence in this behalf expended.

Martin Lorance for the use &c Plt.)   In Debt
       Against   )
William Steel ..... Deft.   ) This day came the parties by
) their attornies and thereupon
came a Jury of good and lawful men To Wit, Henry J. Cooper, Baker P. Potts, Matthew Cunningham, Charles Edwards, Edward Marks, Sterling Graves, Stephen Reading, Jacob Cochran, Marshall Moody, John D. Riddle, William Maxwell & Robert Paine, who being elected tried and sworn well and truly to try the issue aforesaid between the parties in this case upon their (p-65) oaths do say that the defendant hath not paid the debt in the Writing obligatory in the declaration mentioned and that he hath not set off as the plaintiff in his replications hath alledged and they do assess the plaintiffs damages by occasion of the detention of said debt to thirteen dollars besides costs. It is therefore considered by the court that the plaintiff recover against the defendant the sum of two hundred & thirty one dollars and Eighty cents the amount of his debt aforesaid together with his damages aforesaid in form aforesaid by the Jury aforesaid and his costs by him about his suit in this behalf expended.

William Norwood Plt.   )   In Debt
       against   )
John E. Mayfield .. Deft.) This day came the parties by their
) attornies and thereupon came a Jury
of good and lawful men Towit, Henry J. Cooper, Baker P. Potts, Matthew Cunningham, Charles Edwards, Edward Marks, Stirling Graves, Stephen Reading Jacob Cochran, Marshall Moody, John D. Riddle, William Maxwell & Robert Paine who being elected tried and sworn the truth to speak upon this issue joined between the parties in this case upon their oaths do say that the defendant hath not paid the debt in the Writing obligatory in the declaration mentioned and that he hath no sett off as the plaintiff in his replication hath alledged, and they do assess the plaintiff damages by occasion of the detention of said Debt to two dollars & seventy five cents besides costs. It is therefore considered by the court that the plaintiff recover of the Defendant the sum of one hundred & twenty one dollars the amount in form aforesaid in form aforesaid by the Jurors aforesaid assessed and his costs by him about his suit in this behalf expended.

Jarrett Menefee Plt.) In Debt
    Against)
Vaulton Childers Deft.)
) This day came the parties by their attorneys and thereupon came a Jury of good and lawful men Towit, Henry J. Cooper, Baker P. Potts, Matthew Cunningham, Charles Edwards, Edward Marks, Stirling Graves, Stephen Reading, Jacob Cochran, Marshall Moody, John D. Riddle, William Maxwell & Robert Paine who being elected tried and sworn the truth to speak upon the issue joined between the parties in this case upon their oaths do say that the defendant hath not paid the debt in the writing obligatory in the declaration mentioned and that he hath no sett off as the plaintiff in his replication hath alledged and they do assess the plaintiffs damages by occasion of (p-66) the detention of said defendant to Fifty five dollars twenty eight and one fourth cent besides costs. It is therefore considered by the court that the plaintiff recover of the defendant the sum of Five hundred & sixty seven dollars twenty four and one half cents the amount of his debt aforesaid together with his damages aforesaid in form aforesaid by the Jurors aforesaid assessed and his costs by him about his suit in this behalf expended.

Larkin Mayfield to the use &c Plt.) In Debt
    Against)
Elisha B. Mayfield . . . Deft.)
) This day came the parties by their attornies and thereupon came a Jury of good and lawful men Towit, Henry J. Cooper, Baker P. Potts, Matthew Cunningham, Charles Edwards, Edward Marks, Marshall Moody, John D. Riddle, Stirling Graves, Stephen Reading, Jacob Cochran, William Maxwell & Robert Paine who being elected tried and sworn the truth to speak upon the issue's joined between the parties in this case upon their oaths do say that the defendant hath not paid the debt in the Writing obligatory in the declaration mentioned and that he hath no sett off as the plaintiff in his replication hath alledged, and they do assess the plaintiff damages by occasion of the detention of said debt to twenty five dollars besides costs. It is therefore considered by the court that the plaintiff recover of the defendant the sum of five hundred dollars the amount of his debt aforesaid together with his damages aforesaid in form aforesaid by the Jurors aforesaid assessed and his costs by him about his suit in this behalf expended.

A Power of Attorney from George Dumgarner to Robert Lockhart was produced in court and the execution thereof proven by the oaths of John H. Camp one of the witnesses thereto.

Willis S. McLaurine Esquire who was appointed at the last term of this court to take a list of taxable property and polls in Captain McCormacks Company for the year 1824 made return thereof which was ordered to be recorded.

The commissioners who were appointed to settle with Fountain Lester guardian of Alfred White made return of said settlement which is ordered to be recorded.

The commissioners who were appointed to settle with Fountain Lester guardian of Newton White made return of said settlement which is ordered to be recorded.

P-67   Tuesday 17th February 1824

Cargell McLemore Assee &c Plt.)   In Debt
    Against   )
Stephen Samuel . . . Deft) This day came the parties by their
) attornies and thereupon came a Jury of good and lawful men Towit, Henry J. Cooper, Baker P. Potts, Matthew Cunningham, Charles Edwards, Edward Marks, Stirling Graves, Stephen Reading, Jacob Cochran, Marshall Moody, John D. Riddell, William Maxwell & Robert Paine who being elected tried and sworn the truth to speak upon the issue joined upon their oaths do say that the defendant hath not paid the debt in the writing obligation in the declaration mentioned as the plaintiff in his replication hath alleged and they do assess the plaintiffs damages by occasion of the detention of said debt to Ten dollars besides costs. It is therefore considered by the court that the plaintiff recover of the defendant the sum of one hundred & sixty four dollars and fifteen cents the amount of his debt aforesaid together with his damages aforesaid in form aforesaid by the Jurors aforesaid assessed and his costs by him about his suit in this behalf expended.

William & J. Montgomery Merchants &c. Plts.) In Debt
    Against   )
William Sheppard and Andrew M. Ballentine Defts.) This day came the
) parties by their attornies and thereupon came a Jury of good and lawful men Towit, Henry J. Cooper, Baker P. Potts, Matthew Cunningham, Charles Edwards, Edward Marks, Stirling Graves, Stephen Reading, Jacob Cochran, Marshall Moody, John D. Riddell, William Maxwell, & Robert Paine who being elected tried and sworn the truth to speak upon the issue joined upon their oaths do say that the defendants have not paid the debt in the Writing obligatory in replication have alleged and they do assess the plaintiffs damages by occasion of the detention of said debt to one dollar and fifty cents besides costs. It is therefore considered by the court that the plaintiffs recover of the defendants the sum of sixty six dollars & ninety cents the amount of their debt aforesaid together with the damages aforesaid in form aforesaid by the Jurors aforesaid assessed and their costs about their suit in this behalf expended.

A Power of attorney from Joshua Rickman to Joshua Rickman was produced in court and the execution thereof acknowledged by the said Joshua Rickman and ordered to be certified.

P-68   Tuesday 17th February 1824

William & Jonathan Montgomery Merchants &c Plts.) In Debt
    Against   ) This day came the
Nathaniel Young & James Perry   Defts.) parties by their
) attornies and thereupon came a Jury of good and lawful men Towit, Henry J. Cooper, Baker P. Potts

Matthew Cunningham, Charles Edwards, Edward Marks, Stirling Graves, Stephen Reading, Jacob Cochran, Marshall Moody, John D. Riddell, William Maxwell & Robert Paine, who being elected tried and sworn well and truly to try the issue joined between the parties in this case upon their oaths do say that the defendants have not paid the debt in the Writing obligatory in the declaration mentioned and that they have no sett off as the plaintiffs in their replications have alledged and they do assess the plaintiffs damages by occasion of the detention of said debt to one dollar and twenty six cents besides costs.

It is therefore considered by the court that the plaintiffs recover of the defendants the sum of sixty three dollars and fourteen cents their damages aforesaid together with their damages by the jurors aforesaid in form aforesaid by the jurors aforesaid assessed and their costs by them about their suit in this behalf expended.

William Walker Plts.) In Debt
  Against)
Thomas Compton .. Deft.) This day came the parties by their attornies and thereupon came a Jury of good and lawful men Towit, Henry J. Cooper, Baker P. Potts, Matthew Cunningham, Charles Edward, Edward Marks, Stirling Graves, Stephen Reading, Jacob Cochran, Marshall Moody, John D. Riddell, William Maxwell and Robert Paine who being elected tried and sworn well and truly to try the issue joined between the parties in this case upon their oaths do say that the defendant hath not paid the debt in the writing obligatory in the declaration mentioned as the plaintiff in his replication hath alleged and they do assess the plaintiffs damages by occasion of the detention of said debt to six dollars and fifty cents besides costs. It is therefore considered by the court that the plaintiff recover of the defendant the sum of two hundred dollars the amount of his debt aforesaid together with his damages aforesaid in form aforesaid by the jurors aforesaid assessed and his costs by him about his suit in this behalf expended.

Thomas McKissack Admr. &c Plt.) In Debt
  Against)
Mary Kirk Thomas Guthrie and) Defts.) This day came the parties
Herrod Fowlks) by their attornies and
) thereupon (p-69) came
a jury of good and lawful men Towit, Henry J. Cooper, Baker P. Potts, Matthew Cunningham, Charles Edward, Edward Marks, Stirling Graves, Stephen Reading, Jacob Cochran, Marshall Moody, John D. Riddell, William Maxwell, Robert Paine, who being elected tried and sworn well and truly to try the issue joined between the parties in this case upon their oaths do say that the defendant have not paid the debt in the writing obligatory in the declaration mentioned mentioned as the plaintiffs in his replication hath allege and they do assess the plaintiffs damages by occasion of the detention of said debt to fifteen dollars besides costs. It is thereupon considered by the court that the plaintiffs recover of the defendants the sum of Eighty seven dollars and twenty five cents the amount of his debt aforesaid togeth with his damages aforesaid in form aforesaid by the jurors aforesaid assess and his costs by him about his suit in this behalf expended.

Thomas McKissack Admr. &c. Plt.) In Debt
  Against)
Ralph Graves & Charles Perkins Defts.)

This day came the parties by their attornies and thereupon came a Jury of good and lawful men towit, Henry J. Cooker, Baker P. Potts, Matthew Cunningham, Charles Edward Marks, Stirling Graves, Stephen Reading, Jacob Cochran, Marshall Moody, John W. Riddle, William Maxwell, & Robert Paine who being elected tried and sworn well and truly to try the issue joined between the parties in this case upon their oaths do say that the defendants have not been paid the debt in the Writing obligatory in the declaration mentioned as the plaintiff in his replication hath alleged and they do assess the plaintiffs damages by occasion of the detention of said debt to six dollars & seventy cents besides costs. It is therefore considered by the court that the plaintiff recover of the defendants the sum of one hundred and two dollars thirty one & one fourth cents the amount of his debt aforesaid together with his damages aforesaid in form aforesaid by the Jurors aforesaid assessed and his costs about his suit in this behalf expended.

William & J. Montgomery Merchants &c Plt.) In Debt
   Against)
Elisha B. Mayfield Deft.) This day came the parties by their attornies and thereupon came a Jury of good & lawful men To wit, Henry J. Cooper, Baker P. Potts, Matthew Cunningham, Charles Edwards, Edward Marks, Stirling Graves, Stephen Reading, Jacob Cochran, Marshall Moody, John D. Riddell, William Maxwell & Robert Paine who being elected tried and sworn well and truly to try the issue joined between the parties in this (p-70) case upon their oaths do say that the defendant hath not paid the debt in the Writing obligatory in the declaration mentioned and that he hath no sett off as the plaintiffs in their replication have alleged an they do assess the plaintiffs damages by occasion of the detention of said debt to . . . . four dollars and fifty . . . . cents besides costs. Is therefore considered by the court that the plaintiff recover of the defendant the sum of sixty five dollars eighty one and one fourth cents the amount of their debt aforesaid together with their damages aforesaid by the Jurors aforesaid in form aforesaid and their costs by them about their suit in this behalf expended.

Francis Lynch . . . Plaintiff) Debt
   Against)
Thomas Compton . . Defendant) This day came the parties by their attornies and thereupon came a Jury of good and lawful men To wit, Henry J. Cooper, Baker P. Potts, Matthew Cunningham, Charles Edwards, Edward Marks, Stirling Graves, Stephen Reading, Jacob Cochran, Marshall Moody, John D. Riddell, William Maxwell and Robert Paine, who being elected tried and sworn well and truly to try the issues joined between the parties in this case upon their oaths do say that the defendant hath not paid the debt in the Writing obligatory in the declaration mentioned as the plaintiff in his replication hath alleged and they do assess the plaintiff damages by occasion of the detention of said debt to three dollars seventy five cents besides costs. It is therefore considered by the court that the plaintiff recover of the defendant the sum of two hundred and twenty five dollars the amount of the debt aforesaid together with his damages aforesaid by the Jurors in form aforesaid assessed and his costs by him about his suit in this behalf expended.

William Thrower Assignee & Plt.) Debt
   Against)
Edward D. Jones . . . . Deft.) This day came the parties by their

attornies and thereupon came a Jury of good and lawful men To Wit, Henry J. Cooper, Baker P. Potts, Matthew Cunningham, Charles Edward, Edward Marks, Stirling Graves, Stephen Reading, Jacob Cochran, Marshall Moody, John D. Riddle, William Maxwell & Robert Paine who being elected tried and sworn well and truly to try this issue joined between the parties in this case upon their oaths do say that the defendant hath not paid the debt in the writing obligatory in the declaration mentioned as the plaintiff in his repication hath alleged and they do assess the plaintiff by occasion of the detention of said debt to eight dollars besides costs. It is therefore (p-71) considered by the court that the plaintiff recover of the defendant the sum of one hundred and fifteen dollars and sixty three cents the amount of his debt aforesaid together with his damages aforesaid in form aforesaid by the Jury aforesaid assessed and his costs by him about his suit in this behalf expended.

William & J. Montgomery Merchants &c. Plaintiff)   In Debt
　　　　　　　　Against　　　　　　　　　　　　) This day came the
Benjamin Carter and James K. Murrah Defendants) parties by their
　　　　　　　　　　　　　　　　　　　　　　　　) attornies and there-
upon came a Jury of good and lawful men To Wit, Henry J. Cooper, B. P. Potts, Matthew Cunningham, Charles Edwards, Edward Marks, Stirling Graves, Stephen Reading, Jacob Cochran, Marshall Moody, John D. Riddell, William Maxwell, and Robert Paine, who being elected tried and sworn well and truly to try the issue joined between the parties in this case upon their oaths do say that they find said issue in favor of the plaintiff and that they find the balence of the debt of the writing obligatory in the declaration mentioned to be one hundred & seventy eight dollars sixty two and a half cents and they do assess the plaintiffs damages by occasion of the detention thereof to three dollars & twenty five cents besides costs It is therefore considered by the court that the plaintiffs recover of the defendants the balance of their debt aforesaid together with their damages aforesaid in form aforesaid by the Jurors aforesaid assessed and their costs by them about their suit in this behalf expended.

The Sheriff of this County returned into court the names of the following persons Summoned to attend as Grand & petit Jurors at this term an a venire facias which issued presentment to an order of the last term of this court To wit, Charles Edwards, Edward Marks, Joseph Reed, John Young Jr., Jerald Irby, Jacob Cochran, Samuel Perkins, John D. Riddell, William Maxwell, Marshall Moody, John Black, Simpson H. White, Stephen Reading, Stirling Graves, Ephraim A. Young, Nathan Bass, George Bowers, Baker P. Potts, John Butler, Henry J. Cooper, John E. Holden, Charles Mayers Senr., Matthew Cunningham & Jarret Young of whom Marshall Moody foreman, John Young Jr., John E. Holden, Stirling Graves, Joseph Reed, Simpson H. White, Matthew Cunningham, Stephen Reading, Baker P. Potts, John D. Riddell, Charles Myers, Senr., Henry J. Cooper, and William Maxwell, were elected empannelled and sworn a Grand Jury of Inquest for the body of this County who having received this charge withdrew to consider of their presentment.

Thomas W. McKnight a constable of this County was sworn to attend on the Grand Jury at this Term.

P-72 Tuesday 7th February 1824

Andrew Burne &) Plaintiffs)   In Debt
William Patton)
   Against
Kennan McMullen Defendant

This day came the parties by their attornies and thereupon came a Jury of good and lawful men To wit, Henry J. Cooker, Baker P. Potts, Matthew Cunningham, Charles Edwards, Edward Marks, Stirling Graves, Stephen Reading, Jacob Cochran, Marshall Moody, John D. Riddell, William Maxwell & Robert Paine, who being elected tried and sworn well and truly to try the issue joined between the parties in this case upon their oaths do say that the defendant has not paid the debt in the writing obligatory in the declaration mentioned as the plaintiff in his replication hath alleged and they do assess the plaintiffs damages by occasion of the detention of said debt to Eleven dollars & seventy four cents besides costs.

It is thereupon considered by the court that the plaintiff recover of the defendant the sum of one hundred & twenty seven dollars and eighty cents the amount of his debt aforesaid together with his damages aforesaid in form aforesaid by the Jurors aforesaid assessed and his costs about his suit in this behalf expended.

James Wilkinson Plaintiff)   In Debt
   Against
Samuel Y. Anderson &) Defts.
Henry J. Cooper)

This day came the parties by their attornies and thereupon came a Jury of good and lawful men to wit, Simpson H. White, Baker P. Potts, Matthew Cunningham, Charles Edwards, Edward Marks, Stirling Graves, Stephen Reading, Jacob Cochran, Marshall Moody, John D. Riddell, William Maxwell & Robert Paine, who being elected tried and sworn well and truly to try the issue joined between the parties in this case upon their oaths do say that the defendants have not paid the debt in the Writing obligatory in the declaration mentioned as the plaintiff in his replication has alleged and they do assess the plaintiffs damages by occasion of the detention of said debt to fifteen dollars and fifty cents besides costs. It is therefore considered by the court that the plaintiffs recover of the defendant the sum of two hundred & forty eight dollars the amount of his debt aforesaid together with his damages aforesaid in form aforesaid by the Jurors aforesaid assessed and his costs about his suit in this behalf expended.

P-73   Tuesday 17th February 1824

Gilbert D. Taylor the) Plts.)   Original
use of John Taylor))   Attachments
   Against
Daniel Rapelje & William Smith) Defts.
Surviving partners of the late firm)
of Laurence Rapelje &c.)

On motion of the plaintiffs by his attorney at it appearing to the satisfaction of the court now here that the defendant in this cause are not inhabitants of this State. It is ordered by the court that said defendants appear within six months from this time and replevy the property attached at the suit of said plaintiffs in this case & plead or demur a Judgment final by default will be entered in favor of said plaintiffs against them, and that a copy of this order be published three times in succession in the Nashville Whig a Publick newspaper printed at Nashville.

George W. Campbell Plt.)   In Debt
  Against   )
Eldridge B. Robertson Deft.) A. V. Brown & Alfred M. Harris Arbi-
) trators chosen by the parties in this
cause returned into court the following award to wit, State of Tennessee
Giles County Sc.& Pursuant to the Submission of George W. Campbell of the
one part and Eldridge B. Robertson of the other part refering to us Aaron
V. Brown & Alfred M. Harris the Arbitrators and award & final determination
of the matters in dispute between the said George W. Campbell & Eldridge
B. Robertson in a certain suit in Giles County court where in said George
W. Campbell is plaintiff & said Eldridge B. Robertson is defendant and an
obligation executed by said Eldridge B. & Stirling C. Robertson to the
said George W. Campbell we have this 16th February 1824 in the presence
of the said Eldridge B. Robertson proceeded to examine said obligation &
the other papers in said cause and also to examine the evidence produced
& upon such examinations after having allowed the said Eldridge B. all
such credit as he showed himself entitled to find a balance of $329.78 3/4
cents debt & the further sum of $430.44 cents damage upon said obligation
in favor of said George W. Campbell said balance of debt & damages in full
satisfaction of the said obligation as covnant witness our hands and seals
this 16th February 1824.

                Alfred M. Harris (Seal)
                A. V. Brown (Seal)

And thereupon the parties aforesaid agreed that said award be made the
judgment of the court. It is therefore considered by the court that said
plaintiff recover of said defendant the sum of three thousand two hundred
and ninety one dollars 78 2/3 cents balance of Debt together with the sum
of four hundred & thirty dollars & 44 cents damages occasioned by the detention of said balance of debt so awarded as aforesaid and his costs by
him about this suit in this behalf expended.

P-74 Tuesday 17th February 1824

William Bradshaw Plaintiff)   In Case
  Against   )
Robert Davidson Defendant *) On the application of the plaintiff
) it is ordered that a commission issue
to any two of the Acting Justices of the Peace in and for the County of
Maury to take the deposition of Samuel H. Williams, Josiah Masson, and
Abraham Looney to be read in evidence on the trial of this cause and that
the plaintiff give to the defendance ten days notice of the time and place
for taking said deposition.

  On the 17th day of February 1824 Personally appeared in open court and
being a (court of record by the laws of the State) for said County James
Hamilton a resident Citizen of said County aged sixty seven years who being
first duly sworn according to law doth on his oath make the following decla-
rations in order to obtain the provision made by the Acts of Congress of
the 18th March 1818 and the first of May 1820 that he said James Hamilton
enlisted for the term of three years or during the war about October 1775
at Trenton in New Jersey in the Company Commanded by Col. Maxwell (who was
afterward made a Brigadeer General after his return from Quebec) in the
line of the State of New Jersey on the infrantry continental established
that he continued to serve in said Company to the year 1782 when he was

discharged from said service at Camden in the State of South Carolina that he was in the battle at the Storming of Quebec under General Montgomery and afterward was at the battle of three Rivers where he got a flesh wound in the right leg, he was in the battle of German Town in Pennsylvania in the battle of Monmouth in New Jersey where he got a flesh wound in his left thigh and the ball cut out, at German Town he was shot through the left hand and has a large knot remaining on the back of it from the wound. He was also in the battle at Camden in South Carolina, and that he has no other evidence of his said services now in his power, that he knows of except the Army roll of his Country and in Pursuance of the Act of 1st May 1820 I do solemnly Swear that I was a resident Citizen of the United States on the 18th May 1818 and that I have not since that time by gift, sale or in any manner disposed of any property or any part thereof with intent there by so to deminish it as to bring myself within the provisions of an Act of Congress entitled "An Act to provide for certain persons engaged in the land and Naval Service of the United States in the revolutionary War" Pass on the 18th March 1818 and that I have not nor has any person in trust for me any property or security contracts or debts due to me nor have I any income other than   (p-75)   what is contained in the Schedule hereto annexed and by me subscribed.

his
James   X   Hamilton
Mark

Schedule one blind mare about 9 years old 13½ hands high one indifferent bed and furniture.
his
James   X   Hamilton
Mark

I live with three sons two of lawful age one about 16 years old & has no wife, & one duaghter aged 20 years that lives with a neighbor & one about 17 years old living with him & that he is unable to live or do well without the assistance of his County & that he has never received any pension or lands from any State or from the United States.
his
James   X   Hamilton
Mark

Subscribed and sworn to & declaired on the 17th February 1824 before the court aforesaid now setting - - German Lester Clerk, and it is the opinion of the court that the total amount in value of the property exhibited in the aforesaid schudule is thirty dollars.

Robert Shadden . . . Plt.   )   Petition
    Against   )
John Dickey Admrs. &c Deft.   )   On motion of the defendant by his
)   attorney. It is ordered that the
plaintiff be ruled to give good and sufficient security for the prosecution of this suit on or before the setting of the court on Thursday next or the same will be dismissed at his costs.

Robert Shadden . . . Plt.   )   Petition
    Against   )
Charles Perkins Admr. &c. Deft.)   On motion of the Defendant by
)   his attorney, It is ordered
that the plaintiff be ruled to give good and sufficient security for the

prosecution of this suit on or before the setting of the court on Thursday next or the same will be dismissed at his costs.

John Wellett ... Plt.) In Debt
Against)
Robert Anderson Deft.) On the appication of the defendant It is
ordered that a commission issue to any two of the Acting Justices of the Peace in and for the County of Nelson State of Kentucky to take the deposition of Joseph Burns, William Burns & any other witness or witnesses that he may choose, on giving to the plaintiff in proper person the names of the witnesses & place for taking said deposition at least five days preveous to the time of taking the same .. provided the plaintiff lives in the said County of Nelson.

On the petition of Robert Shadden Jr. ordered that Writs of Certiorari & Supercedias issue to stay proceedings and remove this court the record of a Judgment rendered by Alexander Black Esquire a Justice of the Peace of this County in favor of Silas Gilbert against Robbert Shadden & John Shadden on the 11th day of January 1817 for the sum of forty five dollars (p-76) & costs on the petitioners giving bond and security according to law.

Estill Malone &c Plt.) In Case
against)
William D. Jennings Deft.) This day came the plaintiffs by their
attornies and directs that this suit be dismissed which is ordered by the court accordingly ____ and that the defendant recover of the plaintiffs his costs &c.

Ordered that court be adjourned untill tomorrow morning nine oclock.

                H. Hagen
                A. Black
                William Brown

P-77 Wednesday Morning 18th February 1824

Court met according to adjournment Present Henry Hagen,) Esquires
              Alexander Black) Justices of
              William Brown) the Peace fo
) Giles County

On motion of David A. Smith Gentlemen and it appearing to the Satisfaction of the court that he is over twenty one years of age and that he is a man of honesty, probity, and good moral character which facts are ordered to be certified for the purpose of his obtaining a licence to practice law.

Stirling C. Robertson &) Plts.) Original
Eldridge B. Robertson) Attachments
Against)
Isaac Crow ..... Deft.) Samuel Day a Garnishee in this

case appeared in court and after being first duly qualified the following interrogations were put to him Vizt.

Inter Y. 1st What were you indebted to Isaac Crow at the time of serving the garnishment in this case or at any time since? Answer. I Don't conceive I owed him any thing at that time or since.

Inter. Y. 2. What effects of the said Isaac Crow have you now or had you at the time of serving this Garnishment? Answer. A day or two before the service of the Garnishment Isaac Crow put into my hands a parcel of accounts a note and a constables receipt for the benefit Simeon Marsh to whom he said Crow was indebted two hundred and fifty dollars, which papers I hold for the benefit of the said Marsh, and not of the said Crow, But there was no assignment to said Marsh of said papers nor was he present at the time of the delivery of the papers to me by Crow. The following is a list of the amounts and notes left in my hands by said Crow Viz,

Wilkins Abernathy Acct.	(note taken since by me		$10.25
Benjamin Wheeler Acct.	(Paid to me)		11.00
Robert Gordon ditto	paid to me		$12.63
Jacob Jones ditto	(paid to me)	(5.37½)	6.12½
Thomas Pruitt ditto	(note taken by me)		12.50
Samuel McClanlass	. . . .		27.37½
John Worsham	. . . .		1.25
James C. Maclin	. . . .(note taken by me)		4.75
John Lee	. . . .		8.31½
Jesse McMillan	Clos. by note to me in Crows name		5.87½
Daniel Goodrum	. . . .		12.62½
Allen Jones	. . . .		3.00
Thomas McCollum	. . . .		1.50
John Gordon	. . . .		4.12½
John Harmond & Edwind Harmond & Co.			12.12½

P-78   Wednesday 18th February 1824

Henry Palmer	. . . (Runaway)		$ 4.62½
Richard McGee	. . . .		5.
James Foster	. . . .		1.62½
Patsy Robertson	. . . .		1.75
Daniel Frazer	. . . .		3.00
John Wilson	(Note by me as above)		.80
William McNeese	(Paid to me)		1.50
Claybourne M. Vay	. . . .		6.00
Hiram Meadows	. . . .		7.07
Joshua Nichols	. . . .		1.12½
Robert Park	(Note as above by me)		7.25
Robert Page	. . . .		2.00
James W. Parsons	. . . .		4.50
Chesley Smith	. . . .		.75
James Demsey	. . . .		.25
James McCanlass	. . . .		1.00
John McCullock Note	) All in one note to me"		.62½
David McCullock note	) as before mentioned		7.18 3/4
Thomas Easts Acct.	. . . .		18.93¼
James Farquhar's	) think its paid to Crow)		3
James Hammond	. . . .		6.50
Thomas Graves	. . . .		17.12½
Dewey Smith	. . . .		6

Inter. Q. 3: What debt or effects of the said Isaac Crow do you know of in the hands of any other person? Answer. I know of none except those heretofore mentioned.

A Deed of conveyance from James Perry to John & Joseph H. Hodge for part of the lot No. 38 of the large lots in the Town of Pulaski was produced in court and the execution thereof acknowledged by the said James Perry and ordered to be certified for registration.

An award of arbitrators chosen to settle a matter in controversey between Samuel Shields and Thomas Stewart was produced in court and an agreement of the said Thomas Stewart and Samuel Shields to abide by said award was proven by Patrick Henry Braden and John Dickey two of the subscribing witnesses thereto and ordered to be certified for registration.

The Grand jury returned into court and on the Indictment refered against William P. A. McCabe for an affray with and an assault and battery on the body of Amos David Endorsd. "A true Bill and with Drew to consider of further presentments.

(PAGES TORN OUT FROM 78 to 97)

P-97 Saturday 21st February 1824

James J. Thomas one of the Jurors aforesaid is withdrawn and the cause continued till the next term of this court.

An article of agreement between Silas Flournoy & Joseph Alsup was produced in court and the execution thereof proven by the oath of William H. Field one of the witnesses thereto.

A Deed of conveyance from William C. Flournoy Administrator of the Estate of Silas Floyrnoy decd. to Joseph Alsup for seventy nine acres of land was produced in court and the Execution thereof acknowledged by the said William C. Flournoy admr. as aforesaid and ordered to be certified for registration.

The State . . . Plt.) Upon a presentments for a affraw with an
    Against   ) assault & battery on the body of George
John McKnight Deft.) Hicks.
)
This day came as well the Solicitor General for the State as also the defendant in his proper person and thereupon came the Jury who were sworn well and truly to try the issue of traverse in this case who still say they cannot agree by consent of parties and with the assent of the court Charles Edwards one of the Jurors aforesaid is withdrawn and the cause continued till the next term of this court that a new trial may be had therein.

The Grand Jury returned into court the following Indictment & presentments to wit, the State against Francis Guthrie Edward K. McMillin & Mathis

Sharan for an assault & battery on the body of a negro man slave named Moses the property of Elisha Eldridge also a presentment against William Ponds for an affray with an assault & battery on the body of Robert Wells also a presentment against Henry Harrison for retailing spiritous liquors Also a presentment against David Gipson for retailing spiritous liquors and having nothing farther to present were discharged.

A Deed of conveyance from Robert W. Green to David Bridgeforth for one hundred acres of land was produced in court and the execution thereof proven by the oaths of Samuel R. Anderson and Robert Anderson two of the subscribing witnesses thereto and ordered to be certified for registration.

A Deed of conveyance from Robert W. Green to David Bridgeforth for three hundred acres of land was produced in court and the execution thereof proven by the oaths of Samuel R. Anderson & Robert Anderson two of the subscribing witnesses thereto and ordered to be certified for registration.

Ordered that letters of administration be granted to Nancy Beal on the Estate of Thomas Beal decd. whereupon she took the oath required by law and executed Bond and security according to law.

P-98 Saturday 21st February 1824

Rebeccah Kyle & Clayborne Kyle Admrs. &c.	Original Attachment.
Against	
Thomas Jameson . . . Deft.	This day came the plaintiffs by their attorneys

and the defendant altho solemnly called came not but made default. It is therefore considered by the court that the plaintiffs recover of the defendant the sum of three hundred & four dollars and 10 cents together with the sum of one hundred & twenty two dollars & seventy five cents the damages they have sustained by occasion of the detention thereof and their costs by them about their suits in this behalf expended.

A Mortgage from Hannah Underwood to Lunsford M. Bramlett for certain property therein named was produced in court and the execution thereof proven by the oaths of Thomas Underwood & A. G. Underwood the subscribing witnesses thereto and ordered to be certified for registration.

A Deed of conveyance from Benjamin Wheeler to David McCullock for fifty acres of land was produced in court and the execution thereof proven by the oaths of James Farguhas & Robert Tucker the subscribing witnesses thereto and ordered to be certified for registration.

The Administratrix of the Estate of Thomas Beal decd. returned into court an Inventory of sd. estate which is ordered to be recorded.

Ordered that an order of sale issue to the administratrix of the Estate of Thomas Beal decd. commanding her to advertise and sell the property contained in the Inventory by her this day returned to pay the debts due from the said estate. (at six months credits)

Hannah Underwood Plt.) In Traverse
    Against)
James R. Murrah Deft.) On motion of the plaintiff by her attorney.
) It is ordered by the court that a commission
issue to any two of the Acting Justices of the peace in and for the County
of Limestone & State of Alabama to take the deposition of Thomas Land and
Charles Land and also that a commission issue to any two of the Acting
Justices of the peace in & for the County of Madison & State of aforesaid
to take the deposition of Thompson Wilson and Henry Davidson on the plaintiffs giving to the defendant ten days notice of the time and place of
taking the same, which depositions are to be read in evidence on the trial
of this cause.

P-99 Saturday 21st February 1824

    Edward D. Jones Esquire who was appointed to take a list of taxable
property & polls in Captain Potts Company for the year 1824 made return
of said list which is ordered to be recorded.

    William Brown Esquire who was appointed to take a list of taxable
property and polls company for the year 1824 made return thereof which is
ordered to be recorded.

William Gholson Plaintiff) In Covenant
    Against)
William Watson Defendant) This day came the parties by their attor-
) nies and by consent leave is given each
party to take depositions to be read in evidence on the trial of this cause
and the cause is continued.

    For good reasons shown to the court now here It is ordered that John
Balch be discharged from further attendance as a Juror at this term.

The State Plt.) Upon a presentment for an affray with & an as-
    Against) sault & battery on the body of John Brandon.
George Kirk Deft.) This day came as well the Solicitor General for
) the State as the defendant in his proper person
who being charged on the presentment in this case pleads guilty and because
he will not contend with the State, agrees to submit himself to the Justice
and Mercy of the court. It is therefore considered by the court that he
make his fine to the State to the amount of six and one fourth cents, and
that he pay the costs of this prosecution, and that he be committed to the
custody of the Sheriff of this County till said fine & costs be paid or
give security for the payment of the same, and thereupon Francis Guthrie,
Isaac Mayfield, William Kirk, John W. R. Graves, & Francis Smith come into
court and undertake as security for said Defendant. It is therefore considered by the court that the State recover of the Defendant and Francis
Guthrie, Isaac Mayfield, William Kirk, John W. R. Graves & Francis Smith
his Securities the fine & costs aforesaid.

The State Plt.   )   Upon a presentment for an affray with & an as-
   Against   )   sault and battery on the body of John McKnight
George Kirk Deft.   )   Francis Guthris, Isaac Mayfield, William Kirk,
)   John W. R. Graves & Francis Smith come into
court and undertake as Security for said defendant. It is therefore considered by the court that the State recover of the defendant and Francis Guthrie, Isaac Mayfield, William Kirk, John W. R. Green & Francis Smith. his securities the fine and costs of this prosecution according to the Judgment rendered on a former day of this term.

P-100   Saturday 21st February 1824

Ordered that Robert Buchanan, Charles Buford, James Buford, Isaac Mason & George H. Edwards or any three of them be appointed commissioners to settle with Elisha Eldridge as guardian of the minor children of John Edwards and that they make return of said settlement to the next term of this court.

On the petition of Bonapart Garland in proper person and Peter Garland Daniel Garland, Lowry Garland, Harriett Garland, John Garland, Wester Garland, Julia Ann Garland and Louisa Garland orphan children of Peter Garland decd. by their next friend Edward Garland. It is ordered that a summon issue to John Pate Junr. to appear at the next term of this court and answer said petition by plea or demurres and show cause why he should not be removed from his Guardian ship of said minors and that a copy of said petition accompany said summons.

Ordered that court be adjourned untill Monday morning 10 oclock.

                                                    A. Black
                                                    Thomas Brown
                                                    H. Hagan

P-101   Monday Morning 23rd February 1824

Court met according to adjournment Present Alexander Black, Jas. Paine, Robert Reed, Thos. Marks, Thomas Brown & Wm. B. Pepper, Henry Hagan, John Bramlett, Robert Oliver, Arthur Hicks, John Young, Paul Childs & Arch McKissack Esquires Justices of Peace for the County of Giles.

Ordered that letters of administration on the Estate of Lucy Hicks deceased be granted to Thomas Brown whereupon he took the oath required by law and executed bond and security according to law.

A Deed of conveyance from James W. Camp. to Able Wilson for eighty five acres of land and eighty four poles was produced in court and the execution thereof proven by the oaths of Thomas B. Jones and John Bass the subscribing witnesses thereto and ordered to be certified for registration.

A Deed of conveyance from John Vance to James K. Murray was produced in court and fully proven by the oaths of John Bass another of the subscribing witnesses thereto and ordered to be certified for registration.

A license to keep an ordinary for the term of twelve months and no longer is granted to Thomas B. Jones whereupon he took the oath required by law and Executed Bond and security according to Law.

A Deed of conveyance from Thomas Rivers to John Brooks was produced in court and fully proven by the oath of Able Wilson another of the subscribing witnesses thereto and ordered to be certified for registration.

Ordered that Gilham Harwell be appointed Guardian to Albert G. Harwell Mary Ann Harwell & Sarah Carolin Harwell minor heirs of Buckner Harwell decd. whereupon he having give bond and security as the law directs.

John Bramlett Esquire who was appointed to take a list of taxable property and polls in Captain Simpson H. Whites Company for the year 1824 made return thereof which is ordered to be recorded.

A Deed of conveyance from Lewis H. Brown Sheriff of Giles County to William Banks for half of lot No. 67 in the Town of Pulaski was produced in court and the execution thereof acknowledged by the said Lewis H. Brown Sheriff as aforesaid and ordered to be certified for registration.

Ordered that Henry Loyd be appointed Guardian to Julia C. Woodward and George W. Woodward minor heirs of Jeremiah Woodward decd. whereupon he executed Bond gave security according to Law.

P-102   Monday 23rd February 1824

A License to keep an ordinary for the term of twelve months and no longer is granted to William P. A. McCabe whereupon he took the oath required by law and executed bond and security according to Law.

A License to keep an ordinary for the term of twelve months and no longer is granted to David C. Gibson whereupon he took the oath required by law and executed bond and security according to Law.

Ordered that Stephen Loyd be appointed Guardian to Henry L. Woodward minor orphan of Jeremiah Woodward decd. whereupon he took the oath required by law and executed bond and security according to Law.

John Henderson Esquire who was appointed to take a list of taxable property and polls in Captain Youngs Company for the year 1824 made return thereof which is ordered to be recorded.

Ordered that Robert Anderson who is overseer of the road from Pigeon Roost Creek to Mayfields Mill have under his direction for the purpose of keeping said road in repair the following hands to wit, Robert Anderson's hands and William Mayfield and hands and the mill place and the hands that do or may live at said plantations.

The commissioners who were appointed to settle with Gilham Harwell Executor of Buckner Harwell decd. made return of said settlement which is ordered to be recorded.

A Bill of sale from James Perry to James Buford for certain property therein named was produced in court and the execution thereof acknowledged by the said James Perry and ordered to be certified for registration.

Ordered that Joseph C. Hartin be appointed overseer of the road in the room of Thomas B. Jones removed and that he have the same district of hands.

Ordered that John H. Camp and Henry Hagen Esquires be appointed to take the privy examination of Frances Y. Wells touching the execution of a and of conveyance from Thomas Wells and the said Frances his wife and Robert G. Steel to Nathan Hammet and return the same to the present term of this court.

P-103   Monday 23rd February 1824

Ordered that the County Trustee of this County pay to Lawson Hobson the sum of sixty dollars & fifty cents for keeping Isaac N. Hobson a pauper of this County for twelve months from this time.

Ordered that, that part of the Weakley Creek road which lies near the lands belonging to the heirs of Reece Porter Junr. decd. be opened agreeable to the report of a Jury appointed at the present term of this court at the expence of said heirs when so opened be under the direction of John W. R. Graves to keep the same in repair with the hands under his direction.

It is ordered by the court that the following persons good and lawful men of the County of Giles that is each one of whom is a free white citizen and house holders of said County over twenty one years of age, not an overseer of a road & who hasnot been appointed & served as a Juror in this court for twelve months, to wit, William Jones, Benjamin Williams, Joseph Goode, William H. Moore, Robt. Paine, John McKnight, F. R. Daniel, John Brown, John Brandon, Asa McGee, B. B. Watson, R. H. Allen, John P. Taylor Willis Willsford, John Goff, L. M. Shields, E. M. Massie, Thomas Graves, John Johnsen, William Pullen, William Conner, James Buford, Isaac Mason, Robert Buchanan, Anderton Tucker & John Gordon be Jurors to serve in this court at the next term on the 3rd of Monday in May next, that the clerk deliver a copy of this order to the Sheriff of the County and that he summon said persons to attend and serve accordingly.

Ordered that the Sheriff directed to Summon James Rainey constable of this County to attend at the next Term of this court.

It is ordered by the court that the following persons good and Lawful men of the County of Giles that is each one of whom is a free white male citizen and house holders of said County over twenty one years of age not an overseer of any road who has not served on the venise in the Circuit Cour of said county at the last term thereof and who has no cause to be tried in said court at the next term thereof what is known of by this court, to wit, Archd. McKissack, Anderson Hogan, Arthur Hicks, Robert Read, Robert Oliver, Thomas Brown, John H. Camp, Alexander Black, James Paine, James Dugger, Alexander Thompson, Drusy Smith, John Dabney, Thomas K. Gordon, D. K. McEwin, James McCafferty, Jonathan Moody, Robert Turner Thomas E. Abernathy, Gilham Harwell, George Malone, William W. Woods, Wm. Woods, Charles Buford & John Barnett, be Jurors to serve in the next Circuit court to be holden for said County at the Court house in the Town of Pulaski on the first Monday in August next, that the Clerk deliver a copy of this order to the Sheriff & that he summon said persons to attend and serve as a venire in said Circuit Court accordingly.

Ordered that the Sheriff be directed to summon Amanias Oliver constable of this County to attend at the next Circuit Court.

P-104 Monday 23rd February 1824

Ordered that the County tax for this County for the year 1824 be as follows to wit,

    On each 100 acres of land 18 3/4 cents.
    On each free polls 12½ cents.
    On each slave 25 cts.
    On each Town lot 37½ cents.
    On each Stud horse or Jack 25 cents.
    On each merchants or Pedlers license $5.00
    On each two wheeled Pleasure carriage 1.00
    On each four " " " 2.00

Ordered that the additional County tax for this County for the year 1824 for the pay of Jurors be as follows, to wit, On each 100 acres of land 18 3/4 cents. On each Stud horse or Jack 25 cts. On each Town lot 37½ cents.

Ordered that the additional County tax for this County for the year 1824 for the support of the poor be as follows, to wit, On each 100 acres of land 18 3/4 cents. On each Stud horse or Jack 25 cents. On each Town lot 37½ cen

Ordered that the Several Ordinary keepers in this County for the year 1824 be as follows, To wit,

    For breakfast, dinner & supper   25 cts. each
    " horse to corn & fodder   25 cents.
    " one single horse feed   12½ cents
    " Lodging   12 cents
    " Rum by the half pint . . . . 25 cents.
    " Cogniac Brandy by ditto . . . 25 cts.
    " Peach Brandy by ditto   12½ cents
    " Apple Brandy by ditto   12½ cents
    " Whiskey By ditto   12½ cents.

Ordered that the rate of Ferriage at John Daileys Ferry at Lower Elkton in This County be as follows, Towit,

For man & horse over creek & River	12½ cents.	
" Ditto over river only	12½ cents.	
" Ditto over creek only	12½ cents.	
" Wagon over creek only	6¼ cents.	
" ditto over River & Creek	50	"
" ditto over River only	50	"
" Gig over Creek only	18 3/4	"
" ditto over River & Creek	25	"
" ditto over River only	25	"
" Cart over Creek only	18 3/4	"
" ditto over River & Creek	25	"

P-105

" ditto over River only	25 cents	
" four wheel pleasure carriage		
" " " over Creek only	37 ½	"
" ditto over River & Creek	50	"
" ditto over River only	50	"

This day being 23rd of February 1824 personally apper in open court Isham Brown of said State & County who being solemnly sworn upon oath make the following Statements, To Wit, On the 16th of February 1816 he delivered his property amongst his children as equally as he could, he gave at that time to William Brown his son one hundred acres of land in Giles County worth about five dollars per acre but did not execute a deed of conveyance for the same till the 15th of October 1821. On the 16th of February 1816 he gave to his daughter Nancy Brown the following property To wit, 135 acres of land worth about two dollars per acre twelve head of cattle, five head of sheep 20 head of hogs, one sorrel mare, one bed & furniture worth about two hundred and thirty or forty dollars, But did not execute a bill of sale for the same till the 15th of October 1821. The reason why he did not execute the deed to said William at the time of the gift & the Bill of sale to Nancy at the time of said gift to her was that they were both underage & lived with this affiant, That on the same 16th of February 1816 this affiant gave to his sons George, Abraham & James. To his daughters, Polly Watson, Sally Webb, Lucy Finch, Patsy Creoy & Betsy Brown (all of whom were then of full age) a tract of land each, for which he executed and in 1816 & the property, above mentioned was at the same time given to William & Nancy them minors as aforesaid, this affiants object being to make the shares of his children as equal as he could and he does think that he made them as equal as possible. This affiant further states that on the 1st of March 1814 he sold to Minor Winn & Ambrose Foster 150 acres of land in Giles County for which he executed to them a bond of title, & that one Josiah Phelps perchased the interest of said Foster & Winn in said land and this affiant having a small tract of about 105 acres of borken stony land adjoining said land sold as aforesaid to Foster & Winn sold the same in the year 1820 (as well as he recollects to said Josiah Phelps for the sum of one hundred and twenty dollars, which he believes to be a full and fair price for it. This affiant made a deed to said Phelps on the 8th November 1820 for the land he sold said Phelps as aforesaid & the land he sold said Foster & Winn aforesaid including the whole in one deed. This affiant further states that he has not disposed of any of the property which he had since the 18th of March 1818, except said tract of 105 acres of land herein before mentioned, the property conveyed to said William Brown & Nancy in 1821 having been given to them in 1816 honestly & bona fide this affiant did not consider it his own at any time since said gift and though it has been conveyed since the 18th March 1818, yet said conveyance being made in pursuance of a previous gift, this affiant does not consider said conveyance as the commencement of this (p-106) Title of said William & Nancy to said property. The reason why this affiant did not exhibit a schedule of his property previous to the passage of the Act of the 1st of March 1823 is as follows, to wit, when this affiant made his original declaration he did not know that it was necessary to make out a schedule of his property nor does he believe that there was any law requiring it, as he is at present advised. He caused his papers to be put into the Post Office at Pulaski directed to the Secretary of War & never received any answer from them, or knew what had been done with them, till some time in the month of May 1823 — That not having received any answer from the war department relative to the fact of his application he got Alfred M. Harris Esqr. of Pulaski some time in March 1823 write to the secretary of War for information upon the subject. That this affiant received a letter signed J. E. Edwards dated 25th April 1823 informing him that he was inscribed on the pension list for the West Tennessee agency & a certificate of Pension for him Sent to J. Blair Esqr. at Jonesburough Tennessee on the 2nd of June 1820, This letter conveyed the first information to this affiant that he had of what had been done on his claim — he showed it to Alfred M. Harris who transacted this business first as Judge of the 6th Judicial Circuit & after he resigned as a friend for me, I was told that it would be necessary to make out a schedule of his property under some act of Congress that had been passed as I understand since the date of my original declaration — In pursuance of this counsel this affiant made out a schedule of his property at the 1st court that came on in the County in which he lives after the time that he had been informed it was necessary This affiant hath not as yet received his pension certificate & he believes that the person to whom it was sent is now a member of congress He prays to have his certificate transmitted to him at Pulaski in Giles County & that he may receive his pension as he is in great need.

Isham Brown

Subscribed and sworn to in open court this 23rd day of February 1824.

German Lester Clerk

Ordered that Alfred M. Harris be allowed till next term to return a settlement as guardian of Julia Ann Flournoy.

Ordered that William H. Field be allowed till next term to return a settlement as guardian of Silas Flournoy.

P-107 Monday 23rd February 1824

Ordered that the County Trustee of this County pay to John Laird Esquire the sum of forty dollars to be applied by him to the support of the widow Ellis a pauper of this county.

James Buford Guardian of James & Catharine Moore minor orphans of Somerset Moore decd. returned into court an amount current of his said guardianshi which was ordered to be recorded.

William Wood appeared in open court by his attorney and declined his right of qualifying at this term as a Justice of the Peace for this County It is therefore considered and ordered by the court that said William Wood be not allowed to qualify as a Justice of the Peace for this County at this Term.

Ordered that that part of the Fayettsville road which lies between William Ezells and Rolly Harwells be opened at the expence of Micajah Ezell who petitioned for the alteration, and when so opened be kept in repair by William Hayes the overseer of that part of said road with the hands under his direction.

Ordered that the County Trustee of this County pay to Micajah Ezell the sum of eighty two dollars for building a bridge across crooked creek where the Huntsville road crosses the same, let by commissioners appointed for that purpose at the last term of this court.

Vaulton Childress Plt.   )   In Debt
     Against   )
Willis W. Cole ... Deft.   )   From the Judgment of the court in this
                                              case rendered the defendant prayed an appeal to the honorable the Circuit Court to be held for the County of Giles and having entered into bond & security according to law the same was granted him.

William & Jonathan Plts.)   In Debt
Montgomery Merchants &c   )
    Against   ) From the Judgment of the court in this case
Nathaniel Young) Defts.) rendered the defendant prayed an appeal to
& James Perry)   ) the honorable the Circuit Court to be held
) for the County of Giles and having entered into bond and security according to law the same was granted them.

A Power of Attorney from Sarah Poynor to David Scott was produced in court and the execution thereof acknowledged by the said Sarah Poynor and ordered to be certified.

P-108   Monday 23rd February 1824

Ordered that Davis Brown, Hickman Grubbs, James Abernathy, Elisha Abernathy, Henry Birdsong, Willis S. M. McLaurine & Henry McCoy be appointed a Jury to view that part of the Huntsville road which lies between James Paine farm & upper Elkton and see if in their oppinion it be proper to alter the same and if it be to mark out the same and that they make report to the next term of this court.

The commissioners appointed by an order of the last term of this court to devide a three hundred and sixty and a half acre tract of land and allot to Samuel Smith in right of his wife Jane his distributive share therein in the following words figures and platts Towit,

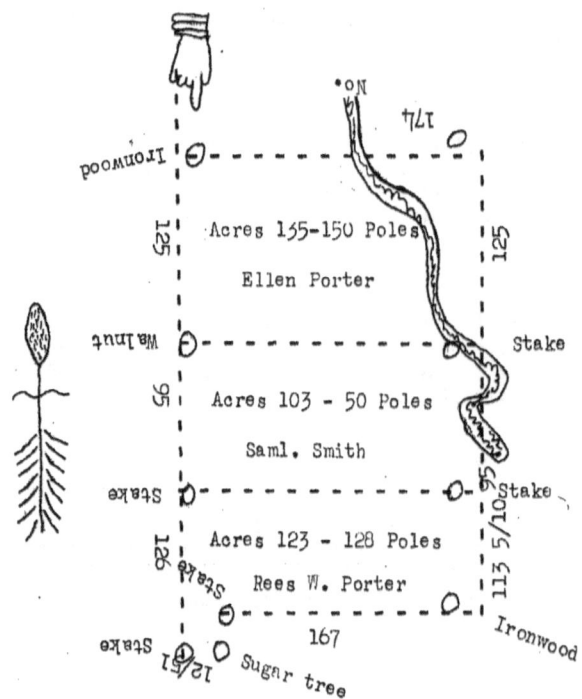

Agreable to a commission from the Worshipfull Court of Giles County to us directed to lay off and set apart to Samuel Smith in right of his wife Jane his proportionable part of three hundred and sixty three acres of land conveyed by Reese Porter Senior Deed. to said minors & after surveying & deviding the aforesaid tract we have allotted to the said Smith in right of his wife Jane the following tract of land & bounded as follows, Towit, Begining one hundred and twenty five poles South of the north West corner of the aforementioned tract of three hundred & sixty three acres at a Walnut and dogwood pointers on the west boundry line of said original tract then south with said boundry line ninety five poles to a stake in field Cherry tree pointer then east one hundred and seventy four poles to a Stake Ironwood & stake pointer thence north ninety five poles to a stake on the bank of Richland Creek thence west one hundred and seventy four poles to the Begining. Containing by estimation one hundred & three acres & fifty poles to which devision and and allotment we do Jointly agree.

Given under our hands and seals this . . . . . day of . . . 1821.

          A. M. McKissack   (Seal)
          A. Black   (Seal)
          Robert Reed   (Seal)
          Robert McLaurine   (Seal)
          Robert Davidson   (Seal)

Which return was ordered to be recorded at full length on the minutes.

Ordered that the commissioners appointed to devide a tract of land Return the distributors of the Estate of Reese Porter Junr., deed be allowed as follows for their services towit,

Archibald McKissack . .	survayor . .	$4.00
Archibald McKissack as commissioners		4.00
Paid Archibald McKissack ditto		4.00
Robert Reed . . . .Ditto		4.00
Robert McLaurine . . Ditto		4.00
Robert Davidson . . Ditto		4.00

Ordered that the County Trustee of this County pay to George Malone, Elisha White, Willis Willsford, James Lester & John Gordon the commissioners who were appointed to Superintend the building of a bridge across Richland Creek on the Prewits Gap road the sum of two hundred dollars a part of which said commissioners are authorised to pay towards their obligation to the undertaker of said Bridge the balance to be applied by them to the best advantage towards lengthening the abutments of said Bridge.

James Perry Esquire Sheriff and collector of the public & County taxes for this County for the year 1823 returned into court his list of Insolvencies for the aforesaid year amounting to twenty two dollars seventy nine and a half cents which was allowed him five Five dollars sixty nine & three fourth cents of which is due to the State and seventy dollars nine & three fourth cents is due to the County.
It is thereupon ordered by the court that certificates issue to the treasure of the State and trustee of the County in order that said Sheriff may receive a credit for the aforesaid sums respectively.

Ordered that Hardy Willsford, George Malone, Elisha White and John Laird be appointed a Jury to view that part of the Prewits Gap road which lies between John Lairds and William Dearings Spring and see if it be proper to turn said road and make report to the next term of this court.

John H. Camp & Henry Hagen Esquires who were appointed to take the privy examination of Frances Y. Wells touching the execution of a deed of conveyance from Thomas Wells & the said Frances his wife and Robert G. Steel to Nathaniel Hamet returned said examination into court and the   (p-110) Said deed together with the examination is ordered to be certified for registration.

it appearing to the satisfaction of the court that Thomas Steel has

failed to comply with the order of this court requiring him to give other and Sufficient security for the true and faithful administration of the Estate of David Steel decd. It is therefore ordered by the court that the order appointing said Thomas Steel administrator of said Estate and the letters of administration which issued to him in conformity to said order be made null and void and of no effect.

Ordered that court be adjourned till tomorrow morning nine Oclock.

A. Black
H. Hagen
Thomas Brown

P-111   Tuesday Morning 24th 1824

Court met according to adjournment, Present Dewey Smith,) Esquires
               Alexander Black) Justices
               James Paine) of the Peace
) in & for the
) County of Giles

Ordered that Charles Buford, Alexander Black, James Patteson, Richard Brandon and Thomas B. Jones or any three of them be appointed commissioners to settle with Thomas McKissack administrator of the Estate of Wilson Jones decd. and that they make return thereof to the next term of this court.

Gray H. Edwards & others ... Plts.) Petition
    Against   )
Thomas McKissack Admr. &c Deft.) On motion of the defendant in
) this case he is allowed untill the next term of this court to file his answer herein.

Robert Shadden Plt.) Petition
  Against   )
John Dickey Admr. &c Deft.) On the application of the plaintiff ordered that a commission issue to any two of the Acting Justices of the Peace in & for the County of Maury to take the deposition of Alfred Donaldson to be read in evidence on the trial of this cause upon his giving to the defendant five days notice of the time and place of taking said deposition.

A Bill of sale from James H. Graves to James S. Conner for certain property therein mentioned was produced in court and the execution thereof acknowledged by the said James H. Graves and ordered to be certified for registration.

James Winters Plaintiff) In Debt
  Against   )
Basil Compton & Isaac Compton) This day came the parties in their
) proper person and the defendants withdrew the plea by them heretofore filed in this case and say they cannot

gainsay the plaintiffs action against them nor but that they do owe him the sum of three hundred and ninety six dollars the debt in the Writing obligatory in the declaration mentioned and that the plaintiff has sustained damages by occasion of the detention of said debt to the amount of thirteen dollars & eighty six cents and agrees that Judgment be entered up against them in favor of the plaintiff for that amount with costs. It is therefore considered by the court that the plaintiff recover against the said defendants the debt aforesaid together with the damages aforesaid in form aforesaid agreed and also his costs by him about his suit in this behalf expended whereupon the plaintiff agrees that execution on this Judgment be stayed the first day of January 1825.

P-112   Tuesday 24th February 1824

Robert Wood Esquire who was appointed at the last term of this court to take a list of taxable property and polls in Captain James L. Hendrys Company for the year 1824 made return thereof which is ordered to be recorded.

Thomas Marks Esquire who was appointed at the last term of this court to take a list of taxable property and polls in Captain Edward M. Brown's Company for the year 1824 made return thereof which is ordered to be recorded.

Ordered that letters of administration on the Estate of David Steel deceased be granted to German Lester whereupon he took the oath required by law and Executed Bond & Security according to law.

Archibald McKissack Esquire who was appointed at the last term of this court to take a list of taxable property and polls in Captain Watson's Company for the year 1824 made return thereof which is ordered to be recorded.

Thomas Harwood Esquire who was appointed at the last term of this court to take a list of taxable property and polls in Captain Kearney's Company for the year 1824 made return thereof which is ordered to be recorded.

Hugh Torrance Assignee & &c. plaintiff)   In Case
            Against)
John Keenan . . . . Defendant)   This day came the parties by
) their attorneys and thereupon
came a Jury of good and lawful men, (To wit) Charles Edwards, Gerald Irby, Mitlington Tidwell, Abednago Moore, Gilham Harwell, Jessee West, Thomas Compton, John J. Barber, Jason Hopkins, William Maultsby, Richard Briggs, and Lewis Conner, who were elected tried and sworn well and truly to try the issues joined between the parties in this case having heard the evidence and argument of counsel retired out of court to consider of their verdict and after some time returned into court, and say they cannot agree by consent of parties said Jurors were permitted to disperse to meet again to morrow morning nine oclock.

P-113 Tuesday 24th February 1824

On the petition of James Perry ordered that Writs of Certiorari and Supercedias issue to stay proceedings and remove to this court the record of a Judgment rendered by John Young Esquire a Justice of the Peace of this County in favor of R. L. Crittenton against said James Perry on the ____ day of _____ 182_ for the sum of sixty four dollars with some interest and costs on the petitioners giving bond and Security according to law.

Harrison Hicks surviving Partner &c.) Plaintiff)
Against)
Ralph Graves and Charles Perkins) Defendant)

In Case

This day came the parties by their attornies and thereupon came a Jury of good and lawful men (Towit) Edward Marks, Nathan Bass, Thomas Davenport, William Hendry, John Black, Richard Bently, Bazil Compton, William Aymett, James I. Thomas, James Hooks, David Reed & Charles Davis, who being elected tried and sworn well and truly to try the issue joined between the parties in this case upon their oaths do say that they find said issue in favor of the plaintiff and assess his damages to four hundred and forty five dollars thirty one and one fourth cents besides costs. It is therefore considered by the court that the plaintiff recover of the Defendant the amount of his damages aforesaid by the Jurors aforesaid in form aforesaid assessed and his costs by him about his suit in this behalf expended, From which Judgment the defendant prayed an appeal to the honorable the Circuit Court to be held for the County of Giles and having entered into Bond and security according to law the same was granted them.

Ralph Graves . . . Plaintiff)
Against)
Nathaniel Alman Defendant)

Motion

This day came the plaintiff by Harris Y. Fields his attornies and moved the court now here for Judgment against the defendant for the sum of twenty two dollars and fifty eight with Interest thereon from the 29th day of July 1820 which he then paid as security for the defendant to John Brown a constable of this County on an execution which issued on a Judgment William M. Beazley recovered against said Nathaniel Alman before Nelson Patteson a Justice of the Peace of this County on the 22nd day of April 1820 and it not appearing to the satisfaction of the court whether said plaintiff was security or principal in said Execution A Jury was empannelled to try that fact, Towit, Edward Marks, Nathaniel Bass, Thomas Davenport, William Henry, John Black, Richard Bentley, Bazil Compton, Nathaniel Graves, William Arnell, James I. Thomas, James Hooks, and David Reed who being duly sworn to Enquire as aforesaid upon their oaths do say that the said plaintiff paid as Security for the defendant the sum of (p-114) Twenty two dollars and fifty eight cents on the 29th day of July 1820 to John Brown a constable of this county on an execution which issued on a Judgment which William M. Beazley recovered against said Alman on the 22nd day of April 1820 before Nelson Patteson a Justice of the peace for the County to the stay of Execution on which said Judgment the said plaintiff became Security for the said defendant the sum of twenty two dollars and fifty eight cents with legal Interest thereupon from the 20th day of July 1820 till Paid and his costs by him about his motion in this behalf expended agreable to an Act of the General assembly in such cases made and provided.

Ralph Graves Plaintiff	Motion
Against	
Nathaniel Alman Defendant	

This day came the plaintiff by Harris & Field his attornies and moved the court now here for Judgment against the defendant for the sum of thirteen dollars twenty four and a half cents with Interest thereon from the 29th day of July 1820 which he then paid as security for the defendant to John Brown a constable of this County on an execution which issued on a Judgment which John Parker recovered against the said Nathaniel Alman before Nelson Patteson a Justice of the Peace of this County on the 22nd day of April 1820 and it not appearing to the satisfaction of the court whether said plaintiff was security or principal in said Execution. A Jury was empanneled to try that fact to wit, Edward Marks, Nathan Bass, Thomas Davenport, William Kendry, John Black, Richard Butler, Basil Compton, Charle Deavers, William Aymett, James I. Thomas, James Hooks and David Reed who being duly sworn to Enquire as aforesaid upon their oaths do say that the said plaintiff paid as security for the said defendant the sum of thirteen dollars twenty four and a half cents on the 29th day of July 1820 to John Brown a constable of this County on an execution which issued on a Judgment which John Parker recovered against said Alman on the 22nd day of April 1820 before Nelson Patteson a Justice of the Peace for this County to the Stay of Execution on which said Judgment the said plaintiff became security for the said defendant. It is therefore considered by the court that the plaintiff recover of the defendant the sum of thirteen dollars twenty four & one half cent with legal interest thereon from the 29th day of July 1820 till paid and his costs by him about his motion in this behalf expended agreable to an Act of this General Assembly in such case made and provided.

P-115 Tuesday February 24 1824

Ralph Graves . . . Plaintiff	Motion
Against	
Nathaniel Alman Defendant	

This day came the plaintiff by Harris & Field his attornies and moved by the court now here for Judgment against the defendant for the sum of Thirty nine dollars fifty four and a half cents with interest thereon from the 29th day of July 1820 which he then paid as security for the defendant to John Brown a constable of this County on an execution which issued an a Judgment which Eli Tidwell recovered against the said Nathaniel Alman before Nelson Patteson a Justice of the Peace of this County on the 22nd day of April 1820 and it not appearing to the satisfaction of the court whether said plaintiff are security or principal in said execution to Jury was empanneled to try that fact, towit, Edward Marks, Nathan Bass, Thomas Davenport, William Hendry, John Black, Richard Bently, Basil Compton, Charles Deavers, William Aymett, James J. Thomas, James Hooks, & David Reed, who being duly sworn to enquire as aforesaid upon their oaths do say that said plaintiff paid as security for the said defendant the sum of thirty nine dollars fifty four and a half cents on the 29th day of July 1820 to John Brown a Constable of this County on an execution which issued on a Judgment which Eli Tidwell recovered against said Alman on the 22nd day of April 1820 before Nelson Patteson a Justice of the Peace for this County to the stay of execution on which said Judgment of said plaintiff became security for the said defendant. It is therefore considered by the court that the plaintiff recover of the said defendant the sum of thirty nine dollars fifty four & a half cents with legal interest thereon from the 29th day of July 1820 till paid and his costs by him about his motion in this behalf expended agreable to an act of the General Assembly in such once made and provided.

Ordered that Court be adjourned untill tomorrow morning 9 oclock.

             A. Black
             H. Hagen
             Thomas Brown

P-116 Wednesday 25th February 1820

Court met according to adjournment Present Alexander Black,) Esquires Justices of the Peace for Giles County.
             Henry Hagen
             Thomas Brown

  On the petition of Richard Bentley it is ordered that Writs of Supercedeas and certiorari issue to Stay proceedings remove to this court the record of a Judgment which Daniel Frazer recovered against said Richard Bentley and Henry Palmer before Richard McGee Esquire a Justice of the Peace for this County on the 16th day of January 1824 for the sum of thirty nine dollars ninty one and three fourth cents and costs on the petitioners giving bond and security according to law.

  On the petition of Richard Bently it is ordered that Writs of Supercedias and Certiorari issue to Stay proceedings & remove to this court the record of a Judgment which Daniel Frazer recovered against said petitioners and Henry Palmer before Richard McGee Esquire a Justice of the Peace for this County on the 16th day of January 1824 for the sum of thirty nine dollars ninety one and three fourth cents and costs on the petitioners giving bond and security according to Law.

Henry Palmer . . . Plt.   )   Certiorari
   Against   )
Sally Maclin   ) This day came the parties by their
Sackfield Maclin Exor.)Dofts.) attornies and thereupon came a
of John Maclin Decd.)   ) Jury of good and lawful men Towit,
) Nathan Bass, Edward Marks, James
J. Thomas, Maddison Riddle, Richard Bentley, Edward K. McMillin, Henry Hester, Thomas Underwood, Martin Griffin, Archibald Storey, Benjamin England & John Kennan, who being elected tried and sworn well and truly to try the matter in controversey between the parties in this case upon their oaths do say that the testator of the defendants in his lifetime was indebted plaintiff the sum of thirty dollars and that the defendant since the death of the said testator unjustly detains the same from said plaintiff. Is therefore on motion of the plaintiff by his attorney considered by the court that the plaintiff recover of the defendants Sterling C. Robertson and James C. Maclin the securities on the certiorari the aforesaid sum of thirty dollars and his costs as well before the magistrate in this court Expended.

(PAGE 117 & 118 TORN OUT)

P-119 Tuesday 26th February 1824

83

Court met according to adjournment Present Alexr. Black,) Esquires
                                   Henry Hagen &   ) Justice
                                   Thomas Brown   ) of the
) Peace of
) Giles County.

A Deed of conveyance from Lewis H. Brown Sheriff of this County to Matthias Shanon for one hundred and ten cents was produced in court and the execution thereof acknowledged by the said Lewis H. Brown Sheriff as aforesaid and ordered to be certified for registration.

William Hendry . . . Plts.   )   Trespass Vi - et
        Against   )   Armis.
Abednego Moore Charles Dever   )
Noely Dever Millirton Tidwell   )   This day came the parties by their
& George Bratton   )   attornies and thereupon came the Jury
)   who were sworn well and truly to try
the issue joined between the parties in this case, who having heard the balance of the argument of counsel retired out of court to consider of their verdict and after some time returned and say they cannot agree By consent of the parties and with the assent of the court Nathan Bass one of the Jurors aforesaid was withdrawn and the cause continued till the next term of this court that a new trial may be had therein.

William & Jonathan Plts.   )   In Debt
Montgomery Merchants &c.   )
        Against   )
Benjamin Carter &)   )   From the Judgment of the court in this
James K. Murrah   ) Defts.   )   case rendered the defendants prayed an
)   appeal to the honorable the Circuit Court
)   to be held for the County of Giles and
having entered into bond and Security according to law the same was granted them.

Hugh Torrence Assee &c. Plaintiff)   In Case
        Against   )
John Kennan . . . . . Defendant   )   On the application of the defendant
)   ordered that a commission issue to
any two of the Acting Justices of the peace in and for the County of Franklin & State of Alabama to take the deposition of William W. Parham to be read in evidence on the trial of this cause upon the defendants giving to the plaintiff Fifteen days notice of the time and place of taking said deposition.

Ordered that the petit Jurors be discharged from further attendance at the present Term.

P-120   Thursday 26th February 1824

Martin Lorance for the use &c Plt.)   In Case
        Against   )
William Steele . . . . . Deft.)   from the Judgement of the court
)   in this case rendered the defendant prayed an appeal to the honorable the Circuit court to be held for

the County of Giles and having entered into bond and Security according to law the same was granted him.

Robert Shadden . . . Plaintiff) Petition
       Against)
Charles Perkins Admr. &c. Defendant) On the affidavit of the
) defendant this cause is
ordered to be continued and that a commission issue to any two of Acting Justices of the Peace in and for the County of Maury to take the depositions of A. W. Donaldson, Sally Donaldson and Mary Donaldson to be read in evidence on the trial of this cause, upon the defendants giving the plaintiff five days notice of the time and place of taking the same.

Thomas McKissack Admr. &c Plaintiff) In Debt
       Against)
Ralph Graves & Charles Perkins Defendants) From the Judgment of the
) court in this case rendered
the defendants prayed an appeal to the Honorable the Circuit Court to be held for the County of Giles and having entered into bond and security according to law the same was granted them.

Edward D. Jones . . . . . . Plt.) In Debt
       Against)
Stephen Anderson & Andrew M. Ballentine) This day came the parties
Executor of the last Will & testement of) by their attornies and
John Samuel Decd. & Thomas Williams & Defts.) thereupon came a Jury of
Anner Samuel Admr. & Administratix of) good and lawful men, Towit,
Anthony Samuel deceased) Charles Edwards, John Parker,
) Featherstone Harwell, Henry
J. Cooper, Hugh H. Williams, Samuel Parsons, William Maltsby, Isaac Crowder, Gray H. Edwards, Charles Duey, William P. Richardson, and Isaac James, who being elected tried and sworn well and truly to try the issue joined between the parties in this case upon their oaths do say that they find the said issue in favor of the plaintiff and that they find the balance of the debt in the writing obligatory in the declaration mentioned to be three hundred & twenty one dollars and Seventy five cents and they do assess the plaintiffs damages by occasion of the detention thereof to Fifty eight dollars and thirty one cents besides costs. It is therefore considered by the (p-121) court that the plaintiff recover of the defendants the balance of their debt aforesaid together with their damages aforesaid in form aforesaid by the Jurors aforesaid assessed and his costs by him about his suit in this behalf expended To be levied of the goods and chattles rights and credits of the Intestate and testator if so much there be if not of the proper goods and chattles lands and tenements of said defendants.

Smith Hunt Guardian & Plt.) In Debt
       Against)
German Lester & Fountain Lester) Defts.

    This day came the parties by their attornies and thereupon by consent of the parties the demurrer of Fountain Lester one of the defendants in this cause to the plaintiffs declaration is withdrawn and said Fountain Lester hath leave to plead the plea of payment at the next term of this Court which is to be tried at the August term succeeding.

85

George Brown & William B. Pepper who were securities for Elisha Eldridge Guardian of the minor children of John W. Edwards filed their petition in writing at the present term of this court praying to be released from their said securityship and the said Elisha Eldridge this day came into court and gave bond with other good and sufficient security for the true and faithful discharge of his duty as guardian of said minors and thereupon the said George Brown & William B. Pepper are released from any future Liability as security aforesaid.

The Commissioners of Pulaski Plt.
    Against
William Ball & the Administrators
of the Estate of Archibald Defts.   Garnishment
Alexander decd.

  On motion of the plaintiffs by attorney and it appearing to the satisfaction of the court now here that said plaintiffs recover against said defendants. On the 23rd of February 1821 in this court a Judgment for the sum of one hundred and Eleven dollars ninety four and a half cents Debt together with the further sum of three dollars and sixty eight cents damages and also the sum of thirteen dollars sixteen and a half cents costs of suit, and that a Pluries Writ of Fiere Facias issued from the Clerks office of this court on the 16th day of December 1823 on said Judgment returned to the present term of this court, upon which the Sheriff hath returned "nothing found, but William P. A. McCab summoned as a Garnishee on the 10th of January 1824. A. M. Harris summoned as a Garnishee on this Si Fa the 18th February 1824." and it also appearing that said Judgment remains wholly unsatisfied and the said Sheriff having summoned Alfred M. Harris as Garnishee (p-122) in said case who being Examined in open court confessed himself indebt to William Ball to the amount of twenty five dollars. It is therefore considered by the court that the plaintiffs recover against said Alfred M. Harris said sum of twenty five dollars and Execution issue for the collection of the Same.

The Commissioners of Pulaski Plts.
    Against
William Ball & the Administrators) Defts. Garnishment
of the Estate of Archibald Alexander decd.

  On motion of the plaintiffs by attorney and it appearing to the satisfaction of the court that said plaintiff recovered against said defendants on the 23rd day of February 1821 in this court a Judgment for the sum of one hundred and eleven dollars ninety four and a half cents debt together with the further sum of three dollars and sixty eight cents damages and also the sum of thirteen dollars sixteen and a half cents, costs of suit, and that a Pluries of Fieri Facias issued from the Clerks office of this court on the 16th day of December 1823 on said Judgment returnable to the present term of this court, upon which the Sheriff hath returned "nothing found, but William P. A. McCabe summoned as a Garnishee on the 10th of January 1824 & A. M. Harris summoned as a Garnishee on this Fi Fa the 18th February 1824 and it also appearing that said Judgment remains wholly unsatisfied, and the said Sheriff having summoned William P. A. McCabe as a Garnishee in said case, who being examined in open court confessed himself indebted to William Ball to the amount of forty one dollars twelve and ahalf cents. It is therefore considered by the court that said plaintiffs recover against said William P. A. McCabe said sum of forty one dollars twelve and a half cents, and that Execution issue for the collection of the same at any time after the first day of May next and not sooner.

    Ordered that court be adjourned till court in course.

                                                      A. Black

                                                     H. Hagen

                                                     Thos. Marks

At a Court of Pleas and Quarter Sessions holden for the County of Giles at the Courthouse of said County in the Town of Pulaski on the third Monday in May being the seventeenth day thereof in the year of our Lord 1824. Present Alexander Black, Drusy Smith, Richard McGee, John H. Camp, John B. Armstrong, Anderson Hogan, James Paine, Thomas Harwood, Archibald McKissack, John Young Senr., William Brown, James Read, Thomas K. Gordon, Thomas E. Abernathy, William Ussery, Edward D. Jones, Robert Oliver, John Laird, John Bramlett, John C. Walker, Hezekiah Jones, Arthur Hicks, John Henderson, William Mayfield & Henry Hagen Esquires Justices of the Peace of said County Residing: German Lester Clerk of said Court & Lewis B. Brown Sheriff of said County.

Ordered that the following tax list be received and the double tax thereon remitted, Towit, David Moore's heirs 141 acres of land.

Ordered that William Watson be appointed overseer of the road in the room of James Woods resigned and that he have the same district of hands.

Ordered that Thomas Brown be appointed overseer of the road in the room of Walter McConnel resigned and that he have the same district of hands.

Ordered that the following tax lists be received and the double tax thereon remitted, Towit, John Nankins 881 3/4 acres of land. 20 black polls. 1 carriage 4 wheel.

Harriet Row
        9 slaves
        1 carriage 4 wheels

A Deed of conveyance from Joseph Armor to Holdman R. Fowler for thirty five acres of land was produced in court and the execution thereof proven by the oaths of Robert Cox & John P. Armor the witness thereto ordered to be certified for registration.

Ordered that Henry Rainey be appointed overseer of the road in the room of Edward York resigned and that he have the same districts of hands.

Jonas B. Jones came personally into court and resigned his office as constable of this County in Giles in Captain John Browns Company.

P-124 Monday May 17th 1824

The Jury who were appointed at the last term of this court to view and mark out that part of the Huntsville road which lies between James Paines farm & upper Elkton made return thereof which was received & confirmed by the court.

The Jury who were appointed at the last term of this court to view that

part of the Prewits Gaps road which lies between John Lairds and William Dearings Spring made report thereof which was received & comfirmed by the court.

The last Will and testament of Joseph Braden decd. was produced in court and proven by the oaths of John B. Armstrong & Alston J. Waters two of the subscribing witnesses thereto and ordered to be recorded and thereupon John G. Brandon & Patrick H. Branden the Executors therein named appeared in court and were qualified & gave bond and security as the law directs.

Ordered that James Hammons, Hezekiah Jones, James Paisley, Anderson Hogan & John Balch or any three of them be appointed commissioners to devide the estate of Robert Hodges decd. into three equal parts and allot Francis Hodges, Polly Hodges & Robert Hodges an equal share of the same and that they make report of said devision & allotment to the next term of this court.

At least five Justices being present Jesse Lamb returned into court one wolf scalp under four months old which was ordered to be burnt.

A Deed of conveyance from John G. Branden & Samuel Davis Executors of the last will & testament of William Martin to Moses Patterson was produced into court for fifty three & one fourth acres of land and the execution thereof acknowledged by the said Executor and ordered to be certified for registration.

Ordered that Robert Williams be appointed overseer of the road in the room of Enoch Davis resigned and that he have the same district of hands.

The last will and testament of William A. Massie decd. was produced in court and proven by the oaths of Aaron Brown & William W. Topp the subscribing witnesses thereto & ordered to be recorded - and thereupon Lewis G. Upshaw one of the executors therein named appeared in court & was qualified & gave bond and security as the law directs.

Ordered that James Kelso be appointed overseer of the road in the room of William B. Hays resigned and that he have the same district of hands.

P-125 Monday 17th May 1824

A Bond from Cornelius Rose to Francis M. Rose for certain purpose therein named was produced in court and the execution thereof acknowledged by the said Cornelius Rose and ordered to be certified for registration.

A Deed of conveyance from Francis M. Rose to Cornelius Rose for one hundred & sixty acres of land was produced in court and the execution thereof acknowledged by the said Francis M. Rose and ordered to be certified for registration.

A Bill of sale from Francis M. Rose to Cornelius Rose for certain property therein contained was produced in court and the Execution there of acknowledged by the said Francis M. Rose and ordered to be certified for registration.

Ordered that the following tax lists be received and the double tax thereon remitted, Towit,

Robert Ross	1 white Poll
	51 acres of land
John Ross	50 acres of land
	1 White Poll

Ordered that James Goldsberry be appointed overseer of the road in the room of Frederick Harwell resigned and that he have the same district of hands.

Ordered that Josiah P. Alexander be appointed overseer of the road in the room of John Newton resigned and that he have the same district of hands

A Deed of conveyance from David Strong to William James for one hundred & sixty acres was produced in court and the execution thereof proven by the oaths of William Ussery & Michael Files the subscribing witnesses thereto and ordered to be certified for registration.

John Pate Guardian to the heirs of Peter Garland decd. returned into Court an account of the hire of the negroes of sd. heirs, which was received by the court and ordered to be recorded.

At least five Justices being present Hardy Benson returned into court one wolf scalp under three months old which was ordered to be burnt.

P-126   Monday 17th May 1824

A deed of conveyance from Isaac H. Williams & Polly his wife to Thomas E. Abernathy for one hundred acres of land was produced in court and the execution thereof proven by the oaths of James Paine & John H. Camp two of the subscribing witnesses thereto to be the Act and deed of said Isaac H. Williams & thereupon John H. Camp & James Paine two of the Acting Justices of the Peace in & for this County were appointed to take the privy examination of Sd. Polly Williams touching the Execution of said deed, who returned said examination which was ordered to be certified for registration.

Ordered that Wilton F. L. Jenkins be appointed overseer of the road leading through Lower Elkton in the room of Larpley Barber removed, and that he have the same district of hands, with the addition of John Cathcart & George Brown.

Ordered that the following tax list be received and the double tax thereon remitted, towit, Mrs. Mary Scott, 1 town lot in Pulaski.

Ordered that the County Trustee of this County pay to Arthur Meaddox a pauper of this County, the sum of forty dollars for his support & maintenance for twelve months from this time.

Ordered that the following tax list be received and the double tax thereon remitted, Towit,

Elizabeth Edwards	150 acres of land
	4 Slaves
Gray H. Edwards	1 White poll
	4 Slaves

An Ordinary licence for the term of one year & no longer is granted to Abbert G. Underwood who took the oath required by law and executed bond & Security as the law directs.

Ordered that William Davenport be appointed overseer of the road in the room of Alexander Tinnen resigned, and that he have the same district of hands.

Ordered that Bartlett Russell be bound an apprenticed to John Huckeby in denture to that effect having been entered into & filed Between the chairman of the court & said Huckeby.

Ordered that James Rainey be appointed constable in Captain Livingston Company whereupon they took the oath required by & executed bond & security according to law.

P-127 Monday 17th May 1824

Ordered that James R. Dickey be appointed constable in Captain Ruff's Company, whereupon he took the oath required by & executed bond and Security according to law.

Ordered that William W. Woods be appointed constable in Captain John Browns Company, Whereupon he took the oath required by & executed bond and security according to law.

Ordered that Daniel Puryear be appointed constable in Captain Whites Company, whereupon he took the oath required by law & executed bond & Security according to law.

Ordered that William Gibson be appointed overseer of the road in the room of James Knox resigned - and that he have the same district of hands.

Henry Hagen was unanimously appointed chairman of this court.

The execution of the last will and testament of Wm. Martin decd. returned into court an Acct. of the sales of said Estate which was ordered to be certified.

Ordered that Homer Rainey be appointed overseer of the road in the room of Richard Briggs resigned and that he have the same district of hands.

Ordered that Seth Williamson be appointed overseer of the road in the room of Levi Sherrill resigned and that he have the same district of hands.

The commissioners who were appointed to settle with the administrator of Peter Bodenhammer decd. made return thereof which is ordered to be recorded.

Ordered that Alexander Black, Fountain Lester & James Perry or any two of them be appointed commissioners to settle with John Dabney admr. of Sarah Hicks decd. & that they make report to the present term of this court.

Ordered that Bever be appointed overseer of the road in the room of Jacob Couch resigned and that he have same district of hands.

John Dabney who is Guardian of the children of Robert Jones rendered an account against his wards which was allowed by the court & ordered to be recorded.

Ordered that Monday next be set apart for County business.

P-128 A Deed of conveyance from Edward D. Jones to Jacob Jones for three hundred acres of land was produced in court & the Execution thereof proven by the oaths of James Rainey & William H. Abernathy two of the subscribing witnesses thereto and ordered to be certified for registration.

Ordered that Samuel Haynes be released from his obligation heretofore taken in this court binding Wesley Wilson to him.

The last will and testament of Godsend Ruff decd. was produced in court and proven by John Wall and David Goodnight the Subscribing witnesses thereto and ordered to be recorded.

A Deed of conveyance from Alexander McDonald to Anderson Hogan for fifteen acres of land was produced in court and the Execution thereof acknowledged by the said Alexander McDonald and ordered to be certified for registration.

Ordered that the County Trustee of this County pay to Elizabeth Edwards the sum of forty dollars for keeping Rebeccah Ruff for twelve months from this time.

Ordered that Alexander Black Esquire purchase a suitable Record Book for the use of the Register of this County & pay for the same out of any monies in his hands as Trustee of this County not other wise approprated.

Ordered that the County Trustee of this County pay to John Manefee the sum of thirty dollars for keeping Jackson Martin a pauper of this County for one year ending at last court.

Ordered that Asa A. Estes be appointed overseer of the road in the room of Daniel Abernathy resigned and that he have the same district of hands.

Ordered that the following lists of taxable property polls be received by the court and the double tax thereon remitted Towit

    Edward Davis 1 Free poll
                    1 Slave
                    216 Acres of land
                    2 Town lots

    James Jossling
                    1 Free poll
                    1 Slave

P-129   Monday 17th May 1824

Ordered the County Trustee of this County pay to Jonathan Moody Esquire the sum of twenty five dollars to be applied by him to the support of Polly Camille a pauper of this County for one year from this time.

A Licence to keep an ordinary for the term of twelve months from this time and no longer is granted to Samuel Davis, who gave bond and security and was qualified as the law directs.

A Bill of Sale from James Slaughter to Claiborne Kyle for certain property therein named was produced in court and the execution thereof acknowledged by the said James Slaughter and ordered to be certified for registrat:

Ordered that Joseph Knox be appointed Guardian of Joseph K. Gibson an orphan of John K. Gibson decd. he having given bond and security as the law directs.

Ordered that George M. Gibson be appointed Guardian of Ann Gibson and John Gibson minor orphans of John K. Gibson decd. he having given bond and security as the law directs.

A Deed of conveyance from Fountain Lester Hearndon Harrolson for sixty eight and a half acres of land in the Western district was produced in court and the execution thereof acknowledged by the said Fountain Lester and ordered to be certified.

Administration on the Estate of Philmer Green decd. is granted to Aaron V. Brown who gave bond and security and was qualified as the law directs.

Rhoda Strichland an orphan Girl is bound an apprentice to Willis Lane, an Indenture to that effect having been entered into between said Lane and the chairman of this court.

The Last will and testement of Nelson Patteson decd. was produced in court and proven by German Lester and Thomas Martin two of the subscribing witnesses thereto, and the codicil thereto proven by the oath of Aaron V. Brown a subscribing witness and said will with the codicil was ordered to be recorded.

Ordered that Alexander Black, Henry Hagen and German Lester be appointed to direct and Superintend an alteration in the upstairs of the court house of this county.

It appearing to the satisfaction of the court now here that James J. Walker late of this county hath departed this life intestate, and that Polly Walker widow of the said decedent relinquishing her right of administration.

P-130 On his Estate William Ussery and thereupon Letters of Administration on the Estate of the said James J. Walker decd. is granted to the said William Ussery who gave bond & security and was qualified as the law directs.

Ordered that Samuel Shields, Peter Ussery & Samuel Perkins be appointed commissioners to lay off and allot to Polly Walker widow of the late James J. Walker decd. so much of his Estate as will be sufficient for the maintainance of herself and Family for one year from the time he departed this life.

A Bill of Sale from John S. Jones and Martha his wife to John Dabney for their interest in two mortgages therein named was produced in court and acknowledged by the said John S. Jones to be his act and deed, and thereupon John Henderson & Richard McGee Esquires two of the acting Justices of the Peace for this County were appointed to take the privy examination of the said Martha Jones touching the execution of said bill of Sale & return the same to the present term of this court.

A Power of Attorneys from Henry Hagen & Catharine his wife, Henry J. Cooper & Pamelia his wife & Letitia Talbott to Isaac Sitler was produced in court and proven to be the act and deed of the said Henry Hagen, Henry J. Cooper & Letitia Talbott by the oath of Lewis H. Brown the subscribing witnesses thereto and thereupon James Paine & Thomas E. Abernathy two of the Acting Justices of the Peace for this County were appointed to take the privy examination of the said Catharine Hagen and Pamelia Cooper touching the Execution of said Power of Attorney & return the same into court instantly and said Justices having returned said examination into court the same was ordered to be certified.

On motion of Jonanna Moss one of the Administrators of Mason Moss decd. and it appearing to the Satisfaction of the Court that at February Term 1820 of this court that the said Joanna Settled with the court her administration of said Estate pursuant to an order made at February 1819 and that upon said settlement John Yancy who was the other administrator & was then dead was charged as administrator with the sum of $181.95 cents the amount of sales, credited by the sum of $142.77½ cents — In which entry the name of Joanna Moss the other administrator is not mentioned, & it appearing to have been the intention of the and the parties that said settlement should also be a settlement of the whole administration of sd. administrators upon sd. Estate, it is ordered that the same be so entered for them.

A Bill of sale from Anthony Fisher to Gilham Harwell for certain property therein named was produced in court and the execution thereof proven by Edward D. Jones the subscribing witness thereto & ordered to be certified for registration.

P-131 Monday 17th May 1824

On the petition of Claiborn Kyle It is ordered that David Bridgeforth, William H. Moore, Ephraim A. Young, David Crouch, William Dailey, Guston Kearney & Burrell Abernathy or any five of them be appointed a Jury to view and mark out a private way from the land belonging to the estate of William Kyle decd. to intersect the Athens road and that they make report to the next term of this court.

Ordered that Samuel Kerr be appointed overseer of the Buck Creek road from the ford of said Creek at Martin Brownings to Collins branch and that he have under his direction the hands on the said part of said road that formerly worked thereon under Thomas Cole.

Ordered that James Shelton be appointed overseer of the Buck Creek road from the ford of said creek at Martin Brownings to the State line and that he have under his direction the hands on the said part of said road that formerly worked thereon under Thomas Cole.

On the petition of Daniel Frazier setting fourth in Writing that he owns the land on the south side of Richland Creek about three miles below Robert Gordons in this County and that the land on the other side of said creek belongs to the heirs of John Samuel decd. and praying that a summons issue to the heirs of said John Samuel to appear and answer said petition, and also that a Jury of view to consist of four honest free holders be appointed to lay off view & value on oath one acre of the land of the sd. Daniel Frazier & also one acre of the land of the said heirs of John Samuel appointed thereto and to report their proceedings thereon to next court & that sd. Daniel Frazier be permitted to erect a mill on said premises. It is ordered by the court that a summon issue according to the prayer of said petition accompanied by a copy of sd. petition and that Stirling Graves, William C. Graves, William Bracken, & William Chapman honest free holders of this County lay off view & value on oath one acre of the land of sd. heirs of John Samuel and also one acre of the land of said Daniel Frazier appointed thereto and report their opinion & proceedings thereon to next court.

A deed of conveyance from James McCafferty to John Brown for one hundred & sixty acres of land was produced in court and the Execution thereof proven by the oaths of R. H. Allen & G. M. Gibson the witnesses thereto & ordered to be certified for registration.

Ordered that court be adjourned untill tomorrow morning nine oclock.

                Wm. Mayfield
                Hezekiah Jones
                A. Black

P-132 Tuesday morning 18th May 1824

Court met according to adjournment present John H. Camp,) Esquires
            Thomas Harwood) Justices
            & Alexr. Black) of the peace
) for the County
) of Giles.

Gilbert D. Taylor for the) Plts.
use of John Taylor
   Against
Daniel Rapelje &
William Smith
Surviving Partners) Defts.
of the late firm of
Lawrence Rapelje & Co.

Original Attachments

This day came the plaintiffs by his attorneys and thereupon came the defendants by their legally constituted Agent, John F. Lawrence, who says that he cannot gainsay the plaintiffs action aforesaid against said defendants do owe said plaintiffs the sum of seven hundred & fifty dollars a part of the debt in the declaration mentioned & the said defendants by their agents aforesaid do agree that Judgment be entered up against them in behalf of said plaintiffs for said sum of $7.50 together with costs of suit and that the property levied upon by virtue of the attachment in this cause be sold, and all rents collected by James Patterson the agent of Sd. Lawrence Rapelye & Co. & which are due from any tenant who may have heretofore, or May now occupy said property shall be paid to said plaintiffs provided that if the amount of such Sale & rents shall exceed said sum of $7.50 & the costs of suit said plaintiffs shall pay over the excess to the assignees of said defendants or their agents. and said plaintiffs after having exhausted said property &

rents shall give a receipt in full against this Judgment & said plaintiffs in proper person agreeing to accept said Judgment upon the above terms, on motion of said plaintiffs by his attorney. It is considered by the court that he recover against said defendants for the use of John Taylor, the sum of $7.50 the debt aforesaid in form aforesaid confessed together with his costs by him about his suit in this behalf expended - To be satisfied according to the terms of the aforesaid agreement.

A Deed of conveyance from Thomas H. Meredith to Elisha Eldridge for three hundred & thirty two acres of land was produced in court & fully proven by the oath of Thomas Martin another of the subscribing witnesses thereto & ordered to be certified for registration.

A Deed of conveyance from Elisha Eldridge Trustee of William Powelll to Alexander Baldridge & Joseph C. Martin for Ten acres of land was produced in court & the execution thereof acknowledged by the said Elisha Eldridge & ordered to be certified for registration.

P-133 Tuesday 18th May 1824

The Sheriff of this County returned into court the names of the following persons summoned to attend as Grand & petit Jurors at this term pursuant to an order of the last term of this court a copy of which issued to the said Sheriff, Towit, William Jones, Benjamin Williams, Joseph Goode, William H. Moore, Robert Paine, John McKnight, T. P. Daniel, John Brown, John Brandon, Asa McGee, B. B. Watson, R. H. Allen, John P. Taylor, Willis Willsford, John Goff, L. M. Shields, E. M. Massie, Thomas Graves, John Johnson, William Pullen, William Conner, James Buford, Isaac Mason, Robert Buchanan, Anderstone Tucker, & John Gordon, of whom James Buford foreman, John Goff, John Johnson, Thomas Graves, Willis Willsford, William Jones, John Brown, Anderston Tucker, William H. Moore, Robert Paine, Isaac Mason, Robert Buckhanan & William Conner were elected empannelled and sworn a Grand Jury of Inquest for the body of this County, who having received their charge withdrew to consider of their presentments.

James Rainey a constable of this County was sworn to attend on the Grand Jury at this term.

Henry Gibson Plaintiff)   Certiorari
   Against   )
John Kennan Defendant) This day came the parties by their attornies
) and thereupon came a Jury of good and lawful men, to wit, Richard H. Allen, Beverly B. Watson, John P. Taylor, William Pullen, Henry Kimbrough, Henry Kerr, John Gordon, Jesse Wells, Archibald Smith, Joseph Alsup, Gatewood Webb & Robert Black, who being elected tried and sworn well & truly to try the matter in controversey between the parties in this case, and having heard the evidence and argument of counsel retired out of court to consider of their verdict after some time returned & say they cannot agree, and thereupon it was agreed by the parties that they be permitted to disperse to meet again tomorrow.

The administrators of the Estate of James J. Walker decd. returned into court an Inventory of sd. Estate which was ordered to be recorded.

The Commissioners who were appointed to Settle with the administrators of Sarah Hicks decd returned sd. settlement into court which is ordered to be recorded.

Ordered that John Dabney be allowed the sum of Fifty four dollars for his serving as administrator of the Estate of Sarah Hicks decd.

The Commissioners who were appointed to settle with the administrators of the Estate of Wilson James deceased returned said settlement into court which is ordered to be recorded.

P-134   Tuesday 18th May 1824

A Deed of conveyance from Alexander McDonald & John McDonald to Edward Davis for twenty two acres of land was produced in court and the execution thereof acknowledged by the said Alexander McDonald & John McDonald and ordered to be certified for registration.

A Deed of conveyance from Alexander McDonald & to William Murrell for Fifteen acres of Land was produced in court and the execution thereof acknowledged by the said Alexander McDonald & John McDonald and ordered to be certified for registration.

A Deed of conveyance from Joseph C. Hartin to George Bowers for ten acres of land was produced in court and the execution thereof acknowledged by the said Joseph C. Hartin and ordered to be certified for registration.

On the petition of Nathan Davis & Joseph Riley who undertook as Security for Thomas McKearly and Patience Caswell Administrators of the Estate of Samuel Caswell deceased. It is ordered that a summons issue to the said Thomas McKearly & Patience Caswell requiring them to appear at the next term of this court to give other and counter security to be approved of by the court in said case & further to be dealt with as the law directs.

Ordered that an order of sale issue to William Ussery administrator of the Estate of James J. Walker decd. commanding him to sell within a reasonable time the personal Estate contained in the Inventory by him this day returned the negro excepted and made return thereof according to Law.

James Perry ... Plt.   )   Certiorari
        Against   )
David Browning Deft.   ) This day Thomas Brown came into court and as-
) sumes upon himself the payment of the attornies
tax fee in this case and thereupon the plaintiff assumes upon himself the balance of the costs and directs that this suit be dismissed, which is by the court ordered accordingly and that the defendant go hence without day and recover of the said Thomas Brown & the plaintiff the part of the costs which have each assumed.

Thomas Henderson Plt.)
    Against)   Original Attachments
William Cannon Admr.) Defts.)
of William Cannon Decd.))
) This day came the parties by
) their attornies and   (p-135)

Thereupon came a Jury of good and lawful men (Towit) Asa McGee, Benjamin Williams, John McKnight, John S. Brandon, Reuben L. Crittenton, Gilliam Harwell, Henry Peden, Elisha Kimbrough, John Abernathy, Hugh Adam's, Henry Harrison & Nathan Davis, who being elected tried and sworn well and truly to try the issue joined between the parties in this case upon their oaths do say that they find said issued in favor of plaintiff, and do assess his damages by occasion of the detention in the Writing obligatory in the declaration mentioned to forty two dollars & Eighty cents besides costs It is therefore considered by the court that the plaintiff recover of the said defendants the sum of one hundred & thirty nine dollars & twelve cents the amount of his debts aforesaid together with his damages aforesaid in form aforesaid by the Jurors afforesaid assessed and his costs by him about his suit in this behalf expended - To be levied of the goods and chattles rights and credits of the intestate in the hands of the administrator to be administered if so much there be if not of the proper goods & chattles & tenements of the said defendants.

    Ordered that court be adjourned untill tomorrow morning Eight oclock.

                                                            H. Hagen
                                                            James Paine
                                                            Hezekiah Jones

P-136   Wednesday Morning 19th May 1824

Court met according to adjournment Present James Paine,)   Esquires Jus-
                                         Hezekiah Jones &)   tices of the
                                         Henry Hagen)   Peace for Giles
)   County.

    Ordered that the following tax lists be received and the double tax there on remitted, Towit,
    The Estate of Thomas H. Meredith deceased,
                                                        740 acres of land Richland Creek.
                                                        120 Acres of land Newton Creek.
                                                        18 slaves
                                                        3 Town lots
    Elisha Eldridge   332 Acres of land Elk River
                                1 White Poll
                                5 Town lots
                                1 slave

Hugh Torrence Plaintiff   )
    Against   )   In Case
John Kennan Defendant   )
)   On affidavit of the defendant it is
)   ordered by the court that this suit
be continued untill the next term of this court and that the defendant pay

the costs which have accrued at this term, and that a commission issue to any two of the Acting Justices of the peace in and for the County of Franklin and State of Alabama to take the deposition of William W. Parkham to be read in evidence on the trial of this cause, and that the defendant give give to the plaintiffs ten days notice of the time & place of taking said deposition.

Thomas Patler Assee &c. Plt.)   Appeal
    Against)
Shadrack Harwell Deft.)

This day came the parties by their attornies and thereupon came a Jury of good and lawful men, Towit, Benjamin Williams, John McKnight, John Black, Asa McGee, Henry Hester, Benton R. White, Jessee West, Joseph Tarkington, John W. Edwards, John Barrett, Joel Callaway, and Patrick R. Smith, who being elected tried and sworn well and truly to try the matter in controversey between the parties in this case upon their oaths do say that the defendant is indebted to the plaintiff the sum of twenty dollars & fifty seven cents Besides costs. * It is therefore considered by the court that the plaintiff recover of said defendant said sum of twenty dollars & fifty seven cents, the amount of his debt aforesaid in form aforesaid by the Jurors aforesaid assessed and also his costs about his suit in this behalf expended.

A Deed of conveyance from John Goff to David C. Gobson for ninety acres of land was produced in court and the execution thereof acknowledged by the said John Goff & ordered to be certified for registration.

P-137   Wednesday 19th May 1824

Henry Gibson Plt.)   Certiorari
    Against)
John Keenan Deft.)

This day came the parties by their attornies and thereupon came the Jury who were sworn well and truly to try the matter in controversey between the parties in this case upon their oaths do say that the defendant is not indebted to the plaintiff anything. It is therefore considered by the court that the defendant go hence without day and recover of the plaintiff his costs as well before the magistrate as in this court expended.

Claiborne Kyle &) Plaintiffs)
Rebeccah Kyle))   Appeal
    Against)
Mary D. Price Defendant)

This day came the plaintiffs by their attorney, who saith they wish no further to prosecute their suit against the Defendant. It is therefore considered by the court that the defendant go hence without day and recover against said plaintiffs her costs as well before the magistrate as in this court expended.

The Grand Jury returned into Court the following Indictments (Towit, The State against Lawson Hobson and John M. Hobson Indictment for an affray with and an assault and battery on the body of David Page, the same against Francis Rose Indictment for an affray with and as an assault and battery on the body of Aaron Wilcookson and withdraw to concider of further presentment.

A Deed of conveyance from John Goff to David C. Gibson for one hundred and three acres of land was produced in court and the execution thereof acknowledged by the said John Goff and ordered to be certified for registration.

The State . . . Plt. Against David C. Gibson Deft.	Presentment for retailing Spirituous Liquors. This day came as well the Solicitor General for the State as also the defendant in proper person, who being charged on the pre-

sentment in this case pleads Guilty, and because he will not contend with the State agrees to submit himself to the Justice & Mercy of the court. It is therefore considered by the court that he make his fine with the State to the amount of one dollar and that he pay the costs of this presentment.

Ordered that Ranson Wells be fined the sum of Five dollars for absenting himself when on the Jury)of William Henry against Abednego Moore & others) without leave of the court.

P-138   Wednesday 19th May 1824

William Henry Plt. Against Abednego Moore Charles Dever Neely Dever Defts Milton Tidwell & George Bratton	Trespass Viets Armies This day came the parties by their attornies and thereupon came a Jury of good and lawful men, Towit, Beverly B. Watson, John S. Brandon, Benjamin Williams, Henry Peden, Thomas Read, David Browning, Gray

H. Edwards, Reuben L. Crittenton, Robert Brooks, William S. Neal, William Pullen, and Ranson Wells - who being elected tried and sworn well & truly to try the issue joined between the parties in this case who having heard part of the evidence were permitted to disperse to meet tomorrow morning nine oclock.

Robert Shadden . . . Plt. Against John Dickey Admr. &c. Deft.	Petition On the affidavit of the plaintiff It is ordered by the court that

this suit be continued untill the next term and that a commission issue to any two of the Acting Justices of the peace in and for the County of Maury this State, to take the deposition of Alfred Donaldson, William Craig, Samuel Craig, Jesse Rogers, & John Wantlin, to be read in evidence on the trial of this cause and that the plaintiff give to the Defendant ten days notice of the time and place of taking said deposition.

Thomas Hudson Against William Cannon Admr. of) Defts. William Cannon Decd.)	Original Attachment This day came the parties by their attornies and thereupon came a Jury of good and lawful men, to-

wit, Asa McGee, Benjamin Williams, John McKnight, John A. Brandon, Reuben L. Crittenton, Gilham Harwell, Henry Peden, Elisha Kimbrough, John Abernathy, Hugh Adams, Henry Harrison & Nathan Davis who being elected tried & sworn well & truly to try the issue joined in this case upon their oaths do say that they find said issue in favor of the plaintiff and assess his damages by occasion of the detention in the writing obligatory in the declaration mentioned to fourteen dollars & forty cents, besides costs. It is therefore considered by the court that the plaintiff recover of said defendant the sum of forty three dollars the amount of his debt aforesaid together with his damages aforesaid in form aforesaid to be levied of the goods & chattles rights & credits of the intestate in the hand of the administrator to be administered if so much then be if not of the proper goods & chattles lands & tenments of the said Defendants.

Ordered that court be adjourned untill tomorrow morning nine oclock.

                Wm. Mayfield
                Hezekiah Jones
                A. Black

P-139 Thursday May 20th 1824

Court met according to adjournment Present Hezekiah Jones,) Esquires
             William Mayfield) Justices
             Alexander Black) of the peace
) for Giles
) County.

Ordered that the following tax lists be received and the double tax thereon remitted, To wit,
      Henry Peden 1 white poll
          3 slaves.

On the petition of William Sawyers ordered that Wits of Certiorari and Supercedias issue to stay proceedings & remove to this court the record of a Judgment rendered by James Paine & Willis S. McLaurine Esquires Justices of the peace of this County in favor of Adam Bell Assee &c. against said William Sawyers on the day of _____ 1824 for the sum of Eighty four dollars with Interest & costs on the petitioners giving bond and security according to law.

The commissioners who were appointed to settle with John Goff administrator of George Goff decd. made return of sd. settlement which is ordered to be recorded.

The Grand Jury returned into court the following Indictments & presentments, Towit, The State Vs David Pace, Indictment for an affray with & an Assault & battery on the body of John M. Hobson the same against John W. Edwards Presentments for an affray with and an assault & battery on the body of James Daily, The same against Thomas Dillon Indictment for an affray with and an Assault & battery on the body of John Vincent - The same against William D. Jennings presentment for an affray with and an assault & battery on the body of James Vincent - and withdrew to consider of further presentments.

A Deed of conveyance from David Wilcockson to Joseph Blair for thirty acres and thirty three polls of land was produced in court and proven by the oaths of Isaac Wilcockson & Andrew Ewings the witnesses thereto and ordered to be certified for registration.

The State . Plt.
Against
Francis M. Rose Deft.

Indictment for an affray with & an assault & battery on the body of Aaron Wilcockson.

This day came as well the Solicitor General for the State as also the defendant in his proper person who being charged on the Indictment in this case pleads guilty and because he will not contend with the State agrees to submitt to the Justice & mercy of the court. It is therefore considered by the court that he make his fine with the State to the amount of one dollar and that he pay the costs of this prosecution and that he be committed to the custody of the sheriff of this County there to remain till sd. fine & costs (p-140) are paid or that he give security for the payment of the same, and thereupon George M. Gibson comes into court & undertakes as security for the said Defendant It is therefore considered by the courts that the State recover of the said defendants & George M. Gibson his security the fine and costs aforesaid.

The State . . . Plt.
Against
Isaac S. Chrisman Deft.

Presentment for an affray with & an assault & battery on the body of Nathaniel Hale.

This day came as well the Solicitor General for the State as also the defendant in his proper person who being charged on the presentment in this case pleads guilty, and because he will not contend with the State agrees to submit himself to the Justice of the court. It is therefore considered by the court that he make his fine with the State to the amount of one dollar and that he be committed to the custody of the Sheriff of this County there to remain till said fine and costs are paid, or that he give security for the payment of the same and thereupon George M. Gibson comes into court & undertakes as security for the said defendant. It is therefore considered by the court that the State recover of the defendant & George M. Gibson his security the fine & costs aforesaid.

Elisha Eldridge Guardian to the heirs of John W. Edwards returned into court an account against his wards which was ordered to be recorded.

The State . . . Plt.
Against
Larkin Mayfield Deft.

Presentment for an affray with & an Assault & battery on the body of Isaac S. Chrisman.

This day came as well the Solicitor General for the State, as also the defendant in his proper person, who being charged on the presentment in this case pleads guilty, and because he will not contend with the State agrees to submit himself to the Justice and Mercy of the court. It is therefore considered by the court that he make his fine with the State to the amount of one dollar, and that he pay the costs of this prosecution and that he be committed to the custody of the sheriff of this County thereto remain till said fine and costs are paid - Or that he give security for the payment of the same, and thereupon Isaac Mayfield comes into court and undertakes as security for the said Defendant. It is therefore considered by the court that the State recover of the defendant & Isaac Mayfield his security the fine and costs aforesaid.

Sterling C. & E. B. Robertson Plt.) Garnishment
Against)
Samuel McCanlass . . . Deft.) By leave of the court this suit
) is continued till next Tuesday.

P-141   Thursday 20th May 1824

The State . . . Plt.   ) Presentment for an affray with & an assault
   Against   ) & battery on the body of William Black.
Robert Anderson Deft.   )
) This day came as well the Solicitor General for the State as also the defendant in his proper person who being charged on the presentment in this case pleads guilty and because he will not contend with the State agrees to submit himself to the Justice & mercy of the court. It is therefore considered by the court that he make his fine with the State to the amount of six and one fourth cents and that he pay the costs of this prosecution, and that he be committed to the custody of the Sheriff of this County there to remain till said fine & costs are paid or that he give Security for the payment of the same, and thereupon Lewis H. Brown comes into court and undertakes as security for the said defendant. It is therefore considered by the court that the State recover of the defendant and Lewis H. Brown his security the fine & costs aforesaid.

On motion of George Bowers upon a petition in writing setting fourth that he is seized in his demusue as in fee of one undivided _____ of a certain tract or parcel of land Situate lying and being in Giles County aforesaid on Elk river containing ten acres be the same more or less, being the same upon which the Mill erected by Doctr. William Purnell is Situated, and butted & bounded as follows, Towit, Beginning at a small Sycamore on the south side of the river on the edge of the lower Bank of said river at the upper ford above the mill, near a log bridge, thence runing east 3½ poles to a lot fence, thence South 14° East 10 poles thence East 3 poles 7 links to a field, thence South 20° East 40 poles to south west corner of a field, thence East 15½ poles to a Scaley bark hickory & beech, thence south 64 poles to Elk river between two lyms & a black oak on the Bant of sd. river, thence up sd. river with its meandas north 48° west 8 poles north 35° west 20 poles - north 22° west 20 poles - north 5° west 20 poles - north 4° west to the Beginning - And that Alexander Baldridge is seized in his demurue as of fee of the other undivided moiety of said land with its appurtenances as a trugant in commerce with said petitioner & praying that a partition of said land with its appertenance be made so as to hold his part thereof in Security, and it appearing to the satisfaction of the court that sd. petitioner has given sd. Alexr. Baldridge more than ten days notice of his intention to make this motion on this day in this court. It is ordered by the court that Jacob Miller, John H. Camp, James Austin, Wilton F. L. Jenkins and Thomas Harwood be commissioners to divide said land with its appertenances into two equal parts according to quantity & quality & make report of their proceedings thereupon to the next term of the court.

P-142   Thursday 20th May 1824

The State Plt.   ) Presentment for an affray with & an assault &
   Against   ) battery on the body of James Pillow.
John Defoe, Deft.   ) This day came as well the Solicitor General

for the State as also the defendant in his proper person who being charged on the presentment in this case pleads guilty, and because he will not contend with the State, agrees to submit himself to the Justice and mercy of the court. It is therefore considered by the court that he make his fine with the State to the amount of one dollar, and that he pay the costs of this prosecution, and that he be committed to the custody of the Sheriff of this County thereto remain till said fine and costs are paid or that he give security for the payment of the same, and thereupon John Pillow comes into court and undertakes as security for the said defendant. It is therefore considered by the court that the State recover of the defendant & John Pillow his security the fine and costs aforesaid.

The State Plt.   ) Indictment for an affray with & an Assault &
   Against   ) battery on the body of James Hardy.
Bailey Davis Deft.   ) This day came as well the Solicitor General for
                         the State as also the defendant in his proper
person, who being charged on the Indictment in this case pleads not guilty, and for his trial puts himself upon his County, and the Solicitor General for the State on the part of the State likewise, therefore let a Jury come who as well &c. to recognize &c and thereupon came a Jury of good and lawful men, Towit, John McKnight, John P. Taylor, Asa McGee, John Roberts, Thomas Butler, William Fogg, Thomas Williams, Willie Boyd, Jesse Hicks, John Anthony, Lewis Ramsey, & Morgan Brown who being Elected tried and sworn well and truly to try the issue of Traverse between the State and said defendant upon their oaths do say that the defendant is guilty in manner and form as he is charged in the Bill of Indictment - It is therefore considered by the court that he make his fine with the State to the amount of six and one fourth cents, and that he pay the costs of this prosecution, and that he be committed to the custody of the Sheriff of this County untill said fine and costs are paid.

The State . . Plt.   ) Indictment for an affray with & an assault &
   Against   ) Battery on the body of John Vincent.
Thomas Dillon Deft.   )
) This day came as well the Solicitor General
for the State as also the defendant in his proper person, who being charged on the Indictment in this case pleads guilty, (p-143) and because he will not contend with the State agrees to submit himself to the Justice and mercy of the court. It is therefore considered by the court that he make his fine with the State to the amount of one dollar, and that he pay the costs of this prosecution and that he be committed to the custody of the Sheriff of this County untill said fine and costs be paid or that he give security of the payment of the same, and thereupon William D. Jennings comes into court and undertakes as security for said defendant. It is therefore considered by the court that the State recover of the said defendant & William D. Jennings his security the fine & costs aforesaid.

Pettway Bond & Co. Plaintiff   )   In Debt
        Against   )
Bernard M. Patteson   )   ) This day came as well the
James Patteson   ) Defendants   ) plaintiffs by their attor-
John Brown & Ralph Graves   )   ) ney as the defendants in
) their proper persons and
said defendants withdraw the pleas by them heretofore filed in this case,

and say they cannot gainsay the plaintiffs actions against them nor but that they do owe them the sum of nineteen hundred dollars a Balance of the debt in the Writing obligatory in the declaration mentioned, and agrees that Judgment be entered up against them for that amount with costs. It is therefore by consent of the plaintiffs attorney, considered by the court that the plaintiffs recover of the defendant the Balance of their debt aforesaid in favor aforesaid agreed and their costs by them about their suit in this behalf expended - From which Judgment the defendants prayed an appeal to the honorable the Circuit Court to be held for the County of Giles and having entered into bond and security according to Law the same was granted them.

The State Plt.) Upon an Indictment for an affray with and an
Against) assault & Battery on the body of John Hobson.
David Pace Deft.)
) This day came as well the Solicitor General for the State as the defendant in his proper person, who being charged on the Indictment in this case pleads guilty, and because he will not contend with the State agrees to submit himself to the Justice and mercy of the Court. It is therefore considered by the court that he make his fine with the State to the amount of one dollar, and that he pay the costs of this prosecution, and that he be committed to the custody of the Sheriff of this County, there to remain till said fine and costs are paid or give security for the payment of the same, and thereupon Andeston Tucker and William Flatt comes into court and undertakes as (p-144) Security for the said defendant. It is therefore considered by the court that the State recover of the defendant and the said Andeston Tucker & William Flatt the fine and costs aforesaid.

William Hendry Plts.) Trespass Vist Armies
Against)
Abednego Moore) This day came the parties by their
Charles Dever) attornies and thereupon the Jury
Neely Dever) Defts. who were empannelled and sworn on
Millenton Tidwell) yestoday, well and truly to try the
& George Bratton) issue joined between the parties in
) this case having heard the balance
of the evidence and aguments of counsil, retired out of court to consider of their verdict after some time returned and say they cannot agree by consent of parties and with the assent of the court said Jurors are permitted to disperse to meet again tomorrow morning.

The State Plt.) Upon an Indictment for an affray with & an as-
Against) sault & battery on the body of James Hardy.
Bailey Davis Deft.)
) James Hardy who was bound at the last term of this court to prosecute and give evidence in behalf of the State against the defendant in this case being solemnly called came not but made default. It is therefore considered by the court that a judgment Ni. Si for the sum of two hundred dollars according to the tenor of his recognizance be entered up against him and that a Scire facias issue against him returnable to the next Term of this court.

The State . . Plt.   )   Upon a presentment for an affray with & an
    Against   )   assault & battery on the body of John Defoe.
James Pillow Deft.   )
)   This day came the Solicitor General for the
State who saith he is unwilling further to prosecute the defendant for
reasons made known to the court now here. It is therefore ordered by
the court that a Nole prosqui be entered in this case, and that the defendant go hence without day.

The State . . Plt.   )   Upon a presentment for an affray with & an
    Against   )   assault & battery on the body of John Defoe.
James Pillow Deft.   )
)   A Nole prosqui having been entered in this
case under the direction of the court It is ordered that Judgment be
entered up against the County of Giles in favor of the several clamants,
on the part of the State for all costs to which they are entitled and that
the Clerk certify the same to the County Trustee for payment.

P-145   Thursday 20th May 1824

It appearing to the Satisfaction of the court now here that Lina Day
wife of Jesse Day formerly Lina Jones a Mulatto woman now residing in the
Town of Pulaski which was born free which fact was ordered by the court to
be certified.

The State . . . Plt.   )   Upon a presentment for retailing Spiritous
    Against   )   Liquors.
Henry Harrison Deft.   )   This day came the Solicitor General for the
)   State who saith he is unwilling further to
prosecute the defendant for reasons made known to the court now here. It
is ordered by the court that a Nole prosqui be entered in this case that
the defendant go hence without day.

The State . . . Plt.   )   Upon a Presentment for retailing Spirituous
    Against   )   Liquors.
Henry Harrison Deft.   )   A Nole Prosqui having been entered in this
)   case under the directions of the court.
It is ordered that Judgment be entered up against the County of Giles in
favor of the several claimants on the part of the State for all costs to
which they are entitled and that the Clerk certify the same to the County
Trustee for payment.

Ordered that Court be adjourned untill tomorrow morning nine oclock.

                                              Joseph Rea
                                              Robt. Oliver
                                              John Young

P-146   Friday 21st May 1824

Court met according to adjournment Present Robert Oliver, Joseph Rae, John
Young, Esquires Justices of the Peace for Giles County.

107

The State . . . Plt.	)	Indictment for an affray & an assault &
Against	)	battery on the body of a Mulatto slave
Mathias Sherron Deft.	)	named Moses.

This day came as well the Solicitor General for the State, as the defendant in his proper person, who being charged on the Indictment in this case pleads not guilty and for trial puts himself upon the County and the Solicitor General for the State on the part of the State, likewise therefore Let a Jury come who as well &c. to recognize &c and thereupon came a Jury of good and lawful men To wit, Richard H. Allen, John Gordon, Archibald Story, John Bass, Philip McCabe, Henry Harrison, David Stockton, Samuel H. Dodson, Thomas Williams, Charles Dever, Archibald Smith, and William Bodenhammer, who being elected tried and sworn well and truly to try the issue of traverse between the State and said defendant, upon their oaths do say that the defendant is not guilty in manner and form as he is charged in the bill of Indictment. It is therefore considered by the court that the defendant be acquitted and discharged from the assault and battery and affray aforesaid and that he go hence without day.

The State Plt.	)	Upon an Indictment for an assault and bat-
Against	)	tery on the body of a negro man slave named
Mathias Sherron Deft.	)	Moses.

The defendant in this case having been acquitted on a trial on the merits by a Jury. It is ordered that Judgment be entered up against the County of Giles in favor of the several claimants on the part of the State for all costs to which they are entitled, and that the Clerk Certify the same to the Trustee of Giles County for Payment.

The State . . . Plt.	)	Upon an Indictment for an assault and bat-
Against	)	tery on the body of a Mulatto man named
Edward K. McMullin Deft.	)	Moses.

This day came as well the Solicitor General for the State and the defendant altho Solemnly called came not but made default. It is therefore considered by the court that a Judgment Ni. Si. for the sum of two hundred and fifty dollars according to the tenor of his recognizance be entered up against him and that a Scire facias issue against him returnable to the next term of this court.

P-147 Friday 21st May 1824

The State . . . Plt	)	Upon an Indictment for an assault & bat-
Against	)	tery on the body of a mulatto man, named
Edward K. McMullen Deft.	)	Moses.

Thomas McKnight who was bound in a recognizance for the appearance of the aforesaid defendant being Solemnly called and required to bring with him the body of said defendant came not neither did he deliver the body of said defendant but made default. It is therefore considered by the court that a Judgment Ni. Si. for the sum of one hundred and twenty five dollars according to the tenor of his recognizance be entered up against him and that a Scire facias issue against him returnable to the next court.

The State . . . Plt.	)	Upon an Indictment for an assault & bat-
Against	)	tery on the body of a Mulatto Man named
Edward K. McMullen Deft.	)	Moses.

William Ball who was bound in a recognizance for the appearance of the aforesaid defendant, being Solemnly called and required to bring him the body of said defendant came not neither did he deliver the body of said defendant but made default. It is therefore considered by the court that a Judgment Ni. Si. for the sum of one hundred and twenty five dollars according to the term of the recognizance be entered up against him and that a Scire Facias issue against him returnable to the next court.

William Hendry Plaintiff Against Abednego Moore Charles Dever Neely Dever Millinton Tidwell } Defts. and George Bratton	))))))	Trespass Vist Armies This day came the parties by their attornies and thereupon came the Jury who were sworn and em-

pannelled well and truly to try the issue joined between the parties in this case who again retired out of court to consider of their verdict, after some time they returned & say they cannot agree by consent of the parties and with the assent of the court said Jurors are again permitted to disperse to meet tomorrow morning nine oclock.

The Grand Jury returned into court the following Indictments, Towit, The State against Joseph H. Hodge for an affray with & an assault and battery on the body of John Coleman - The State against John Coleman for an affray with and an assault & battery on the body of Joseph W. Hodge - The State against Thomas Steel for an affray with and an assault and battery on the body of David Graves, and withdrew to consider of further presentments.

The State . . Plt. Against John M. Hobson Deft.	))))	Upon a Indictment for an affray with & an Assault & battery on the body of David Pace. This day came as well the Solicitor General for the State as also (p-148) the de-

fendant in his proper person who being charged on the Indictment in this case pleads not guilty & for his trial puts himself upon the County and the Solicitor General for the State likewise, therefore let a Jury come who as well &c to recognize &c and therefore came a Jury of good and lawful men Towit, John McKnight, Asa McGee, Joseph S. Ellison, Edward Catlin, Robert Black, Meredith Bunch, John Hill, John Pierce, George Bratton, Gatewood Webb, John Dickey & Reding B. Catlin, who being elected tried and sworn well and truly to try this issue of traverse between the State and said defendant upon their oaths do say that the defendant is guilty of an assault & battery as charged in the several courts in the first court in the indictment.

It is therefore considered by the court that he make his fine with the State to the amount of one dollar and that he pay the costs of this prosecution, and that he be committed to the costody of the Sheriff of this County thereto remain till said issue & costs are paid, From which Judgment the defendant prayed an appeal to the honorable the Circuit Court to be held for the County of Giles which is granted accordingly, and thereupon the defendant and Lanson Hobson acknowledged themselves indebted to the State of Tennessee in the sums following, Towit, The said John M. Hobson in the sum of one hundred dollars and the said Lawson Hobson in the sum of one hundred dollars to be levied of their goods and chattles lands and tenements to the use of the Stat to be void on condition that the said John M.

Hobson make his personal appearance at the next Circuit Court to be held for the County of Giles at the Courthouse in the Town of Pulaski on the first Thursday after the first Monday in August next, and there to answer the State on the above charge and not depart without leave of the said court.

The State Plt.) Upon an Indictment for an affray with & an
Against) assault & battery on the body of David Pace.
John M. Hobson Deft.)
) David Pace came into court and acknowledged himself indebted to the State of Tennessee in the sum of one hundred dollars to be levied of his goods and chattles to be levied of his goods and chattles lands and tenments to the use of the State to be void on condition that he appear at the next Circuit Court to be held for the County of Giles at the Courthouse in the Town of Pulaski, on the first Thursday after the first Monday in August next, and prosecute & give evidence in behalf of the State against the defendant for an affray & assault & battery on the body of the said David Pace and not depart without leave of the court.

P-149   Friday 21st May 1824

An account of the sale of the Estate of Thomas Beal deceased returned and order to be recorded.

The State Plt.) Upon an Indictment for an assault & battery
Against) on the body of a Mulatto man named Moses.
Francis Guthrie Deft.)
) This day came as well the Solicitor General for the State as also the defendant in his proper person who being charged on the Indictment in this case pleads guilty and because he will not contend with the State agrees to submit himself to the Justice & mercy of the Court. It is therefore considered by the court that he make his fine with the State to the amount of one dollar, and that he pay the costs of this prosecution, and that he be committed to the custody of the Sheriff of this County there to remain till said fine & costs are paid, or that he give security for the payment of same and thereupon Lewis H. Brown comes into court and undertakes as security for said defendant. It is therefore considered by the court that the State recover of the said defendant and Lewis H. Brown his security the fine & costs aforesaid.

The State Plt.) Upon an Indictment for an affray with & an
Against) Assault & battery on the body of Joseph M.
John Coleman Deft.) Hodge.
) This day came as well the Solicitor General for the State as also the defendant in his proper person who being charged on the Indictment in this case pleads guilty and because he will not contend with the State agrees to submit himself to the Justice and mercy of the court. It is therefore considered by the court that he make his fine with the State to the amount of one dollar, and that he pay the costs of this prosecution - and that he be committed to the custody of the Sheriff of this county there to remain till said fine & costs be paid.

The State Plt.   ) Upon an Indictment for an affray & An as-
   Against   ) sault & battery on the body of John Coleman.
Joseph H. Hodge Deft.)
) This day came as well the Solicitor General for the State as also the defendant in his proper person, who being charged on the Indictment pleads guilty and because he will not contend with the State agrees to submit himself to the Justice and mercy of the Court. It is therefore considered by the court that he make his fine with the State to the amount of one dollar and that he pay the costs of this prosecution - and that he be committed to the Custody of the Sheriff of this County thereto remain till said fine & costs are paid.

The State Plt.   ) Upon an Indictment for an affray with &
   Against   ) an assault & battery on the body of David
Lawson Hobson Deft.   ) Pace.
) For reasons made known to the court by the
Solicitor   (p-150)   General for the State who saith he wishes no further to prosecute the defendant in this case, It is ordered a Nole Prosqui be entered therein and that the defendant go hence without day.

The State Plt.   ) Upon an Indictment for an affray with &
   Against   ) an assault & battery on the body of David
Lawson Hobson Deft.   ) Pace.
) A Nole Prosqui having been entered in this case under the direction of the court. It is ordered that Judgment be entered up against the County of Giles in favor of the several claimants on the part of the State for all costs to which they are entitled and that the Clerk certify the same to the Trustee of Giles County for payment.

The State Plt.   ) Upon a presentment for an affray with and
   Against   ) an assault & battery on the body of John
Mereday Bunch Deft.   ) Pillow.
) This day came as well the Solicitor General for the State as the defendant in his proper person who being charged on the presentment in this case pleads not guilty and for Trial puts himself upon the County, and the Solicitor General for the State on the part of the State likewise, therefore let a Jury come who as well &c to recognize &c and thereupon came a Jury of good and lawful men, Towit, Richard H. Allen, John Gordon, Gatewood Webb, William Hendry, John Keenan, David Pace, Robert Davitson, Richard Briggs, John W. Graves, Reding B. Gatlin, John McDonald, and John Parker who being Elected tried and sworn well and truly to try the issue of traverse between the State and said defendant upon their oaths do say that the defendant is not guilty in manner & form as he is charged in the bill of Presentment. It is therefore considered by the court that the defendant be acquitted and discharged from the affray and assault and Battery aforesaid and that he go hence without day.

The State Plt.   ) Upon a presentment for an affray with &
   Against   ) an assault & battery on the body of John
Mereday Bunch Deft.   ) Pillow.
) The defendant in this case having been acquitted on a trial on the merits by a Jury, It is ordered that Judgment be entered up against the County of Giles in favor of the several claimants

on the part of the State for all costs to which they are entitled and that the Clerk certify the same to the Trustee of Giles County for presentment.

P-151 Friday 21st May 1824

The State Plt.) Upon a presentment for an affray with &
Against) an Assault & battery on the body of George
John McKissack Deft.) Kirk.
) This day came as well the Solicitor General for the State as the defendant in his proper person, who being charged on the presentment in this case pleads not guilty, and for his trial puts himself upon the County and the Solicitor General for the Stat on the part of the State likewise therefore let a Jury come who as well &c to recognize &c and thereupon came a Jury of good and lawful men, Towit, John Johnson, Thomas Graves, Willis Willsford, John Goff, Wm. Jones, John Brown, William H. Moore, Isaac Mason, William Conner, Charles Myers, John Hill and John Webb, who being Elected tried and sworn well & truly to try the issue of traverse between the State and said defendant upon their oaths do say that the defendant is not guilty in manner & form as he is charged in the Bill of presentment - It is therefore considered by the court that the defendant be acquitted and discharged from the affray & assault & battery aforesaid and that he go hence without day.

The State Plt.) Upon a presentment for an affray with & an
Against) assault & battery on the body of George
John McKissack Deft.) Kirk.
) The defendant in this case having been acquitted on the trial on the merits by a Jury. It is ordered that Judgment be entered up against the County of Giles in favor of the several claimants on the part of the State for all costs to which they are entitled and that the Clerk certify the same to the Trustee of Giles County for Payment.

The State Plt.) Upon a presentment for an affray with & an assault
Against) & battery on the body of Wm. Bodenhammer.
Wm. Ball Deft.) This day came as well the Solicitor General as also the defendant in his proper person, who being charged on the presentment in this case pleads guilty, and because he will not contend with the State agrees to submit himself to the Justice and Mercy of court. It is therefore considered by the court that he make his fine with the State to the amount of one dollar, and that he pay the costs of this prosecution and that he be committed to the custody of the Sheriff of this County there to remain till said fine and costs are paid.

On the petition of Isaac Crow ordered that Writs of certain and Supercedias issue to stay proceedings and remove to this court the record of a Judgment rendered by John Henderson Esquire an Acting Justice of the peace for this County in favor of John B. McCanlass against said Isaac Crow on the day of . . . . . . 1824 for the sum of about nineteen dollars and costs, on the petitioners giving Bond,   (p-152)   (Friday 21st May 1824)   and security as the law directs.

Ordered that court be adjourned untill tomorrow morning 9 oclock.

Joseph Rea
Robert Oliver
A. McKissack

Saturday 22nd May 1824

Court met according to adjournment. Present Robert Oliver) Esquires
Joseph Rea) Justice
Archibald McKissack) of the
) Peace for
) Giles County.

William Polk Plt.) In Covenants
 Against)
David Graves &) Defts.)
Ralph Graves)
) This day came the parties by their
) attornies and thereupon came a Jury
of good and lawful men, Towit, Richard H. Allen, Isaac McGee, John P. Taylor, John McKnight, Nathan Davis, John Dickey, William Foster, Henry J. Cooker, Gatewood Webb, John Goldsberry, John Keenan, & John E. Holden, who being elected tried and sworn well and truly to try the issue joined between the parties in this case upon their oaths do say that the defendants hath not kept and performed their covenants as the plaintiff in his declaration has alleged and they do assess the plaintiffs damages by occasion thereof to two hundred and five dollars, besides costs * It is therefore considered by the court that the plaintiff recover of the said defendants the damages aforesaid by the Jurors aforesaid in form aforesaid assessed and his costs by him about his suit in this behalf expended.

William Bradshaw Plt.) In Case
 Against)
Robert Davidson Deft.) It appearing from the inspection of the Writ
) in this case that this is a case belonging
to the Circuit court of this County & that the papers have been brought
(p-153) into this court by mistake. It is ordered by the court with the assent of the parties in this case that the Clerk give up the papers in this case to the Clerk of the Circuit Court, & it is agreed by the parties that all depositions that have been taken under an order of this court mercy be read upon the trial of the case at the next circuit court of this County, subject only to such legal exceptions as would be if taken under an order and commission of that court.

Samuel H. Williams &) Plts.) In Covenant
David Mitchel Asses. &c)
 Against) This day came the parties
William Mayfield &) Defts.) by their attornies and
Elisha B. Mayfield) thereupon came a Jury of
) good and lawful men, Towit,
Richard H. Allen, Asa McGee, John P. Taylor, John McKnight, Nathan Davis, John Dickey, William Foster, Henry J. Cooker, Gatewood Webb, John Goldsberry, John Keenan & John E. Holden, who being elected tried and sworn well and truly to try the issue joined between the parties in this case upon their oaths do say that the defendants have not kept and performed their covenants as the plaintiffs in their declaration have alleged, and they do assess the plaintiffs damages by occasion of the detention thereof to twelve hundred & sixty seven dollars & ninety five cents besides costs. Therefore it is considered by the court that the plaintiffs recover of said defendants the damages aforesaid by the Jurors aforesaid in form aforesaid assessed and his costs by him about his suit in this behalf expended.

Thomas Hudson . . Plt.)   Original Attachment
   Against)
William Cannon Admr. of)   From the Judgment of the court in this case
William Cannon decd. Defts.) rendered the defendant prayed an appeal to
) the honorable the Circuit Court to be holden
for the County of Giles and having entered into bond and security according
to law the same was granted him.

Thomas Hudson . . Plt.)   Original Attachment
   Against)
William Cannon Admr of) Deft.) From the Judgment of the court in
William Cannon decd.)   this case rendered the defendant
) prayed an appeal to the Honorable
the Circuit Court to be holden for the County of Giles and having entered
into bond and security according to law the same was granted him.

P-154   The Grand Jury returned into court a Bill of Indictment against John
E. Mayfield for an affray with & an assault & battery on the body of Robert
Steel, on which is indorsed a true Bill.

       On motion of Robert L. Cobbs Solicitor General & it appearing to the
satisfaction of the court that the following persons John E. Mayfield,
Joseph H. Hodge, John Coleman, & Robert Steel, have been guilty severally
of an affray and an assault & battery in this county - Leave is given and
it is keenly ordered & directed that said Solicitor Generals prefer a bill
of indictment therefore against each of said persons.

Nicholas R. Smith Plt.)   Original Attachement
   Against)
Dudley Smith Deft.)   This day came the parties by their attornies
) and thereupon came a Jury of good and lawful
men, Towit, John Gordon, Henry Hester, Wilie Boyd, James Hannah, David Read,
Henry Harrison, John Young, Edmund Gatlin, Hugh H. Williams, Samuel H. Dodson,
William H. Wells and Charles Devers, who being elected tried and sworn
well and truly to enquire of damages in this case upon their oaths do say
that the plaintiff hath sustained damages by occasion of the nonperformance
of the assumpsit in the declaration complained of to the amount of one hundred
and eighty dollars besides costs. It is therefore considered by the
court that the plaintiff recover of the defendant the amount of his damages
aforesaid by the Jurors aforesaid in form aforesaid assessed and also his
costs by him about his suit in this behalf expended.

Edmund Shelton Plt.)   Original Attachment
   Against)
Dudley Smith Deft.)   This day came the plaintiff by his attorney
) and moved the court now here to amend his declaration
in this case by inserting the amount of cotton, which privilege
was granted him by the court and the ammendment filed.

P-155   Saturday 22nd May 1824

Edmund Shelton Plt.   )   Original Attachment
　　Against   )
Dudley Smith Deft.   )   This day came the parties by their attornies
)   and thereupon came a Jury of good and lawful
men, to wit, Richard H. Allen, Asa McGee, John P. Taylor, John McKnight, Nathan Davis, John Dickey, William Foster, Henry J. Cooper, Gatewood Webb, John Goldsberry, John Keenan and John E. Holden, who being elected tried and sworn well and truly to Enquire of damages in this case upon their oaths do say that the plaintiff has sustained damages by occasion of the nonperformance of the assumpsit in the declaration complained of to the amount of Two hundred & ninety four dollars Eight & a half cents - besides costs. It is therefore considered by the court that the plaintiff recover of the defendant to the amount of his damages aforesaid in form aforesaid by the Jurors aforesaid assessed and his costs by him about his suit in this behalf expended.

Memorandum, This Judgment is to be credited by ninety dollars Eighteen & three fourth cents, which creditted was due before the attachments in this cause was taken out and allowed by the plaintiffs and by him left out of the amount of his attachment at the time of sueing out the same, Also by twenty five dollars and twenty five cents the amount of Mrs. Stookdons Note - And thereupon it is ordered by court that an order of sale issue to the Sheriff of this County commanding him to sell the property levied on by virtue of the attachment in this case in satisfaction of the aforesaid Judgments in this case, in execution against the goods and chattles lands and tenments of the defendants to satisfy the balance of said Judgment should there be any after the sale of the aforesaid property.

Ordered that Court be adjourned untill Monday Morning Ten oclock.

　　　　　　　　　　　　　　　　　　　　　A. Black
　　　　　　　　　　　　　　　　　　　　　Thomas Brown
　　　　　　　　　　　　　　　　　　　　　Hezekiah Jones

P-156   Monday Morning 24th May 1824

　　Court met according to adjournment Present, Alexander Black, Thomas Brown, Hezekiah Jones, John H. Camp, Thomas Harwood, Thomas Marks, Robert Oliver, Robert Read, Archibald McKissack, John Young, James Dugger, Thomas K. Gordon, Jonathan Moody & Arthur Hicks, Esquires Justices of the peace in and for the County of Giles.

　　A Deed of conveyance from David Kilcrease to Andrew Eding for twenty acres of land was produced in court and the execution thereof proven by the oaths of James McCafferty and John W. Killpatrick the subscribing witnesses thereto and ordered to be certified for registration.

　　Ordered that Matthias Johnson be appointed overseer of the road in the room of Joab Ross resigned and that he have the same district of hands.

　　Ordered that James Hanner be appointed overseer of the road in the room of Josiah Lester resigned and that he have the same districts of hands.

Ordered that the following tax list be received and the double tax thereon remitted, towit,

    Joseph H. Hodge 1 white poll
             2 Slaves
             3 Town lots
    John Hodge   2 Town lots
    J. & John H. Hodge 6 Town lots.

A Deed of conveyance from James Brown to John Moore for Seventy Eight and one fourth acres of land was produced in court and the execution thereof acknowledged by the said James Brown and ordered to be certified for registration.

A Deed of conveyance from Thomas Bigham to Andrew M. Ballentine for four hundred acres of land was produced in court and the execution thereof acknowledged by the said Thomas Bigham and ordered to be certified for registration.

Ordered that John W. Bodenhamer be appointed Guardian of Franklin Bodenhamer, William Bodenhamer, & Sarah Bodenhamer minor orphans of Peter Bodenhamer deceased whereupon he executed bond and security according to law.

Alexander Black Esquire was appointed Chairman of this Court proterm.

P-157 Monday 24th May 1824

Ordered that Thomas McCanlass be appointed to oversee the keeping in repair that part of the road from John Gordons to the fork of the road Mrs. Maclins and to have the hands that now work under him together with the hands in the bounds that formerly worked under Sterling C. Robertson.

A Deed of conveyance from Lewis H. Brown Sheriff of this County to Thomas Goff for one hundred and ninety acres of land was produced in court and the execution thereof acknowledged by the said Lewis H. Brown Sheriff as aforesaid to be his act and deed and ordered to be certified for registration.

A Deed of conveyance from Arthur A. Stewart, Marcus Stewart and Cynthia Stewart to James McCraven for one hundred acres of land was produced in court and the execution thereof partly proven by the oath of Milton Alexander and of the witnesses thereto.

A Deed of conveyance from James McCravan to John Andrews for one hundred and fourteen acres of Land was produced in court and the execution thereof acknowledged by the said James McCraven and ordered to be certified for registration.

A Bill of sale from William Kyle to David Cummings for a certain property therein named was produced in court and the execution thereof proven by the oath of German Lester the subscribing witnesses thereto and ordered to be certified for registration.

At least five Justices being present Featherston Harwell returned into court Two wolf scalps under four months old which were ordered to be burned.

On the petition of James K. Murrah who is Guardian to Pleasant W. Weaver and John W. Weaver minor orphans of William W. Weaver decd. and setting fourth that he has not nor never had any of sd. minors property in his hands, he is discharged and released from his said Guardianship.

Ordered that Beazley Barber be bound an apprentice to Archibald Story an Indenture to that effect having been entered into between said Story and the chairman of this court.

The administrator of the Estate of William Mullinax decd. returned into court an account of the sale of said Estate which is ordered to be recorded.

P-158 Monday 24th May 1824

It is ordered by the court that the following persons, good and lawful men of the County of Giles, that is each one of whom is a free white male citizen and house holder of said County over twenty one years of age, not an overseer of a road and who has not been appointed and served as a Juror in this County for twelve months, to wit, Henry White, Henry Kerr, James Coldwell, Archibald Smith, George Jarret, Alexander Baldridge, William D. Jennings, William Ezell, Henry Croft, Allen Abernathy, Hugh Adams, David Jones, Richard Long, Joshua Horn, James H. Graves, Charles Davis, John W. O. Graves, John R. Abernathy, Henry Miller, Richard Butler, Elisha White, James Walker, Stephen Anderson, Holeman R. Fowler, Daniel Leatherman, be Jurors to serve in this court at the next term, on the third Monday in August next that the Clerk delver a copy of this order to the Sheriff of this County and that he summon said persons to attend and serve accordingly.

Ordered that James K. Murrah constable of this County be summoned by the Sheriff to attend at the next term of this court.

Ordered that James McCravan, John Henderson & James Perry or any two of them be appointed commissioners to settle with Alexander Esselman Administrator of the Estate of William Mullinax decd. and that they make report thereof to the next term of this court.

Ordered that John W. R. Graves with the hands under his direction as overseer work on the road as it now runs from Thomas McKissacks to the ford of Weakley Creek.

Ordered that Simpson H. Whites hands Elizabeth Whites hands, James Smiths, hands, & David Abernathy's hands, work under John Hramlett as overseer of the road.

Ordered that the following tax list be received and the double tax thereon remitted, To wit -

George Hillhouse   1 white poll
                   20 acres of land.

Ordered that an ordinary Licence for the term of twelve months and no longer be granted to Samuel Cox, whereupon he entered into bond and security according to Law and took the oath required by law.

P-159   Monday 24th May 1824

A deed of conveyance from the commissioners of Pulaski to Henry Roberts for part of lot No. 48 in the Town of Pulaski was produced in court and the Execution thereof acknowledged by James Patterson, Elisha Eldridge & Fountain Lester three of said commissioners and ordered to be certified for registration.

Ordered that Archibald McKissack be appointed guardian to Calvin Jones & Thomas M. Jones minor orphans of Wilson Jones decd. whereupon he executed bond and security according to Law.

John Henderson and Richard McGee Esquires acting Justices of the Peace in and for the County of Giles & who were appointed to take the privy examination of Martha Jones touching the execution of a Bill of sale from John S. Jones & said Martha his wife to John Dabney Made return of said examination which together with said Bill of sale is ordered to be certified for registration.

Ordered that William Watson overseer and hands be appointed to work from the Creek near Abe Browns the right hand road to the cross road below Pisgah Meeting house.

Thomas Martin Assee &c. Plt.   )   In Debt
            Against   )
Mary D. Price Jesse Penn   ) Defts.   )   This day came the plain-
Robert Lockhart & Burton R. White)   )   tiff by their attorney
)   and the Defendants altho
solemnly called came not but made default. It is therefore considered by the court that the plaintiff recover of the said defendants the sum of three hundred dollars the debt in the Writing obligatory in the declaration mentioned together with the sum of seven dollars and twenty five cents damages which he has sustained by occasion of the detention thereof and also his costs by him about his suit in this behalf expended.

The Jury who were appointed at the Last term of this court to view and mark out a private way from the land of Bazil Comptons to the Columbia road in this County made report thereof which was received and confirmed by the court.

Ordered that Robert Oliver, Charles C. Abernathy, William B. Pepper, Edmund Shelton & Lewis Brown or any three of them be appointed commissioners to let either by private contract or to the lowest bidder as they may think best, the building of a bridge across Buckhanans Creek on the Huntsville road, and that they be authorised to draw from the County treasure of this County the sum one hundred & fifty   (p-160)   Dollars towards the payment of the same.

Ordered that the road lately viewed and and marked out by a Jury appointed at the last term of this court for that purpose leading from the Tom Bigby road near Stephen Reedings to intersect the dry creek road near Hamilton C. Campbells be opened agreable to the report of said Jury, and that John P. Taylor be appointed to oversee the opening of the same from said Stephen Reddings to the top of the ridge between said Reddings and Isaac Morriss's lane, and that he have under his direction all the hands within three miles of said road north or north east of a line drawn at right angles across said road at the end of his bounds on the ridge above mentioned.

Ordered that Hamilton C. Campbell be appointed overseer of that part of the road lately viewed and marked out (leading from the Little Bigby road near Stephen Redding to the dry creek road near sd. Campbells) which is between said dry creek road and the top of the ridge near Isaac Morriss's and that he have for the purpose of opening the same, all the hands within two miles of said road west or south west of a line drawn at right angles across said road at the end of his bounds on the ridge above mentioned.

Ordered that Isaac Purvis, Samuel Harwell, Robert Read, William Flatt, James Flatt, Charles Davis, William Pratt Junr. or any five of them be appointed a Jury to view that part of the Lawrenceburg road which lies between Isaac Purvis's and the County line and see if it be proper to turn said road, and if in their opinion it be that they mark out the same and that they make report to the next term of this court.

Ordered that James Hannah overseer of the Buck Creek road and the hands under his direction work on the new part of said road near Hezekiah Jone's with the other part of said road over which he is overseer.

Ordered that _____ be adjourned untill tomorrow morning nine oclock.

Jno. H. Camp
Hezekiah Jones
A. McKissack

P-161   Tuesday Morning May 25th 1824

Court met according to adjournment Present John H. Camp,) Esquires
Archibald McKissack) Justices
& Hezekiah Jones) of the peace
) for Giles
) County.

Thomas McKissack Plt.   )   In Debt
    Against   )
Graves Steel & Thomas Steel   )
Admrd. of David Steel Decd.) Defts.) This day came the plaintiff
& James H. Graves   ) by his attorney who saith
) he will not further prose-
          cute this suit. Therefore
it is considered by the court that the defendant go hence without day and
recover of the said plaintiff their costs by him about their said fine in
this behalf expended.

John Penn &c Plaintiff)   Certiorari
    Against   )
John W. R. Graves Defendant) This day came the parties by their at-
) tornies and thereupon came a Jury of
good and lawful men, To wit, Richard H. Allen, Asa McGee, John McKnight,
John P. Taylor, John Keenan, John Bass, Spencer Clack, John Hill, James
Shelton, Gilham Harwell, Isaac James & Robert Davidson, who being elected
tried and sworn well and truly to try the matter in controversy between
the parties in this case upon their oaths do say that the defendant is in
debt to the plaintiff the sum of sixty seven dollars & eight and one half
cents, besides costs. It is therefore considered by the court that the
plaintiff recover of the said defendant, the amount of his debt aforesaid
in form aforesaid by the Jurors aforesaid assessed and his costs by him
about his suit in this behalf expended.

    A Deed of conveyance from Robert Bingham and Thomas Bingham to William
Woods, for one hundred & forty seven acres & one third of an acre was pro-
duced in court and the Execution thereof acknowledged by the said Robert
Bingham & Thomas Bingham and ordered to be certified for registration.

John McAnnally Plaintiff)   In Debt
    Against   )
James Read Defendant   ) This day came the parties by their attornies
) and thereupon came a Jury of good and law-
ful men, Towit, Richard H. Allen, Asa McGee, John P. Taylor John Kennan,
John Bass, Spencer Clack, John Hill, Gilliam Harwell, Isaac James, Robert
Davidson, Peter Satterfield and John Gordon, who being Elected tried and
sworn well and truly to try the issue joined between the parties in this
case upon their oaths do say that the defendant has not paid the debt in
the writing obligatory in the declaration mentioned, as the plaintiff in
his replication has alleged and they do assess his damages by occasion of
the detention of the same to forty (p-162) five dollars besides costs.
It is therefore considered by the court that the plaintiff recover of said
defendant the sum of two hundred and twenty dollars & twenty five cents
the amount of his debt aforesaid by the Jurors aforesaid assessed and also
his costs by his suit in this behalf expended.

Stephen Cole . Plaintiff)   In Debt
    Against   )
Joseph C. Martin Defendant) This day came the parties by their at-
) tornies and thereupon came a Jury of
good and lawful men, towit, Richard H. Allen, Asa McGee, John P. Taylor,
John Keenan, John Bass, Spencer Clack, John Hill, Gilliam Harwell, Isaac

James, Robert Davidson, Peter Setterfield and John Gordon, who being elected well and truly to try the issue joined between the parties in this case upon their oaths, do say that the defendant has not paid the debt in the writing obligatory in the declaration mentioned, and that he has no set off as the plaintiff in his replication has alleged, and they do assess the plaintiffs damage by occasion of the detention of the same to sixteen dollars & fifty cents besides costs. It is therefore considered by the court that the plaintiff recover of the said defendant the sum of Two hundred & eight two dollars & sixty cents the amount of his debt aforesaid in form aforesaid by the Jurors aforesaid assessed and his costs by him about his suit in this behalf expended.

Thomas McKissack Plaintiff) In Debt
Against)
Hugh Torrence &) Defendants)
Ralph Graves)

This day came the parties by their attornies and thereupon came a Jury of good and lawful men, Towit, Richard H. Allen, Asa McGee, John P. Taylor, John Keenan, John Bass, Spencer Clack, John Hill, William Harwell, Isaac James, Robert Davidson, Peter Satterfield, and John Gordon, who being elected well and truly to try the issue joined between the parties in this case upon their oaths do say that the defendants have not paid the debt in the Writing obligatory in the detention mentioned and that they have no set off as the plaintiff in his replication has alleged and they do assess the plaintiffs damages by occasion of the detention of the same to Ten dollars & twenty five cents, besides costs. It is therefore considered by the court that the plaintiff recover of said defendant the sum of one hundred and twenty five dollars the amount of his debt aforesaid in form aforesaid and by the Jurors aforesaid assessed and his costs about his suit in this behalf expended.

P-163   Tuesday 25th May 1824

A Deed of conveyance from William Woods to Rolin McKinney for one hundred & fifteen acres of land was produced in court and the Execution thereof acknowledged by the said William Wood and ordered to be certified for registration.

Hannah Underwood Plt.) In Traverce
Against)
James K. Murrah Deft.)

Upon the application of the plaintiff in this case and she having filed her affidavit herein this cause is ordered to be continued untill the next term of this court and that a commission issue to any two of the Acting Justices of the peace in & for the County of Madison and State aforesaid to take the deposition of Thompson Wilson and Henry Davidson on the plaintiff giving to the defendant ten days notice of the time and place of taking the said deposition and said deposition when taken to be read in evidence on the trial of this cause.

Ordered that the commissioners who were appointed at the last term of this court to settle with John Paul Executor of John Paul decd. be allowed uhtill the next term to file said settlement.

121

Archibald McKissack Assee Plt.) In Debt
      Against)
John McComick . . . Deft.) This day came the parties by their
) attornies and thereupon came a Jury
of good and Lawful men, To wit, Richard H. Allen, Asa McGee, John P. Taylor,
John Keenan, John Bass, Spencer Clack, John Hill, Gilham Harwell, Isaac
James, Robert Davidson, John Gordon and Anderston Tucker, who being elected
tried and sworn well & truly to try the issue joined between the parties in
this case upon their oaths do say that the defendant has not paid the debt
in the writing obligatory in the declaration mentioned, and that he has
no set off as the plaintiff in his replication has alleged, and they do
assess his damages by occasion of the detention of the same to twelve dollars & thirty five cents besides costs. It is therefore considered by the
court that the plaintiff recover of said defendant the sum of one hundred
& thirty dollars the amount of his debt aforesaid together with his damages
aforesaid in form aforesaid by the Jurors aforesaid assessed and his costs
about his suit in this behalf expended.

Thomas C. Porter use &c Plt.) In Debt
      Vs)
William Mayfield Elisha B.) Defts.) This day came the parties by
Mayfield & Thos. McKissack)) their attornies and thereupon
) came a Jury of good and lawful men, to wit, Richard (p-164) McGee, John P. Taylor, John Keenan,
John Bass, Spencer Clack, John Hill, Gilham Harwell, Isaac James, Robt.
Davidson, John Gordon and Anderton Tucker, who being elected tried and
sworn well and truly to try the issue joined between the parties in this
case upon their oaths do say that the defendant have not paid the debt in
the Writing Obligatory in the declaration mentioned and that they have no
set off as the plaintiff in his replicia has alleged and they do assess the
plaintiffs damage by occasion of the detention of the same to twenty two
dollars & fifty cents, besides costs. It is therefore considered by the
court that the plaintiff recover of said defendant the sum of five hundred
dollars the amount of his debt aforesaid together with his damages aforesaid & in form aforesaid by the Jurors aforesaid assessed - and his costs
about his suit in this behalf expended.

The State Plt.) Upon an Indictment for and affray with & an
    Against) assault & battery on the body of Bailey Davis.
James Hodge Deft.) Bailey Davis comes into court and acknowledges
) himself indebted to the State of Tennessee in
the sum of one hundred dollars to be levied of his goods and chattles lands
and tenements to the use of the State, To be void on condition that he make
his personal appearance here on the first Thursday after the third Monday
in August next, and prosecute and give evidence in behalf of the State
against the defendant for an affray with and an assault & battery on the
body of the said Bailey Davis and not depart therefrom without leave of
the court.

Thomas Martin Surviving partner &c Plt.) In Debt
      Against)
Egbert H. Shepperd . . . Deft.) This day came the parties
) by their attornies and
thereupon came a Jury of good and lawful men, Towit, Richard H. Allen, Asa

McGee, John P. Taylor, John Keenan, John Bass, Spencer Clack, John Hill, Gilham Harwell, Isaac James, Robert Davidson, John Gordon, & James Shelton, Who being elected tried and sworn well and truly to try the issue joined between the parties in this case upon their oaths do say that the defendant has not paid the debt in the Writing obligatory in the declaration mentioned and that he has no set off as the plaintiffs in his replication has alleged and they do assess his damages by occasion of the detention of the same to four dollars ninety seven cents besides costs. It is therefore considered by the court that the plaintiff recover of the said defendant the sum of one hundred and eighteen dollars twenty nine cents the amount of his debt together with the damages aforesaid in form aforesaid (p-165) by the Jurors aforesaid assessed and his costs about his suit in this behalf expended.

Sterling C. & Eldridge B. Robertson Plts.) Original Attachment.
    Against) Samuel McCanlass a
Isaac Crow . . . . Deft.) garnishee summoned to
) attend at this term,
came into court and being duly sworn according to Saw depond on his oath in the following, to wit,

Question. Are you indebted to Isaac Crow? Answer, Yes I am indebted to the said Isaac Crow & if his account be just as I have heard I am Indebted to him the sum of twenty three dollars & fifty cents, after my credits against him being allowed. I have no effects of said Crows in my hands, nor do I know of any person who has, neither do I know of any other person who is indebted to him.

Smith Hunt Gdn. &c Plaintiffs) In Debt
    Against)
James Lester and) Defendants) This day came the parties by their
Alexander Black) attorney and thereupon came a Jury
) of good and lawful men, Towit,
Richard H. Allen, Asa McGee, John P. Taylor, John Keenan, John Bass, Spencer Clack, John Hill, Gilham Harwell, Isaac James, Robert Davidson, John Gordon, and James Shelton, who being Elected tried and sworn well and truly to try the issue Joined between the parties in this case upon their oaths do say that the defendants have not paid the debt in the writing obligatory in the declaration mentioned and that they have no set off as the plaintiff in his replication has alleged, and they do assess the plaintiffs damages by occasion of the detention of the same to sixty two dollars & twenty five cents, besides costs. It is therefore considered by the court that the plaintiff recover of the said defendant the sum of three hundred dollars the amount of his debt aforesaid together with his damages aforesaid in form aforesaid by the Jurors aforesaid assessed and his cost about his suit in this behalf expended.

Smith Hunt Adn. &C. Plt.) In Debt
    Against)
German Lester &) Defts.) This day came the parties by their at-
John McCracken) tornies and thereupon came a Jury of
) good and lawful men, Towit, Richard H.
Allen, Asa McGee, John P. Taylor, John Keenan, John Bass, Stencer Clack, John Hill, Gilham Harwell, Isaac James, Robert Davitson, John Gordon &

James Shelton, who being elected tried and sworn well and truly to try the issue joined   (p-166)   between the parties in this case upon their oaths do say that the defendants have not paid the debt in the writing obligatory in the declaration mentioned and that they have no set off as the plaintiff in his replication has alleged and they do assess the plaintiffs damages by occasion of the detention of the same to forty one dollars & fifty cents besides costs - It is thereupon considered by the court that the plaintiff recover of the said defendant the sum of two hundred dollars the amount of his debt aforesaid together with the damages aforesaid in form aforesaid by the Jurors aforesaid assessed and his costs about his suit in this behalf expended.

Thomas Martin Assignee &c Plt.)   In Debt
   Against   )
George Everly . . . . . Deft.   ) This day came the parties by their
) attornies & thereupon came a Jury
of Good and lawful men, Towit, Richard H. Allen, John P. Taylor, Asa Magee, John Hanna, John Bass, Spencer Clack, John Hill, Gilham Harwell, Isaac James, Robert Davidson, John Gordon, and James Shelton, who being elected tried and sworn well and truly to try the issue joined between the parties in this case upon their oaths do say that the defendant hath not paid the debt in the Writing Obligatory in the declaration mentioned, but there remains a Balance of said debt unpaid, to the amount of three hundred and eight dollars and twelve cents, and that the plaintiff hath sustained damages by occasion of the detention of said debt to the amount of one dollar and forty five cents, and that the defendant hath no set off. It is therefore considered by the court that the plaintiff recover of the defendant the Balance of his debt aforesaid together with his damages aforesaid by the Jurors aforesaid in form aforesaid assessed and his costs by him about his suit in this behalf expended.

Thomas Martin Surviving Partner Plt.)   In Debt
   Against   )
John Barnett . . . . . Deft.   ) This day came the parties by
) their attornies and thereupon
came a Jury of good and lawful men, Towit, Richard H. Allen, John P. Taylor, Asa Magee, John Keenan, John Bass, Spencer Clack, John Hill, Gilham Harwell, Isaac James, Robert Davidson, John Gordon, and James Shelton, who being elected tried and sworn well and truly to try the issue Joined between the parties in this case upon their oaths do say that the defendant hath not paid the debt in the writing obligatory in the declaration mentioned as the plaintiff in his replication hath alleged and they do assess the plaintiffs damages by occasion of the detention   (p-167)   Tuesday 25th May 1824, of said debt to three dollars and eight cents Besides costs. It is therefore considered by the court that the plaintiff recover of the defendant the sum of Fifty six dollars and three cents the amount of his debt aforesaid together with his damages aforesaid by the Jurors aforesaid assessed and his costs by him about his suit in this behalf expended.

Thomas Marks Surviving Partner &c Plt.)   In Debt
   Against   )
William Watson . . . . Deft.   ) This day came the parties
) by their attornies and
thereupon came a Jury of good and lawful men, Towit, Richard H. Allen, Asa

Magee, John P. Taylor, Spencer Clack, John Keenan, John Bass, John Hill, Gilham Harwell, Isaac Jones, Robert Davidson, John Gordon & James Shelton who being elected tried and sworn well and truly to try the issue Joined between the parties in this case, upon their oaths do say that the defendand hath not paid the debt in the writing obligatory in the declaration mentioned as the plaintiff in his replication hath alleged, and they do assess the plaintiffs damages by occasion of the detention of said debt to one dollar and fifty cents, besides costs. It is therefore considered by the court that the plaintiff recover of the defendant the sum of Sixty two dollars and nine cents, the amount of his debt aforesaid, together with his damages aforesaid by the Jurors aforesaid in form aforesaid assessed, and his costs by him about his suit in this behalf Expended.

John P. Taylor Plaintiff) In Debt
  Against)
Iasah Couch &) Defendants)
Joshua Horn) This day came the parties by their attornies and thereupon came a Jury of good and lawful men, Towit, Richard H. Allen, Asa McGee, Benjamin S. England, John Keenan, Spencer Clack, John Bass, John Hill, Gilham Harwell, Isaac James, Robert Davidson, John Gordon, and James Shelton, who being Elected tried & sworn well and truly to try the issue joined between the parties in this case upon their oaths do say that the defendants, have not paid the debt in the Writing obligatory in the declaration mentioned as the plaintiff in his replication hath alleged, and they do assess the plaintiffs damages by occasion of the detention of said debt to Five dollars Eighty seven and a half cents, Besides costs. It is therefore considered by the court that the plaintiff recover of the defendant the sum of two hundred and twenty five dollars the amount of his debt aforesaid together with his damages aforesaid by the jurors aforsaid in form aforesaid assessed and his costs by him about his suit in this behalf expended.

P-168 Tuesday 25th May 1824

John Ruff an executor appointed by the last will & testament Godsent Ruff decd. appeared in court and was qualified and gave bond and security according to law.

A Deed of conveyance from Robert Lockhart to Nicholas Fain and Samuel Fain for one third of one half of lot No. 34 in Uper Elkton was produced in court and the execution therefore proven by Stirling H. Lester and Thomas B. Jones two of the subscribing witnesses thereto and ordered to be certified for registration.

A Deed of conveyance from Joseph Alsup to Lewis B. Marks for Fifty nine acres of Land was produced in court & the Execution thereof proven by the oaths of Benjamin Williams & Lewis H. Brown the subscribing witnesses thereto and ordered to be certified for registration.

A Deed of conveyance from John W. R. Graves to Henry Hagen for the benefit of Lewis H. Brown, was produced in court and the execution thereof prove by the oaths of William W. Wood and John Brown the subscribing witnesses thereto and ordered to be certified for registration.

A Power of attorney from William S. Neal to Joseph McIlviane was produced in court and the execution thereof acknowledged by the said William S. Neal & ordered to be certified.

Whereas on the 26th day of November last His excellency William Carroll Esquire Govenor of this State Commissioned William W. Wood to act as a Justice of the Peace for this County, and on motion It is ordered that William Wood be permitted to qualify to said commission, who thereupon appeared in court and took the oaths required by law.

William P. Richardson Plt.)   Petition
      Against)
Samuel Bradley . . Deft.) This day came as well the plaintiff by his
) attornies as the defendant in his proper person, and said defendant failing to give counter security according to the prayer of the plaintiffs petition, and a former order of this court. It is ordered that administration of the Estate of Joseph Bradley decd. be taken from the defendant, and that Joseph Calvert be appointed administrator with the will annexed of the Estate of the said Joseph Bradley decd. in the room (p-169) and Stead of said defendant, and thereupon the said Joseph Calvert came into court and was qualified and gave bond and security according to Law - And it is further ordered and adjudged by the court that the defendant pay the costs of this case, and that Execution be awarded accordingly.

Joseph Calvert . . . Plt.)   Petition
      Against)
Samuel Bradley . . . Deft.) This day came as well the plaintiff by
) his attornies as the defendant in his proper person, and the defendant failing to give counter security according to the prayer of the plaintiffs petition and a former order of this court. It is therefore ordered that administration, with the Will annexed of the Estate of Joseph Bradley decd. be taken from the defendant and that Joseph Calvert the plaintiff be appointed, administrator with the Will annexed of the Estate of Joseph Bradley decd. in the room and Stead of said defendant and thereupon the said Joseph Calvert came into court and was qualified and gave bond and security according to Law - - And it is further ordered and adjudged by the court that the defendant pay the costs of this case and that execution be awarded accordingly.

William Hendry . . . . Plt.)   Trespass Viet Armis
      Against)
Abnego Moore, Charles Dever)
Neely Dever Millenton Tidwell) This day came the parties by their
& George Bratton) attornies and thereupon came the
) Jury who were elected tried and
sworn well and truly upon their oaths do say that the defendants are guilty of the trespass in the plaintiffs declaration complained of, and they do assess the plaintiffs damages by occasion thereof to one hundred dollars besides costs.
    It is therefore considered by the court that the plaintiff recover of the defendants the amount of his damages aforesaid by the Jurors aforesaid assessed together with his costs by him about his suit in this behalf expended.

Ordered that Thomas Harwood, William Brown & John H. Camp be appointed commissioned to settle with Samuel Bradley a former administrator with the Will annexed of Joseph Bradley decd. & that they make report thereof to the next term of this court.

The Grand Jury returned into court and Indictment against Elisha Faris and Elizabeth Tongat for open and notorious Lewdyess on which is indorsed "A true Bill", Also a bill of Indictment against Robert Steele for an affray with an assault and battery on the body of John E. Mayfield on which is indorsed "a true bill" also a bill of Indictment against James Hardy for an affray with & an assault & battery on the body James Hardy on which (p-170) Tuesday 25th May 1824, is indorsed "A true Bill" and having no further presentments to make were discharged as Grand Jurors.

Willie Turner for the use of &c Plt.) Judicial Attachment
      Against)
Hannar Turner . . . Deft.)
) This day came the parties by their attornies and thereupon came a Jury of good and Lawful men, Towit, Richard H. Allen, Asa McGee, John P. Taylor, John Keenan, John Bass, Spencer Clack, John Hill, Gilham Harwell, Isaac James, John Gordon, Robert Davidson & Peter Setterfield, who being elected tried and sworn well and truly to try the issue joined between the parties in this case upon their oaths do say that the defendant hath not paid the debt in the Writing obligatory in the declaration mentioned and they do assess the plaintiffs damages by occasion of the detention of the same to twenty seven dollars, besides costs. It is therefore considered by the court that the plaintiff recover against the said defendant the sum of two hundred & sixty six dollars & Eighty cents the amount of the debt aforesaid together with his damages aforesaid in form aforesaid by the Jurors aforesaid assessed and his costs by him about his suit in this behalf expended.

Thomas Martin) Plt.) In Debt
Surviving Partner &c)
      Against)
William Watson Deft.) From the Judgment of the court in this case rendered the defendant prayed an appeal to the honorable the Circuit Court to be holden for the County Court of Giles, and having entered into bond and security according to law the same was granted him.

Ordered that Thomas Graves be released from all further attendance as Grand or petit Juror at the present Term.

Robert Shadden . . . . Plt.) Petition
      Against)
Charles Perkins Admr. &c Deft.) On this 25th day of May 1824 this cause came on to be heard and was heard upon petition answer and replication before the worshipful John H. Camp, William Mayfield & Hezekiah Jones, Esquires Justices of the Peace for the County of Giles and during the progress of said trial the defendant by his attorney filed his bill of execution to the opinion of the court which was Signed sealed and ordered to be made a part of the record, and said court after having heard the testimony and the argument of counsel in this cause and Mature delibration being thereupon had is of opinion that

said petition is intitled to receive of (p-171) said Defendant the sum of twenty three dollars nine and one half cents the full amount of his distributive share of the Estate of Mary Donalson decd. It is therefore ordered adjudged and decreed by court, now here, that said Robert Shadden recover of said Charles Perkins said sum of twenty three dollars nine and one half cents his distributive share aforesaid and his costs by him about his suit in this behalf expended.

Ordered that court be adjourned untill tomorrow morning nine oclock.

John H. Camp
Hezekiah Jones
Thos. Marks

Wednesday 26th May 1824

Court met according to adjournment Present John H. Camp, Hezekiah Jones, Thomas Marks — Esquires Justices of the Peace for Giles County.

On the petition of David White ordered that Writs of Certiorari and Supercedeas issue to Stay proceedings and remove to the court the record of a Judgment rendered by John H. Camp Esquire an Acting Justice of the Peace for Giles Co. in favor of John Bradley against said David White on the _____ day of _____ 1824 for the sum of ten dollars & costs on the petitioners giving bond and security according to Law.

John Bradley . . . Plt.
Against
William D. Jennings Deft.

In Case

On the application of the plaintiff, and he having filed his affidavit herein this cause is ordered to be continued untill the next term of this court, and that a commission issue to any two of the Acting Justices of the Peace in and for the County of Madison and State of Alabama to take the deposition of George H. Malone, Thomas Gilliam, and others to be read in evidence on the trial of this case upon the plaintiffs giving to the defendant ten days notice of the time and place of taking the deposition of sd. George H. Malone & Thomas Gilliam & Twenty days notice of the time and place of taking the deposition of others if any.

A Bill of sale from William Smith to Lewis H. Brown for certain property therein named was produced in court and the execution thereof proven by the oath of John Bass the witness thereto and ordered to be certified for registration.

P-172 Wednesday 26th May 1824

Thomas Martin Plt.
Against
David Browning Deft.

Certiorari

On motion of the plaintiff this cause is ordered to be continued and an Alias Certiorari is awarded returnable to the next Term of this court.

128

Gilham Harwell Exor. of) Plts.
Buckner Harwell decd.)
    Against
John Boyd . . . . . Deft.

Certiorari

This day came the parties by their attornies and thereupon came a Jury of good and lawful men Towit, John Goff, John Johnson, William H. Moore, Robert Paine, Robert Buchanan, William Conner, Richard H. Allen, John McKnight & Asa McGee who being elected tried and sworn well and truly to try the matter in controversey between the parties in this case, and having heard the evidence and argument of counsel retired out of court to considers of their verdict after sometime returned and say they cannot agree, By consent of the parties and with the assent of the court John Goff one of the Jurors aforesaid was withdrawn, and the cause continued till the next term of this court. that a new trial may be had therein.

    A Bill of sale from Elisha Eldridge Trustee to Lewis H. Brown for certain property therein named was produced in court and the execution thereof acknowledged by the said Elisha Eldridge Trustee and ordered to be certified for registration.

    A Deed of conveyance from Ralph Graves to Charles Perkins for two hundred & fifty three acres of land was produced in court and the execution thereof proven by the oaths of William Graves & John W. Graves the subscribing witnesses thereto and ordered to be certified for registration.

John Clark . . . . Plaintiff
    Against
John Pillow . . Defendant

In Debt

This day came the parties by their attornies and on motion of the defendant this cause is ordered to be continued and that a commission issue to any two of the Acting Justices of the Peace in and for the County of Prince Edward State of Virginia to take the deposition of Joseph Perry & John Foster to be read in evidence on the trial of this cause upon the defendant giving (p-173) (Wednesday 26th May 1824) thirty days notice to Joseph Goode the plaintiffs agent or five days notice to the plaintiff, of the time and place of taking said deposition.

Thomas Lane Plts.
    Against
Nathaniel Young) Defts.
& John Young)

In Debt

This day came the parties by their attornies and thereupon came a Jury of good and lawful men, Towit, William Pullen, John S. Brandon, Beverly B. Watson, Benjamin Williams, John Gordon, John P. Taylor, Gilham Harwell, Wilie Boyd, William M. Frasure, David Stockton, John Roberts, & Gray H. Edwards, who being elected tried and sworn well and truly to try the issue joined between the parties in this case upon their oaths do say that the defendants have not paid the debt in the writing obligatory in the declaration mentioned, and that they have no set off as the the plaintiff in his replication has alleged and they do assess the plaintiffs damages by occasion of the detention of the same to Eleven Dollars sixty seven & a half cents, besides costs. It is therefore considered by the court that the plaintiff recover of the said Defendant the sum of Four hundred & sixty seven dollars & seventy one cents the amount of his debt aforesaid together with his damages aforesaid in form aforesaid by, the Jurors aforesaid, assessed and his costs about his suit in this behalf expended.

Martin Lane Plt.) In Debt
    Against)
Nathaniel Young) Defts.) This day came the parties by their at-
& John Young)) tornies and thereupon came a Jury of
) good and Lawful men, To wit, William
Pullen, John Brandon, Beverly B. Watson, Benjamin William, John Gordon, John P. Taylor, Gilham Harwell, Wilie Boyd, William M. Frasure, David Stockton, John Roberts, & Gray H. Edwards, who being elected tried and sworn well & truly to try the issue joined between the the parties in this case upon their oaths do say that the defendants have not paid the debt in the Writing Obligatory in the declaration mentioned and they do assess the plaintiffs damages by occasion of the detention of the same to nine dollars besides costs. It is therefore considered by the court that the plaintiff recover of the said defendant the sum of three hundred and sixty dollars & ninety eight cents, the amount of his debt aforesaid together with his damages aforesaid in form aforesaid by the Jurors aforesaid assessed and also his costs about his suit in this behalf expended.

P-174 Wednesday 26th May 1824

Abraham Byler Assee &c Plt.) In Debt
    Against)
George Keltner & George M. Gibson Defts.) This day came the parties
) by their attornies and
thereupon came a Jury of good and lawful men, Towit, William Pullen, John S. Brandon, Beverly B. Watson, Benjamin Williams, John Gordon, John P. Taylor, Gilham Harwell, Wilie Boyd, William M. Frasure, David Stockton, John Roberts, & George H. Edwards, who being elected tried and sworn well and truly to try the Issue Joined between the parties in this case upon their oaths do say that the defendants have not paid the debt in the writing obligatory in the declaration mentioned and they do assess the plaintiffs damages by occasion of the detention of the same to four dollars and eighty seven & a half cents, besides costs. It is therefore considered by the court that the plaintiff recover of the said defendants the sum of Two hundred dollars the amount of the debt aforesaid together with the damages aforesaid in form aforesaid by the Jurors aforesaid assessed and his costs about his suit in this behalf expended.

Richard Briggs Assee &c Plt.) In Debt
    Against)
George Brown . . . . Deft.) This day came the parties by their at-
) tornies and thereupon came a Jury of
good & lawful men, To wit, William Pullen, John S. Brandon, Beverly B. Watson, Benjamin Williams, John Gordon, John P. Taylor, Gilham Harwell, Wilie Boyd, William M. Frasure, David Stockton, John Roberts & George H. Edwards, who being elected tried and sworn, well and truly to try the issue joined between the parties in this cause upon their oaths do say that the defendant hath not paid the debt in the writing obligatory in the declaration mentioned, But that there remains a Balance of sd. debt unpaid to the amount of one hundred and twenty nine dollars & twenty eight cents and that the plaintiff hath sustained damages by occasion of the detention of

said debt to the amount of three dollars & twenty cents besides costs. It is therefore considered by the court that the plaintiff recover of the said defendant the Balance of the debt aforesaid together with his damages aforesaid in form aforesaid by the Jurors aforesaid assessed and his costs about his suit in this behalf expended.

A Deed of conveyance from James H. Pickens to Thomas McKnight, for ninety four acres of land was produced in court and the execution thereof proven by the oaths of A. Black & Thomas Marks (the witnesses thereto) and ordered to be certified for registration.

P-175 Wednesday 26th May 1824

Daniel Frasure Plaintiff   )   In Case
       Against   )
Thomas B. Haysin Defendant   ) This day came the parties by their at-
                                    tornies and thereupon came a Jury of
good and lawful men, Towit, William Pullen, John S. Brandon, Beverly B. Watson Benjamin Williams, John Gordon, John P. Taylor, Gilham Harwell, John Brown, David Stockton, John McKnight, William Jones, and Anderson Tucker, who being elected tried and sworn well and truly to try the issue joined between the parties in this case upon their oaths do say that the defendant is guilty of the trespass in the plaintiffs declaration complained of, and they do assess the plaintiffs damages by occasion thereof to Eighty one dollars & sixty cents, besides costs. It is therefore considered by the court that the plaintiff recover of the said defendant the amount of his damages aforesaid by the Jurors aforesaid in form aforesaid assessed and his costs by him about his suit in this behalf expended.

A Bill of sale from Harrison Hicks to Mary Flournoy for certain property therein named, was produced in court and the execution thereof proven by the oath of James Patterson one of the subscribing witnesses thereto and ordered to be certified for registration.

The administrator of the Estate of David Steel decd. returned into court an Inventory of said Estate which is ordered to be recorded.

Samuel Smith and Jane B. his wife formerly Jane B. Porter and one of the heirs and distributee's of the Estate of Reese Porter, Junr. decd. presented a petition in Writing against John Porter, former Guardian of said Jane B. & who is Guardian of Whitsett Rees & Elinor W. Porter for a Distributive share of said Estate, which petition was granted, and an order made that a summons issue requiring said John Porter to appear at the next Term of this court and answer said petition, and that a copy thereof accompany said Summons.

Gilham Harwell Admr. &c Plt.   )   Certiorari
        Against   )
John Boyd . . . . . Deft.   ) On motion of the Defendant it is ordered
) that Willie Boyd be released from further
liability as Security for the defendant in this case, and thereupon John Boyd Junr. came into court and under takes as security in the room of and Stead of the said Willie Boyd.

P-176 Wednesday 26th May 1824

Henry Crabb Assignee & Plt.)   In Debt
    Against)
Alfred Flournoy) Defts.)   This day came the parties by their at-
& James Perry))   tornies and thereupon came a Jury of
                                                          good and lawful men, Towit, William
Pullen, John S. Brandon, Beverly B. Watson, Benjamin William, John Gordon,
Gilham Harwell, Willie Boyd, William M. Frazer, David Stockton, & John
Roberts; who being elected tried and sworn well and truly to try the issue
Joined between the parties in this case, upon their oaths do say that the
defendants do owe the plaintiff the sum of four hundred dollars the amount
of the debt in the declaration mentioned, and that the plaintiff hath sustained damages by reason of the detention of said debt to ten dollars, besides costs. It is therefore considered by the court that the plaintiff
recover of the defendants the amount of his debt aforesaid together with
his damages aforesaid, and his costs by him about his suit in this behalf
expended.

    Ralph Graves, Graves Hester, Spencer Clark and Archibald McKissack,
presented their petition against Bowler Faris, who was by a former order
appointed Guardian of Hiram Brown, Painelia Brown, Esnely Brown, minor
children of Jestirs Brown decd. at which time the said Graves Hester,
Clark, & McKissack became security for the said Faris, on said Guardianship and praying to be released thereupon, and it is thereupon ordered by
the court that a Summons issue to the Sheriff of this County commanding the
said Faris to appear at the next term of this court, and give other or
counter security's to be approved of by the court, or deliver up to one of
the said securities, or to some other person whom the court may appoint the
Estate of said Orphans and that a copy of said petition accompany sd. Summons.

Stirling C. & Eldridge B. Robertson Plts.)   Original Attachment
            Against)
Isaac Crow - - - - - - - Deft.)   Whereupon came here
                                                         into court Samuel Day
who being considered by the court good and sufficient bail agrees that
Stirling C. & Eldridge B. Robertson in this case, that he shall pay and
satisfy the condemnation of the court or surrender his body in discharge
of the same, or he will do it for him. It is thereupon ordered that the
garnishees in this case summoned be discharged. (177-178 torn out)

P-179 Thursday 27th May 1824

Hugh Torrence . . Plaintiff)   Motion
    Against)
John Edwards - - Defendant)   This day came the plaintiff by his at-
                                      torney and moved the court now here to
enter up Judgment in his favor against said defendant for the sum of one
hundred & two dollars with interest thereon from the 3rd day of May 1824
till this time in consequence of his having been compelled by the Judgment
of the court of Pleas & Quarter Sessions of Giles County, at August Term
1823 to pay to John McCracken that sum as security for said John Edwards
and it not appearing to the court on the face of the note upon which said
Judgement was recovered, that said plaintiff was security for said defenant

therefore let a Jury come who as well &c to recognize &c and thereupon came a Jury of good and lawful men, Towit, William H. Moore, Beverly B. Watson, John S. Brandon, Richard H. Allen, John P. Taylor, John Gordon, Edward Davis, John Keenan, Nathan Davis, John Newton, Charles Edwards, & Ira C. Goff, who being elected tried and sworn to try whether said plaintiff paid said sum of $102. as security for said defendant on the 3rd of May 1824 upon their oaths do say that said plaintiff did pay said sum of $102. on the 3rd day of May 1824, as security for said John Edwards & that plaintiff was compelled to pay the sum in consequence of a Judgment of the County Court of Giles County at August term 1823 in favor of John McCracken against said plaintiff & said John Edwards.

It is therefore considered by the court that the sd. plaintiff recover of said defendant said sum of $102. with interest thereon to be computed at the rate of six per cent per annum from 3rd day of May 1824 (the time of paying the money as aforesaid) till this time - and his costs by him about his motion in this behalf expended.

Archibald McKissack Plt.) In Debt
    Against)
John McCormick Deft.) This day came the parties by their attorneys and thereupon came a Jury of good and lawful men, Towit, William H. Moore, Beverly B. Watson, John S. Brandon, Richard H. Allen, John P. Taylor, John Gordon, Edward Davis, John Keenan, Nathan Davis, John Newton, Charles Edwards & Ira S. Goff, who being elected tried and sworn well and truly to try the issue Joined between the parties in this case, upon their oaths do say that the defendant hath not paid the declaration mentioned, But there remains a Balance of said debt unpaid, to the amount of one hundred & thirteen dollars & thirty four cents, and that hath no set off - It is therefore considered by the court that the plaintiff recover of the said defendant the Balance of his debt   (p-180)   aforesaid together with his damages aforesaid in form aforesaid by the Jurors aforesaid assessed, and his costs by him about his suit in this behalf expended.

A Bill of sale from John Elliott to James H. Pickens for certain property therein contained was produced in court & the execution thereof proven by the oaths of James Leitch the subscribing witness thereto and ordered to be certified for registration.

Mahulda Brown . . . Plaintiff) In Case
    Against)
Archibald McKissack) Defendants) This day came the parties by their
& Thomas B. Haynie) attornies and thereupon came a
) Jury of good and lawful men, Towit
William H. Moore, Beverly B. Watson, John S. Brandon, Richard H. Allen, John P. Taylor, John Gordon, Edward Davis, John Keenan, Nathan Davis, John Newton, Charles Edwards and Ira C. Goff, who being elected tried and sworn well and truly to try the issue Joined between the parties in this case who having heard the evidence were permitted to disperse to meet again tomorrow morning nine oclock.

Edmund Shelton Plt.) Original Attachment
    Against)
Dudley Smith Deft.)

This day came the plaintiff by his attorney, and on motion of the plaintiffs Attorney it is ordered that a Judicial attachment issue against the wife of the defendant for Gabriel Bumpass note to defendant for Eleven Dollars and after allowing all just credits to the judgment by collection of debts and sale of the property that Stephen Loyd administrator of the Estate of Jeremiah Woodward decd. Pay over in Satisfaction of said Judgment The proportionable part of so much thereof as will be sufficient to satisfy the Balance of said Judgment and all costs.

Ordered that Court be adjourned till tomorrow morning nine oclock.

Robert Oliver
Joseph Rea
A. McKissack

P-181 Friday 28th May 1824

Court met according to adjournment Present Archibald McKissack,)
Robert Oliver)
Joseph Roe)
Esquire Justice of the Peace for Giles County.

Ordered that the County Trustee of this County pay to Jesse Marlor the sum of Eleven dollars & seventy five cents as per account filed for guarding Wm. Watson to Lincoln Circuit Court.

Ordered that the following tax lists for the year 1822 be received and the double tax thereon remitted, Towit,

Elisha Eldridge 1 white pole
1 Black "
3 Town lots

Mahulda Brown ... Plt.) In Case
Against)
Archibald McKnight &) Deft)
Thomas B. Haynie))
) This day came the parties by their attornies and thereupon came the Jury who were sworn well and truly to try the issue joined between the parties in this case who having the argument of counsel retired out of court to consider of this verdict after some time returned & say they cannot agree By consent of parties & with the assent of the court William H. Moore one of Jurors in this case was withdrawn and the case continued untill next term of this court that a new trial may be had therein.

William H. Fields Guardian of Silas Flournoy returned into court an account against his said ward which is ordered to be recorded.

Boler Faris comes into court and resigns as Guardian of Hiram Brown, Pamela Brown & Ensly Brown minor orphans of Jethro Brown decd. and thereupon Isaac Smith was appointed Guardian of sd. minors whereupon he entered into bond and security as the law directs.

Isaac Smith Guardian of Hiram Brown, Pamela Brown, Ensley Brown, Minor orphans of Jethro Brown decd. made return of the property belonging to sd. minors which is ordered to be recorded.

Jesse Pum Assee &c Plt.) Certiorari
    Against)
John W. R. Graves Deft.) On motion of the plaintiff by his attorney
) It is ordered that the Judgment heretofore rendered against the defendant for the sum of sixty seven dollars Eighty and one half cents & costs be entered up also against James H. Graves his security in the certiorari.

P-182   Friday 28th May 1824

Abraham Byler Assee & Plt.) In Debt
    Against)
George Keltner &) Deft.)
George M. Gibson)) From the Judgment of the Court in this case rendered the defendant prayed an appeal to the honorable the Circuit Court to be holden for the County of Giles and having executed bond and security according to Law the same was granted them.

John P. Taylor Plaintiff) In Case
    Against)
Jacob Couch &) Defendant)
Joshua Horn)) From the Judgment of the court in this case rendered the defendant prayed an appeal to the honorable the Circuit Court to beholden for the County of Giles, and having Executed bond and security according to Law the same was granted them.

Thomas Lam . . Plt.) In Debt
    Against)
Nathaniel Young)
& John Young) From the Judgment of the court in this case rendered the defendant prayed an appeal to the honorable the Circuit Court to be holden for the County of Giles and having executed bond and security according to Law the same was granted them.

Martin Lam Plt.) In Debt
    Against)
Nathaniel Young) Defts.)
& John Young ( ) From the Judgment of the court in this case rendered the defendant prayed an appeal to the honorable the Circuit Court to be holden for the County of Giles - And having executed bond and security according to Law the same was granted them.

Smith Hunt Gdn. & C. Plt.) In Debt
    Against)
German Lester &) Defts.)
Alexander Black)) From the Judgment of the court in this case rendered the defendant prayed an appeal to the honorable

the Circuit Court to be holden for the County of Giles and having executed bond and security according to Law the same was granted them.

P-183   Friday 28th May 1824

Smith Hunt Gdn. &c Plt.) In Debt
   Against)
German Lester &) Defts.) From the Judgment of the Court in this
John McCracken) case rendered the defendant prayed an
) appeal to the honorable the Circuit Court
to be holden for the County of Giles – And having executed bond and security according to Law the same was granted them.

Elizabeth Brown by her next) Plts.) In Case
Friend Morgan Brown)
   Against) This day came the parties by
Archibald McKissack &) Defts.) their attornies and thereupon
Thomas B. Haynie) came a Jury of good and Lawful
) men, towit, James Buford, John
Johnson, Asa McGee, Robert Paine, Robert Buchanan, William Conner, John Brown, Benjamin Williams, William Pullen, John McKnight, John Goff, Anderson Tucker, who being elected tried and Sworn well and truly to try the issue joined between the parties in this case upon their oaths do say that the defendants are guilty of the traverse and conversion in the plaintiffs declaration complained of and they do assess the plaintiffs damages by occasion thereof to Thirty five dollars & thirty six cents besides costs. It is therefore considered by the court that the plaintiff recover of the said defendant the amount of his damages aforesaid in form aforesaid by the Juror aforesaid assessed and his costs by him about his suit in this behalf expended.

Stephen Hightower Plaintiff) In Debt
   Against)
Ambrose Cobbs Defendant) This day came the parties by their at-
) tornies and thereupon came a Jury of
good and Lawful men Towit, William Jones, Stirling Graves, William C. Graves, Henry M. Newlan, Hanner Turner, Hugh Torrence, David McCullock, William Snow, Adam R. Faris, Daniel Frasure, George H. Edwards, & Archibald Story, who being elected tried and sworn well and truly to try the issue joined between the parties in this case, upon their oaths do say that the defendants has not paid the debt in the writing obligatory in the declaration mentioned, and that he has no set off as the plaintiff in his replication has alleged, and they do assess the plaintiffs damages by occasion of the detention of said debt to one dollar & sixty five cents besides costs. It is therefore considered by the court that the plaintiff recover of the said defendant the sum of one hundred and ten dollars the amount of his debt aforesaid together with his damages aforesaid in form aforesaid by the Jurors aforesaid assessed and his costs by him about his suit in this behalf expended.

P-184   Friday 28th May 1824

Willie Turner for the use &c Plt.) In Debt
   Against)
~~Hanner Turner~~)

136

From the Judgment of the court in this case rendered the defendant prayed an appeal to the honorable the Circuit Court to be holden for the County of Giles, and having executed Bond and security according to Law the same as was granted him.

John P. Taylor Plaintiff)   In Debt
    Against)
Gerald Irby Defendant)

This day came the parties by their attornies and thereupon came a Jury of good and Lawful men, Towit, William Jones, Stirling Graves, William C. Graves, Henry M. Newlin, Hanner Turner, Hugh Torrance, David McCullock, William Snow, Adam R. Faris, Daniel Frasure, Gray H. Edwards, and Archibald Story, Who being elected tried and sworn well and truly to try the issue joined between the parties in this case upon their oaths do say that the defendant has not paid the debt in the writing obligatory in the declaration mentioned and that he has no set off as the plaintiff in his replication has alleged, and they do assess the plaintiffs damages by occasion of the detention of sd. Debt to two dollars & seventy five cents besides costs. It is therefore considered by the court that the plaintiff recover of the sd. Defendant the sum of one hundred & ten dollars and fifty cents, the amount of his debt aforesaid together with his damages aforesaid in form aforesaid by the Jurors aforesaid assessed and his costs about his suit in this behalf expended.

John Brown Assee &c Plt.)   In Debt
    Against)
William H. Moore &) Defts.)
Guston Kearney)

This day came the parties by their attornies and thereupon came a Jury of good and Lawful men, Towit, William Jones, Stirling Graves, William C. Graves, Henry M. Newlin, Hanner Turner, Hugh Torrance, David McCullock, William Snow, Adam R. Faris, Daniel Frasure, George H. Edwards and Archibald Story, who being elected tried and sworn well and truly to try the issue joined between the parties in this case upon their oath do say that the defendant hath not paid the debt in the writing obligatory in the declaration mentioned and they do assess the plaintiff damages by occasion of the detention of sd. debt to six dollars and sixty seven cents besides costs. It is therefore considered by the court that the plaintiff recover of sd. defendant the sum of two hundred (p-185) Friday 28th May 1824, & sixty seven dollars the amount of his damages aforesaid in form aforesaid by the Jurors aforesaid assessed and his costs about his suit in this behalf Expended.

Hendry Hightower)   In Debt
    Against)
Nicholas Holly)
Nicholas Holly Senr.)
& John Holly)

This day came the parties by their attornies and thereupon came a Jury of good and lawful men, Towit, William Jones, Stirling Graves, William C. Graves, Henry M. Newlin, Hanner Turner, Hugh Torrance, David McCullock, William Snow, Adam R. Frasure, Adam R. Faris, Daniel Frasure, Gray H. Edwards and Archibald Story - Who being elected tried and sworn well and truly to try the issue joined between the parties in this case upon their oaths do say that the defendants have not paid the debt in the Writing obligatory in the declaration mentioned, and that they have no set off as the plaintiff in his replication has alleged and they do assess the plaintiffs damages by occasion of the detention of said debt to three dollars and forty five cents besides costs. It is therefore considered by the court that the plaintiff recover of said defendants the sum of one hundred & thirty eight dollars the amount of his debt aforesaid, together with his damages aforesaid in form aforesaid by the Jurors aforesaid assessed and his costs about his suit in this behalf expended.

James Coldwell & William A. Brown)   In Case
Admr. of I. H. Neal decd.   )
   Against   )   This day came the parties by their
William D. Jennings Deft.   )   attornies, and the defendant having
                  filed his affidavit herein this
cause is ordered to be continued, and that a commission issue to any two of the Acting Justices of the peace in and for the County of Charlotte & State of Virginia to take the deposition of John P. Richardson to be read in evidence on the trial of this cause – upon the defendants giving to the plaintiff thirty days notice of the time and place of taking said deposition.

Robert Stewart for the use &c Plt.)   In Case
   Against   )
Lewis H. Brown . . . . Deft.   )   This day came the parties by their
                  attornies and the defendant having
filed his affidavit herein this cause is ordered to be continued and that a commission issue to any two of the Acting Justices of the Peace in & for the County of Monroe & State of Alabama to take (p-186) the deposition of Jabez N. Brown to be read in evidence on the trial of this cause, upon the defendant giving to the plaintiff twenty five days notice of the time and place of taking said deposition.

James C. O. Rally . . . Plt.   )   In Debt
   Against   )
Andrew M. Balentine &   ) Defts.   )   Upon the application of the de-
Stephen Anderson Exorer. of)   )   fendant in this case and they
John Samuel Decd.   )   )   having filed their affidavits
                  herein, this cause is ordered
to be continued – and that a commission issue to any two of the Acting Justices of the peace in & for the County of Maury this State to take the deposition of William Brown to be read in evidence on the trial of this cause upon the defendant giving to the plaintiff five days notice of the time and place of taking said deposition.

Stirling C. Robertson for the use &c Plt.)   In Debt
   Against   )
David McCanlass . . . Deft.   )   This day came the parties
                  by their attornies and
thereupon came a Jury of good and lawful men, Towit, William Jones, Stirling Graves, William C. Graves, Henry M. Newlin, Hanner Turner, Hugh Torrance, David McCollock, William Snow, Adam R. Faris, Daniel Frasure, Gray H. Edwards & Archibald Story, who being elected tried and sworn well and truly to try the issue joined between the parties in this case upon their oaths do say that the defendant has not paid the debt in the writing obligatory in the declaration mentioned and they do assess the plaintiffs damages by occasion of the detention of sd. debt to one dollar and sixty two & a half

cents, besides costs. It is therefore considered by the court that the plaintiff recover of said defendant the sum of one hundred & four dollars & fifty cents - the amount of his debt aforesaid together with his damages aforesaid assessed, and his costs about his suit in this behalf expended.

James Perry Plaintiff) In Debt
    Against)
James H. Wells Thomas) Defts.) This day came the parties by
Wells & William H. Wells)) their attornies and thereupon
) came a Jury of good and (p-187)
Lawful men, Towit, William Jones, Stirling Graves, William C. Graves, Henry M. Newlin, Hanner Turner, Hugh Torrence, David McCollock, William Snow, Adam R. Faris, Daniel Frasure, Gray H. Edwards, & Archibald Story, who being elected tried and sworn well and truly to try the issue joined between the parties in this case upon their oaths do say that the defendants have not paid the debt in the writing obligatory in the declaration mentioned and that they have no set off, as the plaintiff in his replication has alleged, and they do assess the plaintiffs damages by occasion of the detention of sd. defendant the sum of one thousand dollars the amount of his debt aforesaid together with his damages aforesaid in form aforesaid by the Jurors aforesaid assessed and his costs by him about his suit this behalf expended.

Fountain Lester & Stirling Lester) In Debt
Partners &c for the use of &c)
    Against) This day came the parties by
William Wood . . . . . Deft.) their attornies and thereupon
) came a Jury of good and lawful
men, Towit, William Jones, Stirling Graves, William C. Graves, Henry M. Newlin, Hanner Turner, Hugh Torrence, David McCullock, William Snow, Adam R. Faris, Daniel Frasure, George H. Edwards & Archibald Story, who being Elected tried and sworn well and truly to try the issue Joined between the parties in this case upon their oaths do say that the defendant has not paid the debt in the Writing obligatory in the declaration mentioned and they do assess the plaintiffs damages by occasion of the detention of said debt to nine dollars besides costs. It is therefore considered by the court that the plaintiff recover of said defendant the sum of one hundred & six dollars & four and one fourth cents the amount of their debt aforesaid together with their damages aforesaid in form aforesaid by the Jurors aforesaid assessed and their costs by them about their suit in this behalf expended.

From the Judgment of this court in this case, rendered the defendant prayed an appeal to the honorable the Circuit Court to be holden for the County of Giles and having executed Bond and security according to law the same was granted them

P-188 Friday 28th May 1824

The United States plaintiff) In Debt
    Against)
Joel Bruce Defendant) This day came the parties by their at-
) tornies and thereupon came a Jury of
good and lawful men, Towit, William Jones, Stirling Graves, William C. Graves, Henry M. Newlin, Hanner Turner, Hugh Torrence, David McCullock, William Snow, Adam R. Faris, Daniel Frazer, Gray H. Edward & Archibald

Story, who being elected tried and sworn well and truly to try the issue joined between the parties in this case upon their oaths do say that the Writing obligatory in the declaration mentioned is not the Act and deed of the defendant, as in pleading he hath alleged. It is therefore considered by the court that the defendant go hence without day and recover of the plaintiff his costs by him about his defence in this behalf expended.

James H. Graves Plaintiff) In Debt
    Against)
James Lynch Defendant) This day came the parties by their attorneys, and thereupon the defendants attorney tendered a Bill of executions which was signed and sealed, and ordered to be made a part of the record in this case and thereupon came a Jury of good and lawful men, Towit, William Jones, Stirling Graves, William C. Graves, Henry M. Newlin, Hanner Turner, Hugh Torrance, David McCullock, William Snow, Adam R. Faris, Daniel Frazer, Gray H. Edwards & Archibald Story, who being elected tried and Sworn well and truly to try the issue joined between the parties in this case upon their oaths do say that the defendant hath not paid the debt in the writing obligatory in the declaration mentioned as the plaintiff in replication hath alleged and they assess the plaintiffs damages by occasion of the detention of said debt to three dollars eighty seven and one half cents besides costs. It is therefore considered by the court that the plaintiff recover of the defendant the sum of one hundred and ninety two dollars & seventy five cents, the amount of his debt aforesaid together with his damages aforesaid by the Jurors aforesaid in form aforesaid assessed and his costs by him about his suit in this behalf expended.

James H. Graves Plt.) In Debt
    Against)
James Lynch Deft.) This day came the parties by their attornies and thereupon the defendants attornies tendered a Bill of exceptions which was signed and sealed and ordered to be made a part of the record in this case and thereupon came a Jury of good (p-189) (Friday 28th May 1824) and lawful men, Towit, William Jones, Stirling Graves, William Graves, Henry M. Newlin, Hanner Turner, Hugh Terrence, David McCullock, William Snow, Adam R. Faris, Daniel Frazer, Gray H. Edwards & Archibald Storey, who being elected tried and sworn well and truly to try the issue joined between the parties in this case upon their oaths do say that the defendant hath not paid the debt in the Writing obligatory mentioned, and they do assess the plaintiffs damages by occasion of the Detention of said Debt to four dollars & twenty five cents, Besides costs. It is therefore considered by the court that the plaintiff recover of the defendant the sum of two hundred dollars the amount of his debt aforesaid together with his damages aforesaid by the Jurors aforesaid in form aforesaid assessed and his costs by him about his suit in this behalf expended.

Washington G. L. Foley Plaintiff) In Debt
    Against)
James Lynch & Defendants)
Benjamin W. Edwards) This day came the patties by their attornies and thereupon came a Jury of good and lawful men, Towit, William Jones, Stirling Graves, William C. Graves, Henry M. Newlin, Hanner Turner, Hugh Terrence, David McCullock, William Snow, Adam R. Faris, Daniel Frazer, Gray H. Edwards & Archibald Storey who being elected tried and

sworn well and truly to try the issue joined between the parties in this case upon their oaths do say that the defendants hath not paid the whole of the debt in the writing obligatory in the Declaration mentioned but that there remains a balance of said Debt unpaid to the amount of three hundred and thirty Dollars eighteen and three fourth cents and they do assess the plaintiffs damages by occasion of the detention of said balance of said debt to six dollars and sixty cents, besides costs. It is therefore considered by the court that the plaintiff recover of the defendants the balance of his debt aforesaid, together with his damages aforesaid, by the Jurors aforesaid in form aforesaid assessed and his costs by him about his suit in this behalf expended.

Ezekiel Bonner to the use of &c Plt.) In Debt
    Against)
William D. Jennings &) Defts.) This day came the parties by
Josiah E. Maddocks) their attornies and therefore
) came a Jury of good and lawful
men, Towit, William Jones, Stirling Graves, William C. Graves, Henry M. Newlin, Hanner Turner, Hugh Terrence, David McCullock, William Snow, Adam R. Faris, Daniel Frazer, Gray H. Edwards and Archibald Storey, who being elected tried and sworn well an truly to try the (p-190) (Friday 28th May 1824) issue joined between the parties in this case upon their oaths do say that the defendant hath not paid the whole of the debt in the declaration mentioned, But there remains unpaid a balance of said debt to the amount of one hundred and forty four dollars and they do assess the plaintiffs damages by occasion of the Detention thereof to four dollars and thirty two cents. Besides costs It is therefore considered by the court that the plaintiff recover of the Defendants the Balance of his Debt aforesaid together with his damages aforesaid by the Jurors aforesaid in form aforesaid assessed and his costs by him about his suit in this behalf expended.

Homer Rainey to the use of Rhoda Boyd Plt.) In Debt
    Against)
Stephen Anderson & Andrew M. Balentine) This day came the parties
Executors of John Samuel decd. &)) by their attornies & there-
James Rainey, Henry M. Newlin &)Defts.) upon came a Jury of good
Edward D. Jones) and lawful men, Towit,
) William Jones, Stirling
Graves, William C. Graves, Henry M. Newlin, Hanner Turner, Hugh Terrence, David McCullock, William Snow, Adam R. Faris, Daniel Frazer, Gray H. Edwards & Archibald Storey, who being elected tried and sworn well and truly to try the issue joined between the parties in this case upon their oaths do say that they find said issues in favor of the plaintiff and assess his damages by occasion of the detention of said debt to seven dollars and fifty cents, Besides costs. It is therefore considered by the court that the plaintiff recover of the defendant the sum of three hundred dollars the amount of her debt aforesaid together with his damages aforesaid by the Jurors aforesaid in form aforesaid assessed & his costs by him about his suit in this behalf expended.

Lyddall Wilkinson Plaintiff) In Debt
    Against)
John C. Underwood Defendant) This day came the parties by their at-
) tornies and thereupon came a Jury of

good and lawful men, Towit, William Jones, Stirling Graves, William C. Graves, Henry M. Newlin, Hanner Turner, Hugh Terrence, David McCullock, William Snow, Adam R. Faris, Daniel Frazer, Gray H. Edwards & Archibald Storey who being elected tried and sworn well and truly to try the issue Joined between the parties (p-191) (Friday 28th May 1824) in this case, on the plea of Payment on their oaths do say that the defendant hath not paid the debt in the Writing obligatory in the declaration mentioned as the plaintiff in his replication hath alleged.

Ordered that Court be adjourned till tomorrow morning nine oclock.

              James Paine
              Robert Oliver
              Joseph Rea

P-192   Saturday 29th May 1824

Court met according to adjournment, Present Alexander Black)
              Robert Oliver &) Esquires
              Joseph Rea   ) Justices.

Ordered that letters of administration on the Estate of Harrison Hicks decd. was granted to James Buford, who thereupon entered into bond and security and was qualified as the Law directs.

John P. Taylor . . . . Plt.   )   In Debt
  Against   )
Gerald Irby . . . . . Deft.) From the Judgment of the court in this
) case rendered the defendant prayed an appeal to the honorable the Circuit Court to be held for the County aforesaid, and having entered bond and security according to law the same was granted him.

John Brown to the use of &c Plt.)   In Debt
  Against   )
William H. Moore &) Defts.) From the Judgment of the court in
Guston Kearney)   ) this case rendered the defendants
) prayed an appeal to the honorable the Circuit Court to be held for the County of Giles, and having entered into bond and security according to law the same was granted him.

Bonapart Garland and   )   Petition
Peter Garland in proper   )
Person Daniel, Lowry   ) On motion of the plaintiffs by their
Harriet, John Wester,   ) attornies and it appearing to the
Julian & Louisa Garland by their) satisfaction of the court now here,
next friend Edward Garland   ) that the defendant is not an inhabi-
  Against   ) tant of this State. It is therefore
John Pate Junr. . . . . Defendants) ordered by the court that the de-
) fendant appear at the next term of this court, and plead answer or Demurr to the plaintiffs petition, or otherwise the same will be set for trial exparte at the next term of this court

and that a copy of this order be published for three weeks successively in the Town of Columbia Tennessee.

P-193   Saturday 29th May 1824

James H. Graves . . . Plaintiff)   In Debt
    Against   )
James Lynch . . Defendant   )   From the Judgment of the Court in
)   this case rendered the defendant
prayed an appeal to the honorable the Circuit Court to be held for the County of Giles & having entered into bond and security according to Law the same was granted him.

James H. Graves Plaintiff)   In Debt
    Against   )
James Lynch Defendant   )   From the Judgment of the court in this
)   court rendered the defendant prayed an
appeal to the honorable the Circuit Court to be held for the County of Giles, and having entered into bond and security according to Law the same was granted him.

Washington G. L. Foley Plt.   )   In Debt
    Against   )
James Lynch & Benjamin W. Edwards   )   From the Judgment of the court in
)   this case rendered the Defendants
prayed an appeal to the honorable the Circuit Court to be held for the County of Giles and having entered into bond and security according to law the same was granted them.

James Buford Guardian of Nancy Hicks minor orphan of John Hicks decd. returned into court an account against his ward which was ordered to be recorded.

Hardy Hightower Plaintiff   )   In Debt
    Against   )
Nicholas Holly   ) Defendants)   From the Judgment of the court in
Nicholas Holly Jnr.)   )   this case rendered the Defendants
and John Holly   )   )   prayed an appeal to the honorable
)   the Circuit Court to be held for
the County of Giles, and having entered into bond and security according to Law the same was granted them.

Archibald McKissack Assignee &c. Plt.)   In Debt
    Against   )
John McAnninch . . . . Deft.   )   From the Judgment of the
)   Court in this case rendered
the defendant prayed an appeal to the honorable the Circuit court to be held for the County of Giles, and having entered into bond and security according to law the same was granted him.

P-194   Saturday 29th May 1824

Archibald McKissack Plt.) In Debt
    Against)
John McAninch Deft.) From the Judgment of the Court in this
) case rendered the defendant prayed an
appeal to the honorable the Circuit Court to be held for the County of
Giles and having entered into bond and security according to Law the same
was granted him.

Thomas McKissack Admr. & Plt.) In Debt
    Against)
Hugh Torrence & Ralph Graves Defts.) From the Judgment of the court
) in this case rendered the de-
fendant prayed an appeal to the honorable the Circuit Court to be held for
the County of Giles, and having Entered into bond and security according
to law the same was granted.

Thomas Martin . . . Plaintiff) In Debt
    Against)
George Everly . . . . Defendant) From the Judgment of the court
) in this case rendered the de-
fendant prayed an appeal to the honorable the Circuit Court to be held for
the County of Giles, and having entered into bond and security according
to Law the same was granted him.

    A Licence to keep an ordinary for the term of twelve months and no
longer is granted to Robert Gordon, who was qualified and entered into
bond and security according to Law.

Charles Perkins Assignee &c Plt.) Debt
    Against)
Thomas Wells . . . . . Deft.) This day came the plaintiff by
) his attorney and the defendant
altho solemnly called came not but made default. It is therefore considered
by the court that the plaintiff recover of the defendant the sum of one
hundred and twenty five dollars, the amount of the debt in the writing obligatory in the declaration mentioned, together with the sum of one dollar
and eighty one and one fourth cents the damages which he hath sustained
by reason of the detention of said debt, and his costs by him about his
suit in this behalf expended.
    From which Judgment the defendant prayed an appeal to the honorable
the Circuit Court to be held for the County of Giles and having entered
into bond and security according to law the same was granted him.

P-195   Saturday 29th May 1824

Silas Gilbert . . Plaintiff) Certiorari
    Against)
Robert Shadden &) Defendants) This day came the parties aforesaid
John Shadden)) by their attornies and thereupon the
) motion of the plaintiff to dismiss
the certiorari in this case being argued and it appearing to the court,
that Judgment was rendered by Alexander Black Esquire, a Justice of the
Peace for Giles County on the 11th of January 1817 in favor for said

plaintiff against John Shadden & Robert Shadden Senr. for the sum of Fifty five dollars & costs and credited by ten dollars, and that Robert Shadden the petitioner then there became security for the Stay of said Execution according to Act of Assembly in such case made and provided, and there being no complaint in said Petition against the Justices of said Judgment of said Justice of the peace be in all things affirmed and that said plaintiff recover against said John Shadden and Robert Shadden and Robert Shadden Junr. for said certiorari the sum of forty five dollars the amount of the balance of said Judgment of said Justice with Interest thereon to be computed at the rate of twelve and a half per cent per anum from the eleventh day of January 1817 (the time of rendering said Judgment by said Justice as aforesaid) till this time together with his costs by him as well before the Justice of the Peace aforesaid as in this court in this behalf expended.

Stirling C. Robertson to the use of & Plt.) In Debt
        Against)
Samuel McCanlass . . . . . . Deft.) From the Judgment of the
) court in this case rendered the defendant prayed an appeal to the honorable the Circuit Court to be held for the County of Giles & having entered into bond and security according to law the same was granted him.

Ezekiel Bonner to the use of &c Plt.) In Debt
        Against)
William D. Jennings &) Deft.)
Josiah E. Maddox)) From the Judgment of the
) court in this case rendered the Defendants prayed an appeal to the honorable the Certiorari Court to be held for the County of Giles, and having entered into bond and security according to Law the same was granted.

P-196 Saturday 29th May 1824

Jesse Penn Assignee & Plt.) Certiorari
        Against)
John W. R. Graves &) Defts.) From the Judgment of the Court in this
James H. Graves) case rendered the Defendant prayed an
) appeal to the honorable the Circuit
Court to be held for the County of Giles, and having entered into bond and security according to Law the same was granted them.

James Buford Administrator of the Estate of Harrisson Hicks decd. returned into Court an Inventory of said Estate which was ordered to be record

Ordered that an order of sale issue to James Buford Admr. of the Estate of Harrisson Hicks decd. commanding him to sell the property mentioned in the Inventory by him this returned, and make return thereof according to Law

Reuben L. Crittenton Plt.) Certiorari
        Against)
James Perry . . . Deft.) This day came the parties by their

attornies and thereupon the plaintiffs motion to dismiss the certiorari in this case being argued and mature deliberation thereupon being had it is considered by the court that said certiorari be dismissed and that the Judgment of the Justice of the peace be affirmed against the defendant for the sum of sixty four dollars and thirty one cents with Interest thereon to be computed at the rate of twelve and a half per cents per anum from the 20th of January 1824 (the time of rendering the Judgment by the Justice of the Peace) till this time together with the costs as well before the Justice of the Peace as in this court in this behalf expended.

Gray H. Edwards & Susan his wife)) Petition for distributive
Spencer Clack & Loucinda his wife)Plts.) Share.
John Wathall & Parmelia his wife)) This day came the parties
    Against) aforesaid by their attor-
Thomas McKissack . . . . . Deft.) nies and by consent of
) the parties and with the
assent of the court it is ordered by the court that German Lester Esquire Clerk of this court between this time and the next term of this court, take an account of all the monied transactions between the defendant and the heirs of Wilson Jones decd. and that said German Lester, Charles Buford, Richard Brandon, and James Buford, or any two of them between this time and next term of this court value and devide all the shares and other personal Estate of sd. Wilson Jones decd. into five (p-197) (Saturday May 1824) Equal parts, and allot to said plaintiffs one fifth each and to Calvin Jones & Thomas Jones, heirs of sd. Wilson Jones decd. one fifth each and that they or any two of them also devide the amount of money and claims for money that may be found upon the amount to be taken as aforesaid in the hands of sd. Defendant as administrator of sd. Wilson Jones decd. into five equal parts and allot the same in the same manner as they are directed to allot the slaves and other personal property and make report of such valuation and allotment to the next term of this court.

James Perry . . . . . Plt.) In Debt
   Against)
James Wells, Thos.Wells,) Defts.) From the Judgment of this court
& William H. Wells) in this case rendered the de-
) fendant prayed an appeal to the
honorable the circuit court to be holden for the County of Giles and having executed bond and security according to Law the same was granted them.

Charles Perkins Assee. &c Plt.) In Debt
   Against)
Thomas Wells . . . . Defendants) From the Judgment of the court
) in this case rendered the de-
fendant prayed an appeal.

William H. Moore Assee. &c Plt.) In Case
   Against)
Henry J. Croft, Robert Oliver)Defts.) This day came the plaintiff by
and James H. Graves) his attorneys and the defendants
) altho solemnly called came not

but made default. It is therefore considered by the court that the plaintiff recover of the defendant the damages which he has sustained by reason of the nonperformance of the several assumpsits in declaration compalined of, but because it is unknown to the court here what the amount of those damages are. It is ordered that the same be enquired of by a Jury at the next term.

A Deed of conveyance from Alexander McDonald to the Heir of Nathan Henderson decd. and Sally Edwards for thirty five acres of land was produced in court and acknowledged and ordered to be certified for registration.

Ordered that court be adjourned till court in course.

                James Paine
                Robert Oliver
                Joseph Rea

At a court of Pleas and Quarter Session holden for the County of Giles, at the court house of said County in the Town of Pulaski on the third Monday in August (being the sixteenth day thereof in the Year of Our Lord one thousand eight hundred and twenty four - Present Alexander Black, William B. Pepper, Thomas Brown, Robt. Reed, John H. Camp, John Young, Hezekiah Jones, James Dugger, Jonathan Moody, Paul Chiles, Archibald McKissack, John C. Walker, Edward D. Jones, Robert Oliver, Anderson Hogan, Richard McGee, Thomas K. Gordon, Dewey Smith, John Henderson, Henry Hagen, Thomas Marks, and John Bramlett, Esquires Justice of the Peace of said County Presiding German Lester Clerk of said court - Lewis Brown Sheriff of said County.

Ordered that the following tax lists be received and the double tax thereon remitted, Towit, The Heirs of Joseph Moore decd. by Thomas Reed Gdn.
2 Town lots in lower Elkton Francis McNairy 1 white poll. 2 Slaves.

Ordered that John Tuly be appointed overseer of the road in the room of Jacob Luther resigned and that he have the same district of hands.

Ordered that George Brooks be appointed overseer of the road in the room of Isaac Wilcoxson resigned and that he have the same district of hands.

At Least five Justices being present William C. Rainey returned into court one wolf scalp over four months old which was ordered to be burnt.

Ordered that Asa Estes be appointed overseer of the road in the room of Daniel Abernathy resigned and that he have the same district of hands.

Ordered that the following tax lists be received and that double tax thereon remitted, Towit,
William Rainey 107 acres of land Rob. fork
5 slaves.
Arthur Rainey 1 Free poll
William Jones 250 acres of land Elk river
1 Free poll.

P-199 Monday 16th August 1824

Ordered that John Britten be appointed overseer of the road leading up main Bradshaw from the Fayettville Road to the Mile post near David Kerseys, and that he have all the hands now under Thomas Clark, that live in Paul Childs Company for the purpose of working on the said part of said Road.

A Deed of conveyance from William Davis to Thomas Pruitt & Henry Parsins for two hundred and fifty four acres of land was produced in court and the execution thereof acknowledged by the said William Davis and ordered to be certified for registration.

Ordered that the County trustee of this County pay to Robert McDonald the sum of twenty dollars for keeping Mary Miskel for six months from this time.

On the petition of Sundry persons. It is ordered by the court that the road leading from Stephen Redding to Hamilton C. Campbell be discontinued as a Public highway.

Ordered that Thomas Cavenor be appointed overseer of the road in the room of Thomas Stuart resigned, and that he have the same district of hands.

A Deed of conveyance from Thomas K. Gordon to Thomas Lam for one hundred acres of Land was produced in court and the execution thereof acknowledged by the said Thomas K. Gordon and ordered to be certified for registration.

Ordered that Ethen Sawyers be appointed constable in Captain Montgomery's Company whereupon he took the oath required by law and executed bond and security according to Law.

Ordered that Isaac Pervis an invalid be released from working on road.

James McCraven came into court and resigned his office as constable in Captain Nances Company, thereupon it is ordered by the court Presley T. Cox be appointed constable in said Nance's Company in the Stead of sd. James McCraven, he therefore took the oath required by law, and executed bond and security according to Law.

Ordered that Alexr. S. Jones be appointed Guardian to Martha L. McCommack infant Orphan of Masterson C. McCommack deceased whereupon he entered into bond and security according to Law.

P-200 Monday 16th August 1824

The last Will and Testament of Wythe Simms decd. was produced in court, and proven by the oaths of Reuben Freeman, & Willis W. Cole, two of the subscribing witnesses thereto and ordered to be recorded, thereupon John H. Camp the executor therein named appeared in court and was qualified and gave bond and security as the Law directs.

A Deed of conveyance from Alexander McDonald to John Phillips for sixty three fourth acres of land was produced in court and the execution thereof acknowledged by the said Alexander McDonald & ordered to be certified for registration.

A Deed of conveyance from Alexander McDonald to John Phillips for one hundred and five acres of land was produced in court and the execution thereof acknowledged by the said Alexander McDonald and ordered to be certified for registration.

A Bill of sale for certain property therein named from Robert Anderson to Samuel R. Anderson was produced in court, and the execution thereof proven by the oath of David Bridgforth & David R. Cole two of the subscribing witnesses thereto and ordered to be certified for registration.

A Bill of sale from Robert Anderson to Samuel R. Anderson for certain property therein named was produced in court and the execution thereof proven by the oaths of David Bridgforth and David R. Cole two of the subscribing witnesses thereto and ordered to be certified for registration.

A Deed of conveyance from Robert Anderson to Samuel R. Anderson for one hundred acres of land was produced in court and the execution thereof proven by the oaths of David Bridgforth and David R. Cole two of the subscribing witnesses thereto and ordered to be certified for registration.

Ordered that Allen Pitts be appointed overseer of the road in the room of John Wright resigned, and that he have the same district of hands.

P-201   Monday 16th August 1824

Ordered that the County Trustee of this County pay to Richard McGee Thirty dollars for the support and maintainance of Abraham Bogard & wife paupers of this County for twelve months from this time.

A Deed of conveyance from Jonathan Richards to Fountain Lester for one hundred & sixty acres of land was produced in court and the execution thereof acknowledged by the said Jonathan Richards & ordered to be certified for registration.

A Deed of conveyance from Nicholas Browning to Reuben Briggs for fifteen acres of Land was produced in court and the execution thereof acknowledged by sd. Nicholas Browning and ordered to be certified for registration.

The commissioners who were appointed to settle with Alexander Esselman Admr. of William Mullinax decd. made return of said settlement which is ordered to be recorded.

The commissioners who were appointed to divide the Estate of Robert Hodges decd. made report thereof which is ordered to be recorded.

A Deed of conveyance from Lewis H. Brown Sheriff of Giles County to Henry F. Crofts for . . . . acres of land was produced in court and the execution thereof acknowledged by the said L. H. Brown Sheriff as aforesaid and ordered to be certified for registration.

A Deed of conveyance from Alexander McDonald to John P. Taylor for one hundred acres of land was produced in court and the execution thereof proven by the oaths of Richard G. Scoggins & Vincent Tidwell the witnesses thereto and ordered to be certified for registration.

Ordered that William Webb be appointed overseer of the road in the room of Christain Zimmermon resigned, and that he have the same district of hands.

A Deed of conveyance from Littlebury Adams to Reuben Freeman for twenty acres of Land was produced in court & the execution thereof partly proven by the oath of Harris Freeman one of the witnesses thereto.

A Deed of conveyance from Reuben Freeman to James K. Murrah for twenty acres of land was produced in court and the execution thereof acknowledged by the said Reuben Freeman and ordered to be certified for registration.

P-202 Monday 16th August 1824

Ordered that the following tax list be received and the double tax thereon remitted, towit,
      Allen Pitts 75 acres of land
                   1 White Poll
                   2 Slaves.

A Deed of conveyance from George Goats to Fountan Lester for one hundred and sixty acres of Land, was produced in court and the execution thereof acknowledged by the said George Goats and ordered to be certified for registration.

Ordered that John Smith be appointed overseer of the road in the room of Edward Davis resigned and that he have the same district of hands.

At Least five Justices being present Phillip Thomas returned into court one wolf scalp under four months old which was ordered to be Burnt.

A Deed of conveyance from Clement Briggs & Jane his wife & William Briggs & Julia his wife to John G. Claiborn for thirty four and a half acres of land in Brunswick County and State of Virginia was produced in court and the execution thereof acknowledged by the said Clement Briggs & William Briggs to be their act and deed - And Thompson, John H. Camp, and Edward D. Jones, two of the Acting Justices of the peace in and for this County were appointed to take the privy examination of the said Jane Briggs and Julia Briggs touching the execution of said Deed - Who returned said examination which was ordered to be certified for registration.

Ordered that Peggy Davis & John Abernathy be appointed Guardian of Benjamin Davis, Lunatic, & Peggy Davis, Ebby Davis, Robert Davis, Maddison Davis, and Anna Davis, minor children of said Benjamin Davis, whereupon they entered into bond and security.

A Deed of conveyance from Elizabeth Smith to John Whitfield for sixty five acres of Land was produced in court and the execution thereof proven by the oaths of Enoch Simpson & Willis Whitfield two of the witnesses thereto and ordered to be certified for registration.

A Deed of conveyance from George Stanford to Allen Pitts for fifty acres of land was produced in court and the execution thereof proven by the oaths of John McCormick & Ranson Wells the the witnesses thereof & ordered to be certified for registration.

P-203 Monday 16th August 1824

Ordered that Gray Russell be bound an apprenticed to Edward Williamson an Indenture to that effect having been entered into between the chairman of the court and said Williamson.

Ordered that Nancy Russell be bound an apprentice to Hardy H. Halcolmb an Indenture to that effect having been entered into between the Chairman of the court and said Hardy H. Halcomb.

A Deed of conveyance from John Wilson & Catharine Wilson to Margaret Plaster for forty nine acres & thirty five poles of land was produced in court and the execution thereof proven by the oaths of John Hudson & Thomas T. Plaster the witnesses thereto and ordered to be certified for registration.

A Deed of conveyance from John McCracken to Jacob Shall for Lots No. 74 & 75 in the Town of Pulaski was produced in court and the Execution thereof acknowledged by the said John McCracken and ordered to be certified for registration.

Ordered that County Trustee of this County pay to Elizabeth Ruff the sum of Forty dollars for the support & maintainance of Rebeccah Ruff a pauper of this County From May term of this court 1823 to May term 1824.

A Deed of conveyance from Littlebury Melton to William Jones for thirty nine acres & one hundred & fifty six poles was produced in court and fully proven by the oath of David K. McEwin the other witness thereto and ordered to be certified for registration.

Ordered that Samuel Y. Anderson be appointed Guardian of Sarah M. Cannon Lunatic whereupon he entered into bond and security according to law.

A Power of Attorney from John Pate to Richard Briggs for certain perposes therein named was produced in court and the execution thereof acknowledged by the said John Pate and ordered to be certified to be registered.

Ordered that the following tax lists be received and the double tax lists thereon remitted, Towit, Isaac Tidwell 90 acres of land Big Creek.

Ordered that John W. Britten be released from paying tax on a pleasure carriage, which was wronglyfully charged to him, on the tax Book.

P-204 Monday 16th August 1824

It is ordered by the court that the following persons good & Lawful men of the County of Giles, that each one of whom is a free white male citizen and house holder of said County, over twenty one years of age, not an overseer of a road, & who has not been appointed & served as a Juror in this County for twelve months, Towit, John Lee, David Brown, James Abernathy, Thomas Cole, Joseph Young, David Kearsey, Martin B. Wood, William Black, Leander M. Shields, Hardy Willsford, George Gibson, George M. Lock, William May, John McKissack, George Ruff, Robert Black, Quinton Shannon, George Oliver, Larkin Webb, John Bass, Wm. Dailey, Baker P. Potts, Matthew Johnston, John Ruff, Robert Anders, & Elisha Anthony, be Jurors to serve on this court at the next Term on the third Monday in November next that the Clerk deliver a copy of this order to the Sheriff of this County, and that he summon said persons to attend & serve accordingly.

It is ordered by the court that the following persons good and lawful men of the County of Giles, that is each one of whom is a free white male citizen and house holder of said County over twenty one years of age, not an overseer of a road, who has not served on the venue in the Circuit Court of said County at the last term thereof, and who has no cause to be tried in said court at the next term thereof that is known of by this court, Towit, William B. Pepper, Marcus Mitchel, Paul Chiles, John Young, Thomas Marks, John McDaniel, Edward D. Jones, John Bramlett, William Bodenhammer, Richard H. Allen, William Dearing, Richard McGee, Hezekiah Jones, William Ussery, Joseph Nance, Fountain Lester, Samuel Y. Anderson, David W. Porter, William Mayfield, Peter Shannon, Thomas Butler, John H. Camp, Guston Kearny, Spencer Clack, Willis S. McLaurine & Charles Long, be Jurors to serve in the next Circuit Court to be holden for said County, at the court house in the Town of Pulaski on the first Monday in February next that the Clerk deliver a copy of this order to the Sheriff of the County, and that he summon said persons to attend & Serve accordingly.

Ordered that Thomas C. Stone be appointed administrator of the Estate of Francis Hicks deceased - Whereupon he was qualified as the Law directs and gave bond and security according to law.

P-205 Monday 16th August 1824

Ordered that part of the Buck Creek Road which lies near the plantation of Elisha L. Kimbro, which was lately altered and opened by the overseer and hands under his direction be established as a publick highway, and part from which the same is turned to be discontinued.

Ordered that the County Trustee of this County pay to Henry T. Croft the sum of one hundred and nine dollars for the Building a Bridge across Buchanan Creek on the Huntsville road, Let by commissioners appointed for that purpose by an order of the Last term of this court.

Ordered that the County Trustee of this County pay to William H. Field, Thomas B. Jones and Archibald McKissack the sum of Fifty dollars to be applied towards the payment for an alteration of the court house of this County agreed to by this court at the last Term.

Ordered that Henry Hagen and German Lester be appointed to let to the highest bidder the useless lumber in the upstairs of the court house of this County, and that he proceeds of said sale be paid over to the Trustee of this county to be applied to the payment of the County Claims.

Ordered that the Sheriff of this County Summon twelve free holders of this County to enquire of the Idiocy or Lunacy of Judith McCabe of this County and also enquire of the good and chattles lands and tenments and the value thereof Belonging to said Judith McCabe, and that they make report of said Inquest to the next term of this court.

Ordered that the Sheriff of this court Summon twelve free holders of this County, to enquire of the Idiocy or Lunicy of Tabitha Browning of this County, and also enquire as to the property if any and value thereof belonging to said Tabitha Browning, and that they make report of said Inquest to the next term of this court.

Ordered that the County Trustee of this County pay to Charles C. Abernathy and other commissioners appointed by the court to settle with the County Trustee of this County the sum of Five dollars to pay for a Book in which to record their Settlements.

An ordinary licence for the Term of one year and no longer is granted to Benjamin Burk, who was qualified and gave Bond and security as the Law directs.

P-206   Monday 16th August 1824

Ordered that the following tax list be received by the court and the double tax thereon remitted viz,
                Ephram A. Young 1 white poll.
                2 Slaves.

John Ruff Executor of Godsend Ruff, decd. Returned into court an Inventory of the Estate of his testator which was ordered to be recorded.

A Deed of conveyance from Rhoda Croney to Adam Hafner for twenty six acres of land was produced in court and the execution thereof proven by the oaths of John Paine and John Manefee the subscribing witnesses thereto and ordered to be certified for registration.

A Deed of conveyance from Adam Hapner to Johh Rea for twenty six acres of land was produced in court & the Execution thereof proven by the oaths of Reuben Freeman and John Manefee the subscribing witnesses thereto and ordered to be certified for registration.

Ordered that Isaac Williams be appointed Guardian of Mira Williams, Robert Williams, Jane Williams, Nancy Williams, Morris Williams, Lucianda Williams, and Eliza Williams, Minor children of said Isaac Williams for the purpose of receiving their distributive shares of the Estate of William Williams decd

A Deed of conveyance from Fountain Lester to Stephen Redding for one hundred and sixty acres of land was produced in court and the acknowledged by the said Fountain Lester and ordered to be certified for registration.

A Deed of conveyance from Stephen Redding to Fountain Lester for one hundred and sixty acres of land was produced in court and the execution thereof acknowledged by the said Sephen Redding and ordered to be certified for registration.

It appearing to the satisfaction of the court now here that Augusta L. Jones late of this County hath departed this life intestate, and that Jane Jones widow of said decedent, Relinquish her Right of administration on his Estate to Alexander Thompson and Mansfield Husband and the court thereupon appoint the said Alexander Tompson & Mayfield Husband administrators of the Estate of said Augustus L. Jones decd. who thereupon was qualified and gave bond and security as the law Directs.

P-207   Monday 16th August 1824

Ordered that Paul Childs, Daniel Goodman & Thomas Clarke be appointed commissioners to allot to Jane Jones widow of the Late Augustus L. Jones decd. so much of his Estate as will be sufficient for the maintainance of her self and family for one year from the time said decedent departed this life, and that they make return of said allotment to the next term of this court.

Ordered that Dewey Bassham be appointed Guardian of Polly Hodges and Robert Hodges, Infant Orphans of Robert Hodges decd. who gave bond and security as the Law directs.

The last will and Testament of Matthew Muncrief decd. was produced in court and the execution thereof proven by the oaths of Lewis Glaze and David C. George two of the subscribing witnesses thereto and ordered to be Recorded and thereupon David Crook and Larkin Cardin the Executors therein named appeared in court and were qualified and gave bond & Security according to Law.

A Deed of conveyance from Thomas Read to Asa A. Estes for twelve hundred acres of land was produced in court & the Execution thereof acknowledged by the said Thomas Read and ordered to be certified for Registration.

155

Stirling Graves, William C. Graves, William Bricken and William Chapman who were appointed at last term a Jury to view lay off and ascertain the value of one acre of land, on one side of Richland Creek belonging to the heirs of John Samuel decd. and also one achre on the oppisite side of said Creek belonging to Daniel Frazer according to the petition of said Frazer for the purpose of building a mill, made their return into court that they had proceeded to the premises, and valued the land according to order, and that they find one acre of land belonging to the heirs aforesaid to be worth five dollars, and also one acre on the opposite side, to be worth five dollars, and the said Daniel Frazer now here paid into court for the benefit of said heirs the sum of five dollars the valuation of said land. It is therefore ordered and adjudged by the court that the said Daniel Frazer be permitted to Build a Mill according to the petition, and that the Right of said acre of land belonging to said heirs be vested in the said Daniel Frazer his heirs and assigns for ever, provided he should commence building said mill in one year from this time or show some satisfactory reasons to the court for such failure, the said Daniel Frazer Paying the costs that has occured in this case.

Received the above five dollars the 27th August 1821 .

Charles G. Wilcox
Stephen Anderson
Justice Esq.

P-208   Monday 16th August 1824

Ordered that John McNight, Henry Loyd, Samuel McNight, Seth J. Williamson, Edmund Williamsons, and Harbard Harwell, or any five of them be appointed a Jury to view that part of the Fayettsville road which lies between the top of the hill east of Isaac Williams to the County line near Edmund Williamsons and see if it be proper to turn said road and that they make report to the next term of this court.

Ordered that a part of the Lawrence Court house road which lies between Isaac Purvis's and the County line be opened agreable to the report of a Jury appointed at the last term of this court to view and mark out the same and that Zadok Hudson be appointed an overseer to open and keep in repair the same with the hands in the following bounds, Towit, Begining at the mouth of Schoats Creek running up Weakley Creek on the west side to a point opposite the Baptist meeting house thence crossing said Creek so as to include Lawson Hobson and John Buckhanan thence to the County line.

Ordered that Dempsey Taylor be appointed overseer to keep in repair the road called Johnsons road from the Maury County line at the head of Shugar fork crossing big creek at Coldwells Mill to the Lawrence County line, and that he have under his direction for the purpose of keeping the same in repair the hands in the following bounds, Towit, All west of Tomlins Branch to appint opposite Blinds Pond thence to the middle fork of Big creek at the mouth of Allens Powder Mill Branch thence up the same to the Lawrence County line thence with that line to Maury County line.

Ordered that the court be adjourned untill tomorrow morning 9 oclock.

John H. Camp
Thomas Marks
Paul Chiles

P-209 Tuesday 17th August 1824

Court met according to adjournment Present John H. Camp,)
                                   Paul Chiles   ) Esquire Jus-
                                   Thomas Marks   ) tice of the
) peace for Giles
) County.

The Sheriff of this County returned into court the names of the following persons Summoned to attend as grand and petit Jurors at this term pursuant to an order of the last term of this court a copy of which issued to the said Sheriff, towit, Harvy Grant, Alexander Baldridge, William D. Jennings, William Ezell, Henry Croft, Allen Abernathy, Hugh D. Adams, David Jones, Richard Long, Joshua Horn, James H. Graves, Charles Dever, John W. O. Graves, John R. Abernathy, Henry Miller, Richard Bentley, Elisha White, James Walker, Stephen Anderson, Holeman R. Fowler, and Daniel Leatherman, of whom Elisha White foreman, Stephen Anderson, Joshua Horn, Archibald Smith, William Ezell, Allen Abernathy, Henry T. Croft, Hugh Adams, James Coldwell, Alexander Baldridge, Henry White, John W. O. Graves, and George Garret were Elected empannelled and sworn a Grand Jury of inquest for the body of this County, who having received their charge withdrew to consider of their presentment.

James K. Murrah a constable of this County was sworn to attend on the Grand Jury at the present term of this court.

Ordered that Henry Kerr & William D. Jennings be released from serving on the Jury at the present term of this court also that James H. Graves & Daniel Leatherman be released from serving as Jurors of this court untill Thursday next.

A Power of Attorney from Edward M. Brown, Lewis H. Brown, Thomas W. Grubbs, & Lucy D. Grubbs to John Brown for certain property therein named was produced in court and the execution thereof acknowledged by the said Edward M. Brown Lewis H. Brown, & Thomas W. Grubbs, to be their Act & deed, and thereupon John H. Camp & Thomas Marks two of the Acting Justices of the Peace in & for this County, were appointed to take the privy examination of the said Lucy D. Grubbs touching the execution of said Power of attorneys who returned said Examination, which is ordered to be certified.

A Deed of conveyance from Lewis H. Brown to John Brown was produced in court and the execution thereof acknowledged by the said Lewis H. Brown and ordered to be certified.

P-210 Tuesday 17th August 1824

157

Edmund Shelton Plt.) Certiorari
Against)
Nathaniel Young Deft.) On motion of the plaintiff this cause is
) ordered to be continued untill the next
term, and it is further ordered that a commission issue to any two of the
Acting Justices of the Peace of this County to take the deposition of James
Shelton Debencess to be read in evidence on the trial of this cause upon
the plaintiffs giving to the Defendant Five days notice of the time and
place taking said deposition.

A release from David Simms & Dorothy Simms to John H. Camp of certain
property in sd. release mentioned, was produced in court and the Execution
thereof proven by the oaths of John Bass & Samuel Fain the witnesses thereto
and ordered to be certified for registration.

A Power of attorneys from Thomas Martin to Rivers & Larpley for certain
property therein named was produced in court and the execution thereof proven
by the oaths of Thomas P. Jones the witnesses thereto and ordered to be
certified for registration.

A Deed of conveyance from Gabriel Bumpass, Tyree Rodes, Maxamillian H.
Buchanan & Nathaniel Moody commissioners of the Town of Pulaski; to Thomas
Harwell, for lot No. 86 in sd. Town was produced in court and the execution
thereof proven by the oaths of John W. Graves & Thomas D. Davenport two of
the witnesses thereto and ordered to be certified for registration.

A Deed of conveyance from Nathaniel Young to Henry Hagen for two hundred acres of land was produced in court and the execution thereof acknowledged
by the said Nathaniel Young and ordered to be certified for registration.

The Grand Jury returned into court the following indictments Towit, The
State against Everard Grant for an affray with & an assault and battery on
the body of John Humedy, on which is indorsed "A true Bill" The same against
Gerard Long, Milford Long, Willis Terry Wm. D. Jennings & Thomas Dillon,
for an affray with & an assault and Battery on the body of Gabriel W. Payne
& Edwin Harden on (P-211) which is indorsed "A true Bill" and withdrew
to consider of Further presentments.

George M. Ridley ... Plt.) In Debt
Against)
Rebecca Kyle Admrx. &) On the application of the plain-
Claiborn Kyle Admr. of) Defts. tiff It is ordered that the
Wm. Kyle decd.) original Writs in this case be
) answered by striking out the
words "to him they owe &" and adding the word "They" upon the plaintiffs
paying the court of this amendment.

The State .. Plt.) Upon a indictment for an affray with & an as-
Against) sault and battery on the body of Gerard W.
Jerard Long) Payne and Edwin Harden.

Milford Long Defts.) Gabriel W. Payne & John McCormick came into
Willis Terry) court and acknowledged themselves indebted to
Wm. D. Jennings) the State of Tennessee in the Sum of two hund-
& Thomas Dillon) red Dollars each, to be levied of their goods
) and chattles lands and tenments to the use of
the State, to be void on condition that the said Grabriel W. Payne appear
here on the fourth day of the next term of this court and prosecute and
give evidence in behalf of the State against the defendants in this case
and not depart without leave of this court.

Hugh Terrance Plt.)
  Against) In Case
John Keenan Deft.)
) This day came the parties by their attornies
and thereupon came a Jury of good and Lawful
men, Towit, David Jones, Richard Long, Aaron Smith, Claiborn Kyle, Lewis
B. Morris, Philip T. McCabe, John McKnight, Joshua Ruckman, Robert Adams,
Hanner Turner, Morgan Brown, and Jeptha Ezell, who being elected tried and
sworn well and truly to try the issue joined between the parties in this
case upon their oaths do say that the defendant did not assume upon himself
in manner and form as the plaintiff in declaring against him hath alleged
It is therefore considered by the court that the Defendant go hence without
day and recover of the plaintiff his costs by him about his Defence in this
behalf expended. From which judgment the plaintiff prayed an appeal to the
honorable the circuit court to be held for the County of Giles and having
entered into bond & security according to Law the same was granted him.

P-212   Tuesday 17th August 1824

Hannah Underwood plaintiff)
  against) In Traver
James K. Murrah Defendant)
) This day came the parties by their attornies & thereupon came a Jury of
good and Lawful men, Towit, David Jones, Richard Long, Richard Bentley, AAro
Smith, Lewis B. Morris, Phillip T. McCabe, John McKnight, Robert Adams,
Joshua Ruckman, Morgan Brown, John Hamlett and John B. McCanlass, who being
elected tried and sworn well and truly to try the issue Joined between the
parties in this case having heard a part of the evidence and permitted to
disperce to meet again tomorrow morning 9 O'Clock.

Vaulton Childers plaintiff)
  Against) Covenant
Willis W. Cole Defendant)
) This day came as well the plaintiff
by his attorney as the defendant in his
proper person, and said Defendant withdraws the plea by him heretofore
filed in this case, and saith he cannot gainsay the plaintiffs action
against him nor but that the plaintiff hath sustained damages by occasion
of the nonperformance of the covenant in the declaration mentioned to the
amount of three hundred and sixty seven dollars and forty cents, and agree
that Judgment may be entered against him in favor of the plaintiff for that
amount with costs. It is therefore with the consent of the plaintiff considered by the court that the plaintiff recover of the defendant the amount
of his damages, aforesaid in form aforesaid agreed and his costs by him
about his suit in this behalf expended.
  Whereupon the plaintiff by his attorney agrees that execution as on this
Judgment be stayed untill the first day of May next.

James McDonald Plt.   )   Motion
       Against   )
George Vandever Deft.   )   This day came the plaintiff by Jones &
)   Flournoy his attornies and moved the court
now here for Judgment (p-213) against the defendant for the sum of
sixty eight dollars, and eighty three cents which he hath paid as Security
for the defendant and it not appearing to the satisfaction of the court
from the receipt of the constable to whom the same was paid whether the
plaintiff was principal or Security, a Jury was thereupon empannelled to
try that fact Towit, David Jones, Richard Long, Richard Butley, Aaron
Smith, Lewis B. Morris, Phillip McCabe, Robert Adams, Joshua Rickman,
Morgan Brown, Jeptha Ezell, William Jones & John Hamblett, who being Elected
tried and sworn well and truly to enquire as aforesaid upon their oaths do
say that the plaintiff paid on the 6th day of August 1824 to Annanias Oliver
a constable of this County the aforesaid sum of sixty eight Dollars and
eighty three cents as security for the defendant on an execution which issued on a Judgment which Lockhart & White Assee of Fountain Lester recovered
against said George Vandever & James McDonald before .... A Justice
of the Peace for this County on the .....day of.....182...On a note originally executed to Fountain Lester by the said George Vandever and the said
James McDonald his said security, which note was afterwards assigned to the
sd. Lockhart & White--It is therefore considered by the court that the plaintiff recover of the said defendant the aforesaid sum of sixty eight dollars
& eighty three cents together with the costs of this motion.

        Ordered that court be adjourned till tomorrow morning 9 O'Clock.

                                                Richard McGee
                                                John H. Camp
                                                John Young

P-214   Wednesday 18th August 1824

Court met according to adjournment Present John H. Camp,) Esquires Justice
                                   Richard McGee &   ) of the Peace for
                                   John Young   ) Giles County.

        A Bill of sale from John C. Underwood to Thomas Underwood for certain
property therein named was produced in court, the execution thereof proven
by the oaths of Albert Underwood and Virginia Underwood two of the witnesses
thereto and ordered to be certified for registration.

        A Deed of conveyance from Jarret Manefee to Daulton Childress for ......
acres of land was produced in court and the execution thereof proven by the
oaths of Alfred M. Harris & William H. Field the witnesses thereto and is
ordered to be certified for registration.

        A Deed of conveyance from John N. Smith to Enoch Simpson for thirty acres
six & a half poles of land was produced in court and proven by the oaths of
O. T. Stribling, and Wilton F. L. Jenkins the witnesses thereto and ordered
to be certified for registration.

The Grand Jury returned into court an Indictment of the State against Jarret Long, and Thomas Dillon for affray with an assault and battery on the body of Grabriel W. Payne & Edwin Hardin, on which is endorsed" a True Bill" The same against against John Kennedy for an affray with & an assault and battery on the body of Everard Garret on which is indorsed "A true Bill" and withdrew to consider of further presentments.

A Power of attorney from Shadrack Harwell to Benjamin Scoggin for certain purposes therein named was produced in court and the execution thereof acknowledged by the said Shadrack Harwell and ordered to be certified.

A Power of attorney from Shadrack Harwell to Embrier Merrit for certain purposes therein named was produced in court and the execution thereof acknowledged by the said Shadrack Harwell and ordered to be certified.

A Plat and certificate for fifteen acres of land in the name of Ralph Graves and an assignment thereon from Mary Flournoy to James B. Kimbro was produced in court (p-215) and the Execution thereof proven by the oaths of Henry Hagen and Charles C. Abernathy the witnesses thereto and ordered to be certified.

Hannah Underwood Plt.) In Trover
    Against)
James K. Murrah Deft.) This day came the parties by their attornies
) and thereupon came the Jury, who were sworn on yesteday well & truly to try the issue joined between the parties in this case, who having heard the balance of the evidence & part of the argument of counsel were permitted to disperse to meet again tomorrow morning Eight O'Clock.

Ordered that court be adjourned till tomorrow morning Eight O'Clock.

                              John H. Camp
                              Paul Chiles
                              E. D. Jones

P-216 Thursday 19th August 1824

Court met according to adjournment Present John H. Camp) Esquires Justices of the Peace for the County of Giles.
                              Paul Chiles)
                              & Edward D. Jones)

A Deed of conveyance from John T. Westmoreland to William Jones for sixty one and a half acres of land was produced in court and the execution thereof acknowledged by the sd. John T. Westmoreland and ordered to be certified for registration.

A Deed of conveyance from James McCormick to Wythe Simms for two hundred and forty six acres was produced in court and the execution thereof proven by the oaths of John H. Camp one of the witnesses thereto.

The administration of the estate of Philmer Green decd. returned into court an Inventory of the property not perishable of the Estate of sd. Green and of the money's &c Belongins to said Estate which is ordered to be recorded.

The administrator of the Estate of Philmer Green decd. returned into court and Inventory and account of sale of the perishable property belonging to the sd. Estate which is ordered to be recorded.

A Bill of sale from Agatha Garrett Executrix & Greenberry Garrett Executor of Eli Garrett decd. to Lewis Garrett for certain property therein named was produced in court and proven by the oath of Aaron V. Brown one of the witnesses thereto and ordered to be certified for registration.

The State Plt.) Upon a presentment for an affray with & an as-
Against) sault & battery on the body of Robert Wells.
William Pond Deft.)
) This day came as well the Solicitor General for the State, as also the defendant in his proper person who being charged on the presentment in this case pleads guilty and because he will not contend with the State agrees to submit himself to the Justice and mercy of the court –
It is therefore considered by the court that he make his fine with the State to the amount of one dollar and that he pay the costs of this prosecution and that he be committed to the custody of the Sheriff of this County there to remain till said fine and costs are paid, or that he give security for the payment of the same, and thereupon George Bowers comes into court and undertakes as Security for said Defendant. It is therefore considered by the court that the State recover of the defendant & George Bowers his security the fine and costs aforesaid (p-217) (Thursday 19th August 1824) at least five Justices being present John Defee returned into court two wolf scalps under four months old which were ordered to be burnt.

The State Plt.) Upon an Indictment for an affray with & an
Against) assault & battery on the Body of David Graves.
Thomas Steel Deft.)
) This day came as well the Solicitor General for the State as also the defendant in his proper person who being charged on the Indictment in this case pleads not guilty and for the trial puts himself upon the County and the Solicitor General for the State on the part of the State likewise therefore let a Jury come who as well &c to recognise &c thereupon came a Jury of good and lawful men, Towit, William D. Jennings, Isaac Hooks, Joseph Alsup, David Stockton, Felix Goff, Thomas Bratton, John K. Luker, Asa A. Estes, John Elliss, James Burnes, George Bowers, & Edward Garland, who being elected tried and sworn well and truly to try the issue of traverse between the State and said defendant upon their oaths do say that the defendant is not guilty in manner and form as he is charged in the bill of Indictment. It is therefore considered by the court that that the

defendant be acquited and discharged from the affray & assault and battery aforesaid and that he go hence without day.

The State Plaintiff)
Against) Upon a Indictment for an affray with an
Thomas Steel Defendant) assault an battery on the body of David
) Graves.

The Defendant in this case having been acquitted on the trial on the merits by a Jury, It is ordered that Judgment be entered up against the County of Giles in favor of the several claimants on the part of the State for all costs to which they are entitled, and that the Clerk certify the same to the trustee of Giles County for payment.

The State Plt.)
Against) Upon an Indictment for an affray with & an as-
Thomas Steel Deft.) sault & battery on the body of David Graves.
)

Archibald McKissack who was summoned to appear at the present term of this court and give evidence in behalf of the State against the defendant in this case being solemnly called came not but made default. It is therefore considered by the court that the Judgment Ni. Si. for the sum of one hundred & twenty five dollars according to the tenor of said Subpoena be entered up against him and that a Soirefacias issue against him returnable to the next Term of this Court.

A Deed of conveyance from Lewis H. Brown, Sheriff of Giles County to Gabriel Bumpass for two hundred acres of land was produced in court and the execution thereof acknowledged by sd. Sheriff and ordered to be certified for registration.

P-218   Thursday 19th Agust 1824

The State Plt.)
Against) Upon a Indictment for an affray with an
John E. Mayfield Deft.) assault and battery on the body of Robert
) Stelle.

This day came the Solicitor General for the State, and the defendant altho solemnly called came not but made default. It is therefore considered by the court that a Judgment Ni. Si. for the sum of two hundred & fifty dollars according to the tenor of his recognizance be entered up against him and that a Soire facias issue against him and that a Soirefacias issue against him returnable to the next Term of this court.

The State Plt.)
Against) Upon an Indictment for an affray with &
John E. Mayfield deft.) an assault an battery on the body of
) Robert Stelle.

Isaac S. Chrisman who was boung in a recognizance for the appearance of the aforesaid defendant being solemnly called and required to bring with him the body of said defendant, but made default. It is therefore considered by the court that a Judgment Ni. Si. for the sum of one hundred & twenty five dollars according to the tenor of his recognizance be entered up against him and that a Soire facias issue against him returnable to the next court.

The State Plt.   )   Upon a Indictment for an affray with &
    Against   )   an Assault & battery on the body of Robert
John E. Mayfield Deft.   )   Stelle.
)   William Mayfield who was bound in a recog-
nizance for the appearance of the aforesaid defendant being solemnly called
and required to bring with him the body of said defendant but made default.
It is therefore considered by the court that a Judgment Ni Si. for the sum
of one hundred & twenty five dollars according to the tenor of the recognizance be entered up against him, and that a Scire facias issue against
him returnable to the next court.

The State Plt.   )   Upon an Indictment for an affray with & an
    Against   )   assault & battery on the body of Bailey Davis
James Hardy Deft.   )
)   This day came as well the Solicitor General
for the State as also the defendant in his proper person who being charged
on the indictment in this case pleads not guilty and for this trial puts
himself upon the Country and the Solicitor General for the State on the part
of the State likewise, therefore let a Jury come who as well &c. and to
recognize &c and thereupon came a Jury of good and lawful men Towit, William
D. Jenning, Isaac Hooks, Joseph Alsup, David Stookston, Felix Goff, Thomas
Bratton, John K. Luker, Asa A. Estes, John Ellias, James Burnes, George
Bowers & Edward   (p-219)   Garland, who being elected tried and sworn
well and truly to try the issue of traverse between the State and said defendant upon their oaths do say that the defendants guilty in manner & form
as he is charged in the bill of indictments. It is therefore considered
by the court that he make his fine with the State to the amount of one dollar, and that he pay the cost of this prosecution and that he be committed
to the custody of the Sheriff of this County, there to remain till said
fine and costs be paid, or that he give security for the payment of the
same and thereupon Baker P. Potts, comes into court and undertakes as security for said defendants.
    It is therefore considered by the court that the State recover of the
said defendant and Baker P. Potts, his security the fine and costs aforesaid.

The State Plt.   )   Upon an Indictment for an affray with &
    Against   )   an assault & battery on the body of John
Robert G. Steele Deft.   )   E. Mayfield.
)   This day came as well the Solicitor
General for the State as also the defendant in his proper person, who being
charged in the Indictment in this case pleads not Guilty and for his trial
puts himself upon his Country and the Solicitor General for the State on
the part of the State likewise therefore let a Jury come who as well &c to
recognize &c and thereupon came a Jury of good and lawful men, Towit, Elisha
White, Hugh Adams, George Grant, Alexander Baldridge, Henry White, Wm. D.
Jennings, Archibald Smith, Buckner Young, Francis Mabrey, Henry Pende, James
Taylor, & Luke Little - who being elected tried and sworn well and truly
to try the issue of traverse between the State and said Defendant, upon
their oaths do say that said defendant is not guilty in manner & form as he
is charged in the Indictment. It is therefore considered by the court that
the defendant be acquitted and discharged from the affray & assault and
battery aforesaid and that he go hence without day.

The State Plt.	Upon an Indictment for an affray with & an
Against	assault and battery on the body of John E.
Robert G. Steele Deft.	Mayfield.

The defendant in this case having been acquitted on the trial on the meritts by a Jury. It is ordered that a Judgment be entered up against the County of Giles in favor of the several claimants on the part of the State for all costs to which they are entitled, and that the Clerk certify the same to the Trustee of this County for payment.

The Grand Jury returned into court an indictment against Phillip T. McCabe, on which is indorsed "Not a true Bill" and withdrew to consider of further presentmenst.

P-220 Thursday 19th August 1824

The State . . . Plt.	Scire Facias
Against	
Thomas W. McKnight Deft.	This day came as well the solicitor General for the State as the defendant in his

proper person and for reasons shewn to the court by the said defendant. It is ordered that he be discharged from the forfeiture heretofore taken against him. On the payment of all the costs and that execution thereof be awarded against him.

The State Plaintiff	Sci facias
Against	
Thomas Hardy Deft.	This day came as well the Solicitor General for the State as the defendant in his proper person,

and for Reasons shewn to the court by the said defendant it is ordered that he be discharged, from the forfeiture heretofore taken against him on the payment of all costs, and thereupon Baker B. Potts came into court and undertook as security for the defendant for the payment of the costs aforesaid It is therefore considered by the court that the State recover of the said Defendant and the said Baker B. Potts the amount of the costs aforesaid and execution thereof be awarded.

The State Plt.	Upon an Indictment for an affray with & an
Against	assault & battery on the body of John E.
Robert G. Steele deft.	Mayfield.

Alexander Tarpley who was Summoned to attend at this term and give evidence in behalf of the defendant in this case being solemnly called came not but made default.

It is therefore ordered by the court that a Judgment Ni. Si, be entered up against the defendant in favor of the plaintiff for the sum one hundred and twenty five dollars according to his Subpoena, and that a Scire facias issue against him returnable to the next term of this court.

Hannah Underwood Plt.	In Trover
Against	
James K. Murrah Deft.	This day came the parties by their attornies and thereupon came the Jury who were here-

tofore sworn well and truly to try the issue joined between the parties in this case upon their oaths do say that the defendant is guilty of the trover and convertion in the plaintiffs declaration complained of and they do assess the plaintiffs damages by occasion thereof to five hundred and twenty two dollars & fifty cents – Besides costs It is therefore considered by the court that the plaintiff recover of the said defendant the damages aforesaid in form aforesaid by the Jurors aforesaid assessed, and also his costs by her about her . (Page 21 and 22 gone)

P-223 Friday 20th August 1824

John Bradley . . . Plt.   )   In case.
    Against   )
William D. Jennings Deft.   )   On the application of the plaintiff as
)   on his affidavit herein this cause is ordered to be continued, untill the next term of this court and that a commission issue to any two of the Acting Justice of the peace in & for the County of Madison and State of Alabama to take the deposition of said George H. Malone, Thomas Gilliam & others to be read in evidence on the trial of this cause upon the plaintiff giving to the defendant ten days notice of the time and place of taking the deposition of sd. George H. Malone & Thomas Gilliam and twenty days notice of the time and place of taking the deposition of the others if any

The State Plt.   )   Upon an Indictment for an affray with & an
    Against   )   assault & battery on the body of Thomas Steele.
David Jones Deft.   )
                            Thomas Steele came into court and acknowledged himself indebted to the State of Tennessee the sum of one hundred dollars to be levied of his good and chattles lands and tenments to the use of the State, to be void on condition that he appear here on the fourth day of the next term of this court and prosecute and give evidence in behalf of the State against sd. defendant for an affray with and an assault and battery on the body of sd. Steele and not depart without leave of the court.

The State Plt,   )   Upon an Indictment for an affray with & an
    Against   )   assault & battery on the body of John Kennedy
Edward Garret Deft.)   This day came as well the Solicitor General
)   for the State as also the defendant in his proper person, who being charged on the indictment in this case pleads not guilty, & for his trial puts himself upon his Country, and the Solicitor General for the State on the part of the State, likewise therefore let a Jury come, who as well to to recognize &c and thereupon came a Jury of good and lawful men, Towit, Samuel Smith, Isaac Mason, William C. Rainey, John Philips, Beverly Brown, Richard Long, David Jones, William D. Jennings, John B. McCanless, Felix W. Goff, Nathan Hammet, & Morgan Brown who being elected tried and sworn well and truly to try the issue of Traverse between the State and said defendants upon their oaths do say that the defendant is guilty of an assault & battery as charged in the several courts in this indictment & not guilty of an affray as charged in the first court in the first court in the indictments – therefore it is considered by the court that he make his fine with the State to the amount of five dollars and that he pay the costs of this prosecution, and that he be committed to the custody of the Sheriff of this County thereto remain till said fine & costs be paid – or that he give security for the payment

of the same and thereupon George Garrett comes into court an undertakes (p-224) as security for said Defendant.

It is therefore considered by the court that the State recover of said defendant and sd. George Garret his security, the fine & costs aforesaid.

The Grand Jury returned into court a Bill of Indictments of the State against David Green, for an affray with & an assault & battery on the body of Thomas Steele on which is indorsed "A true Bill" Also a Bill of presentment, State against Samuel Day for an affray with & an assault and Battery on the body of James Downing also a Bill of presentments against Alexander McKinney & Lucy Bolling for open court and notorious Lewdness - and withdrew to consider of further presentments.

A Deed of conveyance from William Wells to John McCormick for one hundred and forty five acres of Land was produced in court and the execution thereof acknowledged by the said William Wells and ordered to be certified for registration.

The State Plt.) Upon an Indictment for an affray with & an as-
 Against) sault & battery of the body of Everard Garrett.
John Kennedy Deft.) This day came as well the Solicitor General for
) the State as also the defendent in his proper
person, who being charged on the indictment in this case pleads guilty and because he will not contend with the State and agrees to submit himself to the Justice and mercy of the court. It is therefore considered by the court that he make his fine with the State to the amount of six & one fourth cents and that he pay the costs of this prosecution, and that he be committed to the custody of the Sheriff of this County thereto remain till sd. fine and costs be paid or that he give security for the payment of the same - and thereupon Lewis H. Brown comes into court and acknowledged himself as security for said Defendant - It is therefore considered by the court that the State recover of the defendant and sd. Lewis H. Brown his security the fine and costs aforesaid.

Plency Melton Assee &c. Plt.)   In Debt
 Against)
Alexander S. Jones Deft.) This day came as well the plaintiff by
) his attorney as also the defendant in
his proper person, who says he cannot gainsay the plaintiffs action against him nor but that he doth owe him the sum of of one hundred and thirty dollar debt together with the sum of three dollars & fifty seven & a half cents, the damages which the plaintiff hath sustained by reason of the (p-225) Detention of sd. debt Besides costs. It is therefore considered by consent of plaintiffs attorney by the court that the plaintiff recover of the said Defendants his debt aforesaid together with his damages aforesaid in form aforesaid agreed, and also his costs by him about his suit in this behalf expended - From which Judgment the Defendant prayed an appeal to the honorable the Circuit Court to be held for the County of Giles, and having Executed bond and security according to Law the same was granted him.

The State Plt.)   Upon Scire Facias
 Against)
William Ball Deft.)

167

This day came as well the Solicitor General for the State and the defendant altho Solemnly called came not but made default. It is therefore considered by the court that the Judgment Ni. Si. heretofore taken against him for the sum of one hundred & twenty five dollars be made final against him, and that execution thereof be awarded.

The State . . . . Plt.) Se.
 Against)
Alexander Tarpley Deft.) This day came as well the Solicitor General for the State as the defendant in
his proper person and for reasons shown to the court by the defendant. It is ordered that he be released from the forfeiture taken against him at this term, on the payment of all costs, and that execution for the same be awarded against him.

The Trustee of Waterloo Plt.) In Debt
 Against)
John Paul Executor of)Defts.) This day came the parties by their
John Paul deceased) attornies and thereupon came a
) Jury of good and Lawful men, Towit,
Elisha White, Henry White, Richard Long, Archibald Smith, William D. Jennings Buckner Young, David Jones, Felix W. Goff, Henry Peden, David Stockton, well and truly to try the issue Joined between the parties in this case upon their oaths to say that they find that the defendants testator nor the defendant hath not paid the whole of the Debt in the writing obligatory in the declaration mentioned the plaintiffs in their replication have alledged, but there remains unpaid a Ballance of said debt to the amount of ninety two dollars and seventy five cents, and that the plaintiffs have sustained damages by occasion thereof to amount of four dollars and sixty cents, and that the defendant hath fully administered all & singular the goods & chattles Rights & credits of the said John Paul decd. which have come to his hand to be administered (p-226) Except the sum of forty Eight dollars. It is therefore considered by the court that the plaintiffs recover of the defendant the Balance of their debt aforesaid together with their damages aforesaid by the Jurors aforesaid in form aforesaid assessed and their costs by them about their suit in this behalf expended - to be levied of the goods & chattles rights and credits of the said John Paul Senr., decd. in the hands of said defendant so far as they will go.

Stirling C. & Eldridge Plt. B. Robertson) Original Attach't.
 Against) This day came the
Isaac Crow . . . . Deft.) parties by their at-
) tornies and thereupon
came a Jury of good and lawful men, Towit, John Pillow, Jeptha Ezell, William Sanders, Joseph Alsup, John B. Goldberry, John Hamblett, Robert Adams, David Stockton, David Jones, Allen H. Luker, John K. Luker, and Joseph B. Pillow, who being elected tried and sworn well and truly to try the issue joined between the parties in this case upon their oaths do say that they find said issue in favor of plaintiffs and assess his damages to eighty four dollars and ninety cents, Besides costs. It is therefore considered by the court that the plaintiffs recover of said defendant the damages aforesaid in form aforesaid by the Jurors aforesaid assessed and also their costs by them about their suit in this behalf expended.

Ordered that court be adjourned till tomorrow morning nine oclock.

Paul Chiles
A. McKissack
A. Black

P-227 Saturday Morning 21st August 1824

Court met according to adjournment Present Alexander Black,) Esquires
                                    Archibald McKnight   ) Justices
                                    Paul Chiles   ) of the peace
) for Giles
) County.

Ordered that James Perry, Thomas Martin, & Benjamin Edwards, be appointed commissioners to settle with the Executors of Bethy Manefee decd. and make report to the present term of this court.

The commissioners who were appointed to settle with the executors of Bethy Menefee decd. made report of said settlement which is ordered to be recorded.

The State . . . . Plt.   )   This day came as well the Solicitor
       Against   )   General for the State as the defendant
Archibald McKissack Deft.   )   in his proper person, and for reasons
)   shewn to the court by the defendant.
It is ordered that he be released from the forfeiture taken against him at this term on the payment of all costs, and that execution be awarded against him for the Same.

A Deed of mortgage from Ralph Graves to James Perry & German Lester for certain property therein named was produced in court and the execution thereof proven by the oaths of Henry Hagen and Nathaniel G. Nye the witnesses thereto and ordered to be certified for registration.

Ordered that Alfred M. Harris & Gorman Lester executors of Bethy Menefee decd. be allowed the sum of twenty two dollars and eighty nine cents for the settlement of the said Estate.

A Deed of conveyance from Littleburry Adams to Reuben Freeman for twenty acres of land was produced in court and the execution thereof fully proven by the oath of John Nevarre, the other witnesses thereto and ordered to be certified for registration.

A Bill of sale from Thomas C. Porter to James Perry for certain property therein named was produced in court and the execution thereof proven by the oaths of Nathaniel G. Nye the witnesses thereto and ordered to be certified for registration.

A Bill of sale from Nathaniel Young to James Perry for certain property therein named was produced in court & the execution thereof acknowledged by sd. Young & ordered to be certified for registration.

P-228   Saturday 21st August 1824

A Bill of sale from Nathaniel Young to James Perry for certain property therein named was produced in court & the execution thereof acknowledged by sd. Young & ordered to be certified for registration.

A Deed of conveyance from Nathaniel Young to James Perry for lot No. 26 in Pulaski was produced in court and the execution thereof acknowledged by the said Nathaniel Young and ordered to be certified for registration.

A Bill of sale from Robert G. Steele to James Perry for certain property therein named was produced in court and the execution thereof acknowledged by the said Steele and ordered to be certified for registration.

The State Plt.
Against
John E. Mayfield, deft.

Upon an Indictment for an affray with & an assault & battery on the body of Robert Steele.

This day came as well the Solicitor General for the State as also the defendant in his proper person, who being charged on the Indictment in this case pleads guilty and because he will not contend with the State agrees to submit himself to the Justice and mercy of the court.
It is therefore considered by the court that he make is fine with the State to the amount of one dollar and that he pay the costs of this prosecution, and that he be committed to the custody of the Sheriff of this County there to remain till said fine and costs be paid, or that he give security for the payment of the same, and thereupon William W. Thornton came into court and undertook as security for said defendant - It is therefore considered by the court that the State recover of said John E. Mayfield & William W. Thornton his security the fine and costs aforesaid.

The State Plt.
Against
John E. Mayfield Deft.

Upon an Indictment for an affray with & an assault & battery on the body of R. G. Steele.
This day came as well the Solicitor General for the State as the defendant in his proper person, and for reasons shewn to the court by the defendant It is ordered that he be released from the forfeiture taken against him at this term upon the payment of all costs and that Execution be awarded against him for the same.

P-229   Saturday 21st August 1824

The State . . . . . Plt.
Against
Isaac S. Chrisman Deft.

This day came as well the Solicitor General for the State as the defendant in his proper person, and for reasons shewn to the court by the
defendant. It is ordered that he be released from the forfeiture taken

against him at this term upon the payment of all costs - and that execution be awarded against him for the same.

The State . . . Plt.) This day came as well the Solicitor Gen-
Against) eral for the State as the defendant in
William Mayfield Deft.) his proper person, and for reasons shewn
) to the court by the Defendant It is
ordered that he be released from the forfeiture taken against him at this term, upon the payment of all costs, and that execution be awarded against him for the same.

James Perry for the use of &c Plt.) In Debt
Against)
Alexander S. Jones . . . Deft.) This day came as well the plain-
) tiff by his attorney as also
the defendant in his proper person, who saith he can not gainsay the plaintiffs action against him nor but that he doth owe him the sum of one hundred & fifty nine dollars, Eighty and a half cents Debt together with the sum of five Dollars & fifty nine cents damages which the plaintiff hath sustained by occasion of the detention of sd. debt - Besides costs. It is therefore by consent of plaintiffs attorney considered by the court that the plaintiff recover of said defendant his debt aforesaid, together with his damages aforesaid in form aforesaid agreed, and also his costs by him about his suit in this behalf expended - From which Judgment the defendant prayed an appeal to the honorable the Circuit Court to be held for the County of Giles and having executed Bond and security according to Law the same was granted him.

The Grand Jury returned into court a Bill of Presentment against Bailey Davis & David Stockton for an affray also a Bill of Indictment against William Tinnen for an assault and battery on the body of a slave named Amos and retired to consider of futher presentment.

Ordered that the following tax list be received and the double tax thereon remitted, Towit,
John Childers heirs 1360 acres land, Richland Creek.

P-230   Saturday 21th August 1824

Samuel Smith & wife Plt.) Petition
Against)
John Porter . . . . Deft.) On the application of the Defendant and
) his having filed his affidavit herein
this cause is ordered to be continued, and that a commission issue to any two of the Acting Justices of the peace in & for the County of Logan & State of Kentucky to take the deposition of John Breathith, Cardwell Breathith, Samuel Wilson, & Isaac Browning, also that a commission issue to any two of the Acting Justices of the Peace in and for the County of Maury this State to take the deposition of Joseph Porter, and also that a that a commission issue to any two of the Acting Justice of the Peace in and for the County of Lauderdale and State of Alabama to take the deposition of

Doctor Berry, all of said depositions when taken to be read in evidence on the trial of this cause, upon giving to the plaintiff twenty days notice of the time and place of taking all depositions out of the State and 10 days notice of the time and place of taking those in the State

William Gholson Plaintiff)   In Covenant
Against)
William Watson Defendant) On the application of the defendant and he having filed his affidavit herein, this cause is ordered to be continued - and that a commission issue to any two of the Acting Justice of the peace in and for the County of Madison & State of Alabama to take the deposition of Claxton Lightfoot, & Phillips Lightfoot, and also that a commission issue to any two of the Acting Justice of the peace in and for the County of Lawrence & State of Alabama to take the deposition of John C. Doughtry, all of which depositions when taken to be read in evidence on the trial of this cause, upon giving to the plaintiffs attorney twenty days notice of the time and place of taking said depositions.

William Gholson Plt.)   In Covenant
Against)
William Watson Deft.) On the application of the plaintiff and he having filed his affidavit herein, leave is given him to take the deposition of Kinchen Harris Instanter & when taken to be read in evidence on the trial of this cause.

P-231   Saturday 21st August 1824

Mahulda Brown ... Plt.)   In Case
Against)
Archibald McKissack) Defts.) This day came the parties by their
& Thomas B. Haynie) attornies and thereupon came a Jury
) of good and lawful men, Towit, David Jones, Richard Long, James B. Riggs, Joseph Alsup, Robert Adams, John B. Goldsberry, John Johnson, Frederick Harwell, Quinton Shannon, Samuel Smith, Benjamin Williams and Isaac Crowder, who being elected tried and sworn well well and truly to try the issue joined between the parties in this case upon their oaths do say that the defendants are guilty of the trover and conversion in the plaintiffs declaration complained of and they do assess the plaintiffs damages by occasion thereof to thirty five dollars - Besides costs. It is therefore considered by the court that the plaintiff recover of said defendants the amount of his damages aforesaid in form aforesaid by the Jurors aforesaid assessed and also his costs by her about her suit in this behalf expended.

Thomas Martin) Plt.)   Certiorari
Surviving Partner)
Against)
David Browning Deft.) This day came the parties by their attornies and thereupon came a Jury of good and Lawful men, Towit, David Jones, Richard Long, James B. Riggs, Isaac Mayfield, Joseph Alsup, Robert, Adams John B. Goldsberry, John Johnson, David Stockton, Frederick Harwell, Joseph Rickman, & Quinton Shannon, who being elected tried and sworn well and truly to try the matter in controversy between the parties in this case, upon their oaths do say that the defendant is not indebted to the plaintiff any

thing - It is therefore considered by the court that the defendant go hence without day and recover of the said plaintiff his costs by him about his defence in this behalf expended.

Ordered that court be adjourned untill Monday Morning nine oclock.

H. Hagen
Wm. Pepper
Thos. Marks

P-232 Monday Morning 23rd August 1824

Court met according to adjournment Present, Henry Hagen,) Esquire Justices of
William B. Pepper) the Peace
Thomas Marks) for the
) County of Giles.

Ordered that the following tax list be received by the court and the double tax thereon remitted, Towit, Henry Cross, 330 acres Land
2 slaves
Thomas Brown 70 acres land
1 White Poll
Mason Moss 1 White Poll
Joanna Moss 52 Acres of land
1 Slave.

Robert Stewart for the use for &c Plt.) In Debt
Against)
Lewis H. Brown . . . . Deft.) This day came the parties
) by their attornies and
thereupon came a Jury of good and Lawful men, towit, David Jones, Elisha White, Allen Abernathy, Hugh Adams, Henry T. Croft, Alexander Baldridge, Henry White, Archibald Smith, John W. O. Graves, James Caldwell, Joshua Horn and George Garrett, who being elected tried and sworn well and truly to try the issue joined between the parties in this case, upon their oaths do say that they find said issue in favor of plaintiff and assess his damages by reason of the detention of the debt in this declaration mentioned to sixty one dollars besides costs. It is therefore considered by the court that the plaintiff recover of the defendant the sum of one hundred & fifty seven dollars the balance of his debt aforesaid together with the damages assessed and also his costs about his suit in this behalf expended.

Lyddall Wilkinson Plt.) In Debt
Against)
John C. Underwood Deft.) This day came the parties by their attornies and it appearing to the satisfaction
of the court now here that there is such a record as in said plaintiffs declaration is mentioned. It is therefore considered by the court that said plaintiff recover of said Defendant the sum of nine hundred & seventy eight dollars & sixty two cents the debt in the declaration mentioned at the rate of six per centum per annum from the 6th of October 1823, It being the

time of rendering Judgment by the Circuit Court of Madison County, Alabama in favor of said (p-233) plaintiff against said Defendant and the amount of said Judgment inclusive of costs together with his costs by him about his suit in this behalf expended.

Robert Stewart for the use &c Plt.) In Debt
  Against)
Lewis H. Brown . . . . . Deft.) From the Judgment of the court
) in this case rendered the defendant prayed an appeal to the honorable the Circuit Court to be held for the County of Giles, and having executed a bond and security according to Law the same was granted him.

Smith Hunt Guardian &c Plt.) In Debt
  Against)
German Lester &) Deft.) This day came the parties by their at-
Fountain Lester)   torneys and thereupon came a Jury of
) good and Lawful men Towit, David Jones, Elisha White, Allen Abernathy, Hugh Adams, Henry T. Croft, Alexander Baldridge, Henry White, Archibald Smith, John W. O. Graves, James Coldwell, Joshua Horn & George Garrett, who being elected tried and sworn well and truly to try the issue joined between the parties in this case upon their oaths do say that the defendants have not paid the debt in the writing obligatory in the declaration mentioned as the plaintiff in his replication has alleged, and they do assess the plaintiff damages by occasion of the detention of said debt to Eighty Dollars and ninety six cents besides costs. It is therefore considered by the court that the plaintiff recover of the said defendant the sum of three hundred & sixty eighty dollars five and a half cents the amount of his debt aforesaid together with his damages aforesaid in form aforesaid by the Jurors aforesaid assessed, and also his costs about his suit in this behalf expended - From which Judgment the defendant prayed an appeal to the honorable the Circuit Court to be held for the County of Giles, and having executed bond and security according to Law the same was Granted him.

Alfred M. Harris Plt.) In case
  Against)
James L. Hendry Deft.) This day came the parties by their attornies
) and on motion this cause is ordered to be dismissed at the costs of the Defendant. It is therefore considered by the court that the plaintiff recover of said Defendant his costs about his suit in this behalf expended - The plaintiffs attorney agrees that no tax fee is to be charged.

A Deed of conveyance from James W. Camp to Lewis G. Upshaw for Five hundred & forty three acres & fifty five & three fourth poles of land was produced in court & the execution thereof proven by the oaths of Thomas Harwood (p-234) and Robert B. Harney subscribing witnesses thereto and ordered to be certified for registration.

John L. Smith Plt.) In Debt
  Against)
Lawson Hobson Deft.)

This day came the parties by their attornies and thereupon came a Jury of good and lawful men, Towit, David Jones, Elisha White, Allen Abernathy, Hugh Adams, Henry T. Croft, Alexander Baldridge, Henry White, Archibald Smith, John W. O. Graves, James Coldwell, Joshua Horn, & George Garrett, who being elected tried and sworn well and truly to try this issue joined between the parties in this case upon their oaths do say that the defendant hath not paid the whole of the debt in the declaration mentioned, and that he has no sett off as the plaintiff in his replication has alleged, but that there remains unpaid a Balance of said Debt, to the amount of one hundred and forty dollars, and they do assess the plaintiffs damages by occasion of the detention thereof to five dollars & fifty cents besides costs. It is therefore considered by the court that the plaintiff recover of said defendant the balance of his debt aforesaid together with his damages aforesaid in form aforesaid by the Jurors aforesaid assessed & his costs about his suit in this behalf expended.

A Plat and sertificate of survey for eight and a half acres of land in the name of William Purnell and an assignment there on from William Purnell to John Henderson was produced in court and partly proven by Henry T. Jones one of the witnesses thereto.

A Plat and sertificate of survey for eight and a half acres of land in the name of William Purnell and an assignment thereon from John Henderson to Robert Harney was produced in court and the execution thereof proven by the oaths of Samuel S. Jones & Lewis H. Brown the witnesses thereto and ordered to be certified.

Fortunatus Jones Plt.)   In Debt
    Against)
Enoch Davis Deft.)
                         This day came the plaintiff by his attorney and ordered that this suit be dismissed. It is therefore considered by the court that the defendant go hence without day, and recover of the plaintiff his costs by him about his defence in this behalf expended.

P-235   Monday 23rd August 1824

Alexander Thompson Plt.)   In Debt
    Against)
Daniel Goodrum Deft.)
                         This day came the parties by their attornie and thereupon came a Jury of good and lawful men, Towit, David Jones, Elisha White, Allen Abernathy, Hugh Adams, Henry T. Croft, Alexander Baldridge, Henry White, Archibald Smith, John W. O. Graves, James Coldwell, Joshua Horn, and George Garrett, who being electe tried and sworn well and truly to try the issue joined between the parties in this case upon their oaths do say that the defendant has not paid the debt in the Writing Obligator in this declaration mentioned and that he has no sett off, as the plaintiff in his replication has alleged, and they do assess the plaintiffs damages by occasion of detention of the same to nine dollars & seventy five cents, besides costs. It is therefore considered by the court that the plaintiff recover of said Defendant the sum of three hundred dollars the amount of his debt aforesaid aforesaid, together with

his damages aforesaid in form aforesaid by the Jurors aforesaid assessed and his costs about his suit in this behalf expended.

Alexander Thompson Plt.) In Debt
    Against)
Daniel Goodrum Deft.) This day came the parties by their attornies
) and thereupon came a Jury of good and lawful men, Towit, David Jones, Elisha White, Allen Abernathy, Hugh Adams, Henry T. Crofts, Alexander Baldridge, Henry White, Archibald Smith, John W. O. Graves, James Coldwell, Joshua Horn, & George H. Garrett, who being elected tried and sworn well and truly to try the issue joined between the parties in this case upon their oaths do say that the defendant has not paid the whole of the debt in the Writing obligatory in the declaration mentioned, and that he has no sett off as the plaintiff in his replication has alleged and they do assess the plaintiffs damages by occasion of the detention of said Balance of Debt to ten Dollars & ninety nine cents, besides costs. It is therefore considered by the court that the plaintiff recover of said defendant the sum of Two hundred & ninety four Dollars & sixteen cents the Balance of his debt aforesaid together with his damages aforesaid in form aforesaid assessed and his costs about his suit in this behalf expended.

P-236 Monday 23rd August 1824

    A Plat and certificate of survey for six acres of Land in the name of William Purnell and on an assignment thereon from William Purnell to John Henderson was produced in court and the execution thereof partly proven by the oath of Henry T. Jones one of the witnesses thereto.

    A Plat and certificate of servey for six acres of Land in the name of William Purnell, and an assignment thereon from John Henderson to Robert B. Harney was produced in court and the execution thereof proven by the oaths of Alexander S. Jones & Lewis H. Brown the witnesses thereto & ordered to be certified.

    A Plat and certificate of servey for ninety acres of Land in the name of Lion Thrower and an assignment thereon from Lion Thrower to Thomas E. Abernathy was produced in court and the execution thereof proven by the oaths of Thomas Batte & Henry L. Jones two of witnesses thereto and ordered to be certified.

    A Deed of conveyance from Alexander McDonald to George Brown for forty two acres of land was produced in court and the execution thereof acknowledged by the said Alexander McDonald & ordered to be certified for registration.

John Parks Plt.) In Debt
    Against)
Gidion Pillow Deft.) This day came the parties by their attornies and
) thereupon came a Jury of good and lawful men, Towit, David Jones, Elisha White, Allen Abernathy, Hugh Adams, Henry White, William Ezell, Alexander Baldridge, Archibald Smith, John W. O. Graves,

James Coldwell, Joshua Horn, & George Garrett, who being elected tried and sworn well and & truly to try the issue joined between the parties in that case, upon their oaths do say that the defendant has not paid the debt in the Writing Obligatory in the declaration mentioned, and that he has no sett off as the plaintiff in his replication has alleged, and they do assess the plaintiffs damages by occasion of the detention of sd. debt to six dollars and seventy five cents.

It is therefore considered by the court that the plaintiff recover of said defendant the sum of two hundred and seventy one dollars & five cents the amount of his debt aforesaid together with his damages aforesaid in form aforesaid assessed and also his costs about his suit in this behalf expended. (p-237) From which Judgment the defendant prayed an appeal to the honorable the Circuit Court to be held for the County of Giles and having executed bond and security according to Law the same was granted him.

Thomas Martin Assee &c Plt.) In Debt
    Against)
Jacob Templin / Deft.)
) This day came the parties by their attorneys and thereupon came a Jury of good and lawful men, Towit, David Jones, Elisha White, Allen Abernathy, Hugh Adams, Alexander Baldridge, Henry White, Archibald Smith, John W. O. Graves, James Coldwell, Joshua Horn, George Garrett, & William Ezell, who being elected tried and sworn well and truly to try the issue joined between the parties in this case, upon their oaths do say that the defendant has not paid the debt in the writing obligatory in the declaration mentioned, and that he has no sett off as the plaintiff in his repication has alleged and they do assess the plaintiffs damages by occasion of the detention of said debt to Three dollars & twelve and a half cents, besides costs – It is therefore considered by the court that the plaintiff recover of said defendant the sum of one hundred & fifteen dollars the amount of the debt aforesaid together with his damages aforesaid in form aforesaid by the Jurors aforesaid assessed and his costs about his suit in this behalf expended.

James Dyer for the use &c Plt.) In Debt
    Against)
William B. Brooks Deft.)
) This day came the parties by their attornies and thereupon came a Jury of good and lawful men, Towit, David Jones, Elisha White, Allen Abernathy, Hugh Adams, Alexander Baldridge, Henry White, Archibald Smith, John W. O. Graves, James Coldwell, Joshua Horn, George Garrett, & Wm. Ezell who being elected tried and sworn well and truly to try the issue joined between the parties in this case upon their oaths do say that the defendant not paid the debt in the writing obligatory in the declaration, mentioned – as the plaintiff in his replication has alleged, and they do assess the plaintiffs damages by occasion of the detention of said Debt to three dollars & seventy five cents, besides costs. It is therefore considered by the court that the plaintiff recover of said Defendant the sum of one hundred dollars, the amount of his debt aforesaid together with his damages aforesaid in form aforesaid by the Jurors aforesaid assessed and his costs about his suit in this behalf expended.

Robert Lockhart & Burton) Plts.
White, who sues for the use &c.)
    Against
Henry J. Cooper Deft.)

P-238 This day came the parties by their attornies and thereupon came a Jury of good and lawful men, Towit, David Jones, Elisha White, Allen Abernathy, Hugh Adams, Alexander Baldridge, Henry White, Archibald Smith, John W. O. Graves, James Coldwell, Joshua Horn, George Garrett, & William Ezell who being elected tried and sworn well and truly to try the issue joined between the parties in this case upon their oaths do say that the defendant has not paid the debt in the Writing obligatory in the declaration mentioned, and that he has no sett off as the plaintiffs in their replication has alleged, and they do assess the plaintiffs damages by occasion of the detention of said debt to seven dollars & seventy seven cents - besides costs - It is therefore considered by the court that the plaintiffs recover of said defendant the sum of two hundred & thirty nine dollars & fifty cents the amount of his debt aforesaid together with his damages aforesaid in form aforesaid by the Jurors aforesaid assessed and his costs about his suit in this behalf expended.

Elisha Eldridge & Lunford M. Plts.) In Debt
Bramlett Executor of Thos. H. Meredith)
        Against) This day came the parties
Henry Hagen & James Perry Defts.) by their attornies and
) thereupon came a Jury of
good and lawful men, Towit, David Jones, Elisha White, Allen Abernathy, Hugh Adams, Alexander Baldridge, Henry White, Archibald Smith, John W. O. Graves, James Coldwell, Joshua Horn, George Garrett & William Ezell, who being elected tried and sworn well and truly to try the issue joined between the parties in this case upon their oaths do say that the defendant have not paid the debt in the writing obligatory in the declaration mentioned, and that they have no sett off as the plaintiff in their replication have alleged, and they do assess the plaintiffs damages by occasion of the detention of said debt to seventy one dollars and fifty cents, besides costs. It is therefore considered by the court that the plaintiffs recover of sd. defendants the sum of twenty six dollars - the amount of their debt aforesaid together with their damages aforesaid in form aforesaid, by the Jurors aforesaid assessed, and also their costs about their suit in this behalf expended - From which judgment the defendant prayed an appeal to the honorable the Circuit Court to be held for the County of Giles, and having executed Bond and security according to Law the same was granted them.

Polly Kirk for the use of &c Plt.) In Debt
        Against)
John W. R. Graves & John W. Graves Deft.) This day came the parties
) by their attornies and
thereupon (p-239) came a Jury of good and lawful men, Towit, David Jones, Elisha White, Allen Abernathy, Hugh Adams, Alexander Baldridge, Henry White, Archibald Smith, John W. O. Graves, James Coldwell, Joshua Horn, George Garrett & Wm. Ezell - who being elected tried and sworn well and truly to try the issue joined between the parties in this case upon their oaths do say that the defendants have not paid the debt in the writing obligatory in the declaration mentioned as the plaintiffs in her replication has alleged - and they do assess the plaintiffs damages by occasion of the detention of sd. Debt to three dollars, besides costs - It is therefore considered by the court that the plaintiff recover of sd. Defendants the sum of seventy seven dollars the amount of his debt aforesaid together with her damages aforesaid in form aforesaid by the Jurors aforesaid assessed, and also her costs by her about her suit in this behalf expended.

Robert Lockhart & Burton R. White)) In Debt
Who sues for the use &c) Plt.)
  Against) This day came the parties
John Brown . . . . . Deft.) by their attornies and
             thereupon came a Jury of
good and Lawful men, Towit, David Jones, Elisha White, Allen Abernathy, Hugh Adams, Alexander Baldridge, Henry White, Archibald Smith, John W. O. Graves, James Coldwell, Joshua Horne, George Garrett & William Ezell, who being elected tried and sworn well and truly to try the issue joined between the parties in this case upon their oaths do say that the Defendants has not paid the Debt in the writing obligatory in the declaration mentioned as the plaintiff in their replication has alleged and they do assess the plaintiffs damages by occasion of the detention of said debt to five dollars & thirty cents ---besides costs - It is therefore considered by the court that the plaintiffs recover of said defendant the sum of one hundred & thirty three dollars & twenty six cents the amount of his debt aforesaid together with his damages aforesaid in form aforesaid by the Jurors aforesaid assessed, and also his costs about his suit in this behalf expended.

Samuel & Nicholas S. Faine &) Plts.) In Debt
Alexander Lockhart for the use &c.))
  Against) This day came the parties
Thomas Harwood . . . . Deft.) by their attornies and
             thereupon came a Jury of
good and lawful men, Towit, David Jones, Elisha White, Allen Abernathy, Hugh Adams, Alexander Baldridge, Henry White, Archibald Smith, John W. O. Graves, James Coldwell, Joshua Horn, George Garrett & William Ezell, who being elected tried and sworn well and truly to try the issue joined between the parties in this case upon their oaths do say that the defendant has not paid the debt in the Writing obligatory in the declaration mentioned as the plaintiffs in their (p-240) Monday 23rd August 1824, replication have alleged, and they do assess the plaintiffs damages by occasion of the detention of said debt to twenty four dollars & fifty seven cents, besides the costs - It is therefore considered by the court that the plaintiffs recover of said defendant the sum of two hundred & forty seven dollars the amount of their debts aforesaid together with their damages aforesaid, in form aforesaid by the Jurors aforesaid assessed and their costs about their suit in this behalf expended.

David H. Slater Assee &c Plt.) In Debt
  Against)
William Frazer and) Defts.) This day came the parties by their at-
Daniel Frazer)) tornies and thereupon came a Jury of
             good and Lawful men, Towit, David Jones,
Elisha White, Allen Abernathy, Hugh Adams, Alexander Baldridge, Henry White, Archibald Smith, John W. O. Graves, James Coldwell, Joshua Horn & George Garrett, & William Ezell, who being elected tried and sworn well and truly to try the issue joined between the parties in this case upon their oaths do say that the Defendants have not paid the Debt in the Writing obligatory in the declaration mentioned and that they have no sett off as the plaintiff in his replication has alleged and they do assess plaintiffs damages by occasion of the detention of said debt to three dollars eighty seven and a half cents, besides costs - It is therefore considered by the court that the plaintiff recover of said defendants the sum of one hundred dollars, the amount of said aforesaid together with his damages aforesaid in form aforesaid assessed, and also his costs about his suit in this behalf expended.

A Deed of conveyance from Welton F. L. Jenkins to Thomas Batte for Lot No. 62 in the Town of Lower Elkton was produced in court and the execution thereof acknowledged by sd. Welton F. L. Jenkins and ordered to be certified for registration.

Thomas Harwood this day came into court and resigned as Guardian to George W. Jones, Richard M. Jones, and Mary J. Jones Infant orphans of James Jones decd. and thereupon Henry J. Jones, was appointed Guardian to said Infants of James Jones decd. - Whereupon he executed bond and security as the Law directs.

P-241   Monday 23rd August 1824

Lunsford M. Bramlett Plts.)   In Debt
& Elisha Eldridge Exrs.   )
of Thomas H. Meredith decd.)   This day came the parties by their at-
        Assignee &c   )   tornies and thereupon came a Jury of
        Against   )   good and Lawful men, Towit, David Jones,
Benjamin P. Marlin Deft.   )   Elisha White, Allen Abernathy, Hugh Adams,
)   Alexander Baldridge, Henry White, Archi-
bald Smith, John W. O. Graves, James Caldwell, Joshua Horn, George Garrett & William Ezelle who being elected tried and sworn well and truly to try the issue joined between the parties in this case, upon their oaths do say that the Defendant hath not paid the debt in the Writing obligatory in the declaration mentioned as the plaintiff in their replication hath alleged, and they do assess the plaintiffs damages by occasion of the detention of the said debt to two dollars & forty three cents, Besides costs. It is therefore considered by the court that the plaintiffs recover of the defendant the sum of Eighty one dollars and Eighty one cents, the amount of their debt aforesaid, together with their damages aforesaid in form aforesaid by the Jurors aforesaid assessed and their costs by them about their suit in this behalf expended.

Thomas McKissack Admr. &c Plt.)   In Debt
        Against   )
Isaac Mayfield, Nathaniel Young)   This day came the parties by their
William W. Thornton & William Ball) attornies and thereupon came a
)   Jury of good and lawful men, Towit,
David Jones, Elisha White, Allen Abernathy, Hugh Adams, Alexander Baldridge, Henry White, Archibald Smith, John W. O. Graves, James Coldwell, Joshua Horn, George Garrett and William Ezell, who being elected tried and sworn well and truly to try the issue joined between the parties in this case upon their oaths, do say that the defendants have not paid the debt in the writing obligatory in the declaration mentioned, as the plaintiff in his replication hath alleged and they do assess the plaintiffs damages by occasion of the detention of said debt to four dollars and twenty cents, Besides costs.

It is therefore considered by the court that the plaintiff recover of the defendant the sum of one hundred & ten dollars twelve and a half cents, the amount of his debt aforesaid, together with his damages, aforesaid, by the Jurors aforesaid in form aforesaid assessed, and his costs by him about his suit in this behalf expended.

P-242 Monday 23rd August 1824

John Green Assignee &c Plt.
    Against
Elisha Eldridge & Lumford
M. Bramlett Exrs. of Thos.
H. Meredith decd.

In Debt

This day came the parties by their attornies and thereupon came a Jury of good and lawful men, Towit, David Jones, Elisha White, Allen Abernathy, Hugh Adams, Alexander Baldridge, Henry White, Archibald Smith, John W. O. Graves, James Coldwell, Joshua Horn, George Garrett, & William Ezell, who being elected tried and sworn well & truly to try the issue Joined between the parties in this case upon their oaths do say that the defendants have not paid the debt in the writing obligatory in the declaration mentioned, and that they have no sett as the plaintiff in his replication hath alleged, and they do assess the plaintiffs damages by occasion of the detention of said Debt to seventy five dollars besides costs. It is therefore considered by the court that the plaintiff recover of the defendants the sum of two thousand five hundred & sixty two dollars and nine cents, the amount of his debt aforesaid together with his damages aforesaid by the Jurors aforesaid in form aforesaid assessed and his costs by him about his suit in this behalf expended - From which Judgment the defendant prayed an appeal to the honorable the Circuit Court to be held for the County of Giles and having entered into bond according to Law the same was granted them.

Thomas McKissack Admr. &c Plt.
    Against
William Ball, William W. Thornton, Defts.
Isaac Mayfield & Nathaniel Young

In Debt

This day came the parties by their attornies & thereupon came a Jury of good & Lawful men, Towit, David Jones, Elisha White, Allen Abernathy, Hugh Adams, Alexander Baldridge, Joshua Horn, George Garrett, and William Ezell, Who being elected tried and sworn well and truly to try the issue Joined between the parties in this case upon their oaths do say that the defendants have not paid the Debt in the Writing obligatory in the declaration mentioned as the plaintiff in his replication hath alleged, and they do assess the plaintiff damages by occasion of the detention of said debt to four dollars and twenty five cents Besides costs. It is therefore considered by the court that the plaintiff recover of the Defendants the sum of one hundred and thirteen dollars the amount of his debt aforesaid together with his damages aforesaid by the Jurors aforesaid in form aforesaid assessed and his costs by him about his suit in this behalf expended.

P-243 Monday 23rd August 1824

Josiah S. Johnston . . . . Plt.
    Against
William Ball, Isaac
Mayfield & Joseph H. Rodge Defts.

In Debt

This day came the parties by their attornies & thereupon came a Jury of good and Lawful men Towit, David Jones, Elisha White, Allen Abernathy, Hugh Adams, Alexander Baldridge, Henry White, Archibald Smith, John W. O. Graves, James Coldwell, Joshua Horn, George Garrett & William Ezell, who being elected tried and sworn well and truly to try the issue Joined between the parties in this case upon their oaths do say that they find said issue in favor of the plaintiff and assess his damages by occasion of the detention of the debt in the Writing obligatory in the declaration mentioned to three dollars and twenty cents Besides costs. It is therefore considered by the court that the plaintiff recover of the defendants the sum of one hundred and twenty five dollars the amount of his debt aforesaid together with his damages aforesaid in form aforesaid by the Jurors aforesaid assessed & his costs by him about his suit in this behalf expended.

George M. Ridley Assignee &c Plt.) In Debt
   Against)
Claiborne Kyle Admr. &) This day came the parties
Rebeccah Kyle Admr. & } Defts.) by their attornies and
of the Estate of William Kyle decd.)) thereupon came a Jury
) of good and Lawful men,
Towit, David Jones, Elisha White, Allen Abernathy, Hugh Adams, Alexander Baldridge, Henry White, Archibald Smith, John W. O. Graves, James Coldwell, Joshua Horn, George Garrett & William Ezell who being elected tried and sworn well and truly to try the issue Joined between the parties in this case upon their oaths do say that the defendant have not paid the debt in the writing obligatory in the declaration mentioned as the plaintiff in his replication hath alleged and they do assess the plaintiffs damages by occasion of the detention of said debt to twenty nine dollars and twenty cents, Besides costs. It is therefore considered by the court that the plaintiff recover of the Defendant the sum of one hundred and sixty dollars & two third cents the amount of his debt aforesaid together with his damages aforesaid by the Jurors aforesaid assessed and his costs by him about his suit in this behalf expended - To be levied of the goods and chattles rights and credits of said testators in the hands of said Defendants to be administered if so much thereof they have, but if so much they have not then the costs to be levied of the proper goods and chattles of said Defendant.

P-244 Monday 23rd August 1824

Mr. Shaderack Nye for the use of)) In Debt
Westernberg Accademy) Plt.)
   Against) This day came the parties
Ralph Graves, Nathaniel) Defts.) by their attornies and
Young & James Perry)) thereupon came a Jury of
) good and lawfull men, To-
Wit, David Jones, Elisha White, Allen Abernathy, Hugh Adams, Alexander Baldridge, Henry White, Archibald Smith, John W. O. Graves, James Coldwell, Joshua Horn, George Garrett & William Ezell, who being elected tried and sworn well and truly to try the issue Joined between the parties in this case upon their oaths do say that they find said issue in favor of the plaintiff and assess his damages by occasion of the detention of the debt in the declaration mentioned to sixteen dollars, besides costs. It is therefore considered by the court that the plaintiff recover of said defendant the sum of two hundred & sixty five dollars the balance of his debt aforesaid together with his damages aforesaid in form aforesaid by the Jurors aforesaid assessed, and also his costs about his suit in this behalf expended.

Charles Buford Treasure of the)
Westergberg Accademay) Plt.
   Against) In Debt
James Perry and)
~~Nathaniel Young~~)

This day came the parties by their attornies and thereupon came a Jury of good and lawful men, Towit, David Jones, Elisha White, Allen Abernathy Hugh Adams, Alexander Baldridge, Henry White, Archibald Smith, John W. O. Graves, James Coldwell, Joshua Horn, George Garrett and William Ezell who being elected tried and sworn well and truly to try the issue joined between the parties in this case upon their oaths do say that the defendants have not paid the debt in the writing obligatory in the declaration mentioned as the plaintiff in his replication has alleged, and they do assess the plaintiffs damages by occasion of the detention of said Debt to thirteen dollars besides costs — It is therefore considered by the court that the plaintiff recover of said defendants the sum of one hundred & seventy three dollars & Eighty four cents the amount of his debts aforesaid together with his damages aforesaid in form aforesaid by the Jurors aforesaid assessed and also his costs about his suit in this behalf expended.

James Perry for the use of &c Plt.) In Debt
    Against)
Benjamin P. Maclin Deft.)
) This day came the parties by their attornies and thereupon came a Jury of good and lawful men, Towit, David Jones, Elisha White, Allen Abernathy, Hugh Adams, Alexander Baldredge, Henry White, Archibald Smith, John W. O. Graves, James (p-245) Coldwell, Joshua Horn, George Garrett, and William Ezell — Who being elected tried and sworn well and truly to try the issue joined between the parties in this case upon their oaths do say that the Defendants mentioned as the plaintiff in his replication has alledged, and they do assess the plaintiffs damages by occasion of the detention of said debts to Five dollars besides costs — It is therefore considered by the court that the plaintiff recover of said defendant the sum of one hundred & forty Dollars and eighty six cents the amount of his Debt aforesaid, together with his damages aforesaid in form aforesaid by the Jurors aforesaid assessed and also about his suit in this behalf expended.

Fountain & Sterling H. Lester) Plt.) In Debt
to the use of &c.)
    Against)
Henry J. Cooper . . . . Deft.) This day came the parties by their attornies and thereupon came a Jury of good and lawful men, Towit, David Jones, Elisha White, Allen Abernathy, Hugh Adams, Alexander Baldridge, Henry White, Archibald Smith, John W. O. Graves, James Coldwell, Joshua Horne, George Garrett, and William Ezell, who being elected tried and sworn well and truly to try the issue joined between the parties in this case upon their oaths do say that the defendant has not paid the whole of the Debt in the declaration mentioned, and that he has no sett off as the plaintiffs in their replication have alleged, But that there remains yet unpaid a Balance of said Debt, to the amount of one hundred and two dollars, and Eighty four cents and they do assess the plaintiffs damages by occasion of the detention thereof to four Dollars & 12½ cents besides costs — It is therefore considered by the court that the plaintiffs recover of said Defendant the Balance of their Debt aforesaid together with their damages aforesaid in form aforesaid, by the Jurors aforesaid assessed, and also their costs about their suit in this behalf expended.

John B. Anthony Plt.) In Debt
    Against)
John W. R. Graves))
and John Brown) Defts.)

183

This day came the parties by their attornies and thereupon came a Jury of good and lawful men, Towit, David Jones, Elisha, Allen Abernathy, Hugh Adams, Alexander Baldridge, Henry White, Archibald Smith, John W. O. Graves, James Coldwell, Joshua Horn, George Garrett, and William Ezell — who being elected tried and sworn well and truly to try the issue Joined between the parties in this case upon their oaths do say that the Defendants have not paid the Debt in the Writing obligatory in the Declaration mentioned and that they have no sett off, as the plaintiff in his replication have alleged and they do assess (p-246) the plaintiffs damages by occasion of the Detention of said debt to Four dollars & Twenty five cents besides costs. It is therefore considered by the court that the plaintiff recover of said Defendants the sum of one hundred and fourteen dollars, the amount of his debt aforesaid together with his damages aforesaid by the Jurors aforesaid in form aforesaid, assessed and also his costs about his suit in this behalf expended.

Ordered that William R. Davis be allowed the sum of seven dollars and twenty five cents as per account filed, and that the same be certified to the Trustee of Giles County for payment.

Dewey Smith Esquire a Justice of the peace for this County Tenders in Writing his resignation to the court, which was reviewed and ordered to be entered on the minutes.

Jonathan Moody Esquire a Justice of the peace for this County, Tenders in Writing his resignation to the court which was received and ordered to be entered on the minutes.

The administration of the Estate of James Walker decd. returned into court the sale of said Estate which was ordered to be recorded.

The Commissioners who were appointed to allot to Polly Walker widow of James Walker decd. one years provision out of said James Walker's Estate, made return of said allotment which was ordered to be recorded.

William H. Moody Assee &c. Plt.) In Debt
    Against)
Henry T. Croft, Robert Oliver) Defts.) This day came the parties
& James H. Graves . . . .)) by their attornies and
thereupon came a Jury of good and Lawful men, Towit, David Jones, Elisha White, Allen Abernathy, Hugh Adams, Alexander Baldridge, Henry White, Archibald Smith, John W. O. Graves, James Coldwell, Joshua Horne, George Garrett & William Ezell, who being elected tried and sworn well and truly to enquire of Damages in this case, upon their oaths do say that the plaintiff has sustained damages by occasion of the non performance of the several assumptions in the declaration complained of to four hundred and Eighty five dollars, besides costs. It is therefore considered by the court that the plaintiff recover of said Defendants the amount of the damages aforesaid in form aforesaid by the Jurors aforesaid assessed and his costs about his suit in behalf expended to the honorable the Circuit Court to be held for the County of Giles. and having excuted bond and security according to law the same was granted them.

184

P-247 Monday 23rd August 1824

James C. O. Ralley . . . Plt.
      Against
Andrew M. Balentine &
Stephen Anderson Executors)Defts.
of John Samuel Decd.

In Debts

This day came the parties by their attornies and thereupon came a Jury of good and Lawful Men, Towit, David Jones, Esisha White, Allen Abernathy, Hugh Adams, Henry T. Croft, Alexander Baldridge, Joshua Horn, and George Garrett - who being elected tried and sworn well and truly to try the issue joined between the parties in this case upon their oaths, do say that the defendants do detain from said plaintiff the sum of two hundred dollars the Debt in the Declaration mentioned, in manner and form as said plaintiff in declaring in the behalf hath alleged, and they do assess said plaintiffs damages by reason thereof to seven Dollars and fifty cents - besides costs, and they do further say that said Defendants have not fully administered, all and singular the goods and chattles &c of their said Testators, which hath come to their hand to be administered of said plaintiff in replying hath alleged. It is therefore considered by the court that said plaintiff recover against said Defendant his debt aforesaid together with his damages aforesaid in form aforesaid assessed, and his costs by him about his suit in this behalf expended - To be levied of the goods and chattles rights and credits of said testator in the hands of said Defendants to be administered if so much thereof they have, but if so much thereof they have not then the costs to be levied of the proper goods and chattles of said Defendants.

Ordered that court be adjourned untill tomorrow morning nine oclock.

                                                                    Thos. Harwood
                                                                    Peter Swanson
                                                                     Thos. Marks

P-248 Tuesday 24th August 1824

Court met accordind to adjournment - Present Thomas Marks,
                                            Thomas Harwood   ) Esquires Justices of the peace for the County of Giles.
                                            & Peter Swanson

Ordered that a venditrione exponas issue to the Sherriff of this County, commanding him to advertise and sell according to law, one hundred and five acres of Land being part of a one hundred & sixty acre tract in range No. 2 section No. 1 adjoining the land on which Thos. Rea now lives on the Waters of Big Creek, levied on, on the day of ....1824, as the property of Richard Allen, by Annanias Oliver as constable in and for the County of Giles to Later by an execution which issued on a Judgment, which Jacob Jones recovered against E. B. Mayfield, Thomas B. Haney, Wm. Mayfield and sd. Richard Allen before A. McKissack Esquire a Justice of the Peace for this County, on the 15th day of August 1823 for the sum of ninety six dollars & fifty cents & costs.

The Executors of Joseph Braden Decd. returned into court an Inventory of the Estate of sd. Joseph Braden decd. which was ordered to be recorded.

The executors of Joseph Braden decd. returned into court the sale of the Estate of said Joseph Braden decd. which was ordered to be recorded.

John Clark . . . Plaintiff)   In Debt
    Against   )
John Pillow Defendant   )   This day came the parties by their attor-
) neys and thereupon came a Jury of good and Lawful men, Towit, David Jones, Richard Bentley, Elisha White, Hugh Adams, William Ezell, Henry T. Croft, Alexander Baldridge, Henry White, Archibald Smith, James Coldwell, Joshua Horn, & George Garrett, who being elected tried and sworn well and truly to try the issue Joined between the parties in this case upon their oaths do say that the defendant has not paid the whole of the debt in the writing obligatory in the declaration mentioned, and that he has no sett off - as the plaintiff in his replication has alleged, and they do assess the plaintiffs damages by occasion of the detention of the said balance of the debt to Eleven dollars & sixty two cents besides costs. It is therefore considered by the court that the plaintiff recover of said Defendant the sum of Eighty three dollars & fifty seven cents the balance of his debt aforesaid, together with his damages (p-249) aforesaid in form aforesaid by the Jurors aforesaid assessed and also his costs about his suit in this behalf expended.

Mahulda Brown Plt. . . . Plt.   )   In Debt
    Against   )
Archibald McKnight &) Defts.   )   From the Judgment of the court in
Thomas B. Hainie   )   ) this case rendered the defendant
) prayed an appeal to the honorable the Circuit Court to be held for the County of Giles, and having executed bond and security according to Law the same was granted them.

Robert Lockhart &   Plts.   )   In Debt
Benton R. White for the use &c   )
    Against   )   From the Judgment of the court in
John Brown . . . . Deft.   ) this case rendered the defendant
) prayed an appeal to the honorable the Circuit Court to be held for the County of Giles, and having executed bond and security accordind to Law the same was granted him.

Ordered that William Dearing be appointed Guardian to William Braden, Joseph P. Braden, Felix G. Braden & Jacob F. Braden, Infant orphans of Joseph Braden decd. whereupon he executed bond and security according to Law.

A Plat and certificate of survey for Eighty and a half acres of Land in the name of William Purnell and the assignment thereon from the said William Purnell to John Henderson heretofore proven by the oaths of Henry T. Jones one of the witnesses thereto, was fully proven by the oath of James K. Murrah the other witness thereto, and ordered to be certified.

A Plat and Certificate of survey for six acres of land in the name of William Purnell to John Henderson heretofore proven by the oath of Henry T. Jones one of the witnesses thereto, was fully proven by the oath of James K. Murrah the other witness thereto and ordered to be certified.

Alexander Thompson Plt.)   In debt
    Against)
Daniel Goodrum Deft.)   From the Judgment of the court in this case
)   rendered the defendant prayed an appeal to
the honorable the Circuit Court to be held for the County of Giles, and having executed bond and security accordind to law the same was ganted him.

P-250 Tuesday 24th August 1824

Alexander Thompson Plt.)   In Debt
    Against)
Daniel Goodrum Deft.)   From the Judgment of the court in this case
)   rendered the defendant prayed an appeal to
the honorable the Circuit Court to be held for the County of Giles and havin executed bond and security according to Law the same was granted him.

Ordered that the following tax list be received and the double tax thereon remitted, Towit,
           Keenan McMillin 144 acres of Land
                           1 White poll.

Robert Lockhart & Benton) Plts.
R. White for the use &c.)   In Debt
    Against
Henry J. Cooker . . . Deft.   From the Judgment of the court in
                             this case rendered the defendant
prayed an appeal to the honorable the Circuit Court to be held for the County of Giles, and having executed bond and security according to Law the same was granted him.

Fountain & Sterling H.) Plts.)   In Debt
Lester for the use of &c.)
    Against)   From the Judgment of the court in
Henry J. Cooper)   this case rendered the defendant
                           prayed an appeal to the honorable
the Circuit Court to be held for the County of Giles, and having executed bond and security according to Law the same was granted him.

James Coldwell & William A.) Plts.)   In Case
Brown Admr. of Henry Neal decd.)
    Against)   This day came the parties
William Jennings . . . Defts.)   by their attornies and
                             thereupon came a Jury
of good and Lawful men, Towit, David Jones, Richard Bentley, Elisha White, Hugh Adams, Henry T. Croft, William Ezell, Alexander Baldridge, Henry White, Archibald Smith, John W. O. Graves, Joshua Horn & George Garrett, who being

Elected tried and sworn well and truly to try the issue joined between the parties in this case upon their oaths do say that the Defendant did assume upon himself in manner and form as the plaintiffs in their declaration have alleged, and they do assess the plaintiffs damages by occasion of the non performance of said assumption to one hundred and twenty eight dollars, (p-251) & seventy five cents, besides costs. It is therefore considered by the court that the plaintiff recover of said Defendant the amount of this damages aforesaid by the Jurors aforesaid in form aforesaid assessed, and also their costs about their suit in this behalf expended.

A Deed of conveyance from the heirs of Tyree Harris to William Harris for one hundred & twenty acres of land was produced in court and the execution thereof acknowledged by Alfred M. Harris, Robert S. Harris, Charles C. Abernathy, William W. Wood & Samuel Davis to be their Act and Deed, & proven by the oaths of Lunsford M. Bramlett & William H. Field, two of the witnesses thereto as to Frances P. Harris, & also proven by Henry Hagen, & Alexander Black as to Sarah Childers, and thereupon Henry Hagen and Alexander Black, two of the Acting Justices of the Peace in & for this County were appointed to take the privy examinations of Samuel W. Abernathy, Nany Ann Davis, and Elizabeth Wood, touching the examination of said deed who returned said examination into court which was ordered to be certified.

A Deed of Trust from Ralph Graves to James Perry for certain property therein named was produced in court and the execution thereof proven by the oath of Nathaniel G. Nye one of the witnesses thereto, and ordered to be certified for registration.

The administration of the Estate of Henry Neal decd. returned into court a sale of negroes belonging to said Estate which was ordered to be recorded.

| George M. Ridley Plt. Against Claiborn Kyle Admr. & Rebeccah Kyle Admx. of Wm. Kyle decd. | Defts. | In Debt From the Judgment of the court in this case rendered the Defendants prayed an appeal to the honorable the Circuit Court to be held for |

the County of Giles and having executed bond according to law the same was granted them.

A Deed of conveyance from Alfred M. Harris to Joseph D. Peebles for one hundred and forty acres Land was produced in court and the execution thereof acknowledged by the said Harris & ordered to be certified for registration.

| Samuel & Nicholas Faine & Alexander Lockhart to the use of &c. Against Thomas Harwood . . . . . . Deft. | Plts. | In Debt From the Judgment of the court in this case rendered the defendant |

prayed an appeal to the honorable the Circuit Court to be held for the County of Giles and having executed bond and security according to Law the same was granted him.

P-252   Tuesday 24th August 1824

Bonapart Garland & Peter) Plts.
Garland in proper person)
& Attorney by their next)
friend Edward Garland)
        Against
John Porter Jnr. Gdn. &c. Deft.

Petition

This day came the plaintiffs by their attorney and it appearing to the satisfaction of the Court now here that the Defendants has failed to make his annual returnes or rendered an account of this guardianship as guardian to the heirs of Peter Garland decd. It is ordered that said guardianship be taken from the said defendant and that Thomas K. Gordon be appointed Guardian decd. upon his entering into bond and security as the law directs – and it is further ordered that the defendant pay the costs of this petition – and that execution be awarded accordingly.

Ordered that Thomas Lane, David K. McEwen & John Goff be appointed commissioners to settle with John Pate Junr. former guardian of the heirs of Peter Garland decd. and that they make report of the same to the next term of this court.

Jesse Beazley - - - Plt.
        Against
John Hightower Admr. of) Defts.
Richard Hightower decd.)

In Covenant

This day came the parties by their attornies and thereupon came a Jury of good and lawful men, Towit, James Coldwell, Richard Long, Thomas Rosborough, Jesse West, James Wood, William Pullen, John B. Goldsberry, Joshua Rickman, Alexander Tarpley, John G. Russell, Herrod Foulks, and Littleberry Carter, who being elected tried and sworn well and truly to try the issue joined between the parties in this case upon their oaths do say that the Defendants or his intestate hath not kept and performed their covenants as the plaintiff in his declaration hath alleged, and they do assess the plaintiffs damages by reasons thereof to one hundred & ninety seven dollars, & ninety four cents besides costs. It is therefore considered by the court that the plaintiff recover of the said defendants the amount of his damages aforesaid in form aforesaid by the jurors aforesaid assessed and also his costs about his suit in this behalf expended – to be levied of the goods &c of said intestate in the hands of sd. defendants to be administered if so much thereof he hath, if not then the costs of the proper goods & chattles of said defendants.

George & William Shall Plts.
        Against
Ira C. Goff and John Goff Defts.

In Debt

This day came the parties by their attornies & thereupon the plaintiffs demurrer to the Defendants Plea being argued and mature deliberations thereupon being had by the court, it is ordered that said Demurrer be sustained.

P-253   Tuesday 24th August 1824

George & William Shall Plts.
        Against
Ira C. Goff & John Goff Defendants

In Debt

This day came the parties by their

attornies and thereupon came a Jury of good and Lawful men, Towit, Richard Long, John W. O. Graves, Elnathan G. Brown, Robert S. Harris, Daniel Frazer David W. Porter, Henry T. Kimbrough, Robert G. Steele, Joshua Rickman, Asa A. Estes, David Strocton, & Louis B. Morris, who being elected tried and sworn well and truly to try the issue joined between the parties in this case upon their oaths do say that they find said issue in favor of the plaintiffs, and assess their damages by occasion of the detention of the debt in the declaration mentioned to three dollars & forty five cents besides costs - It is therefore considered by the court that the plaintiffs recover of said defendants the sum of one hundred dollars, the amount of their debt aforesaid, together with their damages aforesaid assessed, and also their costs about their suit in this behalf expended - From which Judgment the Defendants prayed an appeal to the honorable the Circuit Court to be held for the County of Giles - and having executed bond and Security according to Law the same was granted them.

Lewis Brown Plaintiff) Motion
    Against)
Dudley Smith, Defendant) This day came the plaintiffs by Rivers & Tarpley his attornies, and moved the court now here for Judgment against the Defendant for the sum of sixty one dollars seventeen and three fourth cents which he hath paid as security for the defendant, and it not appearing to the satisfaction of the court, whether he was principal or security a Jury was empannelled to try that fact, towit, David Jones, Richard Bentley, Elisha White, Hugh Adams, William Ezell, Henry T. Croft, Alexander Baldridge, Henry White, Archibald Smith, James Coldwell, Joshua Horn, & George Garrett, who being sworn well and truly to enquire as aforesaid upon their oaths do say that that the plaintiff paid the aforesaid sum of sixty one dollars seventeen & three fourth cents on a stay of execution on a Judgment that Hardy Hightower Asse's. &c obtained against the said Dudley Smith before James Dugger, Esquire a Justice of the peace for this County on the 13th day of May 1823 to the stay of execution on which said Judgment the said plaintiff was security for the defendant. It is therefore considered by the court that the plaintiff recover against sd. defendant the aforesaid sum of sixty one dollars and seventeen and three (p-254) fourth cents together with the costs of this motion.

Ordered that court be adjourned untill tomorrow morning 9 oclock.

                                                        Thos. Harwood
                                                        Thos. Marks
                                                        Peter Swanson

                          Wednesday 25th August 1824

Court met according to adjournment, Present Thomas Harwood) Esquires
                                                Thomas Marks) Justices
                                                Peter Swanson) of the
) Peace for
) the County of
) Giles

    Ordered that the following tax list be received and the double tax thereon Towit, Hardy Hightower 603 acres of land, Bradshaw Creek.
Thomas P. Jones 1 free poll. 5 slaves.

Ordered that Asa A. Estes be released from paying tax on Twelve hundred acres of land, which was wrongfully listed to him.

John A. Walker Plt.) Covenant
    Against)
Thomas B. Jones Deft.) This day came the parties by their attorneys
) and thereupon came a Jury of good and lawful men, Towit, Elisha White, James Coldwell, George Garrett, David Jones, Richard Long, Henry White Henry T. Croft, John W. O. Graves, Archibald Smith, Allen Abernathy, William Ezell, and Richard Bentley - who being elected tried and sworn well and truly to try the issue joined between the parties in this case upon their oaths do say that the defendant has not kept and performed the covenants as the plaintiffs in his declaration hath alleged, and they do assess the plaintiffs damages by occasion thereof to two hundred & ninety four dollars, and seventy five cents, besides costs. It is therefore considered by the court that the plaintiff recover of said defendant the amount of his damages aforesaid in form aforesaid by the Jurors aforesaid assessed and also his oaths about his suit in this behalf (p-255) expended - From which Judgment the defendant prayed an appeal to the honorable the Circuit Court to be held for the County of Giles and having Executed bond and security according to Law the same was granted him.

A Deed of conveyance from William Price, George B. Henry, Isaac Price, Esther Neil, Henry Kerr, Guardian, Frances B. Kerr, William P. Kerr, witnesses, McKenzie to Joseph P. Howe & Mary D. Price Guardian for the heirs of James Price deceased for - - - - - - acres of land was produced in court and the execution thereof proven by the oaths of James Coldwell, and Benjamin Burk, the witnesses thereto and ordered to be certified for registration.

A Deed of conveyance from William Wells Senr. to Jesse Wells for seven acres and one hundred & forty poles of Land was produced in court and the execution thereof proven by the oaths of Charles C. Abernathy & Gardner Scoggin the witnesses thereto and ordered to be certified for registration.

James Coldwell & William A.) Plts.) In Debt
Brown Admrs. of Henry Neal decd.))
    Against) From the Judgment of the
William D. Jennings . . . Defts.) court in this case rendered the Defendant
prayed an appeal to the honorable the Circuit Court to be held for the County of Giles, and having executed Bond and Security according to Law the same was granted him.

A Deed of conveyance from James McCormick to Wythe Simms for two hundred and forty six acres of land was produced in court and the execution thereof fully proven by the oaths of Thomas Harwood another of the witnesses thereto and ordered to be certified for registration.

James Perry Plaintiff) In Debt
    Against)
Lester Morris Defendant) This day came the parties by their attornies

and thereupon came a Jury of good & lawful men, Towit, Elisha White, James Coldwell, George Garrett, David Jones, Richard Long, Henry White, Henry T. Croft, John W. O. Graves, Archibald Smith, Allen Abernathy, Wm. Ezell, & Richard Bentley, who being elected tried and sworn well and truly to try the issue joined between the parties in this case, and who having heard the evidence & part of the argument of counsel in this case were permitted to disperse to meet again tomorrow morning 8 oclock.

Ordered that court be adjourned till tomorrow morning 8 oclock.

A. Black
Tho. Harwood
Richd. McGee

P-256 Thursday 26th August 1824

Court met according to adjournment, Present Thomas Harwood, Alexander Black & Richard McGee

In Case

This day came the parties by their attornies and thereupon came the Jury who were sworn on yestoday well and truly to try the issue joined between the parties in this case upon their oaths do all say that the defendant is not guilty in manner and form as the plaintiff in declaring against him hath alleged – It is therefore considered by the court that the defendant go hence without day and recover of the plaintiff his costs by him about his defence in this behalf expended – From which Judgment the plaintiff prayed an appeal to the honorable the Circuit Court to be held for the County of Giles, and having executed bond and security according to Law the same was granted him.

The last Will and testement of Samuel Cox deceased was produced in court and proven by the oaths of James Appleton, Thomas H. Ferguson & James Cox, the subscribing witnesses thereto, and ordered to be recorded. Thereupon Anderson Hogan was appointed administrator, with the will annexed whereupon he was qualified and executed bond and security according to Law.

Gilham Harwell Executor of)
Buckner Harwell decd.   ) Plt.
       Against
John Boyd . . . . . Deft.

In Debt

This day came the parties by their attornies and thereupon came a jury of good and lawful men, Towit, Alexander Baldridge, William D. Jennings, Joshua Horn, Hugh Adams, David L. Jones, Thomas Johnson, Benjamin Williams, William Snow, Joseph Alsup, William Bradley, John G. Russell, & Henry Willeford, who being elected tried and sworn well and truly to try the issue joined between the parties in this case, upon their oaths do say that the defendant has not paid the debt in the writing obligatory in the declaration mentioned, and that he has no sett off as the plaintiff in his replication hath alleged, and they do assess the plaintiffs damages by occasion of the detention of said debt to forty four dollars & fifty cents – Besides costs, It is therefore considered by the court that the plaintiff recover of said Defendant the (p-257) sum of one hundred & fifty three dollars & seventy five cents, the amount of his debt aforesaid together with his damages aforesaid in form aforesaid by the Jurors aforesaid assessed, and also their costs about this suit in this behalf expended.

The last Will and testament of Samuel Parton deceased was produced in court and proven by the oaths of David L. Jones & Joseph Knox, two of the witnesses thereto, and ordered to be recorded - thereupon Armistead Redding the executor therein named appealed in court and was qualified and gave bond and security according to Law.

Ordered that the following tax list be received and the double tax thereon remitted, Towit, Thomas Read 12.00 acres of Land.

James Coldwell & Wm. A. Brown) In Debt
Admr. of Henry Neal decd. Plts.)
    Against) This day came the parties into court
William D. Jennings./ Deft.) and the defendant withdraws his ap-
) peal heretofore prayed and granted
in this cause, and thereupon it is considered and agreed by & between the parties that the Judgment heretofore rendered in this cause shall be reduced to seventy five dollars, the plaintiffs are to pay the costs of their witnesses in this case, and the defendant is to pay the court cost, and that execution in said case is to be staid & not to issue untill after the November County Court except for costs.

Shadrack Nye to the use &c Plt.) In Debt
    Against)
Ralph Graves, Nathaniel) Defts.) From the Judgment of the Court in
Young & James Perry) this case rendered the defendant
) prayed an appeal to the honorable
the Circuit Court to be held for the County of Giles, and having executed bond and security according to Law the same was granted him.

Charles Buford treasurer &c Plt.) In Debt
    Against)
James Perry & Nathaniel Yound Deft.) From the Judgment of the court
) in this case rendered the de-
fendant prayed and appealed to the honorable the Circuit Court to be held for the County of Giles, and having executed bond and security according to Law the same was grant them.

P-258   Thursday 26th August 1824

William Ball Plaintiff) Appeal
    Against) This day came the Deft by his attorney and
James Perry Defendant) the plaintiff being solemnly called came
) not but made default nor is his suit further
prosecuted. It is therefore considered by the court that the defendant go hence without day, and recover of the plaintiff his costs by him about his default in this behalf expended.

Stirling C & Eldridge B. Robertson Plts.)   Motion
            Against   )
Samuel Day - - - - Deft.   )   John Maxwell who was summoned to appear at the
present term of this court and give evidence in behalf of the plaintiffs against the defendant in this case being solemnly called came not bwy made default. It is therefore considered by the court that Judgment Ni. Si. be taken against him for the sum of one hundred twenty five dollars according to the Tennor of the said subpoena and that a Scire facia issue against him returnable to the next term of this court.

Marcus Michell Plaintiff   )   In Case
          Against   )
Lester Morris Defendant   )   This day came the defendant by his attorney and the plaintiff being solemnly
called came not but made default, nor is his suit further prosecuted. It is therefore considered by the court that the defendant go hence without day and recover of the plaintiff his costs by him about his defence in this behalf expended.

Stirling C. & Eldridge R. Robertson   )   Motion
            Against   )
Samuel Day . . . . . Deft.   )   This day came the parties aforesaid by their attornies, and
thereupon it appearing to the court, now here that said Samuel Day, did as constable collect upon execution the following Judgments which had been rendered by Richard McGee Esquire an Acting Justice of the Peace for the County of Giles in favor of said plaintiffs Towit, One against John Maxwell, for nineteen dollars sixty two and a half cents rendered the 23rd day of July 1822, one other against Thomas Dickson for four dollars sixty two and a half cents, rendered the 18th day of October 1822, and one other against John Dickson for one dollar sixty two and a half cents rendered the 18th (p-259) day of October 1822, and that said Defendant hath failed and refused to pay over to said plaintiffs or either of them any part of said money, upon motion of said plaintiffs by attorney this considered by the court that said plaintiffs recover of said Defendants the sum of twenty five dollars eighty seven and a half cents the amount of the Judgments aforesaid with interest on nineteen dollars sixty two & ahalf cents from the 23rd day of July 1822, at the rate of six per cent per annum till this time and with interest upon the balance of said Judgment from the 18th day of October till this time at the rate aforesaid, and their costs by them about their motion in this behalf expended.

Ordered that court be adjourned till tomorrow morning nine oclock.

                                                      Thomas Harwood
                                                      A. Black
                                                      Thos. Marks

Friday Morning 27th August 1824

Court met according to adjournment Present, Alexander Black)   Esquires Justice of the Peace for Giles County.
                                                  Thomas Harwood)
                                                  Thomas Marks   )

Robert Lockhart ... Plt.)   In Covenant
    Against   )
William D. Jennings)   )   This day came the parties by the at-
& James K. Murrah   ) Defts.) tornies to the Defts plea being argued
) and fully understood by the court, now
here. It is ordered by the court that the demurrer be sustained, and that
the defendants answer over by pleading the general issue & go to trial at
the next term.

William Gholson Plaintiff)   In Covenant
    Against   )
William Watson Defendant   )   This day came the parties by their at-
)   tornies and by consent leave is given
each party to take depositions to be read in evidence on the trial of this
cause upon each party's giving to the other thirty days notice of the time
and place of taking all depositions in the State of Virginia Twenty days
notice of the time and place of taking all in this State, also five days
notice of the time and place of taking those in this County.

P-260   Friday 27th August 1824

Nathan Davis &   )   )   Motion
Joseph Riley) Plts)
    Against   )   This day came the plaintiffs by their at-
Thomas McKearly &   )   tornies, and the defendants not appearing
Patiance Criswell) Defts.)   It is ordered that unless said defendants
Admr. & Admx. of   )   appear here on or before the 3rd day of
Nathaniel Criswell decd.)   the next term of this court, and give other
)   and counter security as said admrs. the
court will proceed to take the Estate of said defendants of their hands, &
appoint another administrator or admrs. in their stead.

Robert Shadden ... Plt.   )   Petition
    Against   )
John Dickey Admr. of) Defts.)   This day came the parties by their at-
James Donelson decd.)   tornies, and on motion this cause is
)   ordered to be dismissed at the plain-
tiffs costs — It is therefore considered by the court that the defendants
go hence without day and recover of said defendant his costs by him about
his defence in this behalf expended.

Ordered that Thomas K. Gordon who was appointed at the present term of
this court Guardian to the heirs of Peter Garland decd. be allowed until
the next term to give bond and security as such Guardian.

A deed of conveyance from John Dickey to William Wood for Seventy four
acres and sixty three poles of land was produced in court and acknowledged
by said John Dickey and ordered to be certified for registration.

The administrator of the estate of Harrison Hicks decd. returned into
court the sale of said Estate which was ordered to be recorded.

James Dyer for the use &c. Plt.   )   In Debt
   Against   )
William Brooks . . . Deft.)   From the Judgment of the court in
)   this case rendered the defendant
prayed an appeal to the honorable the Circuit Court to be held for the
County of Giles - and having executed bond and security according to Law
the same was granted him.

Stirling C. & Eldridge B. Robertson Plts.   )   Motion
   Against   )
Samuel Day . . . . Deft.   )   From the Judgment of the
)   court in this case ren-
dered, the defendant prayed an appeal (p-261) to the honorable the Circuit Court to be held for the County of Giles and having executed bond and
security according to Law the same was granted him.

Gray H. Edwards & wife   )   Petition
and others   )
   Against   )
Thomas McKissack Admr. &c. Deft.   )   Ordered that that part of the
)   order made by this court at the
)   last term which appointes German
Lester Esqr. Clerk of this court to take an account of all the monied transactions between the defendant and the heirs of Wilson Jones decd. be received
and that he report the same to the next term of this court.

  Ordered that court be adjourned untill court in course.

                    Thomas Harwood
                    A. Black
                    Thos. Marks.

P-262 At a Court of Pleas and Quarter Sessions holden for the County of Giles, at the Court house in the Town of Pulaski, on the third Monday in November (being the fifteenth day thereof in the year of Our Lord one thousand eight hundred and twenty four:- Present Alexander Black, Robert Oliver, Henry Hagen, John Bramlett, Thomas Brown, William B. Pepper, Anderson Hogan, John Henderson, Willis S. McLaurine, Robert Read, Archibald McKissack, John H. Camp, James Paine, William Brown, William Woods, John Young, Paul Childs, Joseph Rea, Thomas Marks, Thomas K. Gordon, Peter Swanson, Arthur Hicks, and Richd. McGee, Esquires Justices of the peace of said County, Presiding German Lester, Clerk of said Court & Lewis H. Brown, Sheriff of said County.

A Deed of conveyance from Andrew Erwin to Daniel Boatright for one hundred and five acres of land was produced in court and the Execution thereof proven by the oaths of William H. McCrory and John English the witnesses thereto and ordered to be certified for registration.

A Deed of conveyance from Thomas Smith to George Everly for lot No. 58 in the Town of Pulaski was produced in court and the execution thereof proven by the oaths of Ralph Graves & John Keenan the witnesses thereto, and ordered to be certified for registration.

Nathaniel Williams Guardian of the minor heirs of Henry Scales made return as said Guardian, which was received by the court and ordered to be recorded.

Ordered that Nathaniel Williams be released from all future responsibility as Guardian of the minor children of Henry Scales.

Ordered that George Rice be appointed overseer of the road in the room of John Williams resigned, and that he have the same district of hands.

Ordered that William Bradley be appointed overseer of the road in the room of Thomas W. Grubbs resigned and that he have the same district of hands.

The Administrator of the Estate of Matthew Muncrief decd. returned into court an Inventory of said Estate which was ordered to be recorded.

A Deed of conveyance from Benjamin Nabers to Henry Melton for one hundred & thirty five acres of land was (p-263) produced in court and the execution thereof proven by the oaths of James Paine & Robert Brooks the witnesses thereto, and ordered to be certified for registration.

A Deed of conveyance from Benjamin Nabers to to Robert Brooks for one hundred and thirty five acres of land was produced in court and the execution thereof proven by the oaths of James Paine & Henry Melton, the witnesses thereto, and ordered to be certified for registration.

Ordered that the following tax list be received and the double tax thereon remitted, Towit, The Heirs of James Hainey Deceased.
150 acres of land Richland Creek.
George W. L. Marr   160 acres land Big Creek.

Ordered that John Neal be appointed overseer of the road in the room of William Rivers resigned, and and that he have the same district of hands.

Ordered that the County Trustee of this County pay to Hezekiah Jones the sum of forty three dollars & fifty cents for the support and maintainance of Jediah Purnell a pauper of this county, for twelve months from this time.

A Deed of conveyance from William Polk to Coleman Harwell, George Davenport, Lewis Williamson & Levi Sherrell for Thirteen Hundred & ninety seven acres of land, was produced in court and proven by the oaths of Lewis Garrett Junr. & Thomas W. McKnight two of the witnesses thereto, and ordered to be certified, for registration.

Ordered that the County Trustee of this County pay to Lewis H. Brown Sheriff of this County the sum of Fifty dollars for his exofficio services for one year prior to this time.

Ordered that Samuel Farmer be appointed overseer of the road in the room of Thomas McCanlass resigned and that he have the same district of hands.

Ordered that Peter Swanson be appointed Guardian to Peter Garland, Lowry Garland, Hamlitt Garland, John Garland, Wester Garland, Julia Ann Garland & Louisa Garland, Infant orphans of Peter Garland decd. whereupon he executed bond & security as the Law directs.

A Deed of conveyance from Richard Bentley and Daniel Bentley to Silas L. Veatch for sixty acres of land was produced in court and the execution thereof proven by the oaths of Henry Livingston & William Swaine the witnesses thereto, and ordered to be certified for registration.

P-264   Monday 15th November 1824

The last Will and testament of Ann Daniel Decd. was produced in court and proven by the oaths of Philip Bruce and Early Benson two of the subscribing witnesses thereto and ordered to be recorded - Thereupon Joseph Goode one of the executors therein named appeared in court and was qualified and gave bond and security as the Law directs.

Ordered that Achillis Samuel be bound an apprenticed to Stephen Samuel An Judgment to that effect having been entered into between the chairman of the Court and the said Stephen Samuel.

Ordered that John McKnight, Henry Loyd, Samuel McKnight, Lewis Williamson, Seth J. Williamson, Edmund Williamson, and Harbard Harwell, or any five of them be appointed a Juror to view that part of the Fayettsville road which lies between the top of the hill East of Isaac Williams to the County line near Edmund Williamson and see if it be proper to turn said road & that they make report thereof to the next term of this court.

A Bill of sale from Ann McCabe and William Edgare to William P. A. McCabe for certain property therein contained was produced in court and the execution thereof proven by the oaths of Peter Swanson & Richard H. Allen the witnesses thereto, and ordered to be certified for registration.

The Executor of the Estate of Samuel Paxton decd. returned into court a sale of said Estate which was ordered to be recorded.

Ephriam M. Massie, James H. Graves, & James Perry, who were commissioned by his Excellency the Governor of this State to Act as Justice of the Peace in and for this County, appeared in court and were qualified as the Law directs.

Ordered that the County Trustee of this County pay to Robert Reed Esquire the sum of sixty dollars to be laid out by him for the support and maintainance of William Harris & wife paupers of this County for one year from this time.

Ordered that John Dabney, John C. Walker, James Leitch, James Perry, & John Henderson, or any three of them be appointed commissioners to value and devide the Estate of Joseph Braden, decd. between the heirs & Legatees of said Braden Decd. and that they make report thereof to the next term of this court.

Ordered that John Dabney, John C. Walker, James Leitch, James Perry & John Henderson, or any three of them be appointed commissioners to allot to Elinor Braden widow of Joseph Braden decd. one years provisions out of said Josephs Estate and that they make report thereof to the next term of this court.

P-265 Monday 15th November 1824

A Deed of conveyance from Aaron Brown to John H. Rivers & William W. Rivers for two hundred acres of land was produced in court and the execution thereof fully proven by the oath of James H. Deaver the other witness thereto and ordered to be certified for registration.

Ordered that John McCormick be appointed constable in Captain McCormicks Company, whereupon he was qualified and gave bond and security as the Law directs.

Ordered that John Webb be appointed overseer of the road in the room of Fountain Lester resigned, and that he have the same district of hands.

Ordered that Benjamin Williams be appointed constable in Captain Crofts Company whereupon he was qualified and gave bond and security as the Law directs.

Ordered that William H. Moore be appointed overseer of the road in the room of David Bridgforth resigned - and that he have the same district of hands.

Ordered that Charles Buford, James Buford, David Porter, Richard Brandon, John W. O. Graves, & Archibald McKissack or any five of them be appointed a Jury to view that part of the road commencing at the mouth of Moores Creek at the Bridge on the Pulaski Road running up said Creek to where Stephen Samuel now lives & on to intersect the Florence road, the nearest and best way, & see if it be proper to establish said road, and make report thereof to the next term of this court.

Ordered that Samuel Day be appointed constable in Captain Frazers Company - Whereupon he was qualified and gave bond and security as the Law directs.

Henry Laird came into court and resigned his office as constable in Captain Lairds Company, whereupon Henry Willeford was appointed constable in sd. Captain Lairds Company in the stead of said Henry Laird, who was qualified and gave bond and security as the Law directs.

James K. Murrah came into court and resigned his office as constable in Captain Bass Company - Whereupon William Rose was appointed constable in said Captain Bass Company in the stead of sd. James K. Murrah - who was qualified and gave bond and security as the Law directs.

Ordered that Ulysses Samuel be bound an apprenticed to Ethelbert Samuel an Indenture to that effect having been entered into between the chairman of the court, and said Ethelbert Samuel.

P-266   Monday 15th November 1824

Ordered that John Black be appointed overseer of the road in the room of John Ross resigned - and that he have the same district of hands.

Ordered that Michael Biles be appointed overseer of the road in room of Ephriam M. Mafee resigned - and that he have the same district of hands.

Ordered that Monday next be set apart for County Business.

A Deed of conveyance from Armistead Redding Executor of the Estate of Samuel Paxton Decd. to Samuel Day for one hundred and eighteen acres of land was produced in court and the execution thereof acknowledged by the said Armistead Redding Executor as aforesaid and ordered to be certified for registration.

The Execution of the Estate of Samuel Cox decd. returned into court and Inventory of said Estate which was ordered to be recorded.

An Ordinary Licence for the term of twelve months and no longer is granted to Thomas P. Estes, who was qualified and gave bond and Security as the Law directs.

The last will and testement of William New decd. was produced in court and proven by the oaths of John Young & Lewis Smith, Two of the subscribing witnesses thereto, and ordered to be recorded - Thereupon Pleasant New was appointed administrator with the Will anexed, whereupon he was qualified and executed bond and security according to Law.

Ordered that County Trustee of this County pay to William B. Forwalt, the sum of Five dollars for fixing the stove pipes in the court house of this County.

On petition it is ordered that Robert Anderson, David Maxwell, Robert Tennen, Thomas P. Estess, David Abernathy, Simpson H. White, and Matthew Johnston, or any five of them be appointed a Jury to view and mark out a road the nearest and best way from the Shelbyville road, near Thomas P. Estes where said road crosses the main branch or fork of Pigeon Roost Creek from thence to Parks Baileys Mill, from thence the nearest & best way to intersect a road that leads by Tyree Rodes's to Mayfield's Mill, and that they make report to this court on Monday next.

Ordered that Tobitha Browning an Idiot and pauper of this County be let to the lowest bidder on Monday next for her support and maintainance for twelve months from this time - It appearing to the Satisfaction of the court, from the report of a Jury appointed at Last court for the purpose that she had no goods or chattles lands or tenments for her said support and maintainance.

P-267 Monday 15th November 1824

On application of Thomas Clark It is ordered that Daniel Goodrum, Robert Clark, David Kearsey, Paul Chiles, Samuel Haines, Mayfield Husband, and James Robertson, or any five of them be appointed a Jury to view that part of the road which runs through said Clarks Plantation and see if it be proper to alter the same agreable to the wishes of said Clark and make report thereof to the next term of this court.

On petition it is ordered that, that part of the Fayettsville road which lies between Leatherwood Creek and Littleburry Webbs be altered to run where it formerly did, and that Asa A. Estes oversee the opening and keeping in repair the same with the hand under his direction.

Ordered that Court be adjourned untill tomorrow morning nine oclock.

                A. Black
                A. McKissack
                John Bramlitt

P-268 Tuesday Morning 16th November 1824

Court met according to adjournment Present Alexander Black) Esquires Justice of the Peace for Giles County.
               Archibald McKissack
               John Bramlitt

Benjamin Long, William Long & James K. Murrah) Plts.
    Against
Simpson H. White Deft.

In Case

This day came the parties by their attornies, and on motion of the plaintiffs this casue is ordered to be dismissed. It is therefore considered by the court that the defendant recover of the plaintiffs his costs by him about his defence in this behalf expended.

On the petition of Isaac S. Crisman ordered that Writs of Certiorari and Super cedias issue to stay proceedings and remove to this court the record of a Judgment rendered by Archibald McKissack Esquire an Acting Justice of the Peace for Giles County in favor of William Risner on the 23rd day of November 1823 for the sum of forty five dollars & forty seven cents & costs, on the petitioners giving bond and security as the law directs.

The Sheriff of this County returned into court the names of the following persons Summoned to attend as grand and petit Jurors at this term pursuant to an order of the Last term of this court a copy of which issued to the said Sheriff of Giles County, Towit, David Brown, James Abernathy, Thomas Cole, Joseph Young, David Kearsey, John Lee, Martin B. Wood, William Black, Leander M. Shields, Hardy Willsford, George Gibson, George W. Look, William May, John McKissack, George Rice, Robert Black, Quinton Shannon, George Oliver, Larkin Webb, John Bass, William Dailey, Baker P. Potts, Matthew Johnson, John Ruff, Robert Anderson, and Elisha Anthony, of whom George Oliver foreman, George Rice, Joseph Young, John McKissack, James Abernathy Matthew Johnson, Elisha Anthony, George W. Look, Thomas Cole, David Kearsey, William Dailey, William May, and Robert Black, were elected empannelled and sworn a grand Jury of inquest for the body of this County: who having receive their charge withdrew to consider of their presentments.

Thomas B. Haynie a constable of this county was sworn to attend on the grand Jury at the present term of this court.

P-268   Tuesday 16th November 1824

Ordered that an order of sale issue to Anderson Hogan administrator with the Will annexed of Samuel Cox decd. commanding him to sell such of the personal property belonging to said Estate as is not specially bequeathed in the Will of said Decendants, and that he make return thereof according to Law.

At Least five Justice being present Thomas Graves returned into court One wolf Scalp over four months old, which was ordered to be burnt.

Gilham Harwell Executor of &c. Plt.   )   Certiorari
    Against   )
John Boyd . . . . . . Deft.   )   This day came the parties by
)   their attornies, and on motion this cause is ordered to be dismissed at the cost of defendant.
It is therefore considered by the court that the plaintiff recover of said Defendant his costs about his suit in this behalf expended - except the plaintiffs witnesses, who he himself is to pay.

William Ball Plt.   )   In Case
    Against   )
John Mayfield Deft.   )   This day came the Defendant by his attorney,
)   and the plaintiff being Solemnly called came not but made default, nor is his suit further prosecuted. It is therefore considered by the court that the Defendant go hence without day and recover of the plaintiff his costs by him about his defence in this behalf expended.

William Ball . . Plt.   )   In Case
    Against   )
Stephen Mayfield Deft.   )   This day came the Defendant by his attorney,
)   and the plaintiff being solemnly called came not but made default, nor is his suit further prosecuted. It is therefore considered by the court that the defendant go hence without day and recover of the plaintiff his costs by him about his defence in this behalf expended.

A Deed of conveyance from Lunsford M. Bramlitt to James W. Wheeler for one hundred & fifty two & a half acres of land was produced in court and the execution thereof acknowledged by the sd. Lunsford M. Bramlitt and ordered to be certified for registration.

Samuel S. Smith &   ) Plts.   )   Petition
Jane B. Smith his wife)   )
    Against   )   This day came the parties by their
John Porter Guardian &c. Deft.)   attornies & by consent this cause
)   is ordered to be continued, at the cost of the Defendant, and that a commission issue to any two of the Acting Justices   (p-270)   of the Peace in & for the County of Maury this State to take the Deposition of Joseph B. Porter, also that a commission issue to any two Acting Justice of the Peace in & for the County of Logan & State of Kentucky to take the Deposition of Spencer Curd and Samuel Owens, all of

which depositions when taken are to be read in evidence on the trial of this cause upon the Defendant giving to the plaintiffs ten day notice of time and place of taking the depositions, of sd. Joseph B. Porter & twenty days notice of the time and place of taking the deposition of sd. Spencer Curd, and Samuel Owens.

An ordinary License for the term of one year & no longer is Granted to James Patteson who was qualified and gave bond and security as the Law directs.

John Bradley . . . Plt.   )   In Debt
    Against   )
William D. Jennings Deft.   )   On the affidavit of the Defendant it is
)   ordered that the trial of this cause
be continued and postponed untill the next term of this court.

John Willit - - - Plaintiff   )   In Debt
    Against   )
Robert Anderson Defendant   )   Whereupon comes here into court David
)   Bridgforth, Samuel R. Anderson, &
William H. Moore, who undertook as Bail for Robert Anderson the defendant aforesaid came into court and Surrendered the Body of said defendant and are thereupon exhonorated and discharged from their obligations.

A Deed of trust from Moses Pullen to William Lee & John Pate Senr. for certain property therein named was produced in court and the execution thereof proven by the oaths of David C. Gibson and James Rainey the witness thereto, and ordered to be certified for registration.

A Deed of conveyance from Thomas Willis to Willis S. McLaurine, and Robert McLaurine, for one hundred and sixty seven acres of land was produced in court and the execution thereof acknowledged by sd. Thomas Willis and ordered to be certified for registration.

William Ussery administrator of the Estate of James J. Walker decd. returned into court a sale of said Estate which is ordered to be recorded.

A Deed of conveyance from John W. Graves to Thomas Davenport for one hundred and thirteen & half acres of land was   (p-271)   produced in court and the execution thereof acknowledged by the sd. John W. Graves and ordered to be certified for registration.

At least five Justices being present Samuel Harwell produced into court one wolf scalp over four months old which was ordered to be burnt.

A Deed of conveyance from William Price to Wilton F. L. Jenkins for thirty six acres of land was produced into court and the execution thereof partly proven by the oaths of Ulyssus McKenzie one of the witnesses thereto and ordered to be certified.

Thomas Williams & Anner) Plts.   )   In Debt
Samuels Admr. of Anthony)   )
Samuel Deod.   )   )   This day came as well the plaintiffs
        Against   )   by their attornies, as also the de-
Robert Fenner .. Deft   )   fendant in his proper person, and
)   said defendant withdraws the pleas
heretofore filed in this case, and saith he cannot gainsay the plaintiffs
action against him nor but that he doth owe them the sum of one hundred and
Eighty one dollars and sixty two and a half cents, the Debt in the writing
obligatory in the declaration mentioned, and that the plaintiffs have sustained damages by reason of the detention of said debt, to the amount of
three dollars & sixty two cents, and agrees that Judgment may be entered
against him in favor of the plaintiffs debts considered by the court that
the plaintiffs recover of the said defendant the amount of his debt aforesaid together with his damages aforesaid in form aforesaid, agreed and also
their costs about their suit in this behalf expended - From which Judgment
the defendant prayed to the honorable the Circuit Court to be held for the
County of Giles, and having executed bond and security according to Law
the same was granted him.

William Gholson Plt.   )   In Covenant
        Against   )
William Watson Deft.   )   This day came the parties, by their attornies,
)   and by consent this cause is ordered to be
continued as on affidavit of the defendants he paying the costs of this
term - and that a commission issue to any two of the Acting Justice of the
Peace in and for the County of Madison State of Alabama to take the depositions of Claxton Lightfoot and Philip Lightfoot, also that a commission
issue to any two of the Acting Justices of the Peace in the County of Lawrence & State of Alabama to take the deposition of John C. Doughtry, and
also that a commission issue to any two of the Acting Justices of the Peace
in and for the County of Lauderdale & State of Alabama to take the depositio
of Benjamin Ingram, and also that a commission issue to any two of   (p-272)
the Acting Justice of the Peace in and for the County of Wilks and State of
Georgia to take the deposition of Gray Mabrey, all of which depositions
when taken to be read in evidence on the trial of this cause upon the Defendants giving to the plaintiffs agent James Perry ten days notice of the
time & place of taking the Deposition in the State of Alabama & Twenty five
days notice of the time and place of taking the deposition in the State of
Georgia aforesaid.

        A Bond from Davis Kilcrease to Robert McDonald was produced in court and
the Execution thereof proven by John McDonald, the subscribing witnesses
thereto, and ordered to be spread at full length upon the minutes of the of
this court which bond is in the words & figures, Towit, know all men by thei
presents that I Davis Kilcrease and held and firmly bound unto Robert Mc-
Donald in the same of two hundred Dollars, which Payment well and truly to
be made, I bind myself my heirs sealed with my seal this 18th of August 1823
The condition of the above obligation is such that the said Kilcrease for
the consideration of Eighty dollars in hand paid hath sold the said McDonald
fifteen acres of Land on the East side of sugar Creek the same located by
said McDonald and sold to a Mr. Hogan who resides on the same, nor should
the said Davis Kilcrease make a Deed in fee simple if applied to in six
months or after then - the above obligation to be void else to remain in
force.
Tests - John McDonald   Davis Kilcrease (Seal)

A Deed of conveyance from William Sawyers to Charles Simpson for one hundred & four acres of land was produced in court and the execution thereof acknowledged by the said William Sawyers and ordered to be certified for registration.

Ordered that the following tax list be received by the court and the double tax thereon remitted, Towit, John Smothers. 1 One Lot in Pulaski No. 13.

A Bill of sale from John W. R. Graves & Ralph Graves to James Conner & Lewis Conner for certain property therein named was produced in court and the execution thereof acknowledged by the said John W. R. Graves & Ralph Graves & ordered to be certified for registration.

The Grand Jury returned into court an Indictment of the State against Daniel Puryear for an affray with & an assault and battery on the body of John Philips on which is endorsed "A true Bill" and withdrew to consider of further presentments.

P-273   Tuesday 16th November 1824

A Deed of conveyance from Thomas Duty to James W. Wheeler for twenty acres & forty Eight poles of Land was produced in court and the execution thereof proven by the oaths of Archibald McKissack the subscribing witness thereto, and ordered to be certified for registration.

Robert Lockhart Plt.) In Covenant
Against)
William D. Jennings &) Defts.) This day came as well the parties by
James K. Murrah) their attorney, as also the Defend-
) ant in their proper person's and
said Defendants withdrew the Plea by them heretofore filed in this case, and say they cannot gainsay the plaintiffs Action against them, nor but that he hath sustained damages by occasion of the breaking of the covenant in the declaration complained of to two hundred and forty six dollars and sixty three cents, and agree that the plaintiff may have Judgment against against them for that that amount, with costs.
It is therefore considered by the court that with the assent of the plaintiff that he recover of the defendants the amount of his damages aforesaid in form aforesaid agreed and his costs by him about his suit in this behalf expended.

Ordered that court be adjourned untill tomorrow morning 9 oclock.

A. McKissack
John Bramlett
Wm. B. Pepper

P-274   Wednesday Morning November 17th 1824

Court met according to adjournment Present Archibald McKissack,)
                              John Bramlett and   ) Esquires
                              William B. Pepper   ) Justice
) of the
) Peace for
) Giles County.

William Ball Plt.   )   Appeal
   Against   )
John G. Russell Deft.   )   This day came the Defendant by his attorney,
)   and the plaintiff being Solemnly called came
not but made default, nor is his suit further prosecuted – It is therefore
considered by the court that the defendant go hence without day and recover
of the plaintiff his costs by him about his defence in this behalf expended.

Hannah Underwood Plt.   )   In Case
   Against   )
Lydall Wilkinson Deft.   )   This day came the parties by their attornies,
)   and on petition of the plaintiffs attorney
leave is given him to amend the declaration filed in this case upon her
paying the costs of the amendment.

William Ball Plt.   )   Certiorari
   Against   )
Ralph Graves Deft.   )   This day came the defendant by his attorney,
)   and the plaintiff being solemnly called came
not but made default, nor is his suit further prosecuted – It is therefore
considered by the court that the defendant go hence without day and recover
of the plaintiff his costs by him about his defence in this behalf expended.

James H. Maury Assee Plt.)   In Debt
    Against   )
William H. Moore Deft.   )   This day came the parties by their attornies
)   and thereupon came a Jury of good and Law-
ful men, Towit, Lander M. Shields, Davis Brown, Larkin Webb, Martin B. Wood,
Quinton Shannon, John G. Russell, Samuel Pearson, George Bowers, Ulysses Mc-
Kenzie, William Webb, James Conner, & Spencer Clack, who being Elected tried
and sworn well and truly to try the issue joined between the parties in
this case upon their oaths do say that the defendant has not paid the whole
of the debt in the Writing obligatory in the declaration mentioned and that
he has no sett off as the plaintiff in his replication hath alleged, and
they do assess the plaintiffs damages by occasion of the detention of said
Balance of Debt to twenty seven dollars & fifty four cents besides costs.
(p-275)   It is therefore considered by the court that the plaintiff recover of the sd. Defendant the sum of two hundred & twenty seven dollars
the Balance of his debt aforesaid together with his damages aforesaid in
form aforesaid by the Jurors aforesaid assessed, and also his costs about
his suit in this behalf expended – From which Judgment the Defendant prayed
an appeal to the honorable the Circuit Court to be held for the County of
Giles, and having executed bond and security according to law the same was
granted him.

207

George & William Shall Merchants &c. Plts.) In Debt
    Against)
Marcus Mitchell...Defts.) This day came the parties
) by their attornies, and
thereupon came a Jury of good and Lawful men, Towit, Leander M. Shields, Davis Brown, Larkin Webb, Martin B. Wood, Quinton Shannon, John G. Russell, Samuel Pearson, George Bowers, Ulysses McKenzie, William Webb, William H. Moore, and Spencer Clack, who being elected tried and sworn well and truly to try the issue joined between the parties in this case upon their oaths do say that the Defendant has not paid the Debt in the writing obligatory in the Declaration mentioned, as the plaintiffs in their replication have alleged, and they do assess the plaintiffs damages by occasion of the detention of sd. debt to three dollars & twelve cents, besides costs. It is therefore considered by the court that the plaintiffs recover of said Defendant the sum of one hundred & fifty six dollars & eighty six & a half cents the amount of his Debt aforesaid together with his damages aforesaid in form aforesaid by the Jurors aforesaid assessed and also their costs about their suit in this behalf expended.

Peter Bass . . . Plt.) In Debt
    Against)
Adam R. Faris &) Defts.) This day came the parties by their at-
Isaac S. W. Cook) tornies, and thereupon came a Jury of
) good and Lawful men, Towit, Leander
M. Shields, Davis Brown, Larkin Webb, Martin B. Woods, Quinton Shannon, John G. Russell, Samuel Pearson, George Bowers, Ulysses McKenzie, William Webb, William H. More, and Spencer Clack who being elected tried and sword well & truly to try the issue joined between the parties in this case upon their oaths do say that the defendants have not paid the debt in the writing obligatory in the declaration mentioned and that they have no sett off as the plaintiff in his replication has alleged, and they do assess the plaintiffs damages by occasion of the detention of sd. Debt to seven Dollars & seventy five cents - besides costs.

It is therefore considered by the court that the plaintiff recover of the sd. Defendants the sum of one hundred & twenty five dollars the amount of his debt aforesaid together with his damages aforesaid in form aforesaid by the Jurors aforesaid assessed, and also his costs by him about his suit in this behalf expended.

P-276 Wednesday 17th November 1824

Tyree Rodes . . . Plt.) In Debt
    Against)
Jonathan Ford Deft.) This day came the parties by their attornies
) and thereupon came a Jury of good and Law-
ful men, Towit, Leander M. Shields, Davis Brown, Larkin Webb, Martin, B. Woods, Quinton Shannon, John G. Russell, Samuel Pearson, George Bowers, Ulysses McKenzie, William Webb, William H. Moore, & Spencer Clack, who being elected tried and sworn well and truly to try the issue joined between the parties in this case, upon their oaths do say that the defendant has not paid the Debt in the writing obligatory in the Declaration mentioned as the plaintiff in his replication has alleged, but that their remains a Balance of said Debt yet unpaid to the amount of two hundred and fourteen dollars & sixty nine cents and they do assess the plaintiffs damages by occasion of the detention of said Balance of Debts to Ten dollars & seventy cents, besides costs. It is therefore considered by the court that the

plaintiff recover of said Defendant the Balance of his Debt aforesaid, together with his Damages aforesaid in form aforesaid by the Jurors aforesaid assessed and his costs about his suit in this behalf expended.

Tyree Rodes . . . Plt.
    Against
Jonathan Ford Deft.

In Debt

This day came the parties by their attornies and thereupon came a Jury of good and Lawful men, Towit, Leander M. Shields, Davis Brown, Larkin Webb, Martin B. Wood, Quinton Shannon, John G. Russell, Samuel Pearson, George Bowers, Ulyssus McKenzie, William Webb, William H. Moore, & Spencer Clack, who being elected tried and sworn well and truly to try the issue joined between the parties in this case upon their oaths do say that the Defendant has not paid the debt in the Writing obligatory in the declaration mentioned as the plaintiff in his replication has alleged and they do assess the plaintiffs damages by occasion of the detention of said Debt to twelve Dollars - besides costs:- It is therefore considered by the court that the plaintiff recover of said Defendant the sum of two hundred & twenty five dollars, the amount of his debt aforesaid, together with his damages, aforesaid, in form aforesaid by the Jurors aforesaid assessed, and his costs about his suit in this behalf expended.

Edward D. Jones Plt.
    Against
James H. Graves Deft.

In Case

This day came the parties by their attornies and thereupon came a Jury of good and lawful men, Towit, Leander M. Shields, (p-277) Davis Brown, Larkin Webb, Martin B. Wood, Quinton Shannon, John G. Russell, Samuel Pearson, George Bowers, Ulysses McKenzie, William Webb, William H. Moore & Spencer Clack, who being elected tried and sworn well and truly to try the issue joined between the parties in this case upon their oaths do say that they find said issue in favor of the plaintiff and assess his damages to one hundred & ten dollars & fifty cents besides costs - It is therefore considered by the court that the plaintiff recover of the said Defendant the amount of his damages aforesaid in form aforesaid by the Jurors aforesaid assessed and his costs about his suit in this behalf expended.

John C. McLemore Assee &c Plt.
    Against
William Perry . . . . Deft.

In Debt

This day came the parties by their attornies, and thereupon came a Jury of good and Lawful men, Towit, Leander M. Shields, Davis Brown, Larkin Webb, Martin B. Wood, Quinton, Shannon, John G. Russell, Samuel Pearson, George Bowers, Ulysses McKenzie, William Webb, William H. Moore & Spencer Clack, who being elected tried and sworn well and truly to try this issue joined between the parties in this case upon their oaths do say that the defendant has not paid the debt in the Writing obligatory in the Declaration mentioned as the plaintiff in his replication has alleged, and they do assess the plaintiff in his replication by detention of the sd. debt to twenty five dollars, besides costs.

It is therefore considered by the court that the plaintiff recover of the sd. Defendant the sum of four hundred & Eighty dollars the amounts of his debts aforesaid, together with his damages aforesaid in form aforesaid by the Jurors aforesaid assessed, and his costs by him about his suit in this behalf expended.

John C. McLemore Assee &c Plt.)   In Debt
    Against)
Martin Davenport ... Deft.)   This day came the parties by their
) attorneys and thereupon came a Jury
of good and Lawful men, Towit, Leander M. Shields, Davis Brown, Larkin Webb, Martin B. Wood, Quinton Shannon, John G. Russell, Samuel Pearson, George Bowers, Ulyses McKenzie, William Webb, William H. Moore, & Spencer Clack, who being elected tried and sworn well & truly to try the issue joined between the parties in this case upon their oaths do say that the Defendant has not paid the debt in the writing obligatory in the Declaration mentioned as the plaintiff in his replication has alleged and they do assess the plaintiffs damages by occasion of the detention of sd. Debt to fifteen dollars & fifty cents, besides costs. It is therefore considered by the court that the plaintiff recover of the sd. defendant, the sum of three hundred dollars the amount of his debt aforesaid, together with his damages aforesaid in form aforesaid by the Jurors aforesaid assessed, and his costs by him about his suit in this behalf expended.

P-278   Wednesday 17th November 1824

John C. McLemore Assee &c Plt.)   In Debt
    Against)
Abraham Shuler .... Deft.)   This day came the parties by thier
) attornies, and thereupon came a
Jury of good and Lawful men, Towit, Leander M. Shields, Davis Brown, Larkin Webb, Martin B. Wood, Quinton Shannon, John G. Russell, Samuel Pearson, George Bowers, Ulysses McKenzie, William Webb, William H. Moore & Spencer Clack, who being elected tried and sworn well and truly to try the issue Joined between the parties in this case upon their oaths do say that the Defendant hath not paid the debt in the Writing obligatory in the declaration mentioned, and that he has not sett off as the plaintiff in his replication has alleged, and they do assess the plaintiffs damages by occasion of the Detention of sd. debt to nine dollars, besides costs. It is therefore considered by the court that the plaintiff recover of the sd. defendant the sum of two hundred dollars the amount of his debt aforesaid, together with his damages aforesaid in form aforesaid by the Jurors aforesaid, assessed, and his costs by him about his suit in this behalf expended.

John C. McLemore Assee &c Plt.)   In Debt
    Against)
Abraham Shuler Deft.)   This day came the parties by their
) attornies and thereupon came a Jury
of good and Lawful men, Towit, Leander M. Shields, David Brown, Larkin Webb, Martin B. Wood, Quinton Shannon, John G. Russell, Samuel Pearson, George Bowers, Ulysses McKenzie, William Webb, William H. Moore, & Spencer Clack, who being elected tried and sworn well and truly to try the issue joined between the parties in this case upon their oaths do say that the defendant has not paid the debt in the writing obligatory in the declaration mentioned, and that he has no sett off as the plaintiff in his replication as alleged, and they do assess the plaintiffs damages by occasion of the detention of sd. debt to Three dollars & fifty cents - besides costs. It is therefore considered by the court that the plaintiff recover of said Defendant the sum of one hundred and fifty dollars the amount of his debt aforesaid together with his damages aforesaid, in form aforesaid

by the Jurors aforesaid assessed, and his costs by him about his suit in this behalf expended.

The Administrators of the Estate of Augusta L. Jones returned into court an account of sale of said Estate which is ordered to be recorded.

P-279   Wednesday 17th November 1824

The commissioners who were appointed to allot to the widow of Augustus L. Jones Decd. one years provisions out of said Augustus L. Jones Estate, made return of said allotments into court which is ordered to be recorded.

Ordered that Letters of Administration on the Estate of Samuel Caswell decd. be granted to Patience Caswell, Whereupon she entered into bond and security and was qualified as the Law directs.

Edmund Shelton Plt.   ) Certiorari
  Against   )
Aaron Smith &   )Defts.   ) This day came the parties by their attornies
Nathaniel Young)   ) and thereupon came the defendant Young by
) his attorney moved the court now here to
Quash the proceedings in this case as to him for want of Indictment in the Justice of the Peace who rendered the Judgment, which motion after solemn argument, and mature deliberation thereupon being had by the court it is ordered that said motion be sustained.

Edmund Shelton Plaintiff   ) Certiorari
  Against   )
Aaron Smith Defendant   ) This day came the parties by their attornies
) and thereupon came a Jury of good and Lawful men, Towit, John Bass, Davis Brown, Larkin Webb, Leander M. Shields, Martin B. Wood, William Webb, Jesse West, Samuel P. Hicks, James P. Hicks, Isaac Crowder, and James S. Conner, who being elected tried and sworn well and truly to try the matter in controversey between the parties in this case upon their oaths do say that the defendant is indebted to the plaintiff the sum of sixty three dollars and twenty cents, Besides costs. It is therefore considered by the court that the plaintiff recover of said defendant the amount of his debt aforesaid together with his costs by him about his suit in this behalf expended as well the Justices of the Peace as in this court.

John Brown Assignee &c Plt.   ) In Debt
  against   )
Thomas Rosborough Deft.   ) This day came the parties by their
) attornies, and thereupon came a
Jury of good and lawful men, Towit, Leander M. Shields, Davis Brown, Larkin Webb, Martin B. Wood, Quinton Shannon, George Bowers, Ulysses McKenzie, John G. Russell, Samuel Pearson, William Webb, William H. Moore, & Spencer Clack, who being elected tried and sworn well and truly to try the issue Joined between the parties in this case upon their oaths   (p-280) do say that they find the issue in favor of the defendant, and that the defendant owes the plaintiff the sum of three Hundred and thirty seven dollars and

and fifty cents, and they do assess the plaintiffs damages by occasion of the detention thereof to forty two dollars and fifty cents, Besides costs. It is therefore considered by the court that the plaintiff recover of the defendant the amount of his debt aforesaid, together with his damages aforesaid in form aforesaid by the Jurors aforesaid assessed, and his costs by him about this suit in this behalf expended.

George Hass . . . . Plaintiff) Motion
    Against)
Thomas Johnston Defendant) This day came the plaintiff by David
) A. Smith his attorney and moved the
court now here for Judgment against the defendant for the sum of twenty one dollars and forty nine cents which he hath paid a co security for said defendant, and thereupon came a Jury of good and lawful men, Towit, John Bass, Davis Brown, Larkin Webb, Leander M. Shields, Quinton Shannon, Martin B. Wood, Edward Shelton, William Jones, James Shelton, George Bowers, William Webb, & Archibald Smith, who being elected tried and sworn well and truly to inquire in this case upon their oaths do say that on the 14th day of May 1819, Peter Powell Thomas Johnston & George Hoss undertook as Co. Security for William Brown to Andrew Tunbeam for the sum of three hundred dollars due the first day of September 1819, and that a Judgment for Debt, damages, and costs, amounting to three hundred & thirty six dollars & fifty eight cents founded on the aforesaid bond to Turnbeam was satisfied by Peter Powell and sd. George Hoss on the 10th day of April 1820, and that they find the amount which said plaintiff paid for sd. Defendant as his Co. Security on the sd. 10th day of April 1820, was Fifty six dollars & nine cents, which with interest thereon till the 10th day of November 1824 amounts to the above sum of seventy one dollars & forty nine cents. It is therefore considered by the court that the plaintiff recover of said defendant the aforesaid sum of seventy one dollars & forty nine cents together with the costs of this motion.

Thomas McKissack Plt.) In Debt
    Against)
Graves Steele German) This day came the parties by their
Lester Admr. &c. James Defts.) attornies, and thereupon came a
H. Graves & Archibald McKissack) Jury of good and Lawful men, Towit,
) John Bass, David Brown, Larkin Webb,
Leander M. Shields, Quinton Shannon, Martin B. Wood, Edward Shelton, (p-281) William Jones, James Shelton, George Bowers, William Webb & Archibald Smith, who being elected tried and sworn well and truly to try the issue joined between the parties in this case upon their oaths do say that the defendants have not paid the debt in the Writing obligatory in the declaration mentioned as the plaintiff in his replication has alleged, and they do assess the plaintiffs damages by occasion of the detention of sd. debt to thirty four dollars - Besides costs. It is therefore considered by the court that the plaintiff recover of the said defendants the sum of two hundred & Eighty three Dollars, the amount of his Debt aforesaid, together with his damages aforesaid in form aforesaid by the Jurors aforesaid assessed, and his costs by him about his suit in this behalf expended - To be levied of the goods and chattles lands and tenments of the said Graves Steele, James H. Graves, & Archibald McKissack and of the goods & chattles right & credits of the Estate of David Steele decd. in the hands of German Lester Admr. &c to be administered.

Ordered that Court be adjourned untill tomorrow morning 9 oclock.

H. Hagen
A. McKissack
John Bramlett

P-282   Thursday Morning 18th November 1824

Court met according to adjournment Present Henry Hagen,) Esquires Justice
Archibald McKissack) of the Peace
John Bramlett) for the County
) of Giles.

The State Plt. Against Samuel Day Deft.	Upon a Presentment for an affray with & An assault & battery on the body of James Downing.

This day came as well the Solicitor General for the State as also the Defendant in his proper person, who being charged on the presentment in this case pleads guilty, and because he will not contend with the State agrees to submit himself to the Justice and mercy of the Court.

It is therefore considered by the court that he make his fine with the State to the amount of one Dollar, and that he pay the costs of this prosecution and that he be committed to the custody of the Sheriff of this County thereto remain till said fine & costs are paid.

The State Plt. Against James Lane, Deft.	Upon an Indictment for an affray with & an assault & battery on the body of Abraham Irvine.

For reasons made known to the court by the Solicitor General for the State, who saith he wishes no further to prosecute the Defendant in this case. It is ordered that a Nole prosequi be entered therein, and that the defendant go hence without day.

The State Plt. Against James Lane Deft.	Upon an Indictment for an affray with & an assault & battery on the body of Abraham Irvine.

A Nole Prosequi having been entered in this case under the direction of the court. It is ordered that Judgment be entered up against the County of Giles in favor of the Several claimants on the part of the State for all costs to which they are entitled, and that the Clerk certify the same to the trustee of Giles County for payment.

The State . . . . Plt. Against Edward K. McMillin Deft.	Scire facias

This day came as well the Solicitor General for the State, and the Defendant altho solemnly called came not but made default. It is therefore considered by the court that the Judgment Ni. Si - heretofore taken against him for the sum of two hundred and fifty dollars be made final against him and that execution thereof be awarded.

The Grand Jury returned into court a presentment against Samuel King for an affray with & an Assault & battery on the body of William Finney & withdrew to consider of further presentments

P-283   Thursday 18th November 1824

The State Plt.   )   Upon an Indictment for an affray with & an as-
   Against   )   sault & battery on the body of Thomas Steele.
David Graves Deft.   )
)   This day came as well the Solicitor General for
the State as also the defendant in his proper person, who being charged on
the Indictment in this case pleads not guilty, and for the trial puts himself upon the Country and the Solicitor General for the State on the part
of the State likewise, therefore let a Jury came, who as well &c to recognize &c and thereupon came a Jury of good and lawful men, Towit, John Bass,
Martin B. Wood, Davis Brown, Leander M. Sheilds, Larkin Webb, Charles Edwards, Daniel Frazier, George Everly, John G. Russell, Jesse West, John
Walthall & Quinton Shannon, - who being elected tried and sworn well and
truly to try the issue of Traverse between the State and sd. Defendant,
upon their oaths do say that the Defendant is guilty in manner and form as
he is charged in the Indictment. It is therefore considered by the court
that he make his fine with the State to the amount of Six and one fourth
cents, and that he pay the costs of this prosecution and that he be committed to the custody of the Sheriff of this County there to remain till
said fine & costs be paid.

The State Plt. Plt.   )   Upon an Indictment for an affray with & an
   Against   )   assault & battery on the body of John Phillips
Daniel Puryear Deft.   )
)   This day came as well the Solicitor General
for the State as also the Defendant in his proper person who being on the
Indictment in this case pleads guilty, and because he will not contend with
the State agrees to submit himself to the Justice & mercy of the court -
It is therefore considered by the court that he make his fine with the
State to the amount of one Dollar and that he pay the costs of this prosecution and that he be committed to the Custody of the Sheriff of this County
there to remain till said fine and costs are paid.

Samuel S. Smith &   )   Petition
Jane B. Smith his wife   )
       Against   )   This day came the parties by their
John Porter Guardian &c Deft.   )   attornies, and by consent leave is
)   given each party to take depositions
both in and out of this State, which when taken are to be read in evidence
on the trial of this cause upon the Defendant giving to the plaintiffs &
the plaintiffs giving to the Defendant ten days notice of the time and place
of the taking depositions in this State, and twenty days notice of the time
and place of taking those out of this State.

On motion it is ordered that the order which was made at the Last Term
of this court appointing commissioners to settle with the Estate of Joseph
Bradley decd. be received, and that said commissioners be allowed untill
next court to make return of said settlement.

P-284 Thursday 18th November 1824

Simeon Hensley Plt.　　　)　　　　Original Attachment
　　Against　　　　　　　)
Anthony Taylor &)Defts.　)　This day came the plaintiff by his attorney
Henry Taylor　　)　　　　)　and the defendant altho solemnly called
　　　　　　　　　　　　　)　came not but made default. It is therefore
considered by the court that the plaintiff recover of the Defendant the sum
of one hundred & five dollars, the amount of the debt in the Writing obligatory in the Declaration mentioned, together with the sum of five dollars
and twenty five cents, the damages which he hath sustained by reason of
the detention of said debts, and his costs by him about his suit in this
behalf expended - Ordered that an order of sale issue to the Sheriff of this
County commanding to expose to sale the property which was Levied on by virtue of the original attachment in this case.

John Webb Plt.　　　　　)　　　　 Motion
　　Against　　　　　　　)
Joseph Rea &　)Defts.　　)　This day came the parties by their attor-
John Warren　)　　　　　)　nies, and by consent this cause is ordered
　　　　　　　　　　　　　)　is ordered to be dismissed as the costs of
plaintiff. It is therefore considered by the court that the Defendant go
hence without day and recover of the plaintiff their costs by them about
their defence in this behalf expended.

　　　Ordered that a venditioni exponas issue to the Sheriff of the County
commanding him to advertise & sell according to Law one hundred and sixty
nine acres of land, adjoining James Hannas with boundry line, levied on on
the 25th day of October 1824 as the property of John Boyd Senior by Jos.
White Constable of Giles County to satisfy an execution which issued on a
Judgment which John Boyd Junior recovered against him sd. John Boyd Senior
before Hezekiah Jones Esquire a Justice of the Peace for this County on the
23rd day of October 1824 for the sum of Eighty nine dollars, fifty one & a
half cents & costs.

The State ... Plt.　　)　Upon a presentment for an affray with an as-
　　Against　　　　　　)　sault & battery on the body of John Gilliam.
Benjamin Tutt Deft.　　)

　　　Benjamin Tutt, and Hansford Tutt, comes into
court and acknowledges themselves indebted to the State of Tennessee in the
Sum of one hundred Dollars each to be levied of their goods and chattles
lands & tenments to the use of the State to be void on condition that said
Benjamin Tutt appear here on the first Thursday after the third Monday in
February next and answer the State upon a presentment for an affray with &
an　(p-285)　Assault and Battery on the body of John Gilliam, and not
depart therefrom without leave of this court.

The State Plt.　　　　　)　Upon a Presentment for an affray with Bailey
　　Against　　　　　　　)　Davis.
David Stockton Deft.　　)

　　　David Stockton and James Coldwell comes into
court and acknowledges themselves indebted to the State of Tennessee in the
sum of one hundred Dollars, each to be levied of their goods and chattles

215

lands and tenments to the use of the State to be void on condition that the said David Stockton appear here on the first Thursday after the third Monday in February next, and answer the State upon a presentment for an affray with Bailey Davis, and not depart therefrom without Leave of the Court.

Benjamin White Plt.) In Case
Against)
John Gregory . . Deft.) This day came the parties by their attor-
) nies, and on motion this suit is ordered
to be dismissed. Each party paying his own costs.

The State Plt.) Upon a presentment for an affray with David
Against) Stockton.
Bailey Davis Deft.)
) This day came as well the Solicitor General for the State as also the Defendant in his proper person who being charged on the presentment in this case pleads not guilty and for his trial puts himself upon his country, and the Solicitor General for the State on the part of the State likewise, therefore let a Jury come who as well &c to recognize &c and thereupon came a Jury of good and lawful men, Towit, Quinton Shannon, Davis Brown, Larkin Webb, Martin B. Wood, Leander M. Shields, Nathan Davis, Herrod Foulks, Thomas Wilkinson, Charles Edwards, William W. Thornton, George I. Jourdan, & Willis W. Cole, who being elected tried and sworn well & truly to try the issue of Traverse between the State and sd. Defendant upon their oaths do say that said Defendant is not guilty in manner & form as he is charged in the presentment - It is therefore considered by the court that the Defendant be acquitted and discharged from the affray aforesaid, and that he go hence without day.

The State Plt.) Upon a presentment for an affray with David
Against) Stockton.
Bailey Davis Deft.)
The Defendant in this case having been acquitted on the trial on the merits by a Jury - It is ordered that a Judgment be entered up against the County of Giles in favor of the Several claimants, on the part of the State for all costs to which they are entitled, and that the Clerk certify the same to the Trustee of the County for payment.

P-286 Thursday 18th November 1824

The State . . . Plt.) Upon an Indictment for an affray with &
Against) an assault & battery on the body of Gabl.
William D. Jenning Deft.) W. Paine & Edwin Hardin.
)
This day came as well the Solicitor General for the State as allso the Defendant in his proper person, who being charged on the Indictment in this case pleads not guilty, and for the trial puts himself upon his County and the Solicitor General for the State on the part of the State Likewise, therefore let a Jury come, who as well &c to recognize &c and thereupon came a Jury of good & Lawful men, Towit, George Oliver, George Rice, Joseph Young, John McKissack, Matthew Johnson, Elijah Anthony, George W. Lock, Thomas Cole, David Kearsey, William Dudley, William May, & Robert Black,

who being elected tried and sworn well and truly to try the issue of Travers between the State and said Defendant upon their oaths do say that sd. Defendant is guilty in manner and form as he is charged in the Indictment aforesaid whereupon the Defendant moved the court now here for a rule to be entered to shew cause why a new trial should be had in this case which was granted.

The State .. Plt. Against Enoch Reynolds Deft.	Upon a Recognizance for Bastardy.

This day came the defendant, and Hugh Bratton, John W. O. Graves, William W. Thornton and Larkin Mayfield and acknowledged themselves indebted to the State of Tennessee in the sum of Five hundred dollars to be levied of their goods and chattles lands & tenments to the use of the State to be void on condition that they or either of them keep free from charge to this county a Bastard child said to have been begotten by the defendant on the body of Patsey ....Bratton of this County, and thereupon it is considered by the court that the defendant pay the costs of this prosecution, and that he be committed to the Custody of the Sheriff of this County thereto remain till said costs be paid or untill he give security for the payment of the same, and thereupon Thomas Bratton came into court and undertook as security for the defendant for the payment of the costs aforesaid.

Larkin Mayfield Plt. Against Robert G. Steele &) Defts. Nathaniel Steele	Motion

This day came the plaintiff by Lunsford M. Bramlett his attorney and moved the court now here for Judgment against the Defendants for the sum of Eighty five dollars & ninety two cents which they had paid as security for them, and it not appearing to the satisfaction of the court from the face of the Execution and receipts produced in court whether the plaintiff was principal or security, a Jury was thereupon empannelled to try the fact, Towit, John Bass, Martin B. Wood, (p-287) Davis Brown, Leander M. Shields, Larkin Webb, Charles Edwards, John Walthall, Joseph Calvert, Spencer Clack, Benjamin Jordan, William W. Thornton, And George Everly, who being sworn well and truly to enquire as aforesaid upon their oaths do say that Larkin Mayfield, the said plaintiff together with Thomas Steele was security for the Stay of a Judgment recovered by Alfred Flournoy against Robert G. Steele & Nathan Steele on the 8th day of February 1822 for the sum of seventy five dollars & costs, and it appearing to the satisfaction of the Court that the sd. plaintiff has paid as such security the sum of ninety five dollars & ninety two cents, for the satisfaction of an execution aforesaid on sd. Judgments. It is therefore considered by the court that he recover of the said Robert G. Steele & Nathaniel Steele the principals in sd. Execution and Judgments the sum of Eighty three dollars Eighteen & three fourth cents, it being the principal and interest paid by sd. plaintiff as security for sd. Defendant together with the costs of this motion.

Larkin Mayfield Plt. Against Thomas Steele Deft.	Motion

This day came the plaintiff by Lunsford M. Bramlett his attorney and moved the court now here for Judgment against the Defendant for the sum of Forty one dollars & fifty nine cents which he has paid as Co security for Thomas Steele in a Judgment recovered by Alfred Floyrnoy against Robert G. Steele & Nathaniel Steele, and it not appearing to the satisfaction of the court from the face of the Judgment, that the said plaintiff and defendants were securities a Jury was thereupon empannelled to try that fact, towit, John Bass, Martin B. Wood, Davis Brown, Leander M. Shields, Larkin Webb, Charles Edwards, John Walthall, Joseph Calvert, Spencer Clack, Benjamin Jordan, William W. Thornton, & George Everly, who being sworn well and truly to enquire as aforesd. upon their oaths do say that the said plaintiff and Defendant were securities for the stay of a Judgment & Execution recovered on the 8th day of February 1822 for the sum of Seventy five Dollars & costs of suit by Alfred Flournoy against Robert G. Steele and Nathaniel Steele, and it appearing to the satisfaction of the court that the plaintiff paid the sum of ninety five dollars & ninety two cents, the whole of sd. Judgment & Execution on the 7th day of January 1823. It is therefore considered by the court that the plaintiff recover of the Defendant & co security the sum of Forty one dollars & fifty nine cents, it being the principal & interest of the one half paid as security in the Judgment of sd. Floyrnoy against Robert G. Steele & Nathaniel Steele and also the costs of this motion.

Ordered that Court be adjourned untill tomorrow morning nine oclock.

H. Hagen
Tos. K. Gordon
A. McKissack

P-288 Friday Morning 19th November 1824

Court met according to adjournment Present Henry Hagen) Esquires Justice
Thos. K. Gordon &) of the Peace for
Archibald McKissack) Giles County.

Lewis H. Brown Plt.   )   In Case
    Against   )
William Shall &)Defts.   )   The Referees to whom was refered the
Gerald Irby   )   )   Settlement of this case returned into
)   court the following awards, towit,
We the Arbitrætors chosen by L. H. Brown & Gerald Irby to settle a certain Matter in controversy wherein said Brown is plaintiff & G. Irby & W. Shall are Defts. in the worshipful the County Court of Giles County, award that said Brown be & is authorised to redeem the share in dispute upon paying to said Irby the amt. of the purchase money at execution sale with 10 per cent per annum there on & the amt. of E. B. Mayfield account with William Shall amounting to forty one Dollars & 79 cents given under our hands & seals this 19th November 1824.

A. S. Jones (Seal)
A. Black   (Seal)
E. D. Jones (Seal)

Whereupon the plaintiff comes into court assumes all costs and orderes that this suit be dismissed which is done accordingly.

The State ... Plt.) An Indictment for an affray with & an
　　Against   ) assault & battery on the bodies of Gabl.
William D. Jennings Deft.) W. Paine & Edwin Hardin.

For reasons made known to the courts by the Solicitor General for the State who saith he wishes no further to prosecute the Defendants in this case, It is ordered that a Nole prosequi be entered in this case, and that the Defendant go hence without Day.

The State Plt.   ) Upon an Indictment for an affray with & as-
　　Against   ) sault & battery of the bodies of G. W. Paine
W. D. Jennings Deft.) & Edwin Hardin a Nole prosqui having been
) entered in this case, under the directions
of the court. It is ordered that Judgment be entered up against the County of Giles in favor of the Several Clamants, on the part of the State for all costs to which they are entitled, and that the Clerk certify the same to the Trustee of Giles County for payment.

The administration of the Estate of Jordon Hicks decd. returned into court an account of the sale of sd. Estate which is ordered to be recorded.

P-289   Friday 19th November 1824

The State Plt.   ) Upon an Indictment for an affray with & an as-
　　Against   ) sault & battery on the body of Gabl. W. Paine
Melford Long Deft.) & Edward Hardin.

For reason made known to the Court by the Solicitor General for the State, who saith he wishes no further to prosecute the Defendant in this case, It is ordered that a nole prosqui be entered therein and that the defendant go hence without day.

The State Plt.   ) Upon an Indictment for an affray with & an as-
　　Against   ) sault & battery of the body of G. W. Paine and
Melford Long Deft.) Edwin Hardin.

A Nole Prosqui having been entered in this case under the direction of the court. It is ordered that a Judgment be entered up against the County of Giles, in favor of the several claimants, on the part of the State, for all costs to which they are entitled and that the Clerk certify the same to the Trustee of Giles County for payments.

The State Plt.   ) Upon a presentment for an affray with & an
　　Against   ) assault & battery on the body of James Dailey.
John W. Edwards Deft.)
)   John W. Edwards, Robert G. Steele and
) Millinton Tidwell, comes into court and ack-
nowledges themselves indebted to the State of Tennessee in the sum for fifty dollars, each to be levied of their goods and chattles lands and tenments to the use of the State to be void on condition that the said John G. Edwards appear here on the first Thursday after the third Monday in February next,

and answer the State upon a presentment for an affray with & an assault,& battery on the body of James Dailey, and not depart without leave of the court.

The State Plt.) Upon an Indictment for an assault & battery
Against) on a slave named Amos.
William Tinnen Deft.)
) For reasons made known to the Solicitor
General for the State, who saith he wishes no further to prosecute the Defendant in this case. It is ordered that a nole prosqui be entered therein, and that the Defendant go hence without day.

The State Plt.) Upon an Indictment for an assault & battery
Against) on a Slave named Amos.
William Tinnen Deft.)
) A Nole prosqui having been entered in this
case under the direction of the court it is ordered that a Judgment be entered up against the County of Giles in favor of the Several Claimants on the part of the State, for all costs to which they are entitled, and that the Clerk certify the same to the Trustee of Giles County for payments.

P-290   Friday 19th November 1824.

John Bradley ... Plt.)   In Case
Against)
William D. Jennings Deft.) On the application of the plaintiff as
) on the affidavits ordered that a commission issue to any two of the Acting Justices of the Peace in and for the County of Madison & State of Alabama to take the deposition of George H. Malone, Thomas Gilliam & others to be read in evidence on the trial of this cause upon the plaintiffs giving to the Defendant ten days notice of the time and place of taking the deposition of sd. George H. Malone & Thomas Gilliam & twenty days notice of the time and place of taking the depositions of others if any.

Partrick H. Braden Assee &c Plt.)   Certiorari
Against)
William Parker .. Deft.) This day came the parties by their
) attornies, and the plaintiffs attorney moved the court for reasons shown to dismiss the cause, and after having heard the argument of counsel it is ordered that this cause be dismissed.

It is therefore considered by the court that the plaintiff recover of the defendant his costs by him about his suit in this behalf expended.

The Grand Jury returned into court the following indictments and presentments, Towit, The State Vs William Tinnen for an assault & Battery on the body of a slave named Amos, on which is indorsed "Not a true Bill" Same against Thomas B. Jones for retailing Spirituous Liquors, Same against Henry Harrison for retailing Spirituous Liquors, Same against Wm. P. A. McCabe for retailing Spirituous liquors, same Vs Jonathan Ford for an affray with & an assault & battery on the body of Thomas Baker, same against

............for failing to keep the road in repair which lies between Capt. Marcus Mitchells & Buckhannans Creek, same against John Bramlett for failing to keep the road in repair of which he is overseer – and having no other presentments to make were discharged.

Ordered that John Bass, Leander M. Shields, Davis Brown, Larkin Webb, & Martin B. Wood be excused from further attendance as petit Jurors at this term.

A Bill of sale from Joseph H. Hodge to Jacob Shall & William Shall for certain property therein mentioned was produced in court and the execution thereof proven by the oaths of Adam R. Faris, & Albert Yergers, the witnesses thereto and ordered to be certified for registration.

P-291. Friday 19th November 1824.

The State – Plt.) Upon an Indictment for an affray with & An
 Against   ) assault & battery on the body of Thomas Baker.
Jonathan Ford Deft.)
) Thomas Baker comes into court and acknowledges himself indebted to the State of Tennessee in the sum of one hundred dollars, to be levied of their goods and chattles lands and tenments to the use of the State to be void on condition that he appear here on the first Thursday after the third Monday in February next to prosecute and give evidence in behalf of the State, upon an Indictment against sd. Deft. Jonathan Ford for an affray with an assault & battery on the body of Thomas Baker & not depart with out leave of court.

Ordered that an order of sale issue to the administrator of the Estate of John Yancy Decd. commanding him to sell so much of the negros property as will be sufficient to satisfy the Debt against the said Estate, and make report thereof as the law directs.

The State Plt.) Upon a presentment for retailing Spiritous
 Against   ) Liquors.
Thomas P. Jones Deft.)
) For reasons made known to the court by the Solicitor General for the State who saith he wishes no further to prosecute the defendant in this case It is ordered that a nole prosqui be entered therein, and that the defendant go hence without day – and no costs to be taxed in this case.

The State Plt.) Upon a presentment for retailing Spriitous
 Against   ) Liquors.
Henry Harrison Deft.)
) For reasons made known to the court by the Solicitor General for the State, who saith he wishes no further to prosecute the defendant in this case. It is ordered that a Nole prosqui be entered therein, and that the defendant go hence without day, and no costs to be taxed in this case.

221.

The State Plaintiff	)	Upon a Presentment for retailing
Against	)	Spiritous Liquors.
William P. A. McCabe Deft.	)	

For reasons made known to the court by the Solicitor General for the State, who saith he wishes no further to prosecute the defendant in this case. It is therefore ordered that a Nole prosqui be entered therein, and that the defendant go hence without day and no cost to be taxed in this case.

The State Plt.	)	Upon a presentment for failing to keep the
Against	)	road in repairing.
John Bramlett Deft.	)	

This day came as well the Solicitor General for the State as also the Defendant in his proper person, who (p-292) being charged on the presentment in this case pleads guilty, and because he will not contend with the State agrees to submitt himself to the Justice and mercy of the Court. It is therefore considered by the court that he make his fine with the State to the amount of six and one fourth cents, and that he pay the costs of this prosecution, and that he be committed to the custody of the Sheriff of this county there to remain till sd. fine and costs are paid.

Ordered that Court be adjourned untill tomorrow morning nine oclock.

                                                                         Thomas K. Gordon
                                                                         John Bramlett
                                                                         E. D. Jones

                        Saturday morning 20th November 1824

Court met according to adjournment Present Thos. K. Gordon	)	Esquires
Edward D. Jones	)	Justices
John Bramlett	)	of the
	)	Peace for
	)	Giles County

James Perry ... Plaintiff			In Debt
Against			
Ralph Graves, John Brown,	)		This day came the parties
William W. Thornton, Marcus	) Defts.		by their attornies, and on
Mitchell & James Patteson	)		motion of the plaintiffs
			attorney it is ordered that

his suit be dismissed, Therefore it is considered by the court that the Defendants recover of the plaintiff their costs by them about their defence in this behalf expended.

A Deed of conveyance from Nathaniel Young to James Patteson for lot No. 6 in the Town of Pulaski of the Large Lots was produced in court and the Execution thereof acknowledged by the said Nathaniel Young, and ordered to be certified for registration.

Page #222
BLANK

George & William Shall Merchants &c Plts.)   In Debt
        Against   )
Marcus Mitchel . . Deft.   )   From the Judgment of the
)   court in this case rendered the Defendant prayed an appeal to the honorable the Circuit Court to be held for the County of Giles, and having executed bond and security according to Law the same was granted him.

P-293   Saturday 20th November 1824

     A Deed of conveyance from John Paul Executor of John Paul Decd. To Samuel B. Keenan for Lot No. 3 in the Town of Pulaski was produced in court, and the execution thereof proven by the oaths of Collins S. Tarpley, and William A. Maulthby, the witnesses thereto and ordered to be certified for registration.

Hannah Underwood Plt.   )   In Debt
       Against   )
Lydall Wilkinson Deft.   )   On the application of the plaintiff It is
)   ordered that a commission issue to any two of the Acting Justice of the Peace in and for this County to take the deposition of Albert G. Underwood Defencessee, also that a commission issue to any two of the Acting Justices of the Peace in & for the County of Limestone & State of Alabama to take the deposition of John H. Matthews, also that a commission issue to any two of the Acting Justices of the peace in & for the County of Madison and State of Alabama to take the Deposition of Alfred T. Jones, all of which are to be read in evidence on the trial of this cause, upon the plaintiff giving to the Defendants attorney ten days notice of the time and place of taking the Deposition of Alfred G. Underwood & fifteen days notice of the time and place of taking the deposition of sd. John H. Matthews & Alfred T. Jones, and on motion of the Defendants attorney as on affidavits. It is ordered that a commission issue to any two of the Acting Justices of the Peace in and for the County of Madison & State of Alabama to take the depositions of John Silvers, George S. Smith, Nathaniel Baker, John T. Mills, George T. Jones, Joseph Jones, and Samuel Ragland, and that a commission issue to any two of the Acting Justice of the Peace in & for the County of Limestone & State aforesaid to take the depositions of Barnett Tatum, Mary Tatum, Archibald Dandridge, William Dandridge, Elvira Dandridge, and William Seallions all of which depositions to be read in evidence on the trial of this casue, and that the defendant give to the plaintiff fifteen days notice of the time and place of taking the same.

Ralph Graves Plt.   )   Motion
    Against   )
Isaac Mayfield Deft.   )   This day came the plaintiff by Harris & Field
)   his attornies, and moved the court now here for Judgment against the Defendant for the sum of ninety six dollars & thirty three cents, with interest thereon at the rate of six per centure per annum from the 18th day of February 1824 which he has paid as security for him, and it not appearing to the satisfaction of the court, whether the plaintiff was principal or security a Jury was therefore empannelled to try that fact, towit, Quinton Shannon, George Everly, Spencer Clack,   (p-294) Shadrack Harwell, Harry Scales, Hugh H. Williams, Joseph Alsup, Joseph McDonald, Simpson H. White, Andrew Gordon, Jesse Crittendon, & John Crittindon,

who being sworn well and truly to try the facts aforesaid upon their oaths do say that said plaintiff did on the 18th day of February 1824 pay as co security for the defendant the sum of ninety six dollars & thirty three cents, on an execution which issued, on a Judgment that William Ranks Assee. &c recovered against John Keenan & Henry Hagen, Ralph Graves & Isaac Mayfield, his security in the Giles Circuit Court at the August term 1823,. It is therefore considered by the court that the plaintiff recover of the defendant the aforesaid sum of ninety six dollars & thirty three cents, with legal interest thereon from the 18th day of February 1824 till paid together with the costs of the motion.

Gray H. Edwards & Susan his wife)   Petition for distributive Shares.
Spencer Clack & Lucinda his wife)
John Walthall & Pamelia his wife)
Vs)   On motion of the said plaintiffs by
Thomas McKissack Deft.)   their attorneys and it appearing to
)   the satisfaction of the court now
)   here, that this court did at May
term 1824 by consent of the parties aforesaid order that German Lester Clerk of this Court between that time and the next ensuing term of said Court take an account of all the monied transactions between the defendant and the heirs of Wilson Jones decd. and that the said German Lester, Charles Buford, Richard Brandon, & James Buford, or any two of them between that time and sd. next ensuing term of sd. court, value and devide all the slaves and other personal Estate of sd. William Jones decd. into five equal shares and allot to the said plaintiffs one fifth each and to Calvin Jones & Thomas Jones heirs of sd. Wilson Jones Decd. one fifty each, and that they or any two of them also defide the amount of money and claims for money that may be found upon the account to be taken as aforesd. in the hands of the sd. Defendant as Admr. of sd. Wilson Jones decd. and it further appearing to the court, now here that German Lester Esquire having failed to make the report of the amount of all the monied transactions between the defendant and the heirs of said Wilson Jones decd. at the term next succeeding sd. May term 1824 of this court as regained by sd. order it was at August term 1824 of this court, on the motion of the plaintiffs by their attorney, Ordered by the court that the sd. orders made at the May term 1824 of sd. court, so far as it related to the appointments of the said German Lester Esq. to take an account of all the monied transaction between the defendant and the sd. heirs of Wilson Jones Decd. be received and that said German Lester report   (p-295) (Saturday 20th November 1824) Such accounts to the next ensuing term of this court - And it further appearing to the satisfaction of the court now here, that German Lester, Charles Buford, Richd. Brandon, & James Buford, who or any two of whom were appointed as aforesaid to value & devide all the Slaves and other personal Estate of sd. Wilson Jones Decd. into five equal parts, and to allot the same as aforesaid and also to devide the money and claims for money which were in the hands of sd. Defendants as administrator of sd. Wilson Jones decd. so far as they could do so without the accounts of the sd. German Lester Esqr. which was to have been taken as aforesd. and it further appearing to the court now here, that sd. report so made as aforesd. which is in the words & figures following Towit, we the undersigned appointed by an order of Giles County Court at May term 1824 commissions to devide the money and negroes belonging to the Estate of Wilson Jones decd. after Examining the claims for money due the Estate we find that on the settlement of the Estate by commissions appointed to make the same a balance due the Estate from Thomas McKissack admr. &c. to the amount of six thousand three hundred & Eighty seven dollars seventy five and a half cents. That since sd

Settlements he hath received from William McKissack on account of Debts put in the hands of said Wm. McKissack for collection his bond for the sum of four hundred & ninety four dollars, forty five and a half cents, both of which accounts when added together makes six thousand Eight hundred & Eighty two dollars & twenty one cents by deviding the same into five equal parts makes each part thirteen hundred & seventy six dollars forty four & one fifth cents that sd. Admr. accounts against Spencer Clark in Wright of his wife Lucinda in Money and other articles, on account of their part the sum of Eight hundred and ninety four dollars and sixteen cents having a balance due in money and notes not yet due the sum of four hundred & Eighty two dollars twenty eight & one fifth cents to John Walthall & wife he hath paid in money & other articles the sum of eight hundred & seventy nine dollars & fifty eight cents leaving a Balance as above the sum of four hundred & ninety six dollars Eighty six & one fifth cents to Gray H. Edwards & Susan his wife has paid in money & other articles the sum of seven hundred & forty three dollars twenty & three fourth cents, leaving a balance as above the sum of six hundred & thirty three dollars twenty three & a half cents for Calvin Jones he has expended money & other districts the sum of one hundred & seventy five dollars forty three & three fourth cents leaving a balance as above the sum of twelve (p-296) hundred & one dollar & half cent. For Thomas Jones he has expended money and other articles the sum of Forty five Dollars & sixty eight cents, leaving a Balance as above the sum of thirteen hundred & thirty dollars seventy six & one fifth cents, and further we have presentments to sd. order valued the slaves belonging to sd. Estate and divided them as following, Towit,

To John Walthall & wife Pamelia we have alloted the following:

Jacob	$5.00
Leathy	5.00
Lem	4.50
Old Jimy	3.50
	$ 18.00

They to pay to Spencer Clack and Lucinda his wife thirty three dollars
To Gray H. Edwards & Susan his wife one hundred & thirteen dollars –
To Calvin Jones sixty eight dollars –
To Thomas Jones thirteen dollars –
To Spencer Clak & wife Lucinda we have alloted the following slaves, Towit,

Yellow Jimy	$ 5.00
Aggy	1.00
Anderson	3.00
Madison	1.40
Amos	5.00
	$ 15.40

And to receive from John Walthall & wife thirty three dollars.
To Gray H. Edwards & wife Susan we have alloted the following slaves Towit,

Jack	5.50
Mathy	4.50
Amy	2.25
Sally	1.50
John	.85
	$ 14.60

And to receive from John Walthall & wife one hundred & thirteen dollars.

To Calvin Jones we have alloted the following slaves, Towit,

Leak	$ 4.50
William	2.25
Charlott	1.60
Martha	1.00
Abram	5.70
	$ 15.05

And to receive from John Walthall & wife sixty eight dollars.

P-297

To Thomas Jones we have alloted the following slaves, Towit,

Willis	$ 5.10
Phebe	4.00
Stanford	2.75
Granderson	2.25
Franklin	1.50
	$ 15.60

And to receive of John Walthall & wife thirteen dollars.

Given under our hands this 12th day of August 1824.

Signed

German Lester
Richard Brandon
Charles Buford

Was made in proper time but omitted to be entered at the Last term of this court through mistake.

It is ordered by the court that said report be recd. at this present term as of the Last term of this court.

George H. Edwards & Susan his wife)
Spencer Black & Lucinda his wife) Plts.
John Walthall & Parmelia his wife)
        Vs
Thomas McKissack Deft.

Petition for distributive shares.

Best remembered that on the 20th day of November 1824 the above cause came on to be heard and was heard upon Bill answer replication & testimony, and the report of German Lester, Richard Brandon & Charles Buford, herein before recorded before the worshipful Thomas K. Gordon, Edward D. Jones, & John Bramlett Esquires, Justices of the Peace in and for the County of Giles, and it appearing to the court that Wilson Jones late of the County aforesaid departed this life intestate leaving the above named plaintiffs and Calvin Jones & Thomas Jones his heirs at law, and leaving considerable personal estate, and that Thomas McKissack the above named Defendant administered in due form of law upon the Estate of sd. Wilson Jones decd. and took into possession the personal property belonging to the same, and it also appearing to the satisfaction of the court now here that at May term 1824 of sd. court it was by consent of the parties aforesaid, ordered by the court that German Lester, Charles Buford and Richard Brandon and James Buford or any two of them value & devide all the slaves and other personal Estate of said Wilson Jones decd. into five equal parts, and allot to the said plaintiffs one fifth each, and Calvin Jones & Thomas Jones heirs of sd. Wilson Jones decd. one fifty each, and that they or any two of them also divide the amount of money and claims for money that might be found in the hands of sd. Defendants as administrators as aforesaid into five equal parts, and allot the same in the same manner as they were directed to allot the slaves & other personal property, and it further appearing to the court that German Lester, Richard Brandon, (p-298) and Charles Buford, three of the persons to whom sd. order was directed as aforesaid and in pursuance thereof divide & allot said slaves & other personal Estate & the amount of money and claims for money so far as they were informed agreeably to the derictories of said order and that their report thereupon has been returned to this court and ordered to be received & is recorded.

It is thereupon ordered adjourned and decreed that said report so for as it relates to the division of the slaves belonging to the Estate of the sd. Wilson Jones decd. be in all things affirmed - and it further appearing to the satisfaction of the court, now here, that the time that sd. report was made as aforesaid Defendant was entitled to a credit against the monied account in sd. report mentioned to the amount of seventeen hundred & twenty nine dollars & seventy five cents which was not allowed him by German Lester, Richd. Brandon, & Charles Buford, and which account is as follows Towit, Commission on $10195,-9¼ cents at 5 per cent.

$. 509.75

Boarding Miss Susan Jones 4 years at $50.		200.00
" " Calvin Jones six years at Do		300.00
" " Thomas Jones six years at Do		300.00
Keeping negro woman & children returned by the person who hired.		250.00
Paid for two attornies $90		90.00
Paid John McKissack for going to North Carolina on the benefit of the Estate.		$ 80.00

It is therefore ordered adjudged and decreed by the court that said account be allowed as a credit to said defendant against the monied account reported against him as aforesd. and that the credit be applied against the monies shares allotted by said report as aforesd. in the following manner against the monied accounts of Spencer Clack & Lucinda his wife as reported as aforesd. there is to be a credit of one hundred and Eighty five dollars and ninety five cents leaving a balance of two hundred & ninety six dollars thirty three & one fifth cents against the monied account of Gray H. Edwards and Susan his wife as reported as aforesd. there is to be a credit of three hundred and eighty five dollars & ninety five cents leaving a balance of two hundred and forty seven dollars twenty eight & ⅔ cents against the monied accounts of John Walthall and Pamelia his wife as reported as aforesd. there is to be a credit of one hundred & eighty five dollars & ninety five cents leaving a balance of three hundred & ten dollars ninety one & one fifth cents against the monied accounts of Calvin Jones as reported as aforesd. there is to be a credit of Four hundred & Eighty five dollars ninety five cents leaving a balance of seven hundred and fifteen dollars, five and a half cents against the monied accounts of Thomas Jones as reported as aforesd. there is to be a credit of (p-299) Four hundred & Eighty five dollars & ninety five cents leaving a balance of eight hundred & forty four dollars one & one fifth cents. It is therefore further ordered adjudged and decreed by the court, now here, that said plaintiffs separately recover against against said defendant the Slaves that have been respectively alloted them as aforesd. if they can or may be had, but if they or any of them cannot be had then that sd. plaintiffs separately recover against sd. defendant the value of such as cannot be had as as-certained by sd. report and that said plaintiffs also recover of sd. defendant the respective accounts in money due them which has been ascertained and set fourth in this decree together with their costs by them about their suit in this behalf expended.

Ordered that court be adjourned untill Monday morning nine oclock.

                                                A. Black
                                                E. D. Jones
                                                H. Hagen

P-300   Monday Morning 22nd November 1824

Court met according to adjournment Present - John H. Camp, Henry Hagen, Alexander Black, William B. Pepper, John Bramlett, Hezekiah Jones, William Wood, James H. Graves, Robert Read, Archbald McKissack, James Dugger, William Brown, & Thomas Marks, Esquires Justice of the Peace in & for the County of Giles.

A Bill of sale from German Lester to Sarah Massie, for certain property therein specified was produced in court and the execution thereof acknowledged by the sd. German Lester & ordered to be certified for registration.

The last Will and testement of Jesse Penn decd. was produced in court and proven by the oaths of Robert B. Harney and George I. Jordan the subscribing witnesses thereto and ordered to be recorded - thereupon Lewis G. Upshaw the executor therein named appeared in court and was qualified and gave bond and security as the Law directs.

The last will and Testement of John Williams decd. was produced in court and proven by the oaths of Charles C. Abernathy & William B. Pepper the subscribing witnesses thereto and ordered to be recorded - thereupon Mildred B. Williams and Benjamin Williams the Executors therein named appeared in court and were qualified, and also gave bond and security as the Law directs.

Ordered that Alexander Black, Fountain Lester, James Patteson, Henry J. Cooper and Henry Hagen, or any three of them be appointed commissioners to settle with James Woodfin Guardian of Caroline V. Woodfin decd. and that they make report of sd. settlement to the next term of this court.

On petition it is ordered that Robert Anderson, David Maxwell, Robert Fenner, Thomas P. Estes, John Bramlett, Simpson H. White, and Matthew Johnson or any five of them be appointed a Jury to view and mark out a road the nearest and best way from the Shelbyville road near Thomas P. Estes where said road crosses the main branch or fork of Pigeon roost Creek, from thence to Parks Baileys Mill, from Thence the nearest & best way to intersect a road that leads by Tyree Rodes to Mayfields Mill and that they make report thereof to the next term of this court.

Ordered that Alexander Black, German Lester & Henry Hagen be appointed commissioners to settle with the Executors of John (p-301) Samuel, Decd. and that they make report of sd. settlement to the next term of this court.

Ordered that Joseph McDonald, John McDonald, Thomas Marks, James McDonald, & Tilman R. Daniel or any three of them be appointed commissioner to devide the personal Estate including the negroes of the Estate of Gardner Harwell decd. and that they make report thereof to the next term of this court.

Ordered that the County Trustee of this County pay to Lewis H. Brown Sheriff of Giles County, the sum of nine dollars, for wood furnished the court for twelve months past.

A Bill of sale from Sarah Massie to German Lester for certain property therein Specified was produced in court and the execution thereof proven by the oath of John Hawkins the witness thereto, and ordered to be certified for registration.

Ordered that John I. Montgomery be appointed overseer of the road in the room of William M. Shields resigned and that he have the same district of hands.

Ordered that Robert Green be appointed overseer of the road in the room of Archibald McDonald resigned, and that he have the same district of hands.

A Power of attorney from William Purnell to Lewis H. Brown for certain purposes therein mentioned was produced in court and the execution thereof Partly proven by the oath of Benjamin Carter one of the witnesses thereto.

A Deed of conveyance from Lewis H. Brown Sheriff of Giles County to George Bowers for Lot No. 51 in the Town of Upper Elkton was produced in court and the Execution thereof acknowledged by the said Lewis H. Brown Sheriff as aforesaid and ordered to be certified for registration.

A Deed of conveyance from William Purnell by Lewis H. Brown to Benjamin Carter for Lot. No. 50 in the Town of Upper Elkton was produced in court and the Execution thereof acknowledged by the said Lewis H. Brown and ordered to be certified for registration.

Ordered that the County Trustee of this County pay to Thomas Browning the sum of thirty seven dollars & Eighty seven & a half cents for the support and maintenance of Tobitha Browning a Poor Idiot of this County for twelve month from this time.

Ordered that John Manefee be appointed overseer of the road from Upper

Elkton to the State line in the direction to Huntsville and that he have the hands that formerly worked on sd. part of sd. road.

P-302   Monday 22nd November 1824

A Deed of conveyance from Micajah Ezell & John Newton to Littleberry Webb for thirty acres of land was produced in court and the execution thereof acknowledged by the said Micajah Ezell & John Newton and ordered to be certified for registration.

A Deed of conveyance from Reuben Freeman to James Breys for twenty six acres of land was produced in court and the Execution thereof acknowledged by the sd. Reuben Freeman & ordered to be certified for registered.

Ordered that William Samuel be appointed overseer of the road in the room of Sterling Graves resigned and that he have the same district of hands.

On motion of Timothy Ezell who is Guardian to Isaac Johnston, he is released from sd. Guardian ship Whereupon Robertson D. Parrish was appointed Guardian to the sd. Isaac Johnston - and gave bond and Security as the law directs.

Ordered that Berry Dearing be appointed Guardian to Mahulda Nichols infant orphan of . . . . . Nichols decd. who Executed bond and security as the law directs - in the Stead of William Mayfield.

Ordered that letters of administration of the Estate of Zenas Martin decd. be granted unto Jordon Massie & James Martin, who executed bond and security and were qualified as the Law directs.

The administrators of the Estate of Zenas Martin decd. returned into court the inventory of sd. Estate which was ordered to be recorded.

Ordered that an order of sale issue to the Administrators of the Estate of Zenas Martin decd. commanding them to sell the property specified in the inventory of the Estate of sd. Zenas Martin decd. and that they make report thereof to the next term of this court.

Ordered that Richard H. Allen be appointed Guardian to Judith McCabe who gave bond & security and was qualified as the law directs.

A Power of Attorney from Lewis G. Upshaw Executor of &c to William Wilson for certain purposes therein mentioned was produced in court and the execution thereof proven by the oaths of William Topp & Collin S. Tarpley, the witnesses thereto and ordered to be certified.

P-303   Monday 22nd November 1824

    A Plat and certificate in the name of Josiah Davidson was produced in court and an assignment thereon from said Davidson to John Blue was proven by the oaths of Benjamin Holland & Tillman Holland, the witnesses thereto, and ordered to be certified.

    Ordered that the order of this court made on Monday last binding Ulysse Samuel to Ethelbert Samuel be received, and the sd. Ethelbert Samuel be released from his obligations entered into on this behalf.

    A Deed of conveyance from Alexander McDonald to Thomas Bettis for one hundred acres of land was produced in court and the execution thereof acknowledged by the sd. Alexr. McDonald and ordered to be certified for registration.

    A Deed of conveyance from Stephen Lee to James McDonald for one hundred and fifteen acres of land was produced in court and the Execution thereof proven by the oaths of John G. McDonand & Alexander McDonald two of the witnesses thereto, and ordered to be certified for registration.

    A Deed of conveyance from James McDonald to Lewis Garrett for one hundred and fifteen acres of land was produced in court and the execution thereof acknowledged by the sd. James McDonald and ordered to be certified for registration.

    A Deed of conveyance from Thomas Bettis to Lewis Garrett for one hundred acres of land, was produced in court and the execution thereof proven by the oaths of Richard G. Scoggin & Charles G. Wilcox, the witnesses thereto, and ordered to be certified for registration.

    Ordered that the County Trustee of this county pay to Robert Read the sum of thirty one dollars for the support and maintenance of Nancy Wilson a pauper of this County for twelve months from this time.

    Ordered that Elisha White be appointed overseer of the road in the room of George Malone resigned, and that he have the same district of hands.

    Ordered that the County Trustee of this County pay to William R. Davis Jailor, the sum of twenty five dollars for sweeping the courthouse for twelve months past.

    Ordered that the County trustee of this County pay to William R. Davis Jailor the sum of four dollars & twenty five cents as per his account filed.

    A Deed of Trust from John Underwood to Nathan Young & Albert G. Underwood for certain property therein Specified was   (p-304) Monday 22nd

November 1824, produced in court on the execution thereof acknowledged by the sd. John C. Underwood, and ordered to be certified for registration.

It is ordered by the court that the following persons, good and Lawful men of the County of Giles, that is each one of whom is a free white male citizen and house holder of said County, over twenty one years of age not an overseer of a road, & who has not been appointed and served as a Juror in this court for twelve months, Towit, Jacob Jones, James Lester, Jeremiah Parker, John E. Holden, David Maxwell, Jesse Pullen, Richard Briggs, Michael Biles, John Fry, Thomas Brown, Isaac S. Christman, Levi Read, James Johnston Larkin Moore, Jesse Marlow, George I. Jordon, Beverly Brown, Alexander Tarpley, Joseph McDonald, Edward M. Brown, James McKnight, Partrick Smith, Edmund Shelton, William P. Richardson, James Ford & Sterling Graves, be jurors to serve in this court at the next term on the third Monday in February next that the clerk deliver a copy of this order to the Sheriff of this County, and that he summon said persons to attend and serve accordingly.

Ordered that James H. Graves Esquire be appointed to take a list of taxable property and polls in Captain John Browns Company for the year 1825 and that he make return thereof to the next term of this court.

Ordered that William Wood Esquire be appointed to take a list of taxable property and polls in Captain Whites Company for the Year 1825, and that he make return thereof to the next term of this court.

Ordered that James Perry Esquire be appointed to take a list of taxable property and polls in Captain Frazers Company for the year 1825 and that he make return thereof to the next term of this court.

Ordered that John Hudson Esquire be appointed to take a list of taxable property and polls in Captain Nances Company for the year 1825, and that he make return thereof to the next term of this court.

Ordered that William Ussery Esquire be appointed to take a list of taxable property and poles in Captain Montgomerys Company for the year 1825, and that he make return thereof to the next term of this court.

Ordered that John B. Armstrong Esquire be appointed to take a list of taxable property & poles in Captain Lairds Company for the year 1825 and that he make return thereof to the next term of this court.

P-305 Monday 22nd Monday 1824

Ordered that Thomas K. Geordon Esquire be appointed to take a list of taxable property & poles in Captain Livingstons Company for the year 1825, & that he make return thereof to the next term of this court.

Ordered that Peter Swanson Esquire be appointed to take a List of taxable property & poles in Captain Ruffs Company for the year 1825 & that he make return thereof to the next term of this court.

Ordered that Joseph Rea Esquire be appointed to take a list of taxable property & poles in Captain Gibsons Company for the year 1825 & that he make return thereof to the next term of this court.

Ordered that Arthur Hicks Esquire be appointed to take a list of taxable property & poles in Captain Hendrys Company, for the year 1825 & that he make return thereof to the next term of this court.

Ordered that Archibald McKissack Esqr. be appointed to take a list of taxable property & poles in Captain Thorntons Company for the year 1825, & that he make return thereof to the next term of this court.

Ordered that Hezekiah Jones Esquire be appointed to take a list of taxable property & poles in Captain Gooch's Company, for the year 1825, and that he make return thereof to the next term of this court.

Ordered that Thomas Brown Esquire be appointed to take a list of taxable property & poles in Captain Potts Company for the year 1825 & that he make return thereof to the next term of this court.

Ordered that William B. Pepper Esquire be appointed to take a list of taxable property & poles in Captain Crofts Company for the year 1825 & that he make return thereof to the next term of this court.

Ordered that James Dugger Esquire be appointed to take a list of taxable property & poles in Captain Edward M. Browns Company, for the year 1825 return thereof to the next term of this court.

Ordered that Paul Chiles Esquire be appointed to take a list of taxable property & poles in Captain Chiles Company, for the year 1825 & that he make return thereof to the next term of this court.

Ordered that James Paine Esquire be appointed to take a list of taxable property & poles in Captain McCormicks Company for the year 1825, & that he make return thereof to the next term of this court.

Ordered that John H. Camp Esquire be appointed to take a list of taxable property & poles in Captain Bass's Company for the year 1825, & that he make return to the next term of this court.

P-306   Monday 22nd November 1825

Ordered that Thomas E. Abernathy Esquire be appointed to take a list of taxable property & poles in Captain Kearneys Company for the year 1825, & that he make return thereof to the next term of this court.

Ordered that the money appropriated at last court for the support of ....Maddox a pauper of this County, be placed in the hands of William P. Richardson instead of Samuel Jordan as directed by said order.

Ordered that the hands of Miller B. Brooks, Daniel McCollum, and Duncan Brown be added to the hands heretofore allotted to Buckner Madry overseer of a part of the Old Shoemakers ferry road, and that said Madry with the hands under his directions oversee and keep in repair that part of the Huntsville Road which lies between the fork south of James Paines and the top of the ridge, at the crossing of the part from James Paine's to Bethesda Meeting house in addition to that part of the Shoemaker's ferry road, over which he is at present overseer.

A Power of Attorney from George Funderburke to William Haile was produced in court and the Execution thereof acknowledged by the said George Funderburke and ordered to be certified.

Ordered that Daniel Puryear be appointed overseer of the road in the room of Alexander Tinnen removed, and that he have the same district of hands, and in addition thereto for the purpose of keeping said road in repair the hands of Robert Rankin, John Porter, James Carroll, Alexander Tinnen, William Bever, and half of Tyree Rodes hands.

James Hester . . . Plt.   )   Motion
      Against   )
John W. R. Graves Deft.   ) This day came the plaintiff by Rivers &
) Tarpley his attornies and moved the
court now here for Judgment against the defendant for the sum of seventy one dollars nineteen and three fourth cents which he hath paid as security for the defendant and it not appearing to the satisfaction of the court, whether he was principal or security a Jury was empannelled to try that fact Towit, John Newton, John Marlow, Isaac Mason, Levi Read, William Pullen, James Shelton, Nelly C. Dever, John Black, William Maxwell, Henry Scales, Littleberry Webb, and Thomas Read, who being sworn well and truly to enquire as aforesaid upon their oaths do say that on the 9th day of November Inst. the plaintiff paid to James L. Hendry a constable of this County the sum of seventy one dollars nineteen and three fourth cents on account of a Judgment which David Baker obtained against the (p-307) Defendant before Archibald McKissack Esquire a Justice of the peace of this County, on the 6th day of February 1824, execution on which said Judgment was stayed by the plaintiff. It is therefore considered by the court that the plaintiff recover of the Defendant the aforesaid sum of seventy one dollars, nineteen & three fourth cents with legal interest thereon from the 9th day of November Inst. till paid together with the costs of this motion.

Charles Devers Plaintiff   )   Motion
      Against   )
Abednego Moore, Defendant   )

This day came the plaintiff by Harris & Field, his attorneys and it appearing to the satisfaction of the court on inspecting the record that at the May term 1824 William Henry recovered a Judgment against the said plaintiff and the said defendant and Millinton Tidwell, Neely Davis, & George Bratton Jointly for the sum of one hundred Dollars & costs of Laite and that said plaintiff hath paid for sd. Defendant as his co Defendant the sum of thirty dollars and ninety eight cents, said defendants part of said Judgments and costs.

It is therefore considered by the court that the plaintiff recover of sd. Defendant the said sum of thirty dollars and ninety eight cents – Together with the costs of this motion.

Charles Devers Plt.) Motion
Against)
Millinton Tidwell Deft.) This day came the plaintiff by Harris & Field his attornies and it appearing to the satisfaction of the court on inspecting the record that at May Term 1824 William Henry recovered a Judgment against the said plaintiff and the said defendant and Abednego Moore, Neely Devers & George Bratton Jointly for the sum of one hundred dollars and costs of suit and that said plaintiff hath paid for sd. defendant as his co defendant the sum of thirty dollars and ninety eight cents said defendants part of sd. Judgment and costs.

It is therefore considered by the court that the plaintiff recover of sd. Defendant the said sum of thirty dollars and ninety eight cents together with the costs of the motion.

Charles Devers Plt.) Motion
Against)
George Bratton Deft.) This day came the plaintiff by Harris & Field his attornies and it appearing to the satisfaction of the court on inspecting the record that at the May term 1824 William Henry, recovered a Judgment against the said plaintiff and the sd. Defendant and Abednego Moore Neely Devers & Millinton Tidwell, jointly for the sum of one hundred dollars & cost of suit and that sd. plaintiff hath paid for sd. Defendant as his co defendant the sum of thirty dollars and ninety eight cents, said Defendants part of sd. Judgment and costs. It is therefore considered by the court that the plaintiff recovered of sd. Defendant the said sum of thirty dollars ninety eight cents together with the costs of this motion.

P-308 Monday 22nd November 1824

Thomas McKissack Plt.) Motion
Against)
William Mayfield &) Defts.)
Elisha B. Mayfield)) This day came the plaintiff by Jones & Flournoy, his attornies and moved the court, nowhere for Judgment against the defendants for the sum of five hundred and seventy four dollars and seventy seven and a half cents, which he hath paid as security for sd. defendants and it not appearing to the satisfaction of the court from the inspection of the record whether sd. plaintiff was principal or security a Jury was therefore empannelled to try that fact, towit, Edward Davis, William May, William Smith, Nathan Davis, John Brown, John Newton, Robert G. Steele, Levi

Reed, Reuben Freeman, John W. O. Graves, Isaac Mason, and Francis Smith - Who being sworn well & truly to enquire as aforesd. upon their oaths do say that the plaintiff paid to Lewis H. Brown, Sheriff of this County the sum of five hundred & seventy four dollars & seventy seven & an a half cent as security for said defendant on an execution which issued on a Judgment which Thomas C. Porter recovered against them at the May term 1824 of this court the plaintiff being security for the Defendants on the note on which said action at the instance of said Porter was foundered -

It is therefore considered by the court that the plaintiff recover of sd. Defendants the aforesaid sum of five hundred & seventy four dollars & seventy seven and a half cents together with the costs of this motion.

A Deed of conveyance from Richard H. Allen to Isaac S. Chrisman for seventeen acres of land was produced in court and the execution thereof acknowledged by the sd. Richard H. Allen and ordered to be certified for registration.

Ordered that court be adjourned untill tomorrow morning nine oclock.

                    H. Hagen
                    E. D. Jones
                    A. Black

P-309 Tuesday Morning 23rd November 1824

Court met according to adjournment Present Alexander Black) Esquires Justices of the peace in and for the County of Giles.
                Edward D. Jones
                Henry Hagen

Ordered that Caty Cox Senr. be appointed Guardian Pendent Lite of Catey Cox Jurn.

John C. Marlow & Hanna his wife)   Petitioned for the legecies and distributive shares.
Isaiah Hogan & Celia his wife) Plts.
Caty Cox Jnr. by his
    Against   This day the plaintiff by their solicitors filed in open court their petition against the defendant which
Anderson Hogan Admr. with the) Defts.
Will Annexed Saml. Cox decd.)

was granted, and it is thereupon ordered by the court that a summon issue to the defendant together with a copy of said petition.

The Account of German Lester against the Estate of Wilson Jones decd. for the sum of two dollars and fifty cents for one days service as commissioner in valueing and devidiing out the slaves &c among the Distributors of sd. estate and making out a report of said devision was allowed by the court, and ordered to be paid out of any monies in the hand of the Admrs. of said Estate.

A Deed of conveyance from Wm. Wood to Parks Baily for one hundred and eleven acres & 102 polls of land was produced in c urt and the execution thereof acknowledged by sd. Woods and ordered to be certified for registration.

John McCracken Plt.) Petition
    Against)
Mary D. Price Gdn. &c Deft.) This day the plaintiff by Harris &
) Field his attornies filed in court
his petition against the defendant which was granted, and it is thereupon ordered by the court that a summon issue to the deft together with a copy of said petition.

    Ordered that court be adjourned till court in course.

                                          Thomas Marks
                                          James H. Graves
                                          William Woods

P-310

At a Court of Pleas and Quarter Session holden for the County of Giles at the Courthouse of said County in the Town of Pulaski on the third Monday in February, being the twenty first day thereof, in the year of our Lord one thousand eight hundred & twenty five, Present - Alexander Black, Joseph Rea, Hezekiah Jones, Paul Chiles, William Wood, Thomas K. Gordon, John H. Camp, William Urssery, James Perry, John Laird, John B. Armstrong, John C. Walker, Edward D. Jones, Henry Hagen, James Dugger, John Henderson, Ephram M. Massie, Arthur Hix, Robert Read, James H. Graves, Thomas Batte, Thomas E. Abernathy, Anderson Hogan, Thomas Marks, John Young and John Bramlett Esquires Justices of the Peace of said County.
Presiding - German Lester Clerk of said County & Louis H. Brown Sheriff of said County.

Ordered that Lewis B. Marks be appointed overseer of the road in the room of Nathaniel Graves resigned and that he have the same district of hands.

Ordered that Joseph Hicks be appointed overseer of the road in the room of William Brown resigned, and that he have the same district of hands.

A Deed of conveyance from Alexander W. Scott to George White for Ten A. .... Acres of land was produced in court and the execution thereof proven by the oaths of James R. Dickey and James McCutchen two of the witnesses thereto, and ordered to be certified for registration.

Ordered that Alexander Black, Henry Hagen, and Fountain Lester be appointed commissioners to settle with the administrators of the estate of John Jones decd. and that they make return thereof to the next term of this court.

Ordered that Hartwell Harwell be appointed overseer of the road in the room of William F. Brown, resigned and that he have the same district of hands.

A Deed of conveyance from Thomas D. Deavers part to John Fogg for one hundred & thirteen & a half acres of land, was produced in court and the execution thereof proven by the oaths of Matthew Deavers part & James W. Wheeler, two of the witnesses thereto, and ordered to be certified for registration.

P-311 A Deed of conveyance from Matthew Cunningham to Nathaniel Carter for one hundred acres of Land was produced in court and the Execution thereof acknowledged by the said Matthew Cunningham and ordered to be certified for registration.

The Administrators of the Estate of Zenas Martin decd. returned into court an account of the sale of the Estate of sd. Martin which is ordered to be recorded.

239

Ordered that James Paine, Willis S. McLaurine, and Duncan Brown be appointed commissioners to settle with the administrators of the Estate of Jeremiah Woodward decd. and that they make return thereof to the next term of this court.

Ordered that William Maxwell be appointed overseer of the road in the room of John Bramlitt resigned and that he have the same district of hands.

Ordered that Williamson C. Rainey be appointed overseer of the road in the room of James Adkins resigned, and that he have the same district of hands.

Ordered that Clayton Tarpley be appointed overseer of the road in the room of Hartwell Harwell, resigned, and that he have the same district of hands.

Ordered that Edward Bledsoe be appointed overseer of the road in the room of Keenan McMillin resigned, and that he have the same district of hands.

Ordered that David McEwen be appointed overseer of the road in the room of Owen Smith resigned and that he have the same district of hands.

Ordered that Robert A. Hewitt be appointed overseer of the road in the room of Boyd Wilson resigned, and that he have the same district of hands.

The Execution of the Estate of Jesse Penn decd. returned into court an Inventory of said Estate which is ordered to be recorded.

Ordered that John Holly be appointed overseer of the road in the room of Amos Richardson resigned, and that he have the same district of hands.

P-312   Monday 21st February 1824

A Deed of conveyance from John Kimbrol to John P. Kimbrol, Elizabeth Kimbrol, & others for twenty acres of land was produced in court and the Execution thereof acknowledged by the said John Kimbrol & ordered to be certified for registration.

A Deed of conveyance from James Madry to Thomas Young for Forty six and a Quarter acres of land was produced in court and the Execution thereof proven by the oathes of John Halley and Andrew Brown the subscribing witnesses thereto and ordered to be certified for registration.

A Deed of conveyance from Willis Willsford to John English for Eighty seven and three tenth acres of land was produced in court and the execution thereof acknowledged by the said Willis Willsford and ordered to be certified for registration.

A Deed of conveyance from Robert R. Alsup to Thomas Young for three hundred & forty acres of land was produced in court and the execution thereof proven by the oaths of John Kennedy & John Holley the subscribing witnesses thereto and ordered to be certified for registration.

A Deed of conveyance from Peter Ussery to William James and William Ussery for one acre of land for the use of Robertson Fork Church was produced in court and the Execution thereof acknowledged by the said Peter Ussery & Ordered to be certified for registration.

A Deed of conveyance from Peter Ussery to William Ussery for two hundred & sixty four acres of land was produced in court and the execution thereof acknowledged by the sd. Peter Ussery and ordered to be certified for registration.

A Deed of conveyance from William Biles to John Goodman for fifty eight acres of land was produced in court and the execution thereof proven by the oaths of Peter Ussery & Wm. Ussery the witnesses thereto and ordered to be certified for registration.

A Bill of sale from Elizabeth Williams to Polly Williams for certain property therein specified was produced in court and the Execution thereof proven by the oath of Davis Brown one of witnesses thereto and ordered to be certified for registration.

P-313 Monday 21st February 1825.

A Bill of sale from Elizabeth Williams to Catherine Williams for certain property therein specified was produced in court and the execution thereof proven by the oath of Davis Brown one of the witnesses thereto and ordered to be certified for registration.

The Administrator of the Estate of John Jones decd. returned into court an account of the sale of sd. Estate which is ordered to be recorded.

Ordered that the County Trustee of this County pay to John Laird Forty dollars for the support and Maintenance of Mary Ellis a pauper of this County for the term of twelve months from this time.

A Deed of conveyance from Hardy Hightower to Levi Sherrill for ten acres of land was produced in court and the execution thereof proven by the oaths of Edmund Lumpkins & John Ellis the witnesses thereto and ordered to be certified for registration.

A Deed of conveyance from Stirling Robertson to Nathan Farmer for one hundred acres of land was produced in court and the execution thereof proven by the oaths of Alexr. Thomas & Samuel McCanlass the witnesses thereto and ordered to be certified for registration.

A Deed of conveyance from James Derr to Amos Richardson for seventeen acres of land was produced in court and the execution thereof proven by the oaths of Alexr. Thompson & Saml. McCanlass the witnesses thereto and ordered to be certified for registration.

A Deed of conveyance from Alexander McDonald & John McDonald & Josiah Stafford for fifteen acres of land was produced in court and the Execution thereof acknowledged by the sd. Alexr. McDonald & John McDonald and ordered to be certified for registration.

Ordered that Letters of Administration on the Estate of Matthew J. Black decd. be granted unto Elizabeth Black & Wm. D. Black whereupon they executed bond and security as the Law directs.

The administrators of the Estate of Matthew J. Black decd. returned into court an Inventory of sd. Estate which is ordered to be recorded.

Ordered that an order of sale issue to the administrators of the Estate of Matthew J. Black decd. commanding them to sell the personal Estate of sd. Decendant the negro excepted & make report to next court.

P-314 Monday 21st February 1824

Ordered that Robert B. Harney, Lewis G. Upshaw & John Nelson be appointed to allot to Elizabeth Black widow of Matthew J. Black decd. so much of the Estate of sd. decedent as will be sufficient for the maintenance of herself and family for one year from the time said Matthew J. Black departed this life and that they make return of said allotment to the next term of this court.

Ordered that John Brown be appointed overseer of the road in the room of William W. Woods resigned and that he have the same district of hands.

A Deed of conveyance from John Boyd to Jeremiah Barnes for one hundred and sixty nine acres of land was produced in court and the execution thereof proven by the oaths of David A. Gooch, & John Boyd Junr. the subscribing witnesses thereto and ordered to be certified for registration.

A Deed of conveyance from Alexander McDonald to Phelps Smith for thirty acres of land was produced in court and the Execution thereof acknowledged by the said Alexander McDonald and ordered to be certified for registration.

Ordered that Charles Devers be appointed overseer of the road in the room of Robert McLaurine resigned and that he have the same district of hands.

Ordered that Littleberry Webb be appointed overseer of the road in the room of Asa A. Estes resigned and that he have the same district of hands.

Ordered that Senior McLene be appointed overseer of the road in the room of John Andrews resigned and that he have the Same district and that he have the same hands.

A Bill of sale from Thomas Richardson to John Dabney, for a negro therein named was produced in court and the Execution thereof acknowd. by the said Thomas H. Richardson and ordered to be certified for registration.

A Deed of conveyance from Roland Hunnicut to Caleb White for 80 acres of land was produced in court and the execution thereof proven by the oaths of Asa McGee and James Paisley the subscribing witnesses thereto and ordered to be certified for registration.

A Deed of conveyance from Allen Williams to Tillman Holland for one hundred and forty two acres was produced in court and the execution thereof proven by the oaths of Thomas E. Abernathy and Sidney S. Holland the witnesses and ordered to be certified for registration.

P-315   Monday 21st February 1825

Ordered that John Wood be appointed overseer of the road in the room of John W. Bodenhamer resigned and that he have the same district of hands.

Ordered that Soloman Bassham be appointed overseer of the road in the room of John Randall resigned and that he have the same district of hands.

Alfred M. Harris Guardian of Julia Ann Flournoy returned into court an acct. of the Estate of his ward which was ordered to be recorded.

The last will and testament of Henry House decd. was produced in court and the execution thereof proven by the oaths of Nathan Bass and Burgess Burkett two of the subscribing witnesses thereto and ordered to be recorded. And thereupon William Owen the Executor therein named came into court and was qualified and gave bond and security according to Law.

A Deed of conveyance from John B. Stribbling to Archbald Bassham for thirty six acres of land was produced in court and the execution thereof proven by the oaths of Dewey Bassham and James Appleton the subscribing witnesses thereto and ordered to be certified for registration.

A Deed of conveyance from Alexander Stinson to Allen Lawyers for two hundred acres of land was produced in court and the Execution thereof acknowledged by the said Alexander Stinson and ordered to be certified for registration.

A Deed of conveyance from George W. Campbell to Alexander Stinson for one hundred and nine acres and one hundred and fifty five poles of land was produced in court and the Execution thereof proven by the oaths of Alexander Essleman and Allen Sawyers the subscribing witnesses thereto, and ordered to be certified for registration.

Ordered that John Clark be appointed overseer of the road in the room of Robert Griggs resigned and that he have the same district of hands.

Ordered that the County Trustee of this County pay to Robert Hunnicut the sum of seventy five dollars for keeping Cheatham a pauper of this County for fifteen months from this term.

Ordered that Samuel Davis be appointed overseer of the road in the room of John Webb resigned and that he have the same district of hands.

P-316   Monday 21st February 1825

Ordered that the County Trustee of this County pay to Robert McDonald the sum of twenty five dollars for the support and maintenance of Elizabeth Miskell a pauper of this county for six months.

A Deed of conveyance from Alexander Thompson to Mores Read for one hundred and fifty acres of land was produced in court and the Execution thereof proven by Samuel McCanlass and John Maxwell the Subscribing witnesses thereto and ordered to be certified for registration.

At least five Justices being present Joseph Wood produced in court one wolf scalp over four months old which was ordered to be burnt.

Ordered that Jacob Shall, Fountain Lester and John H. Rivers, be appointed commissioners to settle with John Pate former Guardian of the minor children of Peter Garland decd. and that they make return to the present term of this court.

A Deed of conveyance from Lewis Garrett to James McDonald for one hundred acres of land was produced in court & the execution thereof acknowledged by the said Lewis Garrett and ordered to be certified for registration.

A Deed of conveyance from Lewis Garrett to James McDonald for one hundred and eight acres of land was produced in court and the Execution thereof acknowledged by the said Lewis Garrett and ordered to be certified for registration.

Ordered that the County Trustee of this County pay to Mason Garrison the sum of thirty three dollars for the support of himself and family for one year from this time.

A Deed of conveyance from George Davenport to Elizabeth Westmoreland for one hundred & twenty five acres of land was produced in court and the Execution thereof proven by the oaths of Tilman R. Daniel, and Charles Neal the subscribing witnesses thereto and ordered to be certified for registration.

The last will and testament of Susan Walker decd. was produced in court and the Execution thereof proven by the oaths of William Ussery, and Presley T. Cox, the subscribing witnesses thereto & ordered to be recorded.

P-317 Monday 21st February 1825

James Buford resigned as Guardian of James Moore, and thereupon the court appointed Larkin B. Moore guardian of said Minor who gave bond and security as the law directs.

Richard Bentley was Elected constable in Captain Livingston Company, who gave bond and security, and was qualified as the law directs.

Esquire C. Erwin was elected constable in Captain Montgomerys Company, who gave bond and security and was qualified as the law directs.

Joshua S. Hayle was Elected constable in Captain Gibsons company, who gave bond & security, and was qualified as the law directs.

Richard Long was Elected constable in Captain Hendrys Company, who gave bond and security and was qualified as the law directs.

James Perry Esquire who was appointed at the last term of court to take a list of taxable property & polls in Captain Frazers Company for the year 1825 made return thereof which was ordered to be recorded.

Thomas E. Abernathy who were appointed at the last term of this court to take a list of taxable property and polls in Captain Kearnesy Company for the year 1825 made return thereof which was ordered to be recorded.

William Usery Esquire who was appointed at the last term of this court to take a taxable list of property and polls in Captain Montgomerys Company for the year 1825 made return thereof which was ordered to be recorded.

John Henderson Esquire who was appointed at the last term of this court to take a list of taxable property and polls in Captain Nance's Company for the year 1825 made return thereof which was ordered to be recorded.

John B. Armstrong, Esquire who was appointed at the last term of this court to take a list of taxable property and polls in Captain Laird's

Company for the year 1825 made return thereof which was ordered to be recorded.

Ordered that Samuel Farmer be appointed overseer of the road in the room of Thomas McCanlass resigned and that he have the same district of hands.

P-318 Monday 21st February 1825

Jesse Allen who was commissioned by his Exellency the Governor of this State to Act as a Justice of the Peace in and for this County appeared in court and was Qualified as the Law directs.

Ordered that Granville Pillow be appointed overseer of the road from the Little Bridge road near Lyree Rodes to Mayfields Mill in the room of Tyree Rodes resigned and that he have the same district of hands.

Ordered that William Bever and Alexander Tinnen be taken from the hands allotted to Daniel Puryear.

Ordered that that part of the road which lies near the plantation of Thomas Clarke be open agreable to the report of a Jury appointed to view the same at the Expence of said Clarke, and when so opened be under the direction of said Clarke to keep the same in repair with the hands under his direction.

Ordered that the County Trustee of this County pay to Robert L. Cobbs Solicitor General of this district the sum of Fifty dollars for his Ex officio services for twelve months.

Ordered that the County Trustee of this County pay to German Lester Clerk of this Court the sum of forty dollars for his ex officio services for one year prior to this time, also the sum of twenty five dollars for recording the tax list for the year 1824.

Administration on the Estate of John S. Jones decd. is granted to Martha Jones and William H. Jones, who were qualified and gave bond and security as the law directs.

Ordered that an order of sale issue to Martha Jones, & William H. Jones, administrators of the Estate of John S. Jones decd. commanding them to sell the perishable part of said Estate and make return thereof according to law.

Ordered that Buckner Abernathy, Benjamin Jones, and Alexander Esselman be appointed commissioners to allot to Martha Jones widow of John S. Jones decd. so much of his Estate as will be sufficient to maintain herself and family for one year from the time said John S. Jones departed this life and that they make return of said allotment to the next term of this court.

P-319   Monday 21st February 1824

Ordered that Henry Hagen, Alexander Black and German Lester be appointed to settle with James Buford administrator of the Estate of John Hicks decd. and that they make return of said settlement to the next term of this court.

The Court proceeded to Class the Magistrates of this County, agreable to an act of the Legislature of this State in the following manner, towit, Class Number one, Composed of Esquires John Henderson, William Wood, James Perry, Thomas Brown, John B. Armstrong, Alexander Black, Anderson Hogan, Robert Reed & John H. Camp to hold the present term of this court. Class Number two composed of Esquires Paul Chiles, Arthur Hicks, Robert Oliver, Hezekiah Jones, Edward D. Jones, Joseph Rea, Thomas Batte, James Paine, Peter Swanson & James McCafferty to hold the next May term of this court, Class Number three composed of Esquires Richard McGee, Jesse Allen, Thomas Marks, Willis S. McLaurine, John C. Walker, Thomas K. Gordon, James Dugger, William B. Pepper & Archibald McKissack and Ephraim M. Massey, to hold the next August term of this court.
Class Number four Composed of Esquires Thomas E. Abernathy, James H. Graves, Thomas Harwood, Henry Hagen, John Young, John Laird, William Brown, William Usery and William Mayfield to hold the next November term of this court.

A Plat and certificate of survey in the name of William Fall and an assignment thereon to Peter Swanson was produced in court, and proven by Jonathan Moody a subscribing witness thereto and ordered to be certified.

Joseph Rea Esquire who was appointed at the last term of this court to take a list of taxable property and polls in Captain Gibson's Company for the year 1825 made return thereto which was ordered to be recorded.

A Licence to keep an ordenary for the term of twelve montsh and no longer was granted to Henry Harrison who was qualified and entered into bond & seourity according to Law.

Ordered that Monday next be set apart for County Business.

P-320   Monday 21st February 1824

A Deed of conveyance from John Clarke to Amos Richardson for one hundred and twenty acres of land was produced in court and the Execution thereof acknowledged by the said John Clarke and ordered to be certified for registration.

A Deed of conveyance from the heirs of James Haynie decd. to Andrew Gordon for one hundred and fifty acres of land was produced in court and the Execution thereof acknowledged by Elisha Haynie Executor and Samuel Wilson.

Peggy Pankey, Joseph Wilson and Joel May parties to said deed, and thereupon William Wood and Thomas K. Gordon Esquires acting Justices of the Peace for this County were appointed to take the privy Examination of Ann Wilson touching the Execution of said deed and return the same into court instanter and said Justices thereupon proceed to take said Examinations, and return the same into court, the same was ordered to be certified for registration.

A Deed of conveyance from George M. Gibson to Walter Look for seventy one acres of land was produced in court and the Execution thereof acknowledged by the said George M. Gibson and ordered to be certified for registration.

A Licence to keep an ordinary for the term of twelve months from the date here of and no longer granted to James W. Wheeler who was qualified and gave bond and security according to Law.

A Deed of conveyance from Richard Briggs to Elizabeth Samuel for part of lot No. 50 in the town of Pulaski was produced in court and the Execution thereof acknowledged by the said Richard Briggs and ordered to be certified for registration.

The Administration of the Estate of John S. Jones decd. returned into court an Inventory of said Estate which was ordered to be recorded.

Ordered that Archibald McKennon be appointed overseer of the road in the room of John Abernathy resigned and that he have the same district of hands.

Ordered that Williamson C. Rainey be appointed overseer of the road in the room of James Adkins resigned and that he have the same district of hands.

Ordered that Joseph Hicks be appointed overseer of the road in the room of William Brown resigned and that he have the same district of hands.

P-321 Monday 21st February 1824.

On the petition of John B. Armstrong it is ordered that David K. McEwin, Shand Golightly, Owen Smith, Daniel Evans, Richard Evans, Martin McCall, and Turner Brimer or any five of them be appointed a Jury to view that part of the Columbia road which lies near sd. John B. Armstrongs dwelling house and see if it then be proper to turn said road and make return thereof to the present term of this court.

Ordered that the County Trustee of this County pay to John Kenedy the sum of seven dollars for the purpose of purchasing a sledge hammer & crow bar for the use of the road over which he is overseer.

Ordered that John P. Taylor be appointed overseer of the Little Tom Bigby road from the Ford of Big Creek at the ten mile post, to the eight mile post on sd. road, and that he have them under his directions for the purpose of keeping the same in repair the hands of Henry Miller, Jesse Allen, Daniel Cameron, and Jacob Luther thence to sd. Miller's to include all the hands in sd. Bounds.

Ordered that Jonathan Moody be appointed overseer of the Little Tombigby road from the ten mile post to the upper and of Jacob Luthers former bounds on said road and that he have under his directions for the purpose of keeping the same in repair all the hands in the bounds of the road over which Jacob Luker was formerly overseer except the hands in the bounds alloted to John P. Taylor by an order of the present term of this court.

Ordered that David K. McEwin overseer of the road have under his direction the hands of the following persons, Towit, James Douglass, John Follis, John Evans, Thornton Evans, Franklin Evans, George Brownlow, William Brownlow, John Cook, Owen Smith & Sd. Ewin.

Ordered that Spencer Clack, James Coldwell, John Snipes, Edward Davis, Henry Kerr, James Ford & John Whitfield or any five of them be appointed a Jury to view that part of the Florence Road which lies near John Tucker's and Hugh Campbells & see if it be proper to turn said road in the following manner beginning at the west end of John Tucker's lane leaving Hugh Campbells plantation on the right of said road and make report to the present term of this court if practicable if not to the next term of this court.

Ordered that Hugh Bratton, Daniel F. Moore, Archibald Bassham, Bradley Phifer, Walter Aday, John Black & Owen Hardy or any five of them be appointed a Jury to view and alter the Florence road to take off from the old road on the hill by Asa McGees, and to intersect sd. road at Daniel F. Moore's and make report thereof to the next of this court.

P-322   Monday 21st February 1825

Ordered that Robert Ross, Asa McGee, Thomas Cole, David Jones, James Hammons, Owen Hardy and Joseph Cowan, be appointed a Jury to view that part of the Florence road which lies between the top of the hill at the head of Moore's Creek & Hugh Brattons and see if be proper to turn said road and that they made report to the next term of this court.

Ordered that Daniel Purpyear, William Pullen, William Wood, Jesse West, Alexander Rosenbum, Simpson H. White, and Jesse Pullen or any five of them be appointed a Jury to view that part of the Prewits Gaps's road which lies near Samuel Dodson's plantation begining at Saml. Dodson's and leaving his house to the right crossing Pigeon Roost Creek at Elisha Dodsons thence running up the Creek so as to intersect the old road at the most convenient points and that they make report to the present term of this court.

Ordered that James Leitch, John Laird, Edward D. Jones, George Malone & Elisha White or any three of them be appointed commissioners to direct the personal Estate of Martin Lane decd. and that they make return of said division to the next term of this court.

Ordered that Richard McGee, Stephen Anderson, William Chapman, Benjamin Smith, S. Hensley, Josiah Alexander, Thomas P. Estes or any five of them be appointed a Jury to view that part of the Shelbyville road which lies near the improvement of William Snow and see if it be proper to turn sd. road & that they make report thereof to the next term of this court.

Ordered that Henry Hagen, Alexander Black & Archibald McKissack be appointed commissions to settle with Wm. Mayfield administrators of the Estate of . . . . . . Nichols decd. and that they make report thereof to the next term of this court.

Ordered that that part of the Fayettsville road which lies between the top of the hill east of Isaac Williams & the County line near Edwins Williams be altered agreable to the report of a Jury appointed at the last term of this court, and that Hubbard Harwell, be appointed to oversee and keep in repair the same, and that he have under his directions for that purpose the following district of hands, towit, Morris Webb, & running so as to include Lewis Williams, Seth J. Williamson, George Tucker, Harbert Harwell, & sd. Hubbard Harwell & all the hands included in said bounds.

P-323   Monday 21st February 1825

On the petition of Thomas Hicks it is ordered that Willis Lane to whom Rhoda Strickland by a former order of this court was bound be resigned to come forward on Monday next and show cause why sd. Rhoda Strickland should not be taken from him and bound again to some other person.

The commissioners who were appointed at last court to value & devide the Estate of Joseph Braden decd. made return of sd. division which was ordered to be recorded.

Ordered that Daniel Leatherman, Robert Webb & William Smith or any five of them be appointed a Jury to lay out a road on the Huntsville road running from Columbia to leave sd. road just beyond where there is a dug place & drifts in sd. road and to intersect sd. road about three hundred yards from where it leaves it and that they make report thereof to the next term of this court.

Ordered that Thomas Batte Fountain Lester, John Young, John Dickey, & Ephram M. Massie be appointed commissioners to superintend the education of poor children within the bounds of this County agreeable to an act of the general assembly in that case made and provided.

Thomas K. Gordon Esquire who was appointed at the last term of this court to take a list of taxable property and polls in Captain Livingston's Company for the year 1825 made return of sd. list which is ordered to be recorded.

Peter Swanson Esquire who was appointed at the last term of this court to take a list of taxable property and polls in Captain Bevers Company for the year 1825 made return thereof which is ordered to be recorded.

Paul Chiles Esquire who was appointed at the last term of this court to take a list of taxable property and poles in Captain Chiles Company for the year 1825 made return thereof which is ordered to be recorded.

Ordered that Court be adjourned untill tomorrow morning 9 oclock.

            James Paine
            Jno. H. Camp
            James Perry

P-324 Tuesday Morning 22 February 1825

Court met according to adjournment Present John H. Camp,) Esquires Justice
             William Wood &) of the Peace for
             Alexander Black) Giles County.

The Sheriff of this County returned into court the names of the following persons summoned to attend as grand and petit jurors at this term, Pursuant to an order of the last term of this court a copy which issued to the said Sheriff of Giles County, towit, Jacob Jones, James Lester, Jeremiah Parker, John E. Holden, David Maxwell, Jesse Pullen, Richard Briggs, Michael Biles, John Fry, Thomas Brown, Isaac L. Chrisman, Levi Read, James Johnston, Larkin B. Moore, Jesse Marlow, Beverly Brown, Alexander Tarpley, Joseph McDonald, Edward M. Brown, James McKnight, Patrick R. Smith, Edmund Shelton, William P. Richardson, James Ford, and Stirling Graves - of whom Edmund Shelton, foreman, Larkin B. Moore, Jacob Jones, Edward M. Brown, Joseph McDonald, Alexander Tarpley, Jeremah Parker, Stirling Graves, John E. Holden, Jesse Pullen, Patrick R. Smith, Levi Read and Jesse Marlow, were elected empannelled and sworn a grand Jury of inquest for the body of this County, who having received their charge withdrew to consider of thier presentments.

P-325 Tuesday 22nd February 1825

Thomas W. McKnight a constable of this county was sworn to attend on the Grand Jury at the present term of this court.

Alexander S. Jones Gentleman was appointed solicitor pro term of this court.

A Mortgage from James Patterson to Alfred M. Harris, & Thomas Martin for certain property therein specified was produced in court and the Execution thereof acknowledged by the said James Patterson and ordered to be certified for registration.

A Deed of trust from John Walthall to James Patterson for certain property therein specified was produced in court and the Execution thereof proven by Henry Hagen one of the subscribing witnesses thereto and ordered to be certified for registration.

A Power of attorney from Elizabeth Hardin Guardian of Joshua Hardin to Thomas Jefferson Porter, was produced in court and the Execution thereof acknowledged by the said Elizabeth Hardin and ordered to be certified for registration.

Samuel Smith & wife Plts.) Petition
  Against)
John Porter Guardian &c Deft.) On motion of the Defendant by his
) attorney leave is granted him to amend his answer in this case.

Adam Bell assignee &c Plt.) Certiorari
  Against)
William Sawyers . . . Deft.) This day came the plaintiff in his proper person and directs that this suit be dismissed, which is by the court ordered accordingly, and that the defendant recover of the plaintiff his costs by him about his suit in this behalf expended.

Ordered that William T. Richardson be released from further attendance as a Juror at this term.

A Deed of conveyance from Thomas T. Armstrong to Henry H. Fry for 270 acres of land was produced in court & the Execution thereof proven by the oaths of John Fry & James H. Evans two of the subscribing witnesses thereto and ordered to be certified for registration.

P-326 Tuesday 22nd February 1825

Jerald Irby . . . Plaintiff) In Case
  Against)
Elnathan G. Brown Defendant) This day came the parties by their attornies and thereupon came a Jury of good and lawful men, Towit, James Lester, David Maxwell, Richard Briggs, Thomas Brown, James Johnston, Beverly Brown, James McKnight, John S. Brandon, Henry Hester, Henry T. Butler, Edward Bledsoe & Nathan Davis, who being elected tried and sworn well & truly to try the issue Joined between the parties in this case having heard the Evedence and agreement of counsel retired out of court to consider of their verdict after some time returned and say they cannot agree by consent of parties and with the assent of the court said Jurors are permitted to disperse to meet again tomorrow morning nine oclock.

A Deed of conveyance from Andrew Fay to James Buford for sixteen acres and thirty seven poles of land was produced in court and the execution thereof acknowledged by the said Andrew Fay and ordered to be certified for registration.

A Deed of conveyance from John McAmrich to James Buford for nineteen acres and thirty one poles of land was produced in open court and the Execution thereof proven by the oaths of Henry Hagen and Charles C. Abernathy the subscribing witnesses thereto and ordered to be certified for registration.

A Deed of conveyance from Lewis H. Brown Sheriff of Giles County to Andrew Fay for lotts No. 221 & 227 in the Town of Pulaski was produced in court and the Execution thereof acknowledged by the said Lewis H. Brown Sheriff &c and ordered to be certified for registration.

A Deed of conveyance from John Cox to Andrew Fay for three thousand two hundred and eight acres of land was produced in court and the Execution thereof proven by the oaths of James Patteson the subscribing witnesses thereto and ordered to be certified for registration.

The grand Jury returned into court and on the Indictment prefered against David Stockton for an affray with & an assault & Battery of the body of Baily Davis, Endorsed a true bill, Edmund Shelton foreman of the Grand Jury & withdrew to consider of further presentments.

P-327 Tuesday 22nd February 1825

Samuel H. Williams Plt.   )   Motion
        Against   )
James Lynch . . . Deft.   ) This day came the parties by their attor-
) neys & thereupon came a Jury of good and
Lawful men, Towit, John Fry, Archibald Smith, Asa A. Estes, Elnathan G. Brown, John Abernathy, Samuel Weis, Graves Hester, William Swainey, William A. Maultsby, Silas L. Veitch, Nathaniel Hamet, & John Phillips, who being elected tried and sworn well and truly to try the issue Joined between the parties in this case upon their oaths do say that the defendant hath not paid the debt in the writing obligatory in the declaration mentioned, and that he hath no sett off, as the plaintiff in his replications hath alleged, and they do assess the plaintiffs damages by occasion of the detention of said debt to twenty seven dollars and fifty cents besides costs. It is therefore considered by the court that the plaintiff recover of the defendant the sum of five hundred and fifty dollars the amount of the debt in the writing obligatory in the Declaration mentioned, together with his damages aforesaid by the jurors aforesaid in form aforesaid assessed, and his costs by him about his suit in this behalf expended.

A Deed of conveyance from William Watson to Lewis H. Brown for one hundred and thirty one and a half acres of land was produced in court and the execution thereof proven by the oaths of German Lester and Alexander Black the subscribing witnesses thereto and ordered to be certified for Registration.

The commissioners appointed to settle with James Woodfin Guardian of Caroline V. Woodfin decd. made return of said settlement which was ordered to be recorded.

Hannah Underwood Plt.　　　　　）　　　　　　In Case
　　Against　　　　　　　　　　）
Lyddall Wilkinson Deft.　　　　）　On the affidavit of the defendant attorney
　　　　　　　　　　　　　　　　）　it is ordered that the trial of this cause
be continued and postponed untill the next term of this court and that a
commission issue to any two of the Acting Justices of the Peace in and for
the County of Madison & State of Alabama to take the deposition of William
I. Adair, John W. Tilford, Richard Elliott, William Weedon, Archibald Mc-
Donald, John Silvers, William E. Phillips, & John F. Mills, and that a commission issue to any two of the Acting Justices of the Peace in and for
the County of Limestone & State of Alabama to take the deposition of
Robert M. Richards, Jonathan Warrin, Ruffin Coleman, John Silvers, Elvin
Dandridge, Bennett Tatum and　　(p-328)　Tuesday 22nd February 1825, Mary
Tatum, all of which said depositions are to be read on the trial of this
cause upon the defendants giving to the plaintiff twenty days notice of the
time and place of taking the same.

　　On the Petition of Daniel Puryear for the Division of a tract of land
in Giles County, being of the Waters of Pigeon Roost Creek, which he claims
by purchase from the heirs of Mary Donaldson decd. and it appearing to the
satisfaction of the court that all other claimants as heirs of the said
Mary have been duly notified of this application by a notice inserted in
the Columbia a public paper printed in Columbia Tennessee - It is therefore
considered by the court that William Wood, Samuel H. Dodson, Jesse Pullen,
William Pullen, Simpson H. White, Granville A. Pillow and Thomas Johnston,
be appointed commissioners to lay off divide & assign to said Puryear five
seventh and five eights of an undivided ninth of thirty nine acres of land
begining at a Dogwood and White ash on the east boundry line of a 5000
acre survey that Tyree Rodes lives on the same being the north west corner
of an entry in the name of Woods, Puryear, West and Phillips for 509 acres,
Then east one hundred and fifty eight poles with said 509 acre entry to a
stake corner of the same thence north with said 509 acre entry seventy
five poles to a poplar corner of the same in the south boundary line of a
2000 acre survey made in the name of James M. Lewis, thence west with said
Lewis line one hundred and fifty eight poles to a Beech tree the east
boundary line of the aforesaid 5000 acres thence south with the said line
seventy five poles to the begining and that they make return thereof to
the next Term of this court.

Dudley Smith Plt.　　　　　　　）　　　　　　In Case
　　Against　　　　　　　　　　）
Lewis Brown Deft.　　　　　　　）　This day came the parties by their attornies
　　　　　　　　　　　　　　　　）　and thereupon came a Jury of good and lawful
men, Towit, John Fry, Archibald Smith, Asa A. Estes, Elnathan G. Brown,
John Abernathy, Samuel Weis, Gaves Hester, Wm. Swainey, William A. Maultsby, Silas L. Veatch, Nathaniel Hammett, & John Phillips who being elected
tried and sworn well and truly to try the issue joined between the parties
in this case, upon their oaths do say that they find said issue in favor
of plaintiff and assess his damages to forty eight dollars and forty one
cents damages besides costs.
　　It is therefore considered by the court that the plaintiff recover of
said defendant the damages aforesaid in form aforesaid by the Jurors,
(p-329)　aforesaid, and also his costs by him about his suit in this behalf expended.

Ordered that court be adjourned untill tomorrow morning nine oclock.

John H. Camp
Jas. Paine
Robt. Read

Wednesday 23rd February 1825

Court met according to adjournment Present John H. Camp,) Esquires Justice
James Paine) of the Peace for
James Perry) Giles County.

James Carpenter &)
Nancy Carpenter Admr.)Plts.   In Debt
& Admx. &c.)
    Against)
Anderson Tinsley Deft.   This day came the plaintiffs by their attorney, and district that this suit be dismissed:- Which is done accordingly and that the defendant recover of the plaintiffs his costs by him about his defence in this behalf expended.

Hugh Bratton & Thomas)
Bratton Admrx. &c.) Plts.   Certiorari
    Against
Elizabeth Bratton Deft.   This day came the Defendants by his attorney and its appearing to the court that said plaintiffs hath not entered their appearance in this cause, & said plaintiffs being solemnly called to prosecute their said suit, came not but made default, nor is their suit further prosecuted - It is therefore considered by the court that said defendant depart hence without day and recover of said plaintiffs her costs by her as well with this court as before the Justice of the Peace, about his defence in this behalf expended.

Ordered that James Woodfin be allowed the sum of seventy six dollars and ninety four cents for his services as Guardian of Caroline V. Woodfin.

P-330   Wednesday 23rd February 1825

Larkin Mayfield .. Plt.)   In Case
    Against)
Thomas B. Haynie Deft.)   By consent of the parties and with the assent of the court the matter in controversy between the parties in this case is refered to the final determination of James Buford David W. Porter, Fountain Lester, George H. Edwards, and James W. Wheeler whose award is to be taken as the Judgment of the court in this case.

Saml. H. Williams Assee &c Plt.)   In Debt
    Against)
Samuel Day ... Deft.)   This day came the parties by their attornies, and thereupon came a Jury of good and lawful men, Towit, John Fry, Graves Hester, William Porter, William M. Beazley, Joseph S. Tarkington, John W. Graves, Archibald Smith,

255

John Abernathy, Ambrose Cobbs, William Bradley, Edmund W. Tipton & Elnathan G. Brown, who being elected tried and sworn well and truly to try the issue Joined between the parties in this case upon their oaths do say that the defendant has not paid the debt in the writing obligatory in the declaration mentioned, and that he has not sett off as the plaintiff in his replication hath alledged and they do assess the plaintiffs damages by occasion of the detention of said debt to three dollars besides costs.

 It is therefore considered by the court that the plaintiff recover of said defendant the sum of ninety dollars the amount of his debt aforesaid together with his damages aforesaid in form aforesaid, by the Jurors aforesaid assessed, and also his costs by him about his suit in this behalf expended.

Lewis Brown Plt.) In Debt
 Against)
Dudley Smith Deft.) This day came the parties by their attorneys and thereupon came a Jury of good and lawful men, Towit, John Fry, Graves Hester, William Porter, William M. Beazley, Joseph S. Tarkington, John W. Graves, Archibald Smith, John Abernathy, Ambrose Cobbs, Wm. Bradley, Edmund W. Tipton and Elnathan G. Brown - who being elected tried and sworn well and truly to try the issue joined between the parties in this case upon their oaths do say that the defendants hath not paid the debt in the writing obligatory in the declaration mentioned, as the plaintiff in his replication hath alleged, and they do assess the plaintiffs damages by occasion of the detention of sd. debt to twenty three dollars besides costs.

 It is therefore (p-331) Wednesday 23rd February 1825, considered of the court that the plaintiff recover of said defendant the sum of one hundred & seventy dollars & Eighteen & three fourth cents the amount of his debt aforesaid together with his damages aforesaid, in form aforesd. by the Jurors aforesd. assessed, and also his costs by him about his suit in this behalf expended.

John C. McLemore Assee &c Plt.) In Debt
 Against)
Thomas Brown . . . . Deft.) This day came the parties by their attornies, and thereupon came a Jury of good and lawful men, Towit, John Fry, Graves Hester, William Porter, William M. Beazley, Joseph S. Tarkinton, John W. Graves, Archibald Smith, John Abernathy, Ambrose Cobbs, William Bradley, Edmund W. Tipton & Elnathan G. Brown, who being elected tried and sworn well and truly to try the issue joined between the parties in this case upon their oaths do say that the defendant has not paid the debt in the writing obligatory in the declaration mentioned as the plaintiff in his repication hath alleged and they do assell the plaintiff plaintiffs damages by occasion of the detention of said debt to thirteen dollars & fifty cents damages besides costs.

 It is therefore considered by the court that the plaintiff recover of said defendant the sum of two hundred and fifty nine dollars, the amount of his debt aforesaid, together with his damages aforesaid assessed, and also his costs about his suit in this behalf expended.

Thomas Read Assee &c Plt.) In Debt
 Against)
William Hendry . . . Deft.) This day came the parties by their attorn

and thereupon came a Jury of good and lawful men, Towit, John Fry, Grayes Hester, William Porter, William M. Beazley, Joseph S. Tarkington, John Abernathy, Ambrose Cobbs, William Bradley, Edward W. Tipton and Elnathan G. Brown, who being elected tried and sworn well and truly to try the issue joined between the parties in this case upon their oaths do say that the defendant has not paid the debt in the writing obligatory in the declaration mentioned and that he has no sett off as the plaintiff in his replication hath alleged and they do assess the plaintiffs damages by occasion of the detention of said debt to seventeen dollars & nine cents besides costs. It is therefore (p-332) considered by the court that the plaintiff recover of the defendant the sum of one hundred and thirty two dollars the amount of his debt aforesaid together with his damages aforesd. in form aforesd. by the Juror aforesaid assessed and also his costs about his suit in this behalf expended.

James Paine Esquire who was appointed at the last term of this court to take a list of taxable property & polls in Captain McCormacks Company for the year 1825, made return thereof which is ordered to be recorded.

Dudley Smith Plt.) In Debt
 Against)
Lewis Brown Deft.) From the Judgment of the court in this case rendered the defendant prayed an appeal to the honorable the Circuit Court to be held for the County of Giles, and having executed bond and security according to law the Same was Granted him.

Gerald Irby Plaintiff) In Case
 Against)
Elnathan G. Brown Deft.) This day came the parties by their attornies and thereupon came the Jury who were sworn on yesterday well and truly to try the issue joined between the parties in this case who still say they cannot agree By consent of the parties and with the assent of the court James Lester one of the Jurors in this case was withdrawn and the cause continued untill the next term of this court that a new trial may be had therein.

A Licence to keep an ordinary for the term of twelve months and no longer is Granted to John H. Camp whereupon he executed bond and security and was qualified as the law directs.

Samuel H. Smith . . . Plaintiff) Petition
 Against)
John Porter Gdn. &c Defendant) On affidavit of the defendant in this case the cause is ordered to be continued, and that he pay the costs of the continuance and by consent leave is given each party to take depositions which when taken are to be read in evidence on the trial of this cause upon the plaintiffs giving to the defendant and the defendant giving to the plaintiff ten days notice of the time and (p-333) place of taking all depositions within this State and twenty days notice of the time and place of all those out of the State.

John Porter Guardian of Elenor W. Porter returned an account current against his said Ward which is ordered to be recorded.

Edward R. Fields Plt.)   In Debt
    Against)
Henry Butler Deft.) This day came the parties by their attornies and by consent this cause is ordered to be dismissed at the cost of the defendant –
It is therefore considered by the court that the plaintiff recover of sd. defendant his costs by him about his suit in this behalf expended.

A Power of Attorney from Joel Smith Admr. &c. to Robert Smith for certain purposes therein specified was produced in court and the execution thereof proven by Charles Smith the witness thereto and ordered to be certified for registration.

A Deed of conveyance from Alexander McDonald to Samuel Davis for forty acres of land was produced in court and the execution thereof proven by the oaths of John S. Brandon & Thomas Brown the witnesses thereto and ordered to be certified for registration.

The Grand Jury returned into court and indictment of the State against George Kirk for an affray with and assault & battery on the body of Adam A. Farris, Endorsed a true bill. Edmund Shelton foreman of the Grand Jury Also a bill of presentment against Thomas B. Jones for an affray with and an assault and battery on the body of Lunsford M. Bramlett, and withdrew to consider of further presentments.

Henry Peden Plaintiff)   Appeal
    Against)
Jesse Beazley Defendant) This day came the parties by their attornies and thereupon came a Jury of good and lawful men, Towit, John Fry, James Lester, David Maxwell, Richard Briggs, James Johnston, James McKnight, Beverly Brown, John B. Anthony, Francis H. Mabery, John Keenan, Graves Hester & Thomas Brown who being elected tried and sworn well and truly to try the matter in controversey between the parties in this case upon their oaths do say that the defendant is (p334) indebted to the plaintiff the sum of Eight dollars, besides costs. It is therefore considered by the court that the plaintiff recover of said defendant his debt aforesaid in form aforesaid by the Jurors aforesaid assessed, and also his costs as well before the Justice of the peace as in this court Expended.

Ordered that court be adjourned untill tomorrow morning nine oclock.

                                               James Perry
                                               Anderson Hogan
                                               John H. Camp

Thursday Morning 24th February 1825

Court met according adjournment Present James Perry) Esquires & Justices
Anderson Hogan) of the Peace for
& John H. Camp) Giles County.

The State . . . Plt.) On a presentment for open & notorious
  Against) loodness.
Alexander McKinney Deft.)
) This day came the Solicitor General for
the State who saith he wishes no further to prosecute the defendant in this
case. It is therefore ordered by the court that a nole prosqui be entered
in this case, and that the defendant go hence without day.

The State / Plt.) On a presentment for open and notorious
  Against) loodness.
Alexander McKinney Deft.)
) A Nole prosqui having been entered up in
this case under the directions of the court. It is ordered that Judgment
be entered up against the County of Giles in favor of the several claimants
on the part of the State for all costs to which they are entitled and that
the Clerks certify the same to the trustee of Giles County for payment.

A Power of Attorney from John Butler to Memucan H. Howard for the purpose therein mentioned was produced in court and the execution thereof acknowledged by the said John Butler and ordered to be certified.

P-335   Thursday 24th February 1825

The State Plt.) Upon a presentment for open & notorious Lewd-
  Against) ness.
Lucy Bolling Deft.)
) This day came the Solicitor General for the
State, who saith he wishes no further to prosecute this suit.
It is therefore ordered by the court that a nole prosqui be entered
in this case and that the Defendant go hence without day.

The State Plt.) Upon a presentment for open & notorious Lewd-
  Against) ness.
Lucy Bolling Deft.)
) A Nole Prosqui having been entered up in this
case under the directions of the court. It is ordered that a Judgment be
entered up against the County of Giles in favor of the several claimants
on the part of the State for all costs to which they are entitled and that
the Clerk certify the same to the Trustee of Giles County for payment.

William Gholson Plt.)   Covenant
  Against)
William Watson Deft.)
) This day came the parties by their attornies
and thereupon came a Jury of good and lawful men, Towit, James Lester, David Maxwell, Richard Briggs, John Fry,

Thomas Brown, James Johnston, Beverly Brown, James McKnight, John W. Graves, John Abernathy, John McKnight, and Archibald Smith, who being elected tried and sworn well and truly to try the issue joined between the parties in this case, and having heard the Evidence the Jurors were permitted to disperse to meat again tomorrow morning nine oclock.

The Grand Jury returned into court a Bill of Indictment against Francis Tillotson for an affray with & an assault & battery on the body of Nathan Davis, "A true Bill" same against Theophilus Guthrie for an affray with & an assault & battery on the body of Daniel Puryear Endorsed "A true bill" same against George Kirk for an affray with & an assault & battery on the body of Adam R. Faris same against Lewis Morris for an affray with an assault & battery on the body of Samuel Day same against Lewis Morris for an affray with an assault & battery on the body of German Prim same against Nathan Davis for an affray with & an assault & battery on the body of Francis Tillotson, all endorsed "A true Bill" same against Benjamin England for an affray with & an assault and battery on the (p-336) body of Isaac Reynolds, Endorsed "A true Bill" same against James Rutherford for an affray with & an assault & battery on the body of Balam Bently Endorsed "Not a true Bill" and withdrew to consider of further presentments.

The administrator of the Estate of Anthony Samuel Decd. returned into court and additional Inventory of said A. Samuels Estate which is ordered to be recorded.

An agreement between John C. Walker & James J. Walker was produced in court and the execution thereof proven by the oaths of Joseph Erwin & Michael Biles the witnesses thereto and ordered to be spread at full length upon the minutes -- which agreement is in the following words & figures "Towit" Article of an agreement between John C. Walker of the one part and James J. Walker of the other part which as the peace of land where we live on, the County surveyor is to run a line due north & south across the Land so as to let John C. Walker have one hundred and ten acres on the west end of the line, and so that James J. Walker one hundred acres on the East side of the line, and whereas there is a water Mill & a distilery on the sd. land, But it is to be understood that we have an equal share in each, and it is to be further understood that the Still house spring if in runing the line it should fall on the east side of the line, there is to be an off set made so as to throw it on the west side of the line & the using spring on the Creek if it should fall on the west side of the line, there is to be an off set made so as to throw it on the East side, but if the Still house spring should give out or the water get bad then John C. Walker is to have the benefit of the Creek Spring where they now use water out of, and it is to be further understood that after the death of our mother the sd. line shall be run and the said John C. Walker is to relinquish his title to the land on the East side of the above named line & James J. Walker is to relinquish his title to the land on the west side of the said line, under the penalty of two thousand dollars.
Given under our hands and seals.

                     John C. Walker (Seal)
                     James J. Walker)Seal)

Witnesses: Joseph Erwin
       Michael Biles

P-337   Thursday 24th February 1825

The State ... Plt.   ) Upon an Indictment for an affray with &
        Against   ) an assault & battery on the body of Dan-
Theophilus Guthrie Deft.   ) iel Puryear.

This day came as well the Solicitor General for the State as also the defendant in his proper person, who being charged on the Indictment in this case pleads guilty and because he will not contend with the State agrees to submit himself to the Justice and mercy of the court.

It is therefore considered by the court that he make his fine with the State to the amount of ten dollars, and that he pay the costs of this prosecution, and that he be committed to the custody of the Sheriff of this County thereto remain till said fine and costs be paid.

The State Plt.   ) Upon an Indictment for an affray with & an
    Against   ) assault & battery on the body of Thomas Baker.
Jonathan Ford Deft.   )
) This day came as well the Solicitor General
for the State as also the Defendant in his proper person who being charged on the Indictment in this case pleads guilty and because he will not contend with the State, agrees to submit himself to the Justice and mercy of this court. It is therefore considered by the court that he make his fine with the State to one dollar and that he pay the costs of this prosecution, and that he be committed to the custody of the Sheriff of this County, thereto remain till said fine and costs be paid - or that he give security for the payment of the same - and thereupon James Perry comes into court and undertakes as security for said Defendant.

It is therefore considered by the court that the State recover of said defendant and James Perry his security the fine and costs aforesaid.

Ordered that John C. Walker be appointed administrator with the will anexed for the Estate of Susan Walker decd. whereupon he was qualified, and gave bond and security as the Law directs.

Ordered that William Ussery be appointed Guardian to Charles Walker, Fanny Walker, Coleman Walker, and Jonston Marion Walker minor orphans of James J. Walker decd. whereupon he executed bond and security as the Law directs.

The State ... Plt.   ) Upon an Indictment for an affray with
        Against   ) & an assault & battery on the body of
John Peace &   ) Defts.   ) Isaac Reynolds.
Benjamin England)   )
) Isaac Reynolds & Wm. Reynolds, comes in
to court and acknowledges themselves indebted to the State of Tennessee in the sum of one hundred dollars each to be levied of their goods and chattles lands and tenments to the use of the State to be void on condition that the said Isaac Reynolds appear here   (p-338)   on the first thursday after the third Monday in May next and prosecute and give evidence in behalf of the State against said defendant and not depart without leave of the court.

John McCracken Plt.) Petition
Against)
Mary D. Price Gdn. &c. Deft.) This day the defendant gave bond and
) Counter Security for the Guardian-
ship of John H. Price, and Martha R. S. Price, Easter J. A. Price, Mary
S. A. Price, James H. Price, minor orphans of James Price decd. and thereupon
the said plaintiff is released from all future responsibility as security
for the said defendant as Guardian of said minors, and it is considered by
the court that the plaintiff recover against the defendant his costs about
his suit in this behalf expended.

Gerald Irby . . . . Plt.) In case
Against)
Elnathan G. Brown Deft.) On the affidavit of the defendant It is
) ordered that a commission issue to any
two of the acting Justices of Peace in and for the County of Rutherford in
this State to take the deposition of Harbert Boyles which is to be read in
evidence on the trial of this cause upon the defendant giving to the plaintiff ten days notice of the time and place of taking said deposition.

Ordered that court be adjourned untill tomorrow morning nine oclock.

H. Hagen
A. Black
Jno. H. Camp

P-339   Friday 25th February 1825

Court met according to adjournment Present Alexander Black) Justice of the
John H. Camp) Peace for the
Henry Hagen) County of Giles.

An Ordinary Liscence for the term of twelve months and no longer is granted
to Thomas B. Jones, Whereupon he executed bond and security & was qualified
as the Law directs.

William Gholson Plt.) In Covenant
Against)
William Watson Deft.) This day came the parties by their attornies
) and thereupon came the Jury who was sworn on
a former day of this term to try the issue joined between the parties in
this case, who after having heard the balance of the evidence and part of
the argument of counsel were again permitted to disperse to meet tomorrow
morning 9 oclock.

The State Plt.) Upon a presentment for an affray with & an
Against) assault & battery on the body of Thomas Franks.
Richard Tutt Deft.)
) This day came the Solicitor General for the
State, who saith he wishes no further to prosecute the defendant in this
case. It is therefore considered by the court that a nole prosequi be
entered therein and that the defendant go hence without day.

The State Plt. Against Richard Tutt Deft.	Upon a presentment for an affray with & an assault & battery on Thos. Franks.

A Nole prosqui having been entered up in this case, under the directions of the court. It is ordered that a Judgment be entered up against the County of Giles in favor of the several claimants, on the part of the State for all costs to which they are entitled, and that the Clerk certify the same to the Trustee of Giles County for payment.

The Grand Jury returned into court a Bill of presentments of the State against John King for retailing Spiritous liquors, also a Bill of Indictment, same against Ira C. Goff for gaming, same against James & Caswell Tucker for an affray with & an assault & battery on the body of Joseph Slider same against John Pearce for an affray with & an assault & battery on the body of Isaac Reynolds, all Endorsed "A true Bill" & withdrew to consider of further presentments.

P-340   Friday 25th February 1825

The Commissioners who were appointed to settle with James Buford Administrator of the Estate of John Hicks decd. made return of said settlement which is ordered to be recorded.

Ordered that James Buford Administrator of the Estate of John Hicks decd. be allowed the sum of one hundred & twenty dollars to be paid out of the Estate of sd. Hicks decd. for his services as administrator in settling the same.

Sterling C. Robertson) Plts. Eldridge B. Robertson) Against John Maxwell ... Deft.	Scire Facias

This day came as well the plaintiffs by their attornies, as also the defendant in his proper person, and the said defendant assumes upon himself the payments of the costs in this case and thereupon the plaintiffs attorney releases the defendants from the forfeeties heretofore entered up against him – It is therefore considered by the court that the plaintiff recover against the defendant their costs about their suit in this behalf expended.

For contempt of court by Joseph H. Hodge in the court house while in session. It is ordered that he be fined in the sum of twenty dollars and that he be committed to the common Jail of this County thereto remain untill the adjournment of court this evening at which time the Jailor is ordered to release him from his said confinement.

Ordered that court be adjourned untill tomorrow morning 9 oclock.

H. Hagen
John H. Camp
A. Black

P-341   Saturday 26th February 1825

Court met according to adjournment Present John H. Camp) Esquires Justices of the Peace for Giles County.
                                    Alexander Black)
                                    Henry Hagen)
)

Ordered that a vendition Exponas issue to the Sheriff of this County commanding him to advertise and sell according to Law one hundred & twenty seven acres of Land the property of Asa A. Estes lying on Shoal Creek Giles County part of a five thousand acre tract Granted by the State of North Carolina of Stokely Donaldson. and by him conveyed to James Cannon Maclingberge County N. C. and by sd. Conner to Thos. Reed and from Reed to sd. Estes adjoining the land of James Hanner & others, also one other tract containing nine hundred and sixty two and a half acres part of the above tract of land discribed adjoining the land of Thos. Reed, Collins, Morris, Hannah, also one other tract containing one hundred and ten acres and a half part of sd. five thousand acre tract as above discribed adjoining the Land of Kimbrough, levied on, on the 31st day of December 1824 as the property of said Asa A. Estes by William W. Wood constable Giles County to satisfy an execution which issue on a Judgment which Charles Buford recovered against him sd. Estes before Thomas Marks Esquires a Justice of the Peace for this County on the 27th day of December 1824 for the sum of Twenty dollars & fifty cents & costs.

Ordered that a venditioni Exponas issue to the Sheriff of this County commanding him to advertise and sell according to Law one hundred and twenty seven acres of land the property of Asa A. Estes lying on Shoal Creek Giles County part of a five thousand acre tract Granted by the State of North Carolina of Stokley Donaldson and by him conveyed to James Cannon Macklingberg County N. C. & by sd. Conner to Thomas Reed and from Reed to sd. Estes adjoining the land of James Hannah, & others – Also one other tract containing nine hundred and sixty two and a half acres part of the above tract of land described adjoining the land of Thomas Reed, Collins, Morris, Nanhan, Also one other containing one hundred and ten acres and a half part of sd. five thousand acre tract as above described adjoining the lands of Kimbrough levied on, on the 31st day of December 1824 as the property of said Asa A. Estes by William W. Woods constable of Giles County to satisfy an execution which issued on a Judgment which Samuel McKnight, recovered against him sd. Estes – before Thomas Marks Esquire a Justice of the peace for this County on the 27th day of Desember 1824 for the sum of seventy five dollars & costs.

P-342   Saturday 26st February 1825

Ordered that a venditioni Exponas issue to the Sheriff of this County commanding him to advertise and sell according to law one hundred & twenty seven acres of land the property of Asa A. Estes lying on Shoal Creek Giles County part of the five thousand acre tract Granted by the State of North Carolina to Stockley Donaldson, and by him conveyed to James Cannon Macklingberg County N. C. and by sd. Conner to Thos. Reed and from Reed to Asa A. Estes adjoining the lands of James Hannah and others:- Also one other tract containing nine hundred and sixty two and a half acres part of the above tract of land described adjoining the land of Thos. Reed Collins, Morris, Hannah, also one other tract containing one hundred and ten acres & a half part of sd. five thousand acre tract as above described adjoining the land of Kimbrough, levied on on the 31st day of December 1824 as the property of Asa A. Estes by William W. Woods Constable of Giles County to satisfy an Execution which issued on the Judgment which Thomas Williams recovered against him sd. Estes before Thomas Marks Esquire a Justice of the Peace for this County on the 17th day of December 1824 - for the sum of thirty dollars & 17 cents & costs.

Ordered that a venditioni Exponas issue to the Sheriff of this County commanding him to advertise & sell according to Law, one hundred and twenty seven acres of land the property of Asa A. Estes, lying on Shoald Creek Giles Cty. part of the five thousand acre tract Granted by the State of North Carolina to Stockley Donaldson and by him conveyed to James Conner Macklingberg County N. C. and by sd. Conner to Thomas Reed and from Reed to Asa A. Estes adjoining the lands James Hannah & others - Also one other tract containing nine hundred & sixty two and half acres part of the above tract of land described adjoining Thos. Marks, Collins, Morris, Hannah, Also one other tract containing one hundred & ten acres and a half part of sd. five thousand acre tract as above described, adjoining the lands of Kimbrough levied on, on the 31st day of December 1824 as the property of sd. Asa A. Estes, by Wm. W. Woods Constable of Giles County to satisfy an Execution which issued on a Judgment which Thomas Williams recovered against him sd. Estes before Thomas Marks, Esquire a Justice of the peace for this County on the 27th day of December 1824 - for the sum of seventeen dollars & sixteen cents & costs.

P-343 Saturday 26th February 1825

An Inventory, additional of the Estate of Harrison Hicks decd, returned by the administrator and ordered to be recorded.

James Buford Guardian of James Moore made return as said Guardian which is ordered to be recorded.

James Buford Guardian of Catherine Moore made return as said Guardian which is ordered to be recorded.

James Buford Guardian of Nancy Hicks made return as said Guardian which is ordered to be recorded.

Elisha Eldridge Guardian of the Minor children of John W. Edwards made return as said Guardian which is ordered to be recorded.

A Deed of conveyance from William Price to Wilton F. L. Jenkins, was produced in court and fully proven by James Caldwell the other witness thereto and ordered to be certified for registration.

Elisha Eldridge & Lunsford) Plts.   )   In Covinants
M. Bramlitt Executors of   )   )

265

Thomas H. Meredith)
    Against   )
James Perry . . Deft.)
)

This day came as well the plaintiff by their attorney as also the defendant in his proper person and said defendant withdraws the plea by him heretofore filed and saith he cannot gainsay the plaintiffs actions against him nor but that they have sustained damages by occasion of the non performance of the covenants in the declaration complained of to five hundred & fourteen dollars & five cents - besides costs - It is therefore by consent of the plaintiffs attorney considered by the court that the plaintiff recover against sd. defendant their damages aforesaid in form aforesaid, agreed and also their costs by them about their suit in this behalf expended.

The State Plt.)
    Against   )
Thomas B. Jones Deft.)

Upon an Indictment for an affray with & an assault & battery on the body of L. M. Bramlitt.

This day came as well the Solicitor General for the State as also the defendant in his proper person, who being charged on the Indictment in this case pleads guilty and because the will not contend with the State agrees to submit himself to the Justice & mercy of the court. It is therefore considered by the court that he make his fine with the State to the amount of one dollar & that he pay the costs of this prosecution.

P-344 Saturday 26st February 1825

The State . . . Plt.)
    Against   )
Francis Tillotson Deft.)
)

Upon an Indictment for an affray with & an assault & battery on the body of Nathan Davis.

This day came as well the Solicitor General for the State as also the defendant in his proper person, who being charged on the Indictment in this case pleads guilty and because he will not contend with the State agrees to submit himself to the Justice & mercy of the court.
It is therefore considered by the court that he make his fine with the State to the amount of twenty five cents and that he pay the costs of this prosecution and that he be committed to the custody of the Sheriff of this County thereto remain till sd. fine & costs be paid, or that he give security for the payment of the same, and thereupon Benjamin M. Scoggin comes into court and undertakes as security for said defendant - It is therefore considered by the court that the State recover of sd. defendant & Benjamin M. Scoggins his security the fine and costs aforesaid.

Ordered that John Barnett & Thomas Brown Esquires be appointed commissioners to settle with Thomas Read administrator of the Estate of Francis Moore decd. and that they make return thereof to the next term of this court.

Ordered that John A. Jones be appointed Guardian to Cathrine Cox Infant orphan of Samuel Cox decd. whereupon he executed bond and security as the Law Directs.

The State . . . Plt.)
    Against   )
Benjamin Tutt Deft.)

Upon a presentment for an affray with & an assault & battery on the body of John Gilliam.

This day came the Solicitor General for the State who saith he wishes no further to prosecute the Defendant in this case.

It is therefore considered by the court that a Nole Prosqui be entered therein and that the defendant go hence without day.

The State Plt. Plt.) Upon a presentment for an affray with & an
    Against   ) assault & battery on the body of John Gilliam.
Benjamin Tutt Deft.)

A Nole prosqui having been entered in this case, under the direction of the Several claimants on the part of the State against the County of Giles for all costs to which they are entitled, and that the Clerk certify the same to the Trustee of Giles County for payment.

P-345   Saturday 26th February 1825

A Deed of conveyance from Thomas B. Haynie to William W. Fogg for two hundred & forty & sevententh acres was produced in court and the execution thereof acknowledged by the said Thomas B. Haynie and ordered to be certified for registration.

The State Plt.) Upon an Indictment for an affray with & an
    Against   ) assault & battery on the body of Bailey
David Stockton Deft.) Davis.
)

Bailey Davis, James Coldwell, & John Whitfield, comes into court and acknowledges themselves indebted to the State of Tennessee the said Bailey Davis in the sum of one hundred dollars & the said James Coldwell & John Whitfield in the sum of fifty dollars each to be levied of their goods & chattles lands & tenements to the use of the State - To be void on condition that the said Bailey Davis here on the first Thursday after the third Monday in May next & prosecute & give evidence on behalf of the State against the sd. Defendant & not depart without leave of this court.

A Deed of conveyance from Alexander S. Jones & Hezekiah his wife to Thomas B. Haynie for twenty nine acres and thirty five poles of land was produced in court and the execution thereof acknowledged by the said Alexander S. Jones, - And thereupon Archibald McKissack and Thomas Marks Esquires Justice of the Peace for this County were appointed to take the privy Examination of sd. Hezekiah P. Jones touching the Execution of said deed and return the same into court instanter and sd. Justice proceeded to take said Examination and returned the same into court, the same was ordered to be certified for registration.

A Deed of conveyance from Henry White to William Wood for thirty and three fourth acres of land was produced in court and the Execution thereof acknowledged by the sd. Henry White & ordered to be certified for registration.

The State Plt.) Upon an Indictment for an affray with & an as-
    Against   ) sault & battery on the body of Adam R. Faris.
George Kirk Deft.)

Adam R. Faris & Beverly B. Watson, comes into court & acknowledges themselves indebted to the State of Tennessee the sd. Adam R. Faris in the sum of one hundred dollars & the sd. Beverly B. Watson in the sum of fifty dollars to the use of the State - to be void on conditions that the said Adam R. Faris appear here on the first Thursday after the third Monday in May next to prosecute and give evidence in behalf of the State against said Defendant and not depart without leave of this court.

P-346   The State Plt.
           Against
          George Kirk Deft.

Upon an Idictment for an affray with & an assault & battery on the body of Adam R. Faris & Beverly B. Watson comes into court & acknowledges themselves indebted to the State of Tennessee the sd. Adam R. Faris in the sum of one hundred dollars and the sd. Beverly B. Watson in the sum fifty dollars to be levied of their goods & chattles lands & tenments to the use of the State to be void on condition that the said Adam R. Faris appear here on the first Thursday after the third Monday in May next and prosecute & give evidence in behalf of the State against said Defendant and not depart without leave of the court.

The State Plt.
     Against
John W. Edwards Deft.

Upon a presentment for an affray with & an assault & battery on the body of James Dailey.

This day came as well came as well the Solicitor General as also the Defendant in his proper person who being charged on the presentment in this case pleads not guilty and for his trial puts himself upon his Country and the Solicitor General for the State for the part of the State likewise, therefore let a Jury come who as well &c to recognise &c, Towit, Edmund Shelton, Larkin B. Moore, Jacob Jones, Edward M. Brown, Joseph McDonald, Alexander Tarpley, Jeremiah Parker, John E. Holden, Jesse Pullen, Patrick R. Smith, Levi Read and William W. Fogg, who were elected tried and sworn well & truly to try the issue of traverse between the State and the said Defendant upon their oaths do say that said defendant is guilty in manner and form as he is charged in the presentment It is therefore considered by the court that the make his fine with the State to the amount of one dollar and that he pay the costs of this prosecution and that he be committed to the custody of the Sheriff of this County thereto remain till said fine and costs be paid or untill he give Security for the payment of the same - and thereupon Gray H. Edwards & Isaac Mason comes into court and undertakes as security for sd. Defendant. It is therefore considered by the court that the State recover of sd. Defendant & Gray H. Edwards & Isaac Mason his securities the fine and costs aforesaid.

A Deed of conveyance from Andrew Fay to Gray H. Edwards for three hundred & Eight & a half acres of land was produced in court and the execution thereof acknowledged by said Fay and ordered to be certified for registration

P-347   Saturday 26th February 1825

The State .. Plt.
     Against
David Stockton Deft.

Upon a presentment for an affray with Bailey Davis.

This day came as well the Solicitor General for the State as also the Defendant in his proper person who being charged on the presentment in this case pleads not guilty, and for the trial puts himself upon his Country, and the Solicitor General for the State on the part of the State likewise, therefore let a Jury come &c who as well &c to recognize &c and thereupon came a Jury of good and lawful men, Towit, Richard H. Allen, Edward Marks, Henry White, Simpson H. White, Henry T. Croft, Robert H. Harris, David Reed, Quinton Shannon, Daniel Abernathy, Thomas Wells, John Brown, and Nathaniel Hammet, who being elected tried and sworn well and truly to try the issue of traverse between the State and the said Defendant upon their oaths do say that sd. defendant is guilty in manner and form as he is charged in the presentment. It is therefore considered by the court that he make his fine with the State to the amount of one dollar and that he pay the costs of this prosecution, and that he be committed to the custody of the Sheriff of this county thereto remain till sd. fine and cost be paid, or untill he gives security for the payment of the same, and thereupon John Whitfield and Baker B. Potts undertakes on security for said Defendant –

It is therefore considered by the court that the State recover of sd. Defendant and John Whitfield & Baker B. Potts his Securities the fine & costs aforesaid.

The State Plt.)   Recognizance
   Against   )
John Rawlins Deft.)   This day came the Solicitor General for the
)   State who saith he wishes no further to prosecute the Defendant in this case upon his coming into Court and assuming upon himself the payment of the cost – Thereupon sd. Defendant came into court and assumed upon himself the payment of sd. costs in this case –

It is therefore considered by the court that the State recover of sd. Defendant his costs about his suit in this behalf expended.

The State Plt.)   Peace Recognizance
   Against   )
Bailey Davis Deft.)   Bailey Davis, James Coldwell & John Whitfield
)   comes into court and acknowledges themselves
indebted (p-348) (Saturday 26th February 1824) to the State of Tennessee the said Bailey Davis in the sum of two hundred dollars, and the said James Coldwell & John Whitfield in the sum of one hundred dollars each to be levied of their good and chattles lands & tenments, to the use of the State to be void on condition that the said Bailey Davis does in all things keep the peace towards the citizen of this State Generally & more particularly towards one David Stockton, for the term of three months from this time – and that they pay the costs of this prosecution – It is therefore considered by the court that said State recover of sd. Defendant his costs about his suit in this behalf expended.

The State Plt.)   Peace Recognizance
   Against   )
David Stockton Deft.)   David Stockton, William Rose & Baker B. Potts,
)   comes into court and acknowledges themselves
indebted to the State of Tennessee the said David Stockton in the sum of two hundred dollars, and the sd. William Rose & Baker B. Potts in the sum of one hundred dollars each to be levied of their goods & chattles lands and

tenements to the use of the State – To be void on conditions that the said David Stockton, does in all things keep the peace towards the citizens of this State Generally & more particularly towards one Bailey Davis for the term of three months from this time – And that they pay the costs of this prosecution.

It is therefore considered by the court that the State recover of sd. Defendants his costs about his suit in this behalf expended.

William Gholson Plt.   )   In Covenant
  Against   )
William Watson Deft.   )   This day came the parties by their attorneys
)   and thereupon came the Jury who were sworn
on a former day of this term well and truly to try the issue Joined between the parties in this case who upon their oaths do say that they find said issues in favor of the plaintiff and assess his damages by ocasion thereof to nineteen hundred & forty eight dollars & thirty three cents, besides costs.

It is therefore considered by the court that the plaintiff recover of said defendant the damages aforesaid, in form aforesaid by the Jurors aforesaid, assessed, and also his costs by him about his suit in this behalf expended – whereupon said (p-349) Defendant moved the court now here for a rule to show cause why a new trial should be granted and the same is granted.

Richard H. Allen . . . Plt.)   Motion
  Against   )
William Mayfield &)Defts.   )   This day came the parties by Lunsford
Elisha B. Mayfield)   )   M. Bramlett his attorney and it appearing
)   to the satisfaction of the court
on inspecting the record that At August term 1823 Homer Rainey assee &c. recovered a Judgment against said Defendant & sd. Richard H. Allen & Thomas B. Haynie Jointly for the sum of nine hundred & ninety four dollars & ninety cents & costs of suit and that said plaintiff hath paid for sd. Defendants the sum of Four hundred & sixty dollars as their security said amount being said Allen's half of sd. Judgment his co. security Thomas B. Haynie having paid the balance – It is therefore considered by the court that sd. Plaintiff recover of sd. Defendants the said sum of Four hundred & forty Dollars together with the costs of this motion.

Ordered that court be adjourned untill Monday morning Eight oclock.

William Woods
A. Black
Robert Read

P-350   Monday Morning 28th February 1825

Court met according to adjournment Present Henry Hagen, William Wood Alexander Black, Robert Read, Archibald McKissack, James Dugger, John Young, William B. Pepper, Hezekiah Jones, Thomas Marks, James H. Graves, Paul Chiles, James Perry, James Paine, Jesse Allen, Arthur Hicks, Esquires Justices of the Peace for Giles County.

James Dugger Esquire who was appointed at the last term of court to take a list of taxable property & poles in Captain E. M. Browns Company for the year 1825 made return thereof which is ordered to be recorded.

William Gholson Plt.) In Covernant
Against)
William Watson Deft.) This day came the parties aforesaid by their
) attornies and thereupon the rule of the Defendant to shew cause why a new trial should be had in this cause, being argued and maturely considered & understood by the court - It is the opinion of the court that no new trial ought to be granted in this case.
It is therefore considered by the court that said rule be discharged.

Ordered that William Beazley an orphan boy be bound and apprenticed to Francis H. Mabrey an Indenture to that effect having been entered into between the chairman of this court and said Francis H. Mabrey.

A Bill of sale from Asa A. Estes to Thomas Marks for certain property therein mentioned was produced in court and the execution thereof proven by the oaths of John H. Rivers, the witness thereto and ordered to be certified for registration.

An Inventory of the Estate of Henry House decd. returned into court by Wm. Owen Executor, and ordered to be recorded.

Ordered that an order of sale issue to William Owen, Executor of the Estate of Henry House decd. commanding him to sell the property mentioned in the Inventory of said Estate, and that he make return thereof to the next term of this court.

Ordered that James W. Wheeler be appointed overseer of the road in the room of John W. R. Graves removed and that he have the same district of hands.

P-351   Monday 28th February 1825

William B. Pepper Esquire who was appointed to take a list of taxable property and poles at last court, in Captain Crofts Company for the year 1825 made return thereof which is ordered to be recorded.

A Deed of conveyance from William R. Pepper to John W. Perry for Lots Nos. 80 & 81 in the Town of Pulaski was produced in court and the Execution thereof acknowledged by sd. William B. Pepper & ordered to be certified for registration.

A Deed of conveyance from John W. Perry to Andrew M. Balentine for Lots Nos. 28 39, 80 & 81 in the Town of Pulaski was produced in court and the execution thereof acknowledged by the said John W. Perry and ordered to be certified for registration.

At least five Justices being present Samuel Harwell returned into court one wolf scalp over 4 months old which was ordered to be burnt.

A Deed of conveyance from Simpson H. White to Beverly W. Watson for lot No. 16, in the Town of Pulaski was produced in court and the execution thereof acknowledged by the sd. Simpson H. White and ordered to be certified for registration.

Ordered that Gilliam Harwell, Robert Adam, and Joseph Anthony be appointed commissioners to settle with Nathan Williams Guardian of the minor children of Henry Scales, and that they make return thereof the present term of this court.

Ordered that Featherston Harwell be appointed overseer of the road in the room of James Kelson resigned and that he have the same district of hands.

Hezekiah Jones Esquire who was appointed at the last term of this court to make a list of taxable property and poles in Captain Gootchs Company for the year 1825 made return thereof which is ordered to be recorded.

William Wood Esquire who was appointed at the last term of this court to take a list of taxable property to poles in Captain Granville Pillow's Company for the year 1825 made return thereof which is ordered to be recorded.

P-352   Monday 28th February 1825

The Jury who were appointed at the present term of this court, to view that part of the Prewits Gap road which lies near Samuel Dodson Plantation made their report and thereupon it is ordered by the court that said part of said road be established as a Publick Highway when opened agreable to Law by the said Dodson at his own expence, and when so opened to be kept in repair by William Wood overseer, with the hands under his directions.

Ordered that the apprentice Indenture heretofore entered into between the chairman, of this court and Henry J. Cooper binding Hugh McCabe to said Cooper be seconded and made null & void.

At least five Justices being present Hezekiah Jones Esquire returned into court one wolf scalp over four months old which is ordered to be burnt.

Ordered that the County Trustee of this County pay to Alexander Jones the sum of eight dollars thirty three and one third cents, for acting as Solicitor General pro tin at the present term of this court as his Exofficio services.

On petition it is ordered that Robert Anderson, David Maxwell, Robert Turner, Robert Fenner, Thomas P. Estes, David Abernathy, Simpson H. White and Matthew Johnson, or any five of them be appointed a Jury to view and mark out a road the nearest and best way from the Shelbyville road near Thomas P. Esters, where said road crosses the main Branch or fork of Pigeon roost Creak from thence to Parks Baileys Mill from thence the nearest and best way to intersect the road that leads by Tyree Rodes to Mayfields Mill and that they make report thereof to the next term of this court.

Ordered that the apprentice Indenture heretofore entered into between the chairman of this court and Willis Lane binding Rhoda Strickland to said Willis Lane, be seconded and that said Rhoda Strickland be bound and apprenticed to Thomas Hicks an Indenture to that effect having been entered into between the chairman of this court and said Thomas Hicks.

P-353   Monday 28th February 1825

A Plat and certificate of survey for fifty acres of Land in the name of Archibald Smith and the assignment thereof from the said Archiblad Smith to Edmund Larkin was produced in court and the Execution thereof acknowledged by the said Archibald Smith and ordered to be certified.

John H. Camp Esquire who was appointed at the last term of this court to take a list of taxable property & poles in Captain John Bass's Company for the year 1825 made return thereof which is ordered to be recorded.

Ordered that the County Trustee of this County pay to William Trigg the sum of thirty four dollars for the support and maintenance of David Trigg who is blind for the term of twelve months from this time.

A Plat & certificate of survey for twenty acres of land in the name of David C. Mitchel and the assignment thereon from said David C. Mitchel to Benjamin Mays was produced in court and the execution thereof acknowledged by the said David C. Mitchel and ordered to be certified for registration.

Ordered that Allen Jones be appointed overseer of the road in the room of David Cook resigned and that he have the same district of hands.

Francis Smith &) Plts.	Petition
James Kimbrough)	
Against	This day came the plaintiff by Rivers & Tar-
Jordan Massie &) Defts.	pley their attornies, and filed their petition
James Martin Admr. &c.	which is granted and it is thereupon ordered
	by the court that a summons issue to the De-

fendants, together with a copy of this petition.

Archibald McKissack, Esquire who was appointed at the last term of this court to take a list of taxable property & poles in Captain Thorntons Company for the year 1825 made return thereof which is ordered to be recorded.

Isaac Smith Guardian to the heirs of Jethro Brown Decd. made return as sd. Gdn. which is ordered to be recorded.

P-354   Monday 28th February 1825

Ordered that Isaiah Hogan be appointed overseer of the road in the room of James Shelton removed and that he have the same district of hands.

Ordered that John B. Wilson be appointed overseer of the road in the room of Robert McKnight resigned, and that he have the same district of hands.

The commissioners who were appointed to settle with Nathaniel Williams Guardian to the minor children of Henry Scales made return of said settlement which is ordered to be recorded.

Arthur Hicks Esquire who was appointed to take a list of taxable property & poles in Captain Hendrys Company for the year 1825 made return thereof which is ordered to be recorded.

Ordered that John Pate Junr. Guardian to the heirs of Peter Garland decd. be allowed the sum of fifty four Dollars & thirty four cents for his services as Guardian to sd. heirs.

The commissioners who were appointed to settle with John Pate Junr. Guardian to the heirs of Peter Garland decd. made return of sd. settlement which is ordered to be recorded.

A Deed of conveyance from Asa A. Estes to John E. Holden for lot No. 62 in the Town of Pulaski was produced in court and the execution thereof proven by the oaths of Fountain Lester & Edward W. Rose the witnesses thereto and ordered to be certified for registration.

A Deed of conveyance from Moses Pullen to Patrick H. Braden for one hundred & eighteen acres of land was produced in court and the execution thereof acknowledged by the sd. Moses Pullen and ordered to be certified for registration.

P-355   Monday 28th February 1825

A Deed of conveyance from John Averett to Moses Pullen for one hundred and Eighteen acres of land was produced in court in court and the Execution thereof proven by the oaths of Joab Ross and Jabez L. Carter, two of the witnesses thereto, and ordered to be certified for registration.

Ordered that Matthew Johnson be appointed overseer of the road in the room of Joab Ross resigned, and that he have the same district of hands.

Ordered that the County Trustee of this County procure a crow bar and sledge hammer for the use of overseers of roads in this County, & pay the same out of any monies in his hands not otherwise appropriated, which are to be kept in the Clerks office of this court.

Ordered that Tyree Rodes, William Wood, William Sheppard, David Maxwell, and Elisha White be appointed commissioners to Let the building of a bridge across Haywood Creek, at or near where the Prewits Gap road crosses said Creek, and that they be authorised to draw on the County Trustee for the sum of fifty dollars towards paying for the same.

Ordered that the County Trustee of this County pay to German Lester the sum of twelve dollars for paper furnished by him, for the use of his office not heretofore allowed for several years past.

It is ordered by the court that the following persons, good and Lawful men of the County of Giles that is each one of whom is a free white male citizen and house holder of said County, over twenty one years of age, not overseer of a road, and who has not been appointed and served as a Juror in this County Court for twelve months, towit, Robert Anderson, William B. Brooks, Rolly Harwell, Robert Adams, Samuel Smith, Daniel McCollum, John McCanlass, Aaron Smith, Walter Hill, John Brown, Elisha Kimbrough, Robert Fenner, Thomas Wilkinson, William W. Fogg, James Horn, Amos Grigsby, William Jones, Arthur M. M. Upshaw, Andrew Gordon, Early Benson, John G. Braden, Henry M. Newlin, Henry J. Cooper, John D. Riddle, Claiborne Kyle & Francis Smith, be Jurors to serve in this court at the next term on the third Monday in May next. That the Clerk deliver a copy of this order to the Sheriff of this County and that he summon sd. persons to attend and serve accordingly.

P-356 Monday 28th February 1825

It is ordered by the court that the following persons good and Lawful men of this County of Giles that is each one of whom is a free white male citizen and house holder of said County over twenty one years of age not an overseer of a road who has not served on the venise in the Circuit Court of said County, at the last term thereof, and who has no cause to be tried in said court at the next term thereof, that is known of by this court Towit, Alexander Black, James Dugger, Quinton Shannon, James Paine, Archibald McKissack, Robert Read, John Dickey, Richard Brandon, Robert Oliver, William Bradley, Thomas K. Gordon, Ephriam M. Massie, Joseph Rea, Anderson, Hogan, George Malone, James Perry, Jesse Allen, Thomas Harwood, Abel Wilson, William Brown, Robert McLaurine, John C. Walker, and John Abernathy, be Jurors to serve in the next Circuit Court to be holden for sd. County at the Courthouse in the Town of Pulaski on the first Monday in August next, that the Clerk deliver a copy of this order to the Sheriff of the County and that he summon said persons to attend and serve accordingly.

Ordered that the County tax of this County for the year 1825 be as follows, Towit,

On each one hundred acres of land 18 3/4 cents on each free poll twelve and one half cents. On each Town lot 37½ cents. On each slave twenty five cents. On each Stud horse or Jack 25 cents. On each merchant or peddlers Liscence five dollars. On each two wheel pleasure carriages one Dollar. On each four wheel pleasure carriage two dollars.

Ordered that the additional County tax for this County for the year 1825 for the pay of Jurors be as follows, towit, On each one hundred acres of land Eighteen & three fourth cents. On each Stud horse of Jack 25 cents. On each Town lot 37½ cents.

Ordered that the aditional County tax for this County for the year 1825, for the support of the poor be as follows, towit,

On each 100 acres of land 18 3/4 cents. On each Stud horse or Jack 25 cents.
On each Town lot 37½ cents.

P-357 Monday 28th February 1825

Ordered that the Several ordinary Keepers in this County for the year 1825 be as follows, towit,

```
For Breakfast Dinner & Supper . . . . . . .   25 cents each
For horse to corn & fodder 12 hours           25  "    "
 "  singhe horse feed . . . . . .             12½ "    "
 "  Lodging . . . . . . . .                   12½ "    "
 "  Rum by ½ pint . . . . . .                 25  "    "
 "  Wine  "   "                               25  "    "
 "  Cogniac wine Ditto                        25  "    "
Peach Brandy  "                               12½ "    "
 "  Peach  "    "                             12½ "    "
```

Ordered that the rate of Ferriage at John Daileys Ferry at Lower Elkton in this County be as follows, Towit,

```
For man & horse over Creek & river  . . .   12½ cents
 "   "   Ditto  " over river only . . .     12½  "
 "   "   Ditto  "    over river only.  . .   6¼  "
 "  Wagon over creek only  . . . . .        37½
 "  Ditto over creek & river . . .          50   "
 "  Ditto over river only  . . . .          50   "
 "  Gigg over creek only  . . . . .         18 3/4
 "  Ditto over creek & river  . . . .       25   "
 "  Ditto over river only  . . . . .        25   "
 "  Cart over creek only  . . . .           18 3/4
 "  Ditto over river & creek  . . . .       25
 "  Ditto over river only  . . . .          25   "
 "  four wheel pleasure carriage . . .      25   "
 "  Ditto over river & creek  . . . .       50   "
 "  Ditto over river only  . . . .          50   "
```

On the Petition of Andrew Turnbean Ordered that Daniel Allen, Richard A.

Allen, Richard S. Baile, Nathan Baile, Samuel Farris, Isaac Christman, and Joseph Rea or any five of them be appointed a Jury to view that part of the road leading from Pulaski to Columbia which lies near said Turnbeans plantation & see if it be proper to turn the said road, and make report thereof to the next term of this court.

Ordered that Robert Gordon, Joseph East, John Lee, Stephen Anderson, Thomas Graves, James Taylor, and John Young or any five of them be appointed a Jury to view that part of the road which lies near or opposite Thomas Clarks, & see whether it be best to Establish the road as it formerly run down the Creek, or the road opened lately by a Jury who were appointed for that purpose on petition of sd. Clark and that they make report to the next term of this court.

P-358   Monday 28th February 1825

Ordered that John W. Croft be appointed to overseer of the road in the room of Enoch Davis the former overseer and that he have in addition to his own hands for the purpose of clearing out the same from the Fork east of Austin Smiths to the fork near Long Creek the hands in the following bounds, towit, All on the Indian Creek road to the Elkton road together with all the hands all ready on sd. Elkton road to the top of the ridge East of Isaac Williams, also the hands of Henry Loyds, John Kimbrol, Samuel King, & John Tillman with all the hands included in those bounds.

Ordered that Archibald Smith, John Young Junr, George Nichols, Robert Smith, John Abernathy, Archibald McKennon & John Kennedy or any five of them be appointed a Jury to view that part of the Fayettsville road which runs around John B. McCanlass farm and see if it be proper to turn said part of said road, and that they make report thereof to the next term of this court.

Ordered that Court be adjourned untill tomorrow morning nine oclock.

              H. Hagen
              A. Black
              James Perry

P-359   Tuesday Morning 1st March 1825

Court met according to adjournment Present Henry Hagen) Esquires Justices
             Alexander Black   ) of the Peace for
             James Perry   ) the County of Giles.

Peter Garland Plt.   )
 Against   )   Appeal
Richard Bently Deft.   )
) This day came the Defendant by his attorney
and it appearing to the court, that sd. plaintiff hath not entered his appearance in this cause, and said plaintiff

being Solemnly called to prosecute this suit, came not but made default nor is his suit further prosecuted -

It is therefore considered by the court that the said defendant depart hence without day, and recover of said plaintiff his costs by him as well before the Justice of the peace, as in this court expended.

A Deed of conveyance from John McCracken to Stirling H. Lester for lots No. 132, 133, 134, 135 in the Town of Pulaski, was produced in court and the Execution thereof proven by the oaths of Allen Yerger and John Mims, two of the witnesses thereto and ordered to be certified for registration.

An additional Inventory of the Estate of Philmer Green decd. returned by Aaron V. Brown administrator of sd. Green decd. which is ordered to be recorded.

James Perry . . . . Plt.) Petition
    Against)
James Terrel Admr. of)) This day came the plaintiff by Harri
the Estate of William)Defts.) & Field his attorneys, and filed
Adams decd.) his petition against the Defendants
) which is granted, and it is thereupo
ordered by the court that a summons issue to the defendants together with a copy of said petition.

Samuel H. Williams Plt.) In Debt
    Against)
James Lynch . . Deft.) From the Judgment of the court in this
) case rendered the Defendant prayed an
appeal to the honorable the Circuit Court to be held for the County of Giles - and having executed bond and security according to Law the same was granted him.

P-360   Tuesday 1st March 1825

Thomas Brown Esquire, who was appointed at the last term of this Court to take a list of taxable property and poles in Captain Potts Company for the year 1825 made return thereof which is ordered to be recorded.

Ordered that a vanditiorie Exponas issue to the Sheriff of this County Commanding him to Expose to sale after advertising the same according to law, one hundred and five acres of land, the property of William Parker adjoining the land of James W. Wheeler & the heirs of Reese Porter decd. it being the same on which sd. William Parker now lives - Levied on, on the first day of March 1825 as the property of sd. Wm. Parker by Thomas B. Haynie, a constable of Giles County, to satisfy an Execution - which issued on a Judgment, which Patrick H. Braden recovered against John W. R. Graves & the said Wm. Parker & James H. Graves before Alexander Black, Esquire, a Justice of the Peace for this County on the 26th day of June 1824 for the sum of twenty five dollars & costs.

Ordered that a venditioni Exponia issue to the Sheriff of this County commanding him to avertise & sell according to Law one hundred and five acres of Land the property of William Parker adjoining the land of James W. Wheeler and the heirs of Reese Porter decd. it being the same on which sd. Wm. Parker now lives - Levied on, on the 1st day of March 1825 as the property of sd. William Parker, By Daniel Puryear (p-361) "Tuesday 1st March 1825" a constable of Giles County to satisfy an execution which issued on a Judgment, which William P. A. McCabe, recovered against said William Parker before A. McKissack Esquire a Justice of the Peace for Giles County on the 24th Decr. 1825 for the sum of nineteen dollars & sixty two & a half cents & costs.

Parks Bailey ... Plt.) In Case
 Against)
Ralph Graves &) Defts.) This day came the plaintiff & Defendants
German Lester) by their attornies, and thereupon came a
) Jury of good and Lawful men, Towit, John
Goff, William R. Brown, Elisha Eldridge, Maddison Riddle, Saml. Harwell, John W. Perry, Joseph S. Tarkington, William Lynch, Thomas Porter, William Bird, George Everly, and Francis H. Mabrey, who being elected tried and sworn well and truly to try the issue joined between the parties in this case, upon their oaths do say that they find said issue in favor of plaintiff and assess his damages by occasion thereof to Eleven dollars & twenty cents - besides costs. -

It is therefore considered by the court that the plaintiff recover of said defendant the damages aforesaid in form aforesd. by the Jurors aforesd. assessed and also his costs by him about his suit in this behalf expended.

John Brown ... Plaintiff) Motion
 Against)
William Ball &))
William Mayfield) Defendants) This day came the plaintiff by Rivers
) & Tarpley his attornies and it appear-
) ing to the Satisfaction of the court
on inspecting the record, that at August term 1823 Benjamin Ingram Gdn. &c recovered against said Defendants and John Brown & Isaac Mayfield jointly for the sum of one hundred & twenty dollars & seventy nine cents & costs of suit, and that said plaintiff hath paid for sd. Defendants the sum of Eighty six dollars & thirty two & a half cents - as their security, said amount being said John Browns half of sd. Judgment his co. security Isaac Mayfield, having paid the balance - It is therefore considered by the court that said plaintiff recover of sd. Defendants the said sum of Eighty six dollars & thirty two and a half cents together with the costs of this motion.

P-362 Tuesday 1st March 1825

On motion of Lewis H. Brown, Sheriff of this County, Levi Read was sworn to act as his deputy.

Ordered that James Paine & Robert Paine be appointed commissioners to settle with Thomas Brown, administrator of the Estate of Jordon Hicks decd. and that they make return thereof to the next term of this court.

Archibald McKissack Plt.)   Motion
    Against   )
Nathan Steele . . . Deft.   )   This day came the plaintiff in proper
                                          person and it appearing to the satis-
faction of the court on inspecting the records that at November term 1824
Thomas McKissack Administrator of Wilson Jones, Decd. recovered a Judgment
against Graves Steele, German Lester, Administrator of David Steele, &
James H. Graves & said Plaintiff in this case for the sum of two hundred
& Eighty three dollars & sd. Archd. McKissack paid the sum of one hundred
sixteen dollars & forty two cents for sd. Nathl. Steele as his security
sd. Nathl. Steele was one of the obligers in the note on which the above
Judgment was obtained by the Thos. McKissack Admr. as aforesd. against
said George Steele, German Lester Admr. James H. Graves, & sd. Archd. Mc-
Kissack, said sum of one hundred and sixteen dollars & 42 cents being the
sd. Archd. McKissacks one third of sd. Judgment.

    It is therefore considered by the court that said plaintiff recover
of sd. Defendant the said sum of one hundred & sixteen dollars & forty two
cents together with the costs of this motion.

Hannah Underwood Plt.   )   In Case
    Against   )
Lydall Wilkinson Deft.   )   By concent of parties and on motion of the
                                          plaintiff ordered that a commission issue
to any two of the acting Justices of the peace in and for the County of
Madison & State of Alabama to take the depositions of David Owens, Stirling
Smith, Allen James, John Airs, also that a commission issue to any two of
the acting Justices of the Peace in and for the County Limestone & State
of Alabama to take the depositions of Barnette Tatum & Mary S. Tatum, which
depositions when taken to be read in Evidence on the trial of this cause,
upon the plaintiffs giving to the defendants attorneys twenty days notice
of the time and place of taking said depositions.

P-363   Tuesday 1st March 1825

    The Grand Jury returned into court a Bill of indictment of the State
against Reese A. Porter for a Trespas Veit Armies, Endorsed "A true Bill"
same against Jacob Shall, Indictment for Trespass Veit Armies Endorsed " A
true bill" same against Wm. Rose Indictment for a Trespass Veit Armies,
Endorsed "Not a true Bill" and not having any further presentments or Indictments to make were discharged.

The State . . Plt.   )   Upon an Indictment for a Trespass Veit
    Against   )   Armies.
Reese A. Porter deft.   )
)   This day came the Solicitor General for the
State as also the defendant in his proper person, who being charged on the
Indictment in this case, pleads not guilty, and for his trial puts himself
upon his Country, and the Solicitor General for the State on the part of
the State likewise therefore let a Jury come, who as well &c to recognize
&c and thereupon came a Jury of good and Lawful men, Towit, Samuel Maultsby,
John W. Graves, Daniel Allen, Graves Hester, Jefferson Tarkington, Joseph
S. Tarkington, Jesse West, Edward Bledsoe, James Lynch, Francis Smith,
Nathan Rea, & William P. A. McCabe, who being Elected tried and sworn well

& truly to try the issue and of traverse between the State and said Defendant and having heard the evidence and argument of counsel withdrew out of court to consider of their verdicts, and after some time returned and say they cannot agree by consent of parties and with the assent of the court sd Jurors were permitted to disperse to meet again tomorrow morning nine oclock.

Ordered that the County Trustee of this County pay to John W. Graves, John Abernathy, John McKnight & Archibald Smith, the sum of three dollars each for serving three days each as States Jurors in the case of William Gholson against William Watson and that certificate issue to sd. Jurors for the same.

James H. Graves Esquire who was appointed at the last term of this court to take a list of taxable property & poles in Captain John Browns Company for the year 1825 made return thereof which is ordered to be recorded.

P-364   Tuesday 1st March 1825

The State Plt.) Upon an Indictment for an affray with &
   Against) Assault & battery on the body of P. Til-
Nathaniel Davis Deft.) lotson.

This day came as well the Solicitor General for the State as also the defendant in his proper person, who being charged on the Indictment in this case pleads guilty, and because he will not contend with the State agrees to submit himself to the Justice & mercy of the court - It is therefore considered by the court that he make his fine with the State to the amount of six and one fourth cents and that he pay the costs of this prosecution.

Ordered that Court be adjourned untill tomorrow morning 8 oclock.

                                                           James Perry
                                                           John H. Camp
                                                           Thomas Brown

Wednesday 2nd March 1825

Court met according to adjournment Present John H. Camp) Esquires Justice
                                                        James Perry &) of the Peace for
                                                        Thomas Brown) Giles county.

Gilham Harwell Plt.)   Certiorari
   Against)
John Boyd Deft.) This cause having been dismissed at a former
                      Term of this court by order of Defendants -
It is hereby ordered by the court that the Justice of the Peace who rendered

the Judgment be direct to issue an Execution for the debt, Interest, & costs against sd. Defendant directed to some constable of Giles County & that he be authorised to proceed & collect sd. debt, Interest, & costs of the sd. Defendants immediately.

Thomas Martin)Plt.)   Motion
surviving partner &c)
   Against
James Perry Deft.

On motion of the plaintiff by Jones & Flournoy his attornies and it appearing to the satisfaction of the court that a Writ of Faisai Facias issued from the Clerks office of this court in favor of the above, (p-365) named plaintiff against Archibald Story on the 30th day of August 1823 returnable to the November Term thereof for the sum of one hundred & four dollars, twenty eight cents debts, two dollars sixty two and a half cents damages, together with the sum of Eight dollars & ninety six & a half cents costs of suit, and it further appearing to the satisfaction of the court that said Execution was put into the hands of James H. Graves Deputy Sheriff of James Perry late Sheriff of this County during the time that said Perry was Sheriff as aforesaid, and it further appearing to the court that the said late Sheriff and his said Deputy have failed and refused to pay the money which was collected on the above execution into the Clerks office of sd. court on or before the second day of said November term 1823 or at any time since – It is therefore considered by the court that said plaintiff recover of said James Perry and Fountan Lester, Robert Oliver, Peter Swanson, Charles Buford, William Pullen, John Barnett, Robert Paine, William B. Brooks & Joseph Anthony, his securities, the sum of one hundred & twenty five dollars & seventy four cents & a half, the amount of the debt damages & costs to this time from the 19th August 1823 the time of rendering the Judgment in the aforesaid case, and on motion of said plaintiff. It is therefore further considered by the court that said plaintiff recover of James Perry and his said securities the further sum of fourteen dollars & fifty cents being 02½ per cent on said debt & damages for his damages & costs agreably to an Act of Assembly in such case made & provided.

Robert G. Steele Plt.)   Motion
   Against
Richard McAllilly Deft.

This day came the plaintiff by Rivers & Tarpley his attornies and moved the court now here, for Judgment against the defendant for the sum of forty four dollars & ninety three and three fourth cents with interest thereon from 18th day of May 1821 which is the date of the receipt on which this motion is founded & which he hath paid as security for the Defendant, and it not appearing to the satisfaction of the court whether he was principal or security a Jury was empannelled to try that fact, Towit, Thomas Porter, Francis Mabry, Elisha Eldridge, William Porter, Jesse Marler, John R. Bittick, Gerald Irby, John Mims, John H. Rivers, Samuel Day, Adam Bell, & Samuel Gilliam, who being sworn well & truly to inquire &c as aforesaid, upon their oaths do say that the plaintiffs paid as security for sd. defendant the aforesaid sum of forty four dollars & ninety three & three fourth cents on a Stay of Execution on a Judgment that William Walker obtained against (p-366) said Richard McAllilly before James Terrell Esquire a Justice of the Peace for this County on the . . . . . . 1821 to the Stay of execution on which said Judgment the said plaintiff was Security for the defendant. It is therefore considered by the court that the plaintiff recover against sd. defendant the aforesaid sum of forty four dollars

& ninety three & three fourth cents, with Interest from the 18th day of May 1821 the date of said receipt together with all costs of this motion.

All Business on the several dockets to this term having been finished Except the Jury in the following case of the State Vs Reese A. Porter who cannot agree, the court under this consideration determined to adjourn on this day untill court in course & discharge the Jury in said case.

The State Plt.	Upon an Indictment for a trespass veit
Against	Armies.
Reese A. Porter Deft.	

This day came the Solicitor General for the State as also the defendant and thereupon came the Jury who were sworn on yestoday well and truly to try the issue of traverse between the State & sd. defendant who returned to their room again to consider of their verdict after some time returned and say they cannot agree — It is therefore ordered by the court that they be discharged. To which opinion of proceedings of the court the Solicitor General for the State Excepts & filed his Bill of Exceptions which was signed sealed and enrolled, and made part of the record in this case and sd. Solicitor General prayed an appeal in the motion of a Writ of error to the Circuit Court to be held in Pulaski on the first Monday in August next which was granted.

Ordered that a vanditioni Exponas issue to the Sheriff of this County commanding him to advertise and sell according to law one hundred & five acres of land the property of Wm. Parker adjoining the land of Jas. W. Wheeler & the heirs of Reese Porter decd. it being the same on which said Parker now lives, Levied on, on the 2nd day of March 1825 as the property of sd. Parker by Danl. Puryear constable Giles County to satisfy an Execution which issue on a Judgment which Jos. H. Hodge recorded against sd. Parker before A. McKissack Esqr. a Justice of the Peace of this County on the 25th Decr. 1824 for the sum nine dollars & costs.

P-367   Wednesday 2nd March 1825

The State . . . Plt.	Upon a Indictment for an affray with &
Against	an assault & battery on the body of
Theophilis Gutherie Deft.	Daniel Puryear.

This day came as well the Solicitor General for the State as also the defendant in his proper person and by consent of parties and with the assent of the court the fine which was taken against sd. defendant is released upon his paying the costs whereupon sd. Defendant came into court paid said costs, and was discharged.

Ordered that court be adjourned untill court in course.

Jno. H. Camp
William Wood
James Perry

At a Court of Pleas & Quarter Session holden holden for the County of Giles at the court house of said County in the Town of Pulaski, on the third Monday in May (being the siteenth day thereof) in the year of our Lord one thousand eight hundred & twenty five - Present William B. Pepper Isaac H. Graves, Paul Chiles, Thomas Brown, Archibald McKissack, Alexander Black, Robert Read, William Brown, William Ussery, John Laird, Hezikiah Jones, James Paine, Thomas Batte, John Young, Peter Swanson, Robert Oliver Anderson Hogan, Willis S. McLawrine, Edward D. Jones, John Bramlett & Henry Hagen, Esquires Justices of the Peace of said County, Presiding German Lester Clerk, of said County & Lewis H. Brown Sheriff of sd. County.

Ordered that Lewis G. Upshaw be appointed overseer of the road in the room of Matthew I. Black deceased, and that he have the same district of hands.

Ordered that George Fice overseer of the road have in addition to his former hands the hands of Thomas B. Haynie & Thomas Bratton.

Bernard M. Patteson came into court and resigned as guardian of William Neal Lunatic, whereupon Henry Hagen, Alexander Black, and James H. Graves, were appointed commissioners to settle with said Bernard M. Patteson, and make report thereof to the next term of this court.

Ordered that James H. Neal, be appointed Guardian to William Neal, Lunitic whereupon he was qualified and gave bond and security as the Law directs.

Ordered that letters of administration on the Estate of William H. Wells decd. be granted to Prudence W. Wells and Robert Wells, whereupon they were qualified & gave bond & security as the law directs.

The administrators of the Estate of William H. Wells, deceased returned an Inventory of sd. estate which is ordered to be recorded.

Ordered that an order of sale issue to the administrators of the Estate of William H. Wells decd. commanding them to Expose to sale the property contained in the Inventory of sd. Estate, by them this day returned & that they make report thereof to next term of this court.

P-369 Monday 16th May 1825

Ordered that Joseph Anthony, Thomas Williams & Robert S. Harris be appointed commissioners to allot to Prudence W. Wells widow of William H. Wells decd. one years provisions out of sd. Estate, and that they make report of sd. allotment to the next term of this court.

Ordered that Henry Hagen, Alexander Black, & James H. Graves be appointed commissioners to settle with James Terrill administrator's of the Estate of William Adams decd. and that they make report thereof to the next term of this court.

285

Ordered that James Buford & Archibald McKissack, be appointed commissioners to settle with the administrators of the Estate of Anthony Samuel decd. and that they make report thereof to the next term of this court

Ordered that Robert Caruthers be appointed overseer of the road from John C. Walkers to Robertson Fork and that he keep the same in repair with the following hands, Towit, James Griffin, Joseph Erwin E. C. Erwin, Eli G. Erwin, James Erwin, Keder Nutt, John C. Walker, Arney Caruthers, George Adkins, Rueben Kennedy, James Henderson, Wm. Jones & Saml. Wiser.

Ordered that James L. Hendry be appointed overseer of the road in the room of John W. Bodenhamer removed and that he have the same district of hands.

A Deed of Gift for certain property therein Specified was produced in court from Benjaman Murrell to John S. Murrell and acknowledged by the said Benjamin Murrell and ordered to be certified for registration.

A Bill of sale from Samuel Williamson to John Laird for certain property therein specified was produced in court and the execution thereof proven by the oaths of Martin Laird one of the witnesses thereto and is ordered to be certified for registration.

Ordered that the County Trustee of this County pay to Elizabeth Ruff the sum of Forty dollars for the support and maintanance of Rebeccah Ruff a pauper of this County from the May term 1825 to the May term 1826 of this court.

Ordered that William M. Beazley be appointed overseer of the road in the room of James Hannah resigned and that he have the same district of hands.

P-370 Monday 16th May 1825

Ordered that Willis Lane deliver to this court on Monday next Rhoda Strickland an orphan girl who was at last court bound to Thomas Hicks.

Ordered that Joseph Davis be appointed overseer of the road in the room of John King resigned, and that he have the same district of hands.

A Deed of release & Power of Attorney from Alexander S. Jones to David L. Jones & Rebeccah Jones for certain properties therein mentioned was produced in court and the execution thereof proven by the oath of John Laird one of the witnesses thereto, and ordered to be certified for registration.

A Bill of sale from David K. McEwin to James Lane for certain property therein mentioned was produced in court and the Execution thereof proven by the oath of John Laird one of the witnesses thereto, and ordered to be certified for registration.

A Deed of conveyance from Robert Paine to Edward Shelton for one hundred & thirty five & six tenth acres of land was produced in court and the execution thereof acknowledged by the said Robert Paine, and ordered to be certified for registration.

At Least five Justices being present, Joseph Crabbe returned into court one wolf scalp over four months old which was ordered to be burnt.

Ordered that Elisha Panter be appointed overseer of the road in the room of Samuel H. Griggsby resigned and that he have the same district of hands.

A Deed of conveyance from Alexander McDonald, & John McDonald, to William Maxwell, for fifty nine acres of land in two tracts was produced in court and the Execution thereof proven by the oath of James Hannah & James Shelton the witnesses thereto, and ordered to be certified for registration.

A Deed of conveyance from Peter Swanson to William Anderson for his interest in a tract of land amounting to sixty nine & three fifth acres of land was produced in court, and the execution thereof acknowledged by the said Peter Swanson and ordered to be certified for registration.

P-371 Monday 16th May 1825

A Deed of conveyance from John Birdwell to Thomas Wells, for one hundred & seventy seven acres of Land was produced in court and the Execution thereof acknowledged by the said John Birdwell & ordered to be certified for registration.

A Deed of conveyance from Thomas Wells to Martin Baugh for one hundred & Seventy seven acres of Land was produced in court and the execution thereof acknowledged by the said Thomas Wells and ordered to be certified for registration.

William Dearing Guardian of the minor heirs of Joseph Braden decd. made return as said Guardian which is ordered to be recorded.

Ordered that Charles Simpson be appointed overseer of the road in the room of Buckner Madry resigned and that he have the same district of hands.

A Deed of conveyance from Richard Hightower to Hardy Hightower for one hundred & sixty acres of land was produced in court and the execution thereof fully proven by the oath of J. A. T. Hightower the other witnesses thereto, and ordered to be certified for registration.

Ordered that William Swinney be appointed overseer of the road in the room of Josiah P. Alexander resigned, and that he have the same district of hands.

Ordered that George Perry be appointed overseer of the road in the room of Thomas Brown resigned and that he have the same district of hands.

Ordered that the County Trustee of this County pay to Willis S. Mc-Claurine, the sum of thirty dollars for the support & maintaneance of the wife of Alexander Patton a pauper of this county for the term of twelve months from this time.

A Deed of conveyance from Hardy Hightower to Nicholas Holly for Eighty acres of land, was produced in court and the Execution proven by the oaths of J. A. T. Hightower and John Young, the witnesses thereto, and ordered to be certified for registration.

Ordered that Henry Young be appointed overseer of the road from James Buford to Joseph Anthoney in the room of Wm. H. Wells decd. and that he have the same district of hands.

P-372 Monday 16th May 1825

The last will & testement of John Brandon decd. was produced in court and the Execution thereof proven by the oaths of Robert Read & Beverly B. Watson, two of the witnesses thereto, and ordered to be recorded - and thereupon Richard Brandon was appointed administrator with the will annexed who was qualified and gave bond an security as the law directs.

Ordered that the County Trustee of this County, pay to Samuel Day the sum of six dollars for Expences & guard & carrying Theophilas Guthrie to the public Jail of this County.

Ordered that Edward Bledsoe have in addition to his former hands the hands of John Porters as overseer of the road.

A Deed of conveyance from Alexander McDonald & John McDonald, to James Leath for thirty acres of land was produced in court and the execution thereof acknowledged by the said Alexander & John McDonald and ordered to be certified for registration.

A Deed of conveyance from Alexander McDonald to James Leath for twenty acres of land, was produced in court and the execution thereof acknowledged by the said Alexander McDonald & ordered to be certified for registration.

Ordered that Gray H. Edwards be appointed overseer of the road in the room of John McAmick resigned and that he have the same district of hands.

An Ordinary licence for the term of twelve months and no longer is granted to Samuel Davis whereupon he was qualified and gave bond and security as the Law directs.

Ordered that William Campbell an orphan boy be bound to Enoch Reynolds an Indenture to that effect having been entered into between the chairman of this court & sd. Enoch Reynolds.

Ordered that Monday next be set apart for County business.

P-373   Monday 16th May 1825

Ordered that Annanias Oliver be appointed constable in Captain Edward M. Brown's Company whereupon he was qualified and gave bond and security as the Law directs.

The commissioners who were appointed to allot to Martha Jones widow of John S. Jones decd. one years provisions out of the Estate of sd. John S. Jones decd. made return of said allotment which is ordered to be recorded.

An additional Inventory of the Estate of John S. Jones decd. was returned by the administrators and ordered recorded.

A account of sale of the Estate of John S. Jones decd. was returned by the administrators of sd. Estate and ordered to be recorded.

Ordered that Robert Gordon, Joseph East, John Lee, Stephen Anderson, Thomas Graves, James Taylor and John Young or any five of them be appointed a Jury to view that part of the road which lies near or opposite Thomas Clarks, & see whether it be best to Establish the road as it formerly run and Established by a former order of court or the road lately opened by a Jury who were appointed for that purpose, on petition of sd. Clark and that they make report to the next term of this court.

Ordered that that part of the Florence road which lies between the hill by Asa Magus and intersect F. Moon's be opened agreable to the report of the Jury appointed to view & mark out the same, and that Solomon Bassham oversee the opening and keeping in repair said road with the same hands that worked under John Randall former overseer.

Ordered that that part of the Florence road which lies between the top of the hill at the head of Moons Creek & Hugh Brattons be opened agreable to the report of the Jury appointed to view & mark the same and that Hugh Bratton oversee the opening and keeping in repair said road, with the same hands, that worked under former overseers.

Ordered that James Paisley, William Maxwell, Jeremiah Barnes, Gilbert H. White, James Hanna, James Collins, & Wm. M. Beasley, or any five of them be appointed a Jury to view out a road to begin at the hand of Brattons Creek where the Lambs ferry road crosses said Creek and runs the nearest and best way so as to intersect the Established road from Pulaski to Lambs, Ferry about one half mile above where Hugh Bratton now lives and see if it be proper to establish the same. and make report thereof to the next term of this court.

P-374 Monday 16th May 1825

Ordered that part of the road leading from Pulaski to Columbia which lies near Andrew Turnbeans plantation be opened agreable to the report of the Jury appointed to view and mark out the same at the expence of sd. Turnbean and when opened to be under the direction of William Finer overseer of sd. road to keep the same in repair with the hands under his directions.

Ordered that George M. Gibson, Joseph Brownlow, Jonathan Moody, Jesse Allen, John P. Taylor, George Keltner, Joseph Knox, or any five of them be appointed a Jury to view and mark out a road from George Keltner to Joseph Reas, and that they make report thereof to the next term of this court.

Ordered that court be adjourned till tomorrow morning nine oclock.

A. Black
Jno. H. Camp
Thomas Batte

P-375 Tuesday Morning 17th May 1825

Court met according to adjournment Present Alexander Black) Esquires Justice
John H. Camp, &) of the Peace for
Thomas Batte) Giles County.

Ordered that the County Trustee of this County pay to John Graves the sum of twenty seven dollars for his support and maintenance (a pauper of this county, for the term of twelve months from this time.

A Deed of conveyance from Lewis H. Brown, Sheriff of Giles County to Aaron V. Brown for lots No. 16 in the Town of Pulaski was produced in court and the Execution thereof acknowledged by the said Lewis H. Brown Sheriff as aforesaid and ordered to be certified for registration.

A Bill of sale from Jordon Black to John Nelson, Senr., for certain property therein specified was produced in court and the execution thereof acknowledged by the said Jordon Black and ordered to be certified for registration.

Ordered that Robert Farmer & John Brown who were summoned as Jurors at this term be exhonorated from service as sd. Jurors at this term.

The Sheriff of this county returned into court the names of the following persons summoned to attend as Grand and petit Jurors at this term, Pursuant to an order of the last term of this court a copy of which issued to the said Sheriff of Giles County, towit, Robert Anderson, William B. Brooks, Rolly Harwell, Robert Adams, Samuel Smith, Daniel McCollum, John B. McCanlass, Aaron Smith, Walter Hill, John Brown, Elisha Kimbrough, Robert Farmer, Thomas Wilkinson, William W. Fogg, James Horn, Amos Griggsby, William Jones, Arthur M. M. Upshaw, Andrew Gordon, Early Benson, John G. Braden, Henry M. Newlin, Henry J. Cooper, John D. Riddle, Claiborn Kyle, and Francis Smith, of whom William B. Brooks foreman, John B. McCanlass, Walter Hill, Robert Anderson, John D. Riddle, Robert Adams, Daniel McCollum, Samuel S. Smith, Rolly Harwell, Arthur M. M. Upshaw, William Jones, Claiborne Kyle, & Elisha L. Kimbrough, were elected empannelled, and sworn a grand Jury of inquest for the body of this county, who having received their charge withdrew to consider of their presentments.

Richard Bently a constable of this County was sworn to attend on the Grand Jury at the present term of this court.

P-376 Tuesday 17th May 1825

Elizabeth Phillips Plt.)
    Against)   In Case
John Hawkins Deft.)
) This day came the parties by their attornies and thereupon came a Jury of good and lawful men, Towit, Henry J. Cooper, Andrew Gordon, Francis Smith, William W. Fogg, Henry M. Newlin, Early Benson, Aaron Smith, Henry McKay, John McKnight, Asa A. Estes, John Walthall, & Elnathan G. Brown, who being elected tried and sworn well and truly to try the issue Joined between the parties in this case upon their oaths do say that the defendant has not paid the whole of the debt in the writing obligatory in the declaration mentioned as the plaintiff in her replication has alleged, but that their remains a balance of sd. debt yet unpaid to the amount of one hundred & ninety three dollars & fifty cents together with the sum of thirty six dollars & sixty seven cents damages, besides costs.

It is thereupon considered by the court that the plaintiff recover of the defendant the balance of her debt aforesaid together with her damages aforesaid, by the Jurors aforesaid assessed, and also her costs by her about her suit in this behalf expended.

A Plat and certificate of Servey for two hundred acres of land in the name of Thomas Marks, and the assignment thereof from said Thomas Marks to Wm. H. Moore was produced in court and the execution thereof acknowledged by the said Thomas Marks, & ordered to be certified.

Elizabeth Phillips Plt.) In Debt
    Against)
Thomas B. Jones &) Defts.)
Thomas Harwood)   This day came the parties by their at-
) tornies, and thereupon came a Jury of
) good & lawful men, Towit, Henry J.
Cooper, Andrew Gordon, Francis Smith, William W. Fogg, Henry M. Newlin,
Early Benson, Aaron Smith, Henry McKay, John McKnight, Asa A. Estes, John
Walthall, & Elnathan G. Brown, who being elected tried & sworn well and
truly to try the issue joined between the parties in this case, upon their
oaths do say that the defendant has not paid the debt in the writing obligatory in the declaration, and that they have no sett off as the plaintiff
in her replication has alleged and they do assess the plaintiffs damages
by occasion of the detention of said debt to ten dollars besides costs.
It is therefore considered by the court (p-377) Tuesday 17th May 1825,
that the plaintiff recover of said defendants the sum of one hundred dollars
the amount of his debt afores'd. together with his damages aforesaid in form
aforesaid, by the Jurors aforesaid assessed, and also her costs about her
suit in this behalf expended.

Henry Langtry & Co. Plts.) In Debt
    Against)
James P. Deams Defts.)
)   This day came the parties by their attor-
) nies and thereupon came a Jury of good
and lawful men, Towit, Henry J. Cooper, Andrew Gordon, Francis Smith,
William W. Fogg, Henry M. Newlin, Early Benson, Aaron Smith, Henry McKay,
John McKnight, Asa A. Estes, John Walthall, and Elnathan G. Brown, who being
elected tried & sworn well & truly to try the issue joined between the parties
in this case upon their oaths do say that the Defendant has not paid the
debt in the Writing obligatory in the declaration mentioned and that he has
no sett off as the plaintiffs in their replication has alleged, and they do
assess the plaintiffs damages by occasion of the detention of sd. debt to
thirteen dollars & twenty cents, besides costs.
    It is therefore considered by the court that the plaintiffs recover of
said Defendant the sum of one hundred & Eighty four dollars & sixty one
cents, the amount of his debt aforesaid together with his damages aforesaid
in form aforesaid, by the Jurors aforesaid assessed and their costs about
their suit in this behalf expended.

Henry Langtry & Co. Plts.) In Debt
    Against)
James P. Deams Deft.)
)   This day came the parties by their attor-
) ney and thereupon came a Jury of good &
lawful men, towit, Henry J. Cooper, Andrew Gordon, Francis Smith, William
W. Fogg, Henry Newlin, Early Benson, Aaron Smith, Henry McKay, John Mc-
Knight, Asa A. Estes, John Walthall and Elnathan G. Brown, who being elected
tried and sworn well & truly to try the issue joined between the parties
in this case upon their oaths do say that the Defendant has not paid the
debt in the writing obligatory in the declaration mentioned, and that he
has no sett off as the plaintiffs in their Replication have alleged, and
they do assess the plaintiffs damages by occasion of the detention thereof
to three dollars & forty cents - besides costs.
    It is therefore considered by the court that the plaintiffs recover of
said Defendant the sum of one hundred & seventy eight dollars & seventy six
cents, the amount of his debt aforesaid together with his damages aforesaid,
in form aforesaid by the Jurors aforesaid assessed, and their costs about
~~their suit in this behalf expended.~~

P-378 Tusday 17th May 1825

Patrick M. Braden Plt.) In Debt
    Against)
James H. Pickens Deft.) This day came the parties by their attornies and thereupon came a Jury of good and lawful men, Towit, Henry J. Cooker, Andrew Gordon, Francis Smith, William W. Fogg, Henry M. Newlin, Early Benson, Aaron Smith, Henry McKay, John McKnight, Asa A. Estes, John Walthall, & Elnathan G. Brown, who being elected tried and sworn well & truly to try the issue joined between the parties in this case upon their oaths do say that the defendant has not paid the debt in the writing obligatory in the declaration mentioned as the plaintiff in his replication has alleged, and they do assess the plaintiffs damages by occasion of the detention thereof to five dollars & forty cents - besides costs. It is therefore considered by the court that the plaintiff recover of the defendant the sum of one hundred and twenty dollars, the amount of his debt aforesaid, together with his damages aforesd. in form aforesaid by the Jurors aforesd. assessed, and his costs about his suit in this behalf expanded.

Charles Perkins Plt.) In Debt
    Against)
James H. Pickens, Thos. B.) Defts.)
Haynie & Gerald Irby) This day came the parties by their attornies and thereupon came a Jury of good and lawful men, Towit, Henry J. Cooper, Andrew Gordon, Francis Smith, William W. Fogg, Henry M. Newlin, Early Benson, Aaron Smith, Henry McKay, John McKnight, Asa A. Estes, John Wathall, & Elnathan G. Brown, who being elected tried & sworn well and truly to try the issue joined between the parties in this case upon their oaths do say the Defendants has not paid the debt in the Writing obligatory in the declaration mentioned, as the plaintiffs in his replication has alleged, and they do assess the plaintiffs damages by occasion of the detention thereof to Eight dollars besides costs. It is therefore considered by the court that the plaintiff recover of said Defendants the sum of three hundred & twenty five dollars the amount of his debt aforesaid together with his damages aforesaid, in form aforesaid, by the Jurors aforesaid assessed, and his costs by him about his suit in this behalf expanded.

P-379 Tuesday 17th May 1825

Jacob Shall Assee &c Plt.) In Debt
    Against)
Patrick H. Braden &) Defts.)
Burton R. White) This day came the parties by their attornies and thereupon came a Jury of good and lawful men to wit, Henry J. Cooker, Andrew Gordon, Francis Smith, William W. Fogg, Henry M. Newlin, Early Benson, Aaron Smith, Henry McKay, John McKnight, Asa A. Estes, John Wathall, & Elnathan Brown, who being elected tried & sworn well & truly to try the issue joined between the parties in this case upon their oaths do say that the defendants have not paid the Debt in the writing obligatory in the declaration mentioned, as the plaintiff in his replication has alleged, and they do assess the plaintiffs damages by occasion of the detention thereof to one dollar & seventy five cents besides cost.

It is therefore considered by the court that the plaintiff recover of the Defendants the sum of Eighty seven dollars & Eighty cents the amount of his debt aforesaid together with his damages aforesaid in form aforesaid, by the Jurors aforesaid assessed, and his costs about his suit in this behalf expended.

Benjamin Ingram to the use of &c) Plt.
Against
Gray H. Edwards Deft.

In Debt

This day came the parties by their attornies and thereupon came a Jury of good and lawful men, Towit, Henry J. Cooper, Andrew Gordon, Francis Smith, William W. Fogg, Henry M. Newlin, Early Benson, Aaron Smith, Henry McKay, John McKnight, Asa A. Estes, John Wathall & Elnathan G. Brown, who being elected tried and sworn well and truly to try the issue joined between the parties in this case, upon their oaths do say that the defendant has not paid the Debt in the writing obligatory in the declaration mentioned, and that he has no sett off as the plaintiff in his replication has alleged, and they do assess the plaintiffs damages by occasion of the detention thereof to nineteen dollars & seventy cents besides costs.

It is therefore considered by the court that the plaintiff recover of sd. Defendant the sum of ninety eight dollars & fifty cents, the amount of his debt aforesaid, together with his damages aforesd. in form aforesd. by the Jurors aforesaid assessed & his costs by him about his suit in this behalf expended.

P-380 Tuesday 17th May 1825

James Turk asses. &c. Plt.
Against
Edward W. Tipton Deft.

In Debt

This day came the parties by their attornies and thereupon came a Jury of good and lawful men, towit, Henry J. Cooper, Andrew Gordon, Francis Smith, William W. Fogg, Henry M. Newlin, Early Benson, Aaron Smith, Henry McKay, John McKnight, Asa A. Estes, John Walthall, & Elnathan G. Brown who being Elected tried & sworn well and truly to try the issue joined between the parties in this case upon their oaths do say that the defendant has not paid the debt in the writing obligatory in this declaration mentioned, as the plaintiff in his replication has alleged, and they do assess the plaintiffs damages by occasion of the detention thereof to sixteen dollars & fifty cents, besides costs.

It is therefore considered by the court that the plaintiff recover of sd. defendant the sum of two hundred dollars, the amount of his debt aforesaid, together with his damages aforesaid, in form aforesd. by the Jurors aforesaid, assessed, and his costs about his suit in this behalf expended.

Malcolm Gilchrist Assee &c. Plt.
Against
James Duys & John Manefee Deft.

In Debt

This day came the parties by their attornies and thereupon came a Jury of good and lawful men, towit, Henry J. Cooper, Andrew Gordon, Francis Smith, William W. Fogg, Henry M. Newlin, Early Benson, Aaron Smith, Henry McKay, John McKnight, Asa A. Estes, John Walthall, & Elnathan

G. Brown, who being elected tried & sworn well and truly to try the issue joined between the parties in this case upon their oaths do say that the Defendants have not paid the whole of the Debt in the writing obligatory in the declaration mentioned, and that he has no sett off as the plaintiff in his replication has alleged, but there remains a ballance of sd. debt yet unpaid to the amount of sd. debt of four hundred and seventy five dollars damages, besides costs.

It is therefore considered by the court that the plaintiff recover of sd. defendant the balance of his debt aforesaid together with his damages aforesaid in form aforesaid by the Jurors aforesaid assessed, and also his costs about his suit in this behalf expended.

P-381   Tuesday 17th May 1825

Alexander Tompson) Plt.
to the use &c   )
    Against   )   In Covenant
John Lee . . . Deft.)

This day came the parties by their attornies and thereupon came a Jury of good and lawful men, towit; Henry J. Cooper, Andrew Gordon, Francis Smith, William W. Fogg, Henry M. Newlin, Early Benson, Aaron Smith, Henry McKay, John McKnight, Asa A. Estes, John Walthall & Elnathan Brown, who being elected tried and sworn well and truly to try the issue joined between the parties in this case upon their oaths do say that they find said issue in favor of the plaintiff and assess his damages by occasion of the non performance of the covenant in the declaration mentioned to six hundred and seventy nine dollars & twenty six cents, besides costs.

It is therefore considered by the court that the plaintiff recover of said Defendant the damages aforesaid, in form aforesaid, by the Jurors aforesaid assessed, and also his costs about his suit in this behalf expended.

Alexander Thompson Plt.   )
    Against   )   In Covenant
John Lee . . . . . Deft.)

This day came the parties by their attornies, and thereupon came a Jury of good and lawful men, towit, Henry J. Cooper, Andrew Gordon, Francis Smith, William W. Fogg, Henry M. Newlin, Early Benson, Aaron Smith, Henry McKay, John McKnight, Asa A. Estes, John Walthall & Elnathan G. Brown, who being elected tried & sworn well and truly to try the issue joined between the parties in this case upon their oaths do say that they find said issue in favor of the plaintiff and assess his damages by occasion of the non performance of the covenant in the declaration mentioned to Eight hundred and Eighteen dollars – besides costs.

It is therefore considered by the court that the plaintiff recover of said Defendant the damages aforesaid, in form aforesaid by the Jurors aforesaid assessed, and also his costs about his suit in this behalf expended.

Alexander Thompson) Plt.
to the use &c.   )
    Against   )   In Covenant
Samuel Haynie Deft)

This day came the parties by their attornies and thereupon came a Jury of good and lawful men, towit, (P-382) (Tuesday 17th May 1825) Henry J. Cooper, Andrew Gordon, Francis Smith, William W. Fogg, Henry M. Newlin, Early Benson, Aaron Smith, Henry McKay, John McKnight, Asa A. Estes, John Walthall, & Elnathan Brown, who being elected tried and sworn well & truly to try the issue joined between the parties in this case upon their oaths do say that they find said issue in favor of the plaintiff and assess his damages by occasion of the non performances of the covenant in the declaration mentioned to one hundred & forty eight dollars, sixty cents & a half besides costs. It is therefore considered by the court that the plaintiff recover of said Defendant the damages aforesaid, in form aforesaid, by the Jurors aforesaid assessed, and his costs about his suit in this behalf expended.

Alexander Thompson) Plt.   In Covenant
to the use &c.)
    Against)
Daniel Goodrum   Deft.) This day came the parties by their attornies and thereupon came a Jury of good & lawful men, Towit, Henry J. Cooper, Andrew Gordon, Francis Smith, William W. Fogg, Henry M. Newlin, Early Benson, Aaron Smith, Henry McKay, John McKnight, Asa A. Estes, John Walthall, & Elnathan Brown, who being elected tried and sworn well & truly to try the issue joined between the parties in this case upon their oaths do say that they find said issue in favor of the plaintiff and assess his damages by occasion of the non performance of the covenant in the declaration mentioned to two hundred and seventy seven dollars, besides costs.

It is therefore considered by the court that the plaintiff recover of said defendant the damages aforesaid, in form aforesaid, by the Jurors aforesaid assessed, and his costs by him, about his suit in this behalf expended.

Coleman Harwell Plt.)   In Debt
    Against)
Henry T. Croft Deft.) This day came the parties by their attornies and thereupon came a Jury of good & lawful men, Towit, Henry J. Cooper, Andrew Gordon, Francis Smith, William W. Fogg, Henry M. Newlin, Early Benson, Aaron Smith, Henry McKay, John McKnight, Asa A. Estes, John Walthall & Elnathan Brown, who being elected tried and sworn well and truly to try the issue joined (p-383) between the parties in this case upon their oaths do say that the defendant has not paid the debt in the writing obligatory in the declaration mentioned as the plaintiff in the replication has alleged and they assess the plaintiffs damages by occasion of the detention thereof to one dollar Eighty seven and a half cent, besides costs. It is therefore considered by the court that the plaintiff recover of the defendant the sum of Eighty four dollars the amount of his debt aforesaid together with his damages aforesaid in form aforesaid by the Jurors aforesaid assessed, and his costs about his suit in this behalf expended.

John Brooks . . . . Plt.)   In Debt
    Against)
Marshall Moody Deft.) This day came the parties by their attornies and thereupon came a Jury of good and lawful men, Towit, Henry J. Cooker, Andrew Gordon, Francis Smith, Wm.

W. Fogg, Henry M. Newlin, Early Benson, Aaron Smith, Henry McKay, John McKnight, Asa E. Estas, John Walthall, & Elnathan Brown, who being elected tried and sworn well and truly to try the issue joined between the parties in this case upon their oaths do say that the defendant defendant has not paid the debt in the writing obligatory in the declaration mentioned and that he has no sett off as the plaintiff in his replication hath alleged, and they do assess the plaintiffs damages by occasion of the detention thereof to Five dollars & sixty two cents, besides costs.

It is therefore considered by the court that the plaintiff recover of sd. defendant the sum of two hundred & fifty dollars - the amount of his Debt aforesaid together with his damages aforesaid, in form aforesaid by the Jurors aforesaid assessed, and also his costs about his suit in this behalf expended.

Thomas Wells Plt.) In Debt
Against)
Robert G. Steele &)Defts.) This day came the parties by their at-
Thomas Steele) tornies and thereupon came a Jury of
) good and lawful men, Towit, Henry J.
Cooper, Andrew Gordon, Francis Smith, Wm. W. Fogg, Henry M. Newlin, Early Benson, Aaron Smith, Henry McKay, John McKnight, Asa A. Estes, John Walthall, & Elnathan G. Brown, who being elected tried and (p-384) sworn well & truly to try the issue joined between the parties in this case upon their oaths do say that the defendant has not paid the debt in the Writing obligatory in the declaration mentioned as the plaintiff in his replication has alleged, and they do assess the plaintiffs damages, by occasion of the detention of sd. debt to twenty one dollars & thirty seven and a half cents, besides costs.

It is therefore considered by the court that the plaintiff recover of said defendant the sum of one hundred & fifty dollars the amount of his debt aforesaid, together with his damages aforesaid in form aforesaid by the Jurors aforesaid assessed, and also his costs about his suit in this behalf expended.

Thomas Wells Plt.) In Debt
Against)
James Yancy Deft.) This day came the parties by their attornies,
) and thereupon came a Jury of good and lawful
men, towit, Henry J. Cooper, Andrew Gordon, Francis Smith, Wm. W. Fogg, Henry M. Newlin, Early Benson, Aaron Smith, Henry McKay, John McKnight, Asa A. Estes, John Walthall & Elnathan G. Brown - who being elected tried and sworn well and truly to try the issue joined between the parties in this case upon their oaths do say that the defendant has not paid the whole of the debt in the writing obligatory in the declaration mentioned, and that he has no sett off as the plaintiff in his replication has alleged, but that there remains a balance of sd. debt yet unpaid, to the amount of two hundred & seventy dollars & seventy five cents, together with the sum of six dollars damages besides costs.

It is therefore considered by the court that plaintiff recover of sd. Defendant the balance of his debt aforesaid, together with his damages aforesaid, in form aforesd. by the Jurors aforesaid assessed and also his costs about his suit in this behalf Expended.

Andrew Fay to the use &c Plt.　) 　　　　　In Debt
　　　　Against　　　　　　　　　　)
Robert Fenner ... Deft.　　　　　) 　　This day came the parties by their
　　　　　　　　　　　　　　　　　) 　　attornies and thereupon came a Jury
of good and lawful men, towit, Henry J. Cooper, Andrew Gordon, Francis
Smith, Wm. W. Fogg, Henry M. Newlin, (p-385) Early Benson, Aaron Smith,
Henry McKay, John McKnight, Asa A. Estes, John Walthall & Elnathan G. Brown,
who being elected tried and sworn well & truly to try the issue joined between the parties in this case upon their oaths do say that the defendant
has not paid the debt in the writing obligatory in the declaration mentioned, and that he has no sett off, as the plaintiff in his replication
has alleged and they do assess the plaintiff damages by occasion of the
detention of the same to four dollars & twenty cents, besides costs.
　　It is therefore considered by the court that the plaintiff recover of
sd. defendant the sum of one hundred & Eighty seven dollars & fifty cents
the amount of his debt aforesd. together with his damages aforesaid in form
aforesaid by the Jurors aforesaid assessed, and also his costs, about his
suit in this behalf expended.

John C. McLemore Assee Plt.　　) 　　　　　In Debt
　　　Against　　　　　　　　　　)
Daniel Culbirth ... Deft.　　　) 　　This day came the parties by their at-
　　　　　　　　　　　　　　　　) 　　tornies and thereupon came a Jury of
good and lawful men, towit, Henry J. Cooper, Andrew Gordon, Francis Smith,
Wm. W. Fogg, Henry M. Newlin, Early Benson, Aaron Smith, Henry McKay, John
McKnight, Asa A. Estes, John Walthall & Elnathan G. Brown, who being elected
tried and sworn well and truly to try the issue joined between the parties
in this case upon their oaths do say that the defendant has not paid the
whole of the debt in the writing obligatory in the declaration mentioned,
and that he has no sett off as the plaintiff in his replication has alleged,
and they do assess the plaintiffs damages by occasion of the detention of
the balance of said debt to four dollars & forty cents, besides costs.
　　It is therefore considered by the court that the plaintiff recover of
said defendant the sum of one hundred & ninety six dollars & Eighty cents
the balance of his debt aforesaid, together with his damages aforesaid in
form aforesd. assessed, and also his costs by him about his suit in this
behalf Expended.

Thomas Martin & Andrew)Plts.　) 　　　　　In Debt
M. Ballentine &c 　　　)　　　)
　　　Against　　　　　　　　　) 　　This day came the parties by their
Graves Hester .. Deft.　　　　) 　　attornies and (p-386) thereupon
　　　　　　　　　　　　　　　　) 　　came a Jury of good and lawful men,
towit, Henry J. Cooper, Andrew Gordon, Francis Smith, Wm. W. Fogg, Henry
M. Newlin, Early Benson, Aaron Smith, Henry McKay, John McKnight, Asa A.
Estes, John Walthall, & Elnathan G. Brown, who being elected tried & sworn
well and truly to try the issue joined between the parties in this case
upon their oaths do say that the defendant has not paid the debt in the
writing obligatory in the declaration mentioned, as the plaintiffs in their
replication have alleged, and they do assess the plaintiffs damages by
occasion of the detention of the same to four dollars & Eighty cents, besides costs. It is therefore considered by the court that the plaintiff
recover of sd. defendant the sum of one hundred and forty eight dollars &
sixty three cents, the amount of his debt aforesaid together with his
damages aforesaid, in form aforesaid by the Jurors aforesaid assessed, and
his costs about his suit in this behalf expended.

Shomas Stephens Assee &c Plt.
    Against
Asa A. Estes, Isaac Mayfield)Defts
& Wm. P. A. McCabe

In Debt

This day came the parties by their attornies and thereupon came a Jury of good and lawful men, Towit, Henry J. Cooper, Andrew Gordon, Francis Smith, Wm. W. Fogg, Henry M. Newlin, Early Brown, Aaron Smith, Henry McKay, John McKnight, David Abernathy, John Walthall & Elnathan G. Brown, who being elected tried and sworn well and truly to try the issue joined between the parties in this case upon their oaths do say that the defendants have not paid the debt in the writing obligatory in the declaration mentioned, as the plaintiff in his replication has alleged, and they do assess the plaintiffs damages by occasion of the detention thereof to one dollar and ninety cents, besides costs. It is therefore considered by the court that the plaintiff recover of sd. defendants the sum of eighty five dollars the amount of his debt aforesaid, together with his damages aforesaid in form aforesd. by the Jurors aforesaid assessed, and also his costs by him about his suit in this behalf expended.

P-387   Tuesday 17th May 1825

Lewis G. Upshaw Executor &c Plt.
    Against
Mary D. Price . . . . . Deft.

In Debt

This day came the parties by their attornies and thereupon came a Jury of good and lawful men, towit, Henry J. Cooper, Andrew Gordon, Francis Smith, Wm. W. Fogg, Henry M. Newlin, Early Benson, Aaron Smith, Henry McKay, John McKnight, David Abernathy, John Walthall, & Elnathan G. Brown, who being elected tried and sworn well and truly to try the issue joined between the parties in this case upon their oaths do say that the defendant has not paid the debt in the writing obligatory in the declaration mentioned and that she has not sett off as the plaintiff in his replication has alleged, and they do assess the plaintiffs damages by occasion thereof to twenty four dollars and seventy five cents, besides costs.
It is there four considered by the court that the plaintiff recover of said defendant the sum of three hundred dollars - the amount of his debt aforesd. together with his damages aforesaid in form aforesd. assessed, and also his costs about his suit in this behalf expended.

Robert W. Graves Assee &c Plt.
    Against
William H. Field . . . . Deft.

In Debt

This day came the parties by their attornies, and thereupon came a Jury of good and lawful men, Towit, Henry J. Cooper, Andrew Gordon, Francis Smith, Wm. W. Fogg, Henry W. Newlin, Early Benson, Aaron Smith, Henry McKay, John McKnight, David Abernathy, John Walthall, and Elnathan G. Brown, who being elected tried and sworn well and truly to try the issue joined between the parties in this case upon their oaths do say that the defendant has not paid the debt in the writing obligatory in the declaration mentioned, and that he has no sett off as the plaintiff in his replication has alleged, and they do assess the plaintiffs damages by occasion thereof to Eleven dollars, besides costs.
It is therefore considered by the court that the plaintiff recover of said defendant the sum of five hundred dollars the amount of his debt

aforesaid, together with his damages, aforesaid in form aforesaid, by the Jurors aforesaid, assessed, and also his costs by him about his suits in this behalf expended.

P-388   Tuesday 17th May 1825

Thomas Martin & Andrew) Plts.
M. Ballentine Merchants &c.)
    Against
James Smith &) Deft.
Leonard Smith)

In Debt

This day came the parties by their attornies and thereupon came a Jury of good and lawful men, Towit, Henry J. Cooper, Andrew Gordon, Francis Smith, Wm. W. Fogg, Henry M. Newlin, Early Benson, Aaron Smith, Henry McKay, John McKnight, David Abernathy, John Walthall, and Elnathan G. Brown, who elected tried and sworn well and truly to try the issue joined between the parties in this case upon their oaths do say that the defendants have not paid the debt in the Writing obligatory in the declaration mentioned and that they have no sett off as the plaintiffs in their replication have alleged, and they do assess the plaintiffs damages by occasion of the detention of sd. debt to three dollars & sixty nine cents, besides costs. It is therefore considered by the court that the plaintiffs recover of said defendant the sum of one hundred & sixty four dollars and thirty seven cents the amount of their debt aforesaid, together with their damages aforesaid in form aforesaid by the Jurors aforesd. assessed and also his costs about his suit in this behalf expended.

John Smith . . . . Plt.)
    Against
William A. Thompson Deft.)

In Debt

This day came the parties by their attornies and thereupon came a Jury of good and lawful men, Towit, Henry J. Cooper, Andrew Gordon, Francis Smith, William W. Fogg, Henry M. Newlin, Early Benson, Aaron Smith, Henry McKay, John McKnight, David Abernathy, John Walthall and Elnathan G. Brown, who being elected tried and sworn well and truly to try the issue joined between the parties in this case upon their oaths do say that the defendant has not paid the debt in the writing obligatory in the declaration mentioned, and that he hath no sett off as the plaintiff in his replication hath alleged and they do assess the plaintiffs damages by reason of the detention of said debt to twenty three dollars besides costs. It is therefore considered by the court that the plaintiff recover of the defendant one hundred and twenty dollars, the amount of his debt aforesaid together with his damages aforesd. & his costs by him about his suit in this behalf expended.

P-389   Tuesday 17th May 1825

George T. Sadler Plt.)
    Against
James Patteson Deft.)

Covenant

This day came the parties by their attornies & thereupon came a Jury of good and lawful men, towit, Henry J. Cooper, Andrew Gordon, Francis Smith, William W. Fogg, Henry M. Newlin, Early Benson, Aaron Smith, Henry McKay, John McKnight, David Abernathy, John Walthall & Elnathan G. Brown, who being elected tried and sworn well and truly to try the issue joined between the parties in this case upon their oaths do say that they find said issue in favor of the plaintiff and assess his damages by reasons of the non performance of the covenant in the declaration mentioned to two hundred and sixteen dollars and fifty cents, besides costs.

It is therefore considered by the court that the plaintiff recover of the defendant the amount of his damages aforesaid, by the Jurors aforesaid in form aforesaid assessed and his costs by him about his suit in this behalf expended.

Thomas Martin date to use &c Plt.) In Covenant
Against)
Claiborn Kyle .... Deft.)

This day came the parties by their attornies and thereupon came a Jury of Good and lawful men, towit, Henry J. Cooper, Andrew Gordon, Francis Smith, Wm. W. Fogg, Henry M. Newlin, Early Benson, Aaron Smith, Henry McKay, John McKnight, Davis Abernathy, John Walthall & Elnathan G. Brown, who being elected tried and sworn well and truly to try the issue Joined between the parties in this case upon their oaths do say that they find said issue in favor of the plaintiff and assess his damages by reason of the non performance of the covenant in the declaration mentioned to one hundred and fifty three dollars, thirty seven and a half cents, besides costs.

It is therefore considered by the court that the plaintiff recover of the defendant, the amount of his damages aforesaid in form aforesaid, by the Jurors aforesaid, assessed, and his costs by him about his suit in this behalf expended.

Letters of administration on the Estate of John Rawlins, decd. are granted to Charles Buford, who was qualified and gave bond and security as the law directs.

Charles Buford administrator of the Estate of John Rawlins decd. returned into court an Inventory of said Estate which was ordered to be recorded.

P-390 Tuesday 17th May 1825

Ordered that an order of sale issue to Charles Buford administrator of the Estate of John Rawlins decd. commanding him to sell the perishable property contained in the Inventory by him this day returned, and also make return thereof according to law.

Ordered that Fountain Lester, James Patteson, and Henry Hagen be appointed commissioners to allot to Caty Rawlins widow of the late John Rawlins decd. so much provisions as will be sufficient for the maintenance of herself and family for one year from the time said John Rawlin departed this life.

Ordered that George Malone, Elisha White and James Leitch be appointed commissioners to settle with Thomas Lane administrator of the Estate of Martin Lane decd. and make return of said settlement to the present term of this court.

James Ridley . . . . . Plt.)   In Debt
    Against
Alfred Flournoy &)
William C. Flournoy)   )   This day came the parties by their
Administrator of   ) Defts.   attorneys and thereupon came a Jury
Silas Flournoy Decd)   of good and lawful men, towit, Henry
)   J. Cooper, Andrew Gordon, Francis
Smith, William W. Fogg, Henry M. Newlin, Early Benson, Aaron Smith, Henry McKay, John McKnight, David Abernathy, John Walthall & Elnathan G. Brown, who being Elected tried & sworn well and truly to try the issue joined between the parties in this case upon their oaths do say that they find said issue in favor of the plaintiff and assess his damages by reason of the detention of the debt in the writing obligatory in the declaration mentioned to fifteen dollars ninety seven and a half cents, Besides costs.

It is therefore considered by the court that the plaintiff recover of the defendant the sum of three hundred and fifty five dollars the amount of his debt aforesaid together with his damages aforesaid by the Jurors aforesaid assessed, and his costs by him about his suit in this behalf expended - to be levied of the goods and chattles rights and credits of the testator in the hands of the said defendants to be administered if so much thereof they have, but if so much thereof, they have not, then the costs to be levied of the proper goods and chattles of said Defendants.

P-391   Tuesday 17th May 1825

James Perry . . . . Plt.   )   In Debt
    Against
James Patteson Executor of the)Defts.   This day came the parties
Estate Nelson Patteson decd.)   by their attorneys and
)   thereupon came a Jury of
good and lawful men, towit, Henry J. Cooper, Andrew Gordon, Francis Smith, Wm. W. Fogg, Henry W. Newlin, Early Benson, Aaron Smith, Henry McKay, John McKnight, Asa A. Estes, John Walthall, and Elnathan G. Brown, who being elected tried and sworn well and truly to try the issue joined between the parties in this case upon their oaths do say that the defendant has paid the debt in the writing obligatory in the declaration mentioned as the plaintiff in his replication has alleged, and they do assess the plaintiffs damages by occasion of the detention of sd. debt to twenty three dollars & ten cents - besides costs.

It is therefore considered by the court that the plaintiff recover of said defendant the sum of fifty five dollars, the amount of his debt aforesaid, together with his damages aforesaid in form aforesaid by the Jurors aforesaid assessed, and also his costs about his suit in this behalf expended - to be levied of the goods and chattles rights and credits of the said testator in the hands of the said defendant to be administered if so much thereof they have, but if so much thereof they have not then the costs to be levied of the proper goods and chattles of said defendant.

John Hawkins to the use &c Plt.) In Debt
    Against)
James Patteson Executor of the)Deft)
Estate of Nelson Patteson Decd.))   This day came the parties by
)   their attorneys and thereupon
                                                     came a Jury of good and law-
ful men, towit, Henry J. Cooper, Andrew Gordon, Francis Smith, Wm. W. Fogg,
Henry M. Newlin, Early Benson, Aaron Smith, Henry McKay, John McKnight,
David Abernathy, John Walthall, and Elnathan G. Brown, who being elected
tried and sworn well and truly to try the issue joined between the parties
in this case upon their oaths do say that they find said issue in favor
of the plaintiff and assess his damages by occasion of the detention of
the debt in the writing obligatory in the declaration mentioned to forty
six dollars & twenty five cents - besides costs.

    It is therefore considered by the court that the plaintiff recover of
the said defendant the sum of one hundred & twenty five dollars the amount
of his debt aforesaid, together with his damages aforesaid in form aforesd.
by the Jurors aforesd. assessed and also his costs about his suit in this
behalf expended to be levied of the goods & chattles rights and   (p-392)
credits of the said testators in the hands of the said Defendants to be
administered if so much thereof they have, but if so much they have not,
then the costs to be levied of the proper goods and chattles of said defendant.

Hannah Underwood Plt.) In Case
    Against)
Tydall Wilkinson Deft.)   On application of the plaintiff and having
)   filed affidavit herein ordered that a com-
mission issue to any two of the Acting Justices of the Peace in and for
the County of Giles to take the deposition of Lucy Underwood to be read
on the trial of this case upon plaintiff giving to Defendants attorney
five days notice of the time and place of taking said depositions and the
cause continued untill the next term of this court.

Hannah Underwood Plt.) In Case
    Against)
Lydall Wilkinson Deft.)   On motion of Defendants attorney ordered
)   that a commission issue to any two of the
Acting Justices of the Peace in & for the County of Madison & State of
Alabama to take the deposition of William J. Adair, John W. Tilford, Rich-
ard Elliott, William Weedon, Archibald McDonald, John Silvers, Wm. E.
Philips, & John F. Wells, and that a commission issue to any two of the
Acting Justices of the Peace in and for the County of Madison and State
of Alabama to take the deposition of Robert M. Richards, Jonathan Warren,
Ruffin Coleman, John Silvers, Elvira Dandige, William Dandage, and May
Tatum all of which said depositions are to be read on the trial of this
cause upon the defendant giving to the plaintiff twenty days notice of
the time & place of taking the same, and also on motion of the plaintiff
ordered that a commission issue to any two of the Acting Justices of the
Peace in and for the County of Madison & State of Alabama to take the
deposition of David Owen, Stirling Smith, Allen James, John Airs, also
that a commission issue to any two of the Acting Justices of the Peace in
& for the County Limestone & State of Alabama to the deposition of Barnett
Tatum & Mary S. Tatum, which depositions when taken to be read in evidence
on the trial of this cause upon the plaintiffs giving to the Defendant attorney twenty days.

                 (Pages gone from 392 to 397)

P-397 Wednesday 18th May 1825

Charles Perkins ... Plt.)   In Debt
    Against)
James H. Pickens, Thomas B.)Defts.) From the Judgment of the court
Haynie, & Gerald Irby) in this case rendered the de-
) fendant prayed an appeal to
the honorable the Circuit Court to be held for the County of Giles, and having executed bond and security according to law the same was Granted them.

John Hamlett Plt.)   In Covenant
    Against)
Giddeon Pillow Deft.) This day came the parties by their attornies
) and thereupon came a Jury of good and lawful
men, towit, Henry J. Cooper, Thomas Wilkinson, Andrew Gordon, Francis Smith, Wm. W. Fogg, Henry M. Newlin, Early Benson, Aaron Smith, Benton R. White, Archibald Smith, Beverly B. Watson, & John Porter, who being elected tried and sworn well & truly to try the issue joined between the parties in this case upon their oaths do say they find said issue in favor of the plaintiff and assess his damages by reason of the non performance of the covenant in the declaration mentioned to thirty four dollars, and Eighty seven and a half cents, besides costs -

It is therefore considered by the court that the plaintiff recover of sd. defendant the damages aforesaid, in form aforesaid by the Jurors aforesaid assessed, and also his costs, about his suit in this behalf expended.

William Gholson Plt.)   In Covenant
    Against)
William Watson Defet.) Lewis H. Brown a Garnishee in this case ap-
) peared in court, and after being first duly
qualified the following interogations were put to him (Viz) Question 1st What sum or sums are you indebted to Wm. Watson, or were you at the time of the service of this Garnishment -

Answer, In February last I gave my note with Thomas Marks & John Brown securities to Wm. Watson for five hundred & fifty dollars payable in notes on good solvent men in Giles County, payable on or before the 25th December 1825, which notes were to be due at that time - Beverly B. Watson a Garnishee in this case appeared in court and after being first duly sworn, the following interogations were put to him, (Viz) Question 1st What sum or sums are you indebted to Wm. Watson or were you at the time of the service of (p-398) this Garnishment, Answer In February 1825 I gave my note to Wm. Watson, for about twenty five dollars due the 25th December 1825 I was security for Wm. Watson to Nathan Rea for the sum of ninety dollars payable 25th December 1825, I do not know whether said ninety dollars is in one or two notes. I do not know whether I want security to sd. note or notes, before the service of this Garnishment or notes - and if there were two notes, I do not know whether they were due at the same time or not. I also was security for Wm. Watson to Richard Brandon for $32. payable 25th December 1825 which note was executed about the 18th April.

I also went security for sd. Williams Watson to Rhoda Smith for sixty five dollars, payable 25th December 1824 upon which suit has been brought Judgment obtained & the execution stayed - To secure myself on account of the above securityships I received from Wm. Watson the following notes and

accounts, towit, One on Wm. Ball for 47½ cents, in favor of Wm. Watson, due 1st May 1824 one on John Davis in favor of same for 25 cents, due 1st May 1823, One on Wm. Brown in favor of same for two dollars & fifty cents due the 25th December 1825 the name of Wm. Watson & R. Watson written on the back of it. One on Henry Phenix & Thomas Underwood in favor of same for $19.25 cents due 10th November 1825 indorsed as aforesaid.
One on Dixon Brown & Robert McLaurine in favor of same for Eight dollars 95 3/4 cents due 19th August 1825, endorsed as last aforesd. One on Robert McLaurine in favor of same for $15 the due 25th December 1825 indorsed as last aforesd. and on the back of it is also indorsed that the same may be discharged in cash notes, due on or at the time the note came due. One on Charles Myers & Beverly B. Watson in favor of same for $9.75½ cents, due 19th August 1825 indorsed, Wm. Watson, & R. Watson.
One on Charles Myers, in favor of same for $5.18 3/4 cts. to be discharged by Smiths work upon application indorsed as last aforesd. One on John S. Brandon, & B. B. Watson in favor of same for $6.50 cts. due 19th August 1825; indorsed as aforesaid one on Robert McLaurine, & Dixon Brown in favor same for $6.13 3/4 cents due 19th August 1825, indorsed as aforesd. One on Robert Davison in favor of same for $13. in cash notes on good solvent men in Giles County due the 25th December 1825 indorsd. as aforesaid one on Thomas Underwood & Henry Phenix (p-399) in favor of same, for $10 37½ cents due 19th August 1825, endorsed as aforesaid one on Daniel Puryear in favour of same for $15 in current Bank notes, due 25th December 1825 indorsed as aforesaid, one on George W. Look, & B. B. Watson in favour of same for $6.40 cents due 19th August 1825 endorsed as aforesaid also an account against Langford Fitzgerald in favor of same for $12 for twition of scholars, also an account against Tobitha Condra in favour of same for $12 for same, which notes and accounts are to be mine if I have the money above mentioned comes due - Question 2nd What property of Wm. Watsons had you in your possession at the time of the service of this Garnishment or have you at this time - Answer I had a lot in the Town of Pulaski, which I purchased of Wm. Watson in the morning of the day Judgment was obtained against Wm. Watson by Wm. Gholson - Queston 3rd Did you not receive the money which you paid for 1st lot of Wm. Watson - Answer, I did Robert Watson a Garnishee in this case appeared in court and after being first duly Qualified the following interogations were put to him, towit, Question 1st What were you indebted to William Watson at the time of serving the garnishment in this case, or are now indebted to him. Answer I bought some property of Wm. Watson, at a sale in February last to the amount of one hundred and fifty odd dollars and gave my note to him payable some time in August next no part of which said note I have yet paid - I have understood from William Watson, that he has traded my note. I think he gave me that in formation before the service of the Garnishment, But did not say to whom he had traded nor did I ask him, But has since told me he had traded it to Silas Webb, with whom I am not acquainted, But have often heard of him by William Watson, but from no other person that I distinctly recollect at this time, nor do I know where he lives I am a Brother of Wm. Watsons & live with him.

Ordered that Court be adjourned untill tomorrow morning nine oclock.

Thomas Batte
James Paine
Peter Swanson

P-400   Thursday 19th May 1825

Court met according to adjournment Present Thomas Batte) Esquires Justice
                                            James Paine) of the Peace of
                                            Peter Swanson) for Giles County.

John Hamlett ... Plt.)   In Covenant
    Against   )
Giddion Pillow Deft.)
)   From the Judgment from the court in this
                          case rendered the defendant prayed an appeal to the Honorable the Circuit court to be held for the County of Giles, and having executed bond and security according to law the same was granted him.

Samuel S. Smith & Wife Plts.)   Petition
    Against   )
John Porter Gdn. &c Deft.   )
) On motion of the plaintiffs this cause
                                is ordered to be continued till next court, and it is also ordered that a commission issue to any two of the acting Justices of the Peace in & for the County of Lylard and State of Missouri to take the deposition of William Y. C. Ewing which when taken is to be read in evidence on the trial of this cause upon the plaintiff giving to the defendant thirty days notice of the time and place of taking said depositions.

John Abernathy Assee &c Plt.)   In Debt
    Against   )
Robert Oliver .... Deft.   )
)   This day came the parties by their
                                 attornies and thereupon came a Jury of good and lawful men, Towit, Aaron Smith, Early Benson, Henry M. Newlin, Wm. W. Fogg, Francis Smith, Andrew Gordon, Thomas Wilkinson, Henry J. Cooker, William Pullen, Stirling H. Lester, Robert McCullough, & George Everly - Who being elected tried and sworn well and truly to try the issue joined between the parties in this case upon their oaths do say that they find said issue in favor of the plaintiffs and assess his damages by reason of the non performance of the condition of the bond in the declaration mentioned to twenty six hundred & twenty six dollars and Eighty seven and a half cents besides costs.

P-401   Thursday 19th May 1825

Henry McAnnick and William Fogg comes into court and acknowledges himself indebted to the State of Tennessee in the sum of two hundred & fifty dollars to be levied of their goods and chattles, lands and tenments to the use of the State to be void on condition that the said Henry McAnnick, appear here on Friday next, and prosecute and give evidence, & the said Wm. Fogg, to give evidence on behalf of the State against William Wood & others overseers of the Prewit Cap road from Pulaski to Maury County line, and not depart without leave of the court.

John McKinney comes into court and acknowledged himself indebted to the

State of Tennessee in the sum of two hundred dollars to be levied of his goods and chattles lands and tenments to the use of the State to be void on condition that the said John McKinney appear here on Friday next, and give evidence on behalf of the State against William Wood & others, overseers of the Prewit Gap road from Pulaski to Maury County Line, and not depart without leave of the court.

The State . . . Plt.) Upon an indictment for an affray with an as-
  Against) sault & battery on the body of George Watson.
Thomas Franks Deft.)
) George Watson & Isaac Reynolds comes into court and acknowledges themselves indebted to the State of Tennessee in the sum of one hundred dollars each to be levied of their goods & chattles lands and tenments to the use of the State to be void on condition that the said George Watson appear here on the first Thursday after the Third Monday in August next & prosecute & give evidence on behalf of the State against said Defendant for an affray with and an assault & battery on the body of sd. George Watson & not depart without leave of this court.

A Power of attorney from Sarah Massie to Thomas Cowls Esquire for certain property therein specified was produced in court and the Execution thereof proven by the oaths of Robert P. Tunstale & John A. Upshaw, two of the witnesses thereto, and ordered to be certified.

Ordered that Thomas Lane Thomas K. Gordon, James Leitch, Elisha White, & John Laird or any three of them be appointed commissioners to settled with George Malone & (p-402) (Thursday 19th May 1825) Jame Woodfin Executor of George Woodfin decd. & that they make report to the next term of this court.

The Grand Jury returned into court an Indictment of the State against Thomas Franks for an affray with & an assault and battery on the body of George Watson Endorsed, a true bill, also an Indictment of the same against Tillman R. Daniels for an affray with & an assault & battery on the body of Amanias Oliver Endorsed "A true bill" also an Indictment of the State aginst Annania Oliver for an affray with & an assault & battery on the body of Thomas R. Daniels Endorsed "A true bill" and withdrew to consider of further prosecutions.

The State . . . . Plt.) Indictment for an assault & battery on the
  Against) body of T. R. Daniel.
Annanias Oliver Deft.)
) John McCormack comes into court and acknowledges himself indebted to the State of Tennessee in the sum of one hundred dollars to be levied of his goods and chattles lands and tenments to the use of the State, to be void on condition that he appear here on the first Thursday after the third Monday in August next and prosecute and give evidence on behalf of the State against said Defendant for an affray with & an assault & battery on the body of Annanias Oliver, and not depart without leave of this court.

P-403 Thursday 19th May 1825

307

Hugh Bratton comes into court and acknowledges himself indebted to the State of Tennessee in the sum of one hundred dollars to be levied of his goods and chattles lands and Tenments to the use of the State to be void on condition that the said Hugh Bratton appear here on the first Thursday after the third Monday in August next and prosecute and give evidence on behalf of the State against Peter Allsup overseer of the road and not depart without leave of the court.

The State Plt.) Upon a presentment for an affray with & an as-
    Against   ) sault & battery on the body of William Finnry.
Samuel King Deft.)
) This day came the Solicitor General for the
State as also the defendant in his proper person who being charged on the presentment in this case pleads guilty and because he will not contend with the State agrees to submit himself to the Justice and mercy of the court. It is therefore considered by the court that he make his fine with the State to the amount of one dollar and that he pay costs of this prosecution.

The State Plt.) Upon an Indictment for an affray with & an as-
    Against   ) sault & battery on the body of Isaac Reynolds.
John Pearce Deft.)
) This day came the Solicitor General for the
State as also the Defendant in his proper person who being charged on the Indictment in this case pleads Guilty and because he will not contend with the State agrees to submit himself to the Justice and mercy of the court. It is therefore considered by the court that he make his fine with the State to the amount of twelve and a half cents, and that he pay the costs of this prosecution and that he be committed to the custody of the Sheriff of this County there to remain till said fine & costs be paid, or that he give security for the payment of the same, and thereupon Beverly B. Watson comes into court and undertakes as security for sd. defendant. It is therefore considered by the court that the State recover of said defendant and Beverly B. Watson his security, the fine and costs aforesaid.

A Deed of conveyance from Beverly B. Watson to Aaron V. Brown for lot No. 16 in the Town of Pulaski, was produced in court and the execution thereof acknowledged by the said Beverly B. Watson and ordered to be certified for registration.

P-404   Thursday 19th May 1825.

A Deed of Gift from David K. McEwin to William L. McEwin, & Sarah C. McEwin, for certain property therein Specified was produced in court and the execution thereof fully proven by the oath of Rebeccah McEwin the other witnesses thereto, and ordered to be certified for registration.

Robert Smith Assee &c Plt.)
    Against   )   In Debt
Joseph Luker and) Defts.)
Elnathan G. Brown)   )
) This day came the parties by their attornies and thereupon came a Jury of

Good and lawful men, Towit, William R. Brown, Lewis R. Morris, Beverly B. Watson, Henry Peden, John B. McCanlass, John Abernathy, John W. Croft, Francis H. Mabrey, Wm. B. Brooks, John McKnight, Daniel Abernathy and Bailey Davis, who being elected tried and Sworn well and truly to try the issue joined between the parties in this case, upon their oaths do say that the defendants have not paid the Debt in the writing obligatory in the declaration mentioned and that he has no sett off as the plaintiff in his replication has alleged, and they do assess the plaintiff damages by occasion of the detention of said debt to two dollars and twenty five cents. besides costs – It is therefore considered by the court that the plaintiff recover of said defendant the sum of one hundred dollars, the amount of his debt aforesaid together with his damages aforesaid in form aforesd. by the Jurors aforesaid assessed, and also his costs about his suit in this behalf expended.

William Wells Plt.) In Case
    Against)
Benjamin W. Edwards) Deft.)
& James Lynch) This day came the parties by their attornies and thereupon came the Jury of good and lawful men, Towit, William R. Brown, Lewis B. Morris, Beverly B. Watson, John Abernathy, John W. Croft, Francis H. Mabrey, Henry Penden, John B. McCanlass, William B. Brooks, John McKnight, Daniel Abernathy and Bailey Davis, who being elected tried and sworn well and truly to try the issue joined between the parties in this case, upon their oaths do say that they find said issue in favor of the plaintiff and assess his damages by occasion of the non performance of the (p-405) Thursday 19th May 1825, assumpsit in the declaration mentioned to the amount of one hundred & forty dollars besides costs.

It is therefore considered by the court that the plaintiff recover of said Defendant the damages aforesaid in form aforesaid by the Jurors aforesaid assessed, and also his costs about his suit in this behalf expended.

Henry Hagen . . . Plt.) In Covenant
    Against)
James Z. Maclin &)Defts.)
Benjamin P. Maclin) This day came as well the plaintiff by his attorney as also the defendants in their proper persons and said defendants sat they cannot gainsay the plaintiffs actions against them nor but that they do owe him the sum of one hundred and Eighty two dollars & seventy cents the damages which he hath sustained by reason of the non performance of the covenant in the declaration mentioned, besides costs.

It is therefore by consent of plaintiff considered by the court that the plaintiff recover of said defendants the damages aforesaid in form aforesaid agreed, and also his costs by him about his suit in this behalf expended – and that execution be stayed untill 25th December 1825.

A Deed of conveyance from James Z. Maclin to Benjamin P. Maclan for one thousand acres of land was produced in court an the execution thereof proven by the oaths of James Patteson and William Maclin, the witness thereto, and ordered to be certified.

The State . . . Plt.) Upon an Indictment for an affray with &
    Against) an assault & battery on the body of Bailey
David Stockton Deft.) Davis.

309

This day came the Solicitor General for the State and the Defendant, altho solemnly called came not but made default – It is therefore considered by the court that a Judgment Ni Si for the sum of two hundred and fifty dollars, according to the tenor of his recognizance be entered up against him, and that a Scire Facias issue against him returnable to the next term of this court.

The State Plt.) Upon a presentment for an affray with & an
   Against) assault & battery on the body of Bailey
David Stockton Deft.) Davis.
)

Baker P. Potts who was bound in a recognizance for the appearance of the aforesaid defendant being Solemnly called and required to bring with him (p-406) Thursday 19th May 1825, the body of said defendant, But made default. It is therefore considered by the court that a Judgment Ni - Si for the sum of one hundred and twenty five dollars according to the tenor of his recognizance be entered up against him, and that a Scire Facias issue against him returnable to the next court.

The State Plt.) Indictment for an affray with & an assault
   Against) & battery on the body of Bailey Davis.
David Stockton Deft.)
)

Bailey Davis, Jesse Hicks & Nathaniel Young comes into court and acknowledges themselves indebted to the State of Tennessee in the sum of one hundred dollars each to be levied of their goods and chattles lands and tenments to the use of the State, to be void on condition that the said Bailey Davis appear here of the first Thursday after the third Monday in August next to prosecute & give evidence on behalf of the State against and said Defendant & not depart without leave of the court.

Ordered that court be adjourned untill tomorrow morning 9 oclock.

                                            A. Black
                                            James Perry
                                            W. B. Pepper

P-407 Friday Morning 20th May 1825

Court met according to adjournment Present Alexander Black) Esquire Justice
                                        James Perry and) of the Peace
                                         William B. Pepper) for the County
) of Giles.

The State Plt.) Upon an Indictment for an affray with & an
   Against) assault & battery on the body of German
Louis B. Morris Deft.) Prim.

This day came the Solicitor General for the State as also the defendant in his proper person who being charged on the Judgment in this case pleads not Guilty, and for his trial puts himself upon his country and the Solicitor General for the State on the part of the State likewise therefore let a Jury came who as well &c to recognize &c and thereupon came a Jury of good and lawful men, Towit, Aaron Smith, Early Benson, Henry M. Newlin, William W. Fogg, Francis Smith, Andrew Gordon, Thomas Wilkinson, John Abernathy, Meredith Bunch, Beverly B. Watson, Robert G. Steele, & Simpson H. White, who being elected tried and sworn well & truly to try the issue of traverse between the State and said defendant upon their oaths do say that said Defendant is not guilty as is charged in the Indictment. It is therefore considered by the court that the defendant be acquitted and discharged from the affray and assault & battery aforesaid, and that he go hence without day.

The State Plt.
 Against
Louis B. Morris Deft.

Upon an Indictment for an affray with & an assault & battery on the body of German Pin.

The Defendant in this case having been acquitted on a trial on the merits by a Jury. It is ordered that Judgment be entered up against the County of Giles in favor of the several claimants, on the part of the State for all costs to which they are entitled, and that the Clerk certify the same to the Trustee of Giles County for payment.

John C. McLaurine Assee &c Plt.
 Against
Daniel Cutbirth . . . . Deft.

In Debt

From the Judgment of the court in this case rendered the defendant prayed an appeal to the honorable the Circuit Court to be held for the County of Giles and having entered into bond & security as the Law directs the same was granted him.

P-408 Friday 20th May 1825

The Grand Jury returned into court the following Indictments & presentments, Towit, The State against John Menefee for neglect of duty as overseer of the road - same against him John H. Camp, for neglect of duty as overseer of the road, - Same against Edmund Shelton for neglect of duty as overseer of the road, - Same against David Stockton for abstructing navagation, - same against Langford Fitzgerald, - same against Andrew Cole for retailing Spiritous liquors without lecence same against Wm. Watson for an affray with & an assault & battery on the body of Langford Fitzgerald, - same against William D. Black for an affray with & an assault & battery on the body of William A. Brown, - Also presented the Dry Creek road from Pulaski to Columbia, and withdrew to consider of further presentments.

John Brooks Plt.
 Against
Marshall Moody Deft.

In Debt

From the Judgment of the court in this case rendered, the Defendant prayed an appeal to the honorable the Circuit Court to be held for the County of Giles, and having executed bond and security as the law directs the same was granted him.

The State Plt.
 Against
Lewis B. Morris Deft.

Upon an Indictment for an affray with & an assault & battery on the body of Samuel Day.

For reasons made known to the court by the Solicitor General for the State who saith he wishes no further to prosecute the Defendant in this case. It is ordered that a nole prosequi be entered therein, and that the defendant go hence without day

The State Plt.) Upon an Indictment for an affray with & an
    Against) assault & battery on the body of Samuel Day.
Lewis B. Morris Deft.)
)

A Nole Prosqui having been entered in this case under the directions of the court. It is ordered that Judgment be entered up against the County of Giles in favour of the several claimants on the part of the State, for all costs to which they are entitled, and that the Clerk certify the same to the Trustee of Giles County for payment.

P-409   Friday 20th May 1825

The State Plt.) Upon an Indictment for Trespass Veit Armies.
    Against)
Jacob Shall Deft.) This day came the Solicitor General for the
) State as also the Defendants in his proper
person who being charged on the Indictment in this case pleads not guilty, and for his trial puts himself upon his country, and the Solicitor General for the State, on the part of the State likewise. Therefore let a jury come who as well &c to recognize &c and thereupon came a Jury of good & lawful men, Towit, Henry J. Cooper, Samuel S. Smith, Henry Peden, Daniel McCollum, John B. McCanlass, Robert Adams, Robert Anderson, Elisha L. Kimbrough, Early Benson, Aaron Smith, Henry McNewlin, and Andrew Gordon who being elected tried and sworn well and truly to try the issue of Traverse between the State and said Defendant and having heard part of the evidence in this case were permitted to disperse to meet again tomorrow morning nine oclock.

                                                            Robert Oliver
                                                            Paul Chiles
                                                            James H. Graves

P-410   Saturday Morning 21st May 1825

Court met according to adjournment Present Robert Oliver) Esquires Justices
                                             Paul Chiles   ) of the Peace for
                                             James H. Graves) Giles County.

The State Plt.) Upon an Indictment for a Trespass Veit Armies.
    Against)
Jacob Shall Deft.) This day came the Solicitor General for the
) State as also the Defendant in his proper person and therefore came the Jury who were sworn on yesterday well and truly to try the issue of traverse between the State and said Defendant, who upon their oaths do say that the defendant is not guilty in manner and form as he is charged in the Indictment.

It is therefore considered by the court that the Defendant be acquitted and discharged from the Trespass aforesd. & that he go hence without day.

The State Plt. Against Jacob Shall Deft.	Upon an Indictment for a Trespass Veit Armies.

The Defendant in this case having been acquitted on a trial on the merits by a Jury, It is therefore considered by the court that a Judgment be entered against the County of Giles in favour of the several claimants, on the part of the State for all costs to which they are entitled that the Clerk certify the same to the Trustee of Giles County for payment.

Andrew Fay use &c Plt. Against Robert Fenner . . . Deft.	In Debt

From the Judgment of the court in this case rendered the Defendant prayed an appeal to the honorable the Circuit Court to be held for the County of Giles and having executed bond and security as the law directs the same was granted him.

Benjamin Ingram, use &c Plt. Against Gray H. Edwards . . . Deft.	In Debt

From the Judgment of the court in this case rendered the Defendant prayed an appeal to the honorable the Circuit Court to be held for the County of Giles and having executed bond and security as the law directs the same was granted him.

P-411 Saturday 21st May 1825

William Wells Plt. Against Benjamin W. Edwards)Defts. & James Lynch)	In Debt

From the Judgment of the court in this case rendered the Defendant prayed an appeal to the honorable the Circuit Court to be held for the County of Giles and having executed bond and security as the law directs the same was granted him..

A Deed of trust from Willis W. Cole to Benjamin Carter, Trustee for Samuel & Nicholas S. Paine was produced in court and the Execution thereof acknowledged by the sd. Willie W. Cole and ordered to be certified for registration.

William Banks Plt. Against Wm. P. A. McCabe Deft.	In Covenant

This day came the parties by their attornies and thereupon came a Jury of good and lawful men, Towit, Thomas Wilkinson, William W. Fogg, Andrew Gordon, Henry M. Newlin, James McDonald, William Giddion, Joseph Luker, Nathan Bass, Francis Smith, Nathan Davis, Robert Wells & Aaron Smith, who being elected tried and sworn well and truly to try the issue joined between the parties in this case upon their oaths do say that they find said issue in favour of the plaintiff and assess his damages by occasion of the non performance of the covenant in the declaration mentioned to two hundred & four dollars & seventy five cents, besides costs.

It is therefore considered by the court that the plaintiff recover of sd. Defendant the damages aforesaid in form aforesaid, by the Jurors aforesaid assessed, and also his costs about his suit in this behalf expended.

Jacob Shall & Wm. Shall Plt.)   Original Attachment
Merchants &c.)
       Against) This day came the parties by their at-
William W. Thornton Deft.) tornies and thereupon came a Jury of
) good and lawful men, towit, Henry J.
Cooper, James Lynch, Elnathan G. Brown, Simpson White, Jason Hopkins, Jefferson, Chambers, Henry Hester, Hugh Long, Enoch Reynolds, Redin B. Gatlin, John McDonald, and Joseph S. Tarkington, who being elected tried and sworn well and truly to try the issue joined between the parties in this case and upon their oaths do say that they find said issue in favour of the plaintiff and assess his damages by occasion (p-412) of the detention in the Writing obligatory in the declaration mentioned to two hundred dollars & nine cents, besides costs. It is therefore considered by the court that the plaintiff recover of said defendant the sum of ninety three dollars thirty nine & three fourth cents the amount of his debt aforesaid together with his damages aforesd. in form aforesaid, by the Jurors aforesaid assessed, and also his cost about his suit in this behalf expended.

Andrew M. Balentine & Thomas)   Appeal
Martin, Merchants &c (use &c))
       Against) This day came the defendant by
Matthew Pate . . . . . Defendant) his attorney and the plaintiff
) being solemnly called came not
but made default, nor is this suit further prosecuted. It is therefore considered by the court that the Defendant go hence without day and recover of the plaintiffs his costs by him about his defence in this behalf expended.

Thomas Martindale, use &c Plt.)   In Debt
       Against)
Claiborn Kyle . . . . . Deft.) From the Judgment of the court in
) this case rendered the defendant
prayed an appeal to the honorable the Circuit Court to be held for the County of Giles, - and having executed bond and security according to law the same was granted him.

The Grand Jury returned into court the following indictments & presentments, towit, The State against Buckner Madra for neglect of duty as overseer of the road, - same against Peter Alsup for obstructing publick highway - Same against William Wood, for neglect of duty as overseer of the road, Same against Jacob Cox for obstructing the publick highway and withdrew to consider of further presentments.

Alexander McDonald Plt.)   In Debt
       Against)
Hugh W. Bratton Deft.) This day came the plaintiff by his attorney
) and the Defendant altho solemnly called
came not but made default, It is therefore considered by the court that the plaintiff recover of the defendant the sum of two hundred & fifty dollars,

the amount (p-413) of the debt in the writing obligatory in the declaration mentioned, together with the sum of five dollars the damages he hath sustained by reasons for the detention of said debt, and his costs by him about his suit in this behalf expended - Execution to be stayed till after August term of this court.

Alexander McDonald Plt.) In Debt
    Against)
Martin Davenport Deft.) This day came the plaintiff by his attorney
) and the Defendant altho solemnly called, came not but made default - It is therefore considered by the court that the plaintiff recover of the defendant the sum of two hundred dollars the amount of the debt in the Writing obligatory in the declaration mentioned together with the sum of four dollars & fifty cents the damages he hath sustained by reason of the detention - of said debt and his costs by him about his suit in this behalf expended The execution in this case is to be stayed untill after the next August term of this court.

Alexander McDonald Plt.) In Debt
    Against)
James Wilson & George Wilson Deft.) This day came the plaintiff by
) his attorney and the Defendant altho solemnly called came not but made default - It is therefore considered by the court that the plaintiff recover of the Defendant the sum of one hundred & fifty dollars, the amount of the debt in writing obligatory in the Declaration mentioned together with the sum of three dollars & thirty five cents, the damages he hath sustained by reason of the Detention of said Debt. And his costs by him about his suit in this behalf expended. The Execution in this case is to be stayed untill after the next August term of this court.

Alexander McDonald Plt.) In Debt
    Against)
William Major's Deft.) This day came the plaintiff by his attorneys,
) and the Defendant altho solemnly called came not but made default. It is therefore considered by the court that the plaintiff recover of the defendant the sum of two hundred dollars the amount of the debt in the writing obligatory in the declaration mentioned together with the sum of four dollars & fifty cents the damages he hath sustained by reason of the detention of said debt, and his costs by him about his suit in this behalf expended.

P-414 Ordered that Court be adjourned untill Monday morning Ten oclock.

                                                          H. Hagen
                                                          A. Black
                                                          W. B. Pepper

Monday Morning 23rd May 1825

Court met according to adjournment, Present, Alexander Black, Henry Hagen, William B. Pepper, Archibald McKnight, James Perry, John Bramlitt,

315

James Dugger, John H. Camp, Thomas K. Gordon, Robert Read, Jesse Allen, and Arthur Hicks, Esquires Justice of the Peace for Gile County.

Ordered that James Ford be appointed overseer of the road in the room of Henry Rainey resigned, and that he have the same district of hands.

A Bill of sale from John Reading to John Brown for certain property therein Specified was produced in court and the execution thereof proven by the oath of James Russel, one of the witnesses thereto, and ordered to be certified for registration.

Ordered that the following tax list be received and the double tax thereon be remitted, towit,

John Hawkins	811½	acres of land.
	17	Black polls.
	1	four wheel carriage.
Harriet Row	9	Black polls
	1	four wheel carriage
Thomas Goff	840	Acres of land
	2	Slaves
	1	Free poll.

A Deed of conveyance from Francis Alexander, Guardian &c to John E. Holden for Lot No. 37 in Pulaski was produced in court and the execution thereof proven by the oaths of James Lynch & Albert G. Underwood the witnesses thereto, and ordered to be certified for Registration.

P-415   Monday 23rd May 1825

Ordered that William W. Fogg be appointed overseer of the road in the room of John McKissack resigned and that he have the same district of hands.

At least five Justices being present, Joel Lane returned into court one wolf scalp over four months old, which was ordered to be burnt.

Ordered that the County Trustee of this County pay to William R. Davis the sum of Eight dollars and Eighteen and three fourth cents, for keeping Isaac N. Hobson, and for articles distroyed by said Hobson White in his possession.

Ordered that the County Trustee of this County pay to William R. Davis the sum of one dollar & seventy five cents for keeping Theophilus Guthrie.

Alexander Thompson, use &c Plt. Against John Lee . . . . Deft.	In Debt From the Judgment of the court in this case rendered the Defendant

prayed an appeal to the honorable the Circuit Court to be held for the County of Giles — And having executed bond and Security as the law directs the same was granted him.

Alexander Thompson, use &c Plt.) In Debt
      Against)
John Lee . . . . Deft.) From the Judgment of the court in
) this case rendered the defendant
prayed an appeal to the honorable the Circuit Court to be held for the County of Giles and having executed bond and security as the law directs, the same was granted him.

Jacob Shall Assee &c Plt.) In Debt
      Against)
Patrick H. Braden &) Defts.) From the Judgment of the court in this
Burton R. White) case rendered the defendant prayed an
) appeal to the honorable the Circuit
Court to be held for the County of Giles, and having executed bond and security as the Law directs the same was granted him.

Ordered that Thomas Williams be appointed overseer of the road in the room of Charles Buford resigned and that he have the same district of hands

P-416   Monday 23rd May 1825

Thomas Martin & Andrew)Plts.) In Debt
M. Balentine Merchant &c)
      Against) From the Judgment of the court in
James & Leonard Smith Deft.) this case rendered the Defendant
) prayed an appeal to the honorable
the Circuit Court to be held for the County of Giles, and having executed bond and security as the Law directs the same was granted them.

Alexander Thompson, use &c Plt.) In Debt
      Against)
Daniel Goodman . . . Deft.) From the Judgment of the court in
) this case rendered the defendant
prayed an appeal to the honorable the Circuit Court to be held for the County of Giles and having executed bond and security as the law directs the same was granted him.

Ordered that Jacob Miller, Thomas Harwood, John Bass, William Menefee, John Carmichael, Samuel Jordon & Samuel Faine, or any five of them be appointed a Jury to view and mark out the Huntsville road leading by Upper Elkton, begining at the Bank of Elk River on the south side and see if it be proper to turn sd. road so as to run on the line dividing the bounds of A. M. W. Upshaw and Elisha Eldridge - and that they make report to the next term of this court.

The commissioners who were appointed to divide the personal Estate of Martin Lane decd. made return of said division which is ordered to be recorded.

317

The commissioners who were appointed to settle with the Estate of Martin Lane decd. made return of said settlement which is ordered to be recorded.

Ordered that James Paine & Robert Paine be appointed commissioners to settle with Thomas Brown, administrators of the Estate of Jordon Hicks decd. and that they make report to the next term of this court.

P-317 : Monday 23rd May 1825

Ordered that James Patteson, John E. Holden, James Lynch, Henry J. Cooper, George Everly, Thomas B. Jones, and Fountain Lester or any five of them be appointed a Jury to view that part of the road leading from the South end of College Street a few feet East along the Margin of the Town of Pulaski, then South with Jason Hopkins line to intersect the Huntsville road, and see if it be proper to turn sd. road and make report to the next term of this court.

The Commissioners who were appointed to settle with Thomas Read administrator of the Estate of Fanny Moore decd. made return of sd. settlement which is ordered to be recorded.

Ordered that the County Trustee of this County pay to Arthur M. Upshaw the sum of forty dollars, for the support and maintenance of Maddox a pauper of this County for Twelve months from this time.

John B. McCanlass Plt.   )   In Debt
        Against   )
John Clark . . . Deft.   )   From the Judgment of the court in this case
)   rendered the Defendant prayed an appeal to
the honorable the Circuit Court to be held for the County of Giles, and having executed bond and security as the Law directs the same was granted him.

Stirling B. Robertson, use &c Plt.)   In Debt
        Against   )
John Clark . . . . Deft.   ) From the Judgment of the Court
) in this case rendered the defendant prayed an appeal to the honorable the Circuit Court to be held for the County of Giles, - and having executed bond and security as the law directs the same was granted him.

Hardy Willsford Guardian of the minor heirs of Joseph Meadows decd. returned an account against his said Wards which is ordered to be recorded.

Ordered that the County Trustee of this County pay to Lawson Hobson the summ of sixty two dollars & fifty cents for the support or maintenance of Isaac M. Hobson, Lunatic, for the term of twelve months from this time conditioned that the sd. Isaac M. Hobson is not at any time run at Large.

P-418   Monday 23rd May 1825

Henry Laugtry &c Plts.   )   In Debt
  Against   )
James P. Deams . . Deft.   )   From the Judgment of the court in this
)   case rendered the defendant prayed an
appeal to the honorable the Circuit Court to be held for the County of
Giles - and having executed bond and security as the law directs the same
was granted him.

Henry Laugtry &c Co. Plt.   )   In Debt
  Against   )
Isaac P. Deams Deft.   )   From the Judgment of the court in this
)   case rendered the Defendant prayed an
appeal to the honorable the Circuit Court to be held for the County of Giles,
and having executed bond and security as the Law directs the same was granted
him.

Ordered that Robert Reed, Archibald McKissack, & Robert McLaurine, be
appointed commissioners to settle with the administrators of the Estate of
Lewis Kirk decd. and that they make report thereof to the next term of this
court.

Richard H. Allen Guardian of Judith McCabe made return of an account
against his said Ward, which is ordered to be recorded.

Ordered that John H. Rivers Esquire be allowed the privilege of occupying the room in the South East corner of the court house on second floor.

Samuel Y. Anderson came into court and resigned as Guardian of Sarah
Cannon.

It is ordered by the court that the following persons good and Lawful
men of the County of Giles that is each one of whom is a free white male
citizen, and house holder of said County over twenty one years of age, not
an overseer of a road and who has   (p-419)   not been appointed and served
as a Juror in this County Court for twelve months, towit, Younger Hobson,
John McAnnick, Gilliam Harwell, Soloman Simmons, Senr., David L. Jones,
Josiah Eaves, Alexander Stinson, William James, Walter Locke, George M.
Gibson, Jonathan Moody, Hugh Long, Samuel Kerr, Robert B. Harney, Reuben
Freeman, Joseph Goode, Thomas Wells, Levi Sherrill, Lewis Williamson, James
McDonald, George Everly, Robert Black, Benjamin M. Scoggins, John B. Goldberry, Jesse West and Henry Phenix, be jurors to serve in this court at
the next term on the third Monday in August next that the Clerk deliver a
copy of this order to the Sheriff of said County and that he summon said
persons to attend and serve accordingly.

Ordered that the Sheriff of this County summon William R. Davis and
Benjamin Williams as constables to attend on the Grand and petit Jurors
at the next term of this court.

Ordered that that part of the road leading from Pulaski to Fayettsville Which runs around John McCanlass farm be opened agreable to the report of the Jury appointed to view and mark out the same, at the expence of sd. John McCanlass and when so opened to be under the directions of John Holley overseer of sd. road, to keep the same in repair with the hands under his directions.

Ordered that Huntsville road running from Columbia to leave said road, and to intersect said road about three hundred yards from it leaves it - be opened agreable to the report of the Jury appointed to view and mark out the same, and when so opened to be under the direction of Christain Zimmermon, Junr. overseer of said road to keep the same in repair with the hands under his directions.

Ordered that Archibald McKissack, Fountain Lester, and James Duford be appointed Judges to Superintend an Election to be held at Pulaski on the first Thursday and Friday in August next for the purpose of Electing a Governor a member of congress and members of the State Legislature.

P-420   Monday 23rd May 1825

Ordered that John Goff, Thomas Lane, & Richard McGee be appointed Judges to Superintend an Election to be held at the house of Martin Lanes, on the first Thursday & Firday in August next for the purpose of Electing a Governor, a member of Congress, and members of the State Legislature.

Ordered that Peter Swanson, Joseph Roe, & Jesse Allen, be appointed Judges to Superintend an Election to be held at the house of Crocket Campbells, on Big Creek on the first Thursday and Friday in August next for the purpose of Electing a Governor and member of Congress, and members of the State Legislature.

Ordered that Anderson, Hogan, Asa McGee, & Benjamin White, be appointed Judges to Superintend an Election to be held at the house of Hugh Bratton on Little Shoal Creek on the first Thursday & Friday in August next for the purpose of Electing a Governor an member of Congress, and members of the State Legislature.

Ordered that Spencer Clack, Burrel Abernathy & Thomas Harwood, be appointed Judges to Superintend an Election to be held as the house of Welton F. L. Jenkins, in Lower Elkton, on the first Thursday and Friday in August next for the purpose of Electing a Governor, a member of congress, and members of the State Legislature.

Ordered that John Young, Paul Chiles & John McKnight, be appointed Judges to Superintend an Election to be held at the house of Samuel McKnight on Bradshaw Creek on the first Thursday & Friday in August next for the purpose of Electing a Governor, a member of congress, and members of the State Legislature.

Upon motion of Rebeccah Jones and Alexander S. Jones, administrators of the Estate of John Jones decd. and it appearing to the satisfaction of the court, now here, that said Estate is indebted to the amount of twelve thousand dollars, and that the personal Estate of the said John Jones decd. is not of value sufficient to pay & satisfy the demands, of the creditors of said Estate, and it also appearing to the satisfaction of the court now here, that there are twelve negro slaves belonging to the Estate of said John Jones decd. which have not been sold by the administrators the value of whom is considered to be sufficient for the payment of said Debts. (p-421) (Monday 23rd May 1825) and it also appearing to the court now here that the said John Jones decd. seized and possessed in his demesne as of fee of one tract of Land containing four hundred & fifty acres more or less, situated lying and being in the County of Giles, and State of Tennessee upon Richland Creek of Elk river, the same being the place upon which John Jones, lived and died, and the place where his widow now lives, and it being the opinion of the court that it is nessary for the purpose of satisfactory demands of the creditors of said John Jones decd. that said negroes and land should be sold by sd. administrators - It is therefore ordered by the court that the sd. administrators sell said negroes & land at publick sale to the highest bidder upon a credit of twelve months and that previously to said sale they gave notice thereof in some news paper printed in the Town of Columbia at least thirty days before said sale, and that said administrators make return of the amount of such sales to the next term of this court.

Ordered that Court be adjourned untill tomorrow morning nine oclock.

Jno. H. Camp
Jas. Perry
H. Hagen

P-422 Tuesday Morning 24th May 1825

Court met according to adjournment Present John H. Camp) Esquires Justice
                                            James Perry &) of the Peace for
                                            Henry Hagen) the County of
) Giles.

Robert W. Greene Assee &c Plt.)   In Debt
     Against   )
William H. Field . . . Deft.   )   From the Judgment of the court in
)   this case rendered the Defendant
prayed an appeal to the honorable the Circuit Court to be held for the County of Giles, and having executed bond and security as the law directs the same was granted him.

State of Tennessee)   Court of Pleas and Quarter Sessions May Term
)   1825.
Giles County   )
)   On this 24th day of May 1825 personally appeared in open court being a court of record for the County of Giles, James Philips, resident in sd. County aged Eighty five years, who being first duly sworn

according to law, doth on his oath make the following declaration in order to obtain the provisions made by the act of Congress of the 18th of March 1818, and and the 1st of May 1820, that he the said James Philips, enlisted for the term of fifteen months, on the . . . . . day of in the year . . . . . . the date not recalled, in the State of Virginia in the Company commanding by Captain John Powell in the Regiment commanded by Colonel John Flood Edwards in the line of the State of Virginia on the continental Establishments, that he continued to serve in the sd. Corps untill the Expiration - of his said term of service, when he was discharged from the said service in the State of Virginia - That he was in no battle except a Battle at the aforesaid place when he was discharged - That he was discharged by Genrl. John Crawford, & has had said discharge accidently consumed by fire and that he has no other evidence now in his power of his said Services - and in pursuance of an Act of the 1st of May 1820, I do Solemnly swear, that I was a resident citizen of the United States on the 18th day of March 1818, and that I have not since that time by gift sale or in any manner disposed of my property, or any part thereof with intent thereby so to diminish it as to bring myself within the provision of an Act of Congress, entitled an act to provide for certain persons engaged in the land and naval services of the United States - in the Revolutionary War - passed on the 18th of March 1818, & that I have not, nor has any person in trust for me, any property or security, contracts or debt, due to me, nor have I any interest other than (p-423) what is contained in the schedule hereto annexed & by me subscribed - Schedule of the property of the above declarant, I am by profession,(or rather when I was able) a cultivator of the earth - I am now altogether unable to pursue my profession, My wife who is near eighty years of age is the only member of my family, she is unable to contribute any thing to my support, as to my property except one bed, & one axe I have nothing.

                 his
              James   X   Philips
                Mark

Sworn to and declared on the 24th May 1825, in open court.

                German Lester Clerk

William Banks Plt.)   In Covenant
 Against   )
Wm. P. A. McCabe Deft.)   From the Judgment of the court in this case
)   rendered the Defendant prayed an appeal to
the honorable the Circuit Court to be held for the County of Giles, and having executed bond and Security as the law directs, the same was granted him.

John Abernathy Plt.)   In Debt
 Against   )
Robert Oliver Deft.)   This day came the parties aforesaid by their
)   attornies and thereupon the plaintiff demurres to the Defendants rejoinder being argued by the court now here fully understood. It is ordered by the court that sd. Demurres be sustained, and that said plaintiff recover against said Defendant five thousand dollars, the debt in the writing obligatory in the declaration mentioned, together with his costs by him about this suit in this behalf expended -
But the same is to be discharged by the payment of the damages by the Jury

in this cause in this court at this term assessed, and his costs by him about his suit in this behalf Expended.

Elizabeth Philips Plt.) In Debt
    Against)
Thomas B. Jones &) Defts   From the Judgment of the court in this
Thomas Harwood) case rendered the Defendants prayed
) an appeal to the honourable the Circuit court to be held for the County of Giles - and having executed bond and security as the Law directs, the same was granted him.

P-424   Tuesday 24th May 1825

William Worsham Plt.) In Case
    Against)
Ira C. Goff ... Deft.) This day came the parties by their
) attornies and thereupon came a Jury
of good and lawful men, towit, Thomas Wilkinson, Henry J. Cooper, Beverly B. Watson, Nathan Davis, William Bodenhamer, John Abernathy, Nathaniel Hammet, Thomas Bratton, Charles C. Abernathy, Henry McAnnick, George Barnes & William Roberts, who being elected tried and sworn well and truly to try the issue joined between the parties in this case upon their oaths do say that they find said issue in favour of the plaintiff, and assess his damages by occasion of the non performance of the cossumpsit in the declaration mentioned to one hundred & two dollars, besides costs.

It is therefore considered by the court that the plaintiff recover of said Defendant the damages aforesaid, in form aforesaid by the Jurors aforesd. assessed, and his costs about his suit in this behalf expended.

A Deed of conveyance from Nathaniel Young to Robert Oliver for fifty acres of land was produced in court and the Execution thereof acknowledged by the said Nathaniel Young and ordered to be certified for registration.

The Grand Jury returned into court the following Presentments, towit, The State against Henry Kimbrough, for obstructing Richland Creek - Same against Daniel Puryear, for neglect of duty as overseer of the road - Same against Matthew Johnston for neglect of duty as overseer of the road & withdrew to consider of further presentments.

John McAnnually Plt.) Sci - Fa -
    Against)
Edward D. Jones & Henry M. Newlin Deft) This day came the plaintiff by
) his attorney and the defendant
being solemnly called came not but made default, and it appearing to the satisfaction of the court that the Scire facias in this cause has been served upon them, and that they were the bail of James Read in the case of John McAnnally against said James Read in this court in which case said McAnnally recovered against said Read, the sum of two hundred & twenty dollars and twenty five cents, together with the sum of forty five dollars damages, and also nine dollars   (p-425)   thirty six and a half cents costs

at May term 1824 of said court as in said Scire facias is mentioned, and it also appearing to the Satisfaction of the court, that a capias adsatisfaci endemu issued upon said Judgment tested the third Monday in August 1824 upon said Judgment in due form of law, and that sd. Ca - Sa was afterward put into the hands of the Sheriff of Giles County, and by him returned to the November term 1824, of sd. court with the following endorsements, towit, that he had not found the body of the said James Read, in his County as his sd. Sci - fa - is presented - It is therefore considered by the court that said John McAnnally recover against said Edward D. Jones & Henry M. Newlin, bail of the aforesd. James Read, the aforesaid debt of two hundred & twenty dollars & twenty five cents together with the sum of forty five dollars damages with interest thereon at the rate of six persent per annum from the last day of May 1824 till this time together with the further sum of nine dollars thirty six & a half cents the costs in said Scia facias, mentioned, and also his costs by him about his suit in this behalf expended.

Ordered that Thomas Martin, James Buford & Charles Buford and Fountain Lester, or any three of them be appointed commissioners to settle with Lunsford M. Bramlitt & Elisha Eldridge, Executors of the Estate of Thomas H. Meredith decd. and that they make return thereof to the next term of this court.

John McAnnally Plt.) Sci - fa -
    Against)
Edward D. Jones &) Defts) From the Judgment of the court in this
Henry M. Newlin)) case rendered the Defendants prayed an
) appeal to the honorable the Circuit
Court to be held for the County of Giles and having executed bond and security as the Law directs, the same was Granted them.

The Grand Jury returned into court an Indictment of the State against Thomas Brown for wounding a horse and having nothing further to present were discharged.

Robert Smith Assee &c Plt.) In Debt
    Against)
Joseph Lucker and) Defts.) From the Judgment of the court in this
Elnathan G. Brown)) case rendered the Defendants prayed
) an appeal to the honorable the Circuit
Court to be held for the County of Giles, and having executed bond & security as the law directs the same was Granted them.

P-426 Tuesday 24th May 1824

William Gholson Plt.) Garnishment
    Against)
Lewis H. Brown Deft.) This day came again the parties by their attornies & thereupon the plaintiff moved the Court now here for Judgment against said Lewis H. Brown for the cash notes which he owes William Watson to be paid on the 25th December next & arengement of Counsel being thereupon had.

It is considered by the court that sd. plaintiff recover of said Lewis H. Brown the sum of five hundred & fifty dollars in cash notes to be paid, on or before the 25th of Decr. next and that he recover of said William Watson his costs by him about his Garnishment in this behalf expended.

William Parker Plt.) Motion
    Against)
John W. R. Graves Deft.) On motion of the plaintiff who suggested
) to the court now here, that he as Security of John W. R. Graves has been compelled to pay to Patrick H. Braden on the 11th May 1825 the Sum of seventy one dollars, and it not appearing to the court by the record produced, that said Parker was security for said John W. R. Graves, It is ordered by the court that a Jury be empannelled to ascertain whether said plaintiff did on the day aforesaid pay the sum aforesd. as Security of said John. W. R. Graves and thereupon came a Jury of good and Lawful men, Towit, William B. Brooks, John B. McCanlass, Robert Anderson, Walter Hill, John D. Riddell, Robert Adams, Daniel McCollum, Samuel S. Smith, Arthur M. M. Upshaw, William Jones, Claiborn Kyle & Elisha L. Kimbrough, who being elected tried and sworn, well & truly to try the facts aforesaid, upon their oaths do say that said sd. plaintiff did on the 11th May 1825, paid said Patrick M. Braden the sum of seventy one dollars as Security for said John W. R. Graves. It is therefore on motion of said plaintiff by Harris S. Fields his attornies considered by the court that said Wm. Parker recover of said John W. R. Graves said sum of seventy one dollars, with interest thereon from the 11th May 1825, till this time, and his costs by him about his motion in this behalf expended.

P-427   Tuesday 24th May 1825

William Gholson Plt.) Garnishment
    Against)
Robert Watson Deft.) This day came again the parties by their at-
) tornies and thereupon the plaintiff moved the court now here for Judgment against said Robert Watson for the sum of one hundred & fifty dollars which he owes Wm. Watson to be paid on 31st day of August 1825, & arangement of council being thereupon had.

It is considered by the court that said plaintiff recover of said Robert Watson the sum of one hundred & fifty dollars to be paid, on the 31st day of August 1825, and that he recover of sd. Wm. Watson, his costs by him about his Garnishment in this behalf expended – Execution to be stayed untill after the 31st August next.

John Abernathy Assee &c Plt.) In Debt
    Against)
Robert Oliver . . . . . Deft.) From the Judgment of the court in
) this case rendered the Defendant prayed an appeal to honorable the Circuit Court to be held for the County of Giles and having executed bond & security as the Law directs, the same was Granted him.

William Gholson Plt.) Garnishment
    Against)
Robert Watson Deft.) From the Judgment of the court in this case

rendered the defendant prayed an appeal to the honorable the Circuit Court to be held for the County of Giles, and having executed bond & Security as the law directs the same was granted him.

Ordered that court be adjourned untill court in course.

H. Hagen

A. Black

E. D. Jones

P-428 At a Court of Pleas and Quarter Sessions holden for the County of Giles at the court house of said County in the Town of Pulaski on the third Monday in August, being the fifteenth day thereof, in this year of our lord, one thousand Eight hundred & twenty five Present William Woods, James Dugger, William Brown, Thomas Harwood, Alexander Black, John Bramlitt, Robert Oliver, Thomas Marks, William B. Pepper, John H. Camp, James McCafferty, Hezekiah Jones, John Young, Paul Chiles, Willis S. McLaurine, William Ussery, Joseph Rea, John B. Armstrong, Edward D. Jones, Thomas Brown, James Perry, Peter Swanson, Robert Read, Thomas Batte, William Mayfield, Richd. McGee, Arthur Hicks, Ephriam M. Massie, Henry Hagen, & Thomas K. Gordon - Esquires Justice of the Peace of said County & Lewis H. Brown Sheriff of said County.

Ordered that the following tax list be received & the double tax thereon remitted, towit,

Jesse Beazley 260½ acres of land
3 Slaves -
Wm. H. Field - 4 Slaves -
1 Free poll
1 two wheel carriage

Silas Flournoy by his Guardian
William H. Field, 200 acres of land Estate of James Jones decd. 200 acres of land Estate of George Rice, 1 white poll.
Stephen Anderson 350 acres of land Estate of John Samuel decd. 210 acres of land.
Nathaniel Douglass 150 acres of land 2 slaves.

Sarah White 110 acres of land
Elizabeth L. Yancy, 250 acres of land
2 slaves
Josiah E. Maddox 174 acres of land
Samuel S. Peak 200 acres of land
Elizabeth Marks 2 Slaves
Rebecca Jones 450 Acres of land
7 Slaves
Charlotte Jones 150 acres of land
4 slaves
James Armstrong 161 Acres of land
1 Slave
William Bruden 100 Acres of land on Robertson Fork Creek.

P-429 Monday 15th August 1825

Ordered that Pascal Tarpley be released from the payment of tax on one thousand acres of land wrongfully listed to him for the year 1825 By the Justice.

Ordered that Reuben Freeman be released as a Jurors at the present term of this court.

Ordered that Robert Paine be appointed overseer of the road in the room of Edward Shelton resigned & that he have the same district of hands with the addition of the hands which live on the plantation of Dr. Charles Perkins.

A Deed of conveyance from Samuel Perkins to John Goodrum for fifty acres of land was produced in court, and the Execution thereof proven by the oaths of William Ussery & William James the witness thereto and ordered to be certified for registration.

A Deed of conveyance from James Neille to William Neille for fifty acres of land was produced in court & the execution thereof acknowledged by the said James Neille & ordered to be certified for registration.

An account of sale of the Estate of Henry Walker decd. was returned into court by the Executor Archer Jordon & ordered to be recorded.

An account of Sale of the Estate of William Wells decd. was returned into court by Robert Wells, administrator & ordered to be recorded.

Jacob Shall & Stirling &)
Lester, Merchants &c.   )   In Case
      Against   )
Josiah Davenport Deft.   )   This day came the parties by their attornies
)   & on motion of the plaintiffs this cause is
)   ordered to be dismissed.

It is therefore considered by the court that the defendant recover of the plaintiffs his costs by him about his defence in this behalf Expended.

Ordered that Tillman R. Daniel be appointed Guardian to Jesse Westmoreland decd. whereupon he executed bond and was qualified as the law directs.

Ordered that Tillman R. Daniel be appointed Guardian to Laban Westmoreland infant orphan of Reuben Westmoreland decd. whereupon he executed bond & was qualified as the Law directs.

P-430   Monday 15th August 1825

Ordered that Tillman R. Daniel Be appointed Guardian to Martha L. Westmoreland infant orphan of Reuben Westmoreland decd. whereupon he was qualified & gave bond & security, as the law directs.

A Deed of conveyance from James Bright & Thomas Philips to Elizabeth Ann Philips, for eighty acres of land was produced in court & the execution thereof proven by the oaths of Thomas W. Grubbs & Jeremiah Gibson the witnesses thereto, and ordered to be certified for registration.

On the petition of Daniel Puryear for the Division of a tract of land in Giles County being on the waters of Pigeon Roost Creek, which he claims by purchase from the heirs of Mary McDonald decd. and it appearing to the Satisfaction of the court that all other claimants as heirs of the said Mary have been duly notified of this application by a notice inserted in the Columbian a publick paper printed in Columbia Tennessee.

It is therefore ordered by the court that William Wood, Samuel H. Dodson, Jesse Pullen, William Pullen, Simpson H. White, Granville A. Pillow, and Thompson Johnson be appointed commissioners to lay off divide & assign to said Puryear five nineths and five eighths, of an undivided nineth of thirty nine acres of land. Begining at a dogwood & white oak on the east boundry line of a 5000 acre Survey, that Tyree Rodes lives on, the same being the north west corner of an Entry in the name of Woods, Puryear, West, & Philips for 509 acres, then East one hundred & fifty eight poles, with said 509 acres entry to a stake corner of the same thence north with said 509 acre Entry seventy five poles to poplar corner of the same in the South boundry line of a 2000 acre survey, made in the name of James M. Lewis, thence north with said Lewis's line one hundred and fifty eight poles to a Beech the east boundry line, of the aforesaid 5000 acres, thence south with the said line, seventy five poles to the Beginning - and that they make return thereof to this or the next term of this court.

On the petition of James Vance ordered that Henry Melton, James Vance, Isaac James, Isaac Majors, Isaac Smith, James Smith & Alexander Buford or any five of them be appointed a Jury of view a road starting at the County line near James Philips crossing Elk river at the Persimmon Island, from thence Upper Elkton, and see if it be proper to to view and mark out the same and make report thereof to the next term of this court.

P-431 Monday 15th August 1825.

Ordered that the hands of William Graves be added to the hands of Lewis B. Marks overseer of the road.

Ordered that Charles C. Abernathy Robert Buchannan, and John McDonald be appointed commissioners to settle with Allen Abernathy and Thomas Marks administrators of the Estate of Austin Smith Decd. & that they make report thereof to the next term of this court.

Ordered that Joseph Anthony, Edward D. Jones & Robert Black or any two of them be appointed commissioners to settle with the administrators of Zanus Martin decd. and that they make report thereof to the present term of this court.

A Deed of conveyance from Thomas Horn to Nancy Horn & Elizabeth Horn for sixty two acres of land was produced in court and the execution thereof proven by the oaths of John P. Taylor and Stephen Redding, the witnesses thereto, and ordered to be certified for registration.

The last will and testament of Martin Lane Decd. was produced in court and the execution thereof proven by the oaths of William Lane and John Gordon (to of the witnesses thereto, and ordered to be recorded. Whereupon Thomas Lane Senr. one of the Executors therein named appeared in court and was qualified, and gave bond and security as the law directs.

Ordered that James Eastman be appointed overseer of the road in the room of Eleazer Purviance resigned, and that he have the same district of hands.

Ordered that Hardy Benson be appointed constable in Captain Benson Company whereupon he executed bond & was qualified as the law directs.

Daniel Puryear came into court and resigned as constable in Captain Fillows Company, whereupon John W. B. Graves, was appointed constable in said Company, who gave bond & Security and was qualified as the law directs.

Ordered that James Hanna be appointed constable in Captain Gooches Company, who gave bond and Security & was qualified as the law directs.

Ordered that Samuel Faires be appointed constable in Captain Tiptons Company who gave bond & Security and was qualified as the law directs.

P-432   Monday 15th August 1825

Ordered that William Brownlow be appointed constable in Captain Ross's Company, who gave bond & security & was qualified as the law directs.

Ordered that John D. Reddell be appointed constable in Captain Hendrys Company, who gave bond & security as the law directs.

An Inventory and account of sale of the Estate of John Brandon decd. returned into court, and ordered to be recorded.

Ordered that William B. Graves be appointed constable in Captain Graves Company, who gave bond & security and was qualified as the law directs.

Ordered that Jesse Marlow be appointed constable in Captain McGees Company who gave bond and security and was qualified as the law directs.

Ordered that the following tax lists be received and the double tax thereon remitted, towit,

```
John P. Hickman    611 acres of land
James Smith        190 acres of land Bradshaw Creek
                   1 slave
                   1 white poll
```

Peter Lemons   150 acres of land.
                    1 Free poll.

A Bill of sale from Richard Jones & Mary Jones to Henry Hagen for certain property therein specified was produced in court & the execution, thereof proven by the oath of Mansfield Husband, the witness thereto, and ordered to be certified for registration.

Ordered that Tilmon R. Daniel Guardian of Jesse Westmoreland Laban Westmoreland & Martin L. Westmoreland, minor orphans of Reuben Westmoreland, decd. advertise and sell according to law the perishable property belonging to sd. minors, and that he make report thereof to the next term of this court.

Alexander Hood Plt.   )   Appeal
    Against   )
Tilmon Holland Deft.   )   This day came the plaintiff by his agent
)   and direct that this suit be discharged at
the costs of the defendant. It is therefore considered by the court that the plaintiff recover of sd. defendant his costs by him about his suit in this behalf expended.

P-433   Monday 15th August 1825

A Bill of sale from Joel Lane to Joseph Braden for certain property therein Specified was produced in court & proven by the oath of Richard H. Allen one of witnesses thereto, & ordered to be certified for registration.

A Deed of conveyance from Archibald Smith to Edward Lumpkin's for sixty two acres of Land was produced in court and the Execution thereof acknowledged by the said Archibald Smith and ordered to be certified for registration.

A Deed of conveyance from Edmund Lumpkins to Archibald Smith for Sixty two & a half acres of Land was produced in court and the Execution thereof acknowledged by the said Edmund Lumpkins & ordered to be certified for registration.

A Deed of conveyance from Edmund Lumpkins to Archibald Smith for forty two acres of land was produced in court and the Execution thereof acknowledged by the said Edmund Lumpkins and ordered to be certified for registration.

Ordered that E. Purvince, Thomas Maxwell, Early Benson, William A. Tompson, Joseph Goode, James Eastman and Hardy Benson or any five of them be appointed a Jury to view & see if it be proper to turn the road about one hundred yards, around Gardner Batte's house, on the road from Elkton to Fayetteville, and that they make report thereof to the next term of this court.

A Deed of conveyance from Samuel Muncrief to William Muncrief for Fifty three & one fourth acres of land was produced in court and the execution thereof acknowledged by the said Samuel Muncrief and ordered to be certified for registration.

Ordered that Joel Lane be appointed overseer of the road in the room of Soloman Tuttle removed from Elk Ridge to Robertson fork, & that he have the same district of hands.

Ordered that the County Trustee of this County pay to Robert McDonald the sum of twenty five dollars for the support & maintenance of Mrs. Elizabeth Miskill a pauper of this county for the term of six months from this time.

P-434   Monday 15th August 1825

Ordered that the County Trustee of this County pay to Richard McGee Esquire the sum of thirty dollars for the support and maintenance of Abram Bogard & wife Paupers of this county for twelve months from this time.

Made Deed of conveyance from Madison McLaurine to the children of William McLaurine for . . . .

A Deed of conveyance from Willis S. McLaurine and Robert McLaurine to Nancy McLaurine and children for one hundred and sixty seven acres of land was produced in court, and the Execution thereof acknowledged by the said Willis S. McLaurine, and Robert McLaurine and ordered to be certified for registration.

A Deed of Gift from Madison McLaurine to the Legal heirs of William McLaurine for certain property therein named was produced in court and the Execution thereof proven by the oath of Fountain Lester and Robert McLaurine the subscribing witness thereto and ordered to be certified for registration.

Ordered that the County Trustee of this County pay to Willis S. McLaurine Esquire the sum of Forty one dollars for the support and maintenance of James Hamilton a pauper of this County for twelve months from this time.

David M. Kerley an orphan boy is bound to Nathan Farmer, an Indenture to that Effect having been entered to file.

Ordered that Stirling Harwell be notified to attend on Monday next to shew cause why Reason Harwell an apprentice boy heretofore bound to him, shall not be taken away from him.

The Jury who were appointed to view a road the nearest & best way from the Shelbyville road near Thomas P. Estes, where said road crosses the main branch or fork of Pigeon roost creek, from thence to Parks Baileys Mill, from thence the nearest and best way to intersect the road leads by Tyree Rodes to Mayfield Mill, made return thereof which is ordered to be established according to the report of said Jury.

Ordered that David Maxwell be appointed to oversee the cutting out the road leading down Pigeon Roost Creek to begin where it intersects the Shelbyville road, near Thomas P. Estes, to (p-435) Elisha Dodsons, and that he have under his direction for that purpose all the hands that live on the waters of Pigeon Roost Creek East of said Columbia Road.

Ordered that William Pullen be appointed to oversee the cutting out a road leading down Pigeon roost creek from Elisha Dodsons to where it is to terminate and that he have under his direction for that purpose all the hands that live on the waters of Pigeon roost Creek west from where the sd. Pullen is to begin.

Ordered that John Phillips, Archibald McKissack, Thomas B. Haynie and Henry Hagen or any two of them be appointed commissioners to settle with the executors of Reese Porter Senr. decd. and that they make report of said settlement to this or the ensuing term of this court.

Ordered that Monday next be set apart for County Business.

John Young who was heretofore appointed School Commissioner according to act of Assembly appeared in court and was qualified and gave bond & security as the law directs.

Ephraim M. Massie who was heretofore appointed School Commissioner according to Act of Assembly appeared in court and was qualified and gave bond & security as the law directs.

Ordered that an order of sale issue to Thomas Brown administrator of the Estate of Jordon Hicks decd. commanding him to advertise & sell according to Law, the land belonging to the said Estate for the purpose of making a division - between the heirs & distributers of sd. Jordon Hicks decd. and that he make report thereof to the next term of this court.

The commissioners who were appointed to settle the Estate of Zanue Martin decd. returned said settlement into court which is ordered to be recorded.

Ordered that Joseph Anthony and Samuel day be appointed administrator of the Estate of Zanue Martin decd. Whereupon they were qualified and gave bond and Security as the Law directs.

Ordered that Samuel Love be appointed Guardian to Francis Martin, Susan Martin & Thomas Martin, minor children of Zanus Martin decd. whereupon he executed bond and security as the Law directs.

P-436   Monday 15th August 1825

Francis Smith & Plts.)   Petition
James Kimbrough   )
    Against   )   This day came the parties by their proper
Jordon Massie & Defts.)   persons, and it appearing to the Satisfaction
James Martin Admrs.   )   of the court that the Petitioners have been
)   released from all future liability as securities for the Defendants. It is therefore ordered by the court that this suit be dismissed, and that the petitioners recover of the defendants their costs by them about their suit in this behalf expended.

Ordered that the following tax list be received and the double tax thereon remitted, Towit,

German Lester   1 Free poll
                    8 Slaves
                    348 Acres of land in 4 tracts
                    5 Town lots
                    1 - 2 wheel pleasure carriage
Thomas Haynes   2 Town lots
Robert C. Foster   1 Town lot
Geo. & Jacob Lindenburgess & others 1 Town lot.
Henry Roberts   6 Town lots.
Bamester Hatchett   4 Town lots.
Peter Bass   4 Town lots.

Deed of conveyance from Thomas Harwood to Thomas Batte for a small parcal of land & four Town lots in Upper Elkton was produced in court and the Execution thereof acknowledged by the said Thomas Harwood and ordered to be certified for registration.

Ordered that court be adjourned untill tomorrow morning nine oclock.

                                        A. Black
                                        Jno. H. Camp
                                        James Dugger

P-437   Tuesday Morning 16th August 1825

Court met according to adjournment Present Alexander Black) Esquire Jus-
                                        John H. Camp   ) tices of the
                                        James Dugger   ) Peace for the
) County of Giles.

The Sheriff of County returned into court the names of the following persons Summoned to attend as Grand and petit Jurors at this term, Pursuant to an order of the last term of this court a copy of which issued to the sd. Sheriff of Giles County, towit, Younger Hobson, John McAnnick, Gilliam Harwell, Solomon Simmons, Jr., David L. Jones, Josiah Eaves, Alexander Stinson, Williams James, Walter Looke, George M. Gibson, Jonathan Moody, Hugh Long, Samuel Kerr, Robert B. Harney, Reuben Freeman, Joseph Goode, Thomas Wells, Levi Sherrell, Lewis Williamson, James McDonald, George Everly, Robert Black, Benjamin M. Scoggin, John B. Goldberry, Jesse West, and Henry Phenix, of whom John Goldberry foreman, Hugh Long, Solomon Simmons Jr., Thomas Wells, George M. Gibson, Gilliam Harwell, William James, Robert B. Harney, Josiah Eaves, Levi Sherrell, Jesse West, Younger Hobson & Lewis Williamson, were Elected Empanneled & sworn a Grand Jury of inquest for the body of this County, who having received their charge withdrew to consider of their presentments.

Benjamin Williams a constable of this County was sworn to attend on the Grand Jury at the present term of this court.

Samuel Y. Anderson, who was heretofore appointed School commissioner according to Act of Assembly, appeared in court and was qualified and gave bond and security as the law direct.

A Bill of sale from James Perry Sheriff of Giles County to German Lester for certain property therein Specified was produced in court and the execution thereof acknowledged by the sd. James Perry as aforesaid and ordered to be certified for registration.

Ordered that Henry Phenix be released from service as a Juror at the present term of this court.

A Bill of sale from James Baugh to German Lester for certain property therein specified was produced in court and the execution thereof proven by the oath of Thomas Martin, the witness thereto, and ordered to be certified for registration.

P-438 Tuesday 16th August 1825

At least five Justices being present William Finn returned into court one wolf scalp under four months old, one over four months old, which were ordered to be burnt.

A Deed of conveyance from Nathaniel Davis to Edward Poteet for thirty acres of land was produced in court and the Execution thereof proven by the oaths of James Patteson & Charles W. Wilcox two of the witnesses thereto and ordered to be certified for registration.

A Deed of conveyance from Edward Poteet & Daniel Ezell to German Lester, for thirty acres of land was produced in court and the Execution thereof

335

proven by the oath of James Patteson and Charles W. Willcox two of the witnesses thereto, and ordered to be certified for registration.

Alexander Black Esquire was elected County Trustee for this County whereupon he was qualified, and gave bond and security as the law directs.

Ordered that James McDonald & Joseph Goode be released from service as Jurors at the present term of this court.

Ordered that the County Trustee of this County pay to Alexander Black the sum of seven dollars & Eighty cents for furnishing agreably to the directions of a former order of this county a crowbar & Stone hammer for the use of this County.

Ordered that the following tax list be received and the double tax thereon remitted, Towit, Jeremiah Parker, 1 Town lot.

John Bradley . . . Plt.   )   In Case
    Against   )
William D. Jennings Deft.) This day came the parties by their attornies and thereupon came a Jury of good and lawful men, Towit, Benjamin M. Scoggin, Robert Black, Robert Brooks, Isaac Chrisman, John R. Abernathy, Ambrose Cobbs, John Abernathy, John Brown, Henry T. Croft, Henry McKay, William Roberts, and Henry Yancy, who being elected tried and sworn well and truly to try the issue joined between the parties in this case and having had the evidence and part of argument of counsel, were permitted to disperse to meet again tomorrow morning nine oclock.

P-439 Tuesday 16th August 1825

On motion of the Solicitor General it is ordered by the court that Judgment be, & is hereby rendered against the County of Giles in behalf of those claiming on the part of the State in the following State cases, the defendants being convicted, and upon execution, nothing being made out of them, towit, at May 1818 State Vs Samuel Croft, 1818, August – State Against Brice M. Mayfield, same against Henry M. Mayfield, 1819, August. Same against William Perry, 1820, February – Same against David Graves, August 1820, Same against John Simpson 1821 May – Same against Andrew Blythe 1822, May – Same against Larkin Mayfield, 1822, August, Same against Martin Adkins Novr. 1822 – Same against Meredith Thacker, Same against Senior Higgs 1823, February – Same against Christaina Mercer, 1823, August – Same against Edward K. McMullin, 1824 February, Same against James Cobbs, Same against John Pillow, and that the Clerk certify the same to the Trustee of this County for payment.

Ordered that court be adjourned untill tomorrow morning 9 oclock.

                                                    James Perry
                                                   Thomas Brown
                                                   A. Black

P-440 Wednesday Morning 17th August 1825

Court met according to adjournment Present James Perry) Esquires Justices
             Thomas Brown) of the Peace for
             Alexander Black) Giles County.

 Samuel Y. Anderson Guardian of Archer White, returned into court an account current against his said ward which is ordered to be recorded.

 A Deed of conveyance from George W. Campbell to Ambrose Yarbrough for twenty Eight acres & one hundred and twenty three and a half poles of land was produced in court and the execution thereof proven by the oaths of Alexander Esselman and Alexander Stinson, the witnesses thereto, and is ordered to be certified for registration.

 The Grand Jury returned into court a Presentment of the State against Francis Mayberry for an affray with & an sault & battery on the body of John W. Graves, also a presentment the same against John W. Graves for an affray with & an assault & battery on the body of Francis Mayberry.

James P. McConnel Plt.)   Appeal
 Against   )
John Maclin Deft.   ) This day came the parties by their attorney
) and thereupon it being suggested to the court
that Judgment was rendered in this case by the magistrate on the 26th day of July 1823, and that an appeal was taken in proper time, and filed in the office, of this court and has been mislaid.
 It is thereupon adjudged & ordered by the court that the case be entered on the docket nunc pro tunce, and that Scire Facias issue against the administrator of John Maclin, returnable to the next term of this court.

John Bradley Plt.   )   In Case
 Against   )
William D. Jennings Deft.) This day came the parties by their
) attornies and thereupon came the Jury
who were sworn on yestoday well & truly to try the issue Joined between the parties in this case, who after having heard the balance of the argument of counsel, retired out of court to consider of their verdict, and after some time returned & say they cannot agree, and by consent sd. Jurors are again permitted to disperse to meet tomorrow morning ten oclock.

P-441 Wednesday 17th August 1825

Hannah Underwood Plt.)   In Case
 Against   )
Lyddall Wilkinson Deft.) This day came the parties by their attor-
) nies and thereupon came a Jury of good
and lawful men, Towit, Alexander Stinson, Walter Locke, George Everly, Edward M. Brown, Samuel S. Smith, Samuel Wise, William Snow, William Mick,

James B. Bostick, Joshua Horne, William Smith, & James Kelly, who being elected tried and sworn well and truly to try the issue joined between the parties in this case, and having heard part of the evidence in this case were permitted to disperse to meet again tomorrow morning nine oclock.

A Bill of sale from Claibourn Kyle administrator of William Kyle decd. to David Cunningham for certain property therein specified was produced in court and the execution thereof proven by the oaths of Thomas Martin the witness thereto and ordered to be certified for registration.

An Inventory of the Estate of John Rawlins decd. returned by Charles Buford Administrator & ordered to be recorded.

A Deed of conveyance from Bernard M. Patteson and Nancy A. Patteson his wife, to Gilbert D. Taylor for one hundred & sixty acres of land was produced in court and the execution thereof acknowledged by the said Bernard M. Patteson and thereupon Henry Hagen & Thomas Brown Esquires, Justices of the Peace for this County were appointed to take the privy examination of said Nancy A. Patteson touching the examination of said deed, and return the same into court instanter.

On the Petition of James H. Pickens ordered that Writs of Certiorari and Supercedeas issue to stay proceedings & remove to this court the record of a Judgment rendered by Joseph Rhea Esquire an acting Justice of the Peace for Giles County in favor of John Mayfield against said James H. Pickens on the 31st day of March 1825, for the Sum of sixty eight dollars & 12½ cents & costs - on the petitioners giving bond and security according to Law.

Aaron Anglin Plaintiff)   In Case
    Against   )
Edward M. Tipton Defendant) This day came the plaintiffs by his
) attorney as also the Defendant in his
proper person who saith he cannot gainsay the plaintiffs action - him nor but that he doth owe him (p-442) the sum of ten dollars & costs.
It is therefore with the assent of the plaintiff considered by the court that the plaintiff recover of said defendant the said sum of ten dollars together with his costs by him about his suit in this behalf expended.

Aaron Anglin Plt.   )   In Covenant
    Against   )
Edmund W. Tipton Deft.) This day came the plaintiff by his attorney
) as also the defendant in his proper person
who saith he cannot gainsay the plaintiffs action against him nor but that he doth owe him the sum of ten dollars besides costs. It is therefore with the assent of the plaintiff, considered by the court, that the plaintiff recover of sd. defendant the said sum of ten dollars in form aforesaid agreed, and also his costs by him about his suit in this behalf expended.

Ordered that court be adjourned untill tomorrow morning nine oclock.

Thomas Brown
W. B. Pepper
James Dugger

P-443   Thursday 18th August 1825

Court met according to adjournment Present Thomas Brown) Esquire Justice
                                            William B. Pepper) of the Peace
                                            James Dugger   ) for Giles County.

Henry Hagen & Thomas Brown Esquires who were appointed on yesterday to take the privy examination of Nancy A. Patteson to a Deed of conveyance from Bernard M. Patteson & sd. Nancy A. Patteson his wife to Gilbert D. Taylor for one hundred and sixty acres of land, this day made return of sd. Examination - and the same is ordered to be certified.

The State Plt.   ) Upon a presentment for an affray with & an
   Against   ) assault & battery on the body of John W.
Francis Mayberry Deft.) Graves.

This day came the Solicitor General for the State, as also the defendant in his proper person who being charged on the presentment in this case pleads guilty, and because he will not contend with the State agrees to submit himself to the Justice and mercy of the court - It is therefore considered by the court that he will make his fine with the State to the amount of six and one fourth cents, and that he pay the costs of this presentment, and that he be committed to the custody of the Sheriff of this County there to remain till said fine & costs be paid, or that he give security for the payment of the same, and thereupon came John W. Graves & Lewis H. Brown, and undertook as security for said defendant. It is therefore considered by the court that the State recover of said Defendant & John W. Graves & Lewis H. Brown his securities the fine and costs aforesaid.

The State Plt.   ) Upon a presentment for an affray with & an
   Against   ) assault & battery of the body of Francis
John W. Graves Deft.) Mayberry.

This day came the Solicitor General for the State as also the Defendant in his proper person - who being charged on the presentment in this case pleads guilty, and because he will not contend with the State agrees to submit himself to the Justice and mercy of the court. It is therefore considered by the court that he make his fine with the State to the amount of six and one fourth cents, and that he pay the costs of this presentment, and that he be committed to the custody of the Sheriff of this County thereto remain till said fine & cost be paid, or that he give security for the payment of the same, and thereupon came Francis Mayberry custody of the Sheriff of this County thereto remain till said find and costs be paid, or that he give security for the payment of the same, and thereupon came Gerald Irby and undertook as security for sd. Defendant, It is therefore considered by the court that the State recover of sd. Defendant and Gerald Irby his security the fine and costs aforesaid.

339

The State Plt.) Upon a presentment for neglect of duty as
   Against   ) overseer of the road.
Buckner Madra Deft.)
) This day came the Solicitor General for the
State as also the Defendant in his proper person who being charged on the
presentment in this case pleads guilty, and because he will not contend
with the State agrees to submit himself to the Justice & mercy of the court.
It is therefore considered by the court that he make his (p-445) fine
with the State to the amount of twelve and a half cents, and that he pay
the costs of this presentment and that he be committed to the custody of
the Sheriff of this County thereto remain till said fine and costs be paid,
or that he give security for the payment of the same and thereupon came
John McCormack, & Richd. H. Blow, and undertook as securitys for said defendants. It is therefore considered by the court that the State recover
of said Defendant and John McCarmack & Richard H. Blow his Securities the
fine & costs aforesaid.

The State Plt.) Upon a presentment for neglect of duty as
   Against   ) overseer of the road -
John Menefee Deft.)
) This day came the Solicitor General for the
State as also the Defendant in his proper person who being charged on
the presentment in this case pleads guilty and because he will not contend with the State agrees to submit himself to the Justice and mercy of
the court.
    It is therefore considered by the court that he make his fine with the
State to the amount of twelve and a half cents, and that he pay the cost
of this presentment.

The State Plt.) Upon a Presentment for neglect of duty as
   Against   ) overseer of the road.
John H. Camp Deft.)
) This day came the Solicitor General for the
State as also the Defendant in his proper person, who being charged on
the presentment in this case pleads guilty and because he will not contend
with the State agrees to submit himself to the Justice and mercy of the
court.
    It is therefore considered by the court that he make his fine with the
State to the amount of twelve and a half cents, and that he pay the costs
of this presentment.

The State Plt.) Upon a Presentment for nelect of duty as
   Against   ) overseer of the road.
Edmund Shelton Deft.)
) This day came the Solicitor General for
the State as also the Defendant in his proper person who being charged
on the presentment in this case pleads guilty & because he will not contend with the State agrees to submit himself to the Justice & mercy of the
court.
    It is therefore considered by the court that he make his fine with the
State to the amount of twelve & a half cents, and that he pay the costs
of this presentment.

P-446   Thursday 18th August 1825.

The State Plt.) Upon an Indictment for an affray with & an
  Against   ) assault & battery on the bodies of W. G. Paine
Jarret Long Deft.) & Ed. Hardin.

This day came the Solicitor General for the State as also the defendant in his proper person, who being charged on the Indictment in this case, pleads guilty, and because he will not contend with the State agrees to submit himself to the Justice and mercy of the court.

It is therefore considered by the court that he make his fine with the State to the amount of Five dollars and that he pay the costs of this prosecution - and that he be committed to the custody of the Sheriff of this County there to remain till said fine and cost be paid, or that he give security for the payment of the same, and thereupon came George I. Jordon who undertook as security for said Defendant.

It is therefore considered by the court that the State recover of sd. Defendant & George I. Jordon his Security the fine & cost aforesaid.

The State Plt.) Upon an Indictment for an affray with & an
  Against   ) assault & battery on the body of Bailey
David Stockton Deft.) Davis.

This day came the Solicitor General as also the defendant in his proper person - who being charged on the Indictment in this case pleads guilty, and because he will not contend with the State agrees to submit himself to the Justice & mercy of the court - It is therefore considered by the court that he make his (p-447) fine with the State to the amount of fifteen dollars, and that he pay the cost of this prosecution, and that he be committed to the custody of the Sheriff of this County there to remain till said fine and costs be paid.

The State Plt.) Upon a presentment for obstructing nava-
  Against   ) gation.
David Stockton Deft.)

This day came the Solicitor General for the State as also the defendant in his proper person, who being charged on the presentment in this case pleads guilty, and because he will not contend with the State agrees to submit himself to the Justice and mercy of the court.

It is therefore considered by the court that he make his fine with the State to the amount of ten dollars, and that he pay the cost of this presentment - and that he be committed to the custody of the Sheriff of this County thereto remain till said fine and costs are paid.

The State Plt.) Sci Fa -
  Against   )
Baker P. Potts Deft.) This day came as well the Solicitor General for the State as also the Defendant in his proper person, and for reasons shewn to the court by sd. defendant it is ordered that he be discharged from the forfeiture heretofore taken against him, on the payment of all costs, and that he be committed to the custody of the sheriff of this county there to remain till sd. costs be paid, or that he give security for the payment of the same and thereupon David Stockton came into court and undertook for sd. Defendant - It is therefore considered by the court that the State recover of sd. Deft & David Stockton his Security the costs aforesaid.

The State Plt. Against David Stockton Deft.	Sci - Fa -

This day came as well the Solicitor General for the State as also the Defendant in his proper person & for reasons shewn to the Court by sd. Defendant it is ordered that he be discharged from the forfeiture heretofore taken against him, on the payment of all costs, and that execution thereof be awarded against him, and that he be committed to the custody of the Sheriff of this County thereto remain till sd. costs be paid - or that he give security for the payment of the same & thereupon came Baker P. Potts, and undertook for sd. Defendant, It is therefore considered by the court that the State recover of sd. defendant and Baker B. Potts his security the costs aforesaid.

P-448 Thursday 18th August 1825

The State Plt. Against William D. Black Deft.	Upon an Indictment for an affray & an assault & battery on the body of William A. Brown.

This day came the Solicitor General for the State as also the defendant in his proper person, who being charged on the presentment in this case, pleads guilty and because he will not contend with the State agrees to submit himself to the Justice and mercy of the court.

It is therefore considered by the court that he make his fine with the State to the amount of twelve and a half cents and that he pay the costs of this presentment.

The State Plt. Against Annanias Oliver Deft.	Upon an Indictment for an affray with & an assault & battery on the body of Tilmon Daniel.

This day came the Solicitor General for the State as also the Defendant in his proper person, who being charged on the Indictment in this case pleads guilty and because he will not contend with the State agrees to submit himself to the Justice and mercy of the court.

It is therefore considered by the court that he make his fine with the State to the amount of twenty five dollars, and that he pay the costs of this prosecution and that he be committed to the custody of the Sheriff of this county thereto remain till said cost & fine is paid, or that he give security for the payment of the same, and thereupon came Lewis B. Marks who undertook as Security for sd. Defendant. It is therefore considered by the court that the State recover of sd. Defendant & Lewis B. Marks, his Security the fine & costs aforesaid.

The State Plt. Against Young Chambly Deft.	Upon an Indictment for disturbing public Worship.

Mansfield Husbands came into court and acknowledged himself indebted to the State of Tennessee in the sum of one hundred dollars to be levied of his goods & chattles lands & tenments to the use of the State to be void on condition that he appear here from day to day at this term and prosecute & give evidence on the behalf of the State against said defendant & not depart without leave of this court.

The State Plt.) Upon an Indictment for an affray with & an
   Against) assault & battery on the body of Bailey Davis.
Davis Stockton Deft.)
) Bailey Davis & Reuben Hardy came into court
& acknowledged themselves indebted to the State of Tennessee each in the
sum of one hundred dollars to be levied of their goods & chattles lands
& Tenments to the use of State to be void on condition that the said Bailey
Davis appear here on the fourth day of our next November Court, & prosecute & give Evidence on behalf of the State against sd. Defendant on above
charge & not depart without leave of the court.

P-449   Thursday 18th August 1825

The State . . . Plt.) Upon an Indictment for an affray with &
   Against) an assault & battery on the body of Isaac
Benjn. S. England Deft.) Reynolds.
)
         This day came as well the Solicitor General for the State as also the defendant in his proper person who being
charged on the Indictment in this case pleads guilty and because he will
not contend with the State agrees to submit himself to the Justice and
mercy of the court.
    It is therefore considered by the court that he make his fine with
the State to the amount of five dollars, and that he pay the costs of
this prosecution - and that he be committed to the custody of the Sheriff
of this county there to remain till said fine & costs be paid.

The State Plt.) Upon a presentment for neglect of duty
   Against) as overseer of the road -
Matthew Johnson Deft.)
) This day came as well the Solicitor General for the State as also the defendant in his proper person - who being
charged on the presentment in this case pleads guilty and because he will
not contend, with the State agrees to submit himself to the Justice &
mercy of the court. It is therefore considered by the court that he make
his fine with the State to the amount of six & one fourth cents, and that
he pay the costs of this presentment.

The State Plt.) Upon an Indictment for making assault on the
   against) body of Henry Steele.
James Simmons Deft.)
     Henry A. Steele came into court and acknowledged himself Indebted to the State of Tennessee, in the sum of one hundred dollars to be levied of his goods & chattles lands and tenments to
the use of the State to be void on condition that he appear here on the
first Thursday after the third Monday in November next and prosecute &
give evidence on behalf of the State against said Defendant on the aforesd.
charge and not depart without leave of the court.

    The Grand Jury returned into court the following Indictments Towit,
The State against David Stockton, for an affray with & an assault & battery on the body of Bailey Davis, on which is indorsed "A true Bill" the

Same against Young Chambly for disturbing publick worship, on which is indorsed "A true Bill." the same against Parsons Evans for feloniarley taking one glass tumbler on which is indorsed "not a true Bill" and withdrew to consider of further presentments.

P-450 Thursday 18th August 1825

William B. & Peter Martin Plts.)   In Debt
    Against   )
Ephriam Evans Deft.   ) This day came as well the plain-
) tiff by their attorney as the
Defendant in his proper person, and said Defendant saith he cannot gainsay the plaintiffs action against nor but that he doth owe them the sum of one hundred dollars the amount of the debt in the Writing obligatory in the declaration mentioned, and that the plaintiffs have sustained damages by reason of the detention of sd. debt to the amount of Five dollars and seventy five cents and agree that Judgment may be entered up against him in favor of the plaintiffs for the amount of said debt and Damages together with their costs - It is therefore with the assent of the plaintiffs considered by the court that the plaintiffs recover of the defendants the amount of their debt aforesaid, together with their damages aforesaid, In form aforesaid agreed and their costs by them about their suit in this behalf expended.

Isaac & James Sitler Plts.   )   In Debt
    Against   )
Henry Goldsberry Deft.   ) This day came as well the plaintiffs
) by their attorney as the Defendant
in his proper person, & said defendant saith he cannot gainsay the plaintiffs action against him nor but that he doth owe them the sum of one hundred and twenty seven dollars and forty cents, the amount of the debt in the writing obligatory in the declaration mentioned, and that the plaintiffs have sustained damages by reason of the detention of said debt to the amount of thirteen dollars & eighty cents, and agrees that Judgment May be entered up against him in favor of the plaintiffs for the amount of said Debt, and Damages together with costs. It is therefore with the assent of the plaintiffs considered by the court that the plaintiffs recover of the defendant the amount of their debt aforesaid, together with their damages aforesaid in form aforesaid, agreed and their costs by them about their suit in this behalf expended, Execution stayed till 25th Decr. 1825.

On motion of Daniel Puryear, and It appearing to the satisfaction of the court that in a petition by the sd. Puryear to this court for the purpose of having petition made in a tract of land lying on Pigeon Roost Creek, containing 39 acres of deed by Wm. Wood to the heirs of Mary Donaldson decd. in which said Puryear claims by virtue of a purchase from said heirs five ninths & five eighths of an undivided ninth of thirty nine acres of land, and that   (p-451) in the petition of said Puryear a mistake in the notes & boundries of said land is made. It is therefore considered & adjudged by the court that the order of February Term 1825 revived at this Term appointing commissioners to make partition of said Land as set out in the notes & boundries of sd. land in said petition contained and assign to said petitioners his part thereof be altered & amended so as to insert in the order the following notes & boundries in the place of those contained in the original order as prayed for in said petitionous petition, (Towit, Beginning at a Stake in Daniel Puryears line, the corner of Puryears land which is a corner to a 509 acre tract then north 75 poles to a poplar corner of a 509 acre survey in the South boundry line of a 2000 acre survey granted to James M. Lewis thence West with Lewis line $83\frac{1}{4}$ poles to a Beech, thence South 75 poles to a hickory in the north boundry line of said 509 acre survey thence east to the Beginning containing 39 acres more or less.

John Bradley .... Plt.) In Case
    Against)
William D. Jennings Deft.) This day came the parties by their
) attornies, and thereupon came the
Jury who were Sworn well and truly to try the issue joined between the parties in this case, who upon their oaths do say that they find said issue in favor of the plaintiff and assess his damages by reason of the Declaration mentioned to two hundred and twenty two Dollars & seventy seven cents — besides costs.

It is therefore considered by the court that the plaintiff recover against said Defendant the damages aforesaid in form aforesd. by the Jurors aforesaid, assessed and also his costs by him about his suit in this behalf expended — From which Judgment the defendant prayed an appeal to the honorable the Circuit Court to be held for the County of Giles, and having Executed bond and Security as the Law directs the same was granted him.

Hannah Underwood Plt.) In Case
    Against)
Lydall Wilkinson Deft.) This day came the parties by their at-
) tornies and thereupon came the Jury who
were sworn on yestoday well & truly to try the issue joined between the parties in this case, and having heard the balance of the evidence and part of the argument of counsel were permitted to dispurse to meet again tomorrow morning Eight oclock.

Ordered that court be adjourned till tomorrow morning Eight oclock.

                                                        H. Hagen
                                                        Thos. K. Gordon
                                                        W. B. Pepper

P-452   Friday Morning 19th August 1825

Court met according to adjournment Present Henry Hagen) Esquire Justice
                                                          Thomas H. Gordon &) of the Peace for
                                                          William B. Pepper) Giles County.

On motion of Lewis H. Brown Sheriff of Giles County, John Brown was sworn to act as his deputy at the present Term of this court.

345

Ordered that the following tax list be received and the double tax thereon remitted, towit,
Elisha Bradley   1 Free poll
Beazley Ingram   1 Free poll
Samuel Hampton)
Thomas Hampton) 239 acre of land
Tarlton Logan 100 acres of land.

Hannah Underwood Plt.   )   In Case
    Against   )
Lydall Wilkinson Deft.   ) This day came the parties by their attor-
) nies and thereupon came a Jury who were
sworn on a former day of this term to try the issue joined between the parties in this case, and having heard the balance of the argument retired out of court to consider of their virdict after some time returned & say they cannot agree and by consent they were permitted to disperse to meet again tomorrow morning nine oclock.

At least five Justice being present James B. Kimbro returned into court, two wolf scalps, under four months old, which were ordered to be burnt.

Ordered that James Gunter be appointed administrator of the Estate of Samuel Gunter, decd. whereupon he entered into bond and security & was qualified as the Law directs.

Heirs of Samuel Cox Plt.   )   Petition
    Against   )
Andreson Hogan Admr. &c Deft.   ) This day came the plaintiffs in
) their proper person and ordered
that this suit be dismissed at their costs - It is therefore considered by the court that the defendant recover of said plaintiffs his costs by him about his defence in this behalf expended.

A deed of conveyance from John McCracken to James Perry for Lot No. 34 in Pulaski was produced   (p-453)   in court and the execution thereof by the oaths of John W. Perry & Edward W. Rose, the subscribing witnesses thereto, and ordered to be certified for registration.

The State Plt.   ) Upon an Indictment for an affray with & an
    Against   ) assault & battery on the body of Wm. Wor-
William Webb Deft.   ) sham.
)
William Worsham came into court and acknowledged himself indebted to the State of Tennessee in the sum of one hundred dollars, to the use of the State to be void on condition that he appear here on the first Thursday after the third Monday in November next, to prosecute & give evidence on behalf of the State against sd. Defendant on the aforesd. charge & not depart without leave of the court.

The Grand Jury returned into court the following Indictments, towit, The State against William Webb for an affray with & an assault & battery on the body of Wm. Worsham on which is indorsed "a true Bill" and withdrew to consider of further presentment.

The State Plt.) Upon an Indictment for Gambling -
   Against)
Ira C. Goff, Deft.) This day came the Solicitor General for the State as also the defendant in his proper person who being charged on the indictment in this case pleads not guilty, and for his trial puts himself upon his country and the Solicitor General for the State Likewise therefore Let a Jury come who as well &c to recognize &c and thereupon came a Jury, Towit, John B. Goldsberry, Hugh Long, Solomon Simmons, Junr., Thomas Wells, George M. Gibson, Wm. James, Robert B. Harney Josiah Evans, Levi Sherrell, Jesse West, Younger Hobson & Lewis Williamson, who being elected tried and sworn well and truly to try the issue of traverse between the State and said defendant who upon their oaths do say that the defendant is not guilty in manner and form as he is charged in the indictment. It is therefore considered by the court that the Defendant be acquitted and discharged from the aforesaid charged, & that he go hence without day.

The State Plt.) Upon an Indictment for gambling.
   Against)
Ira C. Goff Deft.) The defendant in this case having been acquitted on a trial on the merits, by a Jury - It is (p-454) Therefore considered by the court that a Judgment be entered against the County of Giles in favor of the Several Claimants, on the part of the State for all costs to which they are entitled and that the clerk certify the same to the Trustee of Giles County for payment.

The State Plt.) Upon an Indictment for Gambling -
   Against)
Ira C. Goff Deft.) John Pate Junr., who was summoned to attend at this term and give evidence in behalf of the State in this case being solemnly called came not but made default. It is therefore ordered ordered by the court that a Judgment Ni - Si be entered up against the defendant, in favor of the State for the sum of one hundred and twenty five dollars, according to his Subpouna, and that a Scire facias issue against him returnable to the next term of this court.

The State Plt.) Upon an Indictment for disturbing Publick
   Against) worship.
Young Chambley Deft.)
) This day came as well the Solicitor General for the State as also the Defendant in his proper person who being charged on the Indictment in this case, pleads guilty and because he will not contend with the State agrees to submit himself to the Justice and mercy of the court - It is therefore considered by the court that he make his fine with the State to the amount of five dollars and that he pay the costs of this prosecution, and that he be committed to the custody of the Sheriff

of this County there to remain till said fine & cost be paid, or that he give Security for the payment of the same, and thereupon came Aaron Brown, John Abernathy, William C. Flournoy, John H. Rivers, Lewis Smith, & James Appleby, who undertook as security for said Defendant. It is therefore considered by the court that the State recover of said defendant and Aaron Brown, John Abernathy, William C. Flournoy, John H. Rivers, Lewis Smith, & James Appleby, his Securities the fine & cost as aforesaid.

The State Plt.) Upon a presentment for neglect as overseer
   Against   ) of the road.
Daniel Puryear Deft.)
) This day came the Solicitor General for the State who saith he wishes no further to prosecute the Defendant in this case. It is therefore ordered by the court that a nole prosqui be entered in this case, and that the Defendant go hence without day.

P-455 Friday 19th August 1825

The State ... Plt.) Upon a presentment for neglect of duty as
   Against   ) overseer of the road.
Daniel Puryear Deft.)
) A Nole Prosqui having been entered up in this case under the directions of the court. It is ordered that Judgment be entered up against the County of Giles in favour of the several claimants on the part of the State for all costs to which they are entitled, and that the Clerk certify the same to the Trustee of Giles County for payment.

The State Plt.) Upon a presentment for neglect of duty
   Against   ) as overseer of the road.
William Wood Deft.)
) This day came the Solicitor General for the State, who saith he wishes no further to prosecute the Defendant in this case. It is therefore ordered by the court that a nole prosqui be entered in this case, and that the defendant go hence without day.

The State .. Plt.) Upon a presentment for neglect of duty
   Against   ) as overseer of the road.
William Wood Deft.)
) A Nole prosqui having been entered up in this case, under the direction of the court - It is ordered that Judgment be entered up against the County of Giles in favour of the Several claimants on the part of the State, for all costs to which they are entitled, and that the Clerk certify the same to the Trustee of Gile County for payment.

Ordered that court be adjourned till tomorrow morning nine oclock.

                                                                            H. Hagen
                                                                            James Perry
                                                                             W. B. Pepper

P-456   Saturday Morning 20th 1825

Court met according to adjournment Present Henry Hagen) Esquires Justices
                                   James Perry &   ) of the Peace for
                                   Wm. B. Pepper   ) the County of
) Giles.

A Bill of Sale from Josiah Dailey to William B. Pepper for certain property therein in Specified was produced in court and the Execution thereof proven by the oath of A. M. Ballentine (one of the witnesses thereto) and ordered to be certified for registration.

Ordered that the following tax list be received, and that double tax thereon remitted, towit,

Levi Sherrell   1 Free poll.
                       3 Slaves
                       200 acres of land.

John Den Lessee of)Plts.)   In Case
William Kennedy   )   )
    Against   )   On motion of Lunsford M. Bramlitt attorney
Francis Beard Deft.   )   ordered that a Scire facias issue against
)   John Birdwell the plaintiffs securities
in this case, returnable to the next term of this court.

The State .. Plt.   )   Upon a Indictment for wounding a horse.
    Against   )
Thomas Brown Deft.)   Thomas Brown the Defendant and Jeremiah
)   Parker came into court and acknowledged themselves indebted to the State of Tennessee in the sum of two hundred dollars each to be levied of their goods & chattles lands & tenments to the use of the State to be void on condition that the said Thomas Brown appear here on the first Thursday after the the third Monday in November next to answer the State upon an Indictment for wounding a horse, and not depart there from without leave of the court.

William I. Adire Plt.)   In Case
    Against   )
Thomas Underwood Deft.)   This day came the parties by their attorneys, and by consent leave is given each
party to take depositions, both in and out of this State, and that commissions issue accordingly, which depositions, when taken and to be read in evidence on the trial of this cause upon the plaintiff giving to the defendant & the defendant giving plaintiffs attorneys, twenty days notice out & ten days notice within the State, of the time & place of taking said depositions.

P-457   Saturday 20th August 1825

The Commissioners who were appointed to settle with the administrators of the Estate of Anthony Samuel decd. made return of sd. settlement which is ordered to be recorded.

Ordered that a venditioni Exponas issue to the Sheriff of this County Commanding him to expose to sale after giving legal notice, one hundred & thirty five acres of land the property of John R. Biddix levied on, on the 12th day of August 1825, as the property of said John R. Biddix by Thomas B. Hainey a constable of Giles County to satisfy an Execution – which issue on a Judgment which Robert Anderson recovered against said John R. Biddix before Alexander Black Esquire a Justice of the Peace for this county on the fourth day of June 1825 for the sum of sixty dollars & costs.

Dudly Smith Plt.) In Case
Against)
John Butler Deft.) This day came the parties by their attornies
) and by consent this cause is continued untill next court, and on motion of the plaintiff ordered that a commission issue to any two of the Acting Justices of the Peace in & for the County of Lincoln this State to take the deposition of Joseph Greer, which when taken is to be read in evidence on the trial of this case, upon the plaintiffs giving to the defendant five days notice of the time & place of taking said deposition.

Martin Griffin . . . Plt.) In Case
Against)
James Patteson Excr. of)Deft) This day came the parties by their
Nelson Patteson Decd.)) attornies and thereupon came a Jury
) of good and lawful men, Towit, John B. Goldsberry, Hugh Long, Soloman Simmons Junr., Thomas Wells, George M. Gibson, William James, Robert B. Harney, Josiah Evans, Lewis Sherrell, Jesse West, Younger Hobson, & Lewis Williams, who being elected tried and sworn well & truly to try the issue joined between the parties in this case, who after having heard the evidence and argument of counsel retired to consider of their verdict after some time returned & say they cannot afree By consent said Jurors are permitted to disperse to meet again Tuesday morning ten oclock.

Ordered that Thomas Williams administrator of the Estate of Anthony Samuel Decd. be allowed the sum of Sixty five dollars for settleng said Estate.

P-458   Saturday 20th August 1825

Ordered that Bernard M. Patteson be appointed Guardian to William Neal Lunatic, (in the room of James H. Neal decd) whereupon he executed Bond and security as the law directs.

Hannah Underwood Plt.   )   In Case
    Against   )
Lydall Wilkinson Deft.   )
                                 This day came the parties by their attorneys and thereupon came the Jury who were sworn well and truly to try the issue joined between the parties in this case, who still say they cannot agree. By consent of the parties and with the assent of the Court Alexander Stenson, one of the Jurors in the case, this case was withdrawn, and the cause continued untill the next term of this court, that a new trial may be had therein on motion of the defendants attorney ordered that a commission issue to any two of the Acting Justice of the Peace in and for the County of Madison & State of Alabama to take the deposition of William I. Adair, John W. Tilford, Richard Elliott, William Weedon, Archibald McDonald, John Silvers, William E. Phillips, & John F. Mills and that a commission issue to any two of the Acting Justice of the Peace in & for the County of Madison and State aforesaid to the depositions of Robert M. Richard, Jonathan Warren, Ruffus Colemna, John Silvers, Elvira Dandridge, William Dandridge, and that a commission issue to any two of the Acting Justice of the Peace in & for the County of Limestone and State aforesaid to take the Depositions of Barnett Tatum & Mary S. Tatum, all of which depositions are to be read on the trial, of this cause upon the Defendant giving to the plaintiff twenty days notice of the time and place of taking the same - and also on motion of the plaintiff ordered that a commission issue to any two of the Acting Justices of the Peace in & for the County of Madison and State of Alabama to take the deposition of John Airs, David Owen, Stirling Smith, Allen James, and that a commission issue to any two of the Acting Justices of the Peace in and for the County of Limestone and State of Alabama to take the deposition of Barnett Tatum & Mary S. Tatum which depositions, when taken to be read in evidence on the trial of this cause upon the plaintiffs giving to the defendants attorney, twenty days notice of the time & place of taking the same.

    Ordered that court be adjourned till Monday morning ten oclock.

                                                     A. McKissack
                                                     William Wood
                                                     James Dugger

P-459   Monday Morning 22nd August 1825

    Court met According to adjournment Present, Archibald McKissack, William Wood, James Dugger, John Young, Thomas K. Gordon, Alexander Black, Henry Hagen, Wm. B. Pepper, Hezekiah Jones & James Perry, Esquires Justices of Peace for the County of Giles.

    Ordered that the Indentures heretofore entered into between the chairman of this court and Nelson Patteson, binding Robert Riddle to said Patteson be made void, and that said parties be released from all further obligations within said Indenture is continued.

Ordered that the Indenture heretofore entered into between the chairman of this court, and Stirling Harwell binding Ransom Harwell to said Stirling Harwell be made void and that said parties be released from all further obligations that are contained in said Indenture.

A deed of conveyance from Benjamin Burk to John Dailey for twenty five acres of Land was produced in court and the Execution thereof acknowledged by said Benjamin Burk, and ordered to be certified for registration.

A deed of conveyance from George Bowers to John Dailey for one hundred and ninety three acres of land, was produced in court, and the Execution thereof acknowledged by said George Bowers and ordered to be certified for registration.

A Deed of conveyance from John Dailey to George Bowers for fifty six & one fourth acres of land was produced in court and the execution thereof acknowledged by said John Dailey & ordered to be certified for registration.

A Deed of conveyance from Alexander Baldridge to George Bowers for ten acres of land was produced in court and the execution thereof partly proven by the oath of Benjn. Burk (one of the witnesses thereto).

A Deed of conveyance from William Price to George Bowers for forty acres of land was produced in court and the Execution thereof partly proven by the oath of Benjamin Burk (one of the witnesses thereto).

Ordered that James Leath be appointed overseer of the road in the room of Zadock Hudson, resigned and that he have the same district of hands.

Ordered that letters of administration on the Estate of Bennet R. Cody be granted to Price Cody whereupon (p-460) he executed bond & security & was qualified as the law directs.

Price Cody administrator of the Estate of Bennet R. Cody, decd. returned an Inventory of said Estate which is ordered to be recorded.

An Ordinancy Licence for the term of twelve months & no longer is granted to Benjamin Burk whereupon he executed bond and security & was qualified as the law directs.

Ordered that letters of administration on the Estate of Owen Smith decd. be granted to David K. McEwin whereupon he was qualified & gave bond & Security as the law directs.

Ordered that John Laird, George Malone & Wm. Dearing be appointed commissioners to allot to Susan Smith, widow of Owen Smith decd. one years provisions out of Owen Smiths Estate, and that they make report thereof to the next term of this court.

The executor of Martin Lane Senr. Decd. returned into court and Inventory of said Estate which is ordered to be recorded.

It is ordered by the court that the following persons good & lawful men of the County of Giles, that is each one of whom is a free white male citizen and house holder of sd. County over twenty one years of age, not an overseer of the road who has not served on the vinise in this Circuit Court of said County at the last term thereof and who has no cause to be tried in this court at the next term thereof that is known of by this court, towit, David Maxwell, Fountain Lester, James Buford, Thomas Martin, John Young, Hezekiah Jones, William B. Pepper, Peter Swanson, Richard H. Allen, Wm. McGrew, Elisha White, John Gordon, Edward D. Jones, William Ussery, John Dabney, Richard McGee, John Lee, Arnold Zellues, Davis Brown, John H. Camp, Guston Kearney, Lewis G. Upshaw, John Yates, John Buchannan, Beverly B. Watson & Jeremiah Parker be Jurors to serve in the next Circuit Court to be holden for said County at the courthouse in the Town of Pulaski on the first Monday in February next that the Clerk deliver a copy of this order to the Sheriff of this county and that he summon said persons to attend and serve accordingly.

P-461   Monday 22nd August 1825

It is ordered by the court that the following persons good and lawful men of the County of Giles, that is each one of whom is a free white male citizen and house holder of said County, over twenty one years of age, not an overseer of a road, and who has not been appointed and served as a Juror of this County Court for Twelve months towit, Daniel Puryear, James Lester, James Dearing Archibald Crockett, Alexander Esselman, Thomas Graves, Stephen Anderson, Edward M. Brown, James Wilson, Duncan Brown, James Abernathy, John Bass, William H. Moore, Ragen Simpson, Jeremiah Barnes, John Marlow, Charles Buford, James H. Hendry John Hill, H. Crockett Campbell, Joseph Knox, John Goff, Marshall Moody, John P. Taylor, Jeremiah Parker, & Henry J. Cooper be Jurors to serve in this court at the next term, on the third Monday in November next, that the Clerk deliver a copy of this order to the Sheriff of this County, and that he Summon said persons to attend and serve accordingly.

Ordered that the County Trustee of this County pay to Archibald Crockett the Sum of fifty four dollars for the support & maintenance of James Philips & wife paupers of this county, for the term of twelve months from this time.

Ordered that David Pace, James Parchment, John M. Hobson, Robert Yarbrough, William Flatt, Wiley Boyakin, & William Bratt or any five of them be appointed a Jury to view & mark out a road leaving the road that leads from Pulaski to Laurenceburg near David Porters & running up Weakley Creek the nearest & best way in a direction to Mount Pleasant to the County line & that they make report thereof to the next term of this court.

Ordered that William Sheppard, James Lester, John Gordon, William Wood, Daniel Puryear, George Malone & James Buford, or any five of them be appointed a Jury to view the road from Tinnens Mill to the Bridge on Richland Creek & see what alteration is necessary to be made on said road & make report thereof to the next term of this court.

Ordered that Alexander Black & Samuel Y. Anderson be appointed commissioners to contract privately or publickly as they may think proper, the repairing the Bridge over Richland Creek, at Pulaski, & that the same be paid for by the County Trustee.

P-462   Monday 22nd August 1825

Ordered that German Lester and William R. Davis be appointed commissioners to contract publick or privately the repairing of the Gates, Steps, & Railing of the inclosure around the court house, and that the same be paid for by the County Trustee.

The Jury who were appointed to view a road that runs around Gardner Batts farm, made report of same review and said report is received by the court and the road established according to report, and James Eastham overseer is to keep the same in repair with the hands under his directions.

The commissioners who were appointed to allot to Prudence Wells widow of William H. Wells, decd. one years provision out of the Estate of sd. Wm. H. Wells made return thereof which is ordered to be recorded.

A Deed of conveyance from Alexander McCorkle Senr. to Daniel Leatherman for twenty seven acres & twenty five poles of land was produced in court and the Execution thereof proven by the oaths of Thomas Tucker & Clinton Tucker the witnesses thereto, and ordered to be certified for registration.

A Deed of conveyance from Alexander McCorkle Senr. to Thomas Tucker for one hundred and Eleven acres of land was produced in court and the Execution thereof proven by the oaths of Daniel Leatherman & Clinton Tucker the witnesses thereto, and ordered to be certified for registraion.

John Dickey who was heretofore appointed school commissioner according to act of Assembly, appeared in court and was qualified and gave bond and security as the law directs.

Ordered that William P. A. McCabe be appointed overseer of the Columbia road, from his own house to the forks opposite William Giddens and that he have under his direction for the purpose of keeping the same in repair the hands of William Giddens, Samuel Davis, Peter Martin, Joseph H. Hodge, Thomas Wilkinson, John Amis, Francis Wilkinson, & John Wilkinson.

On Petition of John Wood ordered that Writ of Certiorari and supercedeas issue to stay proceedings & remove to this court, the order of a Judgment rendered by William Wood Esquire, An Acting Justice of the Peace for Giles County (p-463) in favor of William S. Gray, against John Wood on the ____ day of ____ 1825 for the sum of fourteen dollars & seventy cents or there about & costs on the petitions giving bond & Security according to Law.

Ordered that Thomas B. Haynie, Bradley Phifer, Elijah Anthony, George Hillhouse, George Rayburn, William H. Ross, & William Terrell, or any five of them be appointed a Jury to view and mark out a road the nearest & best way from the Bratton Hill near the head of Moons Creek to the County line in a direction to Florence & that they make report thereof to the next term of this court.

Ordered that James Patteson, Henry T. Butler, Ralph Graves Senr., John Keenan, and Archibald Story, or any five of them be appointed a Jury to view the road leading from Pulaski to Cross waters, begining at the Town line, on said road, and intersect the same at the mouth of the first lane, on what is called the Polk or Dougherty tract of land running South to the old road and see if it be proper to alter the sd. road to run as aforesd. and that they make report thereof to the next term of this court.

Ordered that court be adjourned till tomorrow morning 9 oclock.

                A. Black
                H. Hagen
                James Perry

P-464 Tuesday Morning 23rd August 1825

Court met according to adjournment. Present Alexander Black) Esquires Justice of the Peace for Giles County.
                 Henry Hagen &
                 James Perry

William H. Field Guardian to Silas Flournoy returned into court an account current against his said Ward, which is ordered to be recorded.

Ordered that William R. Davis Jailor of this County be allowed the sum of one dollar & seventy five cents, as per account filed and the same is ordered to be certified to the Trustee of Giles County for payment.

Ordered that William R. Davis Jailor of this County be allowed the sum of two dollars & fifty cents as per account filed, and the same is ordered to be certified to the Trustee of Giles County for payment.

Ordered that William R. Davis Jailor of the County be allowed the sum of nineteen dollars & seventy five cents as per account filed, and the same is ordered to be certified To the Trustee of Giles County for payment.

Daniel Puryear .. Plt.) In Case
    Against)
Theophilus Guthrie Deft.) This day came the parties by their attorney and thereupon came a Jury of good and lawful men, Towit, Benjamin M. Scoggin, Robert Black, Thomas Underwood, Charles Deavers, Joseph S. Tarkington, John Young Junr., Martin Griffin, Thomas C. Porter, William Snow, Milton G. Haynie, William Maxwell & James Collins, who being elected tried and sworn well & truly to try the issue joined between the parties in this case upon their oaths do say that they find said issue in favor of the plaintiff and assess his damages by reason in the declaration mentioned, to twenty dollars besides costs.

    It is therefore considered by the court that the plaintiff recover of said defendant the damages aforesaid in form aforesd. by the Jurors aforesd. assessed, and also his costs by him about his suit in this behalf expended.

Alexander Hood use &c Plt.) Appeal
    Against)
John Menefee ... Deft.) The Plaintiff not appearing to attend to this cause. It is ordered by the court that the same be dismissed at his cost. It is therefore considered by the court that the defendant recover of the plaintiff his costs by him about his defence in this behalf expended.

P-465   Tuesday 23rd August 1825

Henry Curry use &c Plt.) Appeal
    Against)
John Menefee ... Deft.) The plaintiff not appearing to attend to the cause. It is ordered by the court that the same be dismissed as his costs. It is therefore considered by the court that the defendant recover of the plaintiff his costs by him about his defence in this behalf expended.

John Baskin Assee to the use &c Plt.) In Debt
    Against)
John McCracken ... Deft.) This day came the parties by their attornies and thereupon came a Jury of good and lawful men, Towit, Benjamin M. Scoggins, Robert Black, Thomas Underwood, Charles Deavers, Joseph S. Tarkington, John Young, Junr., Martin Griffin, Albert G. Underwood, William Snow, Milton G. Haynie, William Maxwell, & James Collins, who being elected tried and sworn well and truly to try the issue joined between the parties in this case upon their oaths do say that the Defendant hath not paid the debt in the writing obligatory in the declaration mentioned as the plaintiff in his replication have alleged, and that he has no sett off, and they do assess the plaintiffs damage by occasion of the detention of sd. debt to seven dollars twelve and a half cents, besides costs. It is therefore considered by the court

that the plaintiff recover against the said Defendant the sum of one hundred & twenty dollars the amount of his debt aforesd. together with his damages aforesaid in form aforesaid by the Jurors aforesaid assessed and also his costs by him about his suit in this behalf expended.

Robert W. Green Assee to the use &c Plt.)   In Debt
           Against   )
Alfred Flournoy ... Deft.   )   This day came the parties
)   by their attornies, and thereupon came a Jury of good & lawful men, towit, Benjamin M. Scoggin, Robert Black, Thomas Underwood, Charles Deavers, Joseph S. Tarkington, John Young, Junr., Martin Griffin, Albert G. Underwood, William Snow, Milton G. Haynie, William Maxwell, and James Collins, who being elected tried and sworn well and truly to try the issue joined between the parties in this case upon their oaths do say that the defendant has not paid the debt in the writing obligatory in the declaration mentioned as the plaintiff in his replication has alleged, and they do assess the plaintiffs damages by occasion of the detention of said debt to Fifteen dollars besides costs. It is therefore considered by the court that the plaintiff recover of sd. Defendant the sum of Four hundred dollars the amount of his debt aforesaid, together with his damages aforesd. in form   (p-466)   aforesaid by the Jurors aforesaid, assessed, and also his costs by him about his suit in this behalf expended.

Mason Ford ... Plt.   )   Judicial Attachment
        Against   )
Thomas Underwood Deft.   )   This day came the parties by their attornies
)   and thereupon came a Jury of good and lawful men Towit, Benjamin M. Scoggins, Robert Black, Charles Deavers, Joseph S. Tarkington, John Young, Junr., Martin Griffin, William Snow, Milton G. Haynie, William Maxwell, James Collins, William Roberts & John Westmoreland, who being elected tried and sworn well and truly to try the issue joined between the parties in this case upon their oaths do say that they find said issue in favour of the plaintiff, and assess his damages by reason of the detention of the debt in the declaration mentioned to Eleven dollars & fifty cents besides costs.

It is therefore considered by the court that the plaintiff recover of said defendant the sum of twenty one Dollars & three cents, the debt aforesd. together with his damages aforesd in form aforesd, by the Jurors aforesaid assessed, and his costs about his suit in this behalf expended.

Robert H. Nelson Plt.   )   Judicial Attachment
        Against   )
Thomas Underwood Deft.   )   On the affidavit of the defendant this
)   cause is ordered to be continued, and on motion of said Defendant ordered that a commission issue to any two of the Acting Justice of the Peace in and for the County of Madison and State of Alabama to take the deposition of David Owen, Alfred James, Barnett Tatum & John Philips which when taken to be read in evidence on the trial of this cause upon the defendant giving to the plaintiffs attorney fifteen days notice of the time & place of taking the Same.

Reuben Burton Admr. Plt.   )   Judicial Attachment
    Against   )
Thomas Underwood Deft.   )   On affidavit of the defendant this cause
)   is ordered to be continued and on motion
of said Defendant ordered that a commission issue to any two of the Acting Justices of the Peace in and for the County of Giles, to take the deposition of Rebecca Underwood, which when taken is to be read in evidence on the trial of this cause, upon the Defendant giving to the plaintiffs Attorney five days notice of the time & place of taking the same.

P-467   Tuesday 23rd August 1825

William Carter Plt.   )   Judicial Attachment
    Against   )
Thomas Underwood Deft.   )   On the affidavit of the defendant this
)   cause is ordered to be continued, and
on motion of sd. Defendant ordered that a commission issue to any two of the Acting Justices of the Peace in & for the County of Giles to take the deposition of Rebecca B. Underwood which when taken is to be read in evidence on the trial of this cause upon the defendant giving to the plaintiffs attorney five days notice of the time and place of taking the same.

Robert Weakly . . Plt.   )   In Debt
    Against   )
Robert Davidson Deft.   )   This day came the parties by their at-
)   tornies, and thereupon came a Jury of
good and lawful men, Towit, George Everly, Alexander Stinson, Walter Lock, John Clack, John F. Abernathy, James J. Kelley, Henry Yancy, George Bratton, Jason Hopkins, Stirling H. Lester, William Byrd, and Henry Hester, who being elected tried and Sworn well and truly to try the issue joined between the parties in this case upon their oaths do say that the defendant has not paid the debt in the writing obligatory in the declaration mentioned and that he has no sett off as the plaintiff in his replication has alleged, and they do assess the plaintiffs damages, by occasion of the detention of said debt to Eleven dollars & fifty cents, Besides costs. It is therefore considered by the court that the plaintiff recover of said defendant the sum of one hundred & twenty five dollars & Eighty six cents the amount of this debt aforesaid, together with the damages aforesaid in form aforesd. by the Jurors aforesaid assessed, and also his costs by him about his suit in this behalf expended.

Jacob Shall Assee &c Plt.)   In Debt
    Against   )
Robert Fenner . . Deft.   )   This day came the parties by their attor-
)   nies and thereupon came a Jury of good
and lawful men, Towit, George Everly, Alexander Stinson, Walter Lock, John Clack, John F. Abernathy, James J. Kelley, Henry Yancy, George Bratton, Jason Hopkins, Stirling H. Lester, William Bird, & Henry Hester, who being elected tried and sworn well and truly to try the issue joined between the parties in this case, upon their oaths do say that the defendant has not paid the whole   (p-468)   of the Debt in the writing obligatory in the declaration mentioned, and that he has no sett off as the plaintiff in his replications have alleged, and they do assess the plaintiffs damages by

occasion of the detention of said debt to six dollars & fifty cents, Besides costs. It is therefore considered by the court that the plaintiff recover of defendant the sum of one hundred & five dollars the balance of this debt aforesaid, together with his damages aforesaid assessed also his costs by him about his suit in this behalf expended.

John Gregory Plt.) In Debt
    Against)
Thomas P. Jones Deft.) This day came the parties by their attornies and thereupon came a Jury of good and lawful men, towit, George Everly, Alexander Stinson, Walter Lock, John Clack, Benjamin M. Scoggins, James J. Kelley, Henry Yancy, George Bratton, Jason Hopkins, John McAmerick, William H. Bird, and Henry Hester, who being elected tried & sworn well and truly to try the issue joined between the parties in this case upon their oaths do say that the defendant has not paid the debt in the writing obligatory in the declaration mentioned, and that he has no sett off as the plaintiff in his replication hath alleged, and they do assess the plaintiffs damages by occasion of the detention of said debt, to sixty one dollars and forty cents besides costs. It is therefore considered by the court that the plaintiff recover of the defendant the sum of one hundred and six dollars fifteen and a half cents, the balance of his debt aforesaid together with his damages aforesaid in form aforesaid by the Jurors aforesaid assessed and also his costs by him about his suit in this behalf expended.

Martin B. Wood Plt.) In Debt
    Against)
David McCanlass Deft.) This day came the parties by their attornies and thereupon came a Jury of good and lawful men, towit, Robert Black, John Young, Junr., Martin Griffin, Joseph S. Tarkington, Milton G. Haynie, William Maxwell, James Collier, Charles Deavers, Stirling H. Lester, Bernard M. Patteson, Andrew M. Balentine, and Archibald Storey who being elected tried and sworn well and truly to try the issue joined between the parties in this case upon their oaths do say that the defendant has not paid the debt in the writing obligatory in the declaration mentioned and that he has no sett off as the plaintiff in his replication has (p-469) alleged and they do assess the plaintiffs damages by the occasion of the detention of said debt to three dollars thirty nine cents besides costs.

It is therefore considered by the court that the plaintiff recover of said defendant the sum of one hundred and four dollars, and fifty cents the amount of his debt aforesaid together with his damages aforesaid in form aforesaid by the Jurors aforesaid assessed, and also his costs by him about his suit in this behalf expended.

Alexander McDonald Plt.) In Debt
    Against)
John Tilman Deft.) This day came the parties by their attornies and thereupon came a Jury of good and lawful men, Towit, Robert Black, John Young Junr., Martin Griffin, Joseph S. Tarkington, Milton G. Haynie, William Maxwell, James Collier, Charles Deavers, Stirling H. Lester, Bernard M. Patteson, Andrew M. Balentine and Archibald Story, who being Elected tried and Sworn well and truly to try the issue joined between the parties in this case upon their

oaths do say that the defendant has not paid the debt in the writing obligatory in the declaration mentioned, and that he has no sett off as the plaintiff in his replication has alleged, and they do assess the plaintiffs damages by occasion of the detention of said debt to six dollars & forty cents, besides costs. It is therefore considered by the court that the plaintiff recover of said Defendant the sum of one hundred & Sixty dollars the amount of his debt aforesaid, together with his damages aforesaid, in form aforesaid, by the Jurors aforesd. assessed, and also his costs about his suit in this behalf expended.

Joseph Greer to the use &c Plt.)
    Against)
William Crittenton . . Deft.)
)

In Case

This day came the parties by their attornies and thereupon came a Jury of good & lawful men, Towit, Robert Black, John Young Junr., Martin Griffin, Joseph S. Tarkington, Milton G. Haynie, Wm. Maxwell, James Collier, Charles Deavers, Stirling H. Lester, Bernard M. Patteson, Andrew M. Ballentine & Archibald Story, who being elected tried and Sworn well and truly to try the issue joined between the parties in this case upon their oaths do say that the defendant has not paid the debt in the writing obligatory in the Declaration mentioned, and that he has no sett off as the plaintiffs in his replication has alleged, and they do assess the plaintiffs damages by occasion of the detention of (p-470) said Debt to Five dollars & fifty cents besides costs. It is therefore considered by the court that the plaintiff recover of said defendant the sum of two hundred dollars the amount of his Debt aforesaid together, with his damages aforesaid, in favor aforesaid by the Jurors aforesaid assessed, and also his costs by him about his suit in this behalf expended.

Charles Buford Treasurer of)
Westernburgh Academy Plt.)
    Against)
James Simmons, Henry Hagen)Deft.)
& Elisha Eldridge)

In Debt

This day came the parties by their attorneys and thereupon came a Jury of good and lawful men, Towit, Robert Black, John Young, Junr., Martin Griffin, Joseph S. Tarkington, Milton G. Haynie, William Waxwell, James Collier, Charles Deavers, Sterling H. Lester Bernard M. Patteson, Andrew M. Ballentine & Archibald Story, who being elected tried and sworn well and truly to try the issue joined between the parties in this case, upon their oaths do say that the defendants have not paid the debt in the writing obligatory in the Declaration mentioned, as the plaintiff in his replication has alleged and they do assess the plaintiffs damages by occasion of the Detention of said debt to two dollars & eighty cents besides costs.

It is therefore considered by the court that the plaintiff recover of sd. Defendants the sum of one hundred and forty dollars the amount of this debt aforesaid together with his damages aforesaid, in form aforesaid by the Jurors aforesaid assessed, and also his costs by him about his suit in this behalf expended.

From which Judgment the defendants prayed an appeal to the honorable the Circuit Court to be holden for the County of Giles, and having executed bond and security as the law directs the same was granted them.

Polly Riddle to the use &c Plt.)   In Debt
           Against   )
Thomas Wells . . . . Deft.   )   This day came the parties by their
)   attornies and thereupon came a Jury
of good and lawful men, towit, Robert Black, John Young Junr., Martin
Griffin, Joseph S. Tarkington, Milton G. Haynie, William Maxwell, James
Collier, Andrew M. Ballentine, Charles Deavers, Stirling H. Lester, Barnard M. Patteson, & Archibald Story, who being elected tried and sworn
well and truly to try the issue joined between the parties in this case,
upon their oaths do say that they find said issue in favor of the plaintiff and (p-471) assess his damages by occasion of the detention of
the debt in the declaration mentioned to twenty seven dollars & seventy
five cents besides costs. It is therefore considered by the court that
the plaintiff recover of said defendant the sum of one hundred dollars,
the amount of his Debt aforesaid together with his damages aforesaid in
form aforesaid by the Jurors aforesaid assessed, and also his costs about
his in this behalf expended.

Martin & Ballentine) Plts.   )   In Debt
Merchants &c   )
       Against   )   This day came the parties by their at-
Henry J. Cooper . . Deft.   )   tornies and thereupon came a Jury of
)   good and lawful men, Towit, Robert
Black, John Young Junr., Martin Griffin, Joseph S. Tarkington, Milton
G. Haynie, William Maxwell, James Collier, Charles Deavers, Stirling H.
Lester, Bernard M. Patteson, Andrew M. Ballentine & Archibald Story, who
being elected tried and sworn well and truly to try the issue joined between the parties in this case upon their oaths do say the defendant has
not paid the debt in the writing obligatory in the declaration mentioned,
and that he has no sett off as the plaintiff in their replication have
alleged and they do assess the plaintiffs damage by occasion of the detention of said debt to fourteen dollars & ninety cents besides costs.
    It is therefore considered by the court that the plaintiff recover of
said Defendant the sum of four hundred & twenty eight dollars, & sixty
two cents, the amount of his debt aforesaid, together with his damages
aforesaid, in form aforesaid, by the Jurors aforesaid assessed, and also
his costs by them about their suit in this behalf expended.

    Ordered that Thomas Martin Fountain Lester & James Buford be appointed
commissioners to settle with the Executors of the Estate of Thomas H.
Meredith Decd. and that they make report thereof to the next term of this
court.

    Ordered that Robert Reed, Archibald McKissack & Robert McLaurine be
appointed commissioners to settle with the administrators of the Estate
of Lewis Kirk decd. and that they make report thereof to the next term of
this court.

    A Deed of conveyance from Alexander McDonald to Edmund Gatlin for forty
three acres of land was produced in court and the Execution thereof acknowledged by sd. Alexander McDonald and ordered to be certified for registration

Robert Oliver Assoc &c Plt.)   In Debt
  Against   )
Daniel Frazier Deft.   ) This day came the parties by their at-
) tornies, and thereupon came a Jury of
good & lawful men, Towit, Robert Black, John Young Jr., Martin Griffin, Joseph S. Tarkington, Milton G. Haynie, William Maxwell, James Collier, Charles Deavers, Stirling H. Lester, Bernard M. Patteson, Andrew M. Ballentine & Archibald Story, who being elected tried and sworn well and truly to try the issue joined between the parties in this case upon their oaths, do say that the defendants has not paid the debt in the Writing obligatory in the declaration mentioned, as the plaintiff in his replication has alleged and they do assess the plaintiffs damages by occasion to the detention of said debt to three dollars & thirty seven and a half cents, besides costs.

 It is therefore considered by the court that the plaintiff recover of said defendant the sum of Eighty five dollars & fifty cents the amount of his debt aforesaid, together with his damages aforesaid in form aforesaid by the Jurors aforesaid assessed and also his costs about his suit in this behalf expended.

John McAnnick Plt.   )   In Case
  Against   )
William Maxwell Deft.   ) This day came the parties by their attor-
) nies and thereupon came a Jury of good
and lawful men, towit, Robert Black, John Young Junr., Martin Griffin, Joseph S. Tarkington, Milton H. Haynie, Charles Deavers, Stirling H. Lester, Bernard M. Patteson, Andrew M. Ballentine, George Everly, Alexander Stinson & Thomas C. Porter, who being elected tried and Sworn well and truly to try the issue joined between the parties in this case upon their oaths do say that they find said issue in favour of the plaintiff, and assess his damages by reason of the declaration mentioned to twenty five dollars besides costs. It is therefore considered by the court that the plaintiff recover of said defendant the damages aforesaid, in form aforesaid by the Jurors aforesaid assessed, and also his cost by him about his suit in this behalf expended.

 The Grand Jury returned into court the following presentments, Towit, The State against John W. Edwards & Peter Johnson for an affray with and on assault & battery on the body of each other: The same against Jesse Saunders & Elde Muse for open and notorious Lewdness, & withdrew to consider of further presentments.

P-473   Tuesday 23rd August 1825

Martin Griffin Plt.   )   In Case
  Against   )
James Patteson Exer. of)Deft.) This day came the parties by their
Nelson Patteson Decd.)   ) attornies and thereupon came the
) Jury who were Sworn on a former day
of this term well and truly to try the issue joined between the parties in this case upon their oaths do say that they find said issue in favor of the plaintiff and assess his damages by reasons in the detention mentioned to one hundred and eight dollars & Seventy five cents - besides costs.

It is therefore considered by the court that the plaintiff recover of said defendant the damages aforesaid in form aforesaid by the Jurors aforesaid by the Jurors aforesaid assessed, and also his costs by him about his suit in this behalf expended, to be levied of their goods and chattels rights and credits of the said Testators in the hands of the sd. defendant to be therefore administrated if so much thereof they have, but if so much thereof they have not, then the cost to be levied of the proper goods and chattles of said Defendant.

Ordered that Court be adjourned till tomorrow morning 9 oclock.

H. Hagen
A. Black
A. McKissack

F-474 Wednesday 24th August 1825

Court met according to adjournment Present Henry Hagen) Esquires Justice
              Alexr. Black &) of the Peace for
              Archd. McKissack) the County of
) Giles.

Dudley Smith Plt.)   In Case
 Against   )
John Smith Deft.) This day came the plaintiff by his attorney, and
) the defendant being Solemnly called came not but
made default. It is therefore considered by the court that the plaintiff recover of the Defendant the damages, which he has sustained by reason in the declaration mentioned of but because it is unknown to the court here what the amount of those damages are it is ordered that the same be enquired of by a Jury at the next term.

David Jones . . . Plt.)   In Debt
 Against   )
James Tinnen &)Defts. This day came the plaintiff by his attorney
William Sheppard)   and the Defendant altho solemnly called
) came not but made default - It is therefore considered by the court that the plaintiff recover of said Defendant the sum of one hundred & five dollars the Balence of the debt in the writing obligatory in the Declaration mentioned together with the sum of four dollars & fifty five cents the damages he hath sustained by reason of the detention of said Debt and also his costs by him about his suit in this behalf expended.

James D. Walker Plt.)   Certiorari
 Against   )
Henry Yancy Deft.) This day came the defendant by his attorney, and the plaintiff being called came not but made default, nor is his suit further prosecuted - It is therefore considered by the court that the defendant go hence without day and recover of the plaintiff his costs by him about his defence in this behalf expended.

363

Samuel S. Smith & wife Plt.   )   Petition
        Against   )
John Porter Gdn. &c Deft.   )
)   On motion this cause is ordered to
                                      be continued as on affidavit of
Defendant, he paying the cost of this term, and on motion of plaintiffs
ordered that a commission issue to any two of the Acting Justices of the
Peace for Lillard County Missouri, to take deposition of Wm. Y. C. Ewing
to be read as evidence in this cause upon plaintiffs giving Defendant
thirty days notice of the time and place of taking the same.

P-475 . Wednesday 24th August 1825

A Deed of conveyance from Ethelbert Samuel to George Everly for part
of lot No. 50 in the Town of Pulaski was produced in court and the Execution thereof proven by the oaths of Francis Guthrie & Francis A. Mabrey,
the witnesses thereto and ordered to be certified for registration.

William Gholson Plt.   )   Garnishment
        Against   )
Beverly B. Watson Deft.   )   The defendant by his attorney moved the
)   court to be discharged from the Garnishment in this case which motion was overruled by the court, and the case
continued till next term of this court.

A Deed of conveyance from John E. Holden to William H. Byrd for lot
No. 30 in the Town of Pulaski was produced in court, and the Execution
thereof acknowledged by the said John E. Holden & ordered to be certified
for registration.

Hartwell H. Farris, to the use &c Plt.)   In Debt
        Against   )
Thomas Goodrich ... Deft.   )   This day came the plaintiff
)   by his attorney, and the
defendant altho solemnly called came not but made default - It is therefore considered by the court that the plaintiff recover of said defendant
the sum of two hundred and Eight dollars & 65 cents, the debt in the
writing obligatory in the declaration mentioned together with the sum of
one hundred & thirty two dollars & fifty cents, the damages he hath sustained by reason of the detention of said debt, and also his costs by
him about his suit in this behalf expended.

The Justices of the County   )   )
of Greene & State of North Carolina   ) Plts.)   Scia facias
Suing to the use of James W. Williams)   )
by his Gdn. Catherine Porter   )   )   This day came the plain-
        Against   )   )   tiffs by their attorney,
Thomas B. Haynie Gdn. Pendentolite of) Deft.)   and the defendant al-
Mary E. Porter   )   )   tho solemnly called
)   came not but made default. It is therefore considered by the court that the plaintiff recover
of sd. defendant the sum of Four thousand five hundred & ten dollars the

amount of the Debt & damages in the Judgment in the Scire facias mentioned with interest thereon to be computed at the rate of 6 per cent per annum from the 30th day of May 1823 till paid (the day on which sd. Judgment was rendered) also the sum of ten dollars & thirty four cents, thats amount of the costs that occured in the original suit together with the costs in this behalf expended.

P-476 Wednesday 24th August 1825

Penelope Murphy Plt.) Scire facias
    Against)
Thomas B. Haynie)Deft.) This day came the plaintiff by his
Gdn. of Mary E. Porter)) attorney and the defendant altho
) solemnly called came not but made
default - It is therefore considered by the court that the plaintiff recover of sd. Defendant the sum of two hundred and nine dollars & twenty cents, the amount of the debt & damages in the Judgment in the Scire facias mentioned with interest thereon to be computed at the rate of six per cent per annum from the 30th day of May 1823 till paid (the day of which said Judgment was rendered also the sum of ten dollars & thirty four cents the amount of the costs that occured in the original suit together with the costs in this behalf Expended.

Ordered that court be adjourned till tomorrow morning nine oclock.

                                                          H. Hagen
                                                          James Perry
                                                          A. Black

P-477 Thursday morning 25th August 1825

Court met according to adjournment present Henry Hagen) Esquires Justices
                                               James Perry &) of the Peace for
                                               Alexr. Black) Giles County.

A Deed of conveyance from Robert Bingham & Thomas Bingham to David Weis, for one hundred and fifty eight acres of land was produced in court and the Execution thereof proven by the oaths of William Wood & John Cabe the witnesses thereto and ordered to be certified.

The commissioners who were appointed to settle with the Executors of Thomas H. Meredith decd. made return of a partial settlement of said Estate which is ordered to be certified.

A Deed of conveyance from Robert Bingham, Thomas Green by his agent I. Green, and Thomas Bingham to Charles Chamberlaine for three hundred & forty eight acres of land was produced in court, and the Execution thereof proven by the oath of William Wood and John Cabe, the witnesses thereto, as to Robert Bingham & Thomas Bingham Parties thereto, and ordered to be certified.

A Deed of conveyance from James Paul to William Wood for one hundred & sixty acres of land was produced in court and the Execution thereof, partly proven by the oath of John Cabe, one of the witnesses thereto, and ordered to be certified.

Robert Weakley Plt.)   In Debt
    Against)
Robert Davison Deft.)   From the Judgment of the court in this case
)   rendered the defendant prayed an appeal to the honorable the Circuit Court to be held for the County of Giles and having executed bond and security according to law the same was granted him.

Joseph Greer, to the use &c Plt.)   In Debt
    Against)
William Crittenton Deft.)   From the Judgment of the court in
)   this case rendered the defendant prayed an appeal to the honorable the Circuit Court to be held for the County of Giles, and having Executed bond & security as the law directs the same was granted him.

P-478   Thursday 25th August 1825

Martin Griffin . . . Plt.)   In Debt
    Against)
James Patteson Executor of)Deft.)   From the Judgment of the court
Nelson Patteson Decd.)   in this case rendered the Defendant prayed an appeal to the honorable the Circuit Court to be held for the County of Giles and having executed bond and security as the law directs the same was granted him.

Ordered that Thomas Lane, John Goff, Burton R. White, Thomas K. Gordon, & Jacob Jones, or any three of them be appointed commissioners to settle with Edward D. Jones Administrator of the Estate of William Sims decd. & that they make report thereof to the next term of this court.

The nuncipative will of Robert Anderson decd. was produced in court & James Anderson being present about contesting the same and the Execution thereof proven by the oath of William P. Kirk, Samuel Anderson, & Daniel G. Anderson, the witnesses thereto, and ordered to be recorded, and thereupon Jane Anderson and Samuel Anderson the Executrix & Executor therein named appeared in court and were qualified and gave bond & security as the law directs.

Richard H. Allen Plt.)   Motion
    Against)
James H. Pickens &)Defts.)   This day came the plaintiff by L. M.
Elisha H. Mayfield))   Bramlett his attorney and moved the court for a Judgment for the sum of one hundred and twenty one dollars & 46 cents, which he has paid as security for said defendant as appears to the satisfaction of the court

and from the face of the papers in this case it is therefore considered by the court that the plaintiff recover of the said Defendants the said sum of one hundred & twenty one dollars & 46 cents, debt which he has paid as security as aforesaid, with interest from this date together with the costs of this motion.

Ordered that court be adjourned untill court in course.

H. Hagen

William Wood

A. Black

P-479 At a Court of Pleas & Quarter Sessions held for the County of Giles at the court house of said County in the Town of Pulaski on the third Monday in November (being the twenty first day thereof) in the year of our Lord one thousand Eight hundred & twenty five, Present Alexander Black, Henry Hagen, William B. Pepper, William Wood, Robert Reed, James Paine, Paul Chiles, Anderson Hogan, Willis S. McLaurine, Robert Oliver, Richard McGee, Arthur Hicks, John Bramlitt, Archibald McKissack, Jesse Allen, Hezekiah Jones, John Young, Thomas Harwood, Thomas K. Gordon, Edward D. Jones, John Yancy, Esquires Justices of the Peace for Giles County Presiding - German Lester Clerk of sd. Court & Lewis H. Brown Sheriff of said County.

Ordered that Robert Wells be appointed overseer of the road in the room of Clayton Tarpley resigned, and that he have the same district of hands.

A Deed of conveyance from George W. Campbell to Archibald Crockett, for one hundred and ninety three acres of Land was produced in court and the execution thereof proven by the oaths of Jacob Cochran & Robert Crockett two of the witnesses thereof and ordered to be certified for registration.

A Deed of conveyance from George W. Campbell to Archibald Crockett for thirteen and one half acres of land was produced in court and the execution thereof proven by the oaths of Jacob Cochran & Robert Crockett, two of the witnesses thereto, and ordered to be certified for registration.

A Deed of conveyance from James Davis to Jacob Cochran for fifteen acres & forty eight poles of land was produced in court and the Execution thereof acknowledged by the said James Davis and ordered to be certified for registration.

A Deed of conveyance from Jacob Cochran to James Davis for nine acres of land was produced in court and the Execution acknowledged by the said Jacob Cochran and ordered to be certified for registration.

Ordered that Charles Adkins be appointed overseer of the road in the room of William Watson resigned and that he have the same district of hands.

P-480 Monday 21st November 1825

A Deed of conveyance from Willis Lane & Joel Lane to John Laird for one hundred and thirty one acres and one fourth of Land was produced in court and the Execution thereof proven by the oaths of Joseph Fry & Martin Laird (the witnesses thereto, and ordered to be certified for registration.

Ordered that Sarah Ann Wilson be bound and apprentice to Samuel Shields, an Indenture to that effect having been entered into between the chairman of this court & Samuel Shields.

An Additional Inventory of the Estate of Samuel Paxton decd. returned into court by Armstead Redding Executor, and ordered to be recorded.

A Deed of conveyance from Matthew Wood to John D. Riddell, for the benefit of John W. Bodenhamer for fifty acres of land was produced in court and the Execution thereof proven by the oaths of John D. Riddell, & David Riddell, (the witnesses thereto, and ordered to be certified for registration.

Ordered that the County Trustee of this County pay to Hezekiah Jones the sum of forty three dollars for the support of Judiah Pannell a pauper of this County for the term of twelve months from this time.

Ordered that William Kidd be appointed administrator of the Estate of Elisha L. Kimbrough decd. who was qualified and Executed bond and Security as the Law directs.

An Inventory of the Estate of Elisha L. Kimbrough decd. returned by Wm. Kidd administrator and ordered to be recorded.

Ordered that an order of sale Issue to William Kimbrough decd. commanding him to expose to sale the property mentioned in the Inventory, this day returned and that he make report thereof to the next term of this court.

Ordered that Hezekiah Jones, David Jones & James White be appointed commissioners to allot to Martha Kimbrough widow of Elisha L. Kimbrough decd. one years provisions out of said Elisha L. Kimbroughs Estate, & that they make report thereof to the next term of this court.

P-481 Monday 21st November 1825

A Deed of conveyance from Lewis H. Brown Sheriff of Giles County to Peter Swanson for three thousand acres of land was produced in court and the Execution thereof proven by the oaths of Fountan Lester & Samuel Kercheval (the witnesses thereto) and ordered to be certified for registration.

Ordered that Thomas B. Haynie be appointed overseer of the road in the room of George Rice resigned and that he have the same district of hands.

Ordered that Addison Garrett be appointed overseer of the road in the room of John Neal resigned and that he have the same district of hands.

Ordered that Tyree Rodes, John Gordon, Daniel Puryear, Geo. Malone, Burton B. White, Jesse Allen, & William Pullen, or any five of them be appointed a Jury to view and alter of necessary part of the Columbia Road leading from Tinnens Mill, to the Bridge on Richland Creek, and that they make report thereof to the next term of this court.

Ordered that David W. Porter, James W. Wheeler, James Counce, Samuel S. Smith & John W. O. Graves be appointed a Jury to view that part of the Lawrenceburg road between the mouth of Thomas McKissacks lane to James W. Wheelers lane & see if it be proper to turn said road, and that they make report thereof to the next term of this court.

Ordered that James Paine be appointed overseer of the Shelbyville road leading by his house begining at the Huntsville road, thence through his lane and on to his line adjoining Tilman R. Daniels, and that he keep said road in repair with his own hands.

Ordered that Tilman R. Daniel be appointed overseer of the Shelbyville road from James Paines line near said Daniels to Mount Pisgah and that he have under his direction for the purpose of keeping the same in repair of the following hands, towit, The hands of Francis Wilson, Elizabeth Muncriefs hands, William Muncriefs hands, Jesse Mitchells hands, Henry Sterdivant Joel Wilsons hands, & Tilman R. Daniel hands.

Ordered that Charles Neal be appointed Guardian to Nancy Neal Isaac Neal, Matthias Neal, Rebeccah Neal, his minor children for the purpose of receiving (p-482) (Monday 21st November 1825) their Legacy in the Estate of William Davenport decd & their distributive shares of the Estate of Sarah Davenport, decd. who gave bond and security as the law directs.

Letters of Administration on the Estate of Lenoard Smith decd. was granted to Lewis Smith & John Abernathy, who gave bond and security and were qualified as the law directs.

An Inventory of the Estate of Leonard Smith decd. was returned by Lewis Smith & John Abernathy the administrators and ordered to be recorded.

Ordered that an order of sale Issue to Lewis Smith & John Abernathy Administrators of the Estate of Leonard Smith decd. commanding them to expose to sale the property mentioned in the Inventory, this day returned and that they make report to the next term of this court.

Ordered that John McKnight, John B. McCanlass & Alfred Hightower be appointed commissioners to allot to Martha Smith Widow of Leonard Smith decd. one years provisions out of the sd. Leonard Smiths Estate and that they make report thereof to the next term of this court.

Fountain Lester Guardian to Alfred White made return of an account against his said Ward which is ordered to be recorded.

Fountain Lester Guardian to Newton White made return of an account against his said Ward which is ordered to be recorded.

A Deed of conveyance from Peter Swanson to William B. Robertson for three thousand acres of land was produced in court and the Execution thereof proven by the oaths of Fountain Lester & David J. Moore the witnesses thereto and ordered to be certified for registration.

Ordered that John Rhodes be appointed overseer of the road in the room William H. Moore resigned and that he have the same district of hands.

The Jury who were appointed to view and make out a road commencing at the County line near James Phillips Crossing Elk river at the Persimmon Island from (p-483) thence to Upper Elkton made report thereof which was received by the court and established according to said review, and it is ordered that James Vance be appointed overseer to open the same and that he have under his direction for that purpose all the hands in the Upper Elkton and all others East of the Huntsville road within two miles of the said road.

Ordered that Martha Ann Hemenway be bound an apprenticed to Benjamin Beal an Indenture to that effect, having been entered into between the chairman of this court and said Benjamin Beal.

A Deed of conveyance from Thomas Webb & Rebeccah Webb to Marcus Mitchell for fifteen & two thirds acres of land was produced in court and the Execution thereof acknowledged by the said Thomas Webb and thereupon Edward D. Jones & Robert Oliver Esquires Justices of the peace for this County were appointed to take the privy Examination of said Rebeccah Webb touching the execution of sd. deed and return the same into court instanter and said Justice proceeded to take said examination, and returned the same into court, and the same was ordered to be certified for registration.

The last Will and testament of Abner Rea deceased was produced in court and the execution thereof proven by the oaths of James Kelso & William B. Graves, two of the witnesses thereto, and ordered to be recorded whereupon Jacob Jones & James Wheeler the Executors therein named appeared in court and were qualified and gave bond and security as the law directs.

Ordered that Thomas Compton be appointed in the room of Richard McGee to Superintend the Support and maintenance of Abram Bogard & wife.

A Deed of conveyance from Zebedee Weaver to Jacob Bryan for one hundred

& ninety six acres of Land was produced in court and the Execution thereof proven by the oaths of German Lester & Charles G. Wilcox, the witnesses thereto and ordered to be certified for registration.

Ordered that Jacob Cochran, Archibald Crockett, Joel Lane, Willis Lane, James Douglass, George Malone & David K. McEwin or any five of them be appointed a Jury to view that part of the road leading from Shelbyville to (p-484) Lawrenceberg which runs through the land of Martin McCall, and see if it be proper to turn said road according to the wish of sd. Martin McCall, and that they make report thereof to next term of this court.

Letters of administration on the Estate of Valentine Huff, decd. is granted to Rebecca Huff and David Crook whereupon they Executed bond and security and were qualified as the law directs.

And Inventory of the Estate of Valentine Huff decd. was returned into court by the admr. of said Estate which was ordered to be recorded.

Ordered that an order of sale issue to Rebecca Huff & David Crook Administrator of the Estate of Valentine Huff decd. commanding them to expose to sale the perishable part of said Estate together with two negroes Bun & Nancy, and that they make report thereof to the next term of this court.

Ordered that Willia S. McLaurine Erley Benson & Daniel Leatherman be appointed commissioners to allot to Rebecca Huff, widow of Valentine Huff decd. one years provision out of the Estate of sd. Valentine Huff decd. & that they make report thereof to the next term of this court.

Able Wilson, George M. Gibson, Jacob Jones, John Lee, William McGrew, John B. Goldberry, Beverly B. Watson, John W. Yates, Arnold Zellers, James White, Burton R. White, John Blue, & John Buchannan, Gentlemen who were commissioned by his Excellency the Governor of this State to Act as Justices of the Peace in and for the County, appeared in a court and were qualified as the law directs.

The Commissioners who were appointed to allot one years provisions to Susan Smith widow of Owen Smith decd. made return of said allotment which is ordered to be recorded.

An Inventory of the Estate of Owen Smith decd. was returned by the administrator of said Estate which is ordered to be recorded.

Ordered that an order of sale issue to the Administrator of Owen Smith decd. commanding them to Expose to sale the property specified in the Inventory this day returned, and that they make report to the next term of this court.

P-485   Monday 21st November 1825

Ordered that James Paine, Edward Shelton & Joseph Benson be appointed commissioners to settle with Early Benson, Guardian of Early Reasonover minor orphan of John Reasonover decd. and that they make report to the next term of this court.

A Bill of sale from William P. Richardson to John C. Richardson Clement A. Richardson, Mary Ann L. Richardson, Susannah M. Richardson, Martha E. Richardson & Julia F. Richardson, for certain property therein Specified was produced in court and the Execution thereof proven by the oaths of Isaac McGee and Curtis Terry the witnesses thereto and ordered to be certified for registration.

A Bill of sale from David Crook to Hardy Benson for certain property therein specified was produced in court and the Execution thereof acknowledged by the said David Crook and ordered to be certified for registration.

A Deed of conveyance from Samuel H. Williams to John P. Taylor for one hundred acres of land was produced in court and the Execution thereof proven by the oaths of Fountain Lester & German Lester, the witnesses thereto, and ordered to be certified for registration.

Letters of administration of the Estate of Solomon Simmons decd. is granted to Robert Penner whereupon he executed bond & security and was qualified as the law directs.

Ordered that Jacob Miller, John M. Abernathy, David Maxwell, Wm. Sheppard & William Maxwell or any five of them be appointed commissioners to allot to Mary Simmons widow of Solomon Simmons decd. one years provisions out of sd. Solomon Simmons Estate and that they make report to the next term of this court.

A Deed of conveyance from Joseph H. Hodge, to Albert G. Underwood for lot No. 14 in the Town of Pulaski, was produced in court and the Execution thereof acknowledged by the said Joseph H. Hodge and ordered to be certified for registration.

Ordered that a precinct Election be held at the house of Robert Oliver Esquire.

P-486   Monday 21st November 1825

Ordered that Robert B. Harney, be appointed constable in Captain Potts Company whereupon he was qualified & gave bond and security as the law directs.

Ordered that Joab Ross be appointed constable in Captain Ross company, whereupon he was qualified and gave bond and security as the law directs.

Ordered that the following tax list be received and that double tax thereon remitted, Towit,

Henry White   1 white poll
                  140 Acres of land –
Hartwell H. Brown 1 pleasure carriage.

Ordered that Rebecca Huff be appointed Guardian to William Huff, Sterling Huff, Daniel Huff, Pinckury Huff, Wiley Huff, Early Huff & Parmelia Huff infant orphans of Valentine Huff decd. whereupon she Executed bond & security as the law directs.

A Deed of conveyance from Hugh Weis to Thomas Goff for . . . . . acres of Land was produced in court and the Execution thereof proven by the oaths of Thomas K. Gordon, & David K. McEwin, the witnesses thereto, and ordered to be certified for registration.

Ordered that Thomas B. Haynie be appointed constable in Captain Wheelers Company whereupon he was qualified and gave bond & security as the Law directs.

Ordered that Homer Rainey be appointed Guardian to William Samuel infant orphan of Anthony Samuel decd. whereupon he executed bond & security as the law directs.

An account of sale of the Estate of Henry House decd. returned into court by the administrator of sd. Estate & ordered to be recorded.

Ordered that the return made by George M. Gibson & Joseph Knox Guardian of the minor orphans of John K. Gibson decd. of an account against the said ward be recorded.

Ordered that Monday next be set apart for County Business.

P-487   Monday 21st November 1825

A Deed of conveyance from Samuel R. Anderson to Ephriam A. Young for one hundred acres of land was produced in court and the Execution thereof proven by the oaths of David Bridgeforth & William H. Moore the witnesses thereto, and ordered to be certified for registration.

Ordered that William R. Davis be appointed constable in Captain Lesters

Company whereupon he executed bond and and was qualified as the law directs.

An ordinary licence for the term of one year and no longer is granted to Nathaniel Young, who was qualified and gave bond and security as the law directs.

A Deed of conveyance from Edward D. Jones to Wilfort Faris and Stephen Jones for one hundred and sixty seven and a half acres of land was produced in court and the Execution thereof acknowledged by the said Edward D. Jones, and ordered to be certified for registration.

A Deed of conveyance from John Hightower administrators of the Estate of Richard Hightower decd. to Robert R. Alsup for three hundred & forty acres of land was produced in court and partly proven by John Kennedy one of the subscribing witnesses to said deed.

Ordered that John Pillow, James Pillow, William Terrell, Joseph Pillow, William Maxwell, James J. Kelly, and George Kelly, or any five of them be appointed a Jury to view and mark out a road the nearest and best way from Walter Hills, and runing down Egnews Creek to intersect the Florence road to James B. Kimbroughs, and make report thereof to the next term of this court.

Ordered that William W. Thornton who was Guardian of James W. McKinney be removed from his said guardianship and that Nancy McKinney be appointed Guardian to said James W. McKinney upon her executing bond and security at this term.

Ordered that George Malone, Willis Willsford, & John P. Taylor be appointed commissioners to divide & allot to Bonapart Garland, Daniel Garland, & Peter Garland their distributive shares of the Estate of Peter Garland decd. and that they make report thereof to the next term of this court.

P-488 Monday 21st November 1825

Ordered that the ridge road from Isaac Purviss to the Lawrence County line be discontinued as a public highway, and that the road up the Creek South of the ridge road be established, and that James Leath keep the same in repair with the hands under his direction.

Ordered that the order of the last term of this court for the sale of the real & personal Estate of John Jones decd. be revived so far as relates to the negroes.

A receipt from Allen Pitts & Sarah Pitts to William Burton administrator of the Estate of William Davenport was produced in court, and the

Execution thereof acknowledged by sd. Allen Pitts and thereupon Edward D. Jones & Robert Oliver, Esquires Justices of the Peace in and for this County were appointed to take the privy Examination of said Sarah Pitts touching the Execution of said Rect. and return the same into court instanter, and said Justices proceeded to take said Execution and returned the same into court, and the same is ordered to be certified.

Ordered that Allen Field be appointed Guardian of Rebecca H. Beazley, William O. Beazley, Wytt Y. Beazley, Tilman D. Beazley, Anna B. Beazley, & Polly S. Beazley infant orphant orphans of Burton Beazley decd. in the room of Jesse Beazley removed from sd. Guardianship whereupon he executed bond as the law directs.

Ordered that James McDonald be appointed overseer of that part of the Mount Pisgah road which lies between the Fayetteville road and the corner of John McDonald field, and that he have under his direction for the purpose of keeping the same in repair the hands in the following bounds, towit, To extend East so far as to include Alexr. McDonalds, plantation, thence down the Creek that sd. A. McDonald lives on, including all on the branch that Lewis Garrett lives on, including also James McDonalds farm.

Ordered that William B. Pepper be appointed Guardian to Anna Scales a minor child of Henry Scales, upon his execution bond & security at the present term of this court.

Ordered that court be adjourned untill tomorrow morning 9 oclock.

James Paine
Paul Chiles
Wm. Wood

P-489 Tuesday Morning 22nd November 1825

Court met according to adjournment Present - Richard McGee, James Perry, Henry Hagen, James Dugger, James McCafferty, Thomas K. Gordon, Robert Oliver, Benton R. White, Abel Wilson, James White, Paul Chiles, John Young, Samuel E. Tomlinson, Willis S. McLawrine, Robert Read, Jesse Allen, Jacob Jones, Hezekiah Jones, John Laird, John Blue, William Ussery, Aurther Hicks, John C. Walker, Wm. Brown, Anderson Hogan, John Lee, Alexr. Black, John B. Goldberry, Joseph Roe, Thomas Harwood, Archibald McKissack, James H. Gilmore, Thos. Batte, Wm. Mayfield, John Buchannan, Beverly B. Watson, James Paine, Ephriam Massie, Thomas Brown, Wm. Wood, Wm. McGaw, Geo. M. Gibson, Wm. B. Pepper, John Bramlett, Peter Swanson, John W. Yates, Thomas Marks, Edwd. D. Jones & Arnold Zellum Esquires Justice of the Peace for Giles County.

A Deed of conveyance from John Daley, to Benjamin Burk for lot No. 82 in the Town of Lower Elkton was produced in open court and the Execution thereof acknowledged by the said John Daley and ordered to be certified for registration.

376

Ordered that James Lester be released from serving on the Grand & Petit Jury at the present term of this court.

A Deed of conveyance from Maxamillin H. Buchanan, to Stephen Shelton for forty six acres of land was produced in court & the Execution thereof acknowledged by the said Maxamillin H. Buchanan and ordered to be certified for registration.

The Sheriff returned into court the names of the following persons Summoned to attend as Grand & Petit Jurors at this term Pursuant to an order of the last term of this court a copy of which issued to the sd. Sheriff of Giles County, Towit, Daniel Puryear, James Lester, James Dearing, Archibald Crockett, Alexander Esselman, Thos. Graves, Stephen Anderson, Edward M. Brown, James Wilson, Duncan Brown, James Abernathy, John Bass, William H. Moore, Rodger Simpson, Jeremiah Barnes, John Marlow, Charles Buford, James L. Henry, John Hill, Hamilton C. Campbell, Joseph Knox, John Goff, Marshall Moody, John P. Taylor, Jeremiah Parker, & Henry J. Cooper, of whom John Goff foreman, Duncan Brown, Edward M. Brown, James L. Henry, Daniel Puryear, Stephen Anderson Alexander Esselman, James B. Abernathy, Marshall Moody, Rodger Simpson, Jeremiah Barnes, James Wilson and (p-490) Jeremiah Parker were elected empannelled & Sworn a Grand Jury of inquest for the body of the County, who having received their charge withdrew to consider of their presentments.

John W. Graves a constable of this county, was sworn to attend on the Grand Jury at the present term of this court.

A Deed of conveyance from Alexander McDonald to George Keltnor for sixteen acres of land, was produced in court and the Execution thereof acknowledged by the said Alexander McDonald & ordered to be certified for registration.

A Deed of conveyance from Alexander McDonald to George Keltnor for thirty acres of land was produced in court and the Execution thereof acknowledged by the said Alexander McDonald, and ordered to be certified for registration.

A Deed of conveyance from Thomas Griffin to Thomas Goodman for sixty Eight acres of land was produced in court and the Execution thereof proven by the oaths of William Ussery & Wade Barrett, the witnesses thereto, and ordered to be certified for registration.

A Deed of conveyance from Thomas Goodman to Miller Doggett for sixty Eight acres of land was produced in court and the Execution thereof proven by the oaths of William Ussery & Wade Barrett, the witnesses thereto, and ordered to be certified for registration.

Samuel E. Tomilinson Gentlemen who was commissioned by his Excellency the Governor of this State to act as a Justice of the Peace in & for this County, appeared in court and was qualified as the Law directs.

A Deed of conveyance from John Hightower administrator of Richd. Hightower deed. to Robert R. Alsup for three hundred & forty acres of land was produced in court, and the Execution thereof fully proven by the oaths of Thomas Young, one other witness thereto, and ordered to be certified for registration.

William Ussery and Thomas Batte Esquires came into court and resigned therein office as Justice of the Peace in & for the County of Giles.

P-491   Tuesday 22nd November 1825

A Deed of conveyance from Daniel Allen to Matthew M. Marrow for twelve and a half acres of land was produced in court and the Execution thereof proven by the oaths of Daniel Marrow & Alexander Marrow two of the witnesses thereto, and ordered to be certified for registration.

The State Plt.   )   Upon an Indictment
    Against   )
Joseph Davis Deft.   ) Joseph Slyder & Joseph McDonald came into court
) and acknowledged themselves indebted to the State of Tennessee in the sum of one hundred dollars each to be levied of their goods & chattles lands & tenments to the use of the State to be void on condition that the said Joseph Slyder make his personal appearance on the First Thursday after the third Monday in February next to prosecute and give evidence on behalf of the State against sd. Defendant and not depart without leave of the court.

A Deed of conveyance from Alexander McDonald & John McDonald to Bradly Phifer for thirty acres of land was produced in court and the Execution thereof proven by the oath of James White & Permenus Cox, the witnesses thereto, and ordered to be certified for registration.

Ordered that John Bass be released from serving on the Petit Jury untill Friday morning next.

The commissioners who were appointed to settle with the administrators of the Estate of Austin Smith decd. made return of sd. settlement which was ordered to be recorded.

Ordered that Thomas Marks and Allen Abernathy administrators of the Estate of Austin Smith decd. be allowed the sum of Fifteen dollars, each for their services in settling said Estate.

A Deed of conveyance from Alexander McDonald to John Wells for forty acres of land was produced in court and the Execution thereof acknowledged by the said Alexander McDonald and ordered to be certified for registration.

An Ordinary Licence for the term of twelve months & no longer is granted to James Patteson, whereupon he was qualified and gave bond & security as the law directs.

P-492. Tuesday November 22nd 1825

An ordinary Licence for the term of twelve months & no longer is granted to Thomas P. Estes whereupon he was qualified and gave bond and security as the Law directs.

William B. Pepper who was on yestoday appointed Guardian to Anna Scales, minor of Henry Scales came into court and Executed bond and security as the Law directs.

William Brown who is overseer of a cotton Gin appeared in court and was qualified as an inspector of cotton, and Executed bond & security as the law directs.

At least a majority of the Acting Justices of the Peace in and for the County being present and sitting as a court, the court proceeded by ballott to the Election of a coroner of this County, and upon counting the votes, Joseph Abernathy was found to be duly elected, who thereupon executed bond & security, and was qualified as the law directs.

Ordered that the Sheriff of this County summon twelve free holders of this County to inquire of the Idiocy or Lunacy of Mary Goff, of this County also enquire as to the property if any and value thereof, belonging to sd. Mary Goff, and that they make report of said inquests to the next term of this court.

Ordered that the Sheriff of this County summon twelve free holders of this County to enquire of the Idiocy or Lunacy of David Williams of this County, and also to enquire as to the property if any, and value thereof, belonging to said David Williams, and that they make report of said inquest to the next term of this court.

A Titled bond from David Kilcrease to Matthew Laffoon was produced in court, and the hand writing of said David Kilcrease proven by the oaths of James R. Dickey, & Joseph Rea, witnesses Sworn in Court there being no subscribing witnesses to said bond, and ordered to be spread (p-493) at full length upon the minutes, which bond read in the words & figures following, Towit, "Know all men by the State of Tennessee are held and finely bound unto Matthew Laffoon of Giles County and State aforesaid in the final sum of four hundred & sixty dollars, which payment well and truly to be made I bind myself, my heirs &c Sealed with my seal and dated the seventh of November 1823. The condition of the above obligation is such that where as the said Davis Kilcrease hath this day for the consideration of two hundred & thirty dollars hath bargained and sold unto the said Matthew Laffoon a certain piece or parcel of Land, Situated in

Giles County Head waters of big Creek in range 3 section one, begining on a large beach on the range line 118 poles north of the three mile post, from the south East corner of side section runs West 94 poles and south for complainents containing forty acres including the plantation whereon said Laffoon now lives, now should said Kilcrease convey the same by warrenty titles when complete payment of the money is made, then the above obligation to be void Else to remain in force and Effect.

            Davis Kilcrease (Seal)

Ordered that court be adjourned untill tomorrow morning nine oclock.

            John Laird
            James H. Graves
            Thomas Harwood

P-494 Wednesday 23rd November 1825

Court met according to adjournment Present John Laird) Esquires Justices
           James H. Graves &) of the Peace in &
           Thomas Harwood) for the County of
) Giles.

Bernard M. Patteson Plt.)   In Case
 Against   )
Shadrack Harwell Deft.) This day came the parties in their proper
) persons and by consent this suit is ordered to be dismissed at the costs of the defendant.
 It is therefore considered by the court that the plaintiff recover of said defendant his costs by him about his suit in this behalf expended.

On motion of Lewis H. Brown Sheriff of this County Lewis B. Marks was duly qualified to act as his deputy.

William J. Adire .. Plt.)   Judicial Attachment
 Against   )
Thomas Underwood Deft.) On affidavit of defendant this cause is
) ordered to be continued and postponed untill the next term of this court - and by consent leave is given each party to take depositions both in and out of this State, and that commission issue accordingly, which depositions when taken are to be read in evidence on the trial of this cause upon the plaintiffs giving to the Defendant and defendant giving to plaintiffs attorney fifteen days notice out and ten days notice within the State of the time & place of taking said depositions.

Robert H. Nelson ... Plt.)   Judicial Attachment
 Against   )
Thomas Underwood Deft.)

On the affidavit of the defendant this cause is ordered to be continued, and on motion of said defendant, ordered that a commission issue to any two of the Acting Justices of the Peace in and for the County of Madison & State of Alabama to take the depositions of David Owens, Alfred James, Barnett Tatum & John Philips, which when taken are to be read in evidence on the trial of this cause upon the defendant giving to the plaintiffs attorney fifteen days notice of the the time and place of taking the same.

The Grand Jury returned into court an Indictment of the State against Joseph Davis for an affray with and an assault (p-495) and battery on the body of Joseph Slider & withdrew to consider of further presentments.

Dudly Smith Plt.)   In Case
 Against)
John Butler Deft.) This day came the parties by their attornies
) and thereupon came a Jury of good & Lawful men
Towit, Hamilton C. Campbell, Charles Buford, John Hill, Archibald Crockett, Henry J. Cooper, Jefferson O. Tarkington, George Bowers, Mason Moss, Ambrose Cobb, Albert G. Underwood, William Jackson, & Henry J. Croft, who being elected tried and Sworn well and truly to try the issue between the parties in this case, upon their oaths do say that they find said issue in favor of the defendant.
 It is therefore considered by the court that the Defendant go hence without day and recover of the plaintiff his costs by him about his defence in this behalf expended.

Gerald Irby . . . . Plt.)   In Case
 Against)
Elnathan G. Brown Deft.) This day came the parties by their at-
) tornies and thereupon came a Jury of
good and lawful men, Towit, Charles Buford, Hamilton C. Campbell, Archibald Crookett, John Hill, John W. Fuller, Samuel Craig, John Porter, John L. White, Henry Yancy, John W. Fuller, John Roberts, Henry McAnnick and John Keenan, who being elected tried and sworn well and truly to try the issue joined between the parties in this case, who having heard the evidence were permitted to disperse to meet again tomorrow morning nine oclock.

On motion of Lewis H. Brown Sheriff of Giles County, Levi Reed was duly qualified to act as his deputy.

William Cox, Plt.)   Certiorari
 Against)
John Cox, Deft.) On the affidavit of the plaintiff this cause
) is ordered to be continued, and by consent
leave is given each party to take depositions and that commission issue accordingly, which depositions when taken, are to be read in evidence on the trial of this cause upon the plaintiffs giving to the defendant and the defendant giving the plaintiff ten days notice in this County on in either of the adjoining counties, of the time and place of taking said depositions.

P-496   Wednesday 23rd November 1825

John Pillow Plt.   )   Motion
    Against   )
John Defoe Deft.   )   On motion of the plaintiff by Rivers & Tarpley
)   his attornies, who Suggests the court now here,
that he as security of John Defoe has been compelled to pay to Lewis B.
Marks Deputy Sheriff of Giles County & at the instance of the State of
Tennessee, on the 17th day of September 1824 the sum of twelve dollars
& twenty five cents, and it not appearing to the satisfaction of the court
from the record produced that said John Pillow was security for said John
Defoe. It is ordered by the court that a Jury be empannelled to ascertain
whether said plaintiff did on the day aforesaid pay the sum aforesaid as
security of said John Defore, and thereupon came a Jury of good and lawful
men Towit, Hamilton C. Campbell, Charles Buford, John Hill, Archibald
Crockett, Henry J. Cooper, Jefferson O. Tarkington, George Bowers, Robert
Brooks, Mason Moss, Ambrose Cobbs, Albert G. Underwood, and William Jackson,
who being elected tried and sworn well and truly to try the facts
aforesaid upon their oaths do say that said plaintiff did on the 17th
day of September 1824 pay said Lewis B. Marks, the sum of twelve dollars
and twenty five cents, as security for sd. John Defoe. It is therefore
on motion of sd. plaintiff considered by the court that said John Pillow
recover of sd. John Defoe said sum of twelve dollars & twenty five cents,
with legal interest thereon from the 17th day of September 1824 untill
paid and his costs by him about his motion in this behalf expended.

Matthew Pate Plt.   )   Motion
    Against   )
John Pate Deft.   )   On motion of the plaintiff by Rivers & Tarpley,
)   his attornies who suggests to the court, now
here, that he as security for John Pate, has been compelled to pay to
Danl. Puryear constable of Giles County at the instance of Thomas Graves,
on the 2nd day of April 1825 the sum of eight Dollars & thirty five cents,
and its not appearing to the satisfaction of the court from the record
produced that said Matthew Pate was security for sd. John Pate. It is
ordered by the court that a Jury be empannelled to ascertain whether said
plaintiff do on the day aforesd. pay the sum aforesd. as security of said
John Pate and thereupon came a Jury of good and lawful men, Towit, Charles
Buford, Hamilton C. Campbell, Archibald Crockett, John Hill, John W. Fuller,
Samuel Craig, Samul. S. Smith, John Porter, John L. White, Jeptha Ezell,
Henry Yancy & John Roberts   (p-497)   who being elected tried and sworn
well & truly to try the facts aforesaid upon their oaths do say that said
plaintiff did on the 2nd day of April 1825 pay said Danl. Puryear the sum
of Eight dollars & thirty five cents as security for sd. John Pate - It is
therefore on motion of sd. Plaintiff considered by the court that said
Matthew Pate recover of said John Pate sd. sum of Eight dollars & thirty
five cents with legal interests thereon from 2nd day of April 1825 untill
paid, and his costs by him about his motion in this behalf expended.

Matthew Pate Plt.   )   Motion
    Against   )
John Pate Deft.   )   On motion of the plaintiff by Rivers & Tarpley
)   his attornies, who suggests to the court, now
here, that he as security of John Pate has been compelled to pay to Richard

Bently constable of Giles County at the instance of Wm. Pillow on the 5th day of May 1825, the sum of Eighteen Dollars & seven & three fourth cents, and it not appearing to the satisfaction of the court from the record produced that said Pate was security for sd. John Pate. It is ordered by the court that a Jury be empannelled to ascertain whether said plaintiff did on the day aforesaid pay the sum aforesd. as security for said John Pate, and thereupon came a Jury of good and lawful men, Towit, Charles Buford, Hamilton C. Campbell, Archibald Crockett, John Hill, John W. Fuller, Samuel Craig, Samuel S. Smith, John Porter, John L. White, Jeptha Ezell, Henry Young & John Roberts, who being elected tried and Sworn well & truly to try the fact aforesaid upon their oaths do say that said plaintiff did on the fifth day of May 1825 pay said Richard Bently the sum of eighteen dollars seven and three fourth cents, as security for said John Pate. It is therefore on motion of said plaintiff considered by the court that sd. Matthew Pate recover of said John Pate sd. sum of eighteen dollars seven & three fourth cents with legal interest thereon from the 5th day of May 1825, untill paid and his costs by him about his motion in this behalf Expended.

Ordered that court be adjourned untill tomorrow morning 9 oclock.

                 H. Hagen
                 Thos. Harwood
                 James H. Graves

P-498   Thursday Morning 24th November 1825

Court met according to adjournment Present, Henry Hagen) Esquires Justice
               Thomas Harwood &) of the Peace for
               James H. Graves) Giles County.

 Henry Hagen Esquire who was an Acting Justice of the Peace in and for this County and chairman of this court, came into court and resigned his office of Justice of the Peace & Chairman of this court.

Richard H. Blow Plt.   )   In Case
  Against   )
James Moseley Deft.   ) This day came the parties by their attornies,
) and ordered that this suit be dismissed, at the costs of the Defendant - It is therefore considered by the court that the plaintiff recover of said defendant his costs by him about his suit in this behalf expended.

William Maxwell Plt.   )   Certiorari
  Against   )
John McAnnick Deft.   ) This day came the parties by their attornies,
) and by consent this suit is ordered to be dismissed at the cost of the defendant. It is therefore considered by the court that the plaintiff recover of said Defendant his costs by him about his suit in this behalf expended.

Thomas S. Riddle Plt.) In Case
    Against)
John H. Moore Deft.) This day came the plaintiff by his attorney
) and ordered that this suit be dismissed –
It is therefore considered by the court that the Defendant recover of the plaintiff his costs by him about his defence in this behalf expended.

Ordered by the court that Alexander Black Esquire be appointed chairman pro tem of this court.

The State ... Plt.) Upon a recognizance for Bastardy
    Against)
William B. Smith Deft.) This day came the Solicitor General for the
) State and ordered that this suit be dismissed at the defendants costs. It is therefore considered by the court that the plaintiff recover of Defendant her costs about her suit in this behalf expended.

P-499 Thursday 24th November 1825

Gerald Irby .... Plt.) In Case
    Against)
Elnathan G. Brown Deft.) This day came the parties by their attornies
) and thereupon came the Jury who were sworn on yestoday well and truly to try the issue joined between the parties in this case, who upon their oaths do say that they find said issue in favour of the plaintiff and assess his damages by reason thereof to twenty dollars & twenty five cents, besides costs. It is therefore considered by the court that the plaintiff recover of sd. defendant the damages aforesaid in form aforesd. by the Jurors aforesaid assessed and his costs by him about his suit in this behalf expended.

The State .. Plt.) Upon an Indictment for an affray with &
    Against) an assault & battery on the body of
James Tucker &)Defts.) Joseph Slider.
Caswell Tucker))
) Joseph Slider & James McDonald came into court and acknowledged themselves indebted to the State of Tennessee in the sum of one hundred dollars, each to be levied of their goods and chattles lands & tenments to the use of the State, to be void on condition that the said Joseph Slider appear here on the first Thursday after the third Monday in February next, and prosecute and give evidence on behalf of the State against said Defendants, for an affray with & an assault & battery on the body of sd. Joseph Slider & not depart without leave of the court.

The State Plt.) Upon an Indictment for & affray with & an
    Against) assault & battery on the body of Wm. Worsham.
William Webb Deft.)
) This day came the Solicitor General for the State as also the defendant in his proper person who being charged on the Indictment in this case pleads Guilty and because he will not contend with

the State agrees to submit himself to the Justice and mercy of the court. It is therefore considered by the court that he make his fine with the State to the amount of ten dollars, and that he pay the costs of this prosecution, and that he be committed to the custody of the Sheriff of this County there to remain till said fine & costs be paid, or that he give security for the payment of the same and thereupon came Wm. Bracken and undertook as security for said defendants. It is therefore considered by the court that the State recover of sd. Defendants and Wm. Bracken the fine & costs aforesaid.

P-500 Thursday 24th November 1825

The State . . . Plt.) Indictment for making & assault on the body
    Against   ) of Henry Steele.
James Simmons Deft.)
) This day came the Solicitor General for the
State as also the defendant in his proper person, who being charged on the Indictment in this case pleads guilty, and because he will not contend with the State agrees to submit himself to the Justice & mercy of the court. It is therefore considered by the court that he make his fine with the State to the amount of one dollar & that he pay the cost of this prosecution.

A Deed of conveyance from Charles Perkins to Henry Hagen for sixty three acres of land was produced in court and the execution thereof proven by the oaths of Lewis H. Brown & Nathaniel Young, the witnesses thereto, and ordered to be certified for registration.

A Deed of conveyance from Charles Perkins to Henry Hagen for one hundred & forty eight acres of land was produced in court & the Execution thereof proven by the oaths of Lewis H. Brown & Nathaniel Young, the witnesses thereto, and ordered to be certified for registration.

James Ashmon Admr. of)Plt.) Sciarifacias
Charles Choat decd.)   )
    Against   ) This day came the plaintiff by his at-
Valentine Choate &)Defts.) torney, and it appearing to the Satis-
Philips Parchman   )   ) faction of the court, now here, that
) said plaintiff as administrator as
aforesaid did at September term 1817 of this court of Pleas & Quarter Sessions of Giles County in the State of Tennessee recovered a Judgment against Moses Choate for the sum of one hundred & Eighty four dollars & seventy Eight cents damages together with the sum of one hundred & forty nine dollars & ninety seven & a half cents costs, and it also appearing to the satisfaction of the Court a Capias Adstas fac indemn issued from the Clerks office aforsaid, court on said Judgment tested on the third Monday of February 1824 which was returned at the May Term 1824 of said court, "not found," and where as it also appearing to the Satisfaction of said that Valentine Choate & Philip Prarchman were the Special bail, of said Moses Choate in the above mentioned case of (p-501) James Ashmore administrator &c as Afsd. against Sd. Moses Choate & that since the return of sd. Writ of Capias Adsatis faciaindenu as aforesaid two writs of Sciri facias

have been issued from the clerks office of this court in this cause to the Sheriff of this county directed commanding him to make known to said defendants that they appear in open court & shew cause if any they have why sd. plaintiff should not have Execution against them for the amount afsd. Judgment both of which have been returned "not found" all which appears of record on motion of the plaintiff by his attorney & said Defendants being Solemnly called & coming not or shewing any cause why execution should not be issued against them upon said Judgment according to the prayer of sd. Scire facias. It is considered by the court that sd. plaintiff as admr. as aforesaid have Executed against said defendants, for the amount of said Judgments herein before set fourth, with interest upon the damages aforesd. from the last day of September 1817 at the rate of six pr. cent pr. annum till this time & his costs by him about his Scire facias in this behalf Expended.

James H. Graves Plt.)   Motion
    Against   )
Nathaniel Steele Deft.) On motion of the plaintiff by Harris &
) Field his attornies, who suggests to the court, now here, that he as Security of Nathaniel Steele has been compelled to pay to William C. Mayfield constable of Giles County at the instance of Thomas McKissack on the 3rd day of February 1823, the sum of forty five dollars & twenty five cents, and it not appearing to the Satisfaction of the court, from the record produced that said James H. Graves was security for said Nathaniel Steele - It is ordered by the court that a Jury be empannelled to ascertain whether said plaintiff did on the day aforesaid pay the sum aforesaid as security of said Nathaniel Steele, and thereupon came a Jury of good and lawful men, towit, Alfred Yancey, Henry J. Cooper, Patrick H. Braden, Joseph S. Tarkington, John E. Holden, William Webb, John Davenport, William James, Joel Lane, Thomas Brown, John Goff & James Simmons, who being elected tried and sworn well and truly to try the facts aforesaid upon their oaths do say that said plaintiff did on the 3rd day of February 1823, pay said William C. Mayfield the sum of forty five dollars & twenty five cents as security for said Nathaniel Steele. (p-502) (Thursday 24th November 1825) It is therefore on motion of said plaintiff considered by the court that said James H. Graves recover of said Nathaniel Steele, said sum of forty five dollars & twenty five cents, with Legal interest thereon from the 3rd day of February 1823, untill paid, and his costs by him about his motion in this behalf expended.

Ordered that court be adjourned untill tomorrow morning 9 oclock.

                                                  James Perry
                                                  James H. Graves
                                                  Anderson Hogan

                     Friday Morning 25th November 1825

Court met according to adjournment Present James Perry) Esquire Justice
                                        James H. Graves &) of the Peace for
                                        Anderson Hogan   ) Giles County.

A Deed of conveyance from Henry Hagen to James & Lewis Conner for one hundred & fifty eight acres of land, was produced in court, and the Execution thereof acknowledged by the said Henry Hagen & ordered to be certified for registration.

A Deed of conveyance from Henry Hagen to James & Lewis Conner for sixty three acres of land was produced in court and the Execution thereof acknowledged by the said Henry Hagen and ordered to be certified for registration.

Gerald Irby ... Plt.   )   In Debt
    Against   )
Alnathan G. Brown Deft)   From the Judgment of the court in this case
)   rendered, the Defendant prayed an appeal to
the honorable the Circuit Court to be held for the County of Giles, and having bond & security as the law directs the same was granted him.

A Deed of conveyance from Lewis H. Brown Sheriff of Giles County to Henry Hagen for lot No. 56 in the Town of Pulaski was produced in court and the execution thereof acknowledged by the sd. Lewis H. Brown & ordered to be certified for registration.

P-503   Friday 25th November 1825

Ordered by the court that Henry J. Cooper be released from further service as a petit Juror at this term.

On petition of Leonard Brown ordered that Writs of certiorari & Supercedeas issue to stay proceedings & remove to this court the record of a Judgment rendered by Richd. McGee Esquire an Acting Justice of the peace in & for the County of Giles in favour of Sally Maclin & Z. Maclin against sd. Leonard Brown for costs on the day of 1825 upon the petitioners giving bond & security according to Law.

John G. Braden & Patrick H.)   )   In Debt
Braden Executor of Joseph) Plts.   )
Braden deceased   )   )   This day came the parties by their
    Against   )   attorneys and thereupon came a
Joel Lane .... Deft.   )   Jury of good & lawful men, Towit,
)   Charles Buford, Archibald Crockett,
John Hill, Hamilton C. Campbell, Charles C. Abernathy, Thomas Underwood, Samuel S. Smith, James B. Kimbrough, Charles Deavers, Asa A. Estes, Leonard Brown, & Henry T. Kimbrough who being elected tried and sworn well and truly to try the issue joined between the parties in this case, upon their oaths do say that they find for the defendant.
It is therefore considered by the court that the defendant go hence without day and recover of the plaintiffs his costs by him about his defence in this behalf expended, From which Judgment the plaintiffs prayed an appeal to the honorable the Circuit court to be held for the County of Giles, and having executed bond & security as the law directs, the same was granted them.

The State Plt.) Indictment for an affray with & an assault &
    Against   ) battery on the body of Langford Fitzgerald.
Wm. Watson Deft.)
) This day came as well the Solicitor General for the State as also the Defendant in his proper person who being charged on the indictment in this case pleads not guilty, and for his trial puts himself upon his Country, and the Solicitor General for the State on the part of the State Likewise therefore let a Jury come &c who as well &c to recognize &c & thereupon came a Jury of good and Lawful men, Towit,

P-504 Henry J. Cooper, John E. Holden, John Goff, Edward M. Brown, Daniel McCarmack, Grey H. Edwards, Simpson H. White, Thomas Porter, Larkin B. Moore, John L. White, Moses Preston and Rodgers Simpson, who being elected tried and sworn well and truly to try the issue of traverse between the State and said defendant retired out of court to consider of their verdict, and after some time returned and say they cannot agree. By consent of the parties and with the assent of the court Henry J. Cooper one of the Jurors in this case was withdrawn and the cause continued untill the next term of this court that a new trial may be had therein.

Ordered that court be adjourned untill tomorrow morning nine oclock.

                                                        James Perry
                                                        James H. Graves
                                                       Anderson Hogan

Saturday Morning 26th November 1825

Court met according to adjournment Present James Perry) Esquires Justices
                                                    James H. Graves &) of the Peace for
                                                    Anderson Hogan   ) Giles County.

The State Plt.) Upon an Indictment for obstructing publick high-
    Against   ) way.
Jacob Cox Deft.)
) This day came the Solicitor General for the State as also the defendant in his proper person, who being charged on the indictment in this case pleads not guilty and for his trial puts himself upon his Country, and the Solicitor General for the State on the part of the State Likewise therefore let a Jury come &c who as well &c to recognize &c and thereupon came a Jury of good and lawful men, towit, Charles Buford, Hamilton C. Campbell, Archibald Crockett, John Hill, John Keenan, Robert Harris, Henry Kimbrough, Thomas Underwood, Leonard Brown, William V. Loving, John Loveless, & Archibald Smith who being elected tried and sworn well & truly to try the issue of Traverse between the State and said Defendants upon their oaths do say (p-505) that said Defendant is guilty as is charged in the Indictment.

It is therefore considered by the court that he make his fine with the State to the amount of two dollars & fifty cents and that he pay the costs of this procution, and that he be committed to the custody of the Sheriff of this County thereto remain till sd. fine & costs be paid.

A Deed of conveyance from James Neal to Thomas Hudson for one hundred and a half acres of land was produced in court and the Execution thereof proven by the oaths of Stirling H. Lester & Richard G. Scoggins, two of the witnesses thereto, and ordered to be certified for registration.

An account of sale of the Estate of Samuel Cox decd. was returned by administrators and ordered to be recorded.

A Bill of sale from Henry Hagen to Jacob Shall for certain property therein Specified was produced in court and the Execution thereof acknowledged by the sd. Henry Hagen and ordered to be certified for registration.

A Bill of sale from George W. Locke to Jacob Shall for certain property therein specified was produced in court and the Execution thereof acknowledged by the said George W. Locke and ordered to be certified for registration.

A Bill of sale from Ann Locke to Jacob Shall for certain property therein specified was produced in court and the Execution thereof proven by the oath of John B. Locke one of the witnesses thereto, and ordered to be certified for registration.

A Deed of conveyance from Eliab Vinson to Rodgers Simpson for forty one acres & thirty poles of land was produced in court and the Execution thereof proven by the oaths of William Brown & John W. Graves the witnesses thereto, and ordered to be certified for registration.

The State Plt.) Recognizance
Against)
John R. Biddick Deft.) This day came the Solicitor General for the
) State who suggests to the court now here,
that no person attend for the purpose of prosecuting the defendant in this case thereupon by order of court said defendant is ordered to be discharged.

P-506   Saturday 26th November 1825

Thomas Goff . . . Plt.) In Debt
Against)
Barnard M. Patteson Deft. *) On motion of the Defendant ordered that
) a commission issue to any two of the
Acting Justices of the Peace in & for the County of Laurence & State of Alabama to take the depositions of John Galliger & Thomas M. Farley, which depositions when taken are to be read in evidence on the trial of this cause upon the defendant giving to the plaintiff fifteen days notice of the time & place of taking the Same.

Jesse Bull Plt.) In Case
Against)
Jacob Couch Deft.)
) On motion of the plaintiff ordered that a commission issue to any two of the Acting Justices

of the Peace in & for the County of Person & State of North Carolina, to take the deposition of Isham Edward & R. Vanhook, which depositions when taken are to be read in evidence on the trial of this cause, upon the plaintiffs giving to the defendant twenty five days, notice of the time & place of taking the same.

Thomas Pate to the use &c Plt.)   Appeal
        Against   )
Blackmore H. Pate ... Deft.)   This day came the parties by their
)   attornies, and thereupon came a
Jury of good & lawful men, Towit, Duncan Brown, Edward M. Brown, James L. Hendry, Daniel Puryear, Stephen Anderson, Alexander Essleman, James Abernathy, Marshall Moody, Rodgers Simpson, Jeremiah Barnes, James Wilson, & Jeremiah Parker, who being Elected tried and Sworn well and truly to try the issue of fact in this case retired out of court to consider of the verdict, after some time returned and say they can't agree by consent of parties & with the assent of the court they were permitted to disperse to meet again Tuesday morning ten oclock.

The State ... Plt.   )   Upon a presentment for obstructing Rich-
    Against   )   land Creek.
Henry Kimbrough Deft.)
)   Henry Kimbrough & Lewis H. Brown, came into court & acknowledged themselves indebted to the State of Tennessee in the sum of one hundred dollars each, to be levied of their goods & chattles lands & tenments to the use of the State to be void on condition that said Henry Kimbrough appear here on the first Thursday after the third Monday in February next & answer the State on the aforesaid presentment for obstructing Richland Creek and not depart without leave of this court.

P-507   Saturday 26th November 1825

The State ... Plt.   )   A horse
    Against   )
Thomas Brown Deft.)   Thomas Brown & Jeremiah Parker came into
)   court and acknowledged themselves indebted to the State of Tennessee in the sum of one hundred dollars each to be levied of their goods & chattles lands & tenments to the use of the State to be void on condition that said Thomas Brown appear here on the first Thursday after the third Monday in February next and answer the State on the aforesaid Indictment for wounding a horse and not depart without leave of this court.

The State Plt.   )   Upon an Indictment for wounding a horse.
    Against   )
Thomas Brown Deft.)   Ralph Graves comes into court and acknow-
)   ledges himself indebted to the State of Tennessee in the sum of one hundred dollars, to be levied of his goods & chattles lands & tenments to the use of the State to be void on condition that the said Ralph Graves appear hereon the first Thursday after the third Monday in February next, and prosecute & give evidence on behalf of the State against said Defendant, upon the aforesd. Indictment and not depart without leave of this court.

The State Plt.) Upon an Indictment for making an assault on the
    Against) body of Adam R. Faris.
George Kirk Deft.)

        Adam R. Faris & John E. Holden came into court & acknowledged themselves indebted to the State of Tennessee in the sum of one hundred dollars each to be levied of their good & chattles lands and tenments, to the use of the State to be void on condition that sd. Adam R. Faris appear on the First Thursday after the third Monday in February next to prosecute & give evidence on behalf of the State against said Defendant upon the aforesaid Indictment and not depart without leave of this court.

The State Plt.) Indictment for making an assault on the body of
    Against) Adam R. Faris.
George Kirk Deft.)

        Adam R. Faris & John E. Holden came into court and acknowledged themselves indebted to the State of Tennessee in the sum of one hundred dollars each to be levied of their goods & chattles lands & tenments, to the use of the State to be void on condition that sd. Adam R. Faris appear here on the first Thursday after the third Monday in February next to prosecute & give evidence on behalf of the State against sd. Defendant upon the aforesaid Indictment and not depart with out leave of this court.

P-508   Saturday 26th November 1825

The State Plt.) Indictment for & an assault & battery on the
    Against) body of Wm. Worsham.
William Webb Deft.)

        Ordered by the court that the order made on a former day of this term fining the Defendant in this case ten dollars, be reduced to five Dollars, and that the Defendant make his fine with the State to the amount of five dollars, and that he pay the costs of this prosecution

The State Plt.) Upon Indictment for an affray with & an as-
    Against) sault & battery on the body of L. Fitzgerald.
Wm. Watson Deft.)

        This day came the Solicitor General for the State and the Defendant altho solemnly called came not but made default. It is therefore considered by the court that a Judgment Ni Si, for the sum of two hundred & fifty dollars according to the tenor of his recognizance be entered up against him and that a Scire facias issue against him returnable to the next term of this

The State Plt.) Upon an Indictment for an affray with & an
    Against) assault & battery on the body of Lankford
Wm. Watson Deft.) Fitzgerald.

    Beverly B. Watson who was bound in a recognizance for the appearance of the aforesaid defendant being Solemnly called and required to bring with him the body of said defendant came not but made default. It is therefore considered by the court that a Judgment Ni Si, for the sum of one hundred & seventy five dollars according to the tenor of this recognizance be entered up against him, and that a Scire facias issue against him returnable to the next term of this court.

The State Plt.) Upon an indictment for an affray with & assault
    Against) & battery on the body of Lankford Fitzgerald.
Wm. Watson Deft.)

Lankford Fitzgerald who was recognized to appear here at this term and prosecute and give evidence on behalf of the State against said defendant on the aforesaid Indictment being called Solemnly came not but made default. It is therefore considered by the court that a Judgment Ni Si for the sum of one hundred dollars according to the tenor of his recognizance be entered up against him and that Scire facias issue against him returnable to the next term of this court.

P-509 Saturday 26th November 1825

William P. A. McCabe Plt.) Original Attachment
    Against)
John O. Troutman Deft.) This day came the plaintiff by his attorney and the defendant altho solemnly called came not but made default. It is therefore considered by the court that the plaintiff recover of the defendant the damages he has sustained by reason in the declaration mentioned, but because it is unknown to the court here what those damages are it is ordered that the same be enquired of by a Jury at the next term.

William P. A. McCabe Plt.) Original Attachment
    against)
John O. Troutman Deft.) Edward W. Tipton & Jeremiah Hale, who were summoned to attend as Garnishees at the present term of this court in this case being solemnly called, came not but made default. It is therefore considered by the court that a Judgment Ni Si be entered up against them and that Scire facias issue against them commanding them to appear at the next term of this court this court, and shew cause why they did not appear and answer on oath as Garnishees as aforesaid.

Patterson Crockett Plt.) Motion
    Against)
John Gray Deft.) This day came the plaintiff by Lunsford M. Bramlitt his attorney and it appearing from the inspection of the record to the satisfaction of the court, that at May Session 1821 Daniel Gray assee &c recovered a Judgment against Patterson Crockett, for the sum of one hundred & fifty dollars twelve cents Debt, 75 cents damages & Eleven dollars sixty & one half cents costs, and it not appearing to the satisfaction of the court, now here, from the record produced that said Patterson Crockett was security for said John Gray said sum of money above mentioned and thereupon came a Jury of good & lawful men, towit, Duncan Brown, Edward M. Brown, James L. Hendry, Daniel Puryear, Stephen Anderson, Alexander Esselman, James Abernathy, Marshall Moody, Rodgers Simpson, Jeremiah Barnes, James Wilson,

and Jeremiah Parker, who being elected well & truly to try the facts aforesaid upon their oaths do say that said plaintiff did pay as security for said John Gray the sum of two hundred & fifteen dollars & sixty seven and a half cents. It is therefore on motion (p-510) Saturday 26th November 1825, of said plaintiff, considered by the court that said Patterson Crockett recover of said John Gray said sum of two hundred & fifteen dollars & sixty seven and a half cents, with legal interest thereon from the 15th day of August 1825 untill paid, and his costs by him about his motion in this behalf expended.

Ordered that court be adjourned untill Monday Morning ten oclock.

A. Black
Robert Reed
B. B. Watson

Monday Morning 28th November 1825

Court met according to adjournment Present, Alexander Black, Beverly B. Watson, Robert Reed, Hezekiah Jones, William B. Pepper, George M. Gibson Archibald McKissack, James White, Joseph Rea, James Raines, Thomas Brown, John Blue, William Mayfield, John Buchanan, James Perry, and William Wood, Esquire Justice of the Peace for Giles County.

A Bill of sale from Lester Morris, to Lewis B. Morris for certain property therein specified was produced in court and the Execution thereof acknowledged by the said Lester Morris and ordered to be certified for registration.

Ordered that Hugh Torrence be appointed overseer of the road in the room of Henry Yancey resigned and that he have the same district of hands.

Ordered that an order of sale issue to James Boatright administrator of Daniel Boatright decd. commanding him to sell a negro woman by the name of Winney and her child the property of said Estate that he make report thereof as the Law directs.

Ordered that James Perry, Fountain Lester & James Patteson to be appointed commissioners to settle with Edward D. Jones administrator of the Estate of John Yancey decd. and that they make report thereof to the next term of this court.

P-511 Monday 28th November 1825

A Bill of sale from Henry J. Cooper to Henry Hagen for certain property therein specified was produced in court and the Execution thereof proven by the oaths of Charles C. Abernathy & Richard G. Scoggins the witnesses thereto, and ordered to be certified for registration.

Ordered that Thomas Young be appointed overseer of the road in the room of Seth J. Williamson resigned and that he have the same district of hands.

A Plat & Certificate of survey in the name of John Bass for one hundred & fifty acres of land and the assignment thereon from said John Bass to James Patteson was produced in court and the Execution thereof proven by the oaths of Andrew Fay & Joseph H. Hodge, the witnesses thereto, and ordered to be certified.

Ordered that Anner Samuel and Thomas Williams administrators of Anthony Samuel decd. be allowed a credit of Eleven dollars it being the amount of Abner Rays account, which was wrongfully charged to them on the original settlement.

On the motion of John Abernathy ordered that Robert McKnight, Archibald Smith, Robert Smith, John Young Junr., Archibald McKeenon, John McKnight & Aaron Smith, or any five of them be appointed a Jury to view & alter that part of the road from Gordon's to Huntsville & runing by sd. John Abernathys house commencing at the corner of Robert Smith's grass lot runing Southwardly a short distance & intereseot the same at some convenient point if its found to be practicable, and that they make report thereof to the next term of this court.

A Deed of conveyance from Fountain Lester, James Patteson & Tyree Rodes commissioners of the town of Pulaski to Lawson Hobson for lots Nos. 153-154 & 155 in sd. Town was produced in court and the Execution thereof acknowledged by the said Fountain Lester, James Patteson & Tyree Rodes, and ordered to be certified for registration.

Ordered that Samuel Anderson be appointed overseer of the road in the room of Robert Anderson decd. and that he have the same districts of hands.

P-512 Monday 28th November 1825

Ordered that John Goldsberty, William Brown, William B. Pepper, Marcus Mitchell, Isaac Mason, Hugh Adams, & Charles C. Abernathy, or any five of them be appointed a Jury to view the road so as to straighten it through Marshall Moodys, lane thence to angle to Hartwell Browns lane & see if it be proper to alter the same, and that they make report to the next term of this court.

Ordered that the County Trustee of this county pay to Rodgers Simpson the sum of twenty dollars for the support of clothing John Elder & William Elder paupers of this County, for the turm of twelve months from this time.

Ordered that David Browning be appointed overseer of the road in the room of James Shelton resigned that he have the same district of hands.

Ordered that John H. Rivers be appointed Guardian to Early Reasonover minor orphan of John Reasonover decd. whereupon he executed & security as the law direct.s.

Ordered that Tilman Holland be appointed overseer of the road in the room of Amos Vernon resigned and that he have the same district of hands.

Ordered that the County Trustee of this County pay to Lewis H. Brown Sheriff of this County the sum of fifty dollars for his Exofficio services for twelve months past.

Ordered that Thomas E. Abernathy, Thomas Batte & John Whitfield be appointed commissioners to settle with James Coldwell, & William A. Brown administrators of Henry Neal decd. and that they make report thereof to the next term of this court.

Ordered that Lander M. Shields be appointed overseer of the road in the room of John T. Montgomery resigned, and that he have the same district of hands.

The Jury who were appointed to view & mark out a road leaving the road that leads from Pulaski to Laurenceburg near David Potts & runing up (p-513) Monday 28th November 1825, Weekly Creek the nearest & best way in a direction to Mount Pleasant to the County line, made their report and said road is ordered to be established according to report.

Ordered that James Perry Esquire be appointed chairman of this court.

On the Petition of Daniel Puryear for the division of a tract of land in Giles County, being on the waters of Pigeon Roost Creek, which he claims by purchase by from the heirs of Mary Donaldson decd. and it appearing to the satisfaction of the court that all other claimants as heirs of sd. Mary Donaldson have been duly notified of this application by a notice inserted in the Columbian a paper printed in Columbia Tennessee. It is therefore ordered by the court that William Wood, Samuel H. Dodson, Jesse Pullen, William Pullen, Simpson H. White, Granville A. Pillow, & Thomas Johnson, be appointed commissioners to lay off, divide, & assign to said Puryear five ninths & five eigths of an undivided ninth of thirty nine acres of land, begining at a Stake in Daniel Puryear's line the corner of Puryears land which is a corner to a 509 acre tract then north 75 poles to a popular corner of a 509 acre survey in the South boundry line of a 2000 acre Survey granted to James M. Lewis, thence West with Lewis's line 83¼ poles to a Beach thence south 75 poles to a hickory in the north boundry line of said 509 acre Survey thence East to the begining containing 39 acres more or less, and that they make report thereof to the next term of this court.

Ordered that James Perry, William B. Pepper, & Alexander Black, and Tyree Rodes, be appointed commissioners to let to the lowest bidder the repairing of the windows in the court house, & that they make report &c.

The Jury who were appointed to view the road the nearest & best way from Brattons Hill near the head of Moores Creek to the County line, in a direction to Florance made report, and said road is ordered to be established according to review - and ordered that William Ferrell be appointed to oversee the opening of said road from Brattons hill to the road going to sd. Brattons from Anthony's Mill, and that he have under his direction for that purpose all the following hands, (p-514) Towit, John Raybourn, David Defoe, Thomas White, Elisha Anthony, James Pillow, Jesse Shelton, James Bunch, Richard Pillow, Meredith Bunch, Jefferson Chambers, Able Simpson, George Simpson, John Gordon, Wm. Murrel, W. Phleman, Joseph Pillow, Merrel Stafford & Joel Stafford.

Ordered that Robert Ross be appointed to oversee the opening of the road which leads from Brattons hill near the head of Moores Creek to the County line, in a direction to Florance from the road going to Anthonys Mill from Brattons to the County line, and that he have under his direction for that purpose, all the following hands, Towit, James Gean, Harvey Gean, John Warren, Hannibal Wheeler, George Hillhouse, William H. Ross, Theron H. Ross, Joseph Aidy, Owen Hardy, Bradly Phifer, Wm. Phifer, Chas. Phifer, Joseph Phifer, Tyree Yates and Samuel Yates.

An account of sale of the Estate of John Rawlings decd. returned by administrator & ordered to be recorded.

Ordered that the following tax list be recd. and that double tax thereon remitted, Towit, Robert Ross 15 acres of land
1 White poll.

Ordered that the Sheriff of this County Summon twelve free holders of this County to assess the damages Lawson Hobson has sustained by reason of the road leading from Pulaski to Mount Pleasant by way of Weakley Creek, runing through his cleared land, or that they turn sd. road elsewhere to some convenient place, and that they make report to the next term of this court.

A Deed of conveyance from William Davis to Moses Read for fifty nine acres of Land was produced in court and the Execution thereof proven by the oaths of James Kelso & Larkin S. Webb, the witnesses thereto, and ordered to be certified for registration.

Ordered that Archibald McKissack, Robert McLaurine & Robert Read, be appointed commissioners to settle with the administrators of Lewis Kirk decd. & that they report to the next term of this court.

P-515 Monday 28th November 1825

Ordered that the County Trustee of this County pay to Thomas C. Stone the sum of twenty six dollars and forty cents, for repairing Styles Grates & railings around the court house yard.

Ordered that Hezekiah Jones & James White, Esquires be appointed commissioners to let to the lowest bidder the keeping of Tabitha Browning an Idiot, upon giving fifteen days notice of the time and place, and that they make report to the next term of this court.

Ordered that Edmund Lane be appointed overseer of the road in the room of Joel Lane resigned, & that Archibald Crockett, Jacob Crochran & John Evans be added to his list of hands.

Ordered that Dangerfield Carpenter be bound an apprenticed to Isaac Crowder an Indenture to that effect having been entered unto between the chairman of this court and said Isaac Crowder.

Ordered that John McDonald be appointed Guardian to John Steele infant child of Robert G. Steele whereupon he gave bond & security as the Law directs.

A Deed of conveyance from Hamilton C. Campbell, to James R. Dickey for forty acres of Land was produced in court and the Execution thereof acknowledged by the said Hamilton C. Campbell & ordered to be certified for registration.

Ordered by the court that Willis Lane be permitted to build a mill on Robertson fork of Richland Creek on a tract of sixty five acres of Land owned by said Willis Lane and whereon Benjamin Vick now lives.

A Deed of conveyance from Wilton F. L. Jenkins to John Daly for lots Nos. 41 - 42 - 43 - & 44 in the Town of lower Elkton was produced in court and the Execution thereof acknowledged by the said Wilton F. L. Jenkins and ordered to be certified for registration/

F-516   Monday 28th November 1825

Ordered that Davis Brown & James Abernathy be appointed commissioners to settle with Thomas Brown administrator of the Estate of Jordon Hicks decd. & that they make report to the next term of this court.

Ordered that James P. Hicks be appointed Guardian to Tilman Hicks & Rebecca Hicks infant orphans of Jordon Hicks decd. whereupon he executed bond & security as the Law directs.

Ordered that the County Trustee of this County Pay to Lewis H. Brown the sum of twelve for furnishing & cutting wood for the court, for twelve months past.

Ordered that the County Trustee of this County pay to Lewis H. Brown Sheriff of Giles County the sum of twenty three dollars & forty four cents as per account filed.

Ordered that Stephen Samuel be released from all obligations with respect to an Indenture which was entered into between the chairman of this court & said Samuel binding to him a boy by the name of Achillis Samuel and that sd. Achillis Samuel be delivered to Henry Phenix.

Ordered that Archibald McKissack be appointed administrator of the Estate of John McKissack decd. whereupon he executed bond & security & was qualified as the Law directs.

An Inventory of the Estate of John McKissack decd. returned by Archd. McKissack the Admr. & ordered to be recorded.

Ordered that an order of sale issue to Archd. McKissack commanding him to expose to sale so much of the Estate of John McKissack decd. as will be sufficient to pay his debts, and that he make report thereof as the law directs.

Ordered that the County Trustee of this County pay to Robert Reed the sum of thirty one dollars for the support & maintenance of Nancy Wilson, a pauper of this County for twelve months from this date.

P-517 Monday 28th November 1825

An Inventory of the Estate of Robert Anderson decd. returned by the admr. of sd. Estate and ordered to be recorded.

Ordered that the County Trustee of this County pay to Robert Reed, the sum of Eighty dollars for the support and maintenance of William Harris & Eleanor Harris paupers of this county for twelve months from this time.

Ordered that William Chapman, Wm. Bracheen, Jacob Jones, Benjamin Smith, Simeon Hursby, James McAnse, & Richard Briggs, or any five of them be appointed a Jury to view the road from near Homer Raineys by Daniel Farzer's Mill thence by the widow Rea's thence the most direct way to the Shelbyville road at the plantation whereon William H. Fields now lives, and see if it be proper to open & establish the same, and that they make report thereof to the next term of this court.

Ordered that Fountain Lester, Charles C. Abernathy, & John Philips be appointed commissioners to settle with the Executors of the Estate of Reese Porter Senr. decd. and that they make report to the next term of this court.

Ordered that that part of the road leading from Pulaski to Lambs Ferry which passes by James B. Kimbroughs & which has been heretofore discontinued by order of the court be continued as a private way & mill road.

Ordered that James Buys be appointed cotton inspector in this County. Thereupon he was qualified and gave bond & security as the Law directs.

A Deed of conveyance from the heirs & Legates of Isaac Price decd. to Isaac Price for one hundred & fifty acres of Land was produced in court & the Execution thereof proven by the oaths of James Coldwell and Benjamin Burk the witnesses thereto. and ordered to be certified for registration.

A Deed of conveyance from the Heirs & Legates of Isaac Price Decd. to Esther Neal for one hundred & fifty acres of land was produced in court and the Execution thereof proven by the oaths (p-518) of James Coldwell & Benjamin Burk, the witnesses thereto, and ordered to be certified for registration.

A Deed of conveyance from William Price to Benjamin Burk for thirty Acres of land was produced in court and the Execution thereof partly proven by the oath of Wilton F. L. Jenkins, one of the witnesses thereto, and ordered to be certified.

It is ordered by the court that the following persons good and lawful men of the County of Giles, that is each one of who is a free white male citizen, and house holder of said County, over twenty one years of age not an overseer of a road, and who has not been appointed and served as a Juror of this county court for twelve months, Towit, William Conner, Nathan Davis, Jason Hopkins, John W. Bodenhammer, Wiley Bracken, William Rea, Daniel Morrow, George White, Jesse West, Edward Garland, John McDonald, Thomas McCanlass, John B. McCanlass, Holman R. Fowler, Benjamin Smith, Henry M. Newlin, Wiley Willsford, Richd. S. Stewart, Robert Adams, James Coldwell, Nicholas Jackson, Robert Ross, Joseph Goode, Joshua Rickman, Shadrack Cross, James Vance, & Robert Black, be Jurors to serve in this court at the next term on the third Monday in February next, that the Clerk deliver a copy of this order to the Sheriff of this County, and that he summon said persons to attend and serve accordingly.

Ordered that James Perry Esquire be appointed to take a list of taxable property & polls in Captain Lesters Company for the year 1826 and that he make return thereof to the next term of this court.

Ordered that William Mayfield Esquire be appointed to take a list of taxable property & polls in Captain Wheeler's Company for the year 1826, and that he make return thereof to the next term of this court.

Ordered that Beverly B. Watson Esquire be appointed to take a list of taxable property & polls in Captain Hills Company for the year 1826, and that he make return thereof to the next term of this court.

P-519 Monday 28th November 1825

Ordered that John Buchanan Esquire be appointed to take a list of taxable property & polls in Captain Henrys Company for the year 1826, and that he make return thereof to the next term of this court.

Ordered that Jessee Allen Esquire be appointed to take a list of taxable property & polls in Captain Bevers Company for the year 1826, and that he make return thereof to the next term of this court.

Ordered that George M. Gibson Esquire be appointed to take a list of taxable property & polls in Captain Gibson Company for the year 1826, and that he make return thereof to the next term of this court.

Ordered that Joseph Rea Esquire be appointed to take a list of taxable property & polls in Captain Tiptons Company for the year 1826, and that he make return thereof to the next term of this court.

Ordered that William Woods Esquire be appointed to take a list of taxable property & polls in Captain Pillow Company for the year 1826 and that he make report thereof to the next term of this court.

Ordered that Benton R. White Esquire be appointed to take a list of taxable property & polls in Captain Ross Company for the year 1826, & that he make report thereof to the next term of this court.

Ordered that John Young Esquire be appointed to take a list of taxable property & polls in Captain Chiles Compay for the year 1826, & that he make return thereof to the next term of this court.

Ordered that John Lee Esquire be appointed to take a list of taxable property & polls in Captain Graves Company for the year 1826, & that he make return thereof to the next term of this court.

Ordered that Ephriam M. Massie Esquire be appointed to take a list of taxable property & polls in Captain Nances Company for the year 1826, & that he make return thereof to the next term of this court.

Ordered that Jacob Jones Esquire be appointed to take a list of taxable property & polls in Captain Frazers Company for the year 1826, and that he make return thereof to the next term of this court.

P-520 Monday 28th November 1825

Ordered that Edward D. Jones be appointed to take a list of taxable property & Polls in Captain Deanes Company for the year 1826, & that he make return thereof to the next term of this court.

Ordered that John Laird Esquire be appointed to take a list of taxable property & polls in Captain McCalls Company for the year 1826 & that he make return thereof to the next term of this court.

Ordered that John C. Walker Esquire be appointed to take list of taxable property & polls in Captain Shields Company for the year 1826 & that he make return thereof to the next term of this court.

Ordered that John B. Goldberry Esquire be appointed to take a list of taxable property & polls in Captain Harwells Company for the year 1826 & that he make return thereof to the next term of this court.

Ordered that William Brown Esquire be appointed to take a list of taxable property & polls in Captain Potts Company for the year 1826 & that he make return thereof to the next term of this court.

Ordered that Jas. White Esq. be appointed to take a list of taxable property & polls in Captain Gooches Company for the year 1826, & that he make return thereof to the next term of this court.

Ordered that John Wyart Esquire be apointed to take a list of taxable property & polls in Captain Magus Company for the year 1826 & that he make return thereof to the next term of this court.

Ordered that Able Wilson Esquire be appointed to take a list of taxable property & polls in Captain Bass Company for the year 1826, & that he make return thereof to the next term of this court.

Ordered that Arnold Zellner Esq. be appointed to take a list of taxable property & polls in Captain McCormick Company for the year 1826, & that he make return thereof to the next term of this court.

Ordered that James Paine Esquire be appointed to take a list of taxable property & polls in Captain Benson's Company for the year 1826, & that he make return thereof to the next term of this court.

Ordered that John Blue Esquire be appointed to take a list of taxable property & polls in Captain Moore's Company for the year 1826 & that he make return thereof to the next term of this court.

P-521   Monday 28th November 1826

Ordered that Tyree Rodes Treasurer of the Commissioners of the Town of Pulaski, be allowed five per cent on all monies by him received and paid out from the sale of the Lots in said Town, and that he be allowed the sum of seven hundred and thirty four dollars for his servies as one of the commissioners of said Town all of which is to be paid out of monies arriving from the sale of the Lots in said Town.

Ordered that James Perry, Thomas Martin & German & C. C. Abernathy or any three of them be appointed commissioners to settle with the old commissioners of the Town of Pulaski and that they make return of said Settlement to the next term of this court.

Ordered that Court be adjourned untill tomorrow morning nine oclock.

James Perry
John Bramlett
Thomas Brown

Thursday Morning 29th November 1825

Court met according to adjournment Present James Perry) Esquire Justices
                                           John Bramblett) of the Peace for
                                           Thomas Brown) Giles County.

A Deed of conveyance from Henry Hagen and John E. Holden to Fountain Lester for lot No. 56 of the large lots in the Town of Pulaski, was produced in court and the execution thereof proven by the oaths of James R. Dickey & Richard G. Scoggins, the witnesses thereto, and ordered to be certified for registration.

William Carter Plt.) Judicial Attachment - This day came the
    Against   ) parties by their attornies and thereupon
Thomas Underwood Deft.) came a Jury of good and lawful men, Towit,
                              Charles Buford, Hamilton C. Campbell,
John Hill, Archibald Crockette, William R. Brown, Wm. Rivers, Isaac Mayfield, Asa A. Esters, Jason Hopkins, Ambrose Mayfield, Saml. S. Smith, & John McDonald - who being elected tried & sworn well & truly to try the issue joined between the parties in this case upon their oaths do say that they find said issue in favour of the Defendant - It is therefore considered by the court that the (p-522) Defendant go hence without day and recover of the plaintiff his costs by him about his defence in this behalf expended.

Thomas Pate, to the use of &c Plt.)   Appeal
    Against   )
Blackman H. Pate . . Deft.   ) This day came the parties by
) their attornies and thereupon
came the Jury who were sworn on Saturday well & truly to try the issue joined between the parties in this case who again retired out of court to consider of their verdict, after some time returned and say they cannot agree, by consent of parties and withe the ascent of the court Duncan Brown one of the Jurors in this case was withdrawn and the cause continued untill the next term of this court that a new trial may be had therein.

Reuben Burton Admr. &c Plt.	Judicial Attachment
Against	
Thomas Underwood Deft.	

This day came the parties by their attornies & thereupon came a Jury of good & lawful men, Towit, David W. Porter, Thomas C. Porter, Millinton Tidwell, Jesse Crittenton, Robert C. Steele, John Porter, Simpson H. White, David McCullough, Thomas Bratton, Thomas Webb, Graves Hester, & William Hill, who being elected tried & sworn well & truly to try the issue joined between the parties in this case upon their oaths do say that they find said issue in favour of the defendant – It is therefore considered by the court that the defendant go hence without day and recover of the plaintiff his costs by him about his defence in this behalf expended.

A Deed of conveyance from Wm. Woods to German Lester for fifty seven acres of land was produced in court and the Execution thereof acknowledged by the said William Woods and ordered to be certified for registration.

John A. Jones Guardian of Catey Cox returned an account against his said word which is ordered to be recorded.

P-523 Tuesday 29th November 1825

A Deed of conveyance from Robert Oliver to Henry T. Croft for two hundred & forty acres of land was produced in court and the Execution thereof proven by the oaths of Robert Williams & Hartwell Lucy the witnesses thereto, and ordered to be certified for registration.

A Deed of conveyance from Henry T. Croft to Hartwell Lucy & Robert Williams for sixty acres of land was produced in court and the Execution thereof acknowledged by the said Henry T. Croft & ordered to be certified for registration.

The Governor to the use of &c Plt.	In Debt
Against	
Anderson Hogan Admr.)Defts.	
of Samuel Cox Decd.)	

This day came the parties by their attornies and thereupon came a Jury of good & lawful men, Towit, Charles Buford, Hamilton C. Campbell, John Hill, Archibald Crockette, Larkin B. Moore, Alfred M. Yancy, Jesse Pullen, Asa A. Estes, Wm. P. A. McCabe, John S. Brandon, Ambrose Mayfield, & James Cobbs, who being elected tried and sworn well & truly to try the issue between the parties in this case and having heard the evidence and part of the argument of counsel were permitted to disperse to meet again tomorrow morning nine oclock.

Tilman R. Daniel Guardian of Martha L. Westmoreland made return of the sale of the perishable property of his sd. Ward which is ordered to be recorded.

Tilman R. Daniel Guardian of Jesse Westmoreland made return of the sale of the perishable property of his said ward which is ordered to be recorded.

Tilman R. Daniel Guardian of Laban Westmoreland made return of the sale of the perishable property of his said ward which is ordered to be recorded.

A Deed of conveyance from Tilman R. Daniel Administrator with the will annexed of Reubin Westmoreland decd. to Elizabeth Westmoreland widow of sd. Reubin for one hundred & five & a half acres of land ; (p-524) was produced in court and the Execution thereof acknowledged by the said Tilman R. Daniels Admr. aforesd. and ordered to be certified for registration.

Samuel Y. Anderson Gdn. &c Plt.) In Debt
   Against)
Thomas B. Jones Thomas B.) Defts.) This day came the plaintiff by
Haynie & Nathaniel Young) his attorney as also his defend-
) ants in their proper persons who
say they cannot gainsay the plaintiff action against them, nor but that they do owe him the sum of two hundred & seventy five dollars & Eighteen cents debts - besides costs - It is therefore by concent of the plaintiff considered by the court that the plaintiff recover against the said defendants the debt aforesd. in form aforesaid, confesses and also his costs by him about his suit in this behalf expended - Execution to be stayed untill the next May term of this court.

The Grand Jury returned into court a presentment of the State against Henry Graves, John Redden, & William Bolling, for abstructing publick road, and also an Indictment of the State against James Pillow, for making an assault on the body of Meredith Bunch "Endorsed not a true Bill" and withdrew to consider of further presentments.

Ordered that court be adjourned untill tomorrow morning nine oclock.

                James Perry
                James H. Graves
                John Bramlett

P-525 Wednesday Morning 30th November 1825

Court met according to adjournment Present James Perry) Esquire Justice
              James H. Graves) of the Peace for
              John Bramlett) Giles County.

John Porter Guardian of Reese W. Porter returned into court an account of the property &c of his ward which was ordered to be recorded.

John S. Brandon a tales Juror empannelled and sworn to try a cause in court on yestoday failing to attend at the hour of adjournment and for some time thereafter, is for said failure fined in the sum of $5.00.

The Governor for the use of Baker) Plt.
P. Potts & Jane his wife
    Against
Anderson Hogan Admr. of) Deft.
Samuel Cox decd;

Debt

This day came the parties by their attornies and thereupon the Jury who were empannelled and sworn to try the issue joined between the parties in this case, and having heard the balance of the argument of counsel, upon their oaths do say that they find said issue in favour of the defendant. It is therefore considered by the court that the defendant go hence without day and recover of the plaintiffs his costs by him about his defence in this behalf expended, From which Judgment the plaintiffs prayed an appeal to the honorable the circuit court to be held for the County of Giles, and having entered into bond and security according to law the same was granted him.

Henry Bidleman Plt.
    Against
Henry Peden . . . Deft.

Debt

This day came as well the plaintiff by his attorney as the defendant in his proper person, and said defendant withdraws the plea by him and heretofore filed in this case, and saith he cannot gainsay the plaintiffs action against him nor but nor but that he doth owe him the sum of one hundred and fifteen dollars and fifty cents, the debt in the writing obligatory in the declaration mentioned, and that the plaintiff hath sustained damages by reason of the detention of said debt to the amount of five dollars seventeen and ahalf cents, and agrees that Judgment may be entered up against him in favour of the plaintiff for that amount with costs. It is therefore considered by the court that the plaintiff recover of the defendant the amount of his debt aforesaid together with his damages aforesaid (p-526) in form aforesaid agreed and his costs by him about his suit in this behalf Expended.

George Barnes Plt.
    Against
James Hardin Deft.

Debt

This day came the plaintiff by his attorney and the defendant altho Solemnly called came not but made default. It is therefore considered by the court that th plaintiff recover of the defendant the sum of one hundred & twenty fiv dollars the debt in the Writing obligatory in the declaration mentione also the sum of five dollars the damages which he hath sustained by reason of the detention of said debt, and his costs by him about his suit in this behalf expended.

Joshua Freeman Plaintiff
    Against
William Macklin Defendant

In Debt

This day came the parties by their attornies and thereupon came a Jury of good and lawful men, Towit, John Goff, Duncan Brown, Edward M. Brown,

Daniel Puryear, Stephen Anderson, Alexander Essleman, James Abernathy, Marshall Moody Rodger Simpson, Jeremiah Parker, who being Elected tried and sworn well and truly to try the issue joined between the parties in this case upon their oaths do say that there remains unpaid a balance of the debt in the writing obligatory in the declaration mentioned to the amount of sixty five dollars, and that the plaintiff hath sustained damages by reason of the detention of said debt to the amount of seven dollars twelve and a half cents Besides costs - It is therefore considered by the court that the plaintiff recover of the defendant the balance of his debt aforesaid together with his damages aforesaid by the Jurors aforesaid assessed and his costs by him about his suit in this behalf expended.

Leonard Burford Plt.) In Debt
   Against)
Josiah E. Maddox &)Defts.
William P. Richardson) This day came the parties by their attornies and thereupon came a Jury of good & lawful men, Towit, Charles Buford, Hamilton C. Campbell, John Hill, Archibald Crockett, Larkin B. Moore, Alfred M. Yancy, Jesse Pullen, Asa A. Esters, Samuel S. Smith, John S. Brandon, Ambrose Mayfield, and James Cobbs, who being elected tried and sworn well and truly to try the issue joined between the parties in this case upon (p-527) their oaths do say that the defendant have not paid the debt in the writing obligatory in the declaration mentioned, as the plaintiff in his replication hath alleged, and they do assess the plaintiffs damages by reason of the detention of said debt to Eighteen dollars and twenty five cents besides costs. It is therefore considered by the court that the plaintiff recover of the defendants the sum of three hundred and thirty three dollars his debt aforesaid together with his damages aforesaid by the Jurors aforesaid in form aforesaid assessed & his costs by him about his suit in this behalf Expended.

Dudley Smith Plt.) Writ of Enquiring
   Against)
John N. Smith Deft.) This day came the plaintiffs by his attorney and thereupon came a Jury of good and lawful men, Towit, John Goff, Duncan Brown, Edward M. Brown, Daniel Puryear, Alexander Essleman, Stephen Anderson, James Abernathy, Marshall Moody, Rodgers Simpson, Jeremiah Barnes, James Wilson, & Jeremiah Parker, who being elected tried and sworn well and truly to enquire of damages in this case upon their oaths do say that they do assess the plaintiffs damages by reason of the non performance of the assumsit in the declaration complained of to three hundred & one dollars besides costs - It is therefore considered by the court that the plaintiff recover of defendant the amount of his damages aforesaid by the Jurors aforesaid in form aforesd. assessed and his costs by him about his suit in this behalf expended.

Joshua Horn Plt.) Certiorari
   Against)
Alfred M. Yancy Deft.) Ordered that a motion be entered to dismiss the certiorari in this case.

Ordered that the fine entered up at this term against John L. Brandon for non attendance as a Juror be remitted and that he pay the costs.

Thomas B. Craighead Gentleman who was commissioned by his excellency the Governor of this State, Solicitor General for their distrust appeared in court and was qualified as the Law directs.

P-528   Wednesday 30th November 1825

Thomas Goff......Plt.   )   In Case
    Against   )
Bernard M. Patterson Deft.   )   On the application of the plaintiff
)   it is ordered that a commission issue
to any two of the Acting Justices of the in and for the County of Lawrence and State of Alabama to take the deposition of George B. Balch to be read in evidence on the trial of this cause, and that the plaintiff give to the affidavit fifteen days notice of the time & place for taking said deposition.

An account current of James Terrell Admr. Of the Estate of William Adams deed was returned into court and ordered to be recorded.

On motion of the Solicitor General it is ordered that an Indictment be preferred against Matthew Taylor for an affray with and an assault and battery on the body of James Hooks the offence as charged having been committed in the presence of James H. Graves Esq. a Justice of the Peace for Giles County.

Gilliam Harwell the overseer of a Cotton Gin in this County came into court and was qualified as cotton inspector & gave bond and security as required by Act of Assembly.

The Grand Jury returned into court and on the Indictment preferred against Matthew Taylor for an affray with and an assault and battery on the body of James Hooks. "Endorsed a true Bill" and are thereupon discarged from further attendance at this term Except Edward M. Brown.

Ordered that the Petit Jury be discharged from further attendance at this term Except Charles Buford.

James Perry the overseer of a cotton Gin in this County came into court and was qualified as cotton inspector and gave bond and security as required by Act of Assemby

Ordered that Court be adjourned till tomorrow morning 9 o'clock.
                                      James Perry
                                      James H. Graves
                                      John Bramlett

P-529 Thursday 1st December 1825

Court met according to adjournment Present James Perry) Esquires Justices of the Peace for Giles County.
James H. Graves &
John Bramlett

Elisha Eldridge administrator of the Estate of Thomas Dillon decd. returned into court an account against said Estate which was ordered to be recorded.

George Jones a man of colour came into court and proved to the satisfaction of the court that he is a free man and born free, said George Jones is about twenty Eight years of age about five feet seven inches high, yellow complexion of a stout built, full face, Bushy hair, a scar over the right eye, also one on the left side of uper lip, a small nail on the right fore finger, as tho it had been cut off, a scar across the left fore finger, on the left hand, and one on the back of the head.

Ordered that Court be adjourned untill tomorrow morning 9 oclock.

James Perry
James H. Graves
E. D. Jones

P-530 Friday Morning 2nd December 1825

Court met according to adjournment Present James Perry) Esquire Justices of the Peace for Giles County.
James H. Graves &
Edward D. Jones

William Jackson Plt.   )   Certiorari
    Against   )
Martha Davenport Deft.   ) This day came the parties by their attornies, and thereupon the plaintiffs motion to dismiss the certiorari in this case, being argued, and mature deliberation thereup__ being had it is considered by the court that said certiorari be dismissed, also that the Judgments of the Justice of the Peace be affirmed against the defendant & his security in the certiorari, Thos. D. Cole for the sum of forty nine dollars & 50 cents with interest thereon to be computed at the rate of twelve and a half cents per annum from the 17th August 1825, the time of rendering the Judgment by the Justice of the peace, till this time together with his costs as well before the Justice of the Peace in this court in this behalf expended.

An Account of sale of the Estate of Martin Lane Senr. Decd. returned into court by the Executor of sd. Est. to which was ordered to be recorded.

Ordered that Samuel Hampton be appointed overseer of the road in the room of Edward D. Jones resigned and that he have the same district of hands.

John Birdwell the overseer of a cotton Gin in this County same into Court, and was qualified as Cotton inspector, and qualified and gave Bond and security as the law directs.

Samuel S. Smith & wife Plts.)   Petition
        Against   )
John Porter Gdn. & Deft.   )   By Consent this cause is continued
)   until next court and on affidavit
of defendant, ordered that a commission issue to any two of the Acting Justices of the Peace in & for the County of Tipton and State of Tennessee to take the deposition of John Brown, which when taken to be read on the trail of this cause, upon the defendants giving to the plaintiffs ten days notice of the time and place of taking the same.

P-531   James Perry.... Plantiff   )   In Debt
            Against   )
      James Patterson, Ralph Graves,) Defts.)   As on affidavit of James
      John Brown & Marcus Mitchell   )   H. Graves this cause is
)   ordered to be continued
Until the next term of this court, and on motion of defendants ordered that a commission issue to any two of the Acting Justices of the Peace in & for the County of Davidson & State of Tennessee to take the depositions of Sterling C. Robertson & Eldridge B. Robertson which when taken are to be read in evidence on the trial of this cause, upon Defts. Giving to plaintiffs ten days notice of the time & Place of taking the same.

The State Plt.   )   Indictment for & an assault & battery on
    Against   )   the body of L. Fitzgerald
William Watson) Deft.   )
William Watson)   )   Lewis H. Brown, and Beverly B. Watson came
)   into a court and acknowledged themselves in-
debted to the State of Tennessee the said William Watson in the sum of two hundred & fifty dollars, and that said Lewis H. Brown & Beverly B. Watson, in the sum of one hundred & twenty five dollars each to be levied of their goods & chattles lands & tenments to the use of the State to be void on condition that the said William Watson appear here of the first Thursday after the third Monday in February next, then & there to answer the State on the aforesaid Indictment, and not depart without leave of the court.

Henry Bidleman Plt.   )   In Debt
    Against   )
Henry Peden Deft.   )   From the judgement of the court in this case
)   rendered the defendant prayed an appeal to
the honorable the Circuit Court to be held for the County of Giles and having executed bond & security as the Law directs the same was Granted him.

The State Plt.) Upon an Indct. for & affray with & assault
    Against) & battery on the body of L. Fitzgerald.
Wm. Watson Deft.)
) For reasons shewn to the court the Defendant is released from the forfeiture taken against him at this term, upon the payments of all costs.

Ordered that William R. Davis be allowed $25 for sweeping the court-house for twelve months past.

P-532 Friday 2nd December 1825

The State Plt.) Upon an Indictment for an affray with &
    Against) assault & battery on the body of L. Fitz-
William Watson Deft.) gerald.
)

For reasons shewn to the court, Beverly B. Watson is released from the forfeiture taken against him at this term for failing to produce the body of Wm. Watson upon the payment of all costs.

Reuben Burton Admr. &c Plt.) Original Attachment
    Against)
Thomas Underwood Deft.) From the Judgment of this court in this
) case rendered, the plaintiff prayed
an appeal to the honorable the Circuit Court to be held for the County of Giles, and having executed bond and security as the law directs. the same was granted him.

A Deed of conveyance from Henry F. Steele to Thomas W. McKnight for one hundred & fifty five acres of land was produced in court and the Execution thereof acknowledged by the said Henry F. Steele and ordered to be certified for registration.

William Risener Plt.) Certiorari
    Against)
William Mayfield Deft.) This day came the parties by their attor-
) nies & thereupon the plaintiffs motion
to dismiss certiorari being agreed by counsel and mature deliberations, thereupon being had by the court, It is ordered that the plaintiffs motion to dismiss be sustained, and certiorari dismissed also that the Judgment of the Justice of the peace be affirmed against sd. Defendant & Wm. P. A. McCabe & John Dickey securities in the certiorari for the Sum of fifty five dollars & 67 cents, with interest thereof to be computed at the rate of twelve & a half per cent per annum from the 20th November 1823, the time of rendering the Judgment by the Justice of the peace, untill this time, together with the costs as well before the Justice as in this case in this court expended.

THE END

GILES COUNTY

COUNTY COURT MINUTES VOL. H.

1823-1825

NEW INDEX

Note: Page numbers in this index refer to those of the original volume from which this copy was made. These numbers are carried throughout the copy within parenthesis.

A

Abernathy, Allen 5, 158, 209, 232, 234, 235, 237, 238, 239, 240, 241, 242, 243, 245, 246, 247, 264, 265, 431, 491
" " Buckner, 318
" " Burrell 131, 420
" " Charles C. 27, 30, 159, 205, 215, 251, 255, 300, 326, 424, 431, 503, 511, 517, 521
" " Daniel 128, 198, 347, 404
" " David 158, 266, 352, 387, 388, 389, 390, 391
" " Elisha 108
" " German 521
" " James 108, 204, 268, 461, 506, 509, 516, 526, 527
" " John 25, 59, 138, 320, 327, 328, 330, 335, 356, 358, 363, 400, 404, 407, 427, 438, 455, 482, 511
" " John M. 158, 209, 438, 485
" " John F. 467
" " Joseph 492
" " Samuel W. 251
" " Thomas E. 27, 54, 61, 123, 126, 130, 236, 306, 310, 314, 317, 319, 512
" " Wilkins 77
" " William H. 128
Abraham, George 105
Accademy, Westernburg 244, 470
Adair, William J. 327, 392, 456, 494
Adams, Charles 512
Adams, Hugh 135, 138, 158, 209, 219, 232, 234, 235, 236, 237, 238, 239, 240, 241, 242, 243, 244, 245, 246, 247, 248, 250, 253, 256, 258, 512

Adams, Littleberry 201, 227
" " Luke 63
" " Robert 54, 211, 212, 351, 355, 375, 409, 426, 518
" " William 359, 369, 528
Aday, Walter 321
Adkins, Charles 479
" " James 311
" " John 2
" " Martin 439
Aidy, Joseph 514
Airs, John 362, 392, 458
Alexander, Archibald 50, 121
" " Francis 414
" " Milton 157
Allen, Daniel 357, 363, 491
" " Isaac 1
" " Jesse 31, 318, 319, 321, 350, 356, 374, 420, 479, 481, 489, 519
" " Richard 248
" " Richard A. 357
" " Richard H. 63, 103, 131, 133, 146, 150, 152, 153, 155, 161, 162, 163, 165, 167, 170, 179, 180, 302, 308, 347, 349, 418, 433, 460, 478
Alman, Nathaniel 113, 114, 115
Alsup, Joseph 54, 97, 133, 168, 218, 226, 256, 294
" " Peter 403, 412
" " Robert R. 312, 487, 490
Amis, John 462
Anderson, (Capt.) 29
" " Daniel G. 478
" " Frances 102
" " Jane 478
" " John 314
" " Robert 4, 57, 75, 97, 102, 141, 200, 204, 266, 268, 270, 300, 352, 375, 409, 426, 478, 511, 517

Anderson, Samuel 478, 511
" " Samuel R. 57, 97, 200, 270, 487
" " Samuel Y. 72, 203, 204, 418, 437, 440, 524
" " Stephen 33, 61, 158, 186, 207, 209, 322, 357, 373, 428, 489, 506, 509, 526, 527
" ".William 370
Anglin, Aaron 441, 442
Anthony, Elijah 204, 268, 286, 463, 514
" " John B. 54, 245, 333
" " Joseph 4, 351, 365, 369, 371, 431, 435
Appleby, James 454
Appleton, James 256, 315
Armor, John P. 123
" " Joseph 123
Armstrong, James 428
" " John B. 304, 310, 317, 319, 321, 428
Armstrong, Thomas L. 325
Arnell, William 113
Ashmore, James 12, 500, 501
Atkins, George 369
" " Ira 1
Austin, James 141
Averett, John 355
Aymett, William 113, 114, 115

B

Baker, David 306
" " Nathaniel 293
" " Thomas 290, 291, 337
Balch, John 99, 124
Baldridge, Alexander 132, 141, 158, 209, 219, 233, 234, 235, 236, 237, 238, 239, 240, 241, 242, 243, 244, 246, 247, 248, 250, 253, 256, 259
Ball, Adam 325, 365
" " William 13, 121, 122, 147, 151, 361, 225, 241, 242, 269, 274
Ballentine, Andrew M. 33, 35, 67, 120, 156, 186, 190, 351, 385, 388, 412, 416, 456, 468, 469, 470, 471, 472
Banks, William 101, 294, 411, 423
Barber, John J. 112
Barker, Tarpley 126
Barnes, (Captain) 28
" " George 424, 526

Barnes, Jeremiah 58, 314, 373, 461, 489, 506, 509, 526, 527
" " William 28, 40
Barnett, John 103, 136, 166, 344
Barnett, Joseph F. 54
" " Richard 7
" " Thomas 345
" " Wade 45, 490
Barron, Alexander 63
Basham, Archibald 315, 321
" " Dewey 207, 315
" " Soloman 315, 373
Bass, (Captain) 28, 64, 265, 305, 520
" " John 7, 101, 146, 161, 162, 164, 165, 167, 170, 171, 204, 210, 268, 279, 280, 283, 286, 287, 290, 353, 416, 461, 491, 511
" " Kinchin J. 2
" " Nathan 27, 71, 113, 114, 115, 116, 119, 315, 411
" " Peter 275, 436
Batte, Gardner 433, 462
" " Thomas 1, 7, 28, 61, 64, 236, 240, 310, 319, 323, 368, 374, 375
Battle, Mammouth 74
" " Quebeck 74
Baugh, James 437
" " Martin 437
Beal, Benjamin 483
" " Thomas 149
Beard, Francis 57, 63, 456
Beazley, Anna B. 488
" " Burton 488
" " Jesse 252, 333, 428
" " Polly S. 488
Beasley, Rebecca H. 488
" " Tilman D. 488
" " William 350
" " William M. 113, 114, 330, 331, 369, 373
" " William O. 488
" " Wyatt, Y. 488
Benson, (Captain) 431, 520
" " Early 264, 355, 375, 376, 377, 378, 381, 382, 383, 384, 385, 386, 387, 388, 389, 390, 391, 397, 400, 407, 409, 433, 484, 485
" " Hardy 125, 431, 433, 485
" " Joseph 485
Bentley, Balem 336
" " Daniel 263

Bentley, Richard 5, 48, 113, 115, 116, 209, 212, 213, 248, 250, 253, 254, 255, 263, 265, 317, 359, 375, 497
Betty, Thomas 303
Bevers, (Captain) 323
" " (Captain) 127
" " John 31
" " William 31, 306, 318
Biddix, John R. 365, 467, 505
Bidleman, Henry 525, 531
Bigby, Tom 63
Bingham, Robert 161, 477
" W Thomas 156, 161, 477
Bird, William 361, 467, 468
" " William H. 475
Birdsong, Henry 108
Birdwell, 42, 371, 456, 530
Black, Alexander 1, 3, 6, 7, 24, 25, 31, 32, 35, 53, 54, 55, 56, 59, 61, 62, 63, 64, 75, 77, 100, 102, 103, 109, 110, 111, 115, 116, 119, 122, 123, 127, 128, 129, 131, 132, 138, 139, 155, 156, 174, 182, 192, 195, 198, 226, 227, 257, 259, 261, 262, 267, 268, 299, 300, 310, 319, 322, 324, 338, 339, 340, 341, 355, 356, 358, 359, 360, 368, 369, 374, 375, 406, 407, 414, 428, 436, 437, 438, 439, 440, 457, 461, 464, 473, 747, 476, 478, 479, 489, 490, 510, 513,
" " Elizabeth 314
" " John 11, 12, 27, 37, 44, 45, 71, 113, 114, 115, 136, 126, 306, 321
" " Jordon 375
" " Matthew J. 126, 313, 314, 368
" " Robert 6, 133, 148, 204, 268, 286, 419, 431, 437, 438, 465, 466, 468, 470, 471, 472, 518
" " Thomas 261
" " William 141, 204, 268
" " Wm. D. 313, 408, 448
Blair, J. 106
Blair, Joseph 139
Bledsoe, Edward 311, 326, 363, 372
Blow, Richard H. 498
Blue, John 303, 484, 489, 510, 520
Blythe, Andrew 439
Boatright, Daniel 262, 510
" " James 510

Bodenhammer, Franklin 156
Bodenhammer, Jacob 26
" " John W. 58, 156, 315, 369, 480, 518
" " Peter 58, 127, 156
" " Sarah 156
" " W. 26
" " William 146, 151, 156, 204, 424
Bogard 201, 434, 483
Bolling, Lucy 224, 335
" " William 524
Bond, Pettway 143
Bonner, Ezekiel 189, 195
Bostick, James B. 441
Bowers, George 27, 71, 134, 141, 141, 216, 217, 218, 274, 275, 276, 277, 278, 279, 280, 281, 301, 459, 496
Bowman, Thomas 59
Boyd, John 172, 175, 256, 269, 284, 314, 364
Boyd, Rhoda 190
Boyd, Willie 154, 173, 174, 175, 176
Boykin, Willie 57
Boykin, Wiley 461
Boyles, Charles 12, 16, 23, 33, 48
Boyles, Herbert 388
Bracken, Harriet 62
" " William 131, 499, 517, 518
Braden, Buckner 371
Braden, Elinor 264
Braden, Felix G. 249
" " Jacob F. 249
" " John G. 57, 124, 375, 503
" " Joseph 124, 248, 249, 264, 323, 371, 433, 503
" " Patrick B. 378
" ".Patrick H. 50, 78, 290, 354, 360, 379, 415, 501, 503
" ".William 249, 428
Bradley, Elisha 452
" " John 171, 223, 270, 290, 438, 440, 451
" " Joseph 1, 9, 168, 169
" " Samuel 1, 89, 168, 169
" " William 256, 262, 283, 330, 331, 356
Bradshaw, William 74, 152
Bramlett, John 29, 54, 61, 101, 123, 158, 198, 204, 262, 267, 268, 273, 274, 281, 282, 290, 291, 292, 297, 300, 310, 311, 336, 368, 414, 428, 478, 489, 521, 525, 528, 529
" " Lunsford M. 40, 44, 89, 98, 236, 241, 242, 251, 269, 287,

333, 343, 349, 425, 458, 478, 509
Brandon, John 99, 103, 153, 372, 432
" " John A. 138
" " John G. 124
" " John L. 42, 527
" " John S. 6, 61, 173, 174, 176, 179, 180, 323, 325, 326, 333, 398
" " Patrick H. 124
" " Richard 6, 111, 196, 294, 295, 297, 298, 356, 372, 398
Branch Allens Powder Mill 208
" " Tomlins 208
Bratton, Elizabeth 51, 52, 329
" " George 5, 51, 119, 138, 144, 147, 148, 169, 307, 467, 468,
Bratton, Hugh 1, 51, 52, 54, 286, 321, 322, 329, 373, 374
Bratton, Hugh W. 412, 413
" " James 5, 51
" " John 51
" " Lucinda 51
" " Margaret 51, 52
" " Malinda Hugh 51
" " Patsy 286
" " Peggy 51
" " Thomas 51, 52, 217, 218, 286, 329, 368, 424, 522
" " William 51, 52, 461
Breathith, Cardwell 230
" " John 230
Breys, James 302
Bridge, fourth 4, 57, 97, 131, 200, 265, 270, 487
Bridges, Joseph 4, 37
Briggs, Clement 202
" " Jane 202
" " Julia 202
" " Reuben 201
" " Richard 3, 112, 127, 150, 174, 203, 304, 320, 324, 326, 333, 335, 517
" " William 202
Bright, James 55, 430
Brimer, Turner 321
Britten, John 119
Britten, John W. 203
Brooks, (Captain) 28
Brooks, George 198, 311
" " John 5, 101, 408
" " Miller B. 306
Brooks, Robert 138, 263, 383, 438, 496
" ". William B. 5, 59, 237, 260, 355, 375, 404, 426

Brown, Aaron V. 73, 124, 126, 265, 359, 373, 375, 403, 454
" " Beverly 2, 223, 304, 324, 326, 333, 335
" " David 11, 204, 268, 274
" " Davis 108, 275, 276, 277, 278, 279, 280, 283, 285, 287, 290, 312, 460, 516
" " Dixon 398
" " Duncan 5, 306, 311, 461, 489, 506, 522, 526, 527,
" " Edward M. 7, 29, 112, 209, 305, 324, 346, 350, 373, 441, 461, 489, 504, 506, 509, 526, 527, 528
" " Elizabeth 183
" " Elnathan G. 59, 253, 326, 327, 328, 330, 331, 332, 338, 376, 378, 379, 380, 381, 382, 384, 385, 386, 387, 388, 389, 390, 391, 404, 411, 425, 495, 499, 502
" " Ensley 176, 181
" " George 7, 54, 62, 121, 126, 174, 236
" " Gorde 6
" " Hartwell H. 486 512
" " Henry 32, 61
" " Hiram 176, 181
" " Isaac 181
" " Isham 26, 105
" " Jaby N. 186
" " James 156
" " Jethro 176, 181, 353
" " John 26, 28, 103, 114, 115, 123, 127, 131, 133, 143, 157, 168, 175, 183, 184, 187, 192, 209, 239, 245, 249, 279, 292, 304, 314, 347, 355, 361, 363, 375, 397, 414, 438, 452, 530, 531
Brown, Leonard 503, 504
Brown, Lewis H. 8, 9, 14, 15, 32, 52, 54, 64, 101, 119, 123, 130, 141, 149, 157, 159, 168, 171, 172, 185, 198, 201, 209, 217, 224, 232, 233, 234, 236, 253, 262, 263, 288, 301, 308, 310, 326, 327, 328, 330, 332, 362, 368, 375, 397, 426, 428, 443, 452, 479, 481, 492, 494, 495, 500, 502, 506, 512, 516, 531
" " Mahulda 180, 181, 213, 231, 249
" " Martin 131
" " Morgan 183, 211, 212, 213, 223

Brown, Nancy 105, 106
" " Painelia 176, 181
" " Sam 106
" " Thomas 54, 61, 100, 101,
     103, 110, 115, 116, 119,
     123, 134, 155, 156, 198,
     232, 262, 304, 305, 312,
     319, 324, 326, 331, 333,
     335, 344, 360, 362, 364,
     368, 416, 425, 428, 435,
     439, 440, 441, 442, 443,
     456, 501, 507, 510, 516,
     521
" " William 1, 14, 15, 26,
     54, 61, 63, 76, 77, 99,
     105, 106, 167, 169, 226,
     262, 280, 300, 310, 319,
     356, 368, 428, 489, 492,
     505, 512, 520
" " William A. 185, 250, 255,
     257, 408, 448, 512
" " William F. 55, 310
" " William R. 361, 404, 521
Browning, David 2, 10, 134,
     138, 172, 231, 512
" " Isaac 230
" " John 11
" " Martin 131
" " Nicholas 201, 202
" " Thomas 301
" " Tobitha 205, 266, 301, 515
Brownlow, Joseph 374
" " William 321, 432
Bruce, Joel 188
" " Philip 264
Bryan, Jacob 483
Buford, Alexander 430
" " Charles 100, 103, 196,
     244, 257, 265, 294, 295,
     297, 298, 341, 365, 389,
     390, 415, 425, 441, 461,
     470, 489, 495, 496, 497,
     503, 504, 521, 523, 526,
     528
" " James 30, 100, 102, 103,
     107, 111, 133, 471, 419,
     425
" " Leonard 526
Bull, Jesse 506
Buchanan, John 208, 460, 484,
     489, 510, 519,
" " Maxamillin H. 210, 489
" " Robert 100, 103, 133, 172,
     183, 431
" " William 4

Bumgarner, George 66
Bumpass, Gabriel 9, 180, 210,
     217
Bunch, Benjamin 459, 460, 489,
     517, 518
Bunch, James 2, 36, 37, 514
Bunch, Meredith 33, 148, 150,
     407, 514, 524
Burk, Benjamin 205, 255
Burnes, Andrew 17, 21, 72
" " James 217, 218
" " Joseph 75
" " William 75
Burton, Reuben 466, 522, 532
" " William 488
Burkett, Burgess 315
Butler, Henry 38, 39, 40, 41, 42,
     43, 333
" " Henry T. 326, 463
" " James 294, 295, 297, 317,
     319, 320, 326, 330, 340, 343,
     369, 371
" " John 27, 54, 58, 61, 334,
     457, 495
" " Richard 114, 158
" " Thomas 204
Buys, James 380, 517
Byler, Abraham 174, 182

C

Cabe, John 477
Calloway, Joel 136
Calvert, Joseph 8, 168, 287
Camille, Polly 129
Camp, James W. 101, 233
" " John H. 1, 7, 10, 54, 61,
     64, 66, 102, 103, 109, 123,
     126, 132, 141, 156, 160, 161,
     169, 170, 171, 208, 213, 214,
     215, 216, 262, 300, 305, 310,
     319, 323, 324, 332, 334, 338,
     339, 340, 341, 353, 364, 367,
     374, 375, 408, 414, 421, 422,
     428, 436, 437, 445, 460
Campbell, Crockett 420, 461
" " George 36, 73, 315, 440, 479
" " Hamilton C. 63, 160, 199,
     489, 495, 496, 497, 503, 504,
     515, 521, 523, 526
" " Hugh 321
" " James 56
" " William 372
Cannon, John J. 47
" " Sarah 418

Cannon, William 138
Capps, Benjamin 41
Cerden, Larken 1, 207
Carmichael, John 416
Carpenter, Dangerfield 515
"   "   Hensley 55
"   "   James 329
"   "   Nancy 329
"   "   Richard 3
Carroll, James 306
"   "   William 168
Carter, Benjamin 71, 119, 301, 411
"   "   Jabez L. 355
"   "   Littleberry 252
"   "   Merry 11, 12, 35, 55
"   "   Nathaniel 311
"   "   William 467, 521
Caruthers, Abraham L. 64
"   "   Arney 369
"   "   Robert 379
Carvill, Polly 30
"   " William 30
Caswell, Patience 134
"   " Samiel 134, 279
Cathcart, John 126
Chamberline, Charles 477
Chambers, Edward O. 38
Chambers, Frances 38
Chambers, Jefferson 6, 11, 411, 514
Chambers, Wm. 5
Chambly, Young 454, 448, 449
Chapman, William 131, 207, 322, 517
Cheatem, Emmon 3
Childers, Daulton 214
Childers, John 229
Childers, Sarah 251
Childers, Vaulton 64, 65, 107, 212
Chiles, (Capt.) 29, 305, 323, 519
Chiles, Paul 2, 22, 54, 57, 59, 61, 101, 198, 204, 207, 208, 209, 215, 216, 226, 227, 262, 267, 305, 310, 319, 323, 350, 368, 409, 410, 420, 428, 479, 488, 489
Choat, Chap 12
"   " Charles 500
"   " Moses 500, 501
"   " Valentine 500
Chrisman, Isaac 357, 438
"   " Isaac S. 140
Church, Robertson Fork 312

City Nashville 73
"   " Trenton 74
Clack, John 467, 468
"   "   Lucinda 196, 234, 296, 297, 298
"   "   Spencer 274, 275, 276, 277, 278, 279, 287, 293, 294, 295, 296, 297, 298, 321, 420
Claiborn, John G. 202
Clark, John 172, 315, 320, 417
"   " Robert 267
"   " Spencer 7, 13, 45, 161, 162, 163, 164, 165, 166, 167, 170, 176, 204
"   " Thomas 27, 199, 207, 248, 267, 318, 357, 373
Clarks, 267
Cobb, Ambrose 11, 12, 35, 183, 330, 331, 438, 495, 496
Cobb, James 439, 526
Cobb, Robert L. 54, 154, 318
Cochran, Jacob 25, 27, 58, 64, 65, 66, 67, 68, 69, 70, 71, 92, 479, 483, 515
Cochran, Samuel 58
Cody, Bennet R. 459, 460
Cody, Price 459, 460
Coldwell, James 19, 62, 158, 232, 233, 234, 235, 236, 237, 238, 239, 240, 241, 242, 244, 245, 246, 248, 250, 252, 253, 254, 255, 257, 285, 321, 343, 345, 347, 348, 512, 517, 518
Cole, Andrew 408
Cole, David 200
"   " Stephen 162
"   " Thomas 7, 11, 12, 37, 38, 39, 40, 41, 42, 43, 107, 131, 204, 268, 286, 322
"   " Thomas D. 530
"   " Willis W. 200, 212, 285, 411
Coleman, John 147, 149, 154
"   "   Ruffus 327, 393, 458
Collier, James 468, 469, 470, 471, 472
Collins, James 341, 342, 464, 465, 468
Condra, Tobitha 399
Compton, Bazel 11, 12, 27, 38, 39, 40, 41, 42, 43, 55, 60, 111, 113, 114, 115, 159
"   "   Isaac 60, 111
"   "   Thomas 60, 68, 70, 112, 483
Comby, James W. 12
Conner, Lewis 112, 502
"   "   James 38, 40, 41, 42, 43, 54, 272, 314, 342

Conner, James S. 111, 279
Conner, William 103, 133, 134, 153, 172, 183, 518
Cook, Isaac S. W. 275, 321, 353
" " William H. 56
Cooper, Henry J. 7, 11, 12, 27, 35, 38, 39, 40, 41, 42, 43, 64, 65, 66, 67, 68, 69, 70, 71, 72, 120, 130, 152, 153, 155, 237, 250, 300, 352, 355, 375, 376, 377, 378, 379, 380, 381, 383, 384, 385, 386, 387, 388, 389, 390, 391, 397, 400, 409, 411, 417, 424, 461, 471, 489, 495, 496, 501, 503, 504, 511
" " Pamelia 130
Couch, Isaac 167
Couch, Jack 121,
Couch, Jacob 18, 31, 182, 506
County, Brunswick 202
County, Coldwell 47
County, Franklin 45, 119, 136
" " Giles 18, 19, 20, 21, 35, 46, 52, 64, 73, 101, 103, 105, 107, 108, 113, 116, 122, 123, 136, 139, 143, 145, 146, 148, 150, 151, 153, 156, 159, 170, 171, 192, 193, 194, 195, 196, 197, 198, 201, 204, 211, 217, 219, 227, 232, 237, 284, 289, 297, 300, 304, 309, 310, 324, 328, 329, 332, 334, 339, 342, 355, 359, 360, 368, 375, 392, 397, 400, 408, 412, 414, 415, 417, 418, 422, 425, 428, 437, 440, 443, 451, 452, 454, 455, 459, 461, 464, 470, 474, 479, 481, 489, 493, 496, 497, 502, 504, 510, 513, 516, 525, 528, 532
County, Greene 475
" " Guilford 1
County, Lauderdale 19, 230
County, Lawrence 208, 230, 271, 488, 506, 528
" " Lillard 474
County, Limestone 9, 98, 203, 293, 362, 392, 458
" " Lincoln 6, 181, 457
" " Logan 230, 270
" " Lylard 400
" " Maclingburge 341, 342
" " Madison 98, 162, 171, 223, 230, 271, 290, 327, 362, 458, 466, 494

County, Monroe 185
" " Nelson 75
" " Person 506
" " Prince Edward 172
" " Rutherford 338
" " Tipton 530
" " Wilks 272
Cowan, Joseph 322
Cowls, Thomas 401
Cox, Cathrine 344
" " Caty 309, 522
" " Jacob 504
" " James 256, 523
" " John 326, 495
" " Robert 2, 123
" " Samuel 266, 269, 309, 316, 344, 452, 505, 525, 529"
" " William 495
Crabb, Henry 176
Crabbe, Joseph 370
Craighead, Thomas B. 527
Craig, Samuel 37, 138, 495, 496, 497
Craig, William 138
Crawford, John 422
Cravenor, Thomas 199
Creek, Bradshaw 254, 420, 432
Creek, Brattons 375
Creek, Big 203, 208, 248, 321, 420, 493
Creek, Buchanan 159, 205, 290
Creek, Buck 1, 2, 131, 160
Creek, Crooked 6, 107
Creek, Egnew 6, 487
Creek, Leatherwood 267
Creek, Moons 373, 463
Creek, Moores 265, 513, 514
Creek, Newtons 136
Creek, Pigeon Roast 4, 102, 300, 322, 352, 434, 435, 450, 513
Creek, Richland 109, 131, 136, 207, 229, 263, 421, 424, 461, 481, 506, 515
Creek, Roberson 428, 433, 515
Creek, Schoats 208
Creek, Shoals 5, 341, 342, 420
Creek, Weekley 158, 208, 512, 514
Creek, Yancy 2
Creesy, Bennet 2
Creesy, Patsy 105
Crisman, Isaac 11, 12, 63
Crisman, Isaac L. 324
Crisman, Isaac S. 218, 229, 304, 308
Criswell, Nathan 260
Criswell, Patience 260

Crittendon, Jessee 294, 522
" " John 294
" " Reuben L. 113, 135, 138, 196
" " William 469, 477
Crocket, Archibald 25, 461, 479, 483, 489, 495, 496, 497, 503, 504, 515, 521, 523, 526
" " Patterson 509, 510
" " Robert 479
Croft, (Capt.) 28, 305, 351
" " Henry 158
" " Henry F. 201, 205, 209, 232, 233, 234, 235, 246, 247, 248, 250, 253, 253, 254, 255
" " Henry J. 495
" " Henry T. 1, 17, 18, 347, 372, 382, 438, 523
" " John W. 358, 404
" " Samuel 439
" " Washington 37
Croney, Rhoda 206
Crook, David 207, 484, 485
Cross, Henry 232
" " Shadrack 518
Crow, Isaac 77, 151, 165, 176
Crowder, Isaac 120, 131, 279, 515
Culbirth, Daniel 385, 407
Cummings, David 157
Cunningham, Mathew 27, 47, 64, 65, 66, 67, 68, 69, 70, 71, 72, 311

D

Dabney, John 2, 103, 127, 130, 133, 159, 264, 314, 460
Dailey, James 139, 289, 346
Dailey, John 61, 357, 459, 489, 515
Dailey, Josiah 456
Dailey, William 131, 204, 268
Dandridge, Archibald 293
" " Elvin 327
" " Elvira 293, 392, 458
" " William 293, 458
Daniel, Ann 264
" " F. R. 103
" " J. P. 133
" " Thomas R. 402
" " Tillman R. 301, 316, 402, 429, 430, 444, 448, 481, 523, 524
Davenport, Abner 27
" " George 268, 316
" " John 501

Davenport, Josiah 429
Davenport, Martha 530
" " Martin 277, 413
" " Thomas 113, 114, 115, 270
" " Thomas D. 210
" " William 26, 126, 482, 488
Davidson, Josiah 61
Davidson, Robert 31, 74, 109, 150, 152, 161, 162, 163, 164, 165, 166, 167, 170, 303, 467, 477
Davis, Anna 202
Davis, Bailey 142, 144, 164, 218, 229, 285, 315, 326, 333, 345, 347, 348, 378, 404, 405, 406, 446, 448, 449, 462
" " Benjamin 202
" " Charles 113, 158, 160
" " Ebby 202
" " Edward 128, 134, 179, 180, 202, 308, 321
" " Enoch 124, 234, 358
" " James 25, 479
" " John 202
" " Joseph 370, 491
" " Maddison 202
" " Nancy Ann 251
" " Nathan 134, 135, 138, 152, 153, 155, 179, 180, 260, 285, 308, 335, 344, 364, 411, 424, 438, 518
" " Neely 307
" " Peggy 202
" " Robert 202
" " Samuel 57, 124, 129, 251
" " Tillman R. 432
" " William 199, 246, 514
" " William R. 303, 415, 419, 462, 464, 526, 513
Day, Jesse 145
Day, Lina 145
Day, Samuel 3, 61, 77, 176, 224, 258, 260, 265, 266, 282, 330, 335, 365, 372, 398, 408
Deams, James F. 277, 418
Deane, (Capt.) 520
Dearing, William 57, 124, 204, 249, 249, 282, 302, 371, 460, 461, 489
Deavers, Charles 114, 115, 306, 307, 314, 464, 465, 466, 468, 469, 470, 471, 472, 503
" " James H. 265
" " Matthew 310
" " Thomas D. 310
Defoe, John 36, 142, 217, 496

Dempsey, James 78
Den, John 456
Derr, James 36, 313
Devers, Charles 4, 6, 12, 61,
    119, 138, 144, 146, 147,
    154, 169, 209
" " Neely 306
" " Neely C. 138, 144, 147, 169
Dickey, James R. 127, 310, 492,
    515, 521
" " John 1, 8, 21, 22, 56, 59,
    75, 78, 138, 148, 152, 153,
    155, 260, 323, 356, 460
Dickson, Michael 45
Dickson, Thomas 258
Dillon, Thomas 138, 139, 142,
    214, 529
" " Thomas D. 33
" " Thomas W. 22, 23
Dodson, Elisha 25, 56, 322,
    435
" " George 56
" " Jordon 56
" " Samuel H. 25, 146, 154,
    322, 328, 352, 430, 513
Doggett, Miller 490
Dollon, Thomas 210, 211
Donaldson, A. W. 120
Donaldson, Alfred 21, 32, 111, 138,
    139
" " Betsy 21, 32
" " James 21, 22, 56, 260
" " Mary 21, 32, 120, 171, 328,
    450, 513
" " Polly 21, 32
" " Robert 21, 32
" " Sally 21, 120
" " Stockley 341, 342
Dougherty, ... 463
Douglass, James 483
Douglass, Nathaniel 60, 428
Douglass, John C. 230, 271
Downing, James 224
Dudley, William 286
Duey, Charles 120
Dugger, James 1, 6, 7, 12, 16,
    17, 22, 24, 25, 34, 48, 54,
    61, 156, 198, 253, 300, 305,
    310, 319, 350, 356, 414,
    428, 436, 437, 442, 443,
    458, 459, 489, 518, 519
Dunnegan, Margret 21, 32
" " Martin 32
Duty, Thomas 273
Dyer, James 237, 260

E

East, Joseph 357, 373
" " Thomas 7, 11, 78
Eastman, James 431, 433, 462
Eaves, Josiah 419
" " Mark 55
Edgar, Jesse 19, 58
" " William 264
Eding, Andrew 156
Edmonson, Robert B. 6
" " William 6
Edwards, Benjamin W. 24, 189,
    193, 227, 404, 411
" " Charles 27, 64, 65, 66, 67,
    68, 69, 70, 71, 72, 97, 112,
    120, 179, 180, 283, 285, 287,
" " Elizabeth 126, 128
" " Gray H. 31, 100, 111, 120,
    126, 138, 173, 174, 183, 184,
    185, 186, 187, 188, 189, 190,
    196, 261, 294, 296, 297, 298,
    330, 346, 372, 379, 410, 504
" " Isham 506
" " J. B. 106
Edwards, John 36, 44, 49, 100,
    179
" " John F. 422
" " John G. 289
" " John W. 62, 121, 136, 139,
    140, 289, 343, 346, 472
Edwards, Sally 197
" " Susan 197, 294, 296, 297,
    298
Elder, William 512
Eldridge, Elisha 44, 53, 62, 97,
    100, 121, 132, 136, 140, 159,
    172, 181, 238, 241, 242, 343,
    361, 416, 425, 470, 528, 529
Elk River 136, 416, 421, 430,
    482
Elliott, John 180
" " Richard 327, 458
Ellis, ... 107
" " John 57, 63, 217, 218, 313
" " Nancy 57, 63
Ellison, Joseph S. 38, 39, 40,
    41, 42, 43, 148
England, Benjamin S. 19, 21, 116,
    167, 335, 337, 449
English, John 262, 312
Erwin, Andrew 262
" " Eli G. 369
" " E. C. 369
" " James 369

Erwin, Joseph 336, 369
Esselman, Alexander 158, 201, 315, 318, 440, 461, 489, 506, 509, 526, 527
Estes, Asa A. 198, 207, 217, 218, 253, 254, 267, 314, 322, 327, 328, 340, 341, 342, 376, 377, 378, 379, 380, 381, 382, 383, 384, 385, 386, 391, 434, 492, 503, 521, 523, 526
" " Thomas P. 266, 300, 352
Evans, Josiah 437, 453, 457
" " Parsons 321, 325, 449, 515
Everly, George 35, 165, 194, 262, 283, 293, 400, 417, 419, 437, 441, 463, 467, 468, 472, 475
Ewing, Andrew 139
" " Wm. Y. C. 474
Ezell, Daniel 438
" " Jeptha 210, 211, 213, 226, 496, 497
" " Micajah 59, 107, 302
" " Timothy 30, 302
" " William 6, 187, 158, 209, 236, 237, 238, 240, 241, 242, 243, 244, 245, 246, 248, 250, 253, 254, 255

F

Fain, Nicholas 168, 239, 251
" " Nicholas S. 411
" " Samuel 168, 210, 251, 239, 411, 416
Fall, William 319
Farguhars, James 4, 78, 98
Farley, Thomas M. 506
Farmer, Nathaniel 7, 313, 434
" " Robert 11, 375
" " Samuel 263, 317
Farnswalt, William 266
Farris, Adam R. 183, 184, 185, 186, 187, 188, 189, 190, 275, 290, 335, 345, 346, 507
" " Bowler 176, 181
" " Elisha 169
" " Hartwell H. 475
" " Samuel 357, 431
" " Wilsford 487
Fay, Andrew 346, 384, 410
Felmuth, Jacob 40
Fenner, Robert 26, 271, 300, 352, 355, 384, 410, 467, 485
Ferguson, Thomas H. 256

Field, ... 10, 293, 309, 501
" " Allen 488
" " Edward R. 333
" " Harris Y. 113
" " William H. 43, 45, 49, 64, 97, 106, 181, 205, 214, 251, 387, 422, 428, 464, 517
Finch, Lucy 105
Finn, William 438
Finner, William 374
Finney, William 282, 403
Fisher, Anthony 130
" " William 6
Fitzgerald, 399, 444, 503, 508, 532
Flatt, James 160
" " William 144, 160, 461
Flournoy, ... 212
" " Alfred 35, 44, 49, 287, 390, 469
" " Julia Ann 106, 315
" " Mary 175, 214
" " Silas 97, 106, 181, 390, 428
" " William C. 97, 390, 454
Fogg, John 310
" " William 345, 346, 355, 375, 376, 377, 378, 380, 381, 382, 383, 384, 385, 386, 387, 388, 389, 390, 391, 397, 400, 401, 407, 411, 415
Foley, Washington G. L. 189, 193
Follis, John 321
Ford, James 304, 324, 414
" " Jonathan 276, 290, 291, 337
" " Mason 466
" " Robertson 369
Foster, Ambrose 105
" " James 78
" " John 172
" " Robert C. 436
" " William 152, 153, 155
Fowler, Herrod 68, 252, 285
" " Holman 123, 158, 209, 518
Franks, Thomas 339, 401, 402
Frasure, Daniel 174, 183, 184, 185, 186, 187, 188, 189
" " William 56
" " William M. 173, 174
Frazier (Capt.) 265, 304, 317, 519
" " Daniel 3, 78, 116, 131, 190, 207, 240, 253, 283, 472, 517
" " James 45
" " William M. 176, 240
Freeman, Harris 201
" " Joshan 526
" " Reuben 200, 206, 302, 308, 418, 429, 437

Fry, Captain 29, 55
Fry, Andrew 325
Fry, Henry 325
Fry, John 304, 324, 327, 328, 330, 331, 333, 335
" " Joseph 480
Fuller, John W. 495, 496, 497
Funderburk, George 306

G

Galliger, John 506
Garland, Bonapart 100, 192, 252, 487
" " Daniel 100, 487
" " Edward 100, 192, 217, 218, 219, 252, 263, 518
" " Hamiltt 263
" " Julia Ann 100, 263
" " Julian 192
" " Lewis 263
" " Louisa 100, 192
" " Loury 100, 263
" " Peter 192, 252, 260, 263, 316, 354, 359, 487
" " Wester 100, 263
Garrett, Agatha 216
" " Edward 60, 228
" " Eli 216
" " Everard 214, 224
" " Geenberry 216
" " George 209, 223, 224, 232, 233, 234, 235, 236, 237, 238, 239, 240, 241, 242, 244, 245, 246, 247, 248, 250, 253, 254, 255
" " Lewis 216, 263, 303, 316, 488
Garrison, Mason 56, 316
Gatlin, Edmund 33, 471
Gatlin, Edward 148
" " Reding B. 148, 150, 411
Gean, Harvy 514
" " James 514
George, David C. 207
Gholson, William 99, 230, 259, 271, 335, 339, 363, 397, 399, 426, 427, 475
Gibson, Capt. 305, 317, 319
Gibson, Ann 129
" " David C. 79, 102, 136, 137, 270
" " George 204, 268
" " George M. 63, 129, 131, 140, 174, 180, 320, 374, 419, 437, 453, 457, 484, 486, 489, 510, 519
" " Henry 133, 137

Gibson, Jeremiah 430
" " John 129
" " John K. 5, 129, 486
Giddens, William 411, 462
Gilbert, Silas 75, 195
Gilcrist, Malcolm 380
Gilliam, John 284, 285, 344
" " Samuel 365
" " Thomas 171, 223, 290
Gilmore, James H. 489
Glace, Lewis 207
Goats, George 202
Goff, Felix W. 217, 223, 225
" " George 26, 55, 139
Goff, Ira C. 35, 179, 152, 153, 339, 424, 453, 454
Goff, John 133, 136, 137, 139, 151, 183, 252, 253, 361, 420, 461, 478, 499, 501, 504, 526, 527
" " Mary 492
" " Thomas 11, 12, 157, 414, 486, 506, 528
Goldsberry, Henry 450
" " John 152, 153, 155
" " John B. 231, 226, 252, 437, 453, 457, 484, 489, 520
Golightly, Shand 55, 321
Gooch, (Capt.) 305, 351, 520
" " David A. 314
Goode, Joseph 133, 173, 264, 419, 433, 437, 438, 518
Goodman, Daniel 207, 267
" " John 312
" " Thomas 490
Goodrich, Thomas 475
Goodrum, Daniel 77, 235, 249, 250, 382
" " John 429
Gordon, Andrew 294, 320, 355, 375, 376, 377, 378, 379, 380, 381, 382, 383, 384, 385, 386, 387, 388, 389, 390, 391, 397, 400, 407, 409, 411
" " John 133, 146, 150, 154, 157, 161, 162, 163, 164, 165, 166, 167, 170, 173, 174, 175, 176, 177, 180, 460, 481
" " Robert 131, 194, 199, 152, 160, 262, 357, 373
" " Thomas K. 156, 287, 292, 305, 310, 319, 320, 356, 401, 414, 428, 451, 452, 459, 461, 476, 478, 479, 486, 489, 514

Grant, Everard 120
Grant, George 219
Grant, Harvey 209
Grant, Lewis 17
Graves, Captain 432, 519
" " David 147, 152, 217, 283, 437
" " Henry 524
" " Isaac H. 368
" " James 409, 410
" " James H. 111, 158, 161, 181, 188, 193, 196, 197, 209, 246, 264, 276, 280, 281, 300, 304, 309, 310, 319, 350, 360, 362, 363, 365, 368, 493, 494, 497, 501, 502, 504, 524, 525, 528, 529, 530, 531
" " John 44, 49, 375
" " John W. 210, 238, 270, 330, 331, 335, 336, 440, 443, 449, 505
" " John W. O. 7, 44, 45, 158, 209, 233, 234, 235, 236, 237, 238, 239, 240, 241, 242, 243, 245, 246, 250, 253, 254, 255, 265, 296, 308, 481
" " John W. R. 61, 99, 103, 161, 181, 238, 245, 272, 306, 350, 360, 387, 426, 431
" " Nathaniel 54, 113, 310
" " Oliver 197
" " Philmer 129, 216
" " Ralph 7, 17, 35, 43, 44, 45, 49, 69, 113, 114, 115, 120, 143, 152, 162, 172, 176, 194, 214, 227, 244, 251, 257, 262, 274, 292, 293, 294, 361, 364, 365
" " Sterling 64, 65, 66, 67, 68, 69, 70, 71, 72, 73, 131, 183, 184, 186, 187, 188, 189, 190, 207, 302, 324, 327
" " Thomas 78, 103, 133, 151, 170, 269, 357, 373, 461, 489
" " William 172, 431
Graves, William B. 432, 483
" " William C. 33, 39, 46, 131, 184, 185, 186, 187, 188, 189, 190, 207
Gray, Daniel 509
" John 509, 510
" " William S. 463
Green, David 224

Green, John 45, 242
" " Joseph 457, 469, 477
" " Philmer 359
" " Robert 301
" " Robert S. 465
" " Robert W. 57, 97, 422
" " Thomas 477
Gregory, John 285, 468
Griffin, James 369
" " Martin 116, 459, 464, 465, 466, 468, 469, 470, 471, 472, 473, 478
" " Soloman 369
" " Thomas 490
" " William 369
Grigsby, Amos 355, 375
" " John G. 355
" " Robert 316
" " Samuel H. 370
Grubbs, Hickman 108
" " Lucy D. 209
" " Thomas 1, 209, 262, 430
Gunter, James 452
Gunter, Samuel 452
Guthrie, Francis 30, 97, 99
" " Robert 55
" " Theophilis 335, 367, 372, 415, 464
" " Thomas 68

H
H

Hagen, Cathrine 130
Hagen, Henry 2, 5, 12, 16, 17, 22, 27, 28, 30, 34, 35, 38, 48, 51, 52, 54, 55, 56, 61, 62, 63, 76, 77, 100, 101, 102, 110, 109, 115, 116, 119, 122, 123, 127, 129, 130, 135, 136, 198, 205, 210, 215, 227, 231, 232, 238, 251, 262, 281, 282, 287, 288, 284, 299, 300, 309, 310, 322, 325, 338, 339, 340, 341, 358, 359, 368, 369, 390, 405, 414, 421, 422, 427, 428, 432, 435, 451, 452, 456, 459, 464, 470, 473, 474, 476, 477, 478, 479, 497, 498, 500, 502, 505, 511, 521
Haile, Nathan 357
" " Richard S. 357
" " William 306
Hale, Jeremiah 509
" " Nathaniel 140
Haines, Samuel 267
Hainey, James 263
Halcolmb, Hardy H. 203

Hamilton, George F. 14
" " Hannah P. 14
" " James 74, 75, 434
" " John 44, 45
Hamlett, John 212, 213, 226, 397, 400
Hammet, Nathan 102, 109, 223, 225, 327, 328, 347, 424
Hammons, James 59, 78, 124, 322
Hampton, Samuel 530
Hanison, Henry 5, 97
Hanna, John 166
Hannah, James 7, 11, 160, 284, 341, 342, 369, 370, 373, 431
Hapner, Adam 206
Hardin, Edwin 210, 211, 214, 286, 288, 289, 446
Hardin, Elizabeth 325
" " James 526
" " Joshua 325
Hardy, James 142, 144, 169, 218
" " Owen 2, 321, 322, 514
" " Reuben 448
" " Thomas 220
Harmond, John 77
Harney, Robert 7, 42, 234, 236, 312, 314, 419, 437, 453, 486,
Harris, ... 10, 309, 393, 501
" " Alfred M. 12, 62, 64, 73, 106, 121, 122, 214, 227, 233, 261, 315, 325
" " Eleanor 3, 517
" " Frances P. 251
" " Jordon 47
" " Kitchen 230
" " Robert 504
" " Robert H. 347
" " Robert S. 251, 253, 369
" " Tyree 251
" " William 3, 47, 251, 264, 517
Harrison, Henry 135, 138, 145, 146, 290, 291, 319
Harrolson, Hearndon 129
Hartin, Joseph C. 132, 134, 162
Harwell, Capt. 528
Harwell, Albert G. 101
Harwell, Buckner 30, 101, 102, 172, 256
Harwell, Coleman 263, 382
" " Featherston 120, 157, 351
" " Fredrick 125, 231
" " Gardner 301
" " Gilham 30, 101, 102, 103, 112, 130, 135, 138, 161, 162, 163,
164, 165, 166, 167, 170, 172, 174, 175, 176, 256, 269, 351, 364, 419, 437, 528
Hartwell, Hartwell 54, 310, 311, 322
" " Hubbard 208, 264, 322
" " Mary Ann 101
" " Ransom 459
" " Reason 434
" " Rolly 6, 107, 355, 375
" " Samuel 6, 160, 270, 351, 361
" " Sarah Carolin 101
" " Shadrack 136, 214, 294, 494
" " Stirling 434, 459
" " Thomas 6, 210
Harwood, Thomas 1, 26, 61, 112, 123, 132, 141, 156, 169, 223, 239, 240, 247, 248, 251, 254, 255, 256, 259, 319, 356, 376, 416, 420, 423, 428, 436, 479, 489, 493, 494, 498
Hatchet, Bannester 436
Hawkins, John 123, 301, 376, 391, 414
Hayes, William 6
" " William B. 124
Hayle, Joshua S. 317
Haynes, John 8
" " Samuel 128
Haynie, Elijah 320
" " James 320
" " Milton G. 330, 345, 349, 360, 397, 435, 457, 463, 464, 465, 466, 468, 469, 470, 471, 472, 475, 476, 481, 486, 524
" " Samuel 381
" " Thomas 436
" " Thomas B. 4, 174, 180, 181, 183, 231, 248, 249, 268
Heman, John 13
Hemanway, Martha Ann 483
Henderson, James 310, 317, 319, 369
Henderson, John 61, 102, 123, 130, 151, 159, 234, 236, 249, 262, 254, 264
Henderson, Nathan 197
Henderson, Thomas 47, 134
Hendry, Captain 305, 317, 354, 432
" " James 21
" " James H. 112, 306, 369, 461, 509
" " James L. 4, 19, 233
" " William 4, 113, 115, 119, 144, 147, 150, 169, 331

Henry, George B. 255
" " James L. 489, 506
" " John 519
" " William 44, 45, 137, 138, 307
Hensley, Gabriel 52
" " Simeon 284, 322
Hester, George 327, 328, 330, 331, 333, 336, 385, 522
" " Graves 176
" " Henry 116, 136, 154, 326, 411, 467, 468
" " James 306
Hewitt, Robert A. 311
Hicks, Arthur 1, 4, 6, 54, 61, 101, 103, 123, 156, 262, 305, 310, 319, 350, 354, 414, 428, 479, 489
" " Charlotte 30
" " Francis 61
" " George 97
" " Harrison 43, 49, 61, 113, 175, 192, 196, 260, 343
" " James P. 279, 516
" " Jesse 17
" " John 193, 319, 340
" " Jordon 288, 362, 416, 435, 516
" " Joseph 310, 320
" " Lucy 101
" " Nancy 193, 343
" " Rebecca 516
" " Samuel P. 297
" " Sarah 133
" " Thomas 323, 352, 370, 516
Hightower, Alfred 482
" " Hardy 25, 193, 253, 254, 313, 371
" " Henry 185
" " J. A. T. 371
" " John 252, 487, 490
" " Richard 252, 371, 487, 490
" " Stephen 183
Hill, Capt. 518
" " Brattons 513, 514
" " John 148, 151, 161, 162, 163, 164, 165, 166, 167, 170, 489, 495, 496, 497, 503, 504, 521, 523, 526
" " Walter 355, 375, 426, 461, 487
" " William 522
Hillhouse, George 1, 158, 463, 514
Hobson, Isaac N. 103, 415, 417
" " John 143
" " John M. 137, 139, 147, 148, 461
" " Lawson 103, 137, 148, 149, 150, 208, 234, 417, 511

Hobson, Younger 419, 437, 453, 457, 467,
Hodge, Francis 124
" " James 156, 164
" " John 78, 156
" " Joseph H. 78, 147, 149, 156, 290, 340, 366, 462, 485, 511
" " Joseph W. 147
" " Polly 124, 207
" " Robert 124, 201, 207
Hogan, Anderson 2, 24, 28, 54, 58, 61, 103, 123, 124, 128, 198, 256, 262, 269, 309, 310, 334, 356, 368, 420, 452, 479, 489, 502, 504, 523, 525
Hogan, Celia 309
" " Isiah 309, 354
Holden, John E. 11, 12, 27, 52, 152, 153, 155, 304, 324, 346, 414, 417, 463, 475, 501, 507, 521
Holland, Benjamin 303
" " Tilmon 303, 314, 432, 512
Hollum, Thomas 38, 39, 40, 41, 42, 43
Holly, John 185, 193, 311, 312, 419
" " Nicholas 185, 193, 371
Hood, Alexander 29, 432, 464
Hooks, Isaac 217, 218
" " James 113, 114, 115, 525
Hopkins, Jason 112, 411, 417, 467, 518, 521
Horn, Elizabeth 431
" " James 355, 375
" " Joshua 31, 158, 157, 182, 209, 232, 233, 234, 235, 236, 237, 238, 239, 240, 241, 242, 243, 244, 245, 246, 247, 248, 250, 253, 256, 257, 441, 527
Horn, Nancy 431
" " Thomas 431
Hoss, George 280
House, Baptist 208
" " Bethesda Meeting 306
" " Lawrence Court 208
" " Mariah Meeting 61
" " Pisgah Meeting 159
Houson, John 11
Houston, David 20
Howard, Memucan 334
Howe, Joseph P. 255
Howse, Henry 315, 350, 486
Huckeby, John 126
Hudson, John 203, 304

Hudson, Thomas 47, 138, 153, 505
" " Zadock 208, 459
Huff, Daniel 486
" " Early 486
" " Parmelia 486
" " Pinckury 486
" " Rebeccah 484, 486
" " Sterling 486
" " Valentine 484, 486
" " Wiley 486
" " William 486
Humedy, John 210
Hunnicut, Roland 59, 314
" " Robert 3, 315
" " William 4
Hunt, Smith 121, 165, 182, 183, 233
Hunter, Rebeccah 8
Hurshby, Simeon 517
Husband, Mansfield 206, 267, 432, 448

I

Ingram, Beazley 452
Ingram, Benjamin 271, 361, 374, 410
Irby, Gerald 27, 112, 184, 192, 288, 332, 365, 367, 444, 449, 502
" " Haynie 378
" " Jerald 71, 326
Irvine, Abraham 13, 14, 15, 282
Island, Persimmon 482
Ja
J

Jackson, John 4
" " Nicholas 518
" " William 495, 496, 530
James, Alfred 392, 458, 466, 494
" " Isaac 120, 161, 162, 163, 164, 166, 167, 170, 430
" " William 125, 312, 419, 429, 437, 453, 457, 501
" " Wilson 133
Jameson, Thomas 11, 12, 98
Jarret, George 158
Javis, Henry T. 236
Jenkins, Wilton F. L. 60, 126, 141, 214, 240, 271, 343, 420, 515, 518
Jennings, William D. 58, 64, 76, 139, 143, 158, 171, 185, 189, 209, 210, 211, 217, 218, 219, 223, 250, 286, 288, 290, 438, 440, 451
Johnson, Isaac G. 30
" " James 36
" " John 103, 133, 151, 156, 172, 183, 231
" " Matthew 204, 268, 286, 300, 352, 355, 449
" " Peter 472
" " Richard 3
" " Thomas 256, 430, 513
Johnston, Isaac 302
Johnston, James 304, 324, 326, 333, 335
" " Josiah S. 204
" " Matthew 3, 266, 424
" " Thomas 280, 328
Jones, Alexander 46, 199, 224, 288, 325, 336, 345, 376
Jones, Alfred T. 293
" " Allen, 77, 353, 362
" " Augusta L. 206, 207, 278, 279
" " Benjamin 318
" " Calvin 159, 197, 294, 295, 296, 297, 298
" " Charlotte 428
" " David 158, 209, 211, 212, 213, 223, 225, 226, 231, 232, 233, 234, 235, 236, 237, 238, 239, 240, 241, 242, 243, 244, 245, 246, 247, 248, 250, 253, 254, 255, 332, 474, 480
" " David L. 256, 257, 370, 419, 437
" " Edward D. 9, 13, 25, 26, 29, 32, 34, 54, 56, 61, 64, 70, 99, 120, 123, 128, 130, 198, 202, 204, 215, 216, 276, 288, 292, 297, 299, 309, 310, 319, 322, 368, 425, 427, 428, 431, 460, 478, 479, 483, 487, 488, 489, 510, 520, 529, 530
" " Fortunatus 234
" " George 529
" " George T. 293
" " George W. 240
" " Henry L. 236
" " Henry L. 234, 249
" " Hezekiah 1, 54, 61, 123, 124, 131, 135, 136, 138, 139, 155, 156, 160, 161, 170, 171, 198, 204, 262, 284, 300, 305, 310, 319, 345, 350, 351, 352, 368, 428, 459, 460, 480, 489, 510, 515

Jones, Jacob 77, 128, 248,
    304, 324, 346, 478, 483,
    484, 489, 517, 519
Jones, James 240, 428
Jones, Jane 206, 207
" " John 310, 313, 420, 421,
    488
" " John A. 344, 522
" " John S. 130, 159, 318,
    320, 373
" " Joseph 56, 293
" " Martha 130, 159, 318, 373
" " Mary 240, 432
" " Rebeccah 370, 420, 428
" " Richard 432
" " Richard M. 240
" " Stephen 487
" " Susan 31, 298
" " Thomas 197, 294, 296, 297,
    298
" " Thomas B. 101, 111, 123,
    168, 205, 290, 333, 339, 343,
    376, 423, 524
" " Thomas M. 159
" " Thomas P. 210, 254, 291,
    417, 468
" " William 54, 103, 133, 151,
    159, 175, 183, 184, 185, 186,
    187, 188, 189, 190, 198, 203,
    213, 216, 280, 281, 294, 355,
    369, 375, 426
" " William H. 318
" " Wilson 31, 111, 196, 197,
    261, 284, 295, 297, 298, 309
Joplin, Fanny 7
Jordon, Samuel 285, 287, 300,
    304, 306, 416, 429, 446
Jossling, James 128

K

Kearney, (Captain) 112, 307, 317
" " David 199, 204, 267, 268, 286
" " Guston 4, 131, 192, 204, 460
" " James 59
Keenan, John 35, 38, 45, 49,
    112, 115, 116, 119, 133, 136,
    137, 150, 152, 153, 155, 161,
    162, 163, 164, 165, 166, 170,
    179, 180, 211, 294, 333, 463,
    495, 504
" " Samuel B. 293
Kelley, Cary T. 2, 29
" " George 487
" " James 441, 467, 468, 487
Kelson, James 6, 124, 351, 483, 514

Keltner, George 58, 174, 182,
    374, 490
Kennedy, John 214, 223, 224,
    312, 321, 358, 487
" " Reuben 369
" " William 114, 456
Kercheval, Samuel 481
Kerley, David M. 434
Kernass, (Captain) 28
Kerr, Francis B. 32, 33, 255
" " Henry 133, 148, 209, 255, 321
" " Samuel 131, 419, 434
" " William P. 255
Kidd, William 480
Kilcrease, David 156, 272, 492, 493
" " John W. 156
Kimbrol, Elizabeth 312
" " John 312, 358
" " John P. 312
Kimbrough, Elisha 135, 138, 205,
    355, 375
" " Elisha L. 409, 426, 480
Kimbrough, Henry 133, 424, 304,
    505
" " Henry T. 253, 503
" " James 353, 436
" " James B. 214, 452, 487, 503,
    517
" " Martha 480
" " William 480
King, John 55, 339, 370
" " Samuel 283, 358, 403
Kirk, George 37, 42, 99, 151,
    335, 346, 507
" " Lewis 418, 471, 514
" " Mary 68
" " Polly 238
" " William 99
" " William P. 478
Knox, James 127
" " Joseph 129, 257, 374, 461,
    486, 489
Kyle, Claiborn 11, 19, 98, 129,
    131, 137, 211, 243, 251, 355,
    375, 389, 412, 426, 441
" " Rebeccah 11, 19, 98, 133, 137,
    211, 243, 251
" " William 4, 11, 19, 131, 211,
    243, 251, 441

L

Laffoon, Matthew 492, 493
Laird, Captain 304
" " Henry 59, 265
" " John 1, 6, 7, 13, 29, 54,

55, 61, 107, 109, 123, 124,
310, 313, 317, 319, 322,
368, 369, 370, 401, 460,
480, 489, 493, 494, 520
Laird, Martin 369, 480
Lam, Thomas 182, 192
Lamb, Jesse 124
" " Edmund 515
" " James 13, 14, 282, 370
" " Joel 415, 433, 480, 483,
501, 503, 515
Land, Charles 98
" " Thomas 98
Lane, Martin 3, 7, 173, 322,
390, 416, 420, 431, 460,
530
" " Thomas 7, 173, 252, 390,
401, 420, 431, 478
" " William 431
" " Willis 129, 323, 352, 370,
480, 483, 515
Langers, Allen 315
Lansford, William 1, 408
Larkin, Edmund 353
Lawrence, John F. 132
Laughertry, Henry 377, 418
Leagh, Harriet 21, 32
" " Thomas J. 21, 32
Leath, James 372, 469, 488
Leatherman, David 158
" " Daniel 2, 209, 323, 462,
484
Leatherwood, Creek 267
Leitch, James 180, 264, 322,
390, 401
Lee, John 77, 204, 268, 357,
381, 383, 415, 460, 484,
489, 519
Lee, Stephen 303
Lee, William 3, 270
Lemon, Peter 432
Lester, Captain 487, 518
Lester, Fountain 32, 59, 66,
121, 129, 159, 187, 201,
204, 206, 213, 233, 245,
250, 265, 300, 310, 323,
330, 354, 365, 390, 417,
419, 425, 434, 460, 471,
482, 485, 510, 511, 517,
521
Lester, German 1, 2, 6, 54,
61, 64, 106, 112, 121, 123,
129, 157, 165, 196, 198,
205, 227, 233, 261, 263,
280, 281, 294, 295, 297,
298, 300, 310, 318, 319,
327, 366, 361, 362, 368,
423, 436, 437, 462, 479
483, 485, 552

Lester, James 30, 109, 165, 304,
324, 326, 333, 335, 461, 489
" " Jeremiah 1
" " Josiah 156
" " Sterling H. 168, 187, 245,
250, 400, 429, 467, 468, 469
470, 471, 472, 505
Lewis, James M. 328, 430, 451, 513
Lightfoot, Claxton 230, 232, 271
" " Philips 230, 271
Lindenburgess, Jacob 436
Little, Luke 219
Livingston (Captain) 29, 126,
305, 317, 323
" " Henry 263
" " Henry M. 57
Lock, Ann 505
" " George M. 204, 268, 286, 399,
505
" " John B. 505
" " Walter 320, 419, 437, 441,
467, 468
Lockhart, Alexander 22, 23, 32,
33, 49, 50
Lockhart, Robert 23, 32, 35, 38,
39, 40, 41, 42, 43, 66, 159,
168
" " 213, 237, 239,
249, 250, 251, 259, 273
Long, Benjamin 268
Long, Charles 26, 204
" " Gerald 210, 211
" " Hugh 411, 419, 437, 453, 457
" " Jarret 446
" " Melford 210, 211, 289
" " Richard 158, 209, 211, 212,
214, 223, 225, 231, 252, 253,
254, 255, 317
" " William 268
Looney, Abraham 74
Lorance, Martin 64, 120
Love, Samuel 435
Loveless, John 504
Loving, William V. 504
Lowry, Daniel 192
Loyd, Henry 101, 208, 264, 358
" " Stephen 5, 9, 102, 180
Lucker, Allen H. 226
" " John K. 217, 218, 226
" " Joseph 404, 411, 425
Lumpkin, Edmund 25, 56, 313, 433
Luther, Jacob 198, 321
Lynch, Francis 60, 70
" " James 188, 189, 193, 327,
359, 363, 404, 411, 414, 417,
" " William 361
Mabrey, Francis A. 333, 350, 361,
404, 475
McAllilly, Francis 219

M

Mabrey, Francis A. 333, 350, 361, 404, 475
McAllilly, Francis 219
McAnnally, John 161, 424, 425
McAnnick, Henry 401, 424, 495
" " John 193, 194, 326, 372, 437, 468, 472, 498
McAnse, James 517
McCabe, Alexander 462
" " Ann 264
" " Hugh 352
" " Judith 302, 418
" " Philip 146, 211, 212, 213, 219
" " William P. A. 46, 78, 102, 122, 264, 290, 291, 361, 363, 411, 423, 462, 509, 523
McCafferty, James 2, 6, 28, 61, 103, 131, 156, 319, 428, 489
McCall, (Captain) 520
" " Martin 321, 484
McCanlass, David 186
" " James 78
" " John B. 151, 212, 223, 225, 313, 316, 317, 355, 375, 409, 417, 419, 426, 468, 482, 518
" " Thomas 157, 263
" " Samuel 77, 140, 165, 195
McCarmack (Capt.) 28, 66
" " Daniel 504
" " John 5, 402, 445
" " Marterson C. 49, 199
McCarmick, (Capt.) 305, 332, 520"
" " James 216, 255
" " John 163, 179, 202, 211, 224, 265
McCollum, Daniel 306, 355, 375, 409, 426
" " Thomas 77
McConnel, James P. 440
" " Walter 123
McCork, James 43
McCoy, Henry 108
McCracken, John 35, 165, 179, 183, 203, 309, 338, 359, 452, 465
McCraven, James 157, 199
McCrory, William H. 262
McCullock, David 78, 98, 183, 184, 185, 186, 187, 188, 189, 190
McCullock, John 78
McCullough, David 522
" " Robert 400

McCullum, David 5
McCutchen 310
McDaniel, John 204
McDonald, Alexander 12, 17, 56, 57, 59, 128, 134, 197, 200, 201, 236, 301, 303, 313, 314, 327, 370, 372, 412, 413, 458, 468, 471, 488, 490, 491
" " James 17, 212, 213, 301, 303, 316, 411, 419, 437, 438, 488, 499
" " John 50, 56, 59, 134, 150, 272, 313, 372, 411, 515
" " John G. 303
" " Joseph 294, 301, 324, 346, 491
" " Mary 430
" " Robert 199, 272, 316, 433
McEwin, David K. 103, 203, 252, 311, 321, 370, 404, 460, 486
" " Rebeccah 404
" " Sarah C. 404
McFatter, Archibald 5
McGee, (Captain) 432
McGee, Asa 103, 133, 135, 136, 138, 148, 153, 155, 161, 162, 163, 164, 165, 166, 167, 170, 172, 183, 314, 321, 322, 420
McGee, Ira 59
McGee, Isaac 152, 485
McGee, Richard 54, 61, 78, 116, 123, 159, 201, 204, 213, 214, 255, 256, 258, 259, 268, 319, 322, 420, 428, 434, 460, 479, 483, 489, 503
McGrew, William 460, 484, 489
McIlviane, Joseph 168
McIver, Evander 36
McKay, Henry 376, 377, 379, 380, 381, 382, 383, 384, 385, 386, 387, 388, 389, 390, 391, 438
McKearly, John H. 30
" " Thomas 134, 260
McKenner, John A. 37
McKennon, Archibald 320, 358, 511
McKenzie, Ulysses 271, 274, 275, 276, 277, 278, 279
McKissack, A. M. 48, 109
McKissack, Archibald 13, 20, 28, 31, 34, 61, 101, 103, 109, 112, 123, 152, 156, 159, 161, 163, 176, 179, 180, 181, 183, 193, 194, 198, 205, 217, 227, 231, 248, 262, 265, 280, 281

282, 287, 288, 300, 305,
307, 319, 322, 345, 356, 361,
362, 369, 418, 419, 435, 458,
459, 471, 473, 474, 479, 489,
516
" " John 37, 97, 151, 158, 161,
162, 163, 174, 204, 268, 286,
299, 415, 516
McKissack, Thomas 24, 31, 52, 68,
69, 111, 120, 184, 194, 196,
241, 242, 261, 280, 294, 295,
297, 362, 481, 501
McKissack, William 295
McKnight, Archibald 181, 249,
414
McKnight, James 26, 304, 324,
326, 333, 335
" " John 99, 103, 133, 136,
138, 148, 152, 153, 155,
161, 172, 175, 183, 208,
211, 212, 264, 335, 362,
370, 376, 377, 378, 379,
380, 381, 382, 383, 384,
385, 387, 388, 389, 390,
391, 404, 420, 482, 511
McKnight, Robert 26, 354, 511
" " Samuel 5, 208, 264, 420
" " Thomas 27, 59, 149, 220,
263, 325, 530
McKinney, Alexander 224, 334
" " James W. 487
" " John 401
" " Rolin 163
McLaurine, Madison 434
" " Miller S. 28
" " Robert 5, 6, 31, 61,
109, 270, 314, 356,
398, 418, 434, 471
" " William 434
" " Willis, S. 54, 61, 66,
108, 139, 204, 262, 270,
311, 319, 428, 434, 479,
484, 489
McLemore, Cargell 66
" " John 385
" " John C. 277, 278, 331,
407
McLane, Senior 314
McMillin, Edward 97, 116, 282
" " Jesse 77
" " John 3
" " Keenan 250, 311
McMullin, Edward R. 146, 147,
439
" " Keenan 26, 72
McNairy, Francis 198
McNeese, William 78

Maclin, Benjamin P. 4, 405
" " James C. 77, 116
" " James Z. 8, 405, 503
" " John 7, 46, 116, 440
" " Lockfield 7, 116
" " Sally 7, 47, 116, 503
" " William 8, 405, 526
Madra, Buckner 59, 306, 312,
412, 444
Maddox, Arthur 126
" " Josiah B. 189, 195, 428, 526
" " 306, 497
Mafee, Ephriam M. 266
Malone, Estill 76
" " George 35, 41, 53, 103,
109, 171, 290, 303, 401,
461, 483, 487
" " George H. 223
" " Gerald 481
Marks, Edward 27, 63, 64, 65, 66,
67, 68, 70, 71, 72, 113, 114,
115, 116
" " Elizabeth 428
" " James 16, 17
" " Lewis, B. 168, 310, 431, 448,
494, 496
" " Thomas 1, 5, 29, 51, 52, 53,
61, 101, 112, 122, 171, 198,
204, 208, 209, 231, 232, 247,
248, 254, 261, 262, 300, 301,
309, 310, 319, 341, 342, 345,
350, 376, 379, 428, 489, 591
Marlin, Benjamin P. 241
Marlow, Charles 2
" " Hanna 309
" " Jesse 181, 304, 324, 365, 432
Marlow, John 36, 306, 461, 489
" " John C. 309
Marr, George W. L. 263
Marsh, Simeon 77
Martin 471
" " Francis 435
" " Jackson 128
" " James 302, 358, 436
" " Lewis 16
" " Peter 450, 462
" " Susan 435
" " Thomas 37, 38, 129, 132, 156,
159, 164, 166, 167, 170, 172,
174, 194, 210, 227, 231, 237,
335, 364, 385, 388, 389, 412,
416, 425, 435, 437, 441, 460,
471, 521
" " William 57, 124, 127
" " William B. 42, 450
" " Zanus 302, 311, 431, 435

Massie, Ephriam M. 103, 133,
    264, 310, 319, 323, 356,
    428, 435, 489, 519
" " Jordon 302, 353, 436
" " Sarah 301, 401
" " William 124
Mason, Isaac 13, 55, 100, 133,
    151, 223, 306, 308, 346,
    512
" " Josiah 74
Matthew, John H. 293
Maultsby, Samuel 17, 363
" " William 38, 39, 40, 41,
    42, 43, 112, 120
" " William A. 293, 327, 328
Maxey, Isaiah 15
Maxwell, (Col.) 74
" " David 266, 300, 304, 324,
    326, 333, 335, 352, 355,
    434, 460, 485
" " John 258, 316, 340
" " Thomas 433
" " William 27, 30, 64, 65,
    66, 67, 68, 69, 70, 71, 72,
    306, 311, 370, 373, 464, 465,
    466, 468, 469, 470, 471, 472,
    485, 487, 498
May, Benjamin 353
" " Elisha 349
" " Joel 320
" " William 204, 268, 286, 308
Mayberry, Francis 440, 443
Mayfield, Ambrose 521, 523, 526
" " Brice M. 439
" " Cammell 33
" " Elisha B. 13, 24, 41, 43,
    53, 66, 69, 153, 163, 248,
    288, 308, 478
" " Henry M. 439
" " Isaac 7, 41, 53, 99, 140,
    231, 242, 243, 293, 294,
    361, 386, 521
" " John 269, 441
" " John E. 65, 154, 218, 219, 220
" " Larkin 35, 44, 45, 66, 140,
    286, 287, 330, 437, 439
" " Stephen 269
" " William 1, 4, 24, 29, 35,
    51, 53, 61, 102, 123, 131,
    138, 139, 153, 163, 169, 170,
    204, 218, 229, 248, 302, 308,
    319, 322, 349, 361, 428, 510,
    518, 532
Mayfield, William C. 14, 501
Mayor, Isaac 430
" " William 413
Meadows, Elisha 3

Meadows, Elizabeth 5
" " Hiram 78
" " Joseph 417
Melton, Henry 263
" " Littleberry 203
" " Plency 224
Menefee, Bethy 227
" " Jarratt 65, 214
" " John 61, 128, 206, 301,
    380, 408, 464
" " John E. 228
" " William 461
Mercer, Christaina 439
Meredith, Thomas H. 44, 50, 53,
    132, 136, 238, 241, 242, 343,
    425, 477
Merit, Mary 22, 41
Merrett, Embrier 214
Mick, William 5, 441
Mill, Anthony's 513
" " Baileys's 352, 434
" " Coldwell's 208
" " Hightower's 5
" " Leatherman's 5
" " Mayfields 4, 102, 266, 300,
    318, 352, 434
" " Tinnen's 3, 27, 461, 481
Miller, Aaron 14, 22, 23
" " Henry 158, 209, 321
" " Jacob 141, 416, 485
Mills, John F. 327, 458
Mims,   55, 359, 365
Miskill, Elizabeth 316, 433
Mitchel, David 153
" " David C. 353
" " Jesse 481
" " Marcus 6, 7, 204, 258, 275,
    290, 292, 483, 512
Montgomery, (Capt.) 29, 60, 199,
    304, 317
" " J. 67, 68, 69, 71
" " John 50
" " John I. 301
" " John T. 512
" " Jonathan 107, 119
" " Samuel 56
" " William 50, 67, 68, 69, 71,
    107, 119
Moody, Jonathan 27, 31, 54, 61,
    103, 129, 156, 198, 246, 319,
    321, 374, 419, 437
" " Marshall 7, 27, 64, 65, 66, 67,
    68, 69, 70, 71, 72, 383, 408,
    461, 469, 506, 509, 512, 526, 527
" " Nthaniel 210
" " William H. 246
Moon, F. 373

Moore, (Capt.) 550
Moore, Abednago 112, 119, 138, 144, 147, 168, 169, 307
Moore, Catharine 107, 343
" " Daniel F. 321
" " David 123
" " David J. 482
" " Fanny 417
" " James 20, 107, 317, 343
" " John 55, 156
" " John R. 498
" " Joseph 198
" " Larkin B. 304, 324, 346, 504, 523, 526
" " William H. 7, 103, 131, 133, 151, 172, 179, 180, 181, 184, 192, 197, 265, 270, 274, 275, 276, 277, 278, 279, 461, 482
Morris, ... 341, 342
" " Isaac 32, 63, 160
" " Lester 255, 256, 258, 510
" " Lewis 335
" " Lewis B. 211, 212, 213, 253, 407, 408, 510
" " Lewis R. 404, 407
" " Richard 58
Morrow, Alexander 491
" " Daniel 518
" " Matthew M. 491
Mosely, James 498
Moss, Joanna 130, 232
" " Mason 130, 232, 495, 496
Mullinax, William 157, 158, 201
Muncrief, Elizabeth 481
" " Mathew 207, 262
" " Samuel 5, 533
" " William 433
Murphy, Penelope 476
Murrah, James H. 158
" " James K. 58, 64, 71, 101, 119, 157, 164, 201, 209, 212, 215, 220, 249, 259, 265, 268, 273, 274
Murrah, James R. 98
Murrell, Benjamin 369
" " John S. 369
" " William 134, 514
Muse, Tide 472
Myers, Asher 59
" " Charles 27, 151, 398

N

Nabers, Benjamin 262, 263
Nance, (Capt.) 199, 304, 317
Nance, Daniel 47
Nance, Joseph 204

Narrill 13
Neal, Charles 316, 481
" " Claud 17
" " Henry 62, 250, 251, 255, 257, 263, 512
" " Isaac 481
" " J. H. 185
" " James 368, 505
" " John 481
" " Matthias 481
" " Nancy 481
" " Rebeccah 481
" " William 37, 368, 458
" " William S. 68, 138
Neil, Esther 255
Neille, James 429
" " William 429
Nelson, John 314
" " Robert H. 314, 375, 466, 494
Neverre, John 227
New Pleasant 266
New, William 266
Newlin, Henry M. 7, 183, 194, 184, 185, 186, 187, 188, 189, 190, 335, 375, 376, 377, 378, 379, 380, 381, 382, 383, 384, 385, 386, 387, 388, 389, 390, 391, 397, 400, 411, 424, 425, 518
Newton, John 6, 125, 179, 180, 302, 306, 308
Nicholas, George 358
" " John A. 3
" " Joshua 78
" " Mahulda 302
Nolin, Bird 21
Norwood, William 65
Nutt, Keder 369
Nye, Nathaniel G. 227, 251
" " Shaderack 244, 257

O

Oliver, Annanias 103, 248, 373, 402, 444, 448
" " George 204, 268, 286
" " Robert 28, 53, 54, 61, 101, 103, 123, 145, 146, 152, 156, 159, 180, 181, 191, 192, 197, 198, 242, 262, 319, 356, 365, 368, 400, 409, 410, 423, 424, 427, 428, 472, 479, 483, 488, 489, 523
Owen, David 362, 392, 458, 466, 494
Owen, Samuel 270

Oxford, Able 52

P

Pace, David 137, 139, 143, 147, 148, 149, 150, 461
Page, Robert 78
Paine, Gabl. W. 286, 288, 289, 446
Paine, James 1, 27, 54, 61, 101, 103, 108, 111, 123, 124, 126, 130, 131, 136, 139, 191, 197, 206, 262, 263, 305, 306, 311, 319, 323, 329, 350, 356, 362, 365, 368, 370, 399, 400, 416, 479, 481, 485, 489, 520
Paine, Robert 64, 65, 68, 69, 70, 71, 72, 103, 133, 172, 183, 362, 416, 429
Paisley, James 124, 314, 373
Palmer, Henry 46, 78, 116
Pankey, Peggy 320
Pannell, Giddeon 25
" " Judiah 480
Panter, Elisha 370
Paper, Columbian 513
Park, John 236
Park, Robert 78
Parker, Jeremiah 324, 346, 456, 460, 461, 489, 490, 506, 507, 509, 526, 527
" " John 114, 120, 150
" " William 5, 290, 360, 361, 366, 426
Parkham, William W. 136
Parrish, C. B. 59
" " Robertson D. 302
Parsins, Henry 199
Pearson, James W. 78
" " Samuel 120, 182, 274
Partin, Samuel 257
Pate, Blackmore H. 506, 522
" " John 56, 100, 125, 192, 203, 252, 270, 316, 354, 464, 496, 497
" " Matthew 412, 496, 497
" " Thomas 506, 522
Patler, Thomas 136
Patterson, Benjamin 36
" " Bernard 143, 368, 441, 443, 458, 468, 469, 470, 471, 472, 494, 506, 528
" " James 111, 132, 159, 175, 270, 292, 300, 326, 388, 390, 391, 405, 417, 438, 457, 463, 473, 478, 491, 510, 511, 531
" " Moses 56, 57, 124

Patton, Alexander 371
" " William 72
Paul, James 477
" " John 35, 163, 225, 226, 480
Payne, Gabriel 210, 211, 214
Peden, Henry 138, 139, 219, 225, 333, 404, 409, 531
Peebles, Joseph D. 251
Pellisk, Adam 5
Pendergrift, Lawrence W. 32
Penn, Jessee 159, 181, 196, 300, 311
" " John 161
Pepper, William B. 1, 6, 25, 54, 61, 62, 101, 121, 159, 198, 204, 231, 262, 273, 274, 300, 319, 350, 351, 368, 414, 428, 443, 451, 452, 455, 456, 459, 488, 489, 492, 510, 512, 513
Perkins, Charles 32, 43, 69, 75, 113, 120, 170, 172, 194, 197, 378, 397, 429, 500
" " Clark 49
Perkins, Samuel 27, 71, 429
Perry, James 10, 30, 50, 78, 107, 109, 113, 127, 134, 176, 186, 196, 107, 227, 228, 229, 238, 244, 251, 255, 256, 292, 304, 310, 317, 319, 329, 334, 343, 350, 356, 358, 359, 364, 365, 367, 391, 406, 407, 414, 421, 422, 428, 437, 439, 440, 445, 456, 459, 463, 464, 476, 477, 478, 489, 502, 504, 410, 513, 524, 525, 528, 529, 530, 531
" " John W. 37, 52, 102, 351, 361, 453
" " Joseph 172
" " William 277, 439
Pervis, Isaac 199, 208
Phelps, Josiah 2, 105
Phenix, Henry 398, 419, 437, 516
Phifer, Bradley 321, 491, 463, 514
" " Charles 514
" " Joseph 514
" " William 36, 514
Phillips, Elizabeth 376, 423
Phillips, Elizabeth Ann 430
" " James 422, 423, 430, 461, 482

Phillips, James N. 37
" " John 39, 44, 45, 46, 200, 223, 272, 283, 327, 328, 435, 466, 494, 517
" " Thomas 430
" " William E. 327, 458
Phleman, W. 514
Pickens, James 43
" " James H. 174, 180, 378, 397, 478
Pierce, John 148
Pillow, (Capt.) 431, 519
" " Giddeon 4, 236, 397, 450
" " Granville 318, 328, 351, 430, 513
" " James 36, 142, 144, 487, 514, 524
" " John 10, 142, 153, 172, 226, 248, 439, 489, 496
" " Joseph B. 10, 17, 226, 487, 514
" " Richard 514
" " William 497
" " Willis 8, 36, 37
Pisgah, Mt. 481
Pitts, Allen, 7, 200, 202, 488
" " Sarah 488
Plaster, Margaret 203
" " Thomas L. 203
Poinor, David 1
" " John D. 1
" " Nathaniel 1
" " Sarah 1
Polk, William 152, 263, 463
Pond, Blind's 208
" " William 97, 216
Porter, Catharine 475
" " David 265, 461
" " David W. 5, 6, 61, 204, 253, 330, 481, 522
" " Eleanor W. 31
" " Elinor 175
" " Ellen 108
" " James C. 227
" " Jane 31
" " Jeremiah 304, 438
" " John 4, 26, 31, 130, 175, 252, 269, 283, 306, 325, 332, 333, 337, 339, 400, 474, 495, 496, 497, 522, 525
" " Joseph B. 230, 270
" " Mary E. 475, 476
" " Reese 31, 61, 175, 360, 435, 436, 517

Porter, Reese A. 363, 366
" " Reese W. 108, 109, 525
" " Run 103
" " Thomas C. 24, 53, 163, 308, 361, 365, 464, 472, 504, 522
" " Thomas J. 325
" " William 330
Poteet, Edward 438
Potston, Jones 30
Potts, (Captain) 26, 99, 305, 486, 520
Potts, Baker B. 14, 27, 28, 64, 65, 66, 67, 68, 69, 70, 71, 72, 204, 219, 220, 268, 347, 348, 405, 447, 525
Potts, David 512
Potts, June 525
Powell, John 422
" " Peter 280
" " William 132
Poynor, Sarah 107
Pratt, William 160
Preston, John M. 35
Price, Esther 338
" " George 368
" " Isaac 255, 517
" " James 255, 338
" " James H. 338
" " John H. 338
" " Martha R. S. 338
" " Mary D. 19, 137, 159, 255, 309, 338, 387
" " Mary S. A. 338
" " William 19, 255, 271, 343, 457, 518
Prim, German 335, 407
Pruitt, Thomas 77, 199
Pullen, Jessee 304, 322, 324, 328, 346, 430, 513, 523, 526,
" " Moses 270, 354, 355
" " William 17, 37, 103, 133, 138, 173, 174, 175, 176, 183, 252, 306, 322, 365, 400, 430, 435, 481, 513
Purnell, William 141, 234, 236, 249, 263, 301
Purviance, Eleazer 431, 433
Purvis, Isaac 6, 160
Puryear, Daniel 37, 127, 272, 283, 306, 318, 322, 335, 337, 360, 366, 367, 399, 422, 431, 450, 451, 455, 461, 464, 481, 496, 506, 509, 513, 526, 527

434

R

Ragland, Samuel 293
Raines, James 3, 510
Rainey, Arthur 198
" " Henry 123, 394, 414
" " Homer 7, 11, 12, 43, 127, 190, 486, 517
" " James 44, 49, 103, 126, 128, 133, 190, 270
" " William 10, 198, 223, 311, 320
Randall, John 315, 373
Rankin, Robert 4, 305
Rapely, Daniel 73, 132
" " Lawrence 73, 132
Rawlins, John 347, 389, 390, 441, 514
Ray, Abner 511
Raybourn, George 463
" " John 514
Rea, Abner 483
" " John 206
" " Joseph 54, 61, 145, 146, 152, 180, 181, 191, 192, 197, 262, 284, 305, 310, 319, 356, 357, 374, 420, 428, 441, 489, 510, 519
" " Nathan 363, 398
" " Thomas 248
" " William 63, 518
Read, David 57, 114
" " James 123, 161, 424, 425
" " Moses 316, 514
" " Robert 1, 3, 6, 25, 54, 61, 103, 156, 160, 300, 303, 310, 319, 329, 349, 350, 356, 368, 372, 414, 418, 428, 471, 479, 489, 510, 514, 516, 517
Read, Thomas 138, 306, 331, 342, 344, 417
Reading, John 414, 524
" " Stephen 27, 63, 64, 65, 67, 68, 69, 70, 71, 72, 160
Reasonover, Early 485, 512
" " John 512
Redding, Armstead 257, 266, 480
" " Stephen 199, 206, 431
Reed, David 113, 115, 347
" " Joseph 27, 71
" " Levi 304, 306, 308, 324, 346, 362, 495
" " Robert 6, 9, 27, 28, 31, 32, 34, 35, 37, 38, 58, 59, 61, 198, 262, 264

Reed, Thomas 54, 198, 207, 257
Reynolds, Enoch 286, 372, 411
" " Hugh 57
" " Isaac 336, 337, 339, 401, 403, 449
" " William 337
Rhodes, John 482
Rice, George 37, 262, 268, 286, 428, 481
Richards, Jonathan 201
Richards, Robert 392
" " Robert M. 327, 458
Richardson, Amos 311, 313, 320
" " Clement A. 485
" " John C. 485
" " John P. 485
" " Julia F. 485
" " Martha B. 485
" " Mary Ann L. 485
" " Susannah M. 485
" " Thomas 314
" " William 9
" " William F. 120, 168, 304, 306, 324, 485, 526
" " William T. 325
Rickman, Joseph 231
" " Joshua 67, 252, 253, 518
Riddle, David 480
" " Elisha 36
" " John D. 17, 27, 59, 64, 65, 66, 67, 68, 69, 70, 71, 72, 353, 375, 426, 432, 480
" " Maddison 38, 39, 40, 41, 42, 43, 361
" " Polly 470
" " Robert 459
" " Thomas S. 498
" " William 58
Ridge, Elk 433
Ridley, George M. 211, 243, 251
" " James 390
Riggs, James B. 231
Riley, Joseph 134, 260
Risner, William 262, 532
River, Elk 136, 141, 416, 421, 430, 482
Rivers, ... 210, 253, 353, 361, 365, 496, 497
" " John H. 14, 15, 49, 265, 350, 365, 418, 454, 512
" " Thomas 5, 101
" " William 2, 263, 521
" " William R. 15
" " William W. 265
Road, Athens 131

Road, Bigby 4
" " Bigby Little Tom 318, 321
" " Bigby Tom 160
" " Bradshaw 199
" " Buck Creek 205
" " Columbia 55, 321, 462, 481
" " Elkton 358
" " Dry Creek 160
" " Fayettsville 107, 199, 264, 267, 322, 358
" " Florence 265, 322, 373, 487
" " Huntsville 6, 107, 124, 159, 205, 306, 323, 416, 419, 481, 483, 511
" " Johnsons 208
" " Lambs Ferry 2, 373
" " Laurenceburg 160, 481
" " Pisgah Mt. 488
" " Prewits Gap 109, 124, 322, 352, 355, 401
" " Pulaski 265
" " Shelbyville 266, 300, 352, 434, 481, 517
" " Shoemakers Ferry 306
Roberts, Eldridge B. 16, 17, 23, 33, 36, 37, 48, 73, 77, 140, 165, 176
" " Henry 159, 436
" " John 173, 174, 176, 495, 496, 497
" " William 424, 438, 466
Robertson, Eldridge 226, 258, 260, 340, 531
" " James 267
" " Patsy 78
" " Sterling 313
" " Sterling B. 417
" " Sterling C. 195, 226, 258, 260, 340, 531
" " William R. 482
Robson, Robert 56
Rodes, Tyree 3, 4, 27, 32, 63, 210, 266, 276, 300, 306, 318, 328, 352, 355, 430, 434, 481, 511, 513, 521
Rogers, Jesse 138
" " Joseph 54, 55
Rollins, John 62
Rolly, James C. O. 186, 247
Rosbough, Thomas 252, 279
Rose, Cornelius 125
" " Edward W. 354, 453
" " Francis M. 125, 137, 139
" " William 125, 265
Rosenburn, Alexander 322
Ross, (Capt.) 432, 485, 519

Ross, Joab 156, 355, 486
" " John 125, 261, 266
" " Robert 125, 514, 518
" " Theron H. 514
" " William H. 348, 363, 463, 514
Row, Harriet 123, 414
Ruckner, Joshua 211, 212, 213,
Ruff, (Captain) 29, 55, 127, 305
" " Elizabeth 203, 369
" " Godsend 128, 168, 206
" " John 168, 204, 206, 268
" " Rebeccah 128, 203
Rus, George 204
Russell, Bartlett 126
" " George 203
" " James 31, 414
" " John G. 252, 256, 274, 275, 276, 277, 278, 279, 283
" " Nancy 203
Rutherford, James 336

S

Sadler, George T. 388
Samuel, Achillis 264, 516
" " Anner 120, 271, 511
" " Anthony 22, 43, 58, 271, 336, 369, 457, 486, 571
" " Elizabeth 320
" " Ethelbert 265, 303, 475
" " John 33, 120, 131, 186, 207, 249, 301, 428
" " Stephen 66, 264, 265, 516
" " William 202, 486
" " Ulysses 265, 303
Saunders, Jesse 472
" " Joseph 2
" " William 226
Sawyers, Allen 315
" " Esther 199
" " William 139, 272, 325
Scales, Anna 488, 492
" " Henry 31, 262, 294, 306, 351, 354, 488, 492
Scoggins, (Capt.) 519
" " Benjamin 214, 344, 419, 437, 438, 464, 465, 468
" " Gardner 255
" " Richard G. 303, 521
" " Richard H. 201
" " Richard M. 505, 511
Scott, Alexander N. 310
" " David 107

Scott, Elizabeth 1
" " Joseph 36
" " Mary 126
Scruggs, Thomas 14
Seal, John 27
Seallion, William 293
Setterfield, Peter 6, 161, 162, 170
Shadden, John 75, 195
" " Nancy 21, 32
" " Robert 21, 32, 75, 111, 120, 138, 170, 171, 195, 260,
Shall, George 252, 253, 275, 292
Shall, Jacob 203, 290, 316, 363, 379, 409, 410, 415, 429, 467, 505
" " William 252, 253, 275, 288, 290, 292, 411
Shannon, Matthias 119
" " Quinton 204, 231, 268, 274, 275, 276, 277, 278, 279, 280, 283, 285, 293, 347, 356
Shaw, Jacob 411
Shelton, Edmund 5, 8, 9, 48, 154, 155, 159, 180, 210
" " Edward 279, 280, 281, 304, 324, 326, 333, 346, 370, 408, 429, 445, 485, 514
" " James 7, 161, 164, 165, 167, 210, 280, 306, 354, 370
Sheppard, Egbert 3, 164
" " William 3, 67, 355, 461, 474, 485
Sherrell, Levi 30, 127, 313, 419, 437, 453, 456
" " Lewis 457
Shields, (Captain) 420
" " George 45
" " Joseph 339
" " Leander M. 103, 133, 204, 268, 274, 275, 276, 277, 278, 279, 280, 283, 285, 287, 290, 512
" " Samuel 78, 130, 490
" " William M. 25, 46, 301
Shuler, Abraham 278
Silvers, John 293, 327, 392, 458
Simms, David 60, 210
" " Dorothy 210
" " William 478
" " Wythe 200, 255
Simmons, James 449, 470, 500, 501
" " Mary 485

Simmons, Soloman 419, 437, 453, 457, 485
Simpson, Able 514
" " Charles 272, 371
" " Enoch 202, 214
" " George 514
" " John 47, 439
" " Rogen 461
" " Rodgers 489, 504, 505, 506, 509, 512, 526, 527
Sitler, Isaac 450
" " James 450
Slater, David 250
Slaughter, James 129
Slave, Abram 296
" " Aggy 296
" " Amos 296
" " Amy 296
" " Anderson 296
" " Dun 484
" " Charlotte 296
" " Franklin 297
" " Granderson 297
" " Jack 296
" " Jacob 296
" " John 296
" " Leak 296
Slave, Leathy 296
" " Lem 296
" " Madison 296
" " Martha 296
" " Mathy 296
" " Nancy 484
" " Phebe 297
" " Sally 296
" " Winnie 510
" " William 296
" " Willis 297
" " Yellow Jimy 296
Slyder, Joseph 491, 495, 499
Smith, Aaron 211, 212, 213, 379, 380, 381, 382, 383, 384, 385, 386, 387, 388, 389, 390, 391, 400, 407, 409, 411, 511
" " Archibald 7, 25, 56, 133, 148, 158, 219, 225, 232, 233, 234, 235, 236, 237, 238, 239, 240, 241, 242, 243, 244, 245, 246, 248, 250, 254, 255, 280, 281, 327, 328, 330, 331, 335, 353, 358, 365, 397, 433, 504, 511
" " Austin 5, 46, 358, 431, 491
" " Benjamin 322, 517, 518
" " Charles 333

Smith, Chesley 78
" " David A. 77, 280
" " Dewey 54, 56, 61, 111, 246
" " Druisy 29, 103, 123
Smith, Dudley 8, 9, 48, 52, 78, 154, 180, 253, 328, 330, 332, 457, 474, 495, 527
" " Edward 54
" " Elizabeth 202
" " Francis 17, 99, 308, 353, 355, 363, 375, 376, 379, 380, 381, 382, 383, 384, 385, 386, 387, 388, 390, 391, 400, 407, 411, 436
" " George S. 293
" " Isaac 54, 353, 430
" " Jacob 54
" " James 54, 158, 388, 416, 430, 432
" " James 54, 158
" " Jane B. 175, 269, 283
" " Janie 108
" " Joel 333
" " John 202, 388, 474
" " John L. 57
" " John N. 9, 214, 527
" " John Y. 54
" " Leonard 54, 388, 416, 482
" " Lewis 25, 266, 454, 482
" " Martha 482
" " Nicholas R. 52, 154
" " Owen 10, 311, 321, 460, 484
" " Patrick 304, 324, 346
" " Patrick 136   (R.)
" " Phelps 314
Smith, Porter 530
" " Rhoda 398
" " Robert 6, 333, 358, 425, 511
" " Samuel 31, 108, 175, 223, 230, 231
" " Samuel S. 269, 283, 325, 332, 355, 375, 400, 409, 426, 441, 474, 481, 496, 497, 503, 526
" " Sterling 362, 392, 458
" " Susan 460, 484
" " Thomas 7, 262
" " William 6, 73, 132, 171, 308, 323, 441, 498
Smothers, John 272
Snipe, John 321
Snow, William 183, 184, 185, 186, 187, 188, 189, 190, 256, 322, 441, 464, 465, 466

Stanford, George 202, 297
State, Alabama 19, 45, 98, 119, 136, 171, 185, 223, 230, 232, 271, 290, 293, 294, 327, 362, 392, 466
" " Carolina North 1, 298, 341, 342, 475, 506
" " Carolina South 74
" " Georgia 272
" " Jersey New 74
" " Kentucky 47, 75, 230, 270
" " Missouri 400, 474
" " Pennsylvania 74
" " Tennessee 11, 13, 23, 35, 73, 192, 211, 289, 328, 337, 345, 401, 402, 403, 421, 448, 449, 491, 493, 496, 506, 507, 530, 531
State, Virginia 172, 185, 202, 259, 422
Steadivant, Henry 481
Steele, David 32, 62, 110, 112, 161, 175, 362
" " Graves 161, 280, 281, 262
" " Henry 449, 500
" " Henry F. 26, 532
" " Nathaniel 287, 362, 501, 502
" " Robert 154, 169, 218, 219, 220
" " Robert G. 102, 109, 219, 228, 253, 286, 287, 289, 308, 365, 385, 407, 522
" " Thomas 32, 55, 62, 64, 110, 120, 147, 161, 217, 223, 224, 283, 287
Stegall, Henry 45
Stephens, Thomas 386
Stewart, Arthur 157
" " Cynthia 157
" " Marcus 157
" " Richard S. 518
" " Robert 185, 232, 233
" " Thomas 26, 78, 199
Stinson, Alexander 315, 419, 437, 440, 441, 447, 448, 472
Stockton, David 5, 146, 173, 174, 175, 176, 285, 345, 347, 348, 406, 408, 446, 447, 448, 449
Stone, Robert 127
" " Thomas 204, 515
Story, Archibald 116, 146, 157, 183, 184, 186, 187, 188, 189, 190, 365, 463, 468, 469, 470, 471, 472
Stribling, John B. 316

Stribling, O. J. 214
Strickland, Rhoda 63, 129, 323, 352, 370
Strong, David 125
Swaine, William 263
Swanson, Peter 54, 58, 247, 248, 254, 263, 264, 305, 319, 323, 365, 368, 370, 399, 400, 420, 428, 460, 481, 482, 489
Swiney, William 327, 328, 371

T

Tacker, John 30
Tarkington, Jefferson 363
" " Jefferson O. 495, 496
" " Joseph 136, 330, 331, 361, 363, 411, 464, 465, 466, 468, 469, 471, 472
" " 210, 253, 355, 361, 365, 496, 497
Tatum, Barnett 293, 327, 362, 392, 458, 466, 494
" " Mary 293, 328, 392
" " Mary S. 362, 392, 458
Taylor, Anthony 264
" " Dempsy 208
" " Gilbert D. 62, 73, 132, 441, 443
" " Henry 284
" " Jacob 237
Taylor, James 219, 357, 373
" " John 73, 132
" " John P. 26, 103, 133, 152, 153, 155, 160, 161, 162, 163, 164, 165, 166, 167, 170, 173, 174, 175, 179, 180, 182, 184, 192, 321, 374, 431, 461, 485, 487, 489
" " Mathew 525
" " Sallie 4
" " Tekle, T. 4
Tenner, Lucy 2
" " Robert 2, 266
Terrell, James 359, 366, 369, 528
" " William 463, 487, 513
Terry, Curtis 485
" " Willis 210, 211, 446
Thacker, Meredith 439
Thomas, Alexander 313
" " James I. 113, 114, 115
" " James J. 97
" " Phillip 202
Thompson, Alexander 313, 316, 381, 382, 415, 416
" " And. 202

Thornton, (Captain) 305, 353
" " William W. 7, 17, 35, 38, 39, 40, 41, 42, 43, 44, 45, 61, 228, 241, 252, 285, 286, 287, 292, 411, 487
Thorp, Goodhope 56
Thrower, Lion 236
Thrower, William 70
Tidwell, Eli 115
" " Elias 6
" " Isaac 46, 203
" " Miller 6
" " Millinton 307, 522
" " Milton 112, 119, 138, 144, 147, 169
" " Rode 6
" " Vincent 201
Tilford, Francis 335
" " John W. 327, 392, 458
Tillotson, Francis 344, 364
Tillman, John 358, 469
Tinnen, Alexander 126, 306, 318
" " James 3
" " John 3
" " William 229
Tinsley, 329
Tipton, (Capt.) 431, 509
Todd, John S. 60
Tolbert, Letitia 130
Tomlinson, Samuel E. 489
Tompson, Alexander 103, 206, 235, 249, 250
" " William A. 388, 433
Tongat, Elizabeth 169
Topp, William 124, 302
Torrence, Hugh 45, 112, 119, 136, 162, 176, 183, 184, 185, 186, 188, 189, 190, 194, 211
Town, Camden 74
" " Columbia 183, 192, 328, 357, 374, 408, 419, 421, 430, 513, 521
" " Elkton 104, 108, 124, 126, 168, 198, 240, 301, 357, 416, 420, 430, 433, 436, 483, 489, 515
" " German 74
" " Huntsville 301
" " Fayetteville 419, 433
" " Florance 513
" " Jonesburough 106
" " Lawrenceburg 461, 484, 512
" " Mt. Pleasant 461, 513, 514
" " Pulaski 1, 27, 50, 52, 78, 101, 103, 105, 106, 121, 123,

126, 145, 146, 159, 198,
203, 204, 210, 228, 261,
262, 292, 293, 326, 351,
354, 356, 357, 363, 368,
373, 374, 399, 408, 414,
417, 419, 428, 452, 460,
461, 463, 475, 479, 485,
502, 512, 513, 517
Town, Shelbyville 484
Trigg, David 353
" " William 353
Troutman, John O. 509
Tucker, Anderson 103, 133, 143,
144, 163, 164, 175, 183
" " Caswell 339, 499
Tucker, Clinton 462
" " George 322
" " James 339, 499
" " John 321
" " Thomas 462
" " Robert 98
Tuly, John 198
Turk, James 380
Tunstale, Robert P. 401
Turnbean, 357
Turnbeam, Andrew 280, 357, 374
" " James 22, 37, 41
Turner, Hanner 170, 183, 184,
185, 186, 187, 189, 190, 211
" " Robert 103
" " Willie 170, 184
Tutt, Benjamin 284, 344
" " Hansford 57, 284
" " Richard 339
Tuttle, Solomon 433

U

Underwood, Albert G. 98, 126,
214, 303, 414, 465, 485,
496
" " Hannah 293, 327, 392, 441,
451, 452, 458
" " John H. 190, 214, 232, 303,
304
" " Rebeccah 466, 467
" " Thomas 116, 212, 214, 398,
456, 464, 465, 466, 467, 494,
503, 504, 521, 522, 523
" " Virginia 214
Upshaw, Arthur 355, 375, 416,
417, 426
" " Lewis G. 124, 233, 300, 302,
314, 368, 460
Upshaw, Lewis H. 387
" " John A. 401

Ussery, Peter 130, 312
" " William 25, 32, 34, 37,
38, 45, 61, 123, 125, 130,
134, 204, 304, 310, 312,
316, 317, 319, 337, 428,
429, 489, 490

V

Vance, James 430, 483, 518
" " John 101, 139, 142
Vanderver, George 212
Vanhook, R. 506
Vay, Caybourn M. 78
Veatch, Silas L. 263, 327, 328
Vernon, Amos 61, 512
Vick, Benjamin 515
Viney, Raine 62
Vincent, James 139
Vinson, Elijah 1, 505

W

Walker, Charles 337
" " Coleman 337
" " Fanny 337
" " Henry 429
" " James 134, 158, 209, 246
" " James D. 474
" " James J. 129, 130, 270,
271, 336, 371,
" " John C. 29, 60, 61, 123,
133, 198, 254, 264, 310,
319, 336, 337, 356, 369,
489, 520
" " Johnston M. 337
" " Polly 129, 130, 246
" " Susan 316, 337
" " William 60, 69
Wall, John 128
Walthall, John 283, 287, 294,
295, 296, 297, 298, 325,
376, 377, 378, 379, 380,
381, 382, 383, 384, 385,
386, 387, 388, 389, 390,
391
" " Parmelia 196, 294, 296,
297, 298
Wanttin, John 138
Warren, John 284, 514
" " Johnathan 327, 392, 458
Wartman, Philips 19, 20, 58
Waters, Cross 463
Watson, (Captain) 4, 28, 112
Watson, Alston J. 124
Watson, Benjamin 173, 174, 175

Watson, Beverly B. 133, 138,
    173, 174, 175, 176, 179,
    180, 345, 346, 351, 363,
    372, 397, 398, 403, 404,
    407, 424, 426, 427, 460,
    475, 484, 489, 508, 570
" " George 401, 402
" " Polly 105
" " R. 398, 399, 427
" " William 99, 123, 159, 167,
    170, 181, 230, 259, 271,
    327, 333, 335, 348, 350,
    397, 408, 444, 479, 503,
    500, 531, 532
Weakley, Robert 467, 477
Weaver, John W. 58, 157
Weaver, Pleasant W. 58, 157
" " Samuel W. 58
" " William W. 157
" " Zebedee 483
Webb, Gatewood 133, 148, 150,
    152, 153, 155
" " John 151, 265, 204, 315
" " Larkin 26, 204, 268, 274,
    275, 276, 277, 278, 279, 280,
    283, 285, 287, 290, 514
" " Littleberry 6, 267, 302,
    306, 314
" " Morris 322
" " Rebeccah 483
" " Robert 323, 510
" " Sally 105
" " Thomas 483, 522
" " William 201, 274, 275, 276,
    277, 278, 279, 280, 281, 453,
    499, 501, 508
Weedon, William 327, 458
Weis, David 477
" " Hugh 486
" " John W. 3
" " Samuel 55, 327, 369, 441
Wellet, John 75
Wells, Francis Y. 109
" " James H. 186, 187
" " Jesse 133, 255
" " John 491
Wells, Robert 97, 216, 368,
    411, 429, 479
Wells, Ransom 17, 137, 138
" " Thomas 7, 11, 12, 35, 38,
    39, 40, 41, 42, 43, 102,
    109, 186, 194, 197, 270, 347,
    371, 384, 419, 437, 453, 457,
    470
" " William 154, 187, 197, 224,
    255, 368, 369, 371, 404, 429,
    462

Wesson, Samuel 6
West, Jesse 37, 112, 136, 262,
    279, 283, 293, 419, 437, 453,
    457, 578
Wester, Harriet 193
" " John 192
Westmoreland, Elizabeth 136
" " Jesse 429, 432, 523
" " John 216, 466
" " Laban 429, 432, 523
" " Martha L. 429, 432, 523
" " Reuben 429, 430, 432, 523
Wheeler, (Capt.) 486, 518
" " Benjamin 77, 98
" " Hannibal 514
White, (Captain) 29, 127, 304
White, Alfred 59, 66, 482
" " Archer 440
" " Benjamin 285, 420
" " Benton R. 17, 136, 249, 250,
    397, 439, 519
" " Burton R. 159, 237, 239,
    379, 415, 478, 481, 484
" " Caleb 11, 12, 314
" " Elisabeth 158
" " Elisha 35, 109, 158, 209,
    219, 225, 232, 234, 235, 236,
    237, 238, 239, 240, 241, 242,
    243, 244, 245, 246, 247, 248,
    250, 252, 254, 255, 303, 322,
    355, 390, 401, 460, 500
" " George 518
" " Gilbert H. 373
" " Henry 44, 45, 57, 158, 219,
    225, 232, 233, 234, 235, 236,
    237, 238, 239, 240, 241, 242,
    243, 244, 245, 255, 345, 347,
    468
" " James 284, 480, 489, 491,
    510, 515, 520
" " John L. 495, 496, 497, 504
" " Newton 59, 66, 482
" " Sarah 428
" " Simpson 27, 71, 72, 101, 156,
    266, 294, 300, 322, 328, 347,
    357, 358, 407, 411, 430, 513,
    422
" " Thomas 514
Whitfield, John 26, 202, 345, 347,
    348, 512
" " Willis 202
Whithers, Hugh 64
Whitley, John 37
Wilcox, Charles G. 1, 207, 303,
    430, 483
Wilcoxson, Aaron 137, 139

Wilcoxson, David 139
" " Isaac 139, 198
Wilkinson, Francis 462
Wilkinson, Lydall 190, 232, 274, 274, 293, 327, 362, 392, 441, 451, 452, 458
" " John 462
" " Thomas 7, 44, 45, 50, 72, 128, 285, 355, 375
Willet, John 270
Williams, Allen 314
" " Catherine 313
" " Benjamin 55, 103, 133, 135, 136, 138, 168, 176, 183, 231, 256, 265, 300, 419, 437
" " Edmund 208, 264
" " Edward 203
" " Edwin 322
" " Eliza 206
" " Elizabeth 42, 312
" " David 492
" " Hugh H. 120, 294
" " Isaac 126, 206, 208, 264, 322, 358
" " James Y. 475
" " John 57, 262, 300
" " Lewis 322, 453
" " Lucinda 206
" " Mildred B. 300
" " Morris 206
" " Nancy 206
" " Nathan 31, 262, 351, 354
" " Polly 126, 312
" " Robert 124, 523
Williams, Thomas 7, 120, 146, 271, 342, 369, 415, 457, 511
" " Samuel H. 74, 153, 327, 330, 369, 485
" " William 206
Williamson, Lewis 263, 264, 419, 459
" " Seth 127, 208, 264, 322, 511
Willis, John T. 270
" " Thomas 293
Wilson, Able 101, 356, 484, 489, 520
" " Ann 320
" " Boyd 311
" " Catharine 203
" " Francis 481
" " George 413
" " Henry 98
" " James 413, 461, 489, 506, 509, 526, 527
" " Joel 481
" " John 78, 303
" " John B. 54, 354
" " Joseph 320

" " Nancy 6, 303
" " Thomas 98
" " Thompson 163
" " Sarah Ann 480
" " Samuel 230, 320
" " William 302
" " Wesley 128
Wilsford, Hardy 109, 204, 265, 268, 417
Willsford, Henry 256
Willsford, James 1, 58
Willsford, Willis 15, 103, 109, 133, 151, 312, 487, 518
Winn, Minor 105
Winters, James 111
Woodfin, Caroline V. 300, 327, 329
" " George 402
" " James 41, 53, 300, 327, 329, 402
Woods, Elizabeth 251
" " James 123, 251
" " John 462, 463
" " Martin B. 204, 268, 274, 275, 276, 277, 278, 279, 280, 290, 468
" " Matthew 480
" " Robert 112
" " William 7, 37, 103, 107, 127, 161, 163, 168, 187, 251, 260, 262, 283, 286, 287, 300, 304, 309, 310, 314, 315, 319, 320, 324, 328, 332, 341, 342, 345, 349, 350, 351, 352, 355, 367, 401, 428, 430, 444, 450, 455, 458, 459, 460, 477, 478, 479, 488, 489, 510, 513, 522
Woodward, George W. 101
" " Hannah 7, 180
" " Henry L. 102
" " Jeremiah 5, 9, 101, 102, 311
" " Thomas 7
Worsham, John 77
" " William 424, 453, 499, 508
Wyatt, John 520

Y

Yancy, Alfred M. 501, 523, 526, 527
" " Bartlett 36
" " Elizabeth L. 428
" " Henry 36, 438, 467, 468, 474, 495, 497, 510
" " James 44, 45, 384
" " John 130, 291, 479, 510
" " T. M. 13

Yarbrough, Ambrose 57, 440
" " Robert 57, 461
Yates, John W. 460, 484, 489
" " Tyree 514
" " Samuel 514
Yergers, Albert 290
" " Allen 359
Yokley, Andrew 26
York, Edward 123
Young, (Captain) 29, 102
" " " Archibald 7
" " Buckner 219, 225
" " Ephraim A. 27, 59, 71, 131, 206, 487
" " Henry 371
" " James 487
" " Jarrett 27
Young, John 310, 312, 319, 323, 350, 357, 358, 373, 420, 428, 435, 459, 460, 465, 468, 469, 470, 471, 472, 479, 511

Young, John Jr. 27, 29, 54, 56, 57, 61, 63, 71, 101, 113, 123, 145, 146, 156, 173, 182, 198, 204, 213, 262, 266
Young, Joseph 204, 268, 286
" " Nathaniel 7, 26, 41, 50, 53, 60, 107, 173, 182, 210, 227, 228, 241, 242, 244, 257, 279, 292, 303, 405, 424, 487, 500, 524
" " Thomas 312, 490, 511
" " William Y. C. 400

Z

Zellars, Arnold 460, 484, 489, 520

Zemmerman, Christain 5, 201, 419

THE END

www.ingramcontent.com/pod-product-compliance
Lightning Source LLC
Chambersburg PA
CBHW020635300426
44112CB00007B/122